BT
18.75

The Complete Works of
WASHINGTON
IRVING

Henry A. Pochmann
General Editor

JOURNALS AND NOTEBOOKS

Volume I

Washington Irving
at the age of twenty-two

From an engraving of
the crayon drawing by John Vanderlyn
Paris, 1805

WASHINGTON IRVING

JOURNALS AND NOTEBOOKS

Volume I, 1803-1806

Edited by Nathalia Wright

The University of Wisconsin Press

Madison, Milwaukee, London

1969

Published by the University of Wisconsin Press
Box 1379, Madison, Wisconsin 53701
The University of Wisconsin Press, Ltd.
27–29 Whitfield Street, London W. 1

Printed in the United States of America by
George Banta Company, Inc., Menasha, Wisconsin
Standard Book Number 299–05320–2
Library of Congress Catalog
Card Number 69–16115

ACKNOWLEDGMENTS

The editors of this new edition of the journals and notebooks of Washington Irving are indebted to many persons and institutions. They are under particular obligation to Mrs. A. Duer Irving, of Wilmington, Delaware, for giving her encouragement and assistance and to Mr. Washington Irving, of Providence, Rhode Island, for granting permission on behalf of the heirs of Washington Irving to publish parts of the journals and notebooks first printed in this edition. They wish to thank the many libraries that have so generously allowed the manuscript journals in their collections to be consulted and photographed for use in this edition. Particularly, the editors wish to express their collective thanks to The New York Public Library, Astor, Lenox and Tilden Foundations, and to Mr. James W. Henderson, Chief of The Research Libraries, and Mr. Robert W. Hill, Keeper of Manuscripts, for their generous aid and many courtesies.

The editors of the journals collectively are indebted to the prior work of George S. Hellman, Pierre M. Irving, John F. McDermott, Andrew B. Myers, Clara L. Penny, Barbara S. Simison, William P. Trent, and particularly Stanley T. Williams.

The American Philosophical Society provided the original grant for making the inventory of Irving manuscripts, without which the edition of the journals could hardly have been undertaken. Sleepy Hollow Restorations, whose continuing interest in the Irving edition equals that of the editors themselves, has been helpful in many ways. The Center for Editions of American Authors of the Modern Language Association, through its grant from the National Endowment for the Humanities (National Foundation on the Arts and Humanities), furnished funds for research assistance, travel, and free working time for the editors of the several volumes.

The editor of this first volume of the journals wishes to express her appreciation for permission to consult and make use of Irving journal and notebook manuscripts in their collections to Yale University Library, Fordham University Library, and The New York Public Library.

For kind assistance in transcribing the manuscript the editor wishes to thank the following persons: Professor James F. Beard, of Clark University; Professor Michael Black, of the City College of the City of New York; the late Dr. John Gordan, Curator of The Berg Collection, The New York Public Library; Professor Herbert Kleinfield, of C. W. Post College; Professor Andrew Myers, of Fordham University; and Professor Henry A. Pochmann, of the University of Wisconsin.

The editor also wishes to thank the following persons for kind assistance in securing information in the notes: Dr. Stefano Alberto Policastro, Prince of Manche-Normandia, of Catania, for information regarding Sicilian places and persons; Miss Anna Ravano, of Genoa, for information regarding Genovese persons and places; Baron Matteo Rapisardi di S. Antonio, of Catania, for information from his family archives; Baron Giuseppe Rapisardi di S. Antonio, of Florence, for information regarding several places in Sicily; E. A. Durand, of Tourves, Department of Var, for information regarding several French towns; Professor Richard Beale Davis, of the University of Tennessee, for information regarding Joseph Carrington Cabell and other Virginians; Professor Ben Harris McClary, of Wesleyan College, Macon, Georgia; Miss Jeannette Fellheimer and Miss Sybil Rosenfeld of London, for information regarding places and persons in England; Mrs. Marjorie Sanders, of the University of Tennessee, for assistance in translating Irving's French; Miss Louise Carson, of Carson-Newman College, and Mr. Anthony W. Shipps, of the University of Colorado, for identification of quotations; the Archivists of Bologna, Brussels, Maastricht, Messina, Milan, Nice, Rotterdam, Toulouse, Zurich, and the Departments of Bouches du Rhône, Gard, Gironde, Haute-Saone, Hérault, Lot and Garonne, and Var in France; the mayors of Béziers, Fano, Fondi, Lucerne, Messina, Parma, Reggio Emilia, Savona, Senigallia, and Terracina; the Curators or Conservators of the Museum Calvet in Avignon, the Kunstmuseum in Basel, and the Musées Royaux de Beaux-Arts de Belgique in Brussels, and the Superintendent of the Galleries of Modena and Reggio Emilia in Modena; the Librarians of the State Archives in Berlin, the Biblioteca Universitaria in Genoa and in Catania, the Biblioteca Comunale Laudense Museo Civico in Lodi, the City of Westminster in London, the Biblioteca Ambrosiana in Milan, the State Library in Vienna, the Public Libraries of Canajoharie, Herkimer, Little Falls, Rome, and Utica in New York, and the New York Public Library Theatre Collection; the Curator, Director, Librarian or Secretary of the Grenville County (Ontario) Historical Society, the Massachusetts Historical Society, the New-York Historical Society, and the Schenectady County Historical Society, the Custodian of the Harvard University Archives, and the Curator of Manuscripts of the Virginia Historical Society; the Administrator of the Mensa Arcivescovile, Milan; the Chiefs of the Diplomatic, Legal, and Fiscal and of the Army and Navy Branches of the National Archives; the Manager of the Tourist Information Department, Touring Club Italiano, Milan; and the Vice Consul of the United States Information Service, Naples.

N.W.

University of Tennessee
July 1967

CONTENTS

ILLUSTRATIONS

Figures 1 and 46 are reproduced by permission of the Fordham University Library. Figures 2–4, 6–45, 47, 49, and 50 are reproduced by permission of The New York Public Library, Astor, Lenox and Tilden Foundations. Figures 5 and 48 are reproduced by permission of the Yale Collection of American Literature, The Beinke Rare Book and Manuscript Library, Yale University.

GENERAL INTRODUCTION TO JOURNALS

This edition of Irving's journals and notebooks is planned to appear in five volumes of *The Complete Works of Washington Irving* sponsored by the Center for Editions of American Authors. The journals begin in 1803, Irving's twentieth year, and continue at irregular intervals through his life until 1842. Perhaps the most striking fact about them, besides their intermittent and often fragmentary nature, is their distribution. Most of the journals were written while Irving was traveling. Indeed, he made no journey of any length (on land) of which he did not keep a record, a noteworthy fact, inasmuch as he seemed to need, as a professional writer, a frequent change of scene.

It is also significant that most of Irving's journals were written while he was abroad – a total of twenty-two and a half years. Except for the youthful New York Journal of 1803 and the Western Journal, he apparently kept none during his thirty-two adult years in America: 1806–1815, 1832–1842, 1846–1859. The subject matter of his printed books is correspondingly divided. He wrote only some half dozen books entirely about his native land. The first American writer after the Revolution to come into extended contact with European culture, he did not seem to be consciously a discoverer of that culture. His European journals lack the penetrating analysis of American and European character and also the tension of a strong attraction to, and repulsion by, Europe found in the travel books of Cooper and James and in the European notebooks of Hawthorne. Nor, unlike these authors, did Irving write anything resembling an international novel, in which Americans, confronted with European experience, emerge both losers and gainers. He did, however, in both his journals and his printed works, draw the main outlines of the Old World scene – picturesque, often dangerous, and legendary – whereon in later American literature representatives of the New World repeatedly enact dramas of self-discovery.

About half the original manuscript volumes are journals and notebooks that contain some account of Irving's daily activities; the others are collections of miscellaneous notes, including expense accounts, excerpts from other authors, anecdotes, observations, and reminiscences.

Although the journals and several of the notebooks have more biographical than literary value, their relationship to his other writing is nevertheless significant.

The known dates covered by these volumes are 1803–1806, 1810, 1815, 1817–1833, 1835, and 1840–1843: about half the mature period of Irving's seventy-six year life. The longest sequence of journals covers seven years – from August 1822 to August 1829 – which Irving spent mostly in France, Germany, and Spain (where he served for two and a half years as a member of the American Legation). Next in length comes his account of his first European journey, from July 1804 to about January 1806. The remaining journals represent trips of a few months at most: that which he took as a young man in New York State in 1803, his tour in Wales in 1815, his tour in Scotland in 1817, his trip through the American West in 1832, and his travels from New York to Bayonne in 1842. About a third of the miscellaneous notebooks belong to the period 1817–1823, when he was emerging as a professional writer – the author of *The Sketch Book* and *Bracebridge Hall.* About the same number cannot be dated with certainty.

Washington Irving's nephew, Pierre Munro Irving, notes in the Preface to his *Life and Letters of Washington Irving* (1862) that his uncle "placed in my possession a mass of material, consisting of journals, note-books, diaries at scattered intervals. . . ." It was in the nephew's book that use was first made of the journals and notebooks. The four-volume biography, appearing two decades and more before Irving's literary compeers became the subjects of "official" or "authorized" biographers, in a manner set tone and scope for the others to follow.

But being first in any field often incurs its own drawbacks. Although Pierre M. Irving quoted at some length from his uncle's journals and letters, their separate collection lagged far behind most of the others, presumably on the assumption that the samplings which the official biography provided were sufficient. And so they were until the demands of twentieth-century scholarship encouraged a first generation of serious Irving scholars to supply some of the more significant lacunae in Irving's notebooks and journals.[1]

1. To be enumerated are the following (in chronological order):
Journal, 1803, by Washington Irving, ed. Stanley T. Williams, New York, 1934.
Notes and Journal of Travel in Europe, 1804–1805, by Washington Irving, ed.

Good as they are, they followed varying standards and methods of transcription and editing, besides leaving a considerable gap of some two dozen separate manuscript volumes of miscellaneous journal material. This anomalous situation a half-dozen students of Irving set themselves to rectify when, at an informal meeting during the 1959 sessions of the Modern Language Association, they projected a complete and accurate edition of Irving's journals and letters, to be prepared in accord with modern editorial standards. When the Center for Editions of American Authors was formed, the project was included in the editions sponsored by the Center. The editors' intention has been to produce a text as close as possible to what Irving actually wrote, including his cancellations, insertions, and eccentric variations upon standard spelling, punctuation, and capitalization.

It goes without saying that in adopting the "Editorial Principles" as defined by the Center, the reticences, scruples, and restrictions under which the nineteenth-century editor labored are removed. Pierre M. Irving's constraints to present an image of his uncle in accord with the genteel tradition then in the making and the compulsion under which he felt himself to tidy up the portrait by making judicious deletions, even erasures, and to present an unblemished picture no longer obtain.

William P. Trent. 5 vols. New York, 1921.

Stanley T. Williams, "Washington Irving's First Stay in Paris, [1805]," *American Literature*, II (March 1930), 15–20.

Barbara D. Simison, "Washington Irving's Notebook of 1810," *Yale University Library Gazette*, XXIV (1949), 1–16, 74–94.

The Journals of Washington Irving, from July, 1815, to July, 1842, ed. William P. Trent and George S. Hellman. 5 vols. Boston, 1919.

Notes While Preparing Sketch Book, &c. . . . 1817, by Washington Irving, ed. Stanley T. Williams. New Haven, 1927.

Tour in Scotland, 1817, and Other Manuscript Notes by Washington Irving, ed. Stanley T. Williams. New Haven, 1927.

Journal of Washington Irving, 1823–1824, ed. Stanley T. Williams. Cambridge, 1931.

Myers, Andrew B., "Washington Irving's Madrid Journal, 1827–1828, and Related Letters," *Bulletin of the New York Public Library*, LXII (1958), 217–27, 300–311, 407–19, 463–71.

Journal of Washington Irving, 1828, and Miscellaneous Notes on Moorish Legend and History, ed. Stanley T. Williams. New York, 1937.

Washington Irving Diary: Spain, 1828–1829, ed. Clara L. Penny. New York, 1926.

The Western Journals of Washington Irving [1832–1833], ed. John F. McDermott. Norman, Okla., 1944.

Brief portions of other journals and notebooks were quoted by Stanley T. Williams in his *The Life of Washington Irving*. 2 vols. New York, 1935.

The Irving that appears from a reproduction of the journals as he wrote them presents a far more engaging personality, subject, to be sure, to the common human frailties but also with many admirable traits, alternately succeeding and failing in rising to the occasions that presented themselves. The gaps now first filled in, in so far as the extant manuscripts permit, round out the picture with a wealth of interesting and meaningful detail that presents a better understanding of the man and eventually a sounder interpretation and appraisal of his voluminous writings.

MANUSCRIPTS

Irving's known manuscript journals, travel notes upon which the journals are based, and related miscellaneous notebooks are approximately eighty in number. More than half of them are in the collections of the New York Public Library. Four of these are in the Berg Collection; others are in the Seligman Collection. Those in the Seligman Collection were acquired by Isaac Seligman from Irving Van Wart, a grandnephew of the author. Mr. Seligman, who lived in Tarrytown on the Hudson and for many years owned an estate adjoining Irving's "Sunnyside," had collected Irvingiana all his life and assembled the largest collection of manuscripts, letters, and journals. Named for him, the "Seligman Collection of Irvingiana" was given to the New York Public Library in 1925 by his widow. Her nephew, George S. Hellman, enhanced the collection by adding his own holdings.

The rest of the manuscript volumes are in the Folger Shakespeare Library, Sleepy Hollow Restorations, and the libraries of Fordham University, Harvard University, the Hispanic Society of America, St. John's Seminary in Camarillo, California, the University of Virginia, Washington University in St. Louis, Missouri, and Yale University. Two are unlocated.

The manuscript volumes are relatively small and of various types and sizes. Irving bought the notebooks in which he wrote as he needed them, usually while he was traveling, and thus they are of a size to be conveniently carried, though not uniform. Their subsequent fate has varied, some having been bound by later owners and others remaining in their original covers. Except for the inevitable smudging of penciled passages, they are in a fairly good state of preservation.

EDITORIAL PLAN

Difficult as it is to transcribe even a carefully written manuscript, Irving's handwritten journals present problems that make the attempt impossible. While the editors have made every effort to record what Irving wrote, the condition of some manuscript pages and Irving's careless and eccentric composition produce so many problems which the eye cannot resolve that the only solution is to adopt a set of ground rules, the chief of which is that when a word, character, spacing, construction, or mark of punctuation is debatable, presenting equally defensible alternatives, Irving is given the benefit of the doubt, and the reading is made to conform to normal or accepted usage. In short, the aim has been to provide a reliable text, short of an absolutely literal transcription, which is manifestly impossible, as the sequel will demonstrate.

It does not follow that Irving's errors and inconsistencies are eliminated. Indeed, the aim of the editors, which is to present Irving as faithfully as possible, precludes this possibility. To correct Irving's miscues and normalize his idiosyncrasies would result in a very un-Irvingesque product. The two primary objectives of the editors – fidelity to Irving's text and utility for the reader – are constant but not always compatible aims.

The basic transcription was made from xerox and photostatic copy of the original manuscripts and collated with printed versions where they exist. It was then checked against the original manuscript by the editor and finally by a "new eye" reader. In the meantime it was read against photocopy by the editor, by the managing editor, and by the general editor. Cruces were studied by magnifying devices – not always with gratifying results, except for the reassurance that no available methods or resources were skirted in the effort to retrieve what must be put down as irrecoverable passages. Proofs were read in accord with the specifications of the Center for Editions of American Authors.

Irving's spelling and punctuation are alike arbitrary and erratic. His acquisition, or near-acquisition, of languages (Latin, Dutch, Italian, German, French, and Spanish), far from making him an accomplished speller or linguist, seems merely to have compounded his natural ineptitude. Some of his coinages are novel, as when he used the variants "smoak," smocke," and "schmoke" for "smoke," even after he had become a popular three-book author of international renown. And his method of punctuation (although it seldom leads to positive misconstruction or misreading) was no less idiosyncratic. Generally he was chary in his use of pointing in the journals, but usually (though not always) he left an extra space where ordinarily a comma or some other mark of punctuation would be used to indicate a pause or break. Because of the manifest impossibility of reproducing in print these spaces of varying length, necessary and appropriate marks of punctuation are supplied according to methods detailed below.

Accidentally longer-than-usual spaces between words and between conventionally pointed sentences are not noted, and lines toward the right-hand margin (only rarely toward the left) that Irving left unfilled are also ignored when they have no special significance. On the other hand, spaces left by Irving for names or other information not in hand at the time of writing are indicated by "[*blank*]." These occur chiefly in lists of names of persons whom Irving met on social occasions. No attempt is made to reproduce Irving's irregular spacings between paragraphs, unless the space has a special significance, e.g., to indicate a change of subject matter or to begin a new sequence.

Paragraph indentations are often hard to identify in a wavering left-hand margin, and conversely, the lines on the right side of the page are not consistently filled out. An unfilled line often indicates a sentence end, with or without punctuation. When it does, it is treated according to the method indicated below for terminal punctuation. Occasionally Irving wrote without paragraphing at all. Where the degree of indentation is less than normal, the indentation is observed in accord with the demands of the context, but no indentation is arbitrarily made, i.e., without some justification supplied by the text, except that every new entry following a dateline begins a new line and is indented.

Irving frequently used no pointing at the end of a sentence (particularly when the end of the sentence coincided with the end of the line), and when he did he was as likely to use a dash as a period. This is especially true of portions of the journals that were written on the spot or during brief rest periods while traveling, and with no view to publication, but merely to record his peregrinations, experiences, or daily occupations, so that a kind of telegraphic style sufficed. But even in the journals, or parts of them, that show evidence of having been copied from day-to-day jottings and apparently designed for possible use later, irregularities of punctuation, capitalization, and general orthography are hardly less marked. Usually passages in ink are more legible than those in pencil, but the scrawls of his pen often create problems no less confusing than the smudges of his pencil. Show-throughs of ink from one side of the sheet complicate readings on the other side, and the mirror image made on one page by folding the sheets or closing the journal before the ink on the opposite page had dried interferes with legibility.

The most frustrating part of transcribing Irving's handwriting stems from his whimsical and indiscriminate use of capital and lower-case letters, as much for common as for proper nouns, and occasionally for other parts of speech as well, so that the old-fashioned custom of capitalizing nouns does not explain Irving's peculiar use of capitals. His capital and lower-case formations of letters, particularly "a," "c," "g," "m," "n," "o," "s," "v," and "w" (and occasionally "d," "l," and "t") are often indistinguishable. Their size in relation to following or preceding comparable letters is seldom a clear index to whether a capital or lower-case form is intended, although the initial capitals "B," "F," "H," "I," "J," "K," and "Q," are seldom left in doubt. The conformation of the letter is often more helpful, but in letters like "a," "c," "m," "n," "o," "s," and "r," it is of little use because the formation of lower-case and capital letters is often nearly identical. Place names appear in varying forms, occasionally in successive lines and often on the same page. "Peter," "Paris," "French," and "Italian" are as likely to be lower-case as not. The initial "o" in "o'clock" (almost always without the apostrophe) appears in from pigmy to giant size and usually in the same conformation; whereas "Evg" occurs regularly and becomes routine form regardless of its location in the sentence. The initial flourish with which a capital is likely to begin is an unreliable index, for when it is used (especially in such a letter as "s"), it is used in varying forms – some long, some short, most of them in-between. It is the in-between cases, where the eye cannot decide, that the doubtful cases are resolved in Irving's favor, and the form that usage dictates is rendered. That is, doubtful words that are customarily capitalized are so transcribed, the only exception being those cases in which the letter is clearly a lower-case form – judged so by its distinctive conformation and by comparison with adjacent and comparable characters. In converse cases, where Irving seems to use capitals for normally lower-case words, he is given the benefit of the doubt by transcribing as capital only those letters which are clearly so – all intermediate forms being rendered lower-case.[2]

2. That is, in cases where the confirmation of the letter in question is not significantly distinctive, and when the context indicates a lower-case form, the letter is rendered lower case *unless* it clearly rises as high as, or higher than, the high-rise

In short, Irving's intention, where it can be ascertained, is honored, the exceptions being the instance where his presumed intention (or execution) leaves a doubt – i.e., a clear alternative. In these, Irving is given the benefit of the doubt.

Irving's terminal punctuation, however erratic, as in his frequent use of a dash for a period, is respected. His sentence endings and beginnings are rendered as he wrote them, whether with or without period (or dash) if the succeeding sentence in the same paragraph begins with a capital letter. When the following sentence begins with a small letter, preceded by a period (or dash), it is so rendered. Only when it begins with a small letter and Irving failed to supply a period (or dash) is a bracketed period (sometimes a semicolon) added. No missing punctuation is added at the end of a paragraph.

Similarly, his internal punctuation is respected wherever possible; any necessary marks of punctuation added or changed for clarity are bracketed or footnoted (usually the former). When doubt exists among his uses internally of commas, semicolons, dashes, and periods, Irving is given the benefit of the doubt, the questionable marks being rendered in accord with the demands of the context. If, as is true in a few instances, Irving used a period for a comma or a comma for a period, and the error is corrected, it is noted.

Irving's peculiarities in pointing abbreviations are preserved (for example, "IE" instead of "i.e."), the only exceptions being made in the interest of clarity. In such cases, changes are indicated by brackets or noted. Similarly, Irving's apostrophes for contractions and possessives are reproduced, but they are not added when he omitted them (as he usually did), except in a few instances where the missing apostrophe or the missing letters are necessary for intelligibility. In such cases, they

---

letters in the word. Conversely, if the context calls for a capital, and the letter rises only slightly above adjacent low-rise letters, it is capitalized; it need not reach the height of the high-rise letters. A procedure or decision based on anything short of such measurable differences introduces a new body of inconsistencies and a maze of contradictory and indefensible readings. Even the strictest application of the benefit-of-the-doubt principle within the limits indicated does not obviate Irving's inconsistencies, and is not intended to; but it removes many discrepancies while introducing a minimum of new ones. That is to say, by playing the odds, as it were, some of the guesswork is eliminated, the odds being that more readings will be right than wrong. Given the circumstances and conditions under which the editor labors, this is the most that he can expect. The alternative, which is to make subjective judgments on the basis of variable criteria, would inevitably increase the incidence of error.

are bracketed or noted (usually the former). Participial forms ending in "ed" but often written by Irving without the "e" (and without either an apostrophe indicating the elision or a period denoting an abbreviation) are rendered as he wrote them, – i.e., "servd", rather than "serv'd" or "servd." or "serv[e]d". His colons following abbreviations (usually in connection with titles of books), where modern practice employs periods, are transcribed as written.

Superscript letters (usually in connection with abbreviations) are lowered to the line (except in datelines, where they are silently deleted, according to the principle explained below). When Irving supplied a period after a superscript, the period is preserved, but ordinarily he wrote superscripts without a following period, occasionally using a dash after the superscript to serve the purpose. Underscorings of superscripts (sometimes one, two, or three dots), infrequently and inconsistently used by Irving, are disregarded as mannerisms of no import beyond indicating an abbreviation. Accordingly his intention is honored by silently rendering all such dashes, dots, and underscorings as periods. Thus "M^{r-}", "M$^{\underline{r}}$", "M$^{\underline{\underline{r}}}$", and "M$^{\underset{..}{r}}$" alike become "Mr.", but "M^{r}" (without a period or any of the preceding eccentric additions) is rendered "Mr" (without a period). In rare cases, where difficulty in reading or misreading is likely to occur, missing letters are supplied in brackets.

Datelines are regularized, i.e., uniformly printed flush with the left margin, on separate lines, italicized, with superscripts and end punctuation silently omitted. The essentials are month and day: either or both, when missing and ascertainable, are silently added; if conjectural, they are footnoted. Where Irving supplied, as he sometimes did, the place, such notations as "En route" or "At home" or "Midnight," the name of a special day, and the day of the week, in addition to the month, the date, and the year, the rendition might be "Dresden, At home, Christmas, Wednesday, December 25, 1822" (in this order, regardless of Irving's order), but normally the month and day are deemed sufficient. Place and date appear in the running head. Irving placed the date variously to the left, the right, sometimes in the center, and even within the paragraph, wherever it happened to fall. Often he gave the day of the month only, and sometimes the day of the week only. Regularizing this erratic procedure involves some loss of Irvingesque flavor, but there remains enough of it elsewhere. Moreover, datelines are primarily for convenience in reading and for reference, so that clarity, economy, and uniformity are to be preferred over Irving's eccentricities of form, however quaint. Irving's errors in dates are corrected and noted, but cancellations or corrections that Irving himself made are not noted unless they are especially significant.

Parentheses, dashes, and quotation marks missing from intended pairs are added in brackets. Irving's quotation marks at the beginning of successive lines of a quoted passage are dropped. Missing question marks are added (in brackets) only when their omission would result in misreading.

Carets, which Irving used sometimes to indicate inserted matter, are omitted in favor of the editorial symbols of arrows for the purpose (see list of symbols below), and his use of the long "f" form of "s," usually when the consonant is doubled, is not reproduced.

On the other hand, the ampersand and Arabic numbers are retained wherever Irving used them. The former is used not only for "and" but also in the form of "&c" to indicate *et cetera.* Disjointed writing or the running together of words ("ever thing" and "forgetmenots") are rendered faithfully. His occasional use of the apostrophe with the final "s" to designate a plural is reproduced. Irving seldom used hyphens (almost never at the end of a line, but sometimes at the beginning of the next line), apparently preferring to start anew on the next line rather than carry over part of a word. The same peculiarity obtains in his placement of dashes. Both are treated as if Irving had placed them conventionally.

The care with which the transcription was made and checked repeatedly by four editors justifies the assumption that the printed text attempts to reproduce the original manuscript, eccentricities and absurdities included. In the interest of unencumbered text, missing letters are ordinarily not added and bracketed, and transposed letters are not rectified or noted, unless misreading would result – in which case additions or corrections are made and footnoted. "[*Sic*]" is not used. Certain misspellings occur so frequently as to become routine and not worth noting especially. Similarly, personal names of passing acquaintances, but also of friends and long-time associates, vary from page to page without any consistency. Wherever the correct spelling could be ascertained, it is given in the note of identification and is also found in the index (in the correct form only).

Erasures and significant cancellations (where recoverable) are included in angle brackets. Unrecovered cancellations are marked "<*unrecovered*>" ("<*illegible*>" only when hopelessly irrecoverable).

Some of the cancellations may have been made by someone other than Irving, probably his nephew Pierre M. Irving, in the interest of what he considered propriety. When one or more letters are canceled or written over, the substitution appears immediately after the canceled matter, without an intervening space: for example, "the<ir>re" and "2<7>8." Cancellations which are identical with the substitution, canceled fragments of letters which are illegible, mere slips of the pen, and meaningless false starts (which often occur at the ends of lines and indicate merely that Irving ran out of space and elected to start anew on the next line) are not reproduced. There are many cancellations of these kinds, even in the journals which Irving seems to have written with great care and with more than usual leisure.

A few relatively short passages that are transcribed from printed sources because the original manuscript has disappeared are footnoted.

Numerous marks in the margins and at the beginning and end of passages (often in pencil) – crosses, x's, checks, arrows, vertical and horizontal lines, parentheses, and slashes – are not reproduced, unless they are demonstrably Irving's, as they are in a few cases. Most of them were made by someone other than Irving – presumably earlier owners or editors of the manuscripts, notably Pierre M. Irving, while preparing his uncle's biography. On the other hand, all underlinings presumably Irving's are reproduced as italics.

Vertical rules in tables and lists, as well as meaningless series of dots and dashes, are not reproduced, but the spacings they are designed to indicate are observed.

Whenever possible, proper names are annotated and spelled correctly in the notes. Quotations, allusions, and literary or historical references are identified wherever possible.

Cross references are indicated by date, and should be understood to include both text and relevant notes.

Irving's infrequent footnotes, usually at the bottom of the manuscript page, are printed at the bottom of the page in the same type size as the text, rather than in the smaller type of the editorial notes.

Quotations of poetry in the text are printed in reduced type size when they are known to be from other authors. Irving's own verse is printed in the same type as the text. Quotations are presumed to be Irving's unless otherwise identified.

Catchwords, which occur at irregular or long intervals on a few pages, are not reproduced.

Irving's drawings – on-the-spot sketches of interesting landscapes, unusual architecture, or the quaint and picturesque costumes of country folk – are all noted on the pages where they occur and are reproduced in the pages of illustrations.

Irving did not number the pages of his journals and notebooks, and no systematic numbering has been attempted. The page number is occasionally given, however, for the purpose of locating drawings or miscellaneous notations which are not clearly part of a chronological series of entries. These occur with fair frequency on the covers (inside and outside) and on the end pages of journals. Double-enders (that is, journals written from front to back and then turned around, or up-ended, and written from back to front) are noted, and notes are given to mark where the order was reversed and in some cases resumed.

Irving himself gave titles to only a few of his journals. As an aid to reference the editors have supplied short identifying titles for every journal and notebook. Irving's own titles, when they exist, are printed as part of the text.

INTRODUCTION TO VOLUME I

The journals and notebooks which comprise this volume of the present edition are the first set of the continuing accounts of Irving's activities, and, after "The Letters of Jonathan Oldstyle, Gent." (1802–1803), they are the earliest examples of his writing. Compared to his later journals, these are conspicuous for their length, their use of complete sentences, and their frequent stylistic revisions. They represent not only the opening chapters of his own record of his life, but also the virtual beginning of his career as a writer.

These journals and notebooks cover the events of two trips: one in New York State in 1803 and one in Europe from 1804 to 1806.

NEW YORK JOURNAL, 1803

Irving's first journal records his trip from New York City to Oswegatchie (Ogdensburg), New York, from July 30 to August 30, 1803, in his twentieth year. It was the first long journey he had made. He traveled with the party of J. O. Hoffman, the distinguished New York lawyer in whose office he was reading law and in whose family he was an intimate, and T. L. Ogden, also a prominent New York lawyer, who was Hoffman's first cousin. Hoffman and Ogden had undertaken the journey to inspect their properties in St. Lawrence County, in the western part of the state, and to talk with representatives of the Northwest Fur Company in Montreal, the center of the eastern American fur trade. The other members of the party were Mrs. Hoffman, her stepdaughter Ann, Mrs. Ogden, Eliza Ogden (apparently a cousin of T. L. Ogden's), and, for part of the way, Stephen van Rensselaer of Albany (who went as far as that city), the Englishman Thomas Brandram, and a Mr. Reedy, who seem to have gone as far as Utica. Irving accompanied the Hoffmans and the Ogdens all the way to Montreal and back to New York, but he apparently kept no account of the trip after Oswegatchie.

On the first part of their trip the travelers sailed up the Hudson from New York to Albany, took the stage from Albany to Utica, and from there went by wagon through virtually uninhabited country to Oswegatchie. The wilderness area through which they traveled had been open to settlement for only a few years, and for the last part of their journey they took the first road to be opened north of the Black River, which had first been used only in 1801. After Utica their route took them almost due north, passing through or near the present-day towns of Lowville, Carthage, Antwerp, Heuvelton, and Lisbon to Ogdensburg.

Slight though it is, Irving's first journal merits attention on several counts. It reveals his instinct for recording his experiences while traveling and his enthusiastic response to new scenes and circumstances. An inveterate traveler as it turned out, he was from the beginning a good one. He enjoyed the appurtenances of the road – inns, hosts, local customs and characters (such as the Revolutionary veteran Sammons) – and he took in his stride difficulties of transportation and poor accommodations (like those at the "Temple of Dirt"). He had an eye for scenic prospects, and for all his urbanity, he was excited by physical adventures or the prospect of them: he promptly joined in the pursuit of the doe in the Black River and prepared to protect Ann Hoffman from the rowdy Sharps.

More than any other aspect of traveling, however, Irving enjoyed the companionship of congenial fellow-travelers and whatever social activities the route afforded (on this occasion chiefly the dancing at Ballston Springs). He was, in fact, on his own evidence, a light-hearted and convivial young man, and so he appeared in character during most of his life. The meagerness of his entries at Oswegatchie, Madrid, and Lisbon suggests that the lack of novelty at this point in the expedition left him without incentive to write. His failure to make any entries thereafter may well represent his characteristically spasmodic prosecution of enterprises.

Irving's first journal also reflects his literary inclination. His quotation from Cowper, allusion to Will Boniface, and record of his reading Shakespeare aloud to the ladies are indications of a modest acquaintance with books. His style foreshadows his later writing: general fluency, with particular tendencies toward a pictorial technique in describing landscapes and toward low-keyed satire of pretense and pomposity (such as that exhibited by the clowning Brandram in selecting a cheese). Though his revisions are slight, they indicate that he was conscious of how he was expressing himself.

The subject matter of two groups of entries connects them more particularly with Irving's later writing: the entries referring to his brief stay at Ballston Springs, which is the setting of "Style at Ballston" in *Salmagundi* (1807–1808); and the entries describing the party's route through the backwoods from Utica to Oswegatchie. He did not revisit the American frontier until 1832, when he again traveled to western New York and through several midwestern states; his three books dealing with western America – *A Tour on the Prairies* (1835), *Astoria* (1836), and *The Adventures of Captain Bonneville, U.S.A.* (1837) – were immediately inspired by that later trip. Nevertheless, in the Preface to *Astoria* he noted his own interest in the activities of the great fur companies and of the trappers and traders in "the wild parts" of the continent – "Sinbads of the wilderness" he called them – ever since he had visited Montreal in 1803. Indeed, the germ of all three of these books may be found in his journal account of his first venture, on his way to Montreal, into that wilderness.

EUROPEAN JOURNAL AND NOTES, 1804–1806

The second trip covered by this volume of Irving's journals and notebooks is that which he took in Europe from the summer of 1804 to early 1806, during his twenty-first to his twenty-third year. It is recorded in eight manuscript volumes. Four of these are journals which give his finished account of that trip, from his arrival in Bordeaux to his arrival in London, except for three weeks in Sicily and his stay in Paris. The other four manuscripts consist of two notebooks of sketchy records and expense accounts of his travel from Bordeaux to Genoa, from there to Rome, and on to Altorf; nine loose pages of brief entries made during the first of his four months in Paris; and a notebook containing chiefly expense accounts and a few other brief and fragmentary records of his three months in England and his voyage to New York. Another notebook, containing a record of his trip from Basel to Paris (May 19–24, 1805), stay in Paris, and travel to London (including a section headed "Voyage to England"), some expense accounts, and a reading list (apparently comparable in form to his "Traveling Notes" and its companion notebook) has not been located.[1]

1. In 1936 it was in the possession of William F. Clarke of Scarsdale, N.Y. Passages from it are quoted in PMI, I, 151, and STW, I, 67, 68.

Much of Irving's record of his European trip was written in two versions: the longer journals and the briefer notebooks. When staying one night, or only a short time in one place, he customarily made brief penciled entries, punctuated mostly by dashes, in small manuscript volumes. At places where he stayed for a day or longer he drew on these to make in larger volumes longer, inked entries, with sentences properly constructed, more conventionally punctuated, and frequently revised. Many of his entries in these journals were written in conjunction with letters. When in Naples he began the longer version of his journey to Sicily, but it was never finished; for the period February 12–March 7, 1805, there are only the brief notebooks. Apparently he never attempted to include his stays in Paris and London in his finished account. Even so, the four volumes of this account are the most nearly unified and deliberately written of all his journals.

Irving was now consciously a good traveler, congratulating himself that his north-woods experience of 1803 had seasoned him and boasting that he would not be a Smellfungus like Smollett. He was interested not only in the various accommodations which he found, local customs and characters, and the changing scene, but also the celebrated sights and the buildings and costumes peculiar to Europe.

He was not, however, an altogether systematic traveler. He followed the general route of the Grand Tour, through Italy and north to England, as apparently his brothers wanted him to do, but he adapted his itinerary at various points to his personal pleasure. The longest stops he made (except the month he waited for a proper passport in Nice and the three weeks he was in quarantine in the harbor of Messina) were four months in Paris, three in London, two in Genoa, and one in Bordeaux. The great variety of entertainment in the first two of these cities, the congenial company he found in the third (his friend T. H. Storm, the English Mrs. James Bird and her daughters, and members of the English, French, and Italian nobility), and his pleasant living arrangements in the fourth undoubtedly influenced him to remain so long. He lingered in Marseilles nearly three weeks probably because of the theater and the company of two of his countrymen there, and he cut his visit in Rome to the same length in order to travel north with another, J. C. Cabell. His stay of two weeks in Naples, where he went about with Cabell and Colonel John Mercer, was justified by the number of sights in the area, but his nine days in Syracuse and week in Catania were somewhat more than necessary to see these cities; in both.

his social activity was as extensive as his sight-seeing. Otherwise he stayed only a few days in any one place.

The principal cities which he by-passed – with no noticeable regret – were Florence, which he later said was shut off from travelers with the rest of Tuscany because of a fever in the region, and Venice, which was not on the route he took north, apparently following Cabell's lead. The most unusual portion of his tour was that in Sicily, which lasted some two months; he was among the first Americans to visit that island, the very first apparently to write an account of his travels there.

In his account of all these European travels Irving bestowed most care on his descriptions of the landscape, which he said, in describing an evening in the harbor of Messina, gave him his greatest pleasures. Inspired both by cultivated scenes such as those along the Garonne and the Canal du Midi in southern France, and wild ones like those in the Swiss Alps, he tended to appraise them all by the single criterion of diversity or variety. He had a pronounced taste, however, for what he called the "romantic" and the "picturesque." He continually picked out castles and solitary buildings on hills, which he frequently described in these terms though seldom called by name. He often paused before a prospect in the half-light of early morning and evening, and often listened to vesper bells and hymns. Indeed, the typical Irving landscape, with its softened outlines, faint sounds, and meditative atmosphere, which did not appear in print until *The Sketch Book* (1819–1820), emerges repeatedly in his first European journal.

Irving also devoted a good deal of his European journal to descriptions of cities, particular buildings, and works of art, and to historical facts about the places which he visited. In many of these passages he followed a well-established tradition among travel writers of borrowing extensively from books (most of which he cited) by other travelers and by a few historians: chiefly travelers Tobias Smollett in France, Patrick Brydone and Henry Swinburne in Sicily, Pierre Jean Grosley, John Moore, and Thomas Martyn in Italy, and William Coxe in Switzerland; and historians Pierre Bernardau in Bordeaux and Giuseppe Buonfiglio Costanzo in Sicily. He thus apparently aimed to add a certain weight to his account, perhaps in deference to his brothers' wishes that he should benefit mentally as well as physically from his travels. Yet this desire to please did not drive him to any unusual effort: only in Paris did he make any particular effort to learn the language, and his study of botany there must have been as short-lived as it was out of character. He largely ignored the politics of the emerging empire of Napoleon, except when military maneuvers forced them on his attention.

His interest in tourist attractions was uneven, however, and his care for historical fact imperfect. In his entries in Milan he did not mention Leonardo da Vinci's "Last Supper," and he wrote perfunctory accounts of the ruins in Rome, and even of his ascent of Ætna. Both Bernardau and Buonfiglio Costanzo fell into his hands by accident, and he made highly selective use of them. His knowledge of ancient history and literature was superficial and derived largely from secondary sources. He had, rather, an ear attuned to anecdote, such as the story – false though it was – which he heard about the guillotining of the Baron Valbelle and the true one which he read about the abduction of the Countess Gonzago (neither of whom he properly identified). Legends about the miraculous powers of saints and their relics – "an uncommon bony set of fellows" he called the disciples – afforded him irreverent amusement. He was already, indeed, the Irving who conceived of history as a series of freely borrowed narratives that would provide the reader an escape from the present.

He was most interested, as always, in the people he met. Most of the time he found an agreeable American traveler to join – Dr. Henry in France, Captain John Hall in Sicily, Cabell from Naples to Paris, Thomas Massie and John Gorham from Paris to London – and he eagerly hailed other Americans abroad, particularly T. H. Storm in Genoa and officers of the American fleet at Messina and Syracuse. In such company he attended a good many dances, masquerades, and *conversazioni* in southern Europe. He was equally at home among the nobility of Genoa, Sicily, Naples, and Rome and among members of the lower orders, like Angelina and her family in the mountains above Sestri di Ponente and the Swiss mountaineers; though he appeared blasé, he was obviously curious about the former, and he tended to romanticize the latter. Originals like Dr. Henry, Captain Strong of the ship *Matilda,* and the bandit Giuseppe Musso inspired him to lengthy description. So did the pirates who boarded the *Matilda* off the island of Planosa, giving him his most exciting adventure. But he also produced dozens of vignettes of innkeepers, stage drivers, cicerones, small tradesmen, street performers, petty officials, monks, and pretty girls. He often reported conversations and enlivened his characterizations by quoting (though not always correctly) in other languages, such as the

French of the goiter-afflicted Swiss woman and her daughter Marianne, or in broken English, like that of the Marseilles shoeblacks who called after him and his compatriots, "G<o>d——dam, G——d dam son de bish."

The forty-odd drawings Irving made in the notebooks and journals which comprise this volume reveal his dual interests in the people he met and the romantic aspects of the landscape he saw. There is only one drawing of a rural landscape, and only two of a natural curiosity (the Ear of Dionysus), but there are nine renderings of such scenes as castles and towers and towers within walls. There is one drawing of a waterfront scene and one of a seaport; all the others are of people. With two exceptions (notably a sketch of the group of passengers on the *Remittance* outward bound from London), these are all of individuals: women sitting and reclining, soldiers in uniform, a man with a parrot. The greatest number of these drawings are in the notebooks in which Irving made his brief penciled entries. Obviously most of them were made in haste, but many bring the subject to life (see insert of illustrations for reproductions of the drawings).

The activity which Irving apparently enjoyed most in Europe was attending the theater, of which he had become a devotee in New York. He almost always attended when there was a performance of drama, opera, or ballet in a place where he stopped, even if only for one night, often finding the facilities and the production poor. He was as much interested in the building itself, the staging, and the style of acting. In Paris and London he went almost nightly; only in these cities did he name the pieces which he saw. He complained, especially at first, about the immodesty of French actresses and the artificiality of French acting; and in London he attempted to analyze the technique of the Kembles and others, but succeeded only in giving a personal impression. On the whole, he seemed to regard the theater as a many-sided spectacle, of which the audience was no small part. Thus, with a pen sharpened by satire, he wrote of it in his theatrical contributions to *Salmagundi*.

Irving's European journal also reveals his growing literary consciousness. The quotations and citations are, it is true, from a limited range, chiefly Addison, Beaumont and Fletcher, the Bible, Congreve, Cowper, the Della-Cruscans, Charles Dibdin, Goldsmith, Gray, Nathaniel Lee, James Ogilvie, Ovid, Pope, Mrs. Radcliffe, Shakespeare, Smollett, Spenser, Sterne, Virgil, and Watts. The only one of whom he seemed to have read more than a smattering was Shakespeare; passages from nine of the plays appear. The seven quotations from Addison are all from "A Letter from Italy to the Right Honourable Charles Lord Halifax." He often misquoted, sometimes wrongly ascribed a quotation, and apparently derived most of his classical allusions from travel books. Yet he seemed desirous of giving a literary tone to what he was writing.

Apparently he thought of his European journal itself in relation to publication. Of the letters he sent home at the same time, he wrote his brother Peter, July 7–25, 1804:

> This letter has been written at different times and in different humors . . . . If you find any thing in it, or in any other letters I may write, that you think proper to publish, I beg you will arrange and finish it *handsomely*. It would put a great restraint upon my letter writing if I was obliged to finish every sentence in a manner fit for publication.

The finished nature of much of the writing in his journal, together with its title pages and volume numbers, thus becomes doubly significant. His style, moreover, is decidedly more confident than in his New York journal of 1803. Plans to do anything further with this material, however, languished for many years.

The most obvious literary use which Irving made of the experiences recorded in this European journal – and of the journal itself – was in *Tales of a Traveller* (1824). Though by that time he had traveled in Wales, Scotland, and Germany and further in France, the principal source of the tales was his tour of 1804–1806. The country where he stayed longest at that time – Italy – is the scene of approximately a third of the tales of this volume: the eight which comprise Part III, entitled "The Italian Banditti," and, in Part I, two tales, "The Adventure of the Mysterious Stranger" and "The Story of the Young Italian." "The Adventure of the Mysterious Stranger" is laid in Venice and "The Belated Travellers" somewhere in the Apennines, but the others are laid in cities or specific regions which Irving had visited: five and part of a sixth at or near Terracina, one and part of a second in the mountains above Frascati, and one in Genoa and Naples. Though the tales in "The Italian Banditti" are in the popular romantic banditti or *Räuber* tradition, they owe something as a group to Irving's sight of and sympathy for Musso, his encounter with the *Banditti of the Ocean* on the *Matilda,* and his passage through several bandit-infested regions of southern and central Italy. The detail about the caged head of a murderer in "The

Inn at Terracina" came from his recollection of a similar sight in that town; and the Spanish princess in "The Belated Travellers" who was robbed in the Apennines and later made a pilgrimage to Loreto came from the story of such a robbery which he heard between Foligno and Valcimara, and from his own visit to Loreto. In "The Story of the Young Italian" the villa of Bianca's guardian near Sestri di Ponente and the delightful times Ottavio spent there correspond to the villa of Mrs. Bird and Irving's happy visits to it; and the association of Ottavio with the famous painter in Genoa seems to represent Irving's association with Allston. In this story, too, Irving drew on his journal entries in describing the appearance of Genoa and the wax models of corpses made by the monk near Vesuvius. He also drew on his journal entries in "The Painter's Adventure" for his description of the Roman Campagna.

Irving's European journal is also related, less directly but more significantly, to his first professional publication, *The Sketch Book.* A few distinct echoes of his early journey are detectable in the references to the tranquility of the Atlantic voyage and to the graveyard in Gersau. And although the title, the pseudonym, and the pictorial descriptions of *The Sketch Book* were largely influenced by Irving's association with Allston, C. R. Leslie, and other artists in London in the years immediately preceding its appearance, he drew on memories of his Italian visit of 1805 in his introductory chapter when he compared himself to a landscape painter who had returned from Europe with a sketchbook "crowded with cottages, and landscapes, and obscure ruins," but who had "neglected to paint St. Peter's, or the Coliseum; the Cascade of Terni, or the Bay of Naples; and had not a single glacier or volcano in his whole collection." Actually, not only the type of scenic description in *The Sketch Book* but its whole range of literary genres – reverie, scenic description, character sketch, narrative, historical account – are found in the journal. It might even be said that Irving's criterion of variety or diversity in landscape, first clearly invoked in his description of the European scene in 1804–1805, is in *The Sketch Book* applied to literary composition in such a way as to determine the basic structure of the book. Insofar as *The Alhambra* (1832) is a Spanish sketchbook, though it depends in content on Irving's Spanish travels, in technique it, too, is an outgrowth of his first European journal.

This journal is, finally, a record of Irving's first response to the European scene where he spent many later years and which influenced much of all that he wrote. True, he had not yet visited two of the countries which most affected his writing – Germany and Spain. His later responses, however, were not substantially different from his first. Far from appearing an incipient expatriate, he consorted with Americans at every opportunity, was often homesick, and rejoiced when he reached the southernmost point of his journey at Syracuse and began his return. Like other travelers, he analyzed the national character in the countries which he visited, but in no very penetrating or original way: he was pleased by the politeness yet criticized a superficial gaiety in the French; fumed at the extortion of Italian landlords and servants (whom he dealt with effectually on more than one occasion); warmed to the Swiss because of their love of liberty; exaggerated the Dutch fondness for cleaning and for smoking; took brief umbrage at the indifference of the English but soon appreciated their political liberalism. He was not deeply aroused one way or the other by the spectacle of Roman Catholicism. Nor was he particularly impressed by individual Europeans, even those of literary, artistic, or scientific accomplishment. He often failed to get their names – those of the French explorer J. B. G. M. Bory de Saint Vincent and the Russian painter F. M. Matwejeff, for example – and he misspelled many which he attempted to set down, notably those of Mme. de Staël and the Sicilian naturalist Giuseppe Gioeni. The episode at the inn in Vidauban when, as "an *American Gentleman . . . equal at least* to any engineer general in France," he refused his room to the distinguished scientist J. A. Fabre – though he offered to share it with Mme. Fabre – without troubling to find out who they were, is significant as well as amusing. For all its overtones of Sterne, it affords a glimpse of an early Brother Jonathan, the American innocent abroad with all his confidence, ignorance, and, in practical matters, superiority.

Nevertheless, the Irving who for one reason or another remained out of his country for seventeen years the next time he went abroad, and for four more as minister to Spain, and who dealt with European subject matter in most of his books – this Irving is here. He was by nature, as he himself said, a stroller and a loiterer, and he was often influenced by the actions of others and by chance occurrences. The sources of his inspiration as a writer were in the immediate experience rather than within himself. Had he had a more serious interest in America or in Europe – or in literature – he might have traveled with greater understanding and written with greater depth. As it was, he produced, in effect, a series of sketches inspired by the scene before him, which at their best have all the charm and the suggestive power of that genre.

CHRONOLOGICAL TABLE, 1783–1806

1783: April 3, born in New York City.

1787–1789: attended Mrs. Ann Kilmaster's school.

1789–1797: attended school under Benjamin Romaine.

1797–1798: attended school under Josiah A. Henderson, Jonathan Fiske.

1799–1801: read law in office of Henry Masterton.

1800: summer, visited sisters in Johnstown, N.Y.

1801: summer, read law in office of Brockholst Livingston.

1802–1804: read law in office of J. O. Hoffman.

1802: July, visited sisters in Johnston, N.Y.

1802–1803: November 15–April 23, contributed "Letters of Jonathan Oldstyle, Gent." to the New York *Morning Chronicle.*

1803: July 30–fall?, traveled to Montreal and back in party of J. O. Hoffman, T. L. Ogden, and others.

1804: spring, contributed several comic political sketches or essays to *The Corrector,* edited by his brother Peter.

1804: May 19, sailed from New York for Bordeaux; July 1–August 3, Bordeaux; August 4–October 20, Bordeaux to Genoa (Nice, Sept. 13–Oct. 17); October 20–December 23, Genoa; December 23–January 24, 1805, Genoa to Messina.

1805: January 24–March 5, Sicily; March 6–April 14, Palermo to Naples (Naples, March 7–24) to Rome (Rome, March 27–April 14); April 14–May 24, Rome to Paris; May 24–September 22, Paris; September 22–October 8, Paris to London; October 8–January 17, 1806, London.

1806: January 18, sailed from Gravesend for New York; March 24, arrived in New York.

EDITORIAL SYMBOLS AND ABBREVIATIONS

[roman] Editorial additions

[*italic*] Editorial explanations

< > Restorations of canceled matter

? ? or [?] Doubtful or alternate readings. The former are used within square or angle brackets. The latter is used for a single doubtful word, and appears immediately after the word or character in question, with no intervening space.

unrecovered	Unrecovered word. When more than one word is involved, the fact is indicated ("*three unrecovered words*," or "*two unrecovered lines*").
illegible	Hopelessly unrecoverable word
↑ ↓	Interlinear insertions, above or below the line

Editorial situations not covered by these symbols are explained in the notes.

PMI	Pierre M. Irving, *The Life and Letters of Washington Irving.* 4 vols., New York, 1862–1864.
STW	Stanley T. Williams, *The Life of Washington Irving.* 2 vols., New York, 1935.
WI	Washington Irving.

Other books cited often enough to warrant some form of shorter notation are given full bibliographical identification in the first note in each journal or notebook and short-titled thereafter.

JOURNALS AND NOTEBOOKS

Volume I

NEW YORK JOURNAL, 1803

The manuscript journal is in the Fordham University Library, New York City. It consists of 59 pages, written in brown ink, of a booklet of 168 pages, measuring 7½ × 6¼ inches. The volume was bound in blue morocco in 1899 for Charles Allen Munn, a member of the Grolier Club of New York City. At that time the pages were trimmed slightly, and four leaves were added at the front and two leaves at the back. Pp. [2, 3, 62–168] of the original booklet are blank.

[p. [1] blank except for drawing of a man (Figure 1)][1]

[p. [4], facing first page of journal entries, shows page-size drawing of Ballston Springs][2]

Saturday, July 30, 1803[3]

I sailed from New York for Albany in company with Mr & Mrs. Hoffman. Mr & Mrs Ludlow Ogden Miss Eliza Ogden, Miss Ann Hoffman Mr Brandram & Mr Reedy ↑& Stephen V Rensellaer↓.[4] We sat off

1. A pencil drawing of a man in a long coat and a hat with the notation above it "1780 3 years back."

2. Pasted to p. [4] is an apparently original sepia wash drawing of Ballston Springs by the French landscape painter and engraver Jacques Gerard Milbert (1766–1840). It is signed and the scene identified in English and French, in a hand not Irving's, in brown ink; in a corner of the page, in another hand, in pencil appears "about 1820." Milbert visited Ballston Springs in the summer of 1817, but this drawing is not reproduced in either of his published works on North America. Milbert refers in his *Itinéraire Pittoresque du Fleuve Hudson* . . . (Paris, 1828–1829) to Irving as the author of "The Legend of Sleepy Hollow," but there seems to be no record that they were personally acquainted.

3. Irving wrote "Saturday <August> ↑July↓ 31st. 1803." He continued recording the incorrect day of the month through the entry of Wednesday, August 17 (which he dated August 18). The next entry, that of Friday, August 19 (there is no entry for Thursday), and all the following entries are correctly dated. It is possible that Irving first wrote only the day of the week and later filled in the month and day, since in at least one of the entries – August 7 (written by Irving "Sunday Aug. 8") – the month and day appear to be written with a pen point finer than is used for other writing on the page.

4. The chief members of the party were Josiah Ogden Hoffman (1766–1837), his second wife, the former Maria Fenno (1780–1823), and his daughter Ann (b. 1790) by his first marriage; and Thomas Ludlow Ogden (1773–1844), his wife, the former Martha Hammond, and apparently his cousin, Eliza Ogden (1782–

about 3 Oclock in the after noon and came to anchor in the evening at the enterance of the highlands.

Sunday, July 31[5]

<We> Went ashore with Mr Ogden & Mr Brandram for milk. We found a mean house with a lazy looking fellow seated in the fireplace.

While the woman of the house was <getting the> milking the cows we were entertained by some curious enquiries & speculation of Brandram (who was lately from england.) He declared the man lived in “luxury & disapation” having nothing to do except to work a little on his farm. That he had good milk to drink and rye bread to eat – at the same time Brandram wished he had a *bottle of wine* from on board the sloop that he might cool it in a neighboring spring. As soon as the tide turned we hoisted sail and proceeded through the highlands. The day was delightful. We had a fine view of the magnificent prospects around us and tried the echoes with fowling peices and pistols, at every <?hill?> mountain.

In the afternoon we came to anchor ↑4 miles↓ below Poughkeepsie when Brandram, Stephen Van Rensellaer & myself rowd ashore for milk. We found a tolerable house near the landing. where a Quaker was seated on the stoop <in a ?del?> indulging in a delightful “vacuity of thought[.”][6] we left our bottles here for milk and ascended a long & steep hill in search for Cheese. When we arrived ↑at a house↓ there, Brandram insisted on admission to the dairy to *choose* a cheese <where> and <in the> notwithstanding the profoundness of his

---

1844) (Eugene Augustus Hoffman, *Genealogy of the Hoffman Family,* New York, 1899, pp. 148–49, 205, 277; William Ogden Wheeler, *The Ogden Family in America,* Philadelphia, 1907, pp. 69–70, 189, 110, 111, 213). For other details about them, see above, p. xxvii. Thomas Brandram (1782–1855) was an Englishman, of Lee Grove, Kent, who became a prominent London merchant (E. H. Hart, *History of Lee and its Neighbourhood,* Lee, Kent, England, 1882, pp. 19–23). Reedy was possibly David Reedy of New York, listed in city directories from 1794 to 1801 as an insurance broker; on August 20, 1805, a David Reedy was deeded property in the city by J. O. Hoffman and his wife. Stephen Van Rensselaer (1764–1839), the 8th patroon, occupied the family manor house near Albany. He was co-owner, with J. O. Hoffman, of property in St. Lawrence County, N.Y.

5. Irving wrote “Sunday Aug 1.”

6. William Cowper, *The Task* (1785), IV, ll. 296–98:

> 'Tis thus the understanding takes repose,
> In indolent vacuity of thought,
> And sleeps, and is refreshed.

judgement – he picked out the newest one to the great amusement of the Country people

I then procured a pitcher of cold water and Brandram called for brandy boasting how invaluable & indispensable a liquor it was in this climate. While we sat here enjoying as Brandram called it "Luxury & disappation" a <s>Breeze sprung up and we had to hasten from the house to regain the sloop. When we got on top of the hill a Gun was fired from on board as a signal We then ran down hill full speed and by the time we reached the boat I was quite overcome with fatigue & the cold water I had drank

I exerted my strength however & rowed aboard when I had to go immediately to bed and <was to> felt as if I was almost gone. Owing however to the attentions of my fellow passengers I soon began to recover. Brandram was particuarly busy in shewing the sovreign effects of his "Brandy system" and made me drink a large quantity of his <sovreign> grand specific. It was perhaps owing to this that I soon got over the chills and weakness with which I was seized. but the remedy was a rough one and threw me into a fever for the night.

Monday, August 1[7]

We arrived early this morning at Albany after a passage of about thirty nine hours & put up at the Tontine Coffee house.[8]

I found Mrs Dodge & Sally at Mr Van Vechtens[.] they had lately been at the Springs and intended to remain at Albany for some days and probably take a jaunt to Lebanon.[9]

I saw Bell & Grey at Lewis's. Wetherly & Todd had not yet arrived.[10]

7. Irving wrote "Monday Aug 2."

8. The newest hotel in the city, having been opened in 1798, the Tontine Coffee House was located on State Street and operated at the time by Matthew Gregory (Joel Munsell, *The Annals of Albany,* Albany, 1856, III, 147; IV, 301).

9. Mrs. Dodge was the mother of Richard Dodge whom Irving's oldest sister, Ann Sarah (Sally) Irving (1770–1808), had married in 1788 (STW, II, 254, Table III). They were probably at the home of Abraham Van Vechten (1762–1837), Albany lawyer, at this time state senator and city recorder, and an old friend of J. O. Hoffman. See Hoffman's letter to Van Vechten, October 6, 1796, asking him to take charge of Hoffman's duties at court in Albany since Hoffman could not be present (New York Historical Society). Probably Sally and Mrs. Dodge had been at Ballston Springs and intended to visit Lebanon Springs, another popular watering place southeast of Albany.

10. Bell was possibly William Bell, New York merchant, listed in city directories from 1804 to 1808. A William Bell owned land at this period in Jefferson and Franklin counties (Franklin B. Hough, *A History of Jefferson County in the State of New York,* Albany, 1853, p. 63; Hough, *A History of St. Lawrence and Franklin*

Called on Miss Clinton with a letter from Miss McKnight.[11] but did not find her in I had some conversation with the Governor and Mr Anthony Lamb formerly of New York.[12]

Tuesday, August 2[13]

I sat off with the Ladies for Ballto<w>n Springs[14] Mess[r]s Hoffman & Ogden having agreed to rejoin us at the Springs on Friday. They having for the present to tend court in Albany.

We <went> ↑rode↓[15] along the banks of the Hudson till opposite Troy when we crossed [,] rode thro The flourishing & beautifully situated towns of Troy & Lansingburgh[16] and recrossed at Half Moon point. This is about 10 miles from Albany. While <here som> a light refreshment was preparing we rode to the cohoes[17] about a mile distant. We had only time to view the falls from the Bridge, from whence the scene is high<t>ly picteresque tho the falls seem much more considerable when viewed close by We returned to the house <Where we> and after a light repast set forward on our way to the springs – (about 22 mi distant) where we arrived about half after 6 in the

Counties New York, Albany, 1853, pp. 250–51). Grey was possibly John Gray, New York merchant, listed in city directories from 1803 to 1847/48. A John Gray, broker, appears in directories from 1808 to 1811. "Lewis's" was probably Lewis's Tavern, on State and Pearl Streets, the leading hotel of Albany until the Tontine was built (Munsell, *Annals of Albany,* I, 288, 312). Wetherly was probably a visitor from out of the area since the name does not occur in various lists of New York residents at this period. Todd was possibly William W. Todd of New York, listed in city directories as an accountant from 1803 to 1806 and as a merchant from 1807 to 1811/12.

11. Miss Clinton was presumably one of the daughters of Governor George Clinton (1739–1812), either Elizabeth (1780–1825) or Maria (1785–1829) (Charles B. Moore, "Sketch of the Clinton Family," *The New York Genealogical and Biographical Record,* XIII, 1882, 179). Miss McKnight was possibly a daughter of the Rev. John McKnight, minister of the First Presbyterian Church in New York, 1789–1809 (William B. Sprague, *Annals of the American Pulpit,* New York, 1858, III, 371–75). Irving's baptism is entered in the records of this church, though the ceremony was not performed there (STW, I, 380–81).

12. Anthony Lamb (1771–1855) was a prominent business man of New York and Albany (Munsell, *Annals of Albany,* II, 404; VII, 326; IX, 227). A collection of his papers is in the New York Historical Society.

13. Irving wrote "Tuesday 3d."

14. Ballston Springs.

15. "rode" appears to be in black ink.

16. Since 1901 Lansingburg has been part of the city of Troy.

17. The word "cohoes" is of Indian origin, translated as both "fall of water" and "bend in river"; it refers here to the falls in the Mohawk River where it joins the Hudson. The town at the site is Cohoes.

evening We found Brandram & Reedy already there <they> having sat out some time before <a>us.

Wednesday, August 3[18]

The springs[19] are intollerably stupid owing to the miserable deficiency of female company I took the warm bath this morning and drank the waters which however do not agree with me.

Mr Low[20] is building <an ex> a new house <of> for the accomodation of Boarders[.] it will be very large & on the most commodious style

Our chief amusement was from the queer dress & manners of a Mrs Smith[21] from Boston. This lady is about 55. Some years ago she & her husband began trading in a very small way in Boston, in a little time their obliging & attentive manners & the cheapness of their goods acquired them considerable custom. As their Customers encreased they extended their assortment and having made a handsome fortune they turned their store into a ball room and the upper part into a drawing room decked out in the most gaudy and costly style[.] any young person who wished a ball had but to give them a list of names they would send round invitations & give a supper & ball. They soon attracted the attendance of the fashionable world in Boston who crowded to their entertainments without giving invitations in return. This rage for obliging still continues. Mrs Smith is an original in <look> appearance & manners[.] she dresses <in the> ↑with the↓ most outrageous extravagance. part old & part new fashion In her disposition she is extremely good and possesses an excessive disire to please She will swallow the most barefaced flattery & endeavor to return in kind

18. Irving wrote "Wednesday 4."

19. Irving drew on his visits to Ballston Springs in 1802 and 1803 for his "Style, at Ballston" in *Salmagundi* (1807–1808).

20. Nicholas Low (1739–1826) was a New York merchant and large property owner. He inherited an estate at Ballston Springs, where in 1803 he had built from the Versailles-inspired plans of Andrew Berger, a French political refugee, the elaborate hotel Sans Souci. In 1796 Low, J. O. Hoffman, Richard Harison (see entry of August 8), and William Henderson purchased the so-called Black River Tract in Jefferson County. See Franklin B. Hough, *A History of Lewis County, New York* (Syracuse, 1883), pp. 297–99; Edward F. Grose, *Centennial History of the Village of Ballston Spa* ([Ballston], 1907), p. 67.

21. Only two Smiths not in the laboring class appear in both the 1789 and the 1803 Boston city directories: Abiel, who lived at 6, and later 5, State Street, and William, whose store was at 53 State Street and whose house was on Court Street. Possibly Mrs. Smith was the wife of one of them.

<I had>
as soon as she had sat up for the fine lady she learned to Dance & play on the Harpsicord though 45 years of age

<She> Amidst all her vanity she shews no foolish pride respecting her origin but takes great pleasure in telling how they first entered boston in Pedlars trim <how> &c <th>

This evening we had a very pleasant ball which was opened with a minuet by *Mrs Smith* & Miss Ogden[.] the dance was of course highly amusing

<?I w?> The company broke up about ↑½ after↓ eleven oclock.

Mrs. Smiths dress for the Ball was of muslin with large gold sprigs. A gold ribbon round her waist her hair turnd up over a cushion powderd pomatomed and covered with lace & trinkets. She <carried> was surrounded with an atmosphere of perfume. she carried an enormous Boquet of artificial flowers, in addition to which I presented her with a stylish assortment of poppies Hollihocks & asparagus[.] she was much pleased with my attention & invited me to accompany her to Boston.

Thursday, August 4[22]

We sat out on a jaunt for Saratoga Springs Accompanied by Reedy & Brandram. After tasting of the several springs we partook of a miserable dinner

There were several Ladies at the springs who mounted some high airs & afforded us infinite amusement.

On our return to <Sarato> Ballton we found Mr Hoffman & Mr Ogden had arrived from Albany.

Mr H wished very much to have a sight of Queen Sheba (Mrs Smith) <?wi?>but she was unwell & did not appear – probably in consequence of taking a pitcher full of crem tart: punch[23] the preceding afternoon to reduce her complexion for the Ball

Friday, August 5[24]

We sat off about ½ after 6 this morning in a hired stage for Utica. We rode down the Schenectady rode[25] till in sight of that place and

22. Irving wrote "Thursday 5."

23. Presumably a concoction of cream of tartar and water or milk, operative as a laxative.

24. Irving wrote "Friday 6th."

25. "Ad" is written in pencil over the "de," in a hand apparently other than Irving's.

then turned up the Turnpike to Swartz Tavern[26] about 14 miles from the Springs, where we breakfasted. From Swartz we rode on for Putnams at Trip's hill[27] about <2>14 mile distant[.] on our way we met Dodge[28] in a Chair going to Albany to take Mrs Dodge to Lebanon.

At Trips Hill I hired a horse and rode full speed for <Ut> Johnstown.[29] I had just time to speak a few words to them all and <a>eat something when I had to remount & gallop to Caughnawaga[30] where I rejoined the party.

<?M?>We put up for the night at the Canajoharie Hotel having crossed the river on the Bridge for the sake of putting up there.[31]

We had excellent accomodations and good attendance. In the evening I strolled <in>by moonlight to the banks of the river with my flute but soon received orders to return to the house as the night air was unwholsome

Saturday, August 6[32]

We ↑recrossed the bridge &↓ rode to <?ch?>Cochrans to breakfast about 4 m distant. We found James & Walter Cochran & Gabriel Cooper[33] all at home and were entertained in a very hospitable manner.

26. Probably Swart Tavern, built about 1735 presumably by Adam Swart and still standing in 1967 on the Mohawk Turnpike between Scotia and Amsterdam on the Verf Kill, a small stream (information furnished by the Curator, Schenectady County Historical Society, Schenectady, New York).

27. Possibly Victor Putnam, who emigrated from Holland before 1793 and owned one of the original grants in Montgomery County on the north side of the Mohawk River (Washington Frothingham, *History of Montgomery County*, Syracuse, 1892, pt. 2, p. 105). Trip's Hill is now Tribes Hill.

28. Richard Dodge (1762–1832), the husband of Irving's sister Sarah, was a native of Duchess County. Employed as a surveyor and later, in company with William Irving, in the fur trade, he settled in 1791 at Johnstown (PMI, I, 38, 39).

29. Besides the Richard Dodges, Irving's sister Catherine and her husband, Daniel Paris, lived in Johnstown.

30. Since 1851 the town has been named Fonda.

31. Apparently they crossed the Mohawk River at Palatine Bridge and spent the night at Canajoharie. The inn there, opened in 1777 by John Roof and operated by him and his sons for nearly fifty years, long had a reputation for excellence (Washington Frothingham, *History of Montgomery and Fulton Counties, New York*, New York, 1878, p. 101; newspaper clippings in the Canajoharie Public Library).

32. Irving wrote "Saturday 7."

33. Apparently the party stopped at the family mansion, near Palatine Bridge, of General John Cochrane (1730–1807), Surgeon General and director of the hospitals of the Continental Army. James (1769–1848) and Walter Livingston (1770–1857), his only sons, lived with him at this time. Both were graduates of Columbia, lawyers, and holders of U.S. Army commissions (M. M. Bagg, *The Pioneers of Utica*, Utica, 1877, pp. 439–43). Gabriel Cooper has not been identified.

From Cochrans we sat on for Utica ↑(14 mi from Cochrans)↓ and passing thro the town of little falls we stopped to have one of the horses shoed. While this was doing we went to the tavern nearest the river to see a remarkable painting of the Landlord his wife and child[34] We had much trouble to smother our laughter as the landlady was present.

The picture is an original in its kind & well worth the attention of the traveller We walked on to look at the new locks which are building in the canal.[35] They are of stone and appear to be extremely well built.

We were overtaken by the carriage and remounting we rode to the town of German flats[36] to dinner. This is a handsome town situated in the middle of an extensive plain as level as a table. We put up at a Tavern kept by a man who from his person might make a good representative of Boniface[37]

Our good landlady kept her dinner so late that we had just time to get into Utica before dark.

Sunday, August 7[38]

Utica is a very handsome town seated on the banks of the Mohawk which is here reduced to a very narrow stream. The people about this part of the country are from New England generally, and afford a pleasing <change> contrast in looks and manners to the dutch who are settled on the lower parts of the river.

This morning I went to <church with> presbyterian meeting[39] with Mrs Hoffman. The meeting was an old house that served on week days for a school room. We had a decent moral sermon & were entertained with very good singing. In the afternoon we rode to Whites-

34. Possibly the William Alexander family (1776–1813), who came to Little Falls soon after 1790 (G. A. Hardin and F. H. Willard, *History of Herkimer County, New York,* Syracuse, 1893, pp. 248–50).

35. The canal was built by the Inland Lock Navigation Company to convey boats around the falls in the Mohawk River at this point (*ibid.,* p. 251).

36. This town is now called Herkimer.

37. The man whom Irving compared to Will Boniface, the genial landlord in Farquhar's *The Beaux Stratagem* (1707), was probably Hezekiah Talcott, the operator of Talcott House (Hardin and Willard, *History of Herkimer County,* p. 155).

38. Irving wrote "Sunday Aug 8." "Aug 8." seems to have been written with a finer pen point, probably later.

39. The first Presbyterian church in Oneida County was organized in 1793 (Bagg, *Pioneers of Utica,* p. 91; Bagg, *Memorial History of Utica, New York,* Utica, 1892, pp. 55–57).

town[40] about 4 miles distant a handsome flourishing settlement. We drank tea with Mr Platt[41] here and then returned to Utica. Brandram & Reedy had arrived at Utica just before we set out and had shewn us a patridge they pretended to have shot on the road. The smell however betrayed the time it had been dead. And Mr Hoffman congratulated them on the prospect of an indelgence in "luxury & disappation" when it was cooked.

Monday, August 8[42]

We took an early breakfast and sat out on our route to the Black river.[43] <We were> in two waggons having sent the chief of our baggage in a waggon the preceding afternoon. The roads were very bad and the countery around afforded but little variety of prospect. We were a great part of the time passing through thick woods the under[w]ood being so thick as to prevent our seeing to any extent. When out of the <th>Woods we had nothing to entertain the sight but fields <unbr> undiversified by any great variety of Tree of hill or brook, disfigured with burnt roots & stumps & fallen bodies of trees. We however found sufficient entertainment in the waggon to make the time pass pleasantly along & the jolting of the rugged roads seemed rather to heighten our amusement. We overtook Messrs. Richard Harison Morrice Miller & Abel French[44] who were on horseback on their way to Black river. They accompanied us a little distance & then out-

40. Whitestown, in Oneida County, is a township whose chief community is Whitesboro.

41. Probably Jonas Platt (1769–1834) of Whitesboro, lawyer and politician (Bagg, *Pioneers of Utica,* pp. 567–70; Pomroy Jones, *Annals and Recollections of Oneida County,* Rome, N.Y., 1851, pp. 790–93).

42. Irving wrote "Monday 9th."

43. The road the party traveled had been cut about 1798 by the Castorland Company to open up the Black River lands to French political refugees; it was not a popular route and soon fell into disuse (Hough, *Lewis County,* p. 116). The area through which they passed had been open for settlement for only a decade and was very sparsely inhabited.

44. Richard Harison (1748–1829), New York lawyer, was for several years in practice with Alexander Hamilton (Julius Goebel, ed. *The Law Practice of Alexander Hamilton,* New York, 1964, I, 311). T. L. Ogden had completed his law training in Harison's office. Harison was co-owner with J. O. Hoffman of land in Jefferson and St. Lawrence counties (see nn. 20 and 108). Morris Smith Miller (1780–1824), Utica lawyer, in these years acted as agent for the proprietors of Lowville and Denmark townships, Lewis County (Hough, *Lewis County,* p. 175). Abel French (1765–1843) was a politician and land agent (*ibid.,* p. 175).

In the manuscript the word "Abel" is in pencil.

rode us. We stopt at Humphreys[45] to dine (about [*blank*] miles from Utica) We staid here about two hours & then remounted. I read passages out of Shakespear to the ladies as we were riding & was much entertained with Ann Hoffmans reading several scenes in Romeo & Juliet In the evening we put up at Sheldon's[46] – a very decent log house tavern.

In the course of the evening Mrs Hoffman sung & I accompanied her on the flute.

Tuesday, August 9[47]

We left Sheldons at day light. The roads seemed to grow worse as we proceeded and we were <often> several times obliged to get out of the waggon and walk in places that appeared dangerous.

We breakfasted at <Ran> Ostranders[48] about 10 oclock & again proceeded on our journey. After a fatigueing ride which however was ↑rendered↓ <amusing> less tiresome from the good company in the waggon – we arrived at Hoadleys Tavern close by the high falls in Black river.[49] Here we found our baggage that had been sent on ahead. We here discharged our waggons intending the next day to <go> take boat & go down Black river from the high to the long falls[50] (about 40 miles)

Wednesday, August 10[51]

After an early breakfast we sat off in a waggon to the river which is about 1½ miles off. The road was extremely rugged descending a rocky

45. Possibly Ebenezer Humphry, living in Westmoreland Township, Oneida County, in 1800 (Ralph V. Wood, *Oneida County, New York State 1800 Federal Population Census Schedule: Compilation and Index,* Cambridge, 1962).

46. Probably some of the family of Ezekiel Sheldon, who had settled in 1790 near the present town of Delta, in Western and Lee Townships, Oneida County (Samuel W. Durant, *History of Oneida County, New York,* Philadelphia 1878, pp. 474, 593).

47. Irving wrote "Tuesday 10th."

48. Possibly Moses Ostrander, living in Leyden Township, Lewis County, in 1800 (Hough, *Lewis County,* p. 258).

49. Probably Philemon Hoadley (1764–1811), who came from Westfield, Massachusetts, to Lowville Township, Lewis County, in 1798 and settled on "the old French road" near the "high falls" (*ibid.,* pp. 304, 558). The "high falls" on the Black river are the Lyons Falls.

In the manuscript "Hoadleys" appears first in pencil, then, over the penciling, in ink.

50. The "long falls" are at Carthage.

51. Irving wrote "Wednesday 11th."

hill for most part of the way. We were obliged to walk the greatest part of the distance <we arrived on the banks of the river from and> ↑but were↓ amply repaid for our fatigue by the unexpected beauty of the scenery on our first view of the river. We emerged from a thick woods on to the banks on our right <?our?> we were surprized with a beautiful sheet of water dashing down a mass of rocks from the height of between 40 & 50 feet (it is said to be 60)[.] the water first pours thro a chasm of about 8 or 10 feet wide and pitching about two feet immediately spreads in to a broad & foaming sheet. The river below is broad and tranquil (about 300 yards across) winding along with shores covered with <verd> the most luxurient verdure to the waters edge. <The>

After viewing the fall in every point of view – on one side,[52] we were called to the scow and set off. We had not rowed down half a mile when we missed our Liquor case & found we had left it behind at Hoadleys. We had therefore to send one of the men off to bring it to the landing – in the mean time Mr H & O amused themselves with fishing while I walked up to the falls with the ladies to view them on the north side. The view of them is much finer on this side than on the other. from the Top of the falls you have a fine view of the water above them with the junction of the Deer[53] and Black rivers which form one stream about 4 or 500 yards above the falls[.] you have also a charming prospect down the river. The man having returned with the case we reembarked and proceeded down the river.

The Black river is remarkably <crooked> ↑serpentine↓[.][54] the banks are covered with lofty trees which entirely confine the prospect except now and then in the course of several miles you may pass by a log house round which the land is partially cleared exhibiting a dreary scene of burnt stumps and fallen trunks of trees. The river in many places is very shallow and it requires considerable circumspection to avoid running on a shoal or getting fast <i>on <sun>the sunken trunks of trees which have been blown down into the stream. The water is of a dark color from whence it has derived its name[.] the banks are much frequented by Deer in the evenings and many are shot by the inhabitants. They go after them in a canoe with a candle at the bow and so much is the attention of the deer engaged by the light that

52. The comma is in pencil.

53. "Deer" is in black ink and appears to have been added later in space left for it.

54. "serpentine" is also in black ink.

they will often suffer the canoes to advance within a few feet of them before they attempt to fly. They are therefore easily shot.

We saw their tracks continually along shore as we proceeded.

In the afternoon it began to cloud up very fast and in a short time the rain poured in torrents. We had just stopped by a brook that ran into the river to get some cold water and eat crackers when it began. Some of the party were fishing & weathered the hardest part of the shower As soon as it abated in some degree we bailed out the scow and pushed forwards We sailed the whole afternoon and evening under repeated showers from which we were but partially skreened by a couple of sheets stretched on <w>hoop[55] poles

In the evening <as> we <ha> passed a Deer grazing on the shore which however we did not discover till we had passed it when it made a noise in its retreat out of the water.

About dar<y>k we arrivd within sight of a Log house owned by a Mr <Cook> ↑Puffer↓[56] about 25 miles <from> below the high falls, here we went ashore and procured lodgings for the night. We found a comfortable fire burning by which we dried our clothes and other articles and after eating a supper of milk & crackers & some tea that we had brot along, we retired to a back room (the house consisting only of two rooms) where we had beds spread on the floor and made out to pass the night as comfortably as a numerous regiment of fleas would permit us.

Thursday, August 11[57]

We <sat> embarked early in the morning and had some sport in shooting *at* ducks but had not the good fortune to kill any though <O>Mr Ogden & myself went ashore to get good shots at them. About eleven Oclock we stopd at a Mr Cooks[58] to get our breakfast ready. This was a miserably dirty Log hut consisting of but one room – we however contrived to boil our Tea kettle and being very hungry I made a hearty meal of milk crackers & cucumbers

55. "w" is canceled in pencil.

56. Probably Isaac Puffer (d. 1836), who came from Princeton, Massachusetts, to New York State, lived about ten years in Otsego County, and about 1800 moved to Watson Township, Lewis County (Hough, *Lewis County*, p. 544).

57. Irving wrote "Thursday 12th."

58. The census of electors in Lowville Township in 1807 lists three Cooks: Alexander, Joseph, and Nathan (Hough, *Lewis County*, p. 322).

We had two or three showers of rain in the course of the morning which made it very uncomfortable sailing

In the afternoon it cleared off beautifully and we began to feel in better humour though<t> the scow was still very wet.

On turning a point in the river we were surprized by loud shouting a head which proceeded from two or three canoes in violent motion,[59] the people in them rowing with all their strength.[60] A gun was soon after fired. On approaching a little nearer we perceived something swimming in the water which they were earnestly pursuing[.] this we soon found out to be a deer and we rowed with all our might to *get in at the death.* A canoe in which was a man and woman at last came up with the animal and the woman hit it two or three times on the head with a paddle –[61] in the eagerness of her exertion however she missed her aim and threw a somerset over into the river. While the man was busy getting her aboard and recovering her the deer got away from them and made towards that shore along which we were sailing. We now exerted all our strength to come up with it (as we perceved another canoe endeavoring the same)[.][62] the animal made for shore and we ran ashore immediately & Mr Ogden & myself jumped out. We ran thro the woods along shore a little way when they <ha> called from the scow that the deer had taken again to the river. We stood ready & as it passed Mr Ogden fired and wounded it (it had been also wounded before) The scow then set out in pursuit of it as it swam into the stream. It soon however turned towards the shore where we were stationed. I threw off my coat & prepared to swim after it. As it came near shore a man rushed thro the bushes and sprang into the water. The banks were very steep and he was over his head immediately[.] he floundered about with a large paddle in one hand which impeded his progress while Mr Ogden & myself ran along shore endeavoring to find clubs. Mr Ogden threw one at the Deer[.] when the man who had contrived to get out of the water,[63] sprang in once more & made a

59. The comma is in pencil. The number of penciled alterations in the account of the doe-killing, if made by Irving, suggests that he considered preparing it for publication. He referred to the episode in his "Notes while preparing Sketch Book &c" (1817).

60. The period is in pencil.

61. The dash is in pencil.

62. The parentheses are in pencil.

63. Irving had a period after "water" instead of the comma supplied by the editor.

grasp at the animal he missed his aim,[64] and I jumping after fell on his back and sunk him under water <while> at the same time I caught the deer by one ear and Mr Ogden <?cau[ght]?> seized it by a leg The paddle gentleman had also risen above water & got hold of another leg[.] we drew it ashore when the man immediately dispatched it with a knife. It turned out to be a fine doe. We claimed a haunch for our share permitting the man to keep all the rest. ↑we then took clothes out of our trunks went ashore & stripped ourselves in the woods.↓ The man took it in his canoe to St Michæls[65] a french man who lived about a mile below. on our arrival there we found them busy in flaying & cutting it up. We walked up to the house to see the woman who had fallen over board. She was abed and had got nearly over the accident though she had been <nearly> ↑well nigh↓[66] drowned. We <?ha?> gave her some wine which seemed to do her much good. The house was remarkably clean & neat for a log house and the people (who were french) extremely civil & polite. We set off once more and in the evening <?att?> arrived at Babtists[67] at the head of the long falls – a dirtier house was never seen[.] it is kept by french people and every different room has its peculiar atmosphere. We dubbed it "The temple of Dirt."[68] We contrived to have our venison cooked in a cleanly manner by Mr Ogdens servant and it made very fine Steaks. which after two

64. The comma is in pencil.

65. Louis François de Saint Michel, a Frenchman, believed to have held office under Louis XVI, came to New York in 1798 and soon afterward settled in Croghan Township, Lewis County, on the banks of the Black River. His daughter married another French settler, Louis Marseille. See Hough, *Lewis County,* pp. 163–64, 604. Possibly the couple who contended with the men in Irving's party for the deer were Marseille and his wife.

66. The alteration is in pencil.

67. Jean Baptiste Bossout (1754–1847), commonly known as Battisse, a native of Troyes in France, came to America with General F. W. von Steuben in 1777 and moved about 1798 from the "high falls" to Carthage, where he held an acre of ground and kept a ferry and tavern (Hough, *Jefferson County,* p. 299; Hough, *Lewis County,* pp. 164–65, 604).

68. Before departing the next day Irving penciled over the fireplace the lines

Here Sovereign Dirt erects her sable throne,
The house, the host, the hostess all her own.

They were found several years later by Hoffman and Judge William Cooper, father of James Fenimore Cooper, and Cooper added:

Learn hence, young man, and teach it to your sons,
The wisest way's to take it as it comes (PMI, I, 51).

days <reg> living on crackers & gingerbread – were <fin> highly acceptable.

At night we did not want for plenty of fleas to entertain us

Friday, August 12[69]

We prepared to leave the Temple of Dirt <on> and set out about 60 miles thro the woods to Oswegatchie.[70] We eat ↑ate↓[71] an uncomfortable breakfast for indeed it was impossible to relish any thing in a house so completely filthy. The Landlady herself was perfectly in character with the house. A little squab french woman with a red face, a black wool hat stuck upon her head her hair <dirt> greasy & uncombed hanging about her ears and the rest of her dress and person in similar stile <For an aid> We were heartily glad to make an escape from a house so extremely disgusting. We set off in caravan st<i>yle two waggons for ourselves and another drawn by oxen for our Baggage. Beside our three drivers we had a civil active young fellow by the name of Rockwell[72] to act as guide and <to> assist<ed>[73] in loading unloading &c. &c.

We found the road dreadfully rugged and miry. The horses could not go off of a walk in any part. The road had not been made above a year and the stumps and roots of trees stood in every direction. The waggon in which I rode was driven by a Mr Si↑a↓mmons[74] an honest

69. Irving wrote "Friday 13th."

70. The town was officially named Ogdensburg (see entry of August 16, 1803, n. 100). The road the party traveled, known as the Oswegatchie Road, was the first one north of Black River. It ran from Carthage to Indian River (now Antwerp) to Oxbow to Heuvelton on the Oswegatchie River, a distance of about fifty miles. It was cut with the urging and under the supervision of Nathan Ford, agent for the proprietors of the area (of whom T. L. Ogden was one), who was first to traverse it in the winter of 1801. See Hough, *Jefferson County*, pp. 307–16.

71. "ate" is written in pencil above "eat," which apparently should have been canceled.

72. Possibly Joshua (b. 1774) or Caleb (b. 1779), sons of Joshua Rockwell, who moved with his family from Middletown, Connecticut, to Lewis County in 1795; they were the third white family to settle north of Utica (Henry E. Rockwell, *The Rockwell Family in America*, Boston, 1873, p. 36; Hough, *Lewis County*, pp. 506, 554).

73. "to" and "ed" are canceled in black ink.

74. The word appears in the manuscript as "Simmons" with a penciled "a" above the "i." Apparently the man was the celebrated Joseph Sammons (1751–1816), one of the three sons of Sampson Sammons, prominent Whig of Fulton County at the time of the Revolution. Joseph and another brother were captured by Sir John Johnson when he attacked and burned their father's house in May 1780. They were

country man. He talked considerably of a brother of his who was a member of congress and seemed highly proud of the honor he derived from the relationship. He entertained us very much with an account of Dr Faustus & the Devil and of old *Father Columbus* and his discovering America. He also gave us a long detail of a lonesome journey of his through the woods during the war which he told us was all set in r↑h↓yme[75] by a *Poet* in his neighbourhood and how they made very *mournful humorsome varses.* He repeated us several of them which were <highly> most laughably pathetic.

The driver of the other waggon seemed expert at nothing but tumbling out and running against <logs> stumps of trees.

We were several times obliged to get out of the waggons and walk as the <waggon> road was so bad that the horses could scarcely get along.

As we were riding along we saw Mr Hoffman ahead ta<n>lking to two or three men, one of them had a remarkably striking appearance. He was dressed in light under clothes a red jacket with something like military decorations[.] his bl<c>ack round ha<d>t[76] was stuck on one side of his head & his hair hung <?l?> about his ears in wild disorder[.] he had a bundle Slung over his left shoulder on the end of a cutlass and his countenance was rugged and almost savage. I found out he was a deserter from the english garrison at Montreal and was making over for the Black river. The whole groupe, of which this was the most prominent figure had a singular appearance as they stood Under a twisted tree that grew in the middle of the road. These were the only travellers we met with in the course of the day. We continued our journey for some distance thro thick woods the road hardly <perceptible> ↑to be↓ distinguished from the other parts of the forest. At length the other driver run his waggon against a tree ↑stump↓[77] and

taken to the fortress of Chamblee at St. Johns, Quebec, from which they escaped separately. Both wrote accounts of their wandering in the wilderness, neither of which has been located. See William L. Stone, *Life of Joseph Brant-Thayendanegea* (New York, 1838), II, 75–94; Frothingham, *Montgomery and Fulton Counties,* pp. 144–46; Sophie D. Moore, *Jacob Dunham of Lebanon, Conn., and Mayfield, N.Y.* (Kalamazoo, Mich., 1933), pp. 89–103. Irving may have been referring to Sammons in the notation in his "Notes while preparing Sketch Book &c" (1817), p. [16]: "Old Salmon's story – rescued by the Young Englishman; finds his mother on the point of being denounced for a Witch."

75. A caret and "h" are in pencil.

76. "t" is in pencil.

77. "stump" is written in pencil above "tree," which apparently should have been canceled.

the axle tree gave way. All hands were immediately employed to make another. They singled out a <?hi?>tree and had it down in an instant. We were too impatient to wait for the waggons being ↑to be↓[78] repaired and <ther> walked on. We provided the ladies with walking sticks and on we trudged as we were extremely hungry. We at length came to the place of our destination which was a log hut ↑about 10 miles from the temple↓ owned by Mr Barnes,[79] a brotherinlaw to Rockwell our guide The Hut was very small consisting but of one room. the Fire was made in one end where the earth was left uncovered with boards and there was a large hole left in the roof for the smoke to escape. The sides of the house were in many places open as the spaces between the logs were not well filled up with clay. The house however was clean & neat and after leaving the Temple of Dirt it was delightful The people were very civil and attentive. We had an excellent supper of Tea with venison and ↑boiled↓ corn. Rockwell took his gun and went after patridges but was unsuccessful. at night our hostess stretched a long blanket across the room and divided it into two[.] on one side we spread our mattrass for the ladies and great coats blankets &c. for ourselves The other side was left for the drivers &c. We made out to sleep very soundly

Saturday, August 13[80]

After a very early breakfast we got our things in order to resume our journey. We were sorry to find that one of honest Si↑a↓mmons's[81] horses was lame from a fault in the shoeing. There was no help however, we must proceed. <We> The next log hut was at the distance of 11 miles We intended to endeavor to pass it and reach one 4 miles beyond.

<Af> We were very much annoyed in the morning by Hornets whose nests were disturbed by the horses feet. Several of us were severely stung by them. After riding some distance. We were overtaken by the driver of the other waggon who informed us that the new

78. "to be" is written in pencil above "being," which, together with the "s" of "waggons," apparently should have been canceled.

79. Probably one of the relatives of Major Judah Barnes, who moved with his family from Bristol, Conn., to Lewis County in 1797 (William Richard Cutter, *Genealogical and Family History of Northern New York,* New York, 1910, II, 736; Hough, *Lewis County,* p. 506). A Capt. Rockwell Barnes settled in Gouverneur Township in 1809, but nothing is known about his relationship to the guide Rockwell (Hough, *St. Lawrence and Franklin Counties,* p. 336).

80. Irving wrote "Saturday 14th."

81. "a" is in pencil.

<axelt> axletree which he made the day before was bent, they had therefore to go to work and make another. The ladies <al> got out of that waggon and mounted the one that was whole while the gentlemen proceeded on foot. It began to cloud over very fast and in a short time the rain came down quite briskly. We got under a tree for shelter. We travelled for some distance <wh> in this manner some times stopping under trees when the rain was very hard[.] at length the other waggon rejoined us.

We then got in our former situations and pushed forward. The woods were tiresome from their continued sameness not the least opening to amuse the eye or divert the attention all one cheerless monotony We now and then passed a place where a traveller had passed the night which might be seen from the little shelter of branches he had made for his head and the place where the fire had been kindled at his feet. This is the common way of their sleeping when passing thro the wilderness where no house is near.

We passed by one place where a <wol> Deer had been killed by a wolf as might be seen by the tracks and by the remains of the deer. The rain that fell <had> encreased the badness of the road and the waggon in which I was riding at length stuck fast in the mire and one of the horses laid down refusing to budge an inch further We had therefore to get out as well as we could and travel after the other waggon where the ladies all mounted. The drivers got levers and attemped to raise the <wg> waggon but in vain[.] the horse that had lai<d>n[82] down had no notion of resuming his labor. As the rain was fast encreasing Mr Ogden undertook to drive the waggon in which the ladies were seated.

The road<s> by this time was full of deep mud holes and the waggon proceeded with great difficulty till at last it fairly stuck fast in one where the mud & water almost covered the Horses back. The poor animals were too fatigued to <be able to make sufficient exertion to> extricate it and there was no <other> alternative <than> ↑but↓[83] for the ladies to get out and walk. The rain by this time descended in Torrents. <th> In several parts of the road I had been up to my middle in mud and water and it was equally bad if not worse to attempt to walk in the woods on either side. We helped the ladies

82. "d" is canceled and "n" is written in pencil. The number of alterations of this nature in the account of this day's journey, if made by Irving, suggests that he considered it for publication, then or later.

83. "but" is in black ink.

to a little shed of bark laid on crotches about large enough to hold three when they set down; It had been a nights shelter to some hunter but in this case it afforded no protection, <the shed> one half of it fell down as we were creeping under it and though we spread great coats on the other, they might as well have been in the open air. The rain now fell in the greatest quantity I had ever seen.[84] The wind blew a perfect hurricane. The Trees around <all> shook and bent in the most alarming manner and threatned every moment to fall and crush us. ↑There was↓ Nothing <was seen>[85] now but a scene of confusion. The Ladies <were alarmed> were in the highest state of alarm and entreated that we should walk to <the> ↑a↓ house which we were told was about <a> half a mile distant. We therefore dragged along – wet to the skin wading through mud holes – it seemed as if the whole forest was under water

We passed several old trees that seemed ready to tumble with the blast. The wind however subsided in a few moments[.] had it not it is very probable that some of us would have been crushed. After a most painful walk of half a mile we arrived at the hut. It was a square building 18 feet one way & 16 another[,] the fire place (which was nothing but a large part of the floor left bare and an aperture in the roof over head) took up a fourth part of the room, the spaces between the logs were not filled up and admitted the light ↑& air↓ in every direction. The house was inhabited by a man who had lately came into the country to settle and had left his family in pennsylvania. Every thing therefore was in the rudest style[.] in one corner was a berth raised for a bed and on it <an> a peice of old carpet by way of mattrass – An ↑old↓ chest of drawers laid on their back & shoved under the birth. two or three crazy chairs a rough table & 4 or 5 kegs of rum made up the furniture of this dwelling. Mr Hoffman had walked ahead of the waggon and reached the Hut before the storm commenced, he therefore was dry and able to get things prepared for us against we arrived. We were all soaking wet and had to wait above half an hour for the waggon to come in which were our Trunks that we might change our clothes. At the hut we found beside Mr Hazleton[86] (the owner) two

84. Ann Hoffman described this storm in a letter to her sister Matilda, written from Montreal, August 10, 1803 (STW, I, 387).

85. "There was" is written in pencil; "was seen" is canceled in pencil.

86. Possibly Abner Hazleton, who assisted in surveying the Canton and Lisbon Townships, St. Lawrence County, in 1799 (Hough, *St. Lawrence and Franklin Counties,* p. 274).

men by the name of Sharp[87] who were driving an ox team through to Oswegatchie. They were extremely noisy and boisterous. One of them in particular was the most impudent chattering forward scoundrel I ever <came across> ↑knew↓[88] The waggons at length arrived and we contrived to get on dry clothes. Our Trunks however were <wet> several of them wet through. The drivers entered the house to dry themselves, at this time there were 15 people in this small room[.] the men began to drink immediately and were very noizy in their greetings and welcomings to each other. The Ladies appeared almost ready to give up We had <not> now been two days travelling and had got but 21 miles into the wilderness

Si↑a↓mmons[89] went out to cut some wood and wounded his foot very badly with the axe[.] he entered the hut with his foot bleeding, <and> we endeavored to keep the sight of it from the ladies and got him to go out of doors. Mrs Hoffman however saw it and the sight of it, after the fatigue & trouble of mind & body she had undergone was too much. she fainted away almost immediately. <Nothing could have been worse.> I now gave up all hopes of getting along We were here in a wilderness, no medical aid near, among a set of men rough and some of them insolent (the Sharps) with ladies of delicate minds and constitutions sinking under fatigue and apprehension. I expected every moment to see them sink into Mrs Hoffmans situation, however they stood it surprizingly well. Mrs Hoffman came to<o> in a little while; we got some tea made and with the addition of boiled corn and potatoes enjoyed a comfortable meal.

<In the>

As we were to pass the night in this Hut we began to arrange beds. We made a tolerable one for Mrs Hoffman & Ogden on the berth and drawing out a chest of drawers from under it we placed it along side & spread a mattrass on it for the Girls.

The drivers and the Sharps <got> seated themselves in a corner and began to play cards for liquor, they were very noizy in their amusement, particularly after they had drank considerably. One of the Sharps <in particular> was very boisterous, The ladies were much alarmed and Ann Hoffman was in tears. I drew two chairs beside the Girls bed

87. A John Sharp was in Madrid Township by 1798 and about the same period was described as a "fence viewer" in Lisbon Township; a Peter Sharp, a German, came in 1800 to Lisbon, where he was a constable (*ibid.*, pp. 329, 341).

88. "knew" is in black ink.

89. "a" is in pencil.

and spreading great coats over the backs of them in some measure intercepted the view of the gambling Gentlemen. I stretchd myself on the chairs and passed the night in that situation. Mr Hoffman & Mr Ogden l<a>ying on the floor at the foot of the bed[.] after some time the Gentlemen retired from their amusement almost intoxicated and laying themselves on the floor went to sleep. I never passed so dreary a night in my life, the rain poured down incessantly and I was frequently obliged to hold up an umbrella to prevent its beating <on the ladies> thro the roof on the ladies as they slept, I was awake almost all night and several times heard the crash of falling trees, and two or three time[s] the long dreary howl of a Wolf. I expected to find in the morning the roads totally impassable from the quantity of rain and trees that had fallen.

Sunday, August 14[90]

<After taking a few crackers>

After taking a cracker and glass of wine we prepared to resume our route. We found it impossible to travel the roads with horses and therefore <hired> ↑engaged↓ the Sharps to take our baggage through on their ox cart while the ladies <rode in> should ride in the ox waggon that had hitherto carried our baggage and that the Gentlemen should walk <afoot>.

In this manner we set out and a dreary prospect we had before us, the woods was a continued marsh and as the waggon dragged heavily along to the <horses> ↑oxens↓[91] breasts in water in many places, we were obliged to jump from <limb> ↑trunk↓ to <limb> ↑trunk↓ of dead trees that laid along side of the road, <in> those places where it was not over our knees we generally walked through. Our progress was much impeded by trees that had fallen down in the course of the night and which we had to cut away before we could pass. The day however was very fine and not a cloud to be seen in the morning.

About eleven oclock we reached a Mrs Vromans,[92] a widow woman

90. Irving wrote "Sunday 15th."

91. "oxens" is in black ink. It and all other inserted alterations in this entry seem to have been written at a later date than the rest of the entry.

92. Apparently she lived about where Jefferson and St. Lawrence counties abut. The first settler in this area of Jefferson County – in the village of Oxbow – was a Peter Vrooman who came from Johnstown about 1803 and was still living in 1806 (Hough, *Jefferson County*, pp. 87, 91). It seems likely, however, that the "widow" Vrooman was related to him.

who with two daughters lived in a log hut on the banks of Indian river. <T>Here we stopped to get some bread a tea kettle & other articles as we expected to pass the night in the woods the next hut being too far off for us to reach that day. Having procured the articles we wanted we continued our route <and>[93] after a fatigueing days journey of 11 miles we arrived at our intended quarters. This was a rude kind of hovel about <ten eight> ten feet square formed of logs for the temporary accomodation of hunters. these Cabins are called by the people about here Shanty's[94] – at the front of the hut there was a large tree at the root of which we lighted a fire and put over <it>a little Iron pot which was to <?seve?> serve in quality of tea kettle corn boiler potatoe pot & every thing

We made a hearty supper on boiled corn & potatoes and some bread which we had got at Vromans (our crackers & gingerbread were ruined in the storm). We were much annoyed by the musquitoes and <an> *punkies* or gnats an insect so minute that you cannot see it till it is on your skin where it bites very severely. they were very troublesome to us throughout the Journey We were also much worried by the insolence of the Sharps. One of these was <the most noizy impudent scoundrel I ever came across> ↑particularly familiar and impertinent↓[95] He was continually addressing us in the most <familiar> ↑unceremonious↓[96] and <impertinent> ↑<familiar>↓[97] manner and his <remarks> language was often extremely rude & disrespectful. His brother had less tongue but equal impudence, and when we were eating would help himself off of our table without ceremony.

It was not the least of our inconveniences on this journey that we had to bear with these scoundrels; but we were in their power, as by refusing to go on with us they might have placed us all in a dismal situation.

As we were to sleep in the Shanty <that>this night we endeavored to fit it up in as comfortable a style as possible. We placed trunks &c on the roof (which was flat) to keep the dew from falling on us, and stretched sheets over the sides to keep out the cold air We spread boughs on the floor and laying the mattrass in one part & great coats &c over another we made tolerable beds At the other end we made a

93. "and" is canceled in pencil.
94. The *OED* gives the first appearance in print of "shanty" as 1822.
95. The cancelation and the insertion are both in black ink.
96. "unceremonious" is in black ink.
97. "familiar" is in black ink, canceled in pencil.

large fire and slept with our feet towards it. during the night one or two of the ladies imagined they heard the howling of wolves and were much alarmed but were soon reasoned out of their apprehensions

Monday, August 15[98]

On looking over our stores we found we had but a small loaf of bread & a few potatoes left[.] we were therefore obliged to be <extr> economical <and> as we should not reach any house till evening. We cut the loaf in two and dividing one half had each about a mouthful to eat[.] the potatoes were also boiled and shared. After this breakfast which only served to whet our appetites instead of satisfying them, we pushed forward at our usual snails pace. The travelling was the same as the day before, through deep mud holes over stumps & stones, and we were still obliged to cut our way through fallen trees.

<Having had no breakfast we>

Towards the middle of the day we began to find ourselves very hungry not having had any breakfast and having such constant exercises. We at last came to a fine spring of water and <di> agreed to stop & divide our half <fo> loaf. On <coming> looking for it however we found it was gone, we had either left it behind us at the shanty or the dog had stolen it. We now looked blank enough, we were faint with hunger and <had> yet had to be jolted about several hours before we could satisfy it – luckily we happened to have a pound of flour & some butter with us and the ladies <bega> set themselves to work to make a <cake> couple of small cakes. A fire was made at the root of a tree and they were roasted before it. While they were making one of the drivers had seated himself <at> in a shade and began to amuse himself with the contents of his wallet. he offered me a slice from a junk of raw pork he was eating and I do not know any morcel I ever eat that was so acceptable

having demolished our cakes which were hardly sufficient to stay our Stomachs we <?remounted in the?> again proceeded. Mr Hoffman & Ogden walked a head and were soon out of sight as they wished to reach the house before us and have things in readiness

<Four>Five or <Five>Six hours <at hard> jolting brought [us]

98. Irving wrote "Monday 16th." Apparently the party covered about fourteen miles this day, which with the ten, eleven, eleven, and fourteen Irving recorded for the 12th, 13th, 14th, and 16th respectively, would make up the sixty between Carthage and Ogdensburg.

in sight of the house and no sight could have been more pleasing as we were half famished. We found them all busy in preparing supper for us, and we made a very hearty one. We could have slept sound enough that night had it not been for a few thousand fleas <that had taken up their abode in the house>. As the house did not boast of a brace of rooms we were all obliged to find lodgings in one.

Tuesday, August 16[99]

We had now fourteen miles to <got> go before we reached Oswegatchie.[100] We were six miles from Oswegatchie river which we would have to cross.[101] This would have been a troublesome business had not Judge Ford[102] of Oswegatchie received notice of our coming and <l>sent men to make a raft and assist us in crossing – On crossing the river we found <horses> a couple of horses waiting to take some of us to the Judges. Mr Hoffman & Mr. Ogden each mounted one of them & <took their> Mrs Hoffman & Mrs Ogden rode behind them I staid behind to <co> travel on in the waggon with the girls. This part of the journey seemed more tedious than any so near the end and yet obliged to travel no faster than the lazy pace of oxen

<In> On one part of our road we were assailed by a number of Hornets (a poisonous kind of insect which had frequently annoyed us on the road)[.] two or three of us were stung and the waggon stopped for a moment This was a most fortunate circumstance a<t>s a very large rotten tree fell a little distance ahead of us just about the place where we would have been had we continued on without stopping. We had to ride <into the> out of the road round the tree as it would have detained us too long to cut through it. At last to our <greagh> great

99. Irving wrote "Tuesday 17th."

100. Ogdensburg, on the St. Lawrence River at the mouth of the Oswegatchie River, is on the site of the fort built by the French and later occupied by the British. Colonel Samuel Ogden (uncle of T. L. Ogden and of J. O. Hoffman) purchased Oswegatchie Township in 1792, and settlement was begun in 1796. It was incorporated with St. Lawrence County in 1802 and the settlement named for the owner (Hough, *St. Lawrence and Franklin Counties,* pp. 245, 367–421, 599).

Fifty years later Irving revisited Ogdensburg and wrote his recollections of his first visit in a letter to his niece Sarah (Paris) Storrow, September 19, 1853.

101. The crossing was at Heuvelton.

102. Nathan Ford (1763–1829), a native of Morristown, New Jersey, was, as Samuel Ogden's agent, the virtual founder of Ogdensburg, where he resided the rest of his life. He was the first judge of the County Court of St. Lawrence County (Hough, *St. Lawrence and Franklin Counties,* pp. 578, 589–93).

joy we came in sight of Oswegatchie. The <view> prospect that opened upon us was delightful[.] after riding through thick woods for several days where the eye is confined to a narrow space and <the mind> fatigued with a continual repetition of similar objects, ↑the↓ sight of a beautiful & extensive tract of country is inconceivably enlivening. Close beside the bank on which we rode the Oswegatchie wound along about twenty feet below us. After running for some distance it entered into the St lawrence forming a long point of land on which stood <the> a few houses called the Garrison which had formerly been a fortified place built by the french to keep the indians in awe[.][103] they were now tumbling in ruins excepting two or three which were still kept in tolerable order by Judge ford who resided in one of them and used the others as stores and out houses. We recrossed the <?ferry?> Oswegatchie ↑river↓ to the Garrison as we intended to reside with Judge ford for some time

We found <Mr> The rest of our party there[.] they had arived two or three hours before us. The Judge is a most hospitable open hearted man very lively in his discourse & gentlemanly in his manners[.] his company therefore is highly pleasing.

Wednesday, August 17[104]

Mr Harison from New York and Mr Able French a Gentleman from black river whom we had seen at Utica, arrived at the Garison and added much to our little society. In the morning ↑several of↓ the gentlemen went a fishing but met with indifferent success.

Friday, August 19

This morning Mr Mrs & Miss Ogden left us to go to Madrid[105] (about 15 miles <d>farther down the St Lawrence) where they intended staying three or four weeks as Mr Ogdens lands lay in the neighborhood

After passing through so long a journey with them and having every

103. The fort at the mouth of the Oswegatchie was built, as Fort La Presentation, by Abbé François Picquet as part of a Sulpitian mission in 1749. From 1760 to 1796 it was held by the British, who called it after the river. See *ibid.*, pp. 17, 100, 367.

104. Irving wrote "Wednesday 18th." There is no entry for Thursday and the Friday entry is correctly dated.

105. T. L. Ogden, his brother David A., and their father Abraham, together with J. O. Hoffman, purchased Madrid Township, St. Lawrence County, on June 6, 1796, for $60,000 (*ibid.*, pp. 245, 341, 599–600).

reason to be delighted with their company, it was extremely hard to part and seemed to throw a general damp over the party[.] we agreed however to endeavor to return to New York together. Mr Harison accompanied them part of the way.

In the evening I took a long stroll and fell asleep in a saw mill On waking I was surprized to find it was growing quite dark[.] I hastened home and found that there was a general search making for me in the woods around. Mr Hoffman soon came home to see if I had arrived and finding me there, had a conk[106] shell blown as a signal for the rest to repair home.

PS. Two gentlemen from the Canada side of St Lawrence by the name of Sherwood[107] dined with us to day and gave us an invitation to dinner on Sunday.

Saturday, August 20

Mr French left us early <for> to return to black river[.] he took letters from us which he promised to forward to New York <we amused ourselve>

Mr Hoffman & myself amused ourselves with shooting & fishing during the day.

Sunday, August 21

We crossed the river to dine with a Mr Sherwood & his Brother, two <l>Canada lawyers who lived opposi<d>te Oswegatchie. <We found a>

The elder of the Sherwoods we found a man of good sense and much information

Monday, August 22

We left Oswegatchie for Lisbon[108] one of Mr Hoffmans townships

106. Probably Irving meant "conch."

107. Probably they were Samuel and his younger brother Livius Peters Sherwood (1777–1850), sons of the loyalist Capt. Justus Sherwood of Connecticut. Both were lawyers and politicians. See Thad. W. H. Leavitt, *History of Leeds and Grenville Ontario* (Brockville, Ont., 1879), pp. 19, 73; H. P. Hill, *Robert Randall and the Le Breton Flats* (Ottawa, Ont., [1919]), p. 26.

108. A large tract of land in what became Canton and Lisbon Townships, St. Lawrence County, was acquired by J. O. Hoffman, Stephen Van Rensselaer, and Richard Harison on March 3, 1795, for £5,068.16*s*. (Hough, *St. Lawrence and Franklin Counties,* pp. 245, 328–29, 246, 599).

<where he inted intended> about ten or twelve miles farther down the river We arrived there in the afternoon and took up our residence at the house of Mr Turner,[109] Mr Hoffmans Agent

Tuesday, Wednesday, August 23, 24

remained at <Madrid> Lisbon settling with the tenants, Laying out a town, shooting &c &c.

Thursday, August 25

We sailed <eight> ↑twelve↓ miles down the river to Madrid Mr Ogdens Township where he was engaged in settling with his tenants In the afternoon Mr Hoffman returned to Lisbon Leaving Mrs Hoffman, Ann, & myself at Madrid.

Friday, Saturday, Sunday, August 26, 27, 28

passed away very agreeably fishing shooting &c paying one or two visits to a Mr Paterson[110] on the Canada Side of the river, whom we found very Hospitable & very good company.

Monday, August 29

Hired a horse to take me to Lisbon where Mr Hoffman was. The road was thro woods so thick that it could hardly be distinguished and I was several times lost and obliged to retrace my way. I arrived at Lisbon about one oclock & found Mr Hoffman surrounded by tenants & hard at work. *Amused*[111] myself the rest of the day <fi> writing Bonds & deeds.[112]

Tuesday, August 30

Rode up to Oswegatchie to visit Judge Ford <I dined there> and

109. Alexander J. Turner (d. 1806) came from Salem, Washington County, in February 1800 as agent for the proprietors of Lisbon. He continued in this capacity until 1805, was supervisor from 1801 for several years, and was a judge of the Court of Common Pleas at the time of his death (*ibid.*, pp., 329, 330).

110. Possibly he was Allen Patterson, who owned land along the St. Lawrence River (Irving, *Journal, 1803*, ed. S. T. Williams, New York, 1934, p. 47).

111. "Amused" is underlined in black ink.

112. "In the summer of 1803, Mr. Washington Irving, then a young man, came into the county with some of the proprietors, and remained a short time. His name occurs on several old deeds as a witness" (Hough, *St. Lawrence and Franklin Counties*, p. 402).

found him busily engaged in directing the raising of a court house and in sending off several rafts to Montreal I met with the most friendly & hospitable reception and spent some hours very agreeably

[*The journal breaks off at this point. Irving apparently kept no record of the rest of the journey he and his party made to Montreal and back to New York City, which occupied several weeks. He recorded some of the events of this part of the journey in the Preface to* Astoria *(1836) and in his Autobiographical Notes, January 10, 1843.*]

EUROPEAN JOURNAL, 1804–1805

Volume 1
Bordeaux–Messina

The manuscript journal is in the Manuscript Division of the New York Public Library. It consists of 233 pages, written in ink of several colors, of a vellum-covered booklet of 270 pages, measuring 9 × 7 inches. Pp. [2, 4, 235–69] are blank. Inside the front cover appears the bookplate of Robert Hoe, founder of the Grolier Club.

The color of ink in the main entries changes a number of times in the manuscript, as Irving procured new supplies while traveling. Brown ink was used in the entries from July 1 to August 3; black ink for part of the entry for August 8; gray-black ink for the remainder of August 8 through the entry for August 13; brown for the entries of August 15, 16; black for part of the entry for August 17; brown for the remainder of the entry for August 17 through the entry for August 20; black for the entries for August 22–27; gray or blue for the entry for September 3; brown for the entries of September 8 to December 1; blue for the entries for December 2–21 and for January 23. Certain additional changes in ink (the portions in blue ink of the entries of July 10, 12, 13; August 3, 8, 14, 16, 17, 20; November 13, 14; and the last paragraph of the entry of September 8) indicate that he made additions to and alterations in these entries after he reached Genoa, probably during the nineteen-day quarantine he spent in the harbor of Messina.

[*front cover*]

1804[1]

[*inside front cover blank except for drawings (Figure 2) and bookplate*][2]

[*p. [1] blank except for drawing (Figure 3)*][3]

1. "1804" is written sideways in black ink.

2. The drawings are of a tree, in brown or black ink, and two figures of a man and a profile, all in pencil.

3. The drawing, in pencil, of a waterfront scene may possibly be identified by the notation on the inside of the back cover.

[*p. [3]*]

Journal
of a
Tour thro France, Italy, Sicily.[4]

Washington Irvings Manuscript
115 leaves[5]

Bordeaux, July 1, 1804[6]

My dear Brother

Yesterday morning[7] for the first time I set foot on European land, in this city, after having been forty two days on Ship board. (we set sail from New York the 19th May)[8] Our passage was mild and pleasant, and what the sailors term "a lady's voyage." We were delay'd by head winds and calms, particularly after we entered the Bay of Biscay. <Th> In consequence of these head winds the first land we made was Cape Penas on the coast of Spain. The land rose from the shore into

4. "Journal . . . Sicily" is in blue ink, which may indicate it was written later.

5. "Washington . . . leaves" is in pencil in a different hand; "115 leaves" is written on a slant.

6. On this date Irving wrote a letter to his eldest brother William (1766–1821), which contains some language identical with that in this entry. The entire journal is addressed to William, who, with his third brother, Ebenezer, sponsored the trip, partly in hopes that Washington's health might be benefited. William was a merchant in foreign trade in New York, who engaged in both politics and literature. His home on the Passaic River, Cockloft Hall, was a gathering place for the group of young writers, which included Washington and their brother-in-law J. K. Paulding, who called themselves "The Lads of Kilkenny." William contributed light verse to *Salmagundi* (1807–1808). From 1814 to 1818 he was a member of Congress.

7. From June 30, 1804, to May 14, 1805, Irving kept an account of his expenses in the notebooks containing his "Traveling Notes;" for these accounts see "Traveling Notes, 1804" and "Traveling Notes, 1804–1805." Other notes about his finances during this period are also contained in these notebooks.

8. Irving crossed the Atlantic on the *Rising States,* whose captain was Nathaniel Shaler. He gave a brief account of the passage in his letters to William Irving, June 26 and July 1, 1804, and commended Shaler in his letter to William, August 1, 1804.

vast mountains of rock that lifted their snowy heads far above the clouds. After standing on another tack and losing sight of land we were several days before we made Cordovan light house which we did on the 25 June and anchored the same afternoon in Verdun roads, mouth of the Gironne,[9] where we were obliged to remain <at anchor> three days at quarantine in compliance with a rule observed towards all vessels from America.

The <Ga> Gironne is formed by the junction of the Dordogne and the Garonne <The> which takes place a few leagues below Bordeaux. The Garonne has its source in the Pyrenees and is the river on ↑the banks of↓ which Bordeaux is situated.

Our sail up the river was delightful. At first the river was wide and the land very low but altered as we proceeded and the latter part was charming. The country adjacent is sandy, but is famous for producing the Medoc & other wines that are counted the best in France

The Hills and vales were covered with vineyards of a ↑rich &↓ lively green to which the white walls of the villages and chatteaus afforded a pleasing contrast. Frequently on the Banks of the river <was> ↑were↓ seen <small> cottages embowered in groves of elm's and their white washd walls over run with vines. They <seemed> reminded me of those delightful retreats of rural happiness so often sung by our pastoral poets and had but the muddy Garonne have *rolld a silver wave*[10] I should have pronounced the picture complete

On our arrival we had to parade about the city in a <p> body to the admiralty & municipality offices to have our <names pass> protections &c examined signd seald &c. As there were seventeen passengers of us, all french except myself and several of them pretty looking personages enough you may imagine we made a tolerably amusing procession. These things are not however noticed in france, where they are used to ridiculous sights & manouvres.

9. Gironde.

10. Probably Irving confused ll. 335 and 344 in Alexander Pope, "Windsor Forest" (1713): "The figured streams [of the Thames] in waves of silver roll'd" and "And chalky Wey, that rolls a milky wave."

July 7[11]

I have now been a week in Bordeaux and my ideas begin to collect again, for I assure you they have been quite in a state of derangement since my arrival,[12] from the novelty of my situation.

The letters of introduction[13] I brought for this city have procured me the most hospitable attentions. I am in the family of a Mons Ferrier,[14] an old Gentleman who sometime since was one of the richest and most respectable merchants in this place and for some time Mayor of the city, but a succession of misfortunes ha<ve>s stripped him of most of his property. He has still enough however, to support him in an easy genteel style, his house is <well> handsomely furnished and his table both plentiful and elegant. He has also an estate in the country. The family consists of the old gentleman the old lady & myself besides three servants. They are a most amiable old couple, highly estimated and visited by the most respectable people in Bordeaux. They do not speak english, and their french is free from the barberous Gascon accent & dialect that prevails in this part of france so that I have an excellent opportunity to improve in the language. I am <indebted to the particular rec> admitted in this family as a favor at the particular reccommendation of Dr Ellison[15] formerly of New York now resident here, and I am universally congratulated on my good fortune

11. From July 7 through 25, Irving made the entries in his journal and wrote a letter to his brother Peter. The wording is often identical. For July 7 and 8 the letter seems to have been written first, but for the remaining dates the journal entry seems to have been written first.

12. Irving stayed on June 30 and July 1 at the Hotel Franklin in Bordeaux, where he shared a room with Captain Shaler (Irving to William Irving, July 2, 1804).

13. One was to William Lee, acting U.S. consul, whom he met on July 1, 1804 (Irving to William Irving, July 2, 1804).

14. Jean Ferrière (1741–1813), known as Ferrière-Colck, was a well-to-do, cultivated, and influential citizen of Bordeaux, mayor from 1794 to 1797. At this time he was living at 99 Rue la Trésorerie in a house whose elegant furnishings included a collection of books. His country estate was Le Chateau de la Tour de Gassies, west of the town of Bruges, not far from Bordeaux. His wife was Marie O'Quin, member of an Irish family. See John P. Young, *Washington Irving à Bordeaux* (Niagara Falls, Ont., 1946), pp. 40–53. Presumably Irving moved to the Ferrière house on July 2 (Irving to William Irving, July 2, 1804). He gave a more personal description of Ferrière in his letter to William Irving, August 1, 1804.

15. John Gabriel Ellison (b. 1773), a native of New York, was at this time practicing medicine in the Faubourg des Chartrons, Rue du Couvent 23 (Young, *Irving à Bordeaux,* p. 40). He had been a fellow student of Peter Irving's (Irving to Peter Irving, July 7–25, 1804).

I am gradually becoming accustomed to the looks of Bordeaux. Its narrow streets and high stone buildings no longer appear singular There is a strength and solidity about the houses that gives them an air of dignity we do not find in our light American buildings They are built entirely of a kind of lime stone procured from quarries a few miles down the Garonne. This stone has some qualities that render it very excellent for building – when fresh from the Quarry it is soft and easily cut & shaped, and acquires by ↑age &↓ <a>exposure to the air a considerable degree of hardness. At the same time however it loses that beautiful whiteness <?fl?> that distinguishes it at first and becomes in time black and dirty. This <gives a diss diminishes> ↑injures↓ the looks of their edifices, as they do not think of painting or white washing them on the outside –

The rooms are high, & generally with floors of stone marble or tyle which <with> gives them a delightful coolness in summer, and I am told they are very warm in winter when the floors are covered with carpets. The fronts of their houses are decorated with sculpture and iron raild balconies to the casements

Among the chief antiquities of this place is the Palais Galien.[16] It is the remains of a Roman Ampitheatre built under the reign of the Emperor Galien towards the middle of the third century. It is constructed of the same kind of stone with which Bordeaux is built, intermingled with brick.

Since the revolution the land on which it stands was sold in common with other National property and the purchasers began <bu>demolishing the building to make way for streets and houses. Fortunately however a Gentleman of taste arrived from paris in quality of Prefet of this department and rescued the precious remain of antiquity from entire demolition.[17] The municipality have received a charge to look to its preservation so that there are hopes of its still existing a considerable time. Nothing however stands but part of the bare walls and one of the grand entrances, and it is merely the antiquity that entitles it to notice. This <place> ↑ampitheatre↓ has not <only> served <for>

16. The Palais Gallien was named for the Roman emperor Gallienus. For his description of it Irving drew on Pierre Bernadau, *Annales Politiques, Littéraries et Statistiques de Bordeaux* (Bordeaux, 1803), pp. 147–48.

17. Comte Antoine Claire Thibaudeau (1765–1854), revolutionist and historical writer, was appointed by Napoleon Prefect of the Gironde Prefecture in 1800. He issued the order regarding Palais Gallien in 1801 (Bernadau, *Annales . . . de Bordeaux,* p. 148).

as a place of amusement to the Romans alone In poring over an old book entitled "Cronique Bo<r>urdelaise"[18] I find that about two century's ago some *bon vivants* of the infernal regions used to meet there to amuse themselves An unfortunate chap who I supposed happened to be too knowing for the common run of folks was accused of sorcery, condemnd & executed. Before his death he confessd having been at a meeting of some of these merry devils in the Palais Galien. I regard this ancient pile with peculiar reverance. It stands near my lodgings so that I frequently pass it, and two or three times I have strolld home at night thro its silent ruins, and as I passd under the dark arches of the grand entrance I have almost expected to see an old Roman stalking amid the gloom

The Grand Theatre is a magnificent building and said to be the finest of its kind in Europe[19] The outside is superb but the interior did not answer my expectations. By the interior I mean the audience part, for the grand enterance staircase &c is <magnificent> ↑superb↓. The painting of the audience part is much soild and faded which considerably injures its appearance We complain very much in New York of our Theatre's being badly lighted; in Bordeaux they are far<e> worse, having no light but what is given by a chandalier hung up in the centre. The stage also is not so well lighted as ours.

I have been twice to see La Fond[20] one of the two first tragedians in France. He is performing here for a few nights after which he returns to paris. Tho' I could not understand the language yet I was highly pleased with the Actor. His figure is tall and well made, his face uncommonly expressive – and his voice full and sonorous. The other actors were very indifferent, their gesticulations were violent and their at-

18. Gabriel de Lurbe's *Chronique Bourdelaise* was first published in Bordeaux in 1594–1595. The edition Irving used was that of 1619, also published there (Irving to Peter Irving, July 7–25, 1804). For the reference to sorcerers in the Palais Gallien, however, he was indebted not to de Lurbe, but probably to Bernadau's *Antiquités Bordelaises* (Bordeaux, 1797), a copy of which was owned by Ferrière.

19. Bordeaux's most celebrated edifice, it was built between 1773 and 1780 by Victor Louis.

20. Pierre Lafon (1775–1846), celebrated French actor, made his debut in Paris in 1800. (The other leading French tragedian of the period was F. J. Talma.) Presumably Irving saw Lafon perform on July 3 in Voltaire's *Œdipe* (1718) and on July 5 in La Harpe's *Philoctète*, 1783 (Young, *Irving à Bordeaux*, pp. 311–12). Irving commented more fully on the performances of Lafon which he saw in his letter to Elias Hicks, July 20, 1804.

titudes often straind and unnatural. The Scenery is well executed the dresses rich with great attention to costume.

There are two or three other theatres of inferior merits, one of them called the theatre Française is nearly as large as our theatre, but the actors are miserable.[21] These <inferior> lower order of theatres are great resorts for women of bad character, and are complete hot beds of vice & infamy. In front of one of the meanest a Jack pudding[22] <is> was mounted on a stage endeavoring to attract the multitude by his tricks and jokes

July 9

The people of Bordeaux exercise a liberty of speech that at first surprized me. They make no scruple of talking very freely among themselves concerning the Emperor[23] and his conduct. This I am told is not noticed by the police as long as it is done in private, but should they express their sentiments publicly and endeavor to instill them in the minds of others, they would certainly involve themselves in trouble

In New York <we>you have an idea that France is in a state of agitation and confusion in consequence of the war and the preparations for the invasion. As yet I have seen nothing of the kind. Every thing apparantly goes on with smoothness and regularity. No armed forces are seen parading the streets. No drums or cannons to be heard. All is order and tranquillity and did I not know to the contrary I should think them in peace with all the world.

The merchants appear to be the chief sufferers as I see their vessels laid up in the river totally dismantled of their rigging, and they uni-

21. The theaters in Bordeaux at this time other than the Grand were the Français; the Molière, temporarily closed during the summer of 1804; the Gaîté; and the Union. Somewhat contrary to the impression given by Irving, this was a particularly brilliant period in the history of the Bordeaux theater. See Young, *Irving à Bordeaux,* pp. 305–7. In his letter to Elias Hicks, July 20, 1804, Irving further expressed his opinion of the Théâtre Français. By "our theatre" Irving presumably refers to the Park Theater in New York, which he had frequented (STW, I, 37–40). The only other theater in the city at that time was the Grove, which was open intermittently in 1804–1805. See George C. D. Odell, *Annals of the New York Stage* (New York, 1927), II, 197–200, 202, 244, and *passim.*

22. A buffoon or clown.

23. Napoleon Bonaparte (1759–1821) was proclaimed Napoleon I, Emperor of the French, on May 18, 1804, though he was not crowned until December. England declared war on France in 1803, and from then until late 1805 Napoleon attempted to assemble a fleet for invasion of the island. His maritime policy seriously damaged the commercial life of Bordeaux.

versally complain of want of business. The American vessels crowd the port and enjoy a fine harvest during the contests of Europe. It is only from seeing soldiers posted at the public places that I reccollect I am under a government in a certain degree military. A stranger while he conducts himself with propriety may walk the streets continually & frequent every place of curiosity business or amusement apparantly unnoticed and unknown, but let him once behave ↑in an↓ improper or suspicious manner and he will find his every movement is observed. To this strictness of the police may be ascribed in a great degree the personal security & public tranquillity in France

The roads & highways throughout the country are patrolled by troops of Gens d'armes who visit the different taverns & houses and acquaint themselves with the manner of living and mode of subsistence of the inhabitants. The cities swarm with spies in every direction. In consequence, the streets & lanes may be traversed & the roads and high ways travelled at any time night or day without any danger of depredation or insult Were this not the case every thing might be apprehended from the number of poor people and beggars with which this country abounds.

July 10

It amuses me very much to walk the streets and observe the many ways these people have of getting a living of which we have no idea in America. The fruit women divert me the most, to see them with old fashioned long wasted dresses their arms stuck akimbo, <a> monstrous caps on their head the whole surmounted with a huge basket of fruit, thus decked off they straddle along the pavement bawling out their merchandize in a voice every tone of which is as sharp as vinegar. Beside these we have pedlars shoe blacks, tumblers & savoyards with their musical instruments, at every corner. And now and then we have a <ful> grand concert vocal & instrumental from half a dozen Italian peasant women with fiddles & tamborines.

The streets are entirely free from the broils & boxing matches one would expect in such a medley. A drunken man is rarely seen & generally proves to be some American who has been *enjoying* himself. Our countrymen have got a name for drunkeness among this temperate people, and often when there is any disturbance at a public place of amusement it is common for the French to say – "pho – its only some drunken American or other" This vice which they consider unpardonable among themselves, they <pardon> excuse in an American, they say "it is the custom of his country."

My situation in the family of Mr F is so agreeable that I think of lengthening my stay in this place, beyond what I first intended. I shall then be enabled to <tavel> travel with more pleasure & advantage from having a better acquaintance with the language. I shall escape considerable of the hot weather that prevails at this season in the south of france and what is best of all, about the time I commence my journey the vintage will have began and I shall see the country and inhabitants in their happiest moments – all mirth and festivity.

The weather when I first arrived was uncommonly hot for this climate[.] some of the old inhabitants assure me they have never before experienced such <?hot?> heat in Bordeaux, it has since moderated exceedingly. The heat here is not so oppressive and enervating as in New York and the evenings are cool & delightful There are some very pleasant walks in this city one of which was formerly a vast garden open to the better order of people; since the revolution it has become common to all ranks & is called the Champ de Mars. It no longer contains beds of flowrs &c but there are several fine alleys & groves of trees which render it a delightful promenade.[24] There is also a beautiful walk in ↑the center of↓ one of the public streets called the "Rue Tourney[."] it has three rows of fine elms with stone benches under them and is a very fashionable place of resort in the evening[25]

Amid all the scenes of novelty & pleasure that surround me, I assure you my thoughts often return to <home> New York with the most lively emotions. The idea that I am alone, far from my friends without <an> opportunities of frequent communication "a stranger and a sojourner in the land"[26] often throws a damp over my spirits which I find it difficult to shake off. This however I hope will wear away in time as I become more a "Citizen of the World."[27] Accustomed to be

24. It was laid out between 1746 and 1756 by Louis Urbain Aubert, Marquis de Tourny, Intendant of the province of Guyenne. Enlarged and altered, it is now the Jardin Public.

25. Allées de Tourny.

26. "Stranger and sojourner" is a phrase appearing several places in the King James translation of the Bible; see, for example, Gen. 23:4 and Ps. 39:12.

27. In the antique world this phrase was used by Diogenes Laertius and ascribed to Socrates by Plutarch and Cicero. Among later writers who made notable use of

surrounded by those who took a near interest in my welfare it is a painful thought to indulge, that I am now <?in a?> left to my own self, to work my way among strangers who are indifferent to me and my concerns excepting as far as they can further their own interests.[28]

July 12

Yesterday afternoon I spent most agreeably in viewing one of the finest specimens of Gothic Architecture in France. This was the Cathederal church of St André. It was built by the english when in possession of this city in the eleventh or twelvth century.[29] The style of architecture is said to be extremely similar to that of Westminster Abbey in london[30] and bears about it an air of indiscribable dignity and solemnity The first view of it brought strongly to my reccollection the words of <our immortal bard> Congreve[31]

"How reverend is the face of this tall pile &c"
Whose ancient pillars rear their marble heads
To bear aloft its archd & pondrous roof.
By its own weight made steadfast & immoveable
Looking tranquility it strikes an awe –

It is a vast building, entirely of stone & decoratd with all that profusion of carved work and minute ornament that characterizes the Gothic style. When inside, the lofty <arched> roof of arched work the vast pillars, the windows of painted glass had a *tout ensemble* that awakend awe & veneration The effects of the revolution are descernable in this building. The unhallowed hands of tasteless barbarians have stripped many of the paintings from the walls, have torn the images of the saints from the niches of which they had held quiet possession for

---

it were Francis Bacon, James Boswell, and Oliver Goldsmith in his collection of Chinese letters, *The Citizen of the World* (1762).

28. This sentence, the last on the manuscript page, is in blue ink.

29. The English were in control of Bordeaux from 1154 to 1453, but the church, which was begun about the middle of the twelfth century and essentially completed by the fourteenth century, was not constructed by them. Possibly Irving derived the error from the condensed account in Hiérosme Lopès' *L'Élgise Metropolitaine et Primatiale de Sainct-André de Bordeaux* (1668), a copy of which was owned by Ferrière. See Young, *Irving à Bordeaux*, pp. 179–80.

30. Westminster Abbey was largely built in the thirteenth century in the Gothic style.

31. The cancellation and "Congreve" are in blue ink; the last four lines of the quotation which follows are in blue ink and in smaller script. The quotation is from William Congreve's *The Mourning Bride* (1697), II, i, 8–12.

centuries and have decapitated several of the cardinals who mounted guard over the grand portal. Still however they could not injure materially, the beauty of the main <edifice> Architecture, the undertaking would have required too much labor & time for the patience of a mob. The church has since been cleaned, is undergoing repairs in several places and has again become "the house of prayer."[32] Our company consisted of five[33] and we procured the sexton to shew us the way to the top of one of the grand towers,[34] of which there are two. Our ascent was quite intricate and reminded me of some of those winding & perplexed passages thro which some of the heroes of modern romances wander when prowling about the interior of an old castle. In some places we had to ascend stone stair cases that wound up round towers of about six feet diameter & dimly lighted by narrow apertures in the wall. We then had to pass thro narrow passages in the wall of the church having ↑now & then↓ on one side small square holes that looked into the interior of the building and on the other side similar ones that gave us a peep into the city. In one place our route entered the church and formed a narrow gallery almost as high as the cieling or roof <In another place> from whence we could see the people far below us at their prayers In another place we had to walk on a kind of stone cornice that ran<d> round part of the outside of the edifice. After a great deal of this winding and twisting we at last arrived on the highest *accessable* part of one of the steeples. The view from this place was vast and interesting. Beneath us lay the city presenting a singular *melange* of architecture of different orders & periods Beyond it the beautiful harbor in form of a crescent crowded with the ships of *my country*. And all around in the distance, a level country covered with vineyards, diversified by chateaus and enlivened by the waters of the Garonne.

From the square part of the steeple on which we stood there rose a spire of about an hundred & twenty or thirty feet. it tapered to a point and we could stand <i>on the inside and see to the very top of it as there were no stairs nor any wooden work in the interior. It is built entirely of stone with windows to the very top. And what surprized me was that the walls were not a foot in thickness, this gave it a dangerous

32. This phrase appears in several places in the King James translation of the Bible: Isa. 56:7; Matt. 21:13; Mark 11:17; Luke 19:46.

33. Possibly there were, in addition to Irving, the four members of the Jonathan Jones family (see entry of July 15, 1804, n. 50).

34. The group first ascended the west tower.

appearance, particularly as I observed cracks in several <parts of it> places secured by bars of Iron. There is another spire[35] <of a> ↑exactly↓ similar to this in another part of the church, <th> five or six feet of the top was struck off some time since, by <thunde> lightening. After having remaind here for some time & witnessed a beautiful sunset, we set out to retrace the labyrinth by which we ascended, and arrived safe on terra firma without any bruises or dislocations.

As this was the first gothic building I had seen it made particular impression on my fancy and in fact it was some time before I could recall my eyes from hurrying over the whole & endeavoring to grasp a full view of every part to the more satisfactory manner of deliberate examination. No doubt I give a high colord discription of some objects for every thing is heightend to me by novelty[36]

July 13

The newspapers of france are extremely barren of intelligence and observe the greatest caution about mentioning the designs or actions of Government.[37] Indeed the movements of the executive are conducted with so much secrecy that they are rarely anticipated, nor do the editor[s] of papers dare to indulge themselves in comments or animadversions. One paper in paris the other day entitled the *Publiciste* <having> inserted some conjectures respecting the intentions of France towards Italy. The gazette was immediately stopped and it was with great difficulty it was permitted to go on again, after two days cessation, on condition of changing its editors.[38] This affords a striking contrast to that liberty of the press that prevails in America, where every public measure or public character is attacked with indiscriminate inveteracy in the news papers. In consequence <have> of this silence in the french papers we have but little political news stirring and it is only by vague rumors, we hear what is going on at the seat of Government. The Quid-nuncs of New York hear far more about the

35. This was the east tower, damaged by lightning late in the seventeenth century and restored in 1689.

36. This paragraph, the last on the manuscript page, is in blue ink.

37. Irving made the same complaint about the French newspapers in his letter to Elias Hicks, July 20, 1804.

38. Probably Irving got all this information from the account in the Bordeaux newspaper *Echo du Commerce de Bordeaux* for July 11, 1804 (Young, *Irving à Bordeaux,* p. 211).

concerns of France than her own citizens for those of whom I enquire seem to have nothing but surmises & uncertain reports to give me.[39]

A great part of the polite world of Bordeaux have gone to take the waters of Bagneres,[40] a small town among the Pyrenees famous for its mineral springs, & a fashionable place of resort from different parts of france. The air of that town is said to be cool & salubrious in the midst of summer and its situation among the mountains gives it the advantage of a vast variety of grand & romantic scenery. Probably it is owing to this fashionable desertion that I may attribute the great scarcity of beauty that prevails at Bordeaux, for I have hardly seen a lady since my arrival that I would call handsome. They have also a manner of dressing their heads that I do not admire, They torture the hair into unatural twists & ringlets and lard it over with a profusion of *ancient oil.* My objection to this mode may arise from its reminding me of the greasy locks of the squaws I have seen in Canada. At any rate, it cannot be equal in beauty in the eyes of an unprejudiced person, to light fanciful ringlets of hair dry & elastic, that play with every zephyr. The dress of the french ladies is also unpleasing to me, tho' I was partly prepared for it by the light <ropes> ↑robes↓ of our *transparent elegantees.*[41]

July 14

I have been this evening to visit a garden about three miles out of the city owned by <a> ↑an old↓ gentleman of great property who has his country house there.[42] He is unmarried and <his>takes great pride is[43] in hearing his garden admired It is open to the public at all times, free of expence. The garden is very extensive laid out in the old taste of clipd walks alleys arbors &c. It has a very pretty effect on the eye for the first time, but there is a degree of sameness in the walks &c that soon grows tiresome. The old gentleman has certainly been at a vast expence to please the public, and the least they can do in return

39. "for those . . . give me" is in blue ink.

40. Bagnerès-de-Bigorre.

41. *transparentes élégantes* ("transparent ladies of fashion"). In his letter to Elias Hicks, July 20, 1804, Irving also complained about the scanty attire and the heavy makeup of Frenchwomen.

42. Gabriel Salomon Henriquès belonged to a large mercantile family. His country house, Chateau Raba, in the Talence area near Bordeaux, was begun in 1782 and by 1783 was, with its park, an attraction for travelers. See Young, *Irving à Bordeaux,* pp. 228–30.

43. Presumably Irving intended to cancel the "is" after "pride."

is to admire his works. His garden is a great <reso> place of resort for the lower classes on Sunday, as they can enjoy themselves there free of expence.

<The> Sunday<s in are> ↑is↓ still considered in France as a day of relaxation and amusement, and <none> ↑little↓ of that attention to religious ceremonies that prevaild before the revolution, is observable at present. Tis true however that the churches are again opened and many go there to perform their devotions but they appear to hurry thro them with indifference that they may return to their business, or pleasures. Many of the stores &c are open all Sunday, and the streets are throngd with itinerent merchants as on other days. The theatres gardens & other places of amusement are crowded on Sunday evenings[.] in short it is a perfect holiday. Such of the merchants & principal inhabitants as can afford it have a country house just out of the city, where they retire on Saturday evening with their families and enjoy the air of the country & dust of the roads till the next evening.

July 15

This morning I went with three or four others to view the church of St Michel.[44] After viewing St. André's there is nothing in th<is>e ↑architecture of this↓ church capable of exciting admiration We ascended the <tower> ↑steeple↓ which stands at a little distance from the main body of the church, and enjoyed a very fine prospect from the top of it. The spire, which was of stone & very high, was blown down in a storm about thirty or forty years since,[45] I could not learn if it did much damage in the neighborhood. In a vaulted appartment under this tower are several bodies of persons who have been dead a long time. They have been taken out of the family vaults of the church to make room for fresh corpses The skeletons remain entire and are covered with the skin as dry as parchment.[46] They were ranged about the wall without order & many had fallen to the ground and ↑were↓ trodden[47] to peices. The fellow who bore the light and shewed them to us, handled

44. It was built between the fourteenth and the sixteenth centuries.

45. The damage was done by the hurricane of 1768. The spire was replaced in 1865.

46. Owing to the nature of the soil, corpses interred in an old cemetery on this site were preserved virtually intact. The "momies," as they were called, were long a tourist attraction.

47. "den" is in smaller script.

them & tossd them about without ceremony It reminded me strongly of the gravedigger scene in Hamlet. Here was a true picture of the equality to which death reduces us. persons of all ranks and descriptions crowded promiscuously together, ↑In one corner↓ the body of a belle leaned against that of a beggar and in another <corner one> a <knight> ↑chevalier↓ of the order of St Louis[48] was the intimate neighbor of a common Porter!

After leaving the church we visited the museum. This is an institution commenced since the revolution. The collection is small but very prettily arranged.[49]

In the afternoon I went out of town to dine with Mr Jonathan Jones and his family at their country house.[50] The afternoon passed delightfully. The old gentleman is extremely sociable & good humored, Mrs Jones is very agreeable, & he has two daughters the finest girls I have seen in Bordeaux. The girls talk english tolerably well, dress in the American style considerably and resemble very much the young ladies of New York[.] perhaps this latter circumstance reccommended them more to me than any other for I confess I have not yet got rid of my prejudices in favor of the American girls

<The In walking the pr>

July 17

<In walking the principal streets one is ↑I am↓ very well pleased with the d>

The french ↑trades people↓ display <infinit> a very pretty taste in the arrangements & decorations of their shops &c. This is particularly observable in the shops of the milliners the confectioners and other

48. Louis IX (1214–1279), who became King of France in 1226, was canonized in 1297. The Order of St. Louis was founded by Louis XIV in 1693 for military merit.

49. This establishment was opened in 1801 by Rodrigues and Goethals, who brought together their collections – Rodrigues' of natural history and Goethals' of pictures – in a house in Rue Malby; they separated in 1806 (Young, *Irving à Bordeaux,* p. 208).

50. Jonathan Jones (1748–1835) was a native of Philadelphia and long-time merchant in Bordeaux. He married Jeanne Texier (1765–1829), by whom he had three children: Suzanne, Sally, and Jacques, who were at this time 18, 15, and 9 years old respectively. His residence in the city was 29 Allées de Tourny, a house still in existence in 1946 (at that time it was No. 58). He had two country houses; that which Irving visited on this occasion was 225 l'Avenue Thiers in the Quartier de la Bastide of Bordeaux. See Young, *Irving à Bordeaux,* pp. 53–57.

dealers <of> in fashions and delicacies. The principal streets have a gay look from this circumstance and a stranger is tempted at every turn, to purchase, from the pretty and inviting manner in which the merchandize is spread to view. The trades people also seem to be great adepts in the art of persuasion and with a very little knowledge of the English language and an infinite share of adroitness and insinuation, they can manage to make some of our simple country men purchase a thousand things they have no occasion for.

I was highly amused the other day with a specimen of their ingenuity in this particular. I went to the Exchange[51] with an honest American captain and as the hour of change had not commenced we amused ourselves with walking in a wide lobby that runs round the change room, and on each side of which are arranged *Boutique's* or stalls <of jewellers> of all kinds of merchandize, jewelry millinary literary &c &c ad infin. The captain stopped before one of the Boutiques where a variety of musical instruments were offered for sale <and> to price a very small hand organ, which he thought of purchasing to teach a bird to whistle.

The stall was kept by a pretty little black eyed woman who could make out to prattle a little bad english. She immediately had a dozen instruments spread before the captain. He however did not want one for the present, and we were turning to go away when she begged we would accompany us [her] to a ware house she had close by where she would shew us some fine instruments. The captain turnd to me & wispered with a knowing wink "Dam'me lets go and over haul her trumpery, youl see how she'll try to come along side of us, but the devil a sous[52] do I lay out for her fiddles or music mills." We accordingly accompanied her, to her ware room in the second story of <an>a neighboring house. Here she displayed a fine assortment of organs & hurdy gurdys, played Hail columbia, yankee doodle, got her husband to play on the forte piano, <?unl?> uncorked a bottle of wine & made us drink, in short I cannot tell one tenth of <th>her manouevres but by the help of music & wine and flattery & a pretty face the honest captain was so bewildered that before he got out of the ware room he had bought a large ↑hand↓ organ for 400 liveres[53] (a third more than it

51. The Bourse, on the Place de la Bourse, was laid out between 1738 and 1755 from plans by Jacques Gabriel.

52. The exchange rate at this time was one sou for one cent, as Irving's expense accounts indicate.

53. The exchange rate at this time was one livre for 18½¢, as Irving's expense accounts indicate.

was worth) which he did not know what the devil to do with after he had got it.

July 25

I was witness to a little ceremony the other day that pleased me more than many that I have seen of the kind that were accompanied with infinitely superior shew & grandeur. It was a funeral. An American sailor had been drowned and several of his Brother Tars had assembled to pay the last tribute of respect to his memory The <corps> ↑coffin↓ was carried on a Bier, preceded by the American flag <stretchd> spread horizontally and ↑the corners↓ held by <sai>four sailors, after the corps, the <ensign> [*blank*][54] of the ship was carried in the same manner and was followed by the remainder of the ships <company>. ↑crew.↓ The deceased, I found out had been a great favorite among his messmates – a "fellow of infinite jest," much like Dibdens "Tom Bowling."[55] His loss had been sensibly felt by them, and the <sad> ceremony I had just seen had been dictated by the honest affections of their hearts

Tho I am not one of those who ascribe almost every virtue to the character of a sailor, yet I confess there are often such genuine traits of honest worth displayed by this class of beings, that I do not wonder they gain more credit than they deserve. Removed from intimate intercourse with the world, placed among men <cares> careless and simple in manners as himself, the sailor does not acquire that habit of hypocricy & simulation common in society. He has no need to disguise his feelings or affect a different character than the one he possesses. Of course all his good deeds are spontaneous, his attachments sincere & uninterested. Conscious of no deceit in himself he suspects none in others and displays a frankness and openess of conduct <peculiar> extremely prepossessing. He sets no value on money except as it con-

54. It is not certain what word Irving might have substituted here. Presumably this was a merchant ship and thus "ensign," the term for the national flag flown by naval vessels, was incorrect.

55. The quotation is from Shakespeare's *Hamlet,* IV, iii, 203–4. Tom Bowling is the title character in the elegy written by the English actor, author, and composer Charles Dibdin (1743–1841), reportedly in memory of his brother, which appeared in his *Oddities* (1789–1790). Stanza three contains the lines:

> And then he'd sing, so blithe and jolly,
> Ah, many's the time and oft!

See Charles Dibdin, *A Collection of Songs* (London, 1799), I, 231.

tributes to his pleasure and gratification and < wh the> squanders or gives it way with a freedom that is often mistaken for generosity.

July 29

The most fashionable evening promenade in Bordeaux is the Tourney. This is a walk shaded by three rows of <treess> trees in the centre of one of the principal streets. It presents an entertaining melange of figures & characters. <I often> Whether it is, that I am accustomed to the strange looking beings in New York or not, I cannot say, but it appears to me there <are> is a greater proportion of *outré* objects among the french, than with us. The females dress in three distinct modes indicative of their situations & ranks, tho there are intermediate modes <that> proportioned to the circumstances <& also> of the wearers. Of the Belles you may form some idea from our elegante's in New York tho' they are rather more transparent and uncovered here. The <tradesmen &> daughters of tradesmen & mechanic's, <all> dress very neatly and have a trim appearance, they wear a high cap with a narrow border round the face that has a pretty effect. The servant girls, fruit women &c wear long waists large caps with enormous borders that appear like wings on each side of their heads and at a little distance look like old women. As to the men there is an endless variety in their dress and appearance. <You Beside the variety> You may imagine therefore that a public walk crowded with such a diversity of objects must be amusing to a stranger. But besides these, there are jugglers musicians <mous> and mountebanks of one kind or another continually presenting themselves. I was walking the tourney this evening when I was attracted to the piazza of a handsome coffee house by a number of <p> savoyards male & female who were playing on three or four kinds of instruments and singing, their music was very pretty and the airs simple & sweet after they had finished <the> a girl went round with a little plate to receive the donations of the audience that had collected.

Walking a little farther I encountered another crowd who surrounded a Quack, whose was decorated with stuffed mole skins, a curious sea fish &c and surmounted by a tame hawk[.] he <was> had a rat in a cage which played many tricks at the word of command, after he had collected a sufficient crowd, he opened a box and began to sell his drugs descanting upon the merits of every one of them, and proving them all infallible.

A little further on, a Juggler was playing to another respectable <s>circle, and performing tricks with eggs cards &c His wife danced a hornpipe and two or three of his children tumbled. As soon as they had <went> gone[56] thro their routine of tricks his wife collected a few sous from such of the crowd as appeared most able to give them and then the husband commenced op<p>erating[57] in another branch of his profession. This was as a fortune teller. None of his audience however seemd anxious to peep into futurity, when casting his eyes around he happened to catch a glimpse of me as I stood a little distant from the throng in company with a young french man. The juggler immediately exclaimed, pointing at me, "voilà un homme de bonheur, venez ici Monsieur venez ici."[58] As I had no inclination to have my destiny proclaimed to the world I decamped from his neighborhood as soon as possible.

It is impossible to conceive the various modes the lower orders ↑in europe↓ have of getting a livelihood, unknown in America, nothing is thrown away here, and it is certain that a poor frenchman can live on almost nothing.

August 2[59]

As I intend leaving this place tomorrow I have been all over the city this morning & afternoon to take a farewell look, and to see such objects of curiosity as I had hitherto neglected. <There> In the course of my tour I was in several churches of less note than those I <had> ↑have↓ before mentioned. Some of them are undergoing repairs in those parts that have been injured during the revolution

It is painful to see so many fine specimens of the arts that have been the pride of ages long since passd away, defaced by the blind fury of a misguided populace. In one place I saw the ruins of what had once been a handsome church.[60] The steeple was still standing by itself and will <prop> probably one day or other bring down vengeance on the heads of its persecutors

In the afternoon I visited the church and convent of the Chartreuse.

56. The alteration is in pencil.

57. The alteration is in pencil.

58. "There's a man of good fortune. Come here, Monsieur, come here."

59. Irving drew on this entry in part of his letter to William Irving, August 1–4, 1804.

60. Probably St. Projet, built in the seventeenth and eighteenth centuries, damaged during the French Revolution (Young, *Irving à Bordeaux*, p. 197).

The holy fathers have long since been obliged to evacuate this habitation which at present is <conf> converted into a hospital for Negroes. The church however is still in a good state. It is small but very handsome. The Altar place is the most superb I have seen in Bordeaux. The walls of the church are painted in arches columns Galleries &c. The painting is well executed and makes the place look much larger than<d> it really is. Over the altar is a picture of a singular construction. It represents clouds with surrounding cherubims, the centre is left open and the light is admitted behind in a particular manner. The nearer you approach the picture the more this middle place seems illuminated. This is said to be an emblem of the deity tho' I confess it did not appear a very striking one to me. The lateness of the hour prevented my examining this picture and the rest of the church as much as I wished.[61]

August 3[62]

A delay in getting my passport[63] has prevented my leaving this place to day as I intended. I danced attendance yesterday morning on some <of> *dogs in office*[64] of the municipality and was informed that I must make a request in writing to Mr Le Commissaire Général[65] This I did before three oclock. I was then told I might call the next morning at 11 oclock and they would *see about it.* I represented that I was to depart the next day and any disappointment would be very embarrassing – *Tant pis Monsieur*[66] was the only reply and with this I had to be satisfied. The next morning I went at eleven, had a discription of my

61. The church of St. Bruno was built in the seventeenth century over an ancient Cistercian chapel. Above the altar is a painting of the Assumption by Philippe de Champaigne and over it is a scene such as Irving describes. The opening in the latter picture is still there, but light is no longer admitted through it. The Negroes to whom Irving refers were refugees from the 1791 revolution in St. Domingue. See Young, *Irving à Bordeaux,* pp. 199, 201.

62. Irving drew on this entry in part of his letter to William Irving, August 1–4, 1804.

63. Irving had two passports to leave Bordeaux: one delivered through the police and another delivered through the Chancellor of the city; for the description of him in each, see "Traveling Notes, 1804" (page 461).

64. "Behold the great image of authority: a dog's obeyed in office" (*King Lear,* IV, vi, 163).

65. Pierre Pierre was the Commissaire Général de Police in Bordeaux at this time. A traveler had to present his passport in order to obtain a seat in the diligence. See Young, *Irving à Bordeaux,* p. 19.

66. "So much the worse, Monsieur."

face and person taken and was directed to call at three in the afternoon for my passport. <As I had no disposition to hurry> The dilligence was to sett off at Four and seeing there was a prospect of my being much hurried and fatigued if I persisted in going to day I determined to rest contented till the Dilligence sets off again the day after tomorrow. I was the more willing to do this as <Mes> Mr Colden & Mr S——[67] had just arrived from paris having made a hasty tour thro Italy & Switzerland. I have procured considerable information & advice from them that will be useful on my route. S—— is quite tired of travelling. he says he finds himself a little older than when he sat out, but very little wiser. Two thousand Dollars out of pocket and not two thousand cents worth of improvement in. <He> If however he has not acquired much knowledge in his travels he certainly has not fell into that habit of self importance & affectation common to many young Americans who spend any time in france. If his friends do not find him much better than when he left New York, they will not find him any worse.

Of Mr C—— I can only say he has fully answered the high opinion I had formed of him. He is a gentleman of the worthiest character.

As I am now about quitting Bordeaux it is probably necessary to say something about <the> its history, its founders &c &c[.] on this subject I shall be very brief for my information is chiefly picked out of French books that I cannot read very fluently.[68]

The historians of Bordeaux make some dispute about <the> ↑its↓ first inhabitants. <of> Two opinions seem to have the most advocates. One is that it was founded by the ancient people of Berry (↑the↓

67. Cadwallader D. Colden (1769–1834), New York lawyer and politician, was then in the midst of an eighteen-month sojourn in Europe for his health. His sister was the first wife of J. O. Hoffman. See Edwin R. Purple, "Notes, Biographical and Genealogical, of the Colden Family, and of Some of its Collateral Branches in America," *The New York Genealogical and Biographical Record,* IV (1873), 178–80. Irving wrote a letter from Bordeaux to Colden in Paris, July 5, 1804, and commented on meeting Colden in Bordeaux in his letter to William Irving, August 1–4, 1804.

Henry Hamilton Schieffelin (1783–1865) entered his father's drug business and also began the practice of law in New York in 1805. See Maud Schuyler Clark, comp., *Schieffelin Genealogy* [chart] (1934); *Respice, Adspice, Prospice. One Hundred Years of Business Life 1794–1894* (New York [1894]), pp. 16 ff. Irving commented on meeting Schieffelin and reported examining Schieffelin's European expense accounts in his letter to William Irving, August 1–4, 1804.

68. In the remainder of this entry Irving drew chiefly on Bernadau's *Annales . . . de Bordeaux,* esp. pp. 26, 28, 29, 33, 35, 37, 39, 45, 53. Bernadau gives a list of his authorities on pp. 5–24.

Bituriges Vivisci) who fled before <Caesar> Cæsar when he conquered their territory and took refuge in the midst of marshes on the borders of the Garonne where they formed the first rudiments of a town.

The other opinion makes the first settlement more ancient, and ascribes it to a colony <of Phenicians> who came from Phénicie in Spain and used to trade among the gauls The origin therefore rests in some obscurity and it is of no importance to me to attempt to develope it[.] neither will I dwell upon the etymology of the name which one author thinks derived from the Greek word *Pyrgos* & *cala* and another from latin *Burgus* and *Galate,* both you will perceive have equal claims to <probability> credibility, <and it is almost as> and both are almost as direct & unadulterated derivations as that of *Noah* from *Fohi.*[69]

<at the time the Romans conquered Gaul>

<This> Under the reign of the ↑Roman↓ Emperor Adrian Bordeaux was established the Metropolis of the second Acquitaine, it was brought to a regular plan and surrounded by walls.

At the Beginning of the fifth century the Visigoths made an irruption for the first time into gaul, they held possession of Bordeaux till the commencement of the sixth century when it came under the power of the Kings of France & the dukes of Acquitaine.

During this period it was besieged and taken by the Saracens who were in turn defeated by the french. <it> Some of the Dukes who <suc> afterwards held possession of it in common with the rest of the province of Acquitaine endeavored to become absolute masters independent of the King of france. Charlemagne however <deffeated> defeated the last that made the attempt and it is said caused him to be assassinated The city was successively <raze> ravaged by the Normands the Bretons & the Danes till it was for a while almost abandoned by its former inhabitants. <Som>

Some time about the <year> middle of the twelvth century during the reign of Henry the second it passed <to> into the hands of the English. By these it was held till the year 1453 when it was retaken possession of by the French who have been masters of it ever since. This is a very <p> brief & perhaps incorrect outline of its history.

69. Fo-hi or Foë or Fuh-hi was, according to legend, the first ruler of China. Several details of his story are similar to Noah's, most notably the explanation that he was conceived as his mother was encircled by a rainbow.

It has been the seat of many intestine commotions – the object of many battles & sieges. I was shewn a Gothic gate[70] With two towers remaining perfect where the civil authorities stood a siege against the populace. Adjoining to this gate is a small church,[71] the door of which is nailed full of horse shoes of different ages and constructions. <said to have been> I was told it had formerly been the custom once a year to form a procession to this church and nail a shoe on the door but for why I could not understand. There is a small figure of a horse <cut> carved of stone over this door. The gate is of singular construction. Over it is one or two chambers where it is said their parlement used to set in ancient times. In front of the gate is an old clock & over it a Ball half Black & half gilt that turns upon a pivot & tells the Phazes of the moon.

Bordeaux contains several handsome streets; that of the Chapeau Rouge which leads from the theatre to the Exchange is very handsome, The Rue Tourney is also very fine The Theatre I have already said is a vast superb piece of architecture, there are none in london paris <or> in short in europe to equal it. It is built of the <?wites?> White lime stone used in architecture in Bordeaux. The Port is grand, in form of a crescent, The Buildings in many parts uniform for a great distance and have a noble appearance.

The population of Bordeaux was generally computed at one hundred & twenty or thirty thousand, but it has lately been ascertand that <t> it is not above eighty or ninety thousand. The city has a vast extent along the river, <running> being a compact front of about three

70. Apparently Irving refers to the Porte de la Grosse Cloche or St. Eloi of the Hôtel de Ville, one of the four towers at the angles of the old Hôtel de Ville, built between the thirteenth and fifteenth centuries.

He does not accurately describe the clock, however. Invented in 1756 by the mathematician Paul Larroque, it is in two parts: one on the north face of the belfry, telling the days of the week, and one on the south face, telling the phases of the moon. The ball above the dial is no longer to be seen.

He is also mistaken about the Parliament of the Province of Guyenne, which always sat in the Palais de L'Ombrière, the ancient residence of the dukes of Aquitaine. Possibly in this connection Irving confused the Porte Grosse Cloche with the Porte de Cailhau or Palais, a fifteenth-century edifice which was once the entrance to the Palais de l'Ombrière. See Young, *Irving à Bordeaux,* pp. 177-79.

71. St. Eloi was built in the fifteenth century, named for St. Eloi or Eligius (588–660), a native of Limoges, who was a metal-smith before taking holy orders and who became the patron saint of blacksmiths. The blacksmiths of Bordeaux had their confraternity in this church. The sculptured scene over the door depicts the Saint shoeing a horse whose leg he has cut off; according to legend, he once took this precaution against being kicked, and when finished with the job miraculously reattached the leg to the body. See Young, *Irving à Bordeaux,* p. 198.

miles. <The> It does not however <in the> except in the centre, run back very far from the river.

The wines of Bordeaux are deservedly of great celebrity and afford a vast article of exportation as do likewise its Brandies. The canal of Languedoc[72] is of infinite service in facilitating a communication with the Mediterranean. This is the most frequented port in france – particularly by the Americans who really crowded the harbor while I was there

The Garrone runs by it with extreme rapidity and people are frequently drowned thro carelessness in passing among the ships – which are all obliged to anchor in the current there being no built Quay. American seamen are particularly unfortunate in this particular as they often get intoxicated & fall over board when the swiftness of the river baffles all their attempts to save themselves. Indeed I myself had a narrow escape from a similar fate one evening. <An> A vessel had just arrived from New York and being very anxious to get letters I procured some men to take myself & D. Leffingwell[73] of New York, aboard in a Boat. As it was quite dark they could not see far ahead, and run across the cable of a ship. The current set us on so violently that all our efforts to disengage ourselves were for some time ineffectual and we were beginning to prepare to swim for our lives when the men by a violent exertion got us off just as one gunnel of the boat had reached the <waters> ↑waters↓ edge & began to ship <seas> a sea or two.

W<as>ere sufficient care taken in paving Bordeaux <well>, it would be a very agreeable city; but in dry weather the dust is intolerable and in wet <wh> weather you are equally annoyed with mud. The people are lively and communicative, but my imperfect knowledge of the language prevented me from mingling among them to advantage – and of observing the particular traits of their character.[74]

72. Also called the Canal du Midi, it extends from the Garonne below Toulouse to the Étang de Thau, a distance of 148 miles.

73. Daniel Leffingwell (d. 1804) was a New York merchant and insurance broker, member of the firm of Leffingwell and Dudley, who had come to Bordeaux with a ship of which he was part owner and was being detained by the government because it had touched the English port at Gibraltar. Irving first met him in Bordeaux on July 2, 1804 (Irving to William Irving, July 2, 1804). For other references to Leffingwell by Irving at this time, see his letter to Alexander Beebee, July 20, 1804. See also PMI, I, 66–69

74. The last three paragraphs, covering three quarters of one manuscript page and the whole of another, are in blue ink.

Toulouse, August 8, 1804[75]

I arrived in this <town> city last evening, much fatigued, but highly delighted with my Journey The country has far exceeded my expectations highly as they were raised, and presented a succession of the most beautiful & picturesque scenery. I left Bordeaux on the fifth at four oclock in the afternoon, in the Dilligence The company in the carriage consisted of a little opera singer of considerable celebrity her father and mother, a young french officer, a french gentleman who had just returned from a voyage round the world & myself.[76] The little actress belonged to <Tolo> Toulouse and had been to Bordeaux to perform for a few evening's.[77] The young officer was going to Languedoc to see his relations and the voyager to Agen for the same purpose

The road all the afternoon was sandy and the Country too level to offer much variety[.] at nine oclock we stopped at a small town calld Castres, where we supped[.] after supper we resumed our seats and rode all night. The night was dark and the ride consequently fatigueing. Just before day break we crossd the Garonne at Langon a small town. The Ferriage is by scows, into which the carriages drive the same as those used in America. After crossing the river we found the road hard and good and the country interesting. We continued <to> riding within sight of the river and just at day break passed thro a small village,[78] the inhabitants were still asleep, <at a little v> at one end of the village stood <the> an old Castle in a very ruinous state, One wing of it however was still standing in tolerable condition. It had a most picturesque appearance as the first gleams of morning fell on its mouldering towers. It stood on the <Brow of the river> Brow of a high bank of the river, which glittered at its Base. The <appearance> discriptions of Mrs Radcliffe[79] were brought immediately to my reccollection[.] this would

75. This entry is in an ink apparently black to "The Theatre is a shabby old building," thereafter in gray-black. Irving drew on this entry in his letter to William Irving, August 14–17, 1804.

76. Possibly the opera singer was a Mlle. de Longchamps, member of the group known as L'Athénée of Toulouse. Presumably the French voyager was Jean Baptiste George Marie Bory de Saint-Vincent (1778–1846), French naturalist. See Young, *Irving à Bordeaux,* pp. 21, 129–31.

77. The apostrophe seems to be in pencil.

78. Presumably St. Macaire (see Irving's entry for August 6 in "Traveling Notes, 1804"). The chateau of the town occupied its southwest corner. It was mostly demolished in 1626 but the donjon remained standing until 1837. See Leo Drouyn, "Saint-Macaire et ses Monuments." *Bulletin Monumental,* Ser. 2, VI (1861), 554.

79. Ann (Ward) Radcliffe (1764–1823) was one of the most popular of English

have formed a fine picture for her talents to work upon. The Dilligence passed too fast for me to examine it particularly. <the scenery continued to> After a variety of handsome views rendered particularly so by a charming morning we arrived at the town of Reole, to breakfast

This place was formerly defended by walls & towers[.] they are now however crumbling away and serve but to give the town a ragged and ancient appearance There is an old church & convent ↑that↓ formerly belonged to the Benedictines.[80] The <town> manufactures of the towns are combs and cutlery

After Breakfast I exchanged places for the day with a frenchman who was seated in the *cabriolet*[.] this is a place in front of the Dilligence where three persons can sit. it has a boot, like our Gigs & phaetons, and is open in front with an oil cloth curtain to draw in case of rain. It is a little cheaper than the inside of the carriage, but in the summer I think it is preferable as it commands a view of the country around and is cool and agreeable except when the sun is in front

In this place I found a singular little genius, quite an original[.] his name was *Henry*, a Doctor of Medicine originally of Lancaster in pennsylvania <but for a long time by> ↑by↓ his talk he appear[s] to have been for a long time a citizen of the world.[81] He is about five feet ↑4 inches↓ high, and thick set talks french fluently and has an eternal tongue. He knew every body of consequence. Ambassadors consuls &c were Tom Dick & Harry – intimate acquaintances, The Abby Winkleman had given him a breast pin, Lavater had made him a present of a snuff Box and several authors had sent him their works to read & criticise[82]

He had been this route before and amused me much by his observa-

---

Gothic novelists. In her *Mysteries of Udolpho* (1794) the chateau of M. St. Aubert is located on the banks of the Garonne, and the first and last parts of the action take place in Languedoc.

80. The abbey church of St. Pierre was built about 1200.

81. This person, whose name Irving spells both "Henry" and "Henory," does not seem identifiable through local records and is not mentioned in the records kept at the American consulates in Marseilles and Genoa, where he is known to have been. Henry turned out to be a swindler (see Irving's letter to William Irving, December 20, 1804).

82. Johann Joachim Winckelmann (1717–1768), German archeologist and historian of ancient art, took up residence in Italy in 1755; he was called abbé because of his attachment to the Vatican. Johann Kaspar Lavater (1741–1801), Swiss poet, mystic, and physiognomist, resided in Zurich in his late years.

tions and discriptions. <what> It seems he thought it was necessary for him to be acquainted with every object of importance we passed, to support his character of an intelligent traveller – of course, whenever I enquired respecting any building he had an answer immediately ready, and six times <of> ↑out↓ of ten it was erroneous. A castle he would often mistake for a convent and a manufactory for a church. He however gave me several articles of advice that I expect I shall find useful in travelling. Whenever the Dilligence stopped at any of the small towns to change horses &c we <wou> dismounted and strolled thro the streets talking to every one we met. The voyager could talk english fluently and was much of a Gentleman both in appearance and manners. We found the women very frequently seated outside of their doors at work, and they were always ready to converse.

At Tonneins[83] as we were patroling in this manner we passed a house where a number of Girls were quilting, we immediately returned and accosted them[.] I went into the room and one immediately gave me a needle to work with. The <people> girls (in common with the people in this part of france) spoke the language so barborously that I could not understand what they said. They were highly amused with my bad french and were laughing the whole time we were there. My companions <at la> as I was going away told them I was an *English prisoner* <which> that the young officer had in charge. their merriment immediately gave place to pity, Ah! le pauvre Garçon said one to another, he is merry however, in all his trouble. "And what will they do with him" <sai> enquired a young woman of the *voyager*, "Oh nothing of consequence replied he – Perhaps shoot him or cut off his head." The honest souls seemed quite distressed for me. I happened to mention that I was thirsty and immediately a bottle of wine was placed before me nor could I prevail on them to take any recompense. In short I departed loaded with their good wishes and I suppose furnished a theme of conversation throughout the village

After passing thro Tonniens and riding a few miles we came to the Banks of the River Le Lot at which there is a ferry. From this place we had a fine view of Aigullon a Town situated on an eminence on the opposite side of the river. It had formerly a large chateau[84] be-

83. Irving revisited this town forty-one years later and wrote his recollections of his earlier experiences there to his sister Catherine (Irving) Paris, November 1, 1845.

84. It was the eighteenth-century home of the dukes of Aiguillon.

longing to it <in which the Duke of Aig> which was sold as confiscated property in the time of the revolution and part of it has since been demolished, the walls of the town are also in ruins.

Throughout the country we found the people employed in threshing, harvest having been gatherd some time before. Threshing seems to be completely a *family* peice of business here and all are employed men women and children. They thresh their grain always in the field, and I have seen eight <&>or nine men & women threshing in one spot, they keep excellent time in their motions, as the safety of their heads depends upon it. The women <thro> in this part of the country wear handkerchiefs printed with flowers &c & folded in a particular manner so that a large figure appears on the front of the head & the handkerchief falls down behind with prints resembling lace. Fashions seem to be very permanent here, the daughter dresses like the mother and grandmother and a little distance off you can hardly tell them apart. The masculine labors they go thro in the fields, threshing &c in common with the men, gives them a coarse look and dark complexion directly opposite to beauty and the dresses that they wear, which probably may have been handed down from generation to generation destroy all idea of grace or figure. They however appear to be a gay, contented set of beings that have forgotten that such an idea as *equality* ever existed in France.

At the town of Port St Marie we witnessed a funeral ceremony of an old <pers> man, that was quite new to me. The corps was proceeded by a number of persons habited in white, their faces covered with white veils with two small holes <to permit> for them to see thro. These I was told, were persons called Penetents, who had made a vow to bury the dead and that they always attended in this dress with their faces conceald – They were followed by four priests, and then came the corps in an open coffin habited in similar white robes, and the procession was closed by the relatives & friends of the deceased. They chanted prayers <&> the whole way and had a most solemn appearance.

We put up at <nine> ten oclock at night at Agen a considerable town situated on the Garonne and containing manufactures of silk & woollen. The lateness of our arrival and our early departure prevented my having an opportunity of viewing the place.

In the morning we set forward at three oclock, & breakfasted at

Croquelardit. After leaving this place we continued on for some distance till we arrived at the heights of Moissac. Here I got out and walked up the hills, and never did I see a prospect that gave me more dilight. As the road ascended among the heights a continual succession of prospects presented themselves. To the right, on an eminence stood the ruins of a castle[.] the hill on which it was situated gradually swept down into a delightful valley <?thoro?> through which the Garonne wandered, <sometimes> giving life & animation to the scene. The hills were coverd with vineyards, and small cottages were scatterd in different directions A number of peasant girls mounted on mules, descending the heights, added to the picturesque nature of the scene. The view from the top of the hill, however, baffles all discription. Beautiful vales presented themselves on every side. The eye embraced a vast extent of country, a vast and firtile valley thro which the Garonne pursued its winding course <often> ↑now↓ lost among the trees that fringed its borders and <often it> now breaking upon the view glittering with the sun beams. The country beyond it had the most luxuriant appearances, vineyards, groves & corn fields were mingled together & varied with villages castles & cottages. <The> When I stood upon the height and looked at the enchanting country before me I could not but think of the verses of Watts' that you[85] so much admire

Sweet fields beyond the swelling flood
  <Starend>[86] ↑Stand↓ dressed in living green
So to the Jews old Canaan stood
  While Jordan rolld between &c &c[87]

We continued riding <thro> among these hills for some time, with the most romantic views continually presenting themselves till we came in sight of the Town of Moissac. This was situated in a <small> valley far below us, and be<yond>fore it a small river[88] passed rapidly along. As we wound down the hill the town was seen in different directions and its old towers and battlements had a fine affect from the situation

85. William Irving

86. Irving first wrote "Are," altered it to "Stand"; "nd" is written over "re" in blue ink.

87. The quotation is the second stanza of Isaac Watts, Book II, Hymn 66, in *Hymns and Spiritual Songs* (1707). The first line is "There is a land of pure delight." The final &c's. are in blue ink.

88. The Tarn.

in which they were placed. After crossing the ferry at this town we found ourselves on one of the vast plains of Languedoc. We were the whole afternoon crossing it. The harvest had lately been gathered so that the plain had not a very verdant appearance. It was <dim> sun set when we arrived at this place which is situated at one extremity of the plain, and is built on both sides of the Garonne As I am tired of discription and it is late at night you must excuse any thing very particular about this place. It is by no means to compare with Bordeaux for beauty, tho it has several beautiful walks in its environs It is built entirely of Brick, and the Brick is by no means so handsomely manufactored or so handsomely put together as the Brick in New York. The streets are very narrow & winding. I have been in two or three of the churches which were profusely adorned with pictures & paintings

The Theatre[89] is a shabby old building – you approach to it thro a convent or rather what *was* a convent. The interior of the Theatre is equally poor and the scenery old & tarnished <The> It is lighted the same way as all the french theatres that I have seen, are, by a chandalier hung in the centre & by the <lig> lamps ranged along the front of the stage as with us.

The Capitoul, or City Hall of Toulouse is a handsome building & occupies one side of a tolerable Square.[90] There is a handsome Bridge[91] over the Garonne which commands a fine view up & down the river, with a distant prospect of the Lofty <Appenines> Pyrenees the mountains that divide France from Spain. The Esplanade along the Banks of the Garonne and other walks in the environs of the town are very handsome.

This place was formerly a capital of the Visigoths and has been the seat of many commotions.[92] The Young French officer was very attentive and polite in shewing me the place[.] he had been here before and was acquainted with the Streets &c.

89. The only theater open in Toulouse at this time was the so-called Salle Saint-Martial, named the Théâtre de la Liberté when it was established in 1793. See Jules Chalande, "Histoire Monumentale de l'Hôtel de Ville de Toulouse," *Revue Historique de Toulouse,* XII (1925), 52–53.

90. The Capitole, on the east side of the Place du Capitole, so called because the town magistrates or Capitouls assembled there, was built between 1750 and 1760 by Lambert François Thérèse Cammas.

91. The Pont-Neuf was built between 1543 and 1614.

92. Toulouse was the capital of the Visigoths from 419 to 506 and was the scene of much fighting during the Albigensian Wars (1209–1229).

August 14[93]

The next morning (9th) I took passage on board of a post boat of the canal of Languedoc. I found on board the Little Doctor, who I mentioned before, and a young midshipman who had come by the same Dilligence with me and was going to join his ship at Toulon.

The <Packet> Post boat is drawn by two horses and goes at the rate of ten or twelve leagues a day. The locks are very numerous and every now and then the Baggage was shifted from one boat into another which caused considerable delay. The boats have cabins of nearly their whole length and high enough for a tall man to walk upright in them. The canal winded thro the most delightful plains highly cultivated; the hills gentlely swelling & crowned with villages & castles There is vast quantities of Indian corn raised in these plains, which almost made me fancy myself in my own country

There were two very pretty french girls on board, to whom the little Doctor, (who among his other qualities possesses a world of Galantry) was exceeding attentive and officious. In the afternoon they were leaving the boat to go to their homes in a neighboring town. The Doctor would not let them go without a great many compliments & kept us waiting by his talk. At last as one of the Girls attempted to get away from him <she> he seized her by the gown, she pulld of his hat with his peruque in it, he chased her and she threw the wig into the canal It was a high scene to see the little man fishing for his wig bald headed.

The canal throughout passed thro a variety of the most beautiful scenery. At one time it was higher than the adjacent plain and wound round a bluff of land on which were the ruins of an old castle while below the plain presented a scene of mingled verdures with a beautiful river[94] winding through it. The same river after a while rolls *under* the canal which is conducted over <the> it in an arched aqueduct of stone. It then meandres thro the valley to the right and is lost among distant Hills. At another time it passed <und> by the walls of an old town built on the side of a Hill the old towers of which formed pic-

93. There is no dateline in the manuscript. It is probable on the basis of internal evidence that the account of these events of August 9–14 was written on August 14, after Irving arrived in Montpellier. The entry, to the last paragraph, is in gray-black ink.

94. In this paragraph Irving seems to be describing the portion of his journey from Trèbes to Someil (see his entry of August 10 in "Traveling Notes, 1804"). Between these towns there are three rivers: the Fresquel, the Trapel, and the Orbeil, of which the last is the most important.

turesque objects in the extensive prospect.[95] The sunsets were particularly beautiful. At one place w[h]ere we put up for the night I was delighted with an evening promenade. It was one of those mild lovely evenings common in this Delightful country. The sun sank behind the distant Hills shedding rays of the mildest glory on the surrounding country. A <y> rich yellow gleam was cast upon the <old> mouldring towers of Trebes,[96] (the ↑small↓ town where I put up) The distant hills were tinged with the softest blues & purples and the ↑mistiness of↓ evening blended the valleys into the utmost harmony of tone softening every harsh & discordant feature or color of the landscape and producing a tout ensemble the most mild & enchanting

The canal at one time passes under a hill, the ↑pass is↓ called the *Montagne Percée*. It is said to be four hundred & eighty feet in length[97] <and part> is handsomely arched & part of the way with hewn stone. On the top of the hill are vineyards & cornfields

The Auberges (Inns) at which you stop in going by the Canal are very poor and the people not very attentive. At one of them where we stopped to dine I met an American gentleman & his lady who <had been> ↑were↓ making a tour in france. You should be in my situation, solitary & among strangers of a different <lang> country language & manners to concieve my pleasure at encountering Americans so unexpectedly. Dinner time passed away most rapidly & agreeably. The Lady was handsome & engaging and her husband a very clever fellow They were of Boston. It was with the utmost regret I parted with them.

The Peasantry are a coarse rugged set of beings, ↑some of↓ the men have exceeding sunburnt complexions & black hair and look something like our Indians The women are <d> sturdy masculin<g>e and most disgusting viragos. They are continually scolding and bawl out with the utmost rapidity and violence, accompanying their vulgar & indecent language with distortions and furious gesticulations[98] At one time as I was walking along the banks of the canal I took the liberty

95. The chief towns situated along the Canal du Midi are Baziège, Villenouvelle, Villefranche-de-Lauragais, Castelnaudary (where Irving spent the night of August 9; see his entry for this date in "Traveling Notes, 1804"), and Carcassone, all of which have fourteenth- and fifteenth-century towers or walls.

96. The towers of Trèbes were built by the Gauls.

97. Now called Tunnel de Malpas, it is reckoned about 528 feet long.

98. Irving commented on the peasants in much the same terms in his letter to Alexander Beebee, August 24, 1804.

of gathering some figs from a tree near a house. One of these termagents immediately attacked me with her tongue demanding money for what I had taken; & scolding most horridly – I stood patiently and every time she stopped to take breath shrugged up my shoulders & said *Nong tong paw,*[99] she at last had to give out & left me cursing me for *un miserable anglais.*

At all the towns we passed that were situated near the canal there were great numbers of the women standing <to their> in the water washing clothes. This is done by laying the clothes on a rough stone & beating them with a flat piece of board – a manner <evidently> ↑eminently↓ calculated to benefit the linen manufactories. There appeared a great scarcity of Petticoats among these women one petticoat having often apparently been divided among two or three of them. The Dress of the women is very grotesque[,] a Long waist, red petticoat and woolen hat with a round crown & enormous brim. I generally made my breakfast on bread wine & grapes, in the boat in preference to stopping at the dirty auberges.

After three days & a half sailing on the canal <we> amid a variety of scenery similar to what I have described we <came in> arrived at <Bezies> Beziers. This town is finely situated on a hill and appears very handsome from a distance The cathederal & a convent[100] are very conspicuous & the former is a handsome old building You approach the town over a beautiful Stone bridge of several arches that crosses the river Orbe.[101] A road is cut in a zig zag direction up the side of the Hill and enters one of the gates at the Highest part of the town. From this road you have a grand & extensive view. At your feet are the suburbs of the city by which passes the beautiful river Orbe, running thro a vally the most fruitful & highly cultivated, distributed into vineyards, corn fields & plantations of olives & almonds and high mountains in the distance

I had not time to examine this handsome little town as much as I wished, as I was to set off immediately after dinner on the route to

99. This phrase represents a nasal pronunciation of "Je n'entends pas" ("I don't understand"). Presumably Irving refers to the song in Charles Dibdin's *General Election* (1796), "Monsieur Nongtongpaw," in which an Englishman thinks the phrase is a proper name. See Dibdin, *A Collection of Songs,* V, 32–33.

100. The church of St. Nazaire was built in the twelfth and fourteenth centuries and the adjoining cloister in the fourteenth century.

101. The Pont Vieux, with seventeen arches, was built in the thirteenth century over the River Orb.

Montpellier. The Doctor had agreed with the owner of a Berlin[102] to take <me &> the young midshipman ↑& myself↓ to that place. The owner at first demanded eighteen livres from each of us, but the Doctor who is an old Traveller made him take that sum for *both.* An instance of the extortion of these people. The little Dr I found a most excellent hand to manage these affairs, so that when any demand was made upon me I pretended not to understand & turned them over to the Doctor[.] by this means I escaped much trouble and imposition & the Dr was highly pleased with his employment. I was particularly amused with a scene between him and a woman who owned a cart that had brought our trunks from the canal to the inn. She demanded three times her due, The Doctor refused to give her a farthing more than the just price[.] a violent contest ensued, the Dr pretended to be in a violent passion, and fairly outdid her in talk & gesticulation, so that she was obliged to put up with the price she [he] chose to give. The poor woman when she found that she could not get in a word edge ways began to cry & afterwards swore that if that little man had not have talked so much & so fast she would have had twice as much

The Doctor took a place in the Berlin with us, as far as Meze, a small town on the coast of the Mediteranian. The owner of the Berlin had engaged to have three mules but when we came to set off he had but two. He seemed out of humor from the Doctors having obliged him to make an honest bargain We were dragged along at a snails pace for the driver would not put his mules off of a walk In the evening we put up at Pezenas, a handsome little town with pleasant walks in its environs. Took an agreeable evening promenade.

The next morning (13th) we rose early & resumed our route. The day break was beautiful. The similar scenery as the preceding – vineyards olives almonds & mulberrys &c. After sun rize we arrived on an eminence and for the first time I had a sight of the Mediterranean. The prospect was superb. A vast extent of country lay before me presenting a perfect paradise and beyond it the Mediterranean was seen, smooth and unruffled, with numbers of fishing boats reposing on its bosom. The sun had just gained a little height and <g> cast a gleam of splendor on the glassy ocean. We breakfasted at Meze a small town beautifully situated on the sea shore, & here we parted with the little

102. A four-wheel carriage, having a separate sheltered seat behind the body, invented in Berlin in the seventeenth century.

Doctor who intended taking a fishing boat there to go to Cette a small sea port.

It was with regret I took leave of the little man for he had proved a most amusing character to me. He is an excentric genius, with a great deal of talk & considerable information He possesses the happy faculty of making himself at home every w[h]ere has something to say to every body & is acquainted with any person in five minutes. He has a great flow of spirits much drollery & is very fond of quizzing. He was continually passing himelf off on the Peasants for a variety of characters. Sometimes a Swede sometimes a Turk, now a German & now a Dutchman. With a Farmer he was a Wine merchant, with a Shoemaker, a Tanner, with an officer he was ↑formerly↓ a captain in the American army with others a professor in one of the German colleges & with others a secretary of the American minister who was travelling <to the med> with dispatches to Commodore Preble[103] in the Mediterranean.

He talked four or five languages, told the honest people wonderful stories of his hair breadth scapes among the Turks & the American Indians

In one town he made them believe I was an english prisoner, in another he took the landlady aside told her I was a young mameluke of distinction travelling *incog* & that he was my interpreter. Asked her to bring me a large chair that I might sit cross legged after the manner of my country and desired a long pipe for me that I might smoke perfumes. The good women believed every word, said she had no large chair but she could place two chairs for me and as to a pipe she had none longer than was generally used by the country people The doctor said that would not do and since she could not furnish those articles – she might bring a bottle of her best wine with good bread & cheese & we would eat breakfast

He gave me a variety of servicable advice concerning travelling, and bade me good bye telling me when next we met I might probably find him a conjuror or high german Doctor.

After riding thro a variety of charming views with the Mediterranian frequently presenting itself, we arrived at five oclock at Montpelier.

Here we had no sooner stopped than I was assaild by a regiment of

103. Edward Preble (1761–1807), American naval officer, was in command of the U. S. squadron in the Mediterranean in 1803/1804.

porters, voituriers & servants. Some wanted my trunk, others to know if I wanted a voiture for any other town & others reccommending their several hotels. I repaired to the Hotel du Midi – my trunk was brought to my room by *two* porters one of whom I amply paid, the other insisted on a gratuity & was so clamorous that I had to bundle him head & heels out of the door and slammd it to<o> telling him to go & divide the *spoils* with his brother vagabond.[104]

Montpellier, August 15[105]

Montpellier is said to contain about 30,000 Inhabitants. It is pleasantly situated on an eminence, ↑by↓ which <gives it a free circulation of> ↑it enjoys a free circulation of↓ air & of the sea Breezes. The streets however in the interior, like those of all the French towns I have seen, are very narrow and winding and extremely dirty. The police of the place seem very inattentive to promoting its cleanliness, which, considering it as the resort of so many invalids, I should think ought to be an object of the first attentions. The exterior of the city is handsome, particularly the western side. The walls are old but picturesque & there is a very fine gate ↑on↓ that side[106]

The walks in the environs of the city are extremely pleasant & command fine prospects One in particular is superb, called <the> *La place de Peyrou.*[107] This is a fine extensive terrace surrounded with handsome stone ballustrades, <in the center> At one end is a Beautiful Temple built of white stone with pillars of the Corinthian order. in the middle of it is a fountain of the most limpid water that diffuses a delightful coolness around. Before the temple is a fish pond of the same clear water, tolerably stocked with fish. A grand aqueduct of stone resembling two <pr> bridges, one on top of the other, crosses a valley from a hill at a considerable distance and communicates with the terrace in rear of the temple. This aqueduct conveys the water that supplies the town. The lower part of the aqueduct has about 50 arches,

104. This paragraph, the last on the manuscript page, is in blue ink.

105. This entry and the next are in brown ink. There are several parallels between this entry and Irving's letter to William Irving, August 14–17, 1804.

106. The Porte du Peyrou was built in 1691 by Augustin Charles d'Aviler in honor of Louis XIV.

107. It was begun in 1689 by d'Aviler and finished in 1776. The *chateau d'eau,* or waterworks, at its western end, consisting of a pavilion into which the aqueduct St. Clement empties, was built between 1753 and 1756.

the upper part, nearly three times the number but smaller. The squares & places in the city are decorated with very handsome fountains surmounted with statues &c.

The view from the place de peyrou is extensive and beautiful. You have before you a vast & enchanting plain terminated on one side by Mountains and on the other by the Mediterranean. On a clear day you can see from this place, the alps in one direction & the Pyrenees in an opposite, both at a vast distance.

The theatre[108] is a decent looking building outside, and ↑the interior↓ is finished with much taste and prettiness. It is nearly about the size of our theatre at New York, but the stage is much smaller. The scenery is but indifferent, they have not in any theatre that I have seen in france the facility of shifting the scenery that you observe in our theatre. A scene always stands a whole act & is not shifted till the curtain is down. <Th> One of the peices they were acting in this Theatre when I was there, was a melodrame, a species of play that is very fashionable at present in Paris. At the conclusion of the piece a crown of laurel was thrown <to> on the stage to a favorite actress who had distinguished herself that evening. This <kind of> ↑is a↓ testimony of high approbation, common in France, and when I was at Bordeaux La Fond the famous actor had two thrown to him in the course of one evening.

On returning ↑last night↓ to the Inn, I was surprised & pleased at finding the Little Doctor there. He had dispatched his business at Cette and intended going on to Nice, where he should remain some time for his health. He introduced me this morning to a Mr Walsh of this place, originally an Irishman, but a naturalized citizen of America.[109] He gave us the most open & hospitable reception, and insisted on our dining with him. The afternoon passed most agreeably as the <open> honest hearty welcome of this clever fellow made us perfectly at home in his company.

This day has been the féte of the Assumption. In the evening, I was attracted <to> by a crowd & the sound of music, <to> ↑in↓ one of the principal streets. I found a company of Bakers, who were celebrat-

108. The Théâtre de la Comédie on the Place de la Comédie.

109. Peter Walsh (b. 1779?) had a commercial house in Montpellier and in Cette (now Sète). He was in charge of the American agency in Montpellier in 1805 and applied for the post of U. S. consul, but one was never established there (Letters of Application and Recommendation during the Administration of Thomas Jefferson, RG 59, NA).

ing the holiday with their sweethearts. The men were dressed in pink Jackets & white pantaloons with a sash round their waists and large cockd hats with enormous bunches of colored feathers. The girls wore yellow boddices & white petticoats and a little yellow hat stuck on one side of their heads gave them a very smart <q coque> coquetish appearance, they all held garlands of flowers & were dancing to the music of two or three savoyards. This is a specimen of the liveliness & gaiety of heart that characterized this people before the revolution, but which I am told <is much> has disappeared considerably since. To me however, who did not know them in their most thoughtless days, they still appear all vivacity and affability. This fete of Assumption I am told is celebrated with processions &c in other places but <are n> those are not permitted in towns like Montpellier where a great part of the inhabitants are protestants.

I saw more pretty faces ↑in proportion↓ among the girls of Montpellier than I have seen in any place in france besides. The climate of this place is said to have altered much for the worse in late years[.] the <sp winte> spring & summer are very variable[.] <when> all the while of my stay it was extremely hot. Autumn is the most favorable season.[110]

August 16[111]

I set off in company with the Doctor early this morning for Nismes,[112] in a voiture. between Montpellier and Lunel we met with four conscripts in chains, guarded by two soldiers on horseback. The conscripts are young men who at a certain age are obliged to join the army, and as they sometimes are reluctant to leave their family & friends they are conducted to their regiment in chains & sometimes imprisoned to prevent their escaping.

We dined at Lunel, a small town famous for its white wines. Here I was amused by a quarrel between two upright Postillions who were disputing which was the greatest rogue[.] one charged the other with stealing from the Travellers, he retorted in turn and charged the other with stealing from the <pass> travellers & his master into the bargain.

110. Irving made a similar comment on the climate of Montpellier in his letter to Alexander Beebee, August 24, 1804.

111. Irving drew on this entry in part of his letter to William Irving, August 14–17, 1804.

112. Present-day spelling, Nîmes.

"When Greek meets Greek then comes the tug of war"[113]

We entered Nismes this evening and Drove thro a public place where they were celebrating the Fair of St Roque.[114] Above all assemblages of Discordant noises that I have ever heard, I place a french fair without hesitation.

Drums & trumpets of shewmen & jugglers, whistles & pipes of children braying of Jackasses and as to the clack & confusion of womens tongues, the tower of <Babl> Babel itself could not have presented a more confused chattering.

August 17[115]

The fair is over, to day, but the sound of it is still to be heard. It has supplied all the children in the town with drums, trumpets and whistles and the whole place resounds with them. This was <f> but a trifling fair, but I am told that some of the principal<s> ones, held at <st>large towns and at stated periods, are vast and extremely curious. Had Hogarth ever been present at one of them he would have found an excellent situation for his *enraged musician*[116]

Nismes is placed by some historians 580 Years before Rome and in antient time was a city of great consequence.[117] The inhabitants at present are said to be 40,000. judging from the size of the place I should not thing [think] there were above half the number, but the houses are large and the french have a great faculty of stowing and packing

113. "When Greeks joyn'd Greeks, then was the tug of war" (Nathaniel Lee, *The Rival Queens,* 1677, IV, ii, 137). The line is commonly misquoted as Irving has it. The quotation is in blue ink, inserted between two lines in the manuscript.

114. The feast day of St. Roch (1295–1378?), thought to have been born in Montpellier, is August 16.

115. This entry is in black ink through "It has a noble appe," thereafter to the last paragraph, including the footnote, in brown. There are a few parallels between this entry and Irving's letter to William Irving, August 14–17, 1804, and he evidently drew on it in his letter to Alexander Beebee, August 24, 1804.

116. Hogarth's engraving "The Enraged Musician," first issued in 1741, depicts a violinist holding his hands over his ears while in the street outside his window various persons, from a crying child to an axe grinder, are making harsh noises.

117. On August 17, 1804, Irving purchased in Nîmes for 4 livres, 10 sous, a work he called "Notice Sur. Antiq. Nismes" (see the expense account for this date in "Traveling Notes, 1804"). Though no work with this title has been identified, he apparently drew in this entry on Leon Menard's *Histoire des Antiquités de la Ville de Nismes et de ses Environs,* the chief guide book to the city for many decades, which was first published at Nîmes in 1803 and had many later editions (see especially pp. [3]–6, 14–16, 21, 30, 67, 77, in the 1803 edition).

their carcasses in a very small space so that one of their house[s] would almost people a dozen in america. There are a number of Roman antiquities in this place in good preservation.

The ampitheatre* is a grand ruin and said to be the most perfect one of the kind in France. It is an elipse the grand axis of which is 67 Toises,[118] 3 feet and the smaller 52 toises 5 feet. It has a noble appearance, outside though much ruined and disfigured. The <first> lower part consists of sixty arcades that run round the building and formerly opened into a Piazza[.] the upper story is of the same number of arcades tho the Pillars are of a different order. Several ranges of seats still remain on the inside[.] they are oblong stones of six or eight feet in Length and ↑about↓ two <or> in diameter; and offer a striking contrast to the modern luxury of stuffd seats & leaning places. I believe there was no cement or mortar used in erecting the walls of this immense building. There is mortar at present in several places but it seems to have been put there in more modern times to prevent the places from giving way. The surfaces of the stone where they touch each other are <work> cut very even so as to fit well & to be compact. in many <part> of the highest parts of the walls I saw vast stones of eighteen feet in length. <It is difficult to imagine> The Romans must have had some immense & powerful machine to raise these enormous stones the height of above sixty feet from the ground and to place them in particular situations, besides, they must have been able to raise them with facility, otherwise they would certainly have preferred smaller stones which were more portable. The ampitheatre has suffered more from sieges & fire than from the gradual delapidations of time. Its injuries bear the marks of force and violence rather than the crumbling appearance of decay. It served as a fortress to the Saracen and sustained many assaults To prevent them from again applying it to that use Charles Martel is said to have filled it with faggots to which he set fire in hopes of destroying it. The flames have blackened the walls <and> outside, but the materials were not sufficiently inflamable to be consumed. The arena is crowded with shabby houses of poor people, they have also turned the arcades of the lower story outside into <Botig> Botiques and Dram Shops which prevents the curious examiner from seeing a great part of the construction.

* Supposed to have been built in the <reigh> reign of Antoninus pius.

118. A toise is 6.39459 feet.

In 1786 the King[119] gave orders to demolish these houses and to put the edifice as nearly as possible into its original state. These orders however were never put in execution for the houses still stand there a matter of grievance to every antiquarian.

P.S. It is computed to have been able to contain 17,000 spectators at 20 inches each.[120]

The *Maison Carrée*[121] is the most perfect roman remain I have yet seen, and is spoken of by French artists in the highest manner for the beauty of its proportions and the perfect manner in which it is finished. It is 82 feet long 35 Broad & 37 high, oblong and decorated with columns of the Corinthian order. It is a temple that was consecrated to Caius & Lucius Caesar adopted sons of Augustus. The frize and cornice are ↑sculptured↓ in a very delicate taste. The other chief antiquities are the *Tour magne* <sip> supposed to have formerly been a pharos <tho> much ruined at present. The ruins of a temple of Diana, a roman gate, & two mosaic pavements.[122] What is termed the Fountain of Nismes[123] is superb. <It> ↑The fountain itself↓ rises near the temple of Diana and supplies the whole city with water. But there is a garden near the fountain, which is called by that name, adorned with canals and various water works, erected over the vestiges of some antient roman Bathes These works are of hewn stone, ornamented with statues &c and are <?bo?> objects both of curiosity and admiration.

The streets of Nismes are remarkably dusty. The dust is very light and the least breeze of wind carries it along in clouds. The manufactures of Nismes are silks, silk stockings & some woolens. <Ni A>

119. Louis XVI (1754–1793) became King of France in 1774. The amphitheater was cleared of these houses in 1809.

120. This sentence is inserted between two lines in the manuscript.

121. Built between 20 and 12 B.C., this edifice was dedicated to Caius (d. A.D. 1) and Lucius Caesar (d. A.D. 2).

122. The Tour Magne is 98 feet high and was built about 50 B.C. The so-called Temple of Diana, probably originally a public bath, was built about 25 B.C. The Porte d'Auguste, remaining from an ancient fortification, was built in 15 B.C. Seven mosaics at Nîmes are listed in Menard, *Historie de Nismes,* pp. 68–69; others were discovered in the next few decades. Probably Irving is referring to the two large ones: that in the Rue and Maison de la Calandre Anglaise, found in 1766; and that in the Jardin du Gouverneur, found in 1785; engravings of them appear in the 1814 edition of Menard.

123. The name Fontaine de Nîmes is commonly applied to the whole area at the foot of Mt. Cavalier, in the northwest part of the city, in the midst of which the fountain rises. The nearby Jardin de la Fontaine was created about 1750, incorporating the ruins of a Roman shrine.

A roman Colony was settled at Nismes by Marcus Agrippa Son in Law of Augustus.

By some conversation I had with Dr Henory I had got quite out of conceit of my American protection, it was in writing from the Mayor of New York[124] and he said it was a chance if any of the french officers of Police would be able to read it or would know whether to give credence to the signature of the mayor or not. My French passport also gave a very poor discription of me, and as I was continually mistaken on the road for an Englishman, I began to apprehend I might get into some disagreeable situation with the police before I could reach Marseilles. I was much startled therefore, at Nismes while sitting a supper with several others in the hotel, at the entry of two or three officers of the police with a file of soldiers. They only came however to examine our passports and they passd over mine very lightly. A Young frenchman present was very impertinent to them, knowing that he had a sufficient passport in his pocket. The officers got highly enraged, threatened him with arrest, and one little fellow seemed ready to jump over the table at him. They had <got>, however, a stubborn <piece of workmanship> ↑fellow↓ to manage, for he laughd at their menaces and amused himself with their passionate expressions.[125]

At Nismes I parted once more with the little Doctor, who was so unwell that he could not proceed. He intended to return to <Moot> Montpellier and endeavor to proceed from Cette by water.

I have been two or three times more to look at the *Maison Carrée* and cannot sufficiently admire the sweetness of its constructure and the exquisite taste with which it is finished.[126]

August 19[127]

I left Nismes in the Dilligence for Avignon After riding two posts we came to the small river La Foux, <with the> on the opposite side of which was situated the small town of the same name, having a very picturesque appearance We crossd the ferry and then the country began to change and become more mountainous. We ascended among the heights and rode the most of the afternoon along a ridge of high rocky

124. De Witt Clinton (1769–1828) became mayor of New York in 1803.

125. The alterations in this sentence are in black ink.

126. This paragraph, the last on the manuscript page, is in blue ink.

127. This entry and the next are in brown ink. There are several parallels between this entry and Irving's letter to William Irving, August 26, 1804.

hills from whence we had now and then, delightful prospects of the Distant valleys, offering a charming prospect of verdure & fertility to the rugged barrenness of the mountains. Towards Sun set we came to where the road descended <into the> from the heights, and the view that here broke upon us surpassed every <thing> landscape I had seen in france. At ↑<about>↓ th<e at over ↑the f↓> foot of the hill lay the town of *Villeneuve*[128] thrown in shade by the hill excepting an antient convent of Chartreuse[129] formerly of great wealth & grandeur. This stood on an eminence high above the rest of the town, and the rich gleams of the setting sun, cast upon its towers & battlements of yellowish Stone, rendered it a prominent and interesting object. At a small distance <the> were seen the antient towers & castle of Avignon <glowing in> half buried in trees that are planted round the outside of the walls and reflected in the rhone that passes rapidly by. These towns are situated in one of those enchanting valleys that I have already described, where nature seems to have <f> exerted herself particularly to harmonize the scene and to fit it for the abode of tranquility, & love. The valley is highly cultivated. the Rhone wanders irregularly thro it and is seen to a vast distance forming delightful islands of luxurient fertility The view is bounded by ridges of mountains When I saw it the sun was setting among clouds and here & there threw partial gleams of the mildest radience on the landscape in one place lighting up the walls of an old tower, in another resting in rich refulgence on a distant mountain, while the others were envelloped in the shades of evening After descending from the heights we entered the town of Villeneuve where we quit the Dilligence and left our trunks to be carried to the <?po?> Bureau of the Port at avignon, we then walked to the ferry which was at some distance, where we crossed the Rhone in a scow; on the opposite side we landed under the walls of Avignon <Abo> In our way to the gate of the city we passed under a high cliff, on which is situated the castle in which the popes formerly resided.[130] On top on an old tower or rampart[131] on the brow of the

128. Villeneuve-lès-Avignon.

129. The Carthusian monastery, the Chartreuse de Val de Benediction, was founded in 1356 by Innocent VI.

130. The walls of Avignon, dating from 1350 to 1368, have thirty-nine towers. The Palais des Popes was built between 1335 and 1365 under Popes Benedict XII, Clement VI, Innocent VI, and Urban V and was used as a papal residence until 1411.

131. The ramparts were built between 1355 and 1366 by Innocent VI and Urban V.

cliff, were seated two soldiers, enjoying the setting sun an[d] playing on a french horn & clarinet, Their situation, appearance and music <had a very romantic> was very interesting & seemed to accord with the romantic scenery around.

August 20[132]

Avignon is celebrated in the classic world, for <being> ↑having been↓ the residence of Petrarch and Laura. I was shewn a picture in the portico of the church *de notre dame de dom,* of St George Slaying the Dragon and before him a Lady Kneeling in an attitude of supplication.[133] This <was> is said to be intended for a representation of Petrarch & Laura, the likeness of the former being taken in St George & of the latter in the lady. The painting is so much defaced by time the [that] the countenances & part of the figures are not discernable. The interior of this church was finished in an exquisite taste with carvings, gildings paintings, reliefs &c and has been admired by the most celebrated masters The blind fury of the revolutionary mobs <have> has stripped it of its paintings and scatterd the fine carvings &c in fragments about the floor. The church however is still magnificent, in ruins & worthy the attention of the traveller. The same rash & indiscriminating fanaticism that destroyed this beautiful edifice, has also entirely demolished the church of the Cordeliers which contained the tomb of the fair Laura,[134] so that there is no vestige remaining.

Avignon[135] <fo> was <formerly> ↑antiently↓ held by the Romans, after the destruction of the Empire it went thro many changes and masters. In 1348 it was sold by Joan Queen of Naples to the pope after she had lost her crown & been driven out of Italy[.] for seventy two years this was the seat of the popes till Gregory XI restored that honor

132. Irving drew on this entry in his letters to Alexander Beebee, August 24, 1804, and to William Irving, August 26, 1804.

133. Notre Dame des Doms was built in the twelfth century and altered in the seventeenth century. The fresco in the main portal, alleged to be a portrait of Petrarch and Laura, is by Simone Martini.

134. Laura was buried in the Chapelle de la Croix of the church of the Franciscan convent known as the church of the Cordeliers, which was established in 1390. The structure was demolished during the French Revolution, only the left aisle of the nave remaining. Laura's remains were removed to the Bibliotheque Nationale in Paris in 1793 and have since been lost.

135. Irving apparently drew on some printed account of the history of Avignon in this entry but it has not been identified.

to the Vatican.[136] It is said to contain between twenty & thirty thousand Inhabitants. It formerly boasted a vast number of churches & convents, the bells of which <g> kept a continual jingling – which occasioned Rabelais to give it the name of the *Isle sonnante*,[137] many of these churches still remain, but in a ruinous situation. I observed in most of the towns thro which I have passed, that they are endeavoring to repair the churches & once more put them in a state for worship. This is by order of Bonaparte who is rapidly reestablishing the papal religion. It will be impossible for them however to replace the fine Gothic ornaments the superb paintings & carvings that their senseless fury has demolished.

In avignon was stationed a troop of Gens d'armes. Their horses were the finest that I have seen in france, but the vagabonds do not seem to know how to treat them. I saw one of them cleaning his horse at the Door of the Gendarmerie. It was a beautiful animal & full of spirits. As he was combing it, the horse started, the brute flew in a violent passion to chastise the horse threw large stones at him sufficient to break his ribs and maim him forever. This cruelty to horses is universal among the lower order of French. I have <?watc?> seen <them> ↑<an> a postillion↓ exercise a continual flagellation on two or three poor skeletons of horses, from the time they set out from the post house till they arrived at the place of relay. One fellow in particular between Bordeaux & Toulouse, had four poor animals before the dilligence who had been so constantly used that their flesh was raw wherever it touched the traces, they were lame sick & weary. This however excited no indulgence in the wretch who drove them, he flogged them the more, to make them dread the pain of the whip more than of their sores. At the end of the post he came with hat in hand, <as is the custom among> to beg the customary gratuity given to postillions I ordered him away & told him such a cruel scoundrel as himself diserved to be put in the horses place and made to feel a little of his own discipline.

136. The pope who acquired the title to Avignon was Clement VI (1291–1352), who took office in 1342. Gregory XI (1330–1378), pope from 1370 until his death, moved the papal court back to Rome in 1377–1378, but Irving presumably refers to Gregory XII (*ca.* 1327–1417), pope from 1406 to 1415, whose resignation helped bring to an end in 1417 the succession of antipopes at Avignon.

137. Pantagruel's adventures on "l'isle sonnante" ("the ringing island"), as Avignon is called, are related in *Gargantua et Pantagruel*, Book V (1562–1564), chs. 1–8. Rabelais wrote Books I–IV of this work, but his authorship of Book V is in dispute.

The other passengers likewise refused to give him any thing, and I believe he got a lesson that made more impression than any he had ever recieved as it was addressed not to his heart – but his *pocket.*

I have heard it remarked by some traveller that when <a postillion sets off bef> you set off in any town in france, you must calculate on at least three or four stops before you get out of the town. Some part of the harness gives way, or some buckle is displaced or some strap is out of order. This is an absolute fact. For my part I generally allow two stops to a league and find on an average I am tolerably correct. The french load their horses with <an im> a huge quant[it]y of leather wood brass and iron. An immense stuffd & peaked yoke is placed upon their necks <enough to> and then their whole carcass is covered with straps saddles belts &c studded with brass nails, ornamented with worsted bobs and <rendered both> a profusion of bells that give a most harmonious sound. As these harnesses are of antient date and may have probably <survived thro> flourished for one or two centuries, you may suppose they are not of the strongest texture. They are however, mended with pieces of rope thongs of leather &c &c and it is natural to suppose that a machine so complicated, that depends upon so many minute articles to keep it together, must frequently get out of order.

But <let us> ↑to↓ return to Avignon. On an eminence at one end of the town <is> stands the <ch> castle in which the popes formerly resided. It is a venerable looking old building & very large. Above it is an esplanade[138] on top of the hill from whence the prospect is superb. I was up there at sun rise and took the same stand where I had seen the two soldiers the preceding evening It commanded a considerable view of the town – the walls flanked with square towers that surrounded it, the beautiful walks <that> in the environs, and the rich & fertile valley stretching to a vast extent, with the <ga> Rhone winding in glittering splendor thro it. At a distance was the town of Villineuve with the old <cont> convent of Chartreuse. Below me <I> were boatmen fishermen &c in groups on the shore <talking> joking & laughing tho their voices were almost lost in distance; <and an> three or four arches of an old bridge,[139] that stood in the river with an antique tower on them added to the picturesque beauties around me. The air was pure

138. Promenade du Rocher des Doms.

139. The Pont St. Bénézet, a fortified bridge, was built between 1177 and 1185; half of it was destroyed in 1669.

salubrious & reviving, and I do not know when I have enjoyed a prospect more exquisitely than at this time.

For Beauty of situation and surrounding scenery Avignon is worthy of having been the residence of so celebrated a poet. The variegated loveliness of the <sur> neighboring country is enough to enliven the mind and call forth all the native powers of poetry. It appears to me that Avignon would prove a most favorable residence for the valitudinarian in regard to beauty of landscape and pleasant walks tho I am unacqua<nt>inted to what degree the climate is beneficial in this particular spot.[140]

Marseilles, August 22[141]

I arrived in this city last evening after a tiresome ride of twenty <five>two hours from Avignon. In our way we stopped to dine at Aix, a handsome town with wide clean streets and agreeable public walks. This was a Parliament[142] town under the former Government. <It has some resort> It is often resorted to by invalids on account of its mineral baths which were celebrated in time of the Romans and lost till the beginning of the last century when they were discovered[143] in digging for the foundation of an <E> edifice without the city walls.[144] We did not rest long enough in the town to allow me to examine its buildings or curiosities.

The new city (or rather the new *part*) of Marseilles is well built, the streets regular clean <&> well paved and <of> wide. The old part of the city is villainously filthy the streets narrow and crooked. They have fountains that play in different parts of the city and supply streams of water thro many of the streets yet it is impossible to carry off the vile smells that prevail throughout the place in consequence of all filth & dirt being <emptied> ↑thrown↓ into the streets. With all its beauty therefore, Marseilles is a disagreeable place for an invalid to reside at, who is peculiarly sensible to corrupt air.

140. This paragraph, the last on the manuscript page, is in blue ink.

141. This entry and the next two are in black ink. Irving drew on this entry in his letter to Alexander Beebee, August 24, 1804.

142. The Parliament of Provence was established at Aix by Louis XII in 1501 and existed until 1790.

143. The springs at Aix were rediscovered in 1704, and an edifice for their use was erected the following year.

144. Irving drew in this paragraph on Tobias Smollett, *Travels through France and Italy*, 1766 (*The Works of Tobias Smollett*, ed. W. E. Henley and T. A. Seccombe, Westminster, 1900, XI, 415, 417).

The port of Marseilles is excellently contrived to ensure the safety of vessels. it is oblong with a narrow entrance defended by a fort on each side. The Quay <that> is well paved with bricks laid edgeways, and for the width of two feet next the water, it is paved with square stones.

It is amusing to walk on this Quay and see the variety of beings assembled together of different nations languages & dresses. The Tunisians, Algerines Spaniards, Genoese, Italians & french all mingled together, form a curious medley.

August 25

There are but two American vessels in port, at present. This somewhat surprized me, as Marseilles is most favorably situated for enjoying & almost engrossing the trade of the Mediterranean But I am told that the restrictions laid on commerce by <the cus> duties &c, the impositions & delays of the Custom House & many other inconveniences are rapidly discouraging all trade with this port and induces the Americans to go to Leghorn in preference, as there they are less annoyed & impeded in their trade. Many petitions and complaints have been made to the Government on this head by the Merchants of Marseilles, but the Government is to[o] much engaged in planning victories at present as to attend to such a dull mechanical inglorious affair as commerce.

The taxes and duties are enormous and more felt in Marseilles than in most ports, insomuch that several of the oldest houses have abandoned business rather than be subject to them.

I have met with a very agreeable companion here, in a Mr Appleton, a young gentleman of Boston who came out supercargo of a Brig which he has sent to Naples and awaits her return.[145] He is a young fellow of an excellent disposition good understanding and most amiable manners. After passing thro a considerable tract of country, among strangers of a different <n>language & nation you cannot imagine how grateful it is to encounter a fellow countryman. The heart hails him as a Brother to whom <we>it <are> is entitled to look for friendship – <I>

145. Presumably John Appleton (b. 1758), if he was, as Irving said in his letter to William Irving, August 26, 1804, brother to Thomas Appleton (1763–1840), U. S. consul at Leghorn. John was at one time consul at Calais. See Isaac Appleton Jewett, comp., *Memorial of Samuel Appleton of Ipswich, Massachusetts* (Boston, 1850), pp. 36, 37. Irving also referred to meeting Appleton in his letter to Alexander Beebee, August 24, 1804.

August 27

I was agreeably surprized the other evening on returning to the hotel from a promenade, to find Dr Henory quietly seated in the parlor. It seemd as if the little man had dropped from the clouds, for I had supposed him still at Cette. He told me he had reached there the day after he parted with me at Nismes but found that no vessel would sail <before> in less than two Months, as they would not have a convoy before that time. His complaint encreasing he determined once more to try the Journey by land and after divers misfortunes, the carriage over turning &c he arrived safe at Marseilles. His health is better at present, his spirits have returned and he is ↑again↓ as merry as a cricket.

The Theatre of Marseilles is a neat building of white stone.[146] I went there <f> to see for the first time a French ballet. The Dancing was admirable, but the immodesty of the women who danced rather offended my old fashioned, American ideas of propriety.

As to the french style of acting, it is contrary to all <my> that I have been accustomed to admire. It appears to me a continual violation of nature. Affected positions, strained attitudes, violent and uncouth gestures, and excessive ranting. In their dancing, fighting &c they keep excellent time to the music and are very graceful, of course they are good in pantomime, and, till I get more accustomed to their style of acting or better acquainted with their language, that is the only species of entertainment in which I can be much pleased with them. I must however do them the justice to say that the singing parts of their operas <is>are sometimes very well performed.

Marseilles, like all the other french towns is throngd with beggars. This is a natural consequence of the discouragements & checks commerce has received. I believe the Americans are generally considered the patrons of beggars shoe black[s] fiddlers & pedlars, for never were mortals so harrased with them as we are at the hotel where I lodge & where <the> all the Americans that <are here on business co> come to Marseilles, reside. We can seldom go out but we are escorted by a regiment of ragged boys, who have a knack of rattling off a tune by drumming with both fists on the chin, this causes the mouth to open quick with a peculiar sound & very loud. Our doors are besieged by singing beggars and pedlars with their gilded trumpery, and the shoe blacks thinking to gain our custom by speaking english, run after us in

146. The Grand Théâtre on the Place de la Comédie was built in 1784.

the street with their brushes & blacking <holl> crying "Monsieur, monsieur, G<o>——d dam, G——d dam son de bish son de bish"

September 3[147]

I had anticipated some amusement at the Fair of St Lazare[148] which commenced last week & which I had heard some talk of before. It is however, but a paltry affair, merely calculated for poor people and children. At some of the french fairs where they vend silks and other valuable merchandizes there is generally a vast concourse of people, and great sums of money are expended. Here <how they> ↑the articles of trade↓ were chiefly toys & tin ware, with here and there a little vampd up jewelry. In one stall the owner had a little of every thing collected, and sold his articles indiscriminately at twenty eight sous apiece. I have seen very few shew men & no jugglers at this fair but I expect they do not exhibit much till the last days. Yesterday afternoon Blanchard (the <aeronaut> Æreal navigator who once made an unsuccessful attempt in New York) took a flight in a balloon from a plain <elevated a> in an elevated part of the suburbs.[149] He had prepared the public mind by flaming handbills, announcing that himself & his wife would go up in a grand balloon to which would be attached two smaller ones. Of course all the good people of Marseilles repaired to the hills & high places to see the wonder and had the enemy been nigh they might have played the same trick that yorick relates happened to strassburg "that the enemy marched in at one end of the town as the citizens marched out of the other"[150]

The ↑streets that led to the↓ plain w<ere>as <enclosed by> barricadoed and guarded by soldiers, the tickets of admission were thirty sous. Blanchard had very wisely sold his days profits to some officers of the police for six thousand Livres by which the worthy souls "gained

147. This entry is in black ink through "Here the articles of trade," thereafter in gray-blue.

148. St. Lazarus of Bethany (1st century) was, according to legend, the first bishop of Marseilles.

149. Jean Pierre Blanchard (1750–1809) was the first man to make balloon ascensions in France, England, and America. That which Irving saw was his fifty-seventh. There seems to be no record of his failure in New York. See Léon Coutil, *Jean-Pierre Blanchard Physician-Aéronaute* (Évreux, 1911), pp. [3], 5, 18, 19, 20.

150. According to Slawkenbergius' tale in *The Life and Opinions of Tristram Shandy* (1767) by Laurence Sterne, the French captured Strasburg in this manner: ". . . when they saw the *Strasburgers,* men, women, and children, all marched out to follow the stranger's nose – each man followed his own and marched in" (*The Works of Laurence Sterne,* Oxford, Shakespeare Head Press Ed., 1926–1927, II, 36).

a loss" of about two or three thousand, for though the people of Marseilles were all very willing to see the ascension yet but a small proportion were inclined to spend thirty sous upon their curiosity

The ascension took place, to be sure, but with the trifling variations from the bill, that there was but one balloon instead of three, that it was much smaller than they expected, and not above two thirds filled, that Mr Blanchard went up *solus,* that he ascended to a very inconsiderable height and descended about a mile from the place he started, so that the people one and all with their accustomed ease and politeness pronounced Mr Blanchard "*a foutre*[151] and sent him to the d——l."

On the plain we encountered the American consul Mr Cathalin and his lady and a young fellow who is some relation to him and acts as his chancellor.[152] I have neglected to mention these geniuses before, which is almost unpardonable for they have afforded us a vast deal of amusement at the hotel where I reside.

Cathalin is a small man – a french man but talks <consid> English fluently. <He is well acquainted with his own> He has a great esteem and admiration of his own appearance and qualifications in which <he> good opinion he is a little singular[153] as I believe very few except himself intertain it. Tho' rather of the *simple sort* he has considerable of the Gascon in his composition and wants no trumpeter to proclaim his <good> ↑great↓ deeds as long as he has the use of his tongue Tho affecting an excess of politeness he has very little knowledge of etiquette and gentlemanlike civility.

We had invited him to dine with us at the hotel as there were f<our>ive or six Americans of us. He humd and hawd mysteriously and gave no decided answer; His chancellor, who is a squire worthy <of so great> of the knight he follows, lodges at the hotel and the next day <let us> took each of us aside at different times and let us know as a secret, that the consul intended to dine with us on such a day that

151. A coarse term of contempt; an ass.

152. Etienne (or Stephen) Cathalan, Jr. (d. 1819), a Marseilles merchant (*Tableau Historique et Politique de Marseilles, Ancienne et Moderne,* Marseilles, 1812, p. 55) was commissioned U. S. vice-consul there in 1790, and after 1798 (when consular offices between America and France were revoked) served as commercial agent for all French ports in the Mediterranean. From May 1804 to July 1805 Julius Oliver of Philadelphia served as Cathalan's chancellor. In May 1804 Cathalan also appointed a Mr. Vallette as his secretary, who may be the relative Irving mentioned. See Despatches from U. S. Consuls, Marseilles, RG 59, NA.

153. The rest of this entry has been canceled by lines drawn across two manuscript pages.

he did not wish any parade to be made so had determined to drop in as if by chance and surprize us. This *Secret,* imparted to the whole of us & to the landlady in the bargain[154]

. . . .

liberty of admiring very much a picture <he had> of a lady on the back of his snuff box[.] he told me it was his wife, which I knew before in spite of the egregious flattery of the painter. He told me the painter was a friend of his – a man of great talents and very obliging so that if I wanted any thing done in the minature line, I would do well to employ him. I told him there was a lady in New York whose picture I was very desirous to have, <and that wishd to know if he thought the> that I would give the painter a *discription of her countenance* if he would draw a *likeness* of it for me." <?A?>The consul told me he had no doubt but his friend would do it as he was a skillful man & very *obliging* that he would call on him in the evening & enquire. I thanked him *sincerely* & bidding him good after noon we all sheerd off to find vent for our laughter. This morning he called upon me and told me "he had seen the painter and was sorry to say that he could not paint a *likeness* unless he *could see the lady*"

September 8[155]

I was <to> ↑at↓[156] the theatre the other evening to see for the first time a French ballet.[157] The Scenery, dresses &c were very good, and the dancers delighted me from the beauty and agility of their steps and the elegance of their attitudes. The women were <bress> dressed in a flesh colored habit fitted exactly to their shapes so that it really looked like the skin, over this was a light robe of <orname> white muslin ornamented very tastily but so transparent that their figures were perfectly visible through it and in dancing particularly, were completely exposed. as I was unaccustomed to see women expose themselves thus publicly I felt my American blood mounting in my cheeks on their account and would have been happy to have given them an-

154. A leaf has been removed from the notebook at this point.

155. This entry, to the last paragraph, and subsequent entries through December 1 are in brown ink.

156. The alteration is in pencil.

157. Irving described the dancers in this ballet in much the same terms in his letter to Alexander Beebee, September 18–October 27, 1804.

other petticoat or a thicker robe to cover their nakedness. The audience seemed to look on with perfect indifference not perceiving <t>any thing immodest or improper in it and the ladies regarded with perfect indifference a spectacle at which our American girls could not even peep thro their fans without blushing. These lascivious exhibitions are strong evidences of the depraved morals and <p>licentiousness of the public. The stage which should be employed by "holding the mirror up to nature"[158] to inform the understanding and improve the heart is degraded by performances devoted to sensuality and libertinism.

I have seen no stage in france that I think equals ours in the management of the scenery machinery & other parts of the stage business. The grand theatre at Bordeaux, it is true, did not exhibit much change of scenery while I was there so that I had not suffici<nt>ent opportunity to judge well of its stage management.[159]

September 9

The ascension of Mr Blanchard has introduced a new *play thing* among the *grown children* of Marseilles The Balloon mania has absolutely arisen to an alarming height. Paper balloons are sent up from different parts of the town & from the country seats adjacent every day. This day being Sunday & of course a *holliday* in France They have full opportunity to indulge in all the pleasures of *gas* & *steel filings.* I have counted this afternoon four airballoons up above the city at one time & some of them quite large. The whole town is crazy after them. Happy people – "Pleasd with a feather – tickled with a straw[.]"[160] you forget your national calamities at the sight of any new amusement however trifling.[161]

There are two pleasant walks at Marseilles one thro the centre of the

158. ". . . for any thing so overdone is from the purpose of playing, whose end, both at the first and now, was and is, to hold, as 't were, the mirror up to nature . . ." (Shakespeare, *Hamlet,* III, ii, 20–23).

159. This paragraph, the last on the manuscript page, is in blue, or blue-black, ink.

160. Alexander Pope, *Essay on Man* (1732–1734), II, 275–76:

> Behold the child, by Nature's kindly law
> Pleas'd with a rattle, tickled with a straw.

161. This paragraph is in black ink, the remaining page and a half of this entry in blue; presumably Irving wrote all but the first paragraph after he left Marseilles.

town shaded with fine large trees and the houses on each side well built, the other at one end ascending a hill called mount Bonaparte.[162] In the evenings and on Sundays they are much frequented. The manufactures of Marseilles are gold & silver stuffs laces silk stockings woolens and they export much wine oil and wool. The climate during my stay was very hot, (as it is all summer) but the sea breezes were often refreshing. The valley in which Marseilles is situated is well cultivated and crowded with country seats & gardens.

The Marseillians date the origin of their city from a colony of Phocians, who, they say, founded it about six hundred years before the birth of our Saviour[163] It has some celebrity from the friendship it shewd for Pompey & its strenuous opposition to Caesar

The latter when on his way to Spain to oppose the friends of Pompey, wished to enter Marseilles but the inhabitants resolutely shut their gates against him Enraged at this conduct he immediately invested it by sea and land and shortly after departed to prosecute his designs in Spain leaving the seige under the direction of Trebonius and Decimus Brutus

The situation of Marseilles must have been different in those days from its present one as it is said to have been "coverd on three sides by water & on the fourth only accessible by an isthmus or neck of land" (vide Ferg: Rom: Rep:) & this Isthmus was defended by high walls & towers. The Marseillans were enspirited by the presence of Domitius a Roman pro consul and expected speedy release from Pompey; they were therefore uncommonly persevering & courageous in defence of their city frequently making sallies & burning the works of the besiegers. They had particular engines of extraordinary force with which they discharged arrows or rather beams of wood twelve feet long and proportionally thick which penetrated the works of the besiegers and obliged them to redouble the force of their skreens & walls.

When the town was reduced to th<eir>e last extremity Caesar arrived, accepted their offers of capitulation & took possession of the city treating the inhabitants with great mildness & indulgence –

162. Presumably Irving is referring to the Cours Belsunce, dividing the city into the new and the old parts, and what was then the Boulevard Bonaparte (now the Boulevard Charles Livon) leading to the hill on which now is located the Parc and Chateau du Pharo; the plans for making this area into a memorial of Napoleon did not materialize.

163. In writing the rest of this entry Irving drew on Adam Ferguson, *The History of the Progress and Termination of the Roman Republic* (London, 1783), especially II, 409, 432, 433, 437. The quotation, not altogether accurate, is from II, 432.

September 10[164]

This morning I left Marseilles in company with Dr H[165] we having engaged a voiture to carry us to Nice. We sat off at day break and took a cross road that was in the evening to join the main road from Aix to Nice. The country thro which we passed in the morning was hilly and sterile and cultivated by the assistance of Manure. We rode thro the small town of Oreal; this had formerly been absolutely a horde of Banditti.[166] The People of the Fauxbourgs (suburbs) began by plundring the houses of the Richer Citizens after which they committed depredations on travellers accompanied sometimes with the greatest cruelties. We dined at Jacquel,[167] another town of the same character as Oreal, the inn was dirty & miserable and poverty & filth was observable throughout the town. After dinner we ascended the mountains and found the road so stoney & rugged that we were obliged to get out of the carriage and walk tho the sun was exceeding hot. No houses were to be seen on these heights, but every thing shewed signs of sterility. In one place we passed a long tract of road that wound among rocks & precipices <th> and where the frequent ascents & descents together with the badness of the road itself made it difficult for the carriage to get along. Here our voiturier told us had been numerous robberies & murders committed. The robbers sometimes appearing in troops of twenty or thirty at a time and <plundering> stripping the traveller of every thing, for the state of the road made it impossible for either carriage or horseman to escape by flight

The frequency of these depredations at length occasioned this road to be nearly deserted till the present excellent regulations of the police were carried into execution. Troops of *Gens d'arms* (soldiers in the service of the police) scoured the roads, ferreted out the robbers who were gullotined by dozens and put a complete stop to their enormities so that the road is as safe at present as any other in france and the people since they dear [dare] not *rob,* content themselves with *cheating* the traveller as much as possible.

164. Irving drew on his entries of September 10–26 and October 14 in his letter to William Irving, September 20–October 27, 1804, and on his entries of September 10–12 in his letter to Alexander Beebee, September 18–October 27, 1804.

165. Dr. Henry.

166. Bandits known as "compagnons du soleil" operated among several small towns in the neighborhood of Auriol in the last years of the eighteenth century (information furnished by the Director of the Archives of the Department of the Bouches-du-Rhône, Marseilles).

167. Probably St. Zacharie, the village next after Auriol en route from Marseilles to Tourves.

In the evening we put up at Tourves a small town on the main road from Aix to Nice. Before we arrived at the town we passed the ruins of a magnificent chateau having charming pleasure grounds formerly belonging to a French Baron.[168] He was gullotined in the revolution and his fine seat &c ruined. At supper, at the inn, we had silver spoons with coats of arms engraved upon them, most propably the <coats> spoils of some chateau perhaps of the one above mentioned. This town, like most of the others in Provence, was extremely loathsome from the quantities of manure piled up against the houses which at certain seasons they carry into the fields & spread it about to fertilize the soil. The abominable smells occasioned by these heaps of manure, together with the vileness of the Inns destroy all idea of comfort to a traveller unaccustomed to them. Fortunately for me, my Canada jaunt of last summer has seasoned me in some measure to these disagreeables. When I enter one of those Inns where I am to pass the night, I have but to draw a comparison between it and one of the log hovels into which we were huddled after a fatiguing days journey thro the wood and the inn appears a palace. For my part I try to take things as they come, with cheerfulness, and when I cannot get a dinner to suit my taste I endeavor to get a taste to suit my dinner. I have made a hearty meal <off> of cucumbers & onions off of a dirty table in a filthy log hut on the banks of Black river and I have made as hearty a one in a vile french auberge of a stale fowl that I verily believe had mounted guard on the table a half a score of times. There is nothing I dread more than to be taken for one of the Smellfungii[169] of this world. I therefore endeavor to be satisfied with the things round me when I find there is no use in complaining, and with the master, mistress & servants of the inns when I perceive they have "all the dispositions in the world" to serve me, as Sterne says – "It is enough for Heaven, and ought

168. Presumably the chateau Valbelle, built in 1772 by Joseph Alphonse Omer, Comte de Valbelle d'Oraison (1729–1778), who had numerous other titles. Irving misstated his fate, however: he died of apoplexy while en route to Paris. He was distinguished both as a soldier and a patron of the sciences, the arts, and letters. See *Les Bouches-du-Rhône Encyclopédie Départementale,* IV-2 (Paris, 1931), 483.

169. Laurence Sterne in the chapter "In the Street. Calais" in *A Sentimental Journey through France and Italy* (1768) refers to Tobias Smollett as "Smelfungus" because of his continual objections, in *Travels through France and Italy* (1766), to the accommodations he encountered as a traveler. Smollett was especially outraged by the inns he found on his way from Montpellier to Nice, a route with which Irving's coincided at several points.

to be enough for me."[170] I find indeed an advantage in this, I am attended with more cheerfulness & promptness than those who make the most complaints & curse the waiters.

September 11

In the morning we sat out at day break and after riding sometime in a fog (the country being low & humid) we stopped to breakfast at Brignolles.[171] At first they told us they had nothing to give us to eat but veal just killed, we made out however to get eggs, figs, grapes, cheese, bread <&c> wine &c and made a very comfortable meal.

The country began to grow much more fertile & picturesque. In one place I saw this years fourth crop of oats in great forwardness. Wine is very cheap from the numerous vineyards & abundant vintages They sell last years wine in this part of the country for one *sous* a bottle exclusive of the bottle itself. The wine is harsh at first but in time becomes a very wholesome pleasant table drink & has body sufficient to bear exportation to America. Grapes are 10 sous pr Cwt. – Between Vidauban & Frejus, figs are sold 9 livres pr Cwt. & 10 livres if they are packed up. <The> People come here from Genoa & other places to purchase figs as these parts abound with them. In riding along, whenever we pleased we had at our command a fine regale of grapes & figs from the vineyards & plantations that were along the road. In the afternoon we passed by several places where they were gathering the vintage. They do not celebrate it with that mirth and *gaieté de cœur* here as they do in other parts of france. The song, the dance, the inspiring sound of the pipe and tabor & the hospitable feast are the usual attendants of this happy season in some of the provinces "When Nature is pouring her abundance into every ones lap and every eye is lifted up" "When music beats time to *labor* and her children are rejoicing as they carry in their clusters." There it is really a "joyous riot of the affections"[172] but here it is reduced to a level with the other

170. In Sterne's *Sentimental Journey through France and Italy* the narrator writes of his first interview with his servant La Fleur: "You can shave, and dress a wig a little La Fleur? – He had all the dispositions in the world – It is enough for heaven! said I . . . and ought to be enough for me –" (*Works of Sterne,* IV, 37).

171. Irving's experience at Brignoles was much like that of Smollett as described in *Travels through France and Italy* (*Works of Smollett,* XI, 134–35).

172. In Sterne's *Sentimental Journey through France and Italy* the narrator exclaims: "[T]o travel it through the Bourbonnois . . . in the heyday of the vintage, when Nature is pouring her abundance into every one's lap, and every eye is lifted

rustic employments of plowing, threshing &c. In fact the peasantry throughout the south of france have a stupidity & heaviness of looks and manners that I had not expected to find among a people so celebrated for gaiety. For aught I know they may be very good hearted worthy people for I could not understand their language sufficiently to talk with them. It is a barbarous jargon of french & italian jumbled together in such a manner that neither french nor italian can understand it without the greatest difficulty. A traveller is too apt to form his opinion of the lower class of people, from those that surround him, who are generally postillions guides, servants, cicerones waiters &c &c The most mercenary wretches in existance. If you even make them a present for any little service they have rendered they will generally complain of the smallness of the gratuity and I do not reccollect ever to have been thanked for money I gave in this manner *but once* and that was when for want of small change in my pocket I gave a fellow about six times as much as he deserved for shewing me the inside of a church at Avignon.

I have had three or four sturdy fellows come lumbering up stairs to my chamber at a hotel with my portmanteau which alltogether did not weigh sixty weight, & every one of them demanded a recompense. I gave <the ?ha?> one of them who seemed to have <st> sustained most of the weight a few sous and it was only by threatening to send for a *Gen dArms* that I got rid of the others. ——— ——— ——— ———

In the evening we arrived at Vidauban and as the Inn seemed to have considerable company we took care to choose our rooms immediately <This precaution was well timed for just before supper the hostess came in with a countinance somewhat perplexed and told me that the Engineer general of the Department had just arrived with his lady –[173] that he was *un grand homme* and ought to be well accomodated that he patronized her inn and wished to have my room as it was the best in the inn that therefore she supposed "*monsieur* would have the *bonté*

---

up—a journey through each step of which Music beats time to *Labour,* and all her children are rejoicing as they carry in their clusters. . . . There was nothing from which I had painted out for myself so joyous a riot of the affections, as in this journey in the vintage . . ." (*Works of Sterne,* IV, 142, 147).

173. Jean Antoine Fabre (1748–1834), a distinguished French engineer specializing in the field of hydraulics, was Ingénieur en Chef des Ponts et Chaussées of the Department of Var from 1798 to 1812. His wife at this time was the former Marie Charlotte Eléonore Gautier du Poët (1765–1805) (information furnished by the Director of the Archives of the Department of Var, Draguignan).

to oblige Mr. l Eng: Genl. by giving up his room[."] as I was somewhat piqued at this cavalier request of M. l Eng: Genl. – I replied to the landlady that I was an *American gentleman* & of course considered myself *equal at least* to any engineer general in France and would not give up my room to him if he was[?] to come with all his engines & lay seige to it but that I would have no objection to give[?] a part of my room to the engineer's *lady* The landlady retired much chagrined with my answer but I heard no more from the *grand man* & was sufferd to retain my room without any farther interruption>[174]

September 12

<We sat> We recommenced our route early in the morning and had a fatigu<ng>ing hilly road to traverse The country not very productive except in Figs which were in vast abundance. At half past ten we arrived at the small town of *Frejus.*[175] This town is pleasantly situated near the sea shore and was formerly a place of some trade and importance, it has declined into a state of poverty & insignificance. There are here <th> a few Roman remains[176] viz. an Ampitheatre an Aqueduct which brought water from a neighboring hill –(only a few broken arches remaining) and some crumbling reliques of the antient wall of the town. They are all in a very ruinous condition & are only worthy of curiosity from their antiquity. At this town Bonaparte & his suite landed on his return from Egypt.[177] He debarked without performing Quarantine a crime punishable with death according to the laws of the country which are very strict on vessels from the L<e>avant. He did not remain longer in Frejus than was sufficient to bring his things ashore & procure post horses, & then sat off post haste for paris – spreading astonishment <from> ↑by↓ his unexpected appearance

174. This passage has been inked out in the manuscript, the corresponding passage in the "Traveling Notes, 1804" has been erased, and the account of the same episode in Irving's letter to William Irving, September 20–October 27, 1804, has been inked out. The account in the letter seems to have been copied in large part from the journal.

Possibly Irving was inspired in his reply to the landlady by the concluding chapter in Sterne's *Sentimental Journey through France and Italy,* "The Case of Delicacy," in which a lady and her maid are put in the same bedchamber with the narrator.

175. Irving's description of the town contains faint echoes of Smollett, *Travels through France and Italy* (*Works of Smollett,* XI, 137–38).

176. Julius Caesar finished the port of Fréjus and built a lighthouse, aqueduct, and amphitheater.

177. Napoleon reached Fréjus October 9, 1799, having been unsuccessful in his plan to cut the English route via the Mediterranean to Egypt.

After dining at Frejus we rode for some distance within sight of the Mediterranean and then began to ascend the mountain of *Estrelles*[178] one of the maritime Alpes said to be eight miles over. As the ascent in a little while became steep and laborious we got out and walked. The road wound up the mountain in different directions humoring the ascents and declivities, every now and then we caught a glimpse of the valley we had left – variegated with different plantations, vineyards &c bounded by the distant mountains on one side and on the other by the ocean calm and unruffled.

In one of the highest passages of the mountain we overtook two old women who solicited charity They had been on a pilgrimage to a hermitage among the mountains and were now returning to their native home near Milan in Italy. I was astonished to see two poor infirm old beings who seemed hardly able to support their own weight undertaking so long & toilsome [a] journey *on foot.* We could not understand them sufficiently to know the reason that induced them to make this pilgrimage.

The sunset was rich & lovely. The highest points of the mountains were brightly illuminated while the lower ones were tinged with mellow colors and the distant vallies blended in the softest tones. The evening was calm & serene, the pure breeze of the mountains, loaded with perfumes from the aromatic shrubs & herbs that grew on every side, was refreshing and invigorating. The road had passed the highest eminence and after descending a little continued winding along the heights often on the brink of vast precipices. At length about dusk we arrived at a house where the driver told us we must put up for the night as the next town was a considerable distance off and the road among the mountains too dangerous to think of passing it in the night. I did not at all like the looks of the house, it was large and solitary over hung by part of the mountain and Embowered in thick trees[.] before the door some fellows were seated on a wooden bench drinking wine – they looked as rough as the mountains that surrounded us. On entering the Inn we desired the hostess to shew us to our rooms. She took a candle and we followed her up stairs to one <wing>end of the building where she opened the doors of two rooms in one of which were two and in the other three beds. The rooms would serve as perfect representations of the residence of poverty and sloth. Dirty, without any furniture except one broken chair each[,] no glass in the

178. The Massif de l'Estérel extends from St. Raphael nearly to Cannes.

windows[,] in short every thing had an appearance the most cheerless & forlorn – particularly to weary travellers who had need of comfortable accomodations to recover from their fatigue. We demanded of her to shew us her other rooms, she replied that these were all she had *furnished* and she was sure they were good enough. We were obliged therefore to be content and after a miserable supper we retired to one of the rooms the door of which we <secured as fast> ↑fastned as secure↓ as possible. I confess I did not feel well at ease in this lodging. The wild and solitary situation of the house, the rough looks & manners of the people and their apparent indigence were sufficient to awaken disagreeable sensations particularly as I knew this road had been much infested by robberies within the short space of 18 months or two years. In spight however of these uneasy reflections – of a hard bed and a host of hungry fleas I soon fell asleep and[179]

September 13

– this morning (13th) I had the pleasure of awaking (when the voiturier knocked at the door) neither *robbd nor murdered.*[180] We risumed our seats in the voiture at day break and passed thro a succession of wild & romantic mountain scenery with now and then a view of a distant valley all rendered more charming by the enlivening aid of a <charming> delightful morning. These mountains <are> do not admit of cultivation in general – they are covered with Pines laurels box myrtle tamarisc cypress &c & fragrent herbs & shrubs as Hysop Thyme lavender &c[181] In some parts they afford subsistance to flocks of sheep that are driven upon them when the summer heats have scorched up the valleys We observed flocks of them on some of the distant heights of an admirable whiteness. At length we came again in sight of the Mediterranean and after long and rugged descents gained the valleys. After passing thro the little village of Cannes on the coast, we continued riding within a little distance of the shore having on the other side of us vineyards – figs & olives in luxurient plenty and behind them the Alps grandly terminating the prospect. These mountains as

179. The first sentence of the entry of September 13 follows immediately after this word in the manuscript. Irving may have also written the entry of the twelfth from "After dining at Frejus" after he arrived in Nice; the appearance of the script changes slightly beginning with that phrase.

180. Presumably the italicized words are a quotation, but its source has not been identified.

181. For this list and much of the rest of the entry Irving apparently drew on Smollett, *Travels through France and Italy* (*Works of Smollett,* XI, 139–40).

they approach the sea are by no means to be compared to those of the same chain in the interior (particularly in Savoy & Switzerland) either for height and singularity, they are by no means lofty enough to have snow on the top; but when I passed over them I fancied I could feel a considerable change in the atmosphere and that it was more pure & refreshing than in the valleys. We arrived at antibes about mid day where we dined. This is a small sea port well fortified & garrisoned & formerly the frontier town of France. After leaving antibes we passed thro St. Laurent, a small village where formerly they examined the trunks of travellers before they passed into Italy. Here we crossed the *Var* on a long wooden bridge. The river at this season is nearly dry. It was once the boundary between France & Italy. St. Laurent is said to be celebrated for its fine muscadine wines.

In the evening we arrived at NICE and put up at the Hotel des Etrangers.

Nice, September 14

Having thus happily accomplished my journey thro the *south of France* I felicitated myself with the idea that nothing farther was necessary than to step into a Felucca & be wafted to the <happy> classic shore of Italy! I accordingly waited on the municipality in company with the Doctor to deliver up my passport from Marseilles and obtain another one for Genoa.[182] What was my surprize when the Secretary General[183] having read my passport told me it was impossible for him to grant me permission to depart. That I had come on with a passport such as is given to *suspected persons* and that I must remain here till a better passport came on, or an order from the Grand Judge *at Paris*[184] authorizing my departure. This speech absolutely struck me dumb. The Doctor however, who spoke french far more fluently than <me> ↑I↓ took up my cause and represented my situation, character &c &c in as fair a light as possible offered to pledge himself his property his all that I was veritably an American citizen and had demeaned myself

182. Irving gave an account of his passport troubles in Nice in his letter to Alexander Beebee, September 18–October 27, 1804, using much the same language as is in this entry.

183. The Secrétaire général de la Mairie was a M. Grivel to the end of the French Revolutionary year XII (September 21, 1804), then Jean Baptiste Masseille (information furnished by the Archivist of Nice).

184. Claude Ambroise Régnier (1736–1814), French lawyer and jurist, who held several posts under the government of Napoleon, was Grand Juge de France from 1802 to 1813.

peaceably & properly in france. In short he evinced the most friendly zeal and earnestness in my cause and said every thing he could think of to induce the Secretary General to give me a passport.

The Secretary still made the same reply – it was out of his power – he was amenable to superior authority – or he would do it with the sincerest pleasure but that he would write to the Comissary General of Police at Marseilles inclosing my passport and requesting another that would enable me to proceed He also asured us that if I could procure a reclamation from any of our consuls he would forward me with pleasure the moment it arrived In the mean time he gave me a letter of surety that should grant me the freedom of the <cit> town & protect me from molestation of police officers &c.

By the Doctors advice I immediately wrote to Mr Schwartz & to our consul Cathalan at Marseilles requesting them to represent my case to the Com: Genl: of their city & endeavor to have a good passport sent on immediatily or if there was no other way – to reclaim me as an American citizen[185]

I have also written to a friend & to our consul at Bordeaux requesting them to take the same measures there.[186] Dr Henory leaves this place <for tomorrow> in a day or two and has promised to use his exertions to have me reclaimd at Genoa I have written by him to my friend S——[187] at the latter place and do not doubt but he will exert his friendship to the utmost so that it will be hard if I do not recieve relief from one quarter or another.

September 15

Feeling indisposed after dinner this afternoon I went to my chamber,

185. Schwartz was a partner of Abraham Ogden of New York in the firm of Ogden and Schwartz in Marseilles; according to Irving he was "about thirty" (Irving to William Irving, September 20–October 27, 1804). Irving's letter to Cathalan is dated September 15, 1804. The Commissaire Général de Police in Marseilles at this time was a M. Permion. In reply to a letter from Cathalan of September 18, 1804, Permion replied the next day (2 Complementaire an XII) that he could do nothing about Irving's passport since Irving was in the Department of the Alpes-Maritimes and should therefore apply to the "grand prefet" of that department (Alderman Library, University of Virginia).

186. The friend was Dr. J. G. Ellison. The consul was William Lee (1772–1840), commercial agent for the U. S. in Bordeaux from 1801 to 1816 (William Lee, *A Yankee Jeffersonian,* ed. Mary Lee Mann, Cambridge, Mass., 1958).

187. Thomas Hall Storm, of New York, an "early playmate" of Irving's though somewhat older, was at this time in business in Genoa (PMI, I, 81). In 1805 he was named a U. S. vice-consul there (Despatches of U. S. Consuls, Naples, RG59, NA).

laid down & soon fell asleep. I was suddenly awakened by <a> the noise of some persons entering the room, & found before me an officer of the Police and the Doctor. The former had come to demand my papers to carry before the mayor[188] for some particular reasons – The Dr. told me not to disturb myself – that he would accompany the man & learn what was the occasion of this visit. In about half an hours time I heard the Doctor coming up stairs humming a tune in a hideous manner in a tone of voice like that of Tom Pipes between a *screech & a whistle.*[189] He entered my room with a furious Countenance and throwing himself into a chair, stopped in the middle of his tune & began to curse the police in a most voluble manner nor could I get a word from them [him] till he had consigned every mothers son of them to the infernal regions.

He then let me know that I had been denounced by some scoundrel of a spy, for an *Englishman* which had occasioned the demand for my papers. He had seen the adjoinat of the mayor[190] who spoke English & was very polite; by his representations he had prepossessed him in my favor.

I changed my dress & accompanied the Doctor before the adjoint, who gave me a very civil reception, told me he was sensible of the folly of the suspicions that had been indulged against me, and assured me that my tranquility should not again be disturbed while I remained in Nice. Having recieved my papers from him we <?reat?> returned to the Hotel –

September 17

This morning the Doctor sat sail in a Felucca for Genoa and tho I could not but feel regret at parting with a man whose company was so

188. Louis Chalcédoine Romey was mayor of Nice from April 20, 1804, to May 2, 1808 (information furnished by the Archivist of Nice). On September 15 (28 Fructidor an XII) he wrote the Commissioner of Police requesting the passports of both Irving and Henry, though he did not name them. This letter is the only document relative to Irving in the Nice Archives.

189. Tom Pipes is the former boatswain's mate on the ship of Com. Trunnion, who becomes a traveling companion of Peregrine Pickle in *The Adventures of Peregrine Pickle* (1751) by Tobias Smollett. The phrase underlined by Irving does not occur in the novel, but Tom is repeatedly depicted blowing his whistle, called "a natural genius in the composition of discords" who could imitate "the screeching of a night owl" among other sounds, and said to have a voice when he sang to which "nothing in nature bore the least resemblance" (*Works of Smollett,* V, 79, 80, 115).

190. There were two adjoints of the mayor of Nice in 1804: François de Orestis and Louis Millonis (information furnished by the Archivist of Nice).

agreeable & who had proved himself so much my friend yet I was satisfied on one account as it would facilitate my own departure for I look chiefly to Genoa for effectual assistance. As I did not expect to make any stay at <Genoa> ↑Nice↓ I brought on but one letter of introduction, to Mr Guide one of the principal merchants of this place.[191] Like most french merchants, however, he is too much wrapped up in commercial affairs & too intent on making money to pay much attentions to a stranger from whom he cannot expect *profitable returns.* I make out, however, to pass away the time pretty tolera<r>bly by writing, reading walking &c The maitre de hotel where I reside is a Swiss, with all the honesty & goodness of heart that characterizes his nation.[192] He spares no pains to render my situation agreeable & whenever I walk into the country one of his sons is sent with me as a guide, to shew me the gardens &c. I cannot but laugh at the blackguardisms of the common soldiery with which I am greeted sometimes as I walk the streets. They mistake <?f?> me for an Englishman – indeed half the people in france that are not well informed hardly know but that America appertains to England and that we are in the same situation in regard to them as Scotland or Ireland. Others again place us in quite another quarter of the globe. I was asked the other day at dinner by a well dressd frenchman whether my *province* (for he took the United States to be a mere province) was not a great wine country and whether it was not in the neighborhood of *Turkey* or *somewhere there about*!" Another time I was accosted by a French officer "vous etes Anglais monsieur" said he – "Pardonnez moi" replied I "Je suis des Etats Unis d'Amerique" – "Eh bien – *c'est la même chose*"![193]

September 24

Yesterday was the thirteenth anniversary of the french republic and the commencement of a New Year according to their present calender[194]

191. Presumably Jean Baptiste Guide, listed among those paying a license tax for the exercise of a trade in Nice in 1798–1799; at that time his address was Ile 85, Maison No. 1 (information furnished by the Archivist of Nice).

192. Laurent Stir is listed among those paying a license tax for the exercise of a trade in Nice in 1798–1799; at that time his address was Ile 17, Maison No. 14. His family lived in Nice until 1855 (information furnished by the Archivist of Nice).

193. "You are English, sir." . . . "Excuse me . . . I am from the United States of America." – "Oh well – it's the same thing"!

194. Irving commented on this occasion in much the same terms in his letter to Alexander Beebee, September 18–October 27, 1804.

It was necessary therefore to celebrate it with some rejoicing as we do the fourth of July in America. These national fêtes are seldom kept up with vigor for any length of time among this fickle people. They now wait for a *new batch* of public days, such as the birth day of the Emperor – the anniversary of the coronation &c. But in the present instance as the fête was not absolutely abolished it was requisite *for decencys sake* to make some shew of rejoicing. There was therefore some firing of cannon – some shutting of shops & some shew of holliday aprons. In the Evening the ↑house of the↓ municipality was superbly illuminated with a couple of paper lanthorns in each window and one of the public walks was brilliantly lighted up by ↑½ a dozen↓ tar buckets & pots of turpentine elevated on posts at certain distances by the light of which the soldiery & lower people amused themselves with dancing.

The day passed off with decency and decorum nor did I observe any of that amusement going forward so fashionable among our *mobility*[195] of boxing & cudgeling. The quarrels among the lower class<es> in this country are generally settled by the *tongue* and he that has the most volubility & strongest lungs <general> carries the day.

I never saw a contest of fisty cuffs in france but once, and that was between t[w]o Porters in Bordeaux & they managed it in so clumsy a manner that it was evident they were but novices in the business. Three or four Americans had stopped to enjoy the *fun* but they soon got out of patience on the combattants kicking scratching pulling hair &c – and went off damning them for <?brun?> brutes that did not know how to <fight> ↑box↓ *like men.*

You may wish to know something of Nice, where I am vegetating so very agreeably. It is charmingly situated in a small valley bounded on one side by the sea and on the other by an ampitheatre of Hills which rise gradually and are covered to the top with gardens vineyards olive, orange, lemon, pomgranate trees &c & diversified by handsome white county seats. Behind these hills the Alps rise in more lofty and majestic heights. The highly cultivated state of the valley and hills gives the prospect a luxurient verdure. As most of the trees are evergreens <they flor> retain this appearance all the year. <It is>Properly speaking there is no winter here as the climate is so mild that the fruits and flowers flourish equally well in that season as in the others. It is delightful to walk out into the country and visit the Gardens; the oranges

195. I.e., mob-ility.

& lemons are not yet ripe but there is abundance of grapes figs pomegranates &c Nice is but a small place containing about ten or twelve thousand inhabitants. The houses are neat, built of stone and painted very <neatly> ↑ingeniously↓ in imitation of stucco work arround the doors & windows a manner customary in the Italian towns.

The streets are very narrow and dirty except in the west end of the town (where I reside) where the houses are well <bil> built – generally four stories high & uniform. There is a pleasant walk along the sea shore – on a terrace <raised on the> built on the roofs of a range of small houses – caffés &c. it is paved with small stones over which is laid a thick coat of excellent plaister or cement, so that it is very even & agreeable to the feet. the country also, in the vicinity of the town affords dilightful promenades. The weather is ↑very↓ warm at present but the mornings and evenings are cool & bracing. Musquitoes gnats &c are very troublesome here, but <gn> musquito curtains are universally used for the beds, which prevents their tormenting at night. The chief employments of the inhabitants are making oil wine & cordage. The privateers that infest the coasts have injured very much the commerce of Nice. The <low> common people speak the *Patois* (a Jargon of french & Italian) in the highest degree corrupt so that it is impossible for me to understand them. Nice is defended by some small batteries of cannon and a fort on Monte Albano,[196] a high rocky bluff which <?pre?> terminates the city on the east & runs into the sea <around this bluff there is a road cut which leads to the port which is defend by a mole &c> ↑The port is defended by a mole & does not appear capable of receiving very large vessels.↓ The vessels that I saw in the port were generally Feluccas. & such small craft & one little Brig. At the back of the town runs the river Paglion[197] & empties itself into the sea <at the> west of the town. At present it is almost dry but in rainy seasons – spring time &c it is filld by the snows & floods from the mountains. In this part of the country they raise a great deal of hemp, ↑some↓ rice <baly> barley wheat &c & Indian corn (the latter is raised in great quantities in languedoc – along the Garonne &c <th>neither the stalk nor ears are by any means as large as in America).

The winds are very variable here and in summer there is often much

196. Forte Montalban was built in the sixteenth century by Emanuel Philibert, Duke of Savoy, on the elevation Mont Alban east of the city, but the great promontory which rises from the sea there is Mont Boron.

197. Paillon.

fickleness in the climate which occasions colds pluresies fevers rheumatisms &c In the spring the winds are very keen from passing over the alps which are then coverd with snow The people of Nice are said to be subject to scrophulas rheumatisms scorbutic complaints &c The winters are very mild and peculiarly <beneficial> agreeable to persons suffering under pulmonary complaints – The falls are wet. The climate bad for scorbutic habits. Nice formerly was an Italian town & situated in Piedmont[.] at present it appertains to france, has a french garrison & is the chief place (*chef lieu*) of the department of the Alpes Maritimes. In time of peace vast numbers of English ↑invalids↓ resort here to pass the winter which makes it lively & fashionable[.] at present it is dull & stupid the only public amusement being a wretchedly performed play in a miserable theatre[198] twice or three times a week. A French garrison by no means enliven a place as the officers seem to have but little of that gallantry and spirit of polite amusement that is necessary to promote public diversions &c.

The <letters> accounts I read in the paris papers of the yellow fever's having made its appearance in New York is by no means calculated to raise my spirits which are depressd by <solitude> lonesomeness & chagrin. I have not the hopes of hearing from you or any of my friends while here, as my letters are directed to be forwarded to Italy. this adds to my impatience to get on.

September 26

I have just recieved two or three letters and I cannot express the agreeable revolution they have occasioned in my feelings. They were put into my hands by my landlord just as I returned from one of my solitary morning rambles along the sea shore, where I had been ↑wistfully↓[199] contemplating the ocean & wishing myself on its bosom in full sail to Genoa. The first packet was from my indefatigable friend Dr Henory inclosing a letter from T H S——[200] and a reclamation from our consul, all obtained & dispatched in less than twenty four hours after

198. The only theater in Nice at this time was founded in 1789 by a society of nobles in the city and restored at the time of the Revolution. It occupied the site of the present Opera of Nice on the Boulevard du Midi, now the Quai des États-Unis. No records of the play which Irving saw seem to exist, but a few months earlier, in July 1804, a troup of amateurs, assisted by actresses of the theater, were playing two pieces: *Pygmalion* and *L'Amant Bourru* (information furnished by the Archivist of Nice).

199. "Wistfully" is in pencil above the line.

200. T. H. Storm. For the U. S. consul in Genoa, see n. 369.

his arrival. As to the letter from S—— it <contains> breathes all the warmth of heart & openess of soul that distinguishes that worthy fellow. He expresses his delight & surprize at finding me so near him his sorrow at my embarrassments & regret that his situation will not allow him to haste here & meet me. He urges me to make no delay in coming to him "my dear fellow" says he "you know the offer of *my uncle Toby* to poor sick *le fevre*[201] – with the same honesty of soul I tender the same *in every respect to you.*" I do not know how to express the delightful emotions this letter has occasiond. To meet an old friend so far from home – *and such a friend* too – Heavens – it is an extacy I have been anticipating in all my Journyings in France. Dr Henory speaks highly in his letter of <St> S——'s hospitable and friendly reception of him in consequence of an introductory letter from me – and of the zeal S—— displayed in dispatching my business. In consequence of their united exertions certificates &c a reclamation was immediately procured & as promptly forwarded.

I have also recieved a pacquet from our consul Mr Cathalan at Marseilles representing my case to the Prefet of Nice[202] & urging him to give me a passport for Italy. Thus is my situation happily relieved and I have but to get a passport & then away for Italy & S——.

Evening

"Ye Gods, if theres a man I ought to hate
"Attendance & dependance be his fate.[203]

I never felt the force of these lines of Swift more than I have to day when I have been dancing attendance <of> ↑on↓ Mr Le Secretaire General <?fl?> from morning till night without being able to see

201. In Sterne's *Life and Opinions of Tristram Shandy,* Toby Shandy's offer to the poor lieutenant Le Fever is: "You shall go home directly, *Le Fever* . . . to my house, – and we'll send for a doctor to see what's the matter – and will have an apothecary – and the corporal shall be your nurse; – and I'll be your servant, *Le Fever*" (*Works of Sterne,* II, 215).

202. Marc Joseph de Gratet Dubouchage was Préfet of the Department of the Alpes-Maritimes from 1803 to 1814 (information furnished by the Archivist of Nice).

203. The quotation is not from Swift, as Irving says, but from Abraham Cowley, "Martial. Lib. 2," *The Works of . . . Cowley* (1668), p. 86:

If there be Man (ye Gods) I ought to Hate
Dependance and Attendance be his Fate.

The poem is a paraphrase of Martial, I, lv, though Cowley indicates it is of Martial, II.

him. At last I had to give the reclamation & letter to one of the head clerks to carry them to the prefet or Sec Gen: After <waitting> waiting some time in sanguine hopes, or rather in certainty of a passports being ordered me The clerk returned with with the pleasing intelligence that I <might> must wait "*quelque jours*" (some days) till an answer was received to a letter that had been written to the Comissary General at Marseilles. What this letter is about or why I have to wait for it I cannot concieve, surely the reclamation of our consul is sufficient. I never wanted a knowledge of the language <of> so much as when the clerk brought this answer. I fairly gasped for words. As it was, I gave him my sentiments pretty roundly in the best french I could utter. The <Secrete> Secretary had promised that when a reclamation was presented from our Consul I should be forwarded with pleasure and now that it is obtained supported by a letter from our Consul at Marseilles I am still detained. I am apprehensive they intend to keep me here till the decision of the Grand judge at paris is obtained conformable to the words of my passport. If so, I cannot tell how much longer I may be obliged to rest here. This it is to <be in the> have to deal with *Dogs in office*, however I am in their power and *patience par force* must be my motto.

September 29

I calld the day before yesterday in the morning on Monsieur G——,[204] a french merchant of this place to whom I had brought a letter of introduction and mentioned to him my situation. He desired me to leave my <ref> reclamation &c with him and he would <w> visit the Préfet with whom he was acquainted – and represent my case to him. I calld on him to day and he told me he had seen Mr De Buty the Secretary particulier[205] and that the answer still was that it was not in their power to give me a passport. That they would write immediately to Marseilles for the Passport with which I came on to Marseilles from Bordeaux. and <inclose the same to> and when they recieved it they would send it on to Paris to the Grand Judge and on his decision being sent in my favor they would give me a passport to proceed *with pleasure*. Thus have I the agreeable prospect of waiting here near a month nor do I know even if I will obtain a passport then. I have been

204. J. B. Guide.

205. A M. De Butet was the Secrétaire particular du Préfet (information furnished by the Archivist of Nice).

so repeatedly amused and bantered here with promises and false accounts that my confidence in their veracity is entirely destroyed.

October 5

Nothing has since occurred to alter my situation. The weather has been unsettled & rainy. This morning however was clear & beautiful & I set off very early to visit Ville franche a small town about a league & <an> ↑a↓ half from Nice on the sea shore. We ascended the mountains to the east of the city and after a rugged ascent which however was rendered less fatigueing from the variety of picturesque prospects with which it was enlivened we at length arrived at an Emenence that commanded a charming & extensive view. The sides of the mountain were as a continued Garden, embellished with white country seats &c & they gradually swept down into the beautiful & luxuriently cultivated valley of Nice. The town lay at a distance below us its spires gilded by the first rays of the sun[.] beyond it spread the unruffled Medditeranean speckled here & there with the bark of a fisherman.

The ampitheatre of hills that <form the> surround the valley seemed from the height from which we viewed them to be almost level & like the valley presented to the eye the rich & refreshing verdure of oranges citrons olives & vineyards. Behind them the alps reared their rocky summits and gradually melted into distance. In the *foreground* of the picture the mountain ascended to a <rocky> height steep & rugged – <on which> called Monte Albano on which is seated the Castle of Nice[206]

While we were enjoying the prospect we were overtaken by two polonese noblemen whom I had formed an acquaintance with in Nice and who were going by land on mules to Genoa.

After proceeding together for some time we came to where the road parted, when I to<k>ok leave of them but I could percieve them now & then for a long time as their road wound among the heights. We afterwards descended to Ville franche which is very romantically situated in a small hollow at the foot of the mountains & partly built on the ascent of one of them. Here is a Chateau in which the criminals vagabonds &c of Nice are confined. There is also a good & deep port defended by a mole. On a point that runs out into the sea to the east of

206. The so-called Castle, or Château, of Nice was on a hill west of Mont Alban, where the entire city was located before the fifteenth century. All but the tower was destroyed in 1706. It does not seem possible to identify the noblemen Irving met.

Ville franche is the Fanale or light house of Nice. From Ville franche we returned by water in a small boat to Nice and the pleasantness of the weather made the sail delightful.

October 8

I received a letter from Wm Lee Esqr. our consul at Bordeaux in reply to one I wrote him the 15th. of September. He mentions that he had applied to the Commissary General of Police to rectify my passport but had not yet recieved an answer. He had also written to our minister at Paris[207] requesting him to interest himself in my favor.

October 9

I <walked> took a walk into the country in company with two young physicians one italian the <oft> other french,[208] to examine some roman ruins[209] situated among the mountains at some distance from the town. The ruins consisted of an ampitheatre and a temple of Diana. Of the former some arcades remained in a crumbling condition but the space of the Arena was still distinct & was converted into a little plantation of olive trees which seemed to say that the bloody scenes & contentions that had once reigned there, had given place to peace & tranquility. The temple of Diana has been converted into an habitation for Peasants so that its genuine appearance is much altered Both buildings are constructed with small square stones with layers of thin broad bricks at certain intervals like the ampitheatre at Bordeaux. This has been the scite of some Roman town but from the smallness of the ampitheatre it could not have been very considerable.

October 14

I have recieved a very polite letter from Robt L Livingston Esqr.[210] Son in law of the minister mentioning that a letter had been received

207. Robert R. Livingston (1746–1813), New York statesman, was U. S. minister to France from 1801 to 1804.

208. Probably Antoine Risso (1777–1847), chemist and botanist. In 1801 he was director of the botanic garden of the Central School of Nice and in 1802 a teacher of botany (Georges Mathiat, "Les rues de Nice," II, 567–68, Ms. in the Archives of Nice). Irving gave a fuller description of this man in his entry of October 8 in "Traveling Notes, 1804."

209. They represent the Roman town of Cemenelum at Cimiez, north of Nice.

210. Robert L. Livingston (1775–1843) married Margaret Maria, daughter of Robert R. Livingston, July 10, 1799. From 1801 to 1804 he was his father-in-law's private secretary. See Edwin Brockholst Livingston, *The Livingstons of Livingston Manor* (n.p., 1910), p. 557.

by the minister from Mr Lee of Bordx. and that they had also received sometime since some letters that I had sent on from Bordeaux written by the M[iniste]rs. friends in America which mentioned me particularly That therefore as soon as the minister had heard of my embarrassments he sent a passport immediately to the Grand Judge for his signature and that it would most probably come on by that or the next post. Two couriers however have arrived without the passport.

This morning I went to the cathederal[211] to see grand mass performed in presence of the Prefet & other authorities & the soldiers of the Garrison The cathederal is <a> handsomely decorated in the interior but the paintings of value have been removed and inferior ones substituted. The music of the regiment played at different times during the service. At a signal given by the drum all the soldiery – (who were in the middle of the church) presented arms knelt down and were *supposed* to pray for the space of a moment when at another signal they rose up & shoulderd their muskets. This may have a good effect in habituating the soldiery to have a respect for religion, but it is somewhat whimsical to see *praying* introduced into the manual exercise. In the evening I recieved a visit from Mr Lowel an American Gentleman who arrived last evening on his route to Italy I accompanied him to his lodgings and was introduced to his wife and sister.[212] The sight of some <fellow cou> Americans in this corner of france was cheering & reviving and I experienced the truth of the poets words

> "How with a brothers look a brothers smile
> The stranger greets each native of his isle."[213]

October 17

After five weeks detention wherein I ha<ve>d been continually baffled disappointed and abused with false promises I at length was

211. St. Réparate was built in 1650.

212. John Lowell (1769–1840), Boston lawyer and political writer, had just retired from his profession on account of ill health. He traveled in Europe from 1803 to 1806 in company of his second wife, Rebecca Amory, her sister Mary, and his daughter, Rebecca Amory Lowell. See Ferris Greenslet, *The Lowells and their Seven Worlds* (Boston, 1946), pp. 92, 114; "Memoir of the Family of Amory," *The New England Historical and Genealogical Register,* X (1856), 65.

213. Samuel Rogers, *The Pleasures of Memory* (1792), II, 193–94:

> And, with a brother's warmth, a brother's smile,
> The stranger greets each native of his isle.

Irving also quoted the lines in his letter to Alexander Beebee, September 18–October 27, 1804.

relieved by the passport from Mr Livingston who has behaved to me in a very handsome manner. After arranging <it> matters with the police[214] I sat sail this morning in a Felucca for Genoa. There were seven [of] us from the *Hotel des Etrangers* all french officers excepting a young german who talks english perfectly and myself. In the felucca we found three other officers. They were going to join their regiment which is stationed in the Genoese territories.

The weather was delightful and the sea calm as the Mediterranean most generally is. We coasted along partly sailing & partly rowed always keeping near the shore for fear of the little privateers that infest the coasts (These privateers are <generally> termed always *english* tho very often there is but one englishman aboard & the rest of the crew are made up of Genoese Maltese Spaniards &c They are very unprincipled and are in fact complete pirates)

The shore was a continual succession of mountains rocky & barren yet the lower parts cultivated with great industry so as to resemble a perfect forest of olives, oranges, citrons &c The mountains were skirted with villages towns, <the> which had a most picturesque appearance from the water <many> ↑some↓ of them being perched on the point of precepices that seemed rather as the haunts of eagles than of men.

As there was a little swell in the sea my fellow passengers soon became sea sick and cascaded most violently. Three or four of the officers had never been on the sea before and made such hideous contortions of features that I could not but laugh. One of them eyed me <as> askance with a rueful expression of countenance and said I might laugh if I pleasd – but that he should certainly die before we arrived at Genoa I told him not to be cast down, & drawing a roasted leg of fat mutton out of our provision basket, I asked him if he would not take a slice by way of medicine. The sight of the mutton sent the poor devil to the side of the vessel in a moment and acted like a powerful emetic. One of the officers had been in the french navy and was ashamed to be sea sick. I could percieve however that there was an insurrection in his bowels – he turnd as pale as a ghost but still continued to keep his stomach within proper bounds till a sudden pitch of the vessel overcame all his precautions & he continued vomiting for an half hour. He would not however alow he was sea sick but laid it all to the account

214. Irving gave a more dramatic account of his final interview with the police in his letter to William Irving, September 20–October 27, 1804.

of the breakfast he had eaten and between every strain would exclaim "Ah le villain chocolat<e>!"

We passed the town of Monaco formerly the capital of a small principality of that name. It contains about nine hundred persons and is <very prettil> situated on a flat rock that runs into the sea having a very picturesque appearance.[215] We also passed Vingtamiglia[216] where the Genoese territories commence – Bordighera &c & several villages of <no impot> small importance but very prettily situated in well cultivated spots at the f<oo>eet of the mountains. Towards sun down we arrived at St Remo a town built on the slope of a hill and making a very handsome appearance from the water. As our party was rather large (consisting of ten) we had a difficulty in finding accommodations. There were but two hotels in the place *the Post* & *the Marine hotel* and as the former was the best we went there The Landlord told us he had but one vacant bed in the house, that a number of French troops had filld the town on their way to Genoa. The man I believe was affraid the officers intended to be billeted upon him and he knew they were rather unprofitable lodgers[.] as soon however as they assured him they meant to pay the same as other travellers he reccollected three or four beds were unoccupied. We therefore made out to find lodgings the officers sleeping two in a bed and a mattrass being given to me. two or three of the officers slept at the Marine hotel where they were entertained by a host of fleas. Our[217] own hotel did not afford much matter of congratulation. It was dark and dirty and miserably off for attendance. As soon as we had settled our arrangements for the night and ordered supper I took a walk to see the town in company with the young German and one of the officers. In the lower part of the town the <houses we> streets were narrow but clean but as we ascended they became extremely small dark and intricate winding about in a singular manner and often for considerable distances <passing> having the houses built over them so that they appeared to be vaulted subterraneous passages. The sun never penetrated into these dark places and many of them hardly would admit a feeble twilight. They were so steep that even mules themselves seemed hardly able to travel them. After attaining the summit of the hill we arrived in front of <an>a handsome

215. Apparently Irving drew in this sentence on Smollett, *Travels through France and Italy* (*Works of Smollett*, XI, 257).

216. Ventimiglia.

217. A deleted "Our" appears slightly below "fleas" and indented, as though Irving first intended to begin a new paragraph.

building[218] but whether convent or seminary I could not learn. From hence there is a very fine view of the surrounding country. The hills coverd with vines olives oranges pomegranates &c and interspersed with pretty white country seats. <From> The town swept down from the place where we stood to the ocean and <in> as the weather was clear we could percieve the highlands of Corsica at a great distance. The town of St Remo is well peopled. There are two or three convents for men & women & several churches.[219] I could immediately perceive <that I was in a different> that I had left <fran> the french dominions from the situation of the latter. Unplunderd and the statues pictures &c undefaced by the fury of revolutionary mobs. <In the neighborhood of St Remo is Oneglia a small town that produces excellent oil.>

October 18

Early in the morning we again set sail with a light breeze and delightful weather. We glided pleasantly past the villages of Larma Santa la Riva St Stephano (or St Lorenzo) and came in sight of the flourishing town of Port Mauritio (or Port Maurice)[220] The wind had by this time came ahead and blew rather strong, however we might very easily have beat in to <St>Porto Mauritio but one of the officers was frightned and prevaild upon the Padrone[221] to put back for St Stephano. Here the surf ran so high that we dared not approach the shore but had to cast anchor & get the people of the village to come off to us with a large fishing boat. This they did very cheerfully and when they arrived where the surf broke they jumpd into the water & carried us on their back to land. After this they labored for near an hour in dragging our felucca ashore on the sands as they feared <he> a strong gale of wind. In reward for their goodness and the trouble & fatigue they had

218. Presumably the church or Santuario of Madonna della Costa on the hill above the old city, founded in 1474, reconstructed in 1630. The building in front of it was originally an Augustinian convent, later a hospital for lepers.

219. There were nearly a dozen churches or oratorios in San Remo, the most notable being San Siro, the cathedral dating from the twelfth century. In addition to the Augustinian convent, there were two monasteries: delle Salesiane and delle Turchine. See John Congreve, *Visitor's Guide to San Remo* (San Remo, 1892), pp. 5–7.

220. The vessel passed Arma, Riva Ligure, San Stefano al Mare, and San Lorenzo al Mare, and came in sight of Porto Maurizio.

221. Possibly this was the "Juam Padrone," whose name appears inside the back cover of "Traveling Notes, 1804."

undergone laboring so long in the water I proposed that we should each give them something. This the officers did not appear to relish, and two or three of them strongly opposed it. I was surprized at such meaness so incompatible with the character of soldiers but before we arrived at Genoa I saw several more instances which seemed to corroborate the reputation the french soldiery have, of being very penurious & niggardly. The young German had seconded me very warmly in the proposal & at last to induce the others to join he mentioned the small sum of *twenty sous* about 18 cents. Still however they declined till I declared that I would pay for all of them myself rather than the poor people should go unrewarded. This piqued their pride and they reluctantly paid the money. As there was no prospect of being able to <con> resume our voyage th<is>at day and the village did not offer even tolerable accommodations we determined to walk to Porto Mauritio about three leagues distant and wait there the arrival of our felucca. We therefore engaged two boys to carry our night bags and sat out <to> in the heat of the day. The road is the high way from Nice to Genoa along the sea and is only practicable for mules & asses and indeed I hardly see how they get along it. It is very stoney & rugged, cut along the face of the mountains sometimes ascending like stairs scarcely wide enough for two animals to pass & nothing to secure them in case of a stumble from falling down the precipices into the sea. Those sure footed animals, notwithstanding, traverse them with perfect safety with enormous loads – indeed it is generally observed that mules will pass where men dare not trust themselves. The sun was powerful and the reflection from the face of the mountain renderd it almost insupportable. To add to our vexations the wind sprung up favorably by the time we had accomplished half of our walk & we had the mortification to see that if we had not have turnd back from Porto Mauritio we might have made several more leagues this day.

Porto Mauritio is built on a rocky hill and from the sea makes a handsome shew. Our auberge was below the town on the shore and we were too fatigued to walk up and examine the place. This town & Oneglia another little place about a mile & half distant furnish oil which is said to be the best of the whole Riviera.[222] They have much demand for it. When I arrived at the auberge I found the boy who had carried a small packet for me and a large night bag for one of the officers –

222. Apparently Irving drew in this sentence on Smollett, *Travels through France and Italy* (*Works of Smollett,* XI, 261).

bitterly complaining He had carried the things on his head in the heat of the sun for six miles and in reccompence the officer had given him 10 sous (about eight or nine cents) I could not but express my contempt of such meanness and gave the boy a reward with which he seemed highly delighted. The officer observed that "*Les messieurs Anglaises* were always more rich than wise. that it was not in every ones power to pay equally well." "I replied that I never demanded the labor of other people unless I intended to pay them justly for it and that whenever I could not afford to hire the services of others I always served myself."

I was disgusted at the mean spirit of those officers. They cavild with every inkeeper about his prices tho I was convinced the poor devil charged them at the lowest rate, and they invariably gave the servants nothing but curses for their pains. Our Lodgings at Porto Mauritio w<as>ere miserable and the supper ill cooked and served up in a most slovenly manner.

October 19

Our vessel having arrived over night we set sail this morning at an early hour and continued coasting along within our usual distance from the shore continually amused with the variety of prospect and the continual succession of Towns villages convents, chateaus &c that skirted the mountains & crowned the inferior hills. This chain of mountains that form the Genoese coast is a part of the Grand chain of Appenines that run thro Italy and connect with the alps.

In the middle of the day we passed by the little town of Albenga opposite which stands a small rocky island of the same name on which a vast number of rabbits are said to exist. The country about Albenga produces considerable quantities of hemp.

Just before we passed this Island a shot was fired ahead of us by a small felucca privateer in shore who suspected from the number of us on board that we were one of the little privateers that infest the coast Our Padrone immediately displayed the Genoese flag & haild the privateer. Either they did not see & hear him or their suspicions were very strong for they fired another shot at us which whistled just over our heads. Three or four of the officers immediately poppd into the small hold of the felucca & crammd themselves among the trunks. The Padrone wavd his flag & bawled repeatedly with all his might & they sufferd us to pass without further molestation. In the afternoon at 5 oclock we <passed> arrived opposite Noli where the Padrone would have put in but we insisted upon his continuing on to <Savena> Savona about 3 or 4 leagues further on[.] he consented tho very unwillingly. <The> Cape Noli[223] is a remarkable bluff that rises perpendicular out of the sea to a considerable height & is very difficult to pass when the weather is stormy. The waves have formed caverns in various places and the breakers dashing into them when the wind is high make a noise that is awful even to the felucca men who are in some degree habituated to them.

Some time ago the people of a privateer ascended one of the heights of this cape to <discover> ↑look out↓ if there were any vessels in sight when they discoverd a cavern in the rock with implements for coining &c This had been the working place of a Gang of Coiners who <?whe[re]?> had drove their trade most spiritedly some years ago. Rewards had been offerd by the state for their apprehension & numerous attempts had been made to find out their retreat but all in vain. They had made their fortunes & abandond their hiding place which was thus accidentally discoverd. <It is said that> The coiners have left a monument of industry behind them <in the aperture for It ha> as it must have required infinite labor & patience to make an aperture thro the rock in one place to admit light into their cavern. The town of Noli & the surrounding parts afford fine subjects for the landscape painter being charmingly picturesque.

The breeze which sprung up opposite Noli soon died away and the men had to take to the oars. The evening that succeeded was calm & serene and by the aid of a bright moonlight we could distinguish the white villages churches &c And now and then the vesper bell of some convent situated among the mountains would seem to <?smite?> linger over the calm surface of the sea and to be in perfect unison with the scene. The <sai> men belonging to the felucca were all Genoese & shewed a degree of religious respect that I had lookd in vain for in france.[224] When they heard the bell sound for vespers they stopped rowing pulld of[f] their caps made the sign of the Cross & repeated their *Ave Maria.* About half past seven or eight oclock we arrived at Savona, a large town the port of which is defended by a mole & capable

223. Irving's description of the cape contains a few echoes of Smollett, *Travels through France and Italy* (*Works of Smollett,* XI, 262).

224. The religious nature of the Italian sailors between Nice and Genoa is also noted by Smollett (*ibid.,* p. 263).

of receiving large ships tho I saw nothing there but small craft. Here is an excellent college for the education of youth.[225]

When we entered the port we found every thing silent & on hailing the shore we were informed that the Gates were shut & that we could not be admitted. We now began to wish <wh> we had <?f?> not forced the padrone to continue on to this place. A northerly wind had sprung up which made it quite cold and as we had eat nothing since the morning but dry bread we began to feel quite hungry. Luckily one of the officers was a French Commissary – he demanded to be landed mentioned his rank &c &c and after much dispute and nearly an hours shivering in the cold we were permitted to land.

Here the same difficulty of finding accomodations occurd that we had experienced the whole voyage and I was content to pass the night on a straw bed on which however I slept most soundly.

October 20

We parted from Savona by day light. The city made a beautiful appearance when viewd from the entrance of the harbor and is certainly charmingly situated. We had Genoa now full in view and were <hi> in high spirits at the prospect of a speedy arrival. <We> The shore presented a continual string of villages very close to each other. Albisolla[226] which contains a magnificent palace Novi-Voltri *Sestri di ponente* &c <all making> and among others the small village of Cocorato[227] famous for being the birth place of Christopher Columbus. It is about [*blank*] leagues from Genoa pleasantly on the shore with the mountains gradually rising behind it. After having sailed past several villages in the vicinity of Genoa & adorned with the villas of the Genoese nobility we at length passd the magnificent suburbs calld St Pietra d'Arena & enterd the harbor of Genoa about one oclock. The city had a Striking

225. At this time there were two institutions of public instruction in Savona, the college of the Scuole Pie and that of the Preti della Missione, but they seem to have been considered together; in 1806 they were reported to have a faculty of 13 and a student body of 258. In 1811 they were united in a Collegio Communale. (Information furnished by the Mayor of Savona.)

226. Albisola.

227. Cogoleto, sixteen miles from Genoa. Several small villages in the vicinity of Genoa, where Columbus was born, at one time claimed to have been his birthplace. Irving discussed the matter fully in the Appendix of his *A History of the Life and Voyages of Christopher Columbus* (1828).

appearance to me when I enterd <the> between the moles that guard the harbor and saw the town like an ampitheatre around it. The houses rise one above another in consequence of the hills on which they are built, so that the town shews to a vast advantage & cannot but strike the most indifferent observer.[228] After stopping at the health office & displaying our bills of health we landed at a fine stone Quay and were immediately surrounded by a herd of Porters beggars & vagabonds. Three or four laid hold of my trunk and as I did not speak their language they <would> pretended not to know what I meant when I orderd them to put it down till I collard one of the fellows and one of my fellow passengers interfered & deliverd it into the hands of a public Porter. We were stopped at the gate by a custom house officer who had his little office just by and said our trunks must be examind. I was in company with one of the officers who told the custom house officers that we were french officers and had no need to have our trunks searchd. The <custom> man then hinted that if we would give him *something* he would wave the ceremony. With this I was going to comply when my companion swore I should not, that I was one of the Emperors soldiers and they had no right to demand it.

For my part I said nothing as my English accent would soon have given the lie to his assertion, but I could not but laugh heartily. We were therefore sufferd to pass with a few curses from the custom house officer.

The best hotel in Genoa is the *Hotel de Ville* or rather it is the most fashionable. I was reccommended to the *Hotel di Torri*[229] which I believe is nearly as good[.] at least I was so well satisfied with it that I never thought it worth while to change my lodgings. As soon as I <could> had changed my clothes at the Hotel I calld upon S——[230] and recieved a welcome the most open and friendly imaginable. It is impossible to express the rapture I felt at meeting with <?as?>a particular friend so far from home and after having been so long among strangers

228. Apparently Irving drew in his description of Genoa from the harbor on Smollett, *Travels through France and Italy* (*Works of Smollett*, XI, 265).

229. Irving should have written "de la Ville" and "dei Torri."

230. T. H. Storm. Soon after reaching Genoa, Irving moved in to share Storm's quarters in one of the palaces of the city, in a wing of which the proprietor, "an old Italian princess," Irving called her, still lived (Irving to a brother, *ca.* November 1, 1804).

October 25

Genoa is the capital of the Ligurian or Genoese Republick (antiently called Genua capital of the Ligurian tribes in the time of the Roman republick) It is as I before observed, situated on the side of a hill making a semicircle round the harbor, from whence the best view of it is to be obtained.[231] It is computed to contain about [*blank*][232] Inhabitants. This city is celebrated for the magnificence of its palaces which have obtained for it the title of *Genoa the Superb.*[233] The finest of those palaces are situated in the two principal streets the *Strada Nuovo* and the *Strada Balbi.* These present a continued string of grand buildings on each side of the way – decorated with marbles and some of them painted in fresco on the exterior walls with histories of Battles &c Those streets <hav> are termed by the English the *Streets of Palaces,* and it is said that all Europe cannot furnish streets <of such ↑a↓ continued & uniform> with such a continued succession of magnificent architecture. The narrowness of the streets however prevent the palaces from being seen to advantage for tho they are the two widest in the city yet in general they are not above thirty[234] feet wide. As to the other streets of Genoa – they hardly deserve the names of alleys some of them being but six seven & eight feet wide and I have been obliged to turn back or get into the door of a house to make way for an ass with a pannier on each side that was walking in the middle of the street. The streets <however> are well paved and generally very clean

The city is surrounded by two walls one of which is built round the town itself and the other takes in all the commanding heights <It The> ↑There↓ is a charming ride on horseback on the outer wall, <?con?> as you have prospects of Genoa the harbor & the surrounding country from different points of view.

231. A space precedes "obtained," the first word in the last line of the manuscript page, and "built" appears below the space. Apparently Irving first wrote "built" on the manuscript page by mistake, then properly in the same place on the preceding manuscript page in the entry of October 20.

232. The population of Genoa in 1804 was approximately 212,920 (information furnished by the Director, Direzione Belle Arti del Comune di Genova).

233. Irving may have drawn in this sentence on Pierre Jean Grosley, *New Observations on Italy and its Inhabitants,* tr. Thomas Nugent (London, 1769), II, 342. Apparently he acquired a copy of this work in Genoa (see entry of December 23, 1804).

234. "Thirty" is in blue ink and seems to have been written later than the rest of the passage.

The churches are very rich in marbles fresco & oil painting carvings &c The walls are coverd with <fres> Scripture peices in frescos.

In the church of St Ambrogio[235] are three very fine oil paintings viz. 1. the *Circumcision* by Rubens over the high altar. 2d *St. Ignatius exorcising a demoniac & raising dead children to life* by the same painter but placed in so dark a chaple that <it> the figures cannot be seen except the heads where the lights of the picture are most strongly thrown 3d The *Assumption of the Virgin* a most charming piece by Guido.[236]

The cathederal dedicated to St Laurence is of a Gothic construction.[237] This Saint <was> sufferd martyrdom in Rome in the year 260 and they immediately converted the house where he lodged in Genoa on his way from Spain to Rome into a church. In 985 it was made the cathederal but still bears the name of the saint. Over the Grand entrance is a carved figure of the saint broiling on a gridiron (the manner of his death) and two grotesque looking figures blowing up the fire with small bellows's. The church is incrusted both the inside & the exterior with black & white marble & paved with the same.

The chief treasures of this church were said to be the bones of St John the Baptist preserved in the chapel of the same name and an Emrald dish which was the Genoese share of the plunder of C<a>esaria when that city was capturd by the Crusaders, others say it was presented by Baldwin king of Jerusalem.[238] It has been pretended by some to have been the same dish out of which our Saviour eat at the last supper, (tho if I recollect right the supper was eaten at an Inn where it is not likely they would serve their Guests in Emrald dishes)[.] lastly some affirm that the dish was <part> ↑one↓ of the presents made by Queen Sheba to Solomon. Whoever gave the dish or however great its antiquity

235. It dates from the sixth century, but was rebuilt in 1589 by Pellegrino Tibaldi and Giuseppe Valeriani; the facade was added in the seventeenth century.

236. Guido Reni.

237. The present structure was built in 1100, modified in the thirteenth and fourteenth centuries, and given the dome in 1567.

238. The *Sacro Catino,* preserved in the sacristy, was among the spoils captured by the Genoese and the Pisans in their conquest of Caesarea in 1101 during the First Crusade and kept by the Genoese as their share, all the rest going to the Pisans. It was taken to Paris by Napoleon in 1809 and on its return journey in 1815 was broken. See Augustus J. C. Hare, *Cities of Northern and Central Italy* (New York, 1876), I, 38–39.

Baldwin I (1058?–1118), king of Jerusalem, was brother and successor to Godfrey of Bouillon, who was chosen by the members of the First Crusade king of Jerusalem after its capture in 1099, but who adopted another title.

it must certainly be a precious article for it is said to be 14½ inches in diameter. For my part I <do not> did not see either the Bones of St John or the Dish of King Solomon for I forgot to enquire for either. – The walls of the cathederal were formerly painted in fresco but they have lately been white washd in a desperate fit of cleanliness.

The church of the *Annonciata* is in the square of the same name and is one of the Richest churches of Genoa in marbles & workmanship. It is built at the Expence of the Lomellino family by two brothers of that name. They are said to have differd about the manner in which they should finish the front of the church which has therefore never been compleated.[239]

Over the grand entrance in the interior is a large painting of the last supper by Julius Caesar Procaccino[240] which is very much admired. It is not in a good light and the picture is much darkend by time It is counted one of the chef d'ouvres of that painter.

St. *Maria di Carignano* have [has] two or three good paintings by Procaccino. There are two statues by Puget the famous french sculptor. One of them St Sebastiano is a representation of that martyr bound to a tree & half flead alive, and possesses great merit as does the other which is St Allessandro Pauli.[241] In front of this church is the remarkable bridge of Carignano that joins the hill of the same name to that of Sarzano.[242] It has four arches. is 90 feet high 45 wide & 160 or 170 paces

239. SS. Annunziata del Guastato, founded in the thirteenth century, was built in its present form between 1591 and 1620; it is the most elaborate church in Genoa.

The Lomellini were one of the wealthiest families in Genoa; from 1514 to 1741 they were rulers of the island of Tabarca. In 1591 Lorenzo Lomellino pledged himself and his family to rebuild and decorate the church, but the work was stopped in 1635 because of the failure of his fortune. The façade was added in 1843. See C. DaPrato, *Genova, Chiesa della SS. Nunziata del Guastato* (Genoa, 1899), pp. 28–38. No disagreement between two Lomellino brothers seems to be recorded; Irving may have heard such a story which originated in an attempt to explain the unfinished façade.

240. Giulio Cesare Procaccini (1548?–*ca.* 1626) was a member of a large family of Bolognese painters.

241. The church was begun after 1576 from plans of Galeazzo Alessi and finished about 1600. The paintings by Procaccino are "The Virgin with St. Francis and St. Carlo Borommeo," and "The Holy Family." The statues by the French painter and sculptor, Pierre Puget (1622–1694), are two of four beneath the dome. Alexander Sauli (1534–1593) of Milan, Apostle to Corsica and Bishop of Pavia, was beatified in 1741–1742, but not canonized until 1904. The church was built at the expense of the Sauli family.

242. The Ponte Carignano, built between 1718 and 1724, leads from the site of the church to the Piazza Sarzano.

long. from the top of it you see houses & streets below you.[243] The armory that formerly contained (besides a vast number of stands of arms) – several suits of antient armor & antient implements of war was plunderd by the french when they took possession of Genoa.[244] Some of the mob ran about the streets with helmets on their heads. Two or three of the helmets have been hoisted on liberty poles & transformed to liberty caps and many of them were converted by taylors into chafing dishes to heat their irons on. In which humble occupation I saw many of them employed in different parts of Genoa Several of the suits of armor are hung up in the entrance to the court yard of the Doges palace.[245]

I visited yesterday the Palace of the great Andrea Doria.[246] This is one of the most antient of Genoa and was formerly of great splendor. It is at present deserted & neglected, its possessors residing in palaces less capacious & uncomfortable. The long suites of splendid appartments stripped of their furniture – the rich tapestry faded & torn, had a dreary & melancholy appearance. These are the chief of the churches & palaces I have yet seen tho there are others in Genoa well worthy of attention.

The Theatre[247] is a mean looking building on the outside and the interior is very ill contrived It is very large and high a circumstance extremely unfavorable to the voices of the actors. There are about two hundred boxes which are all hired by the year. <For the accommo>

243. Irving drew on the rest of this paragraph in his letter to William Irving, December 25, 1804–January 25, 1805.

244. The "land arsenal" occupied the former convent of the Sisters of St. Domenico; the "sea arsenal" was the navy yard (*Dizionario Geografico, Storico, Statistico, Commerciale degli di S. M. il Re de Sardegna,* Torino, 1840, VII, 308). The French took possession of Genoa after the battle of Marengo, June 14, 1800, in which Napoleon defeated the Austrian forces.

245. The Palazzo Ducale was begun in 1291, rebuilt in the sixteenth century, and restored after fire in 1777.

246. Andrea Doria (1468–1560), Genoese admiral and statesman, secured the independence of Genoa from the French and ruled it as a republic. The palace, also called the Palazzo del Principe, was presented to him in 1522 by the city; he had it remodelled and ornamented in 1529.

247. Presumably the Teatro Sant'Agostino in the Stradone de Sant'Agostino, the principal one of the three theaters in Genoa at this time, where operas were produced in the carnival season and plays in the autumn. See L. T. Belgrano, *Imbreviature di Giovanni Scriba* (Genoa, 1882), pp. 479–80; *Descrizione di Genova e del Genovesato* (Genoa, 1846), III, 248. A few days later the opera *Le Gelosie Villane* (1776) by Giuseppe Sarti was produced (*Gazzetta Nazionale della Liguria,* November 3, 1804).

Those who have no box seat themselves in that part of the theatre which we call the pit, which has a number of rows of benches with backs to them. The same ticket that admits you here admits you likewise to any other part of the house and you pay about 20 sous for it. The Boxes are partitiond off from each other and only open in front where they generally have curtains ↑by↓ which means they can entirely seclude themselves from the audience. <Sofas & chairs are> They are <g> likewise furnished with sofas, chairs, tables &c and in carnival time it is very common to sup, play at cards &c in the boxes. The stage only is illuminated as the ladies complain that lights placed in the other parts of the theatre *hurt their eyes.* Besides they say if the theatre was illuminated they would have to take pains in dressing themselves whereas at present they can go to the theatre in an undress. Indeed an Italian Theatre is the most accomodating public place <that> immaginable. The scenery is pretty good. My ignorance of the language renderd it impossible for me to judge of the dialogue but the music was very fine. All the <comedies> operas at present exhibited in Genoa are Buffa. (or comic) They in a manner chant all the dialogue which has a singular & unnatural appearance to a stranger. The chief drollery of the piece seemd to lie in the grimaces & whimsical faces & attitudes of one of the performers who exerted his talents in this respect to a most extravagant and unnatural degree yet in spight of the contempt I felt for such buffoonery I could not but laugh at some of his distortions of countenance & figure.

It is forbidden here for the audience to *encore* and I highly approve of the regulation. When any actor sings a song well, or performs a scene with skill <the audience clap on> on his exit the audience continue clapping till he reappears and bows an acknowledgement of their applause This is so frequently done in the course of a play that it becomes fatiguing to one not accustomed to it. <At a public> At the benefit of a performer the theatre is illuminated very brilliantly and a <box or dish is> person (sometimes the actor) stands near the entrance or sits at a table placed there, with a box to recieve the donations of those who enter. The admirers of the performer very often make handsome presents; and without this the benefits would be very inconsiderable, <as those who have boxes are admitted free the same as at other times> ↑from the low price of the tickets.↓

The Genoese women are generally well made with handsome features and very fine black eyes.[248] They are infinitely superior in my opinion to the french women in respect to personal charms. They are much given to intrigue, exceeding amorous and in case of neglect it is said revengeful. As to the latter however it is not so much the case at present as it was formerly. The stilleto is forbidden to be worn and Genoa that was once one of the worst places in Italy for assassinations no longer deserves the character. In this respect an change has taken place all over Italy and the french I believe deserve a great part of the merit of effecting it. <The> Assassinations now are very rare and generally take place among the lower class in their quarrels.

October 26

Yesterday morning made an excursion into the country to visit Sestri a small village about six miles <from> ↑to the west of↓ Genoa. I was in company with Storm and Mr Caffarena[249] an English gentleman; we intended to visit the Lomilleno gardens near Sestri, which are laid out in the English taste and much admired.[250] Our road la<id>y along the shore of the Medditeranean and as we rode along we were presented with a variety of charming prospects. We passd thro the suburbs of St Pietra d'Arena in which are some fine palaces tho much injured by the shot from the English ships when they bombarded Genoa about 5 years since.[251] When we arrived at *Sestri di Ponenti* we stopped to visit at the house of Mrs Bird lady of the English consul.[252] She resides at a

248. Irving commented on Genoese women in some of the same terms in his letter to Andrew Quoz, January 1–20, 1805.

249. In 1805 Edward Caffarena was named by the U. S. consul in Genoa one of two vice-consuls, and from 1807 to 1819 in this capacity he kept all the U. S. consular records in the city (Despatches from U. S. Consuls, Genoa, RG 59, NA).

250. They are at the villa now called Roston, built for Agostino Lomellino in 1760 from designs of Andrea Tagliafichi (*Descrizione di Genova e del Genovesato,* III, 336–37; pictured in *Dimore Genovesi,* Milan, copyright 1956, pp. 157–58).

251. The most notable are Palazzo Scassi or Imperiali and Palazzo Spinola, both by Galeazzo Alessi. After the French took Genoa in 1800, the city was besieged by an English and Neapolitan fleet; the French capitulated but immediately reoccupied the city.

252. James Bird did much of the work for John William Brame, the British consul at Genoa, because of the latter's incapacity. Bird's wife was Brame's daughter. See Consular Reports, F. O. 28/18, Public Record Office, London; *The Dispatches and Letters of Vice Admiral Lord Viscount Nelson* (London, 1846), II, 261, 263, and *passim.* Apparently Irving drew on his several visits to Mrs. Bird's house at Sestri Ponente in "The Story of the Young Italian" in *Tales of a Traveller* (1824).

little distance from Sestri, the house being charmingly situated on <an> a small eminence on the sea shore. I was here introduced to Mrs Bird and her daughters <and a Mrs Walsh who are> and to a Mrs Walsh & her daughters[253] who are on a visit of some weeks at Mrs Birds. The girls were very lively and agreeable. The eldest Miss Bird to the graces of a fine person and beautiful countenance adds the accomplishments of an excellent english education and the attractions of an amiable disposition. The sister Eliza has a goodness of heart and mildness of manner that cannot fail to engage esteem and tho the small pox has unfortunately destroyed her pretensions to beauty, yet it could not deprive her of that good nature that shines in her countenance. The younger sister Harriet is yet quite young but promises to possess the highest accomplishments of mind and person. The daughters of Mrs. Walsh are not very remarkable either in person or manner. As to their mother she is one of those *knowing, notable* kind of women. Has read considerable and sets up for a *woman of Learning* – a dangerous character for a woman to sustain who has not strength of head or delicacy of taste & judgement sufficient to support it. Mrs Bird is a charming woman. <Easy and> Polite without ceremony – attentive and hospitable without being officious and possessd of good sense without the ostentation of it.

Understanding we had come out of town on a ramble she pressd us to return there to dinner to which we consented, having obtaind the consent of the young ladies to accompany us in our visit to the Lomellino garden at Pali.[254] This garden is as I before said, laid out in the english taste and deserves a visit from the traveller who stays any time at Genoa. It has a variety of fine walks, Groves, grottos rivulets, a hermitage, a rustic theatre, a temple &c &c &c and delightful glimpses are caught of the Medditeranean from different parts of the Garden. The society of the ladies rendred our ramble delightful & we did not find our way back to the house till three oclock. Before dinner the ladies entertained us with playing on the Harpsichord and singing in both which they acquitted themselves very handsomely. The dinner hour passed away very merrily, we were all in high spirits and as soon as we left the table we began to dance to the music of the Harpsichord.

253. Possibly they were the wife and daughters of Joseph Walsh, who was recommended by the U. S. consul in Genoa to succeed him in 1805 (Despatches from U. S. Consuls, Genoa, RG 59, NA).

254. Pegli.

It was not till late in the evening that Storm & myself reccollected that we were engaged at Lady Shaftesburys[255] and that we had no time to lose in getting to town. We parted therefore from the ladies with infinite reluctance and set out on our return

The night was dark and rainy and when we arrived at <the> St Pietra d'Arena was found that the city gates was shut and no carriage would be admitted. It raind too hard to think of returning home from the gates on foot as the distance was very far, so we stopped in the little theatre of St Pietra[256] till the rain should subside

The theatre was a miserable little hole and the performance very poor. One of the actresses, a very pretty girl, happened to be an *old acquaintance* of Storms and in the course of the play when she had fainted away and was reclining in a most pathetic situation in an arm chair – Storm pelted her with balls of paper. This had nearly involved us in a quarrel with a couple of French officers[.] however after a few words they thought proper to keep themselves silent. After remaining here an hour the rain ceased and we set out again on our journey homeward, where we arrived after having waded thro mud holes and encounterd various accidents *by flood & field.*[257] It was too late to think of going to Lady Shaftesburys th<is>at evening so we <determined to make the great speed to bed> went to bed highly satisfied with our days amusements.

October 27

Yesterday evening I was introduced by Storm to Lord & Lady Shaftesbury. His Lordship & family are detained here prisoners of war having been arrested <between one &> above a year ago while on their travels. He is one of the richest earls of England his income being 40,000 £ sterling a year. His lordship received a violent injury on the

255. Barbara Webb, daughter of Sir John Webb, married in 1786 Anthony Ashley Cooper (1761–1811), the fifth Earl of Shaftesbury.

256. Presumably it was a private theater since the first public one in San Pier d'Arena (modern spelling) was built in 1833 (*Dizionario Geografico, Storico, Statistico, Commerciale degli di* S. *M. il Re de Sardegna,* XVIII, 594). A few years earlier the English traveler Robert Grey attended opera at the "Theatre Della Crosa" there (*Letters during the Course of a Tour through Germany Switzerland and Italy,* London, 1794, p. 260).

257. Shakespeare, *Othello,* I, iii, 134–35:

> . . . I spake of most disastrous chances,
> Of moving accidents by flood and field.

head by a fall from his horse some years since <and> which produced a derangement of intellect for some time. <Even to> He has never perfectly recovered from the effects of it, exhibiting continually an excentricity in his conversation and manners. He often makes some extravagant observation and expresses his ideas a little wildly. He appears to possess a very good disposition is extremely polite and evinces a continual fear of offending. at the end of ↑almost↓ every remark he makes he seizes you by the hand and exclaims – "My dear Sir – I hope I have not offended you – I may be very wrong in my opinion – but I have not offended you – have I? you'll excuse me, <if> I cannot be certain – but I think – I believe I am not very wrong but I hav'nt given offence – now – have I?" And this whimsical string of expressions is often made after the most trifling <ob>& indifferent observation staring you earnestly in the face & rubbing his forehead with one hand all the while.

His lordship expresses great friendship for the Americans and together with his lady thinks we are advancing rapidly to become the first nation in the world.

Lady Shaftesbury is an affable, charming woman – and still bears the remains of great beauty. She sets you at ease immediately in her presence <by the by> releasing you from all painful ceremoniousness of manner by her sociability. She plays charmingly on the piano and Harp and never requires a second request to play if she is really in a humor for music. They have with them their only child Lady Barbara Ashley Cooper[258] a very pretty girl of about fifteen extremely lively. Great care is taken to instruct her in all the fashionable accomplishments. She talks french & Italian fluently, plays on the piano, harp & Guitar and is very good humord Our reception was very polite an[d] satisfactory Storm being an old acquaintance and favorite of her Ladyship.

November 8

Since writing last, the time has passed very pleasantly away, having been introduced by Storm to some of the first nobility of Genoa. Taken collectively, I cannot speak very highly in praise of them. They seem to be a stupid set of beings without much talents or information. The depressd state of their country and the misfortunes they have undergone may have depressd their spirits and <prevented them from> produced

258. Barbara Cooper (d. 1844) married in 1814 the Hon. William Francis Spencer Ponsonby, created Baron de Manley in 1838.

a change in their manners, tho' as far as I can find from different authors they never were celebrated for much wit & learning. Some among them however are very agreeable – many of them speak english & almost all of them French so that I have no difficulty in conversing with them

We have been out two or three times since to Sestri, and rambled about its romantic environs accompanied by the ladies. We have dined once since with Mrs Bird and met at her house a Mr Alton a Swiss Gentleman who talks english perfectly and a Mr Wilson a Scotch painter who passes for an American and <is> has been above a year in Genoa purchasing paintings &c.[259] The former is an old Batchelor that still retains all his boyish waggery and is very fond of *fun*, the latter a good natured good kind of a fellow & a true *sawney*. Our evenings at Sestri were generally spent in dancing or playing games of sport and delighted me from the resemblance they bore to the pleasant ones I have passd among my female acquaintances in America. As to Storm and myself we were so delighted with the place and its fair inhabitants that we <seldom left> generally slept at the hotel in the town all night & did not get home till late the next day The sober Italians stare at us often with suprize and call us the *wild Americans* They generally remark that the Americans and English are just alike except that the Americans are wilder & have a higher flow of spirits.

Yesterday we paid a visit to Madame Gabriac,[260] a lady of distinction to whom I was introduced some time since. There we found a Signor Moranda[261] an Italian gentleman of Storms acquaintance who speaks english fluently. He proposed that we should accompany him to the country seat of Madame Brignoli[262] at Voltri about ten miles to the west

259. No record of a Mr. Alton seems to be preserved in the archives of Genoa. Andrew Wilson (1780–1848), Scotch landscape painter, lived in Genoa from 1803 to 1806 and again from 1826 to 1846.

260. Marie Elizabeth Célésia, Marquise de Gabriac, daughter of the Genoese diplomat Pierre Paul Célésia, married in 1790 the Marquis de Gabriac of Languedoc (Louis de la Roque, *Armorial de la Noblesse de Languedoc,* Montpellier, 1860, I, 221; II, 432; Nicolas Viton de Saint-Allais, *Nobiliare Universel de France,* Paris, 1872–1878, III, 83). Irving gave a more personal description of her in his letter to William Irving, December 20, 1804.

261. Possibly the chemist of this name who espoused the ideas of the French Revolution; his Christian name is given as Giuseppe by one authority, Felice by another (Antonio Cappellini, *Dizionario Biografico de Genovesi Illustri e Notabili,* Genoa, 1932; V. Vitale, "Onofrio Scassi e la Vita Genovese del suo Tempo," *Atti della Società Ligure di Storia Patria,* LIX, 1932, 25 ff).

262. Anna Maria Gasparda Vincenza Pieri, Marchesa Brignole Sale (1765–1815), was noted for the breadth of her cultural interests and for her liberal political views.

of Genoa on the sea shore. Madame Brignoli has a *Dillitanti theatre* at her country seat and they were to perform <the> Voltaires tragedy of Zaira that evening. We agreed to accompany him in the afternoon. We sat off about four o'clock being accomodated with seats in the carriage of Madame Gennistou[263] sister in law to Madame Gabriac. This lady was one of the ma<d>ids of Honor to the late Queen of France and was a witness to many of the scenes of Blood that took place in paris at the commencement of the revolution. She was present in the room when the head of Madame Lamballe[264] was struck off by the sanguinary mob. The horrid scene had such an effect on her mind as to produce a derangement of intellects from which she was a long time recovering It has subsided into a melancholy that has become habitual & settled. We arrived at the palace of Madame Brignoli sometime after dark I was introduced to her and had an extremely polite reception. She is a woman of a fine person & features and elegant manners and is said to be one of the most intelligent ladies of Genoa. She is one of the richest members of the Brignoli family – (a family of the highest rank in the Genoese republic) We found here a number of the beau monde of Genoa amusing themselves with billiards till the play commenced. After <an>

She established herself in Paris after the death of her husband, and in 1811 was made Contessa dell'Impero by Napoleon. She was lady-in-waiting to the Empress Marie Louise in Olanda and Vienna. See O. Grosso, "Anna Pieri Brignole Sole," *Liguria,* XXVII (March 1960), 23–24, (April 1960), 15–16; Grosso, "L'Aquila Ferita," *Liguria,* XXVII (May 1960), 19–20. See also A. E. Bacigalupi, *Famiglie Nobili e Patrizie di Genova e della Liguria* (n.p., 1900), I, 6. The Brignole Sale villa at Voltri was built in the eighteenth century, the theater being added later. It is pictured in *Dimore Genovesi,* pp. 148–49. The performance put on in the theater by Mme. Brignole and her friends was evidently of an Italian translation of Voltaire's *Zaïre* (1732). Irving drew almost verbatim on this account in his letter to William Irving, December 25, 1804–January 25, 1805.

263. "Gennistou" is in blue ink. The woman was Marie Geronima Célésia, Comtesse de Ginestous, older sister of the Marquise de Gabriac, one of the favorite ladies-in-waiting of the Princess de Lamballe. Mme. Ginestous was in Paris during the imprisonment of the Princess there, but did not witness her execution. After Marie Antoinette's execution in October 1793, Mme. Ginestous took ship for England, en route developed a fever and for the rest of her life suffered alternating states of madness and clarity. See H. de Reinach-Foussemagne, *La Marquise la Lage de Volude* (Paris, 1908), pp. 23, 70, 280–81; B. C. Hardy, *The Princess de Lamballe* (London, 1908), p. 301, *passim.*

264. Marie Thérèse Louise of Savoy-Carignano, Princess de Lamballe (1749–1792), widowed the year after her marriage, was chosen by Marie Antoinette as her chief companion, confidante, and superintendent of the royal household. Intensely unpopular, the Princess was beheaded and mutilated by the Paris mob in the courtyard of La Force prison on September 3, 1792.

passing about an hour in the billiard room we were summoned to the theatre. This is fitted up with much taste & judgement & great expence in one wing of the palace. A place <near the> in front of the stage ↑in what we call the pit↓ is seperated from the other parts of the theatre for the reception of Madame Brignoli's visitors. The rest of the theatre consisting of the back part of the pit and a gallery is free for the country people. Zaira the heroine of the play was performed by Madame Reverolle[265] and was her first attempt at theatric's. She is a lady of much <personal> beauty and <?f?> acquitted herself remarkably well. The hero was represented by the eldest son[266] of Madam Brignoli about 18 years <of>old. tall and well made. His performance was energetic & graceful[.] his voice, tho hardly of sufficient strength & flexibility was however full & manly. As the language of the play was italian I could not judge how he succeeded in the dialogue, but he appeared to give much satisfaction to the audience. The other characters were sustaind tolerably well – Madame Brignoli filld <the> one of the female characters but had not scope to display her <theatric> dramatic powers. After the play we partook of an elegant supper furnished in a room that was decorated to represent a Grotto.

The walls were inlaid with porcelaine in imitation of scales & shells and marine productions were distributed with great taste. The *tout ensemble* was superb and must have required a vast expense. After supper word was brought us that the rain that had fallen in great quantities all the evening together with the floods from the mountains ha<ll>d swelld a small river,[267] which we had to cross on our way to town, to such a degree <that> as to render it very dangerous to pass it in the dark. We were therefore obliged to remain at Madame Brignoli's till morning. To pass away the time we adjourned to another room and danced, between the dances some ladies & gentlemen performed on different instruments & sung. Lady Shaftesbury & Lady Barbara were present[.] the latter was in high spirits & danced with great vivacity. In spight of every endeavor we began to be fatigued & heavy

265. Probably Anna Cicopero, Marchesa Rivarola. See L. M. Levati, *I Dogi di Genova dal 1771 al 1797* (Genoa, 1916), pp. 706–9; M. Staglieno, "Genealogie di Famiglie Patrizie Genovesi," VI, 184 (MS in the Biblioteca Berio, Genoa).

266. Antonio Brignole Sale (1786–1863) became a distinguished statesman and received the title Marchese de Groppoli. In his letter to William Irving, December 25, 1804–January 25, 1805, Irving called him Stefano.

267. Voltri is situated at the mouth of the Ceruso River, and there are several other rivers between there and Genoa.

before day light. Storm fell asleep on a sofa having in vain endeavord to persuade a young lady to let him lay his head in her lap. At length the morning dawnd and <released as> we sat off for home as weary a looking set as ever was seen at the breaking up of a ball. We nodded to one another very sociably the whole ride and once or twice a jolt of the carriage sent all our sleepy heads together.

November 13[268]

Yesterday <we>Storm & myself rode out to Sestri to Mrs Birds with an intention of rambling upon the mountains. We had not been there long before we were joind by Mr Wilson whom the fine weather had likewise induced to visit the country. The ladies consented to accompany us in clambering up the heights, and to shew us such places as commanded the most beautiful prospects. The ascent of the mountains was steep & rugged but we were amply repaid by the variety of views that continually opened upon us. The deep gullies <of> between the mountains were well cultivated and cottages appeard on every side, and thro the mountain vistas we caught fine glimpses of the sea shore and the village of Sestri. From <of of> one of the highest places we could see Genoa <at> in the distance <which ha> its steeples & towers having a very picturesque effect in the landscape On the other side a long stretch of the sea shore with villages palaces &c and behind, the Appenines gradually <sw> rising up <t> in vast rocky heights. While we were at this spot enjoying the charming prospects we were surprized by the sound of some uncouth instrument and looking round we percieved a strange, ragged figure approaching us. He was short & brown, his clothes of the rainbow order and an old woolen cap on his head. His countenance was sturdy and good humord and his black eyes had a peculiar archness of expression. His instrument was a simple piece of reed with three slits that ran half its length and by blowing on this and humoring the reed with his hand he produced sufficient variety of notes to perform a few simple rustic airs.

He advanced towards us with his cap under his arm, <and> played two or three of his tunes and then handed us very good humordly his instrument to examine. We gave him a few sous tho he had not requested them. He did not make any acknowledgements but laughed & appeared mightily pleased. While we were looking at him and his reed

268. This entry is copied almost verbatim into Irving's letter to William Irving, December 25, 1804–January 25, 1805.

he very quitely <pull> ↑took↓ some mushrooms out of his cap & began to eat them raw. He told the ladies his name and said he knew where they lived and would come to their palace and play on his reed under their windows. We afterwards learnd from some peasants that he was foolish, but a harmless innofensive good humord fellow that rambled about in the neighborhood of Sestri and was supported by the peasants.

Advancing a little farther up the mountain we stopped at a peasants cottage built of stone in form of a square tower <& forming a picturesque object> ↑half embowerd in large chestnut trees and↓[269] of a picturesque appearance. Here the ladies told us they had taken shelter one day when a shower of rain had surprized them in one of their rambles and they had been so much delighted with the inhabitants of the cottage as to be induced often to visit them. The family consisted of an old man & his wife, a healthy contented looking couple, <and> three <girls> daughters & two sons. The girls were the handsomest female peasants that I have seen in Italy – or I may say in Europe. One in particular, had a blooming complexion, fine black eyes a beautiful set of teeth and when she smiled, two of the prettiest dimples imaginable.[270] Tho dressed in the coarse rustic manner, there was a neatness & cleanliness about her, seldom to be found among the peasantry excepting on Sundays & hollidays. Her name accorded with her person, and was one of those that we demoninate *romantic* tho one by no means uncommon in Italy – it was Angeli<c>na[271] (IE *little angel*)[272] The inhabitants of the cottage crouded around us seeming much pleased with our visit and delighted to see the ladies. After stopping a little while we sat out to ascend <a little> higher ↑<up>↓ and the pretty Angeli<c>na[273] offerd to accompany us, to guide us to a very pleasant spot.

The place where she led us was a little plain that formd a kind of terrace on the top of one of the heights and commanded the most enchanting views on every side. We remained here a long time before we were satisfied with looking about us, and Angeli<c>na[274] <an> em-

269. The alteration is in blue ink.

270. In his letter to William Irving, December 25, 1804–January 25, 1805, Irving directed that his description of this girl be communicated to James K. Paulding, who in a letter written to him in Bordeaux had asked to be informed if he found such a child of Nature in Italy.

271. "n" is written over "c" in blue ink.

272. The words in parenthesis are in blue ink.

273. "n" is written over "c" in blue ink.

274. "n" is written over "c" in blue ink.

ployed herself in the mean time in gathering flowers for us. We asked her a great many questions to which she answerd with much simplicity and good humor. Tho within six miles of Genoa she had only been there but twice in her life tho she was now eighteen years old. She had all the artlessness of nature and <answ> amused us much with her replies. Mr Wilson asked her, if she had not any sweetheart yet. She replied without hesitation "That she loved Iacimo, and that Iacimo loved her likewise and they <would> were to be married in about a year." We asked her who Iacimo was and she told us he was a young man that lived in Sestri, and that he came to see her very often and that she always saw him when she went to church on Sundays at Sestri that he was a charming young man – a very charming young man (uno amabellissimo Giovonotto)[275]

<We returned>

She appeared to be quite unreserved in her replies, tho she blushed and smild whenever she was talking of Iacimo. We returnd to the cottage to dispatch a loaf of bread which we had brought with us. The good people were very eager to serve us. They handed us benches immediately and produced a pitcher of milk for us to eat with our bread. Good humor and content seemed to <reigh> reign in this happy family and for the first<ime> time I realized in Europe the many poetic pictures I have read of rustic felicity.

Our return down the mountain was by a different route which likewise abounded with beautiful scenery.

The rest of the day & the evening passed away very pleasantly in company with the ladies whose society was of that easy unaffected kind that banishes all disagreeable ceremonius restraint. <From> The house of Mrs Bird, commands an extensive and variegated view. A terrace, particularly, on one wing overlooks a charming prospect. The sea shore and the village of Sestri built along it, at a distance the suburbs of St Pietra d'Arena beyond which rises the ridge of mountain on which is built the wall of Genoa running into the sea and terminated with the high tower or light house. The whole shore and the skirts of the mountains, from the village of sestri to Genoa, is a succession of villages palaces &c interspersed with delightful gardens, behind the Appenines rear their rocky summits. On the other hand is the vast bosom of the Middeterranean speckled with sails of vessels feluccas, fishing boats

275. "that he was . . . Giovonotto)" is in blue ink.

passing & repassing continually – and in another direction is seen the Genoese coast stretching as far as the eye can see, forming a continued chain of rocky mountains at the feet of which the white villages & chateaus brighten in the sun. And between the intervalls of the <brown> grey summits of the Appenines you catch glimpses of the alps at a great distance, covered with eternal snow and shining with reflection of the sun beams. The whole surrounding scenery is of the richest & most charming variety and at sun rise or sun set, is really enchanting.

November 14

<This day we were>

<We dined>

Yesterday we were invited to Mrs Birds to eat *Ravioli* and spend the day. Ravioli is a favorite Genoese dish made of flour and forced meat and is very delicate. Yesterday was the day of St Martins[276] when it is universally eaten by the Genoese the same as [*blank*][277] is on Good friday by the English. They generally invite several of their friends to dine with them & make merry <on that day> and after that day the fashionable world commonly abandon their country residences and return to town The lower classes make it a point to get drunk on the occasion and will often compel persons to do so, who are soberly inclined. The day & evening passed away very agreeably the latter as usual being devoted to dancing. We returned to town early this morning.

At eleven oclock to day, took place the execution of a notorious robber who has for some time made a great noise in europe and was known by the name of *The Great Devil of Genoa.* (Il grande Diavolo)[278]

The real name of this man was Josep<pe>h Musso[279] – he was born in Genoa, of obscure parentage and followed the occupations of a common laborer or peasant till the time the Germans beseiged Genoa. He then enlisted under the German standard and by his bravery acquired some inferior commission. When the <Geno> German Army withdrew from the country he remained behind but being outlawed he did not

276. The feast day of St. Martin of Tours (*ca.* 316–397) is November 11.

277. Presumably Irving meant the hot-cross bun.

278. Irving drew on this entry in his letter to William Irving, December 24, 1804–January 25, 1805.

279. "Josep<pe>h Musso" is in black ink. The man was Giuseppe Musso (1779?–1804) (*Gazzetta Nazionale della Liguria,* November 17, 1804). The description in this newspaper of Musso's behavior on the day of his execution accords with Irving's.

dare to appear in his native city. His military life had inured him to toils & dangers and gave a warlike turn to his disposition. His fortunes were desperate, he had sworn eternal enmity to the French & Bonaparte in particular. <Thus situated he determined to> The whole country was in the hands of his enemies and he could expect no mercy at their hands. Every door to honest subsistence being thus shut against him he determined to have resort to <violence> ↑robbery↓ for a livelihood and <since the> ↑violate those↓ laws which had already sat their faces against <them> ↑him↓.[280] He soon found companions equally desperate with himself and formed a band that in a short time became notorious and dreaded for its intrepid <de> exploits. The Appenines in the neighborhood of Genoa afforded safe retreats for his band from whence they frequently descended to lay travellers under contribution and plunder convoys of merchandize. But their depredations were not entirely confined to these parts – They extended to other parts of Italy and even it is supposed he was often a leader in many signal robberies in Spain. <He was> A favorite scene of his crimes was at the Boquetto[281] a rugged pass over a mountain on the road to Milan. It is the only <carriage> pass by which a carriage can enter or leave the Ligurian republick & is consequently much travelled. Here from the steepness & roughness of the mountain it was impossible for either carriage or horseman to escape from his gang – and robberies were incessant in this spot. His band seldom consisted of above eighteen or twenty – but they were all men of desperate courage & their mode of life had inurd them to hardships & fatigue.

The name of *The Great Devil* (given him in consequence of his incredible exploits) soon became universally dreaded. Troops of soldiers were sent out to take or destroy him but he invariably escaped from their toils. At one time they surrounded him & his comrades on the top of a mountain, but they cut thro their enemies & <effectuated> ↑effected↓[282] their escape. His bodily strength was astonishing & he was equally remarkable for his agility in running – bounding among the rocks & precipices of the mountains like a goat. Another time <he was surrounded by> a company of soldiers surrounded a small hut in which

280. The alteration is in black ink.

281. La Bocchetta.

282. The alteration is in blue ink. The alterations of this nature in the remainder of this entry, if made by Irving, suggest that he considered preparing his account of Musso for publication.

he was sleeping, <and> he leapd out of a window, fought his way thro them & got off unhurt though a volley of musketry was fired at him. There was a considerable degree of discrimination observed by him in his robberies. He never plunderd the poor, but often releived them by the spoils he had taken from the rich. The poor peasants frequently experienced the effects of his bounty and he was careful to cultivate a good understanding with all the peasantry in his neighborhood. He was therefore very secure from being betrayed by them even when they knew his lurking place & large rewards were offerd for his apprehension. His <connexions> relations & friends in Genoa gave him notice of every thing that was carrying on so that he knew when to profit by convoys of merchandize or to escape parties that were sent out <to> in pursuit of him. At one time when a body of soldiers were searching for him in the mountains he was sailing off the harbor in a small boat – Another time an officer of police was sent to insinuate himself into his band & act as a spy. He repaired to the Great Devil & offerd his services as a man who was unfortunate and ill treated by the world – Musso who had information of his intentions turnd to some of his gang who was present & orderd them to lead forth that man and shoot him – The orders were immediately obeyd.

Any person that wished to trade with him for his spoils might rely on his *honor* and safely bring any sum of money to purchase them with. The Great Devil had plunderd a rich convoy of Goods belonging to a mercht. of Genoa. The latter sent his brother to treat for their redemption. Musso gave him a meeting – having his guards stationd at a little distance to prevent surprize. The mercht. offerd him a price very much inferior to the value of the goods – Musso replied "do you think your brother would have sold them at such a miserable rate! – They have become mine by capture <but> ↑and↓ I cannot think of *sacrificing* <them> ↑my goods↓[283] at so inferior a price." The mercht. <was permitted to retire in perfect safety> passed the night in Mussos tent, in consequence of his assurance of safety – in the morning he took leave unmolested altho' he had a large sum of Gold by <?th?> him to make the purchase ↑he afterward returnd with the sum Musso required↓.[284] It would be tiresome to enter into a detail of his manouvres <which> and the many accounts I have heard of ↑his↓ different exploits for sev-

283. The alterations in this sentence are in blue ink.
284. This sentence is in blue ink.

ral years. His robberies & murders had been transacted in different parts of Italy, Germany, France, Spain & portugal and he has been condemnd to death & prices set on his head by different courts in those different territories. After the many regular attempts to apprehend him, the business was effected by a mere accident. He had taken passage from Gibraltar in a vessel bound to Trieste a <town in> port in Germany to the eastward of Venice. While performing Quarentine at Trieste he had a violent Quarrel with the master & swore <violently> that the latter should not live long after they were landed

Intimidated by this menace and by the manner of the person who made it The captain as soon as he landed applied to the proper authorities for protection – mentioning that <the> ↑a↓ Genoese on board of his vessel threatned his life. The magistrate applied to the Genoese consul to become responsible for Musso – The consul was struck with the name and immediately suspected from the discription given that it might be the notorious robber of whom in common with all Genoese authorities – he had been put on his guard. He went on board of the vessel and was confirmed in the opinion He <immediately> ↑instantly↓ had him apprehended & thrown in prison & wrote to Genoa <for> an account of the affair. A company of soldiers were immediately dispatched who brought him to Genoa where he was closely confined ↑in the Tower.↓[285] After an imprisonment ↑of three months↓[286] he was <condemnd> ↑convicted↓[287] & sentenced to be shot. He was brought to the chapel of the prison to have the sentence read to him by <th> a Priest. <An>A gentleman of my acquaintance was at the prison at the time & mentiond to me the particulars. It was friday evening. Musso came skipping down stairs between two soldiers – <in a> with a careless air smoking a pipe & jumping two steps at a time. When the priest read off the sentence he shewed no signs of agitation but replied carelessly ["]*è bene* (very well) – you might as well have sentenced me at first and not kept me three months in prison"

He was then going off but stopped and turning briskly round – "Stop says he – you have forgot to tell me when I am to be shot" The priest replied "on *Monday*" – "Saturday is *one* <Monday> ↑Sunday↓ *two* Monday *three* (replied he counting his fingers) – three days – *è bene*"

285. "in the tower" is in blue ink.
286. "of three months" is in blue ink.
287. The alteration is in blue ink.

and was then again going off very unconcernedly but added "I suppose I may see my sister & relations before I am shot[.]" he was told that could not be granted "Then replied he they will have to drag me to execution for my own feet shall not carry me there." He was then led to the dungeon where the condemnd are confined between the reading & execution of their sentence. He was allowed to see his relations the next day and <on> Sunday – being St Martins when all the Genoese ↑eat↓ *raviole's*, a dish of the kind <h> cooked in the best manner, was given him & they searchd Genoa for a bottle of the finest wine (a bottle of good wine is always given to the condemnd in Genoa before execution) which was furnished by an old princess of my acquaintance.

<The day of> This morning all Genoa was in commotion (I E the lower class) to see <his last> him shot. As the <Govt.> Police was apprehensive an attempt might <have> be made to rescue him by his relations & the peasantry (the latter being highly prepossessd in his favor from the liberality with which he had often distributed his plunder among them) a large body of soldiers were orderd out to guard him to the place of execution.

The streets – windows &c were throngd by spectators. Having in common with the multitude a great curiosity to see this singular man I stationd myself near the gate of the city at which he was to go out – & had a tolerable view of him as he passd. He appeard to be about five feet 8 inches stout & well set of a dark complexion with strong but good features & immense eye brows. He was about 26 years of age. Two priests attended him to whom he appeared to listen <t> very devoutly and he held a small cross between his hands. He was shot on the banks of a small river[288] that runs without the town, and <?f?> sufferd his sentence in a very manly decent manner. I have been particular in my account of this man from his great <cleli> celebrity. An account was published sometime ago in england of his apprehension & execution – and an afterpiece written of which he was the hero.[289] In a better cause he might have distinguished himself to advantage. he certainly possessd superior genius & undaunted courage.

288. The Bisagno.

289. The work to which Irving refers is not certain. A play, "The Great Devil; or, the Robber of Genoa," by Charles Dibdin, was performed at Sadler's Wells in London about 1800; it appears in [John] *Cumberland's Minor Theatre*, XIV (London, n.d. [*ca.* 1837]). There is, however, no particular parallel between Musso and Dibdin's Great Devil, who meets his death when his hiding place is betrayed.

November 16[290]

Yesterday we dined at Lord Shaftesbury's. There were but three or four <strangers> ↑visitors↓ at table beside ourselves, but after dinner in the evening more company came in and violins having been prepared we had a pleasant little dance. The Italians do not equal the french in dancing altho' they have dancing masters of that nation. As there are not many Gentlemen among the nobility who excel in dancing, they are obliged when they give balls to invite merchants clerks, to assist in making up the dances[.] these they call "the dancers of the city." & are considered much in the light of joint stools or arm chairs sometimes used in <one> family dances to make up a set for a cotillion or country dance. Ices & lemonades are handed about at the balls continually – and the italians make no hesitation in eating the former when in a state of the highest perspiration.

December 1

I have been for three or four days past engaged in examining <different> the paintings in several of the palaces. In this employment I was accompanied by a Mr Wilson <a> the <S>Young Scotch man who <has resided for some> I mentioned before as having seen at Mrs Birds. He <?y?> very obligingly acted as cicerone and being acquainted with every painting of merit in Genoa he acquitted himself very well. To enter into a detail of the many fine peices I have seen would be fatiguing[.] among the finest are a *holy family* by Reubens in the palace of Giacomo Balbi.[291] Diogenes looking for an honest man – Rape of the Sabines – Perseus with Medusa's head – <G>Je<s>zabel[292] <by> devourd by dogs – all four by Luca Giordano[293] a painter of great merit. (It is one of the peculiarities of this painter that he continually changes his style in his different paintings.) Magdalene with a

290. Irving drew on this entry in his letter to William Irving, December 25, 1804–January 25, 1805.

291. The palace to which Irving refers is No. 6 Via Balbi, built in the seventeenth century by Bartolomeo Bianco (C. G. Ratti, *Instruzione di Quanto Può Vedersi di Più Bello in Genova,* Genoa, 1780, I, 179 ff.). It was owned by Gacomo Ignazio Balbi (d. 1796) until his death, then by his son Costantino (Staglieno, "Genealogie di Famiglie Patrizie Genovesi," I, 46). A list of the paintings in it in the period when Irving visited it is contained in [Giacomo Brusco?], *Description des Beautés de Gênes et de ses Environs* (Genoa, 1788), pp. 139–45.

292. "J" and "z" are written in blue ink over "G" and "s."

293. Luca Giordano (1632–1705), who spent most of his life in Naples, formed his style on that of Paolo Veronese and Pietro da Cortona.

death's head by Guido &c &c all in the same palace. In the palace of Marcellino Durazzo[294] is an exquisite painting of the Magdalene bathing the feet of our Saviour by Paolo Veronese & in the same palace is a remarkably exact copy of it by another painter. The figure of the Magdalene is peculary fine & interesting – to the left of our Saviour – is an old man said to be the portrait of Paolo Veronese himself.

The appartments in those palaces are superbly furnished – Admission to them is very easy, <A servant> as the family generally reside in appartments less splendid – and only keep these for shew & company. You have but to knock at the hall door & mention that you wish to see the palace and one of the servants immediately attends you thro all the rooms handing you a book in writing that mentions the pictures & the names of the painters – you reward the sevt with a trifling present of two or three livres.[295]

The other morning we breakfasted with Sigr. John Carl di Negri a gentleman of the balbi family.[296] He has built himself a pretty little house <i>on an eminence in the skirts of the city and keeps batchelors hall in a very elegant style. His house commands several beautiful views of the city – the Harbor & the adjacent country – and he has a very well arranged botanical garden around the house. The appartments of his house are painted <by under his> & fitted up according to his own directions & with great taste. A front room that opens to the garden he has <called> ↑named↓ the temple of Apollo from a fresco painting of that deity on the <wall.> cieling – He intends having the Muses painted on the walls and to represent in them nine of the *belles* of Genoa.

This Gentleman talks english very well having been in London some

294. Probably Domenico Giacomo Marcello (or Marcellino) Durazzo (1762–1837) (Staglieno, "Genealogie di Famiglie Patrizie Genovesi," III, 213; *Gazzetta Nazionale della Liguria,* January 1, 1805). His palace, No. 10 Via Balbi, was built about 1650 by Francesco Cantone and Giovanni Angelo Falcone for the Durazzo family. A list of the paintings it contained in the period when Irving visited it is in Thomas Martyn, *A Tour Through Italy* (London, 1791), pp. 58 ff.

295. The exchange rate at this time was one livre for 15½¢, as Irving's expense accounts indicate. Irving drew on this paragraph in his letter to William Irving, December 25, 1804–January 25, 1805.

296. Gian Carlo di Negro (1769–1857), poet and essayist, was famed for his cultural receptions at his villa, La Villetta (Giovanni Casati, *Dizionario degli Scrittori d'Italia,* Milan, [1926], II, 278). The house and garden in the period when Irving visited them are described in *Descrizione di Genova e del Genovesato,* III, 333–34. The relationship of di Negro to the Balbi family has not been determined.

time. He has a library of choice English authors. Among other accomplishments he has the singular one that I have often heard spoken off as being peculiar to the Italians. This is – of making verses extempore. Those gifted <t> with this talent are termed Improvisitori. You appoint them any subject, either an annecdote in history or any present circumstance or object – such as a ladies eyes – a handkerchief &c and they will immediately compose a number of verses on it – very often of much beauty & merit.

December 2–20[297]

<Two in these>

Tho' the Catholic religion has received a great shock in Genoa since the French have had possession of it yet it still retains much of its former pomp & ceremony. There were formerly a vast number of convents in and about the city, most of which are stripped of their property – abandond by their inhabitants and ruined by the mob. Some still exist, but are very poor and the monks are reduced to beggary. Religious processions are not at present <allowed to pass thro> ↑frequent in↓[298] the streets except on particular occasions but are chiefly confined to the churches, as are likewise all their other religious ceremonies. A few mornings since I attended Lady Shaftesbury & Lady Barbara to the church of <S Luca> ↑De Vigne↓[299] to hear a grant [grand] concert that was to be given in honor of some saint. The church <was> is one of the smaller ones of Genoa, but well built & beautifully ornamented with paintings gildings &c. it is hung with red ↑& blue↓[300] damask & the marble pillars that support the roof are covered with the same. ↑I was surprized to see a people of so much taste & judgement disguising the beauty of their church by such gaudy frippery ornaments↓[301] The Orchestra was very numerous and the vocal parts chiefly performed by amateurs. The church music of the Italians is peculiarly fine. <Sometimes a single voice is heard There is a simplicity & grandeur in many of their peices that I admire more than all the affected trillings that I have

297. The manuscript has only "December." Irving drew on this entry, several times verbatim, in his letter to William Irving, December 25, 1804–January 25, 1805.

298. "frequent in" is in blue ink.

299. S. M. delle Vigne was founded in the thirteenth century and rebuilt in the sixteenth century.

300. "& blue" is in blue ink.

301. This sentence is in blue ink.

heard used in> It has a simplicity and Grandeur best calculated to produce the sublime in music – and well suited to the dignity of the place and the solemnity of the occasion. In the churches there are no fixed seats as in ours in America. <Chairs are> rush bottomd chairs are <given> brought to you for the use of which you pay <about a coup> two or three sous. The church was very much crowded and the people huddled together as in a mob. You are continually jostled by people passing to & fro <and> who brush along without any ceremony. Above all the chief annoyance is the swarm of beggars with which the churches are infested You are assailed by them in every direction and they are the most importunate I ever beheld. I have seen them attack an honest Catholic while at prayers and worry him for an half hour till his torpid charity was fairly forced to exert itself. These miserable beings are seen wandering in every part of a church during mass presenting the most loathsome objects – <and> coverd with rags & filth. I <had bee> have often mentiond the number of beggars in france but they are nothing to compare to the multitudes that swarm in Genoa – and yet I am told that in <oth> some other cities of Italy they are still more numerous

The demands upon your charity is incessant in the streets of Genoa – nor will they take a denial tho often repeated but follow you for some time with their importunities. Never have I seen such pictures of abject want & wretchedness as I have witnessed in this place.

A few evenings ago I was in company with the Doge[302] & Cardinal [*blank*][303] at Madame Gabriacs. The evening after I was introduced to the other ↑former↓[304] at his Levee by his nephew Sigr John Baptista Serra.[305] He is a small man of an ordinary countenance – but extremely polite & affable as is likewise his lady. There were present at the Levee a number of the Genoese nobility of both sexes – After the usual articles of conversation the company began to disappear except a few who remained to play cards.

The office of the Doge has undergone much alteration since the revo-

302. Girolamo Durazzo (1739–1809) was the last Doge of Genoa; the office was discontinued when the city was annexed to France in 1805.

303. Probably Giuseppe Spina (1756–1828), who was created cardinal in 1802 and afterwards archbishop of Genoa.

304. "former" is in pencil.

305. Gian Battista Serra (1768–1855) was so enthusiastic a supporter of the French Revolution that he was called "Serra il Giacobino."

lution. He was formerly obliged to remain always at home during the two years he held his station excepting twice a year that he attended particular religious processions At present he has full liberty to go in or out whenever he pleases.

Tho the Doge is the ostensible head of the Ligurian Government yet it is said he is completely gov<d>erned by the M——r of f——ce[306] who is both hated & feard throughout Genoa. He is one of the miscreants that played a principal part in france during the reign of Terror, and gave the casting vote for the death of the king. He was the <first> best friend that Bonaparte had <to> in <his>the commencement of his carreer and was the person that first put him in command. He afterwards imprisoned B—— for some circumstance which I have not learnd. It is said he is merely retained <by P> in favor by B—— thro fear and it is expected that he will one day or other meet with his deserts by his former Protegee.

It is painful to witness the depressd state of the Genoese nobility. Deprived of their titles and stripped of part of their fortunes they fear to shew out with what is left and endeavor to make as little display as possible. They have no handsome carriages – their servants are without livery and themselves dress as plainly[307] as possible. The Genoese nobility have never been highly extolld for talents or information – the greater part of them may not perhaps deserve much eulogium but I have found among them several possessd of very superior abilities – particularly the Serra's of whom there are four brothers[308] nephews of the present Doge, who are all men of brilliant talents. Sigr John Carl Di Negri a gentleman of very handsome poetical <talents> ↑endowments↓ & an *Improvisatore* & several others men of taste & genius.

The Italians are very fond of games of play, such as <forfeit> throwing the handkerchief – passing the ring & forfeits. <among thos> Their favorite one however is called <The Tab> *La Tableau* (the Picture). This requires a good memory & much historical reading to play. One

306. Antoine Christophe Saliceti (1757–1809), Corsica-born French revolutionary, was the French minister to Genoa from 1803 to 1805. He allowed the blame for the Corsican insurrection of 1794 to fall on Bonaparte, who was in consequence imprisoned for thirteen days. See William M. Sloane, *The Life of Napoleon Bonaparte* (New York, 1912), I, 254.

307. "ly" is in blue ink.

308. G. B. Serra had several brothers, but the three to whom Irving refers are evidently Gerolamo (1761–1837), politician and historian; Giancarlo (1760–1813); and Vincenzo (1778–1846), mayor of Genoa and rector of the university.

person is sent out of the room the rest dispose themselves in a group so as to represent some transaction in history such as the death of Cato – Rhemus slain by Romulus[309] &c &c. The person is then calld in and guesses what historical incident it is <made> ↑intended↓ to represent. I have seen this played several times and very rarely have known the person to <fal> fail in guessing. De Negri was particularly good at it and sometimes even sung the subject in extempore verses said to be of much merit.[310]

This winter the Beau monde of Genoa seemed to have conceived a great *penchant* for private Theatric's. The *dillitanti* performances at Madame Brignoli['s] gave rise to this inclination. Her private theater is indeed fitted up with taste & managed very judiciously. the performances possess very considerable merit. Lady Shaftesbury had some private performances at her house but they were intended chiefly as lessons to Lady Barbara. The performers were Lady Barbara & the Miss Spinola's[311] – and some Italian gentlemen. A <The> large hall or saloon served for theatre and a Skreen was placed at one end for the actors to retire behind. Some few friends were admitted as audience and as no great ceremony was observed, we had a great deal of sport & amusement.

As soon as the piece was performd the company began their favorite plays – blind mans buff forfeits &c and the evening passd off merrily. Indeed Lady S has the faculty of making all her visitors feel perfectly at home and banishing all <?re?> disagreeable restraint. Her Ladyship is extremely affable & good humourd and possessd of superior understanding

Her chief attention is directed towards forming the mind & manners of Lady Barbara and studying italian. Lady Barbara <to the> is a very pretty girl of about fifteen and one of the best dispositions I ever knew Her temper appears never ruffled – and there is an artless frankness & simplicity in her that cannot fail to charm. Without unnecessary pride or affectation <she>tho <is> enjoying all the advantages of birth &

309. Cato the Younger committed suicide. Romulus killed Remus in a quarrel.

310. The rest of this entry and the rest of this manuscript (through January 23, 1805) is in blue ink.

311. It does not seem possible to identify these persons, since the Spinola family was very large and had many branches; at least two villas in Sestri Ponente belonged to them, that of Lilla Mari Spinola in the late eighteenth century being especially notable. See [Brusco?], *Description des Beautés de Gênes et de ses Environs*, p. 277.

fortune and possessing superior accomplishments. Lord S amid all his excentricity evinces a good heart & friendly disposition. At times he displays much judgement & information in his conversation tho often blended with singularity of manner. I was extremely delighted with this family, from whom I recieved the most friendly & particular attentions. Their house used to be one of my constant evening resorts as I was ever sure to find amusement there. A few days <before> ago Lord S receivd news from England of the Death of his mother,[312] which put a stop for a while to all visiting at his house as they did not see any company for near a week.

The news of the coronation of Bonaparte arrived laterly at Genoa. The Govt. have been sometime talking of giving a ball in compliment to that *benefactor* of their country. This has been deferred repeatedly and I was somewhat surprized at the delay till I was told by Madame G—— a lady of Distinction & friend of the Doge – that the Govt. was absolutely *too poor to give a ball* – "and it would be a hard thing to have to run in debt" said she "in rejoicing at the success of the very man who has draind our purses." The French minister intends giving a splendid ball on the occasion and indeed he can afford it as he takes care to <pay> be well paid for all his public services. He is in fact a little tyrant in Genoa & no one dare displease him. A noble lady of my acquaintance expressed great unwillingness to attend his ball, "but" said she "I do not *dare* refuse."

As I have often leisure time on hand I now & then stroll into the churches to see the faces of the ladies & to see the church ceremonies performd. There is certainly something very solemn & imposing in the ceremonies of the Roman church. Unwilling as we may be to acknowledge it we cannot deny that forms & ceremonies have a great effect on the <imagination>. ↑feelings in matters of religion↓ To enter a superb & solemnly constructed edifice

> Whose ancient pillars rear their marble heads
> To bear aloft its archd and pondrous roof[313]

gives us a dignified idea of the being to whose honor it is erected. Its long & dimly lighted aisles & vaulted chapels adornd with paintings all pointing out some attribute or action of the deity have an impressive

312. Mary, daughter of the first Viscount Folkestone, the Dowager Lady Shaftesbury, died November 12, 1804.

313. William Congreve, *The Mourning Bride* (1697), II, iii, 9, 10.

appearance while the gloomy grandeur of the whole inspires us with reverence & respect

"Looking tranquility it strikes an awe"[314]

Then the service itself has such an air of pomp & sublimity that I always feel more filld with an exalted Idea of the Deity than at any other time.

The superb altars magnificently decorated and illuminated – The solemn movements of the priests and the humble prostration of the congregation, The full chant of the choir and the pealing sound of the organ swelling thro the archd aisles and dying away <as if ascend> in soft gradations, the incense arising in fragrant columns before the grand altar <and> ↑as↓ if ascending to the "heaven of heavens"[315] a grateful offering of homage – has altogether an effect on my feelings irrisistibly solemn. This perhaps is only an instance how easily an imagination may be heated & led away by form & shew – but in matters of religion I am convinced <the imagination ↑it is the> it↓ is the part most vulnerable, and was I attempting to introduce a new doctrine I should address my attempts chiefly against the imagination. <& fancy>.

The Roman religion however multiplies its saints to such a degree that a poor Catholic I believe is often puzzled in his choice which to apply to, to <vindicate> plead his cause at the high tribunal of heaven Several of them <however> are of particular eminence the same as we have superior Lawyers who are generally applied to on great emergencies. Every day in the year is allotted to some particular saint.

This reminds me of a story of an honest Scotchman <th> who livd in a Catholic family – he was told he must fast the next day as it was *All saints day*[.] to this he had no objection thinking it the least he could do for so respectable an assemblage. A few days after he was told he must fast again – "and wha for" cries he "For <saint> St Andrew" was the answer "Hoot awa mon" replies Sawney "I fast for no St. Andrew[.][316] why the de'el did he keep <out of the way> ↑oot o' the way↓ when I fasted for *a the Saints* in a drove?"

Since the revolution much more liberty & freedom has introduced it-

314. *Ibid.*, l. 12.

315. This phrase occurs several times in the King James translation of the Bible; see, for example, Deut. 10:14, I Kings 8:27; II Chron. 2:16, 6:18.

316. The feast day of St. Andrew (1st century), the patron saint of Scotland, is November 30.

self into the ↑customs &↓ manners of the Genoese. They now permit their daughters to frequent balls and assemblies a thing not known of before the revolution. Young ladies of respectability however are not permitted to walk out or visit without the company of their Father mother gouvernante or some person of the kind and such a thing as a young gentleman gallanting a young lady along the street would be looked upon as exceeding singular. A lady seen alone in the street may safely be concluded to be married or to be a woman of loose character.

I was talking on this subject to a lady of my acquaintance and mentioning the difference of our manners in this respect[317] – that our young ladies walkd the streets entirely alone or in the company of a young gentleman – that they visited in the same manner. That young gentlemen attended them home in the evenings &c &c &c. She was exceedingly surprized but said "it was a mark of the simplicity & honesty of our manners but that it would never do in Italy & france in both which countries the ladies are kept under great restraint."

This is the reason why the ladies are so happy to rush into matrimony without having any affection for their husbands. They merely consider it as a priviliged state where they can indulge themselves with greater freedom. The husband (I E the italian) perhaps conscious of this becomes Jealous of his wife nor do they generally take much pains to hide this passion when it enters into their bosoms. The lady seeing they do not confide implicitly in her virtue thinks herself no longer bound in honor to observe those vows which they will not give her the credit of having an inclination to keep sacred & perhaps from this in some degree arises the notorious unfaithfulness of Italian wives.

December 21[318]

An American ship[319] sailing from this port for Messina in Sicily I have engaged my passage in her. By this means I shall avoid the necessity of travelling thro Italy at this unpleasant season of the year particularly as travelling is much embarrassed by the cordonès (lines of troops) drawn

317. Irving commented on this subject in much the same terms in his letter to Andrew Quoz, January 1–20, 1805.

318. Irving communicated the substance of this entry in his letter to William Irving, November 30, 1804.

319. The *Matilda* of Philadelphia arrived in Genoa September 29, 1804; no other American vessel called for the next nine months at least (Despatches from U. S. Consuls, Genoa, RG 59, NA). See also Irving to William Irving, December 20, 1804.

in different parts to prevent communication from infectious provinces. After making a hasty tour in Sicily I shall cross over to Naples. We were to have saild today but the wind is too violent for the vessel to warp out.

December 23[320]

After having been detaind till to day by a violent storm of wind & snow uncommonly severe for Genoa we set sail from Genoa at 2 oclock with a fine brisk gale. It was with the deepest regret I left this city where I had experienced so many attentions – where I ha<f>d found a friend particularly dear[321] to me and formed a number of most agreeable acquaintances – but th<at>is is the grand misfortune of travelling – no sooner have we become acquainted in any place and began to form an agreeable circle of friends – but we are obliged to tear ourselves away and <once more> again in a manner become alone in the world.

I received the kindest wishes at parting together with particular letters for different parts of Italy for Sicily & Malta with promises that more letters of introduction for Italy should be sent after me to Naples. We passed out of the port with a noble wind. The city rapidly receded – Sestri and its environs – the haunt of many an happy hour broke upon my view and I remaind alternately gazing upon Sestri & Genoa till they faded in the distance and evening vield[322] them even from the sight of the telescope.

"Genoa figurd conspicuously in the time of the Crusades and still bears the red cross as the arms & standard of the Republic. It was then a powerful & important state and by different means had gaind possession of Majorca Minorca Sardinia Corsica Candia Malta Lesbos Smyrna in Asia Minor &c &c Also some places of importance in the Black sea & even the suburbs of Constantinople. Weakend by foreign colonies and conquests it had <to> at length to surrender to Charles VI of France <she> within a century after it had made so formidable an appearance. It afterwards regaind its liberty but again threw itself under protection of Lewis XII and Francis Ist.

320. Irving drew on the second paragraph and the last two paragraphs in this entry virtually verbatim in his letter to William Irving, December 25, 1804–January 25, 1805.

321. Presumably Irving refers to Lady Shaftesbury; see his letter to William Irving, December 25, 1804–January 25, 1805, especially the passage in which he compares her to Mrs. J. O. Hoffman.

322. Read "veiled."

[“]Andrea Doria quitting the french service for that of the Emperor Charles 5 stipulated with that prince for the freedom of his country and gave such laws to his fellow citizens as settled their freedom and strengthend their domestic & external security” (Abridgd from Nugents <tr> observ: on Italy.)[323]

The Genoese erected numerous monuments to the memory of this Great & worthy man – of which I know but one remaining which represents him in the character of Neptune in a fountain in the midst of the Doria Garden. The rest have been destroyd by the hands of the French.

I had observed in different parts of Genoa over the doors of churches, gates &c several links of enormous Iron chains hanging of which I was curious to know the meaning – I was told that in their wars with the Pisans (a long time since) the Genoese fleet had anchord in the harbor of pisa and the pisans had made an Iron chain of vast strength & size which they stretchd across the river & prevented the Genoese either from getting to sea or recieving succors therefrom. In this <dis> unfortunate situation a blacksmith with great resolution undertook to remove the obstacle He plungd in the river – swam under water & with great perseverance cut thro the chain. The Fleet regaind the sea carried the chain in Triumph to Genoa <where it was> ↑and↓ hung ↑it↓ up in the places where it remains to this day. The Blacksmith was asked what reccompence he demanded for so very important a service. He replied he hoped they would take off all tax upon coals – <a thing which was done &> an act was immediately passd to that effect and still remains in force. A Singular instance of moderation in a person who had it in his power to obtain <so> ↑a much↓ ampler <a> reward.

While at Genoa they celebrated the anniversary of the day when in 1746 the common people of Genoa rose against the Austrians who held possession of the city and drove them out of the walls. All Europe was struck with surprize & admiration at the boldness & success of the attempt, as the people were destitute of <arms> warlike instruments.

The revolution was supported <by> with equal energy and the public funds being inadequate to its support the nobility themselves indi-

323. Irving’s preceding paragraph is a loose paraphrase of Grosley, *New Observations on Italy and its Inhabitants,* II, 336. His paragraph “Andrea Doria . . . external security” is a virtual quotation from II, 337. In the rest of this entry he apparently drew further on this work, II, 338, 342, 346, 347. He made most use of it, however, in his entries written between Rome and Milan.

vidually contributed to its maintenance according to their pecuniary abilities

The state has the monopoly of bread at Genoa which is manufactord in a large building which contains a mill oven &c & every convenience for its manufacture. From hence the bakers that vend it in different parts of the city repair to fetch it away in Large Baskets. I was likewise told the state monopolizes the oil and wine which are kept in large barks floating in a bason near the arsenal

There are but two or three galleys at present belonging to genoa. The slaves are generally employed on shore. I have seen them frequently <empl> passing thro the street chaind two and two. They look hearty & well nor is their situation extremely hard.

The Genoese were anciently renownd for their craftiness and want of faith – and the present generation prove that they have inherited in these respects the qualities of their ancestors. It is a saying in Italy that "It takes six Christians to cheat a Jew and six Jews to cheat a genoese but a genoese Jew is a match for the d——l himself."

The sumptuary laws that formerly restricted the dress of the people are no longer observed. The genoese men are not however very remarkable for finery of dress. They follow the french fashions particularly the women. There is one article of female dress, however, which has been handed down from generation to generation and is still retaind by all ranks & fortunes – this is a kind of veil formd of an oblong piece of ↑Lace↓ cambrick, muslin or callico – which is thrown over the head and shoulders and falls down in front. A pretty woman in my opinion looks extremely well in this veil – I have seen a pair of languishing blue eyes from under one of them give the countenance all the air of a beautiful Madonna.

December 24[324]

The fine breeze with which we set out died away towards evening and all night we had but a light zephyr that hardly filld the sails. The ship has a convenient cabin having formerly been employd as a Charleston packet. There are two or three passengers besides myself. – Genoese captains who talk french very well and can give me information in respect to every place we pass having been long engaged in the Messina

324. Irving drew on this entry almost verbatim in his letter to William Irving, December 25, 1804–January 25, 1805.

trade. They sleep in the steerage – so that I have the cabin to myself. The captain[325] is a worthy honest old gentleman who is always in good humor and strives to the utmost to render every thing agreeable to me.

<25th.> This morning we are quite becalmd. The weather is mild and delightful and the clouds of the late storm <g> entirely dis-appeard. The sun rise was peculiarly lovely. A few low morning clouds hung about the horison and were gradually lighted up with ruddy tinges. In a little time the sun emergd in full splendor from the ocean – his beams diffused a blaze of refulgence thro the clouds, of indiscrib-able richness – the curling tops of the waves seemd tip'd with gold – and the snowy summits of Corsica and the opposite Italian shore <shone with> brightned with reflection of his <beams> rays. So en-chanting a scene was sufficient to inspire the poet – nor do I wonder that this climate should <be> ↑have been↓ particularly productive of poetry & romance. Had those happy days continued when the Deities made themselves visible to man and now and then payed ↑him↓ a familiar visit, <?to?> we might have been entertaind by the *raree shew* of Neptune and Ampithrite[326] and all their gay train of Nerieds and Dolphins. Such a morning would have been a noble time for them to have taken a *drive* round their dominions and seen if all was safe after the late stormy weather. But those days of romance are over. The gods are tired of us heavy mortals and no longer admit us to their intimacy. In these dull *matter of fact* days our only consolation is to wander about their once frequented haunts and endeavor to make up by imagination the want of the reality. There is a poetic charm (if I may so express myself –) that difuses itself over our ideas in considering this part of the globe. We regard every thing with an enthusiastic eye – <and a> thro a romantic medium that gives an illusive tinge to every object. Tis like <regardin> beholding a delightful landscape from an eminence, on a <beati> beautiful <evening> ↑sunset↓. A delicious mistiness is spread over the scene that softens the harshness of particular ob-jects – prevents our examining their forms too distinctly – <But> ↑a glow is thrown over the whole↓ that by blending & softning and en-riching – gives the <whole>, ↑landscape↓ a mellowness – ↑a sweet-ness↓[327] a loveliness of coloring not absolutely its own, but derived in a

325. Matthew Strong was killed on his next voyage when his vessel was wrecked (PMI, I, 103).

326. Amphitrite.

327. The alterations from "sunset" to "a sweetness" appear to have been made with a different pen and may have been made at a later date.

great measure from the illusive veil with which it is oerspread. I do not know whether I express myself intelligibly. Those are sensations difficult to be <discribed> ↑explained↓ – <but> they are too exquisitely delicious to bear a cool discription.

1 oclock. We are within sight of <the sm> Gorgona a small Island between Corsica & the main Land. The wind has sprung up ahead and it is gradually clouding over – threatening wet weather – Gorgona affords subsistance to a few fishermen & appears to be hardly any thing but rock.

December 25[328]

My opinion was right, the weather thickend up <before night> ↑before dark↓ and we have had rain all the night. The wind is still a head & we have not yet made the island of Gorgona. So commences *Christmas day* with me. Seated in the cabin writing by the light of a candle with the wind the Rain & the sea making a furious noise without – and the honest captain snoring pretty nearly as loud in his birth at my elbow. How joyfully would I translate myself to New York and spend these hollidays among my friends. I hope however you may have a *merry* day of it and that in toasting distant friends my name may not be forgotten.

Afternoon

The weather <cle> held up before sunrise and has continued clear & pleasant all day tho' it is still clouded over head. The wind remains ahead and our progress is very inconsiderable. We have passd the Island of Gorgona and are near that of Capraia. It is like the former rocky & barren being merely a place of residence for fishermen and Padronè's of small craft that trade from Corsica to the Italian coast. This island formerly belonged to the Tuscan Government but at present appertains to France and is part of the Department of Corsica. We are now opposite Leghorn but too far distant to see the port. The mountains all along the italian coast are coverd with snow and the sun shining on their summits they make a glittering appearance while all the rest of the prospect is in shade.

Head winds or calms are much more fatiguing when in sight of land than out at sea – as by the islands & mountains we percieve the extreme

328. Irving drew on this entry in his letter to William Irving, December 25, 1804–January 25, 1805.

slowness of our progress. The ship is very comfortable but by no means a fast sailer tho' built expressly for a Charlestown packet.

December 26

After a rainy night of head winds we find ourselves this morning, again abreast of the Island of Gorgona the ship having lost way by standing too long to northward. The weather is overcast & rainy but mild & agreeable in other respects.

December 28[329]

Baffling winds & calms have prevaild these two days and keep us beating about between the small islands & Corsica. The weather continues overcast & showery. <We ?hav?> The days are very short and at night we have to take in almost all the sails as the navigation is hazardous. We are now off the Island of Elba.

This is an island extremely mountainous with very little ground for culture. It does not produce sufficient grain for the consumption of its inhabitants but the wine is extremely good & goes to the Leghorn market. ↑<it is> It is white wine↓ It* is situated opposite Tuscany and seperated therefrom by the streights of Piombino. It is in 42 deg. 50 min Latitude of a triangular figure & nearly 100 miles in circumference

The fruits of Elba are said to be excellent tho the soil is shallow. It possesses a valuable Iron mine that supplies all Italy with that metal. On the west side is a high mountain called Della Calamita from the loadstone (in italian calamita) which is frequently found in its neighborhood. ↑This was first discoverd by a peasant who in walking <had his> found himself held by the heels – the loadstone attracting the hob nails in his shoes.↓ Some travellers have asserted that the attraction of the loadstone is <found> <felt> ↑felt↓ at some distance from the island particularly in the Streights of Piombino where it deranges the mariners compass but I was assured by the Genoese captains that were fellow passengers with me – that this assertion was unfounded.

This Island was antiently called by the Greeks Æthalia & by the

* It also produces salt.

329. From December 28, 1804, through January 5, 1805, Irving made the entries in his journal and continued his letter to William Irving of December 25, 1804–January 25, 1805. The wording is often identical. In general the journal entry seems to have been written first.

Romans Ilva. The principal town is Porto Ferraio handsomely built on a rock that forms the bottom of a large circular bay. It was antiently called Portus Argous – from Argos the ship of Jason. It was said that he passed in the Medditerranean & that Medea had occasion to view the enchantress Circé – Homer says in his Oddessy that Jupiter favord that celebrated vessel and permitted it safely to pass by Scylla & Charybdis[330] ↑(vide Swinburne)↓[331] Virgil also mentions that Æneas received a support from the island of Ilva of 3000 men –[332]

Small as it is it was formerly divided between three neighboring potentates viz. The Prince of Piombino the Grand Duke of Tuscany & the King of Naples but at present it appertains to france.

December 29

Early this morning the wind sprung up at the north west. <and> the clouds had dissapeard and the Sun rise was clear & beautiful. Nothing can be more inspiring than such weather after having had several days of calms head winds and rain. We at length effected what we have long been atttempting[333] – the clearing the isle of Elba, and are now passing between it and the Island of Planosa.

The latter is a low flat island of about a league in extent – ↑in Lat. 42.34 long. 9.45 E.↓ It was called by the Romans *Planasia* and is celebrated by the exile & death of Caesar Agrippa. Caesar was the son of Julia & Marcus Agrippa and grandson of Augustus – Julia being Augustus's daughter by his first wife Scribonia whom he afterwards repudiated. Livia the second wife of Augustus by her intrigues ruind Caesar in the affections of his Grandfather who confiscated his estate and banished him to the Isle of Planasia. About eight years after Augustus secretly paid him a visit – which Livia hearing – dreaded that he

330. In *The Odyssey,* XII, Hera guides the *Argo* safely past Scylla and Charybdis because of her love for Jason.

331. Henry Swinburne (1743–1803), English traveler and writer, produced accounts of his travels in Spain and Italy which were both learned and popular. Irving is referring here to Swinburne's *Travels in the Two Sicilies* (London, 1783, 1785). In his description of Elba in this entry he drew fully on this work. I, 30–33, including the erroneous statement that in *The Odyssey* Jupiter is said to have guided the *Argo.*

332. Ilva sent 300, not 3000, men to Aeneas' aid, as recounted in *The Æneid,* X, 173. The correct number is given in Swinburne, *Travels in the Two Sicilies,* I, 30.

333. The first two "t's" are at the end of one line, the third at the beginning of the next.

would be recalld to prevent which she hastned the end of the old Emperor and sent a centurion to kill the young prince – The latter defended himself courageously and fell covered with wounds.[334] – Planosa is uninhabited – it is cultivated by people from Elba who cross over at the proper seasons to <till sew and> sew and reap. It likewise serves as a shelter for small privateers that infest this ocean who lay in wait here <for> & sally out on vessels as they pass <At one end there are some fortifications but not garrisoned.> ↑*These*↓ little privateers are of the kind termed *Picaroons* and are the most unprincipled in the world – plundering from any nation – They are what may be termed the *Banditti of the Ocean.* One of the Genoese captains who is very well informed and communicative, gave me several annecdotes of their depredations and says they have been known to plunder ships – murder the crew & sink the vessel to prevent discovery & punishment. He says the Algerines & Tripolitans are far less formidable as they <seld> do not kill their prisoners unless in case of resistance. The [*sentence breaks off at this point*]

December 30

While I was writing yesterday <↑about 11 oclock↓ some account of the> the above ↑about 11 oclock↓ I was interrupted by one of the Genoese who came into the cabin for the Spy glass saying that there was a *sail* in sight. I immediately went up on deck and saw a small vessel coming off towards us from the Island. The Genoese captain after regarding it thro the glass for a moment turned pale and said it was one of those privateers he had been speaking of. A moment after she fired a gun upon which we hoisted the American flag – another gun was fired as a signal for us to bring to, which we immediately complied with

The Genoese and the captain mate & myself <immediately> went to work to conceal what money or trinkets we had. As to myself I had but a couple of Spanish Doubloons one of which I gave to the Cabin boy and the other to a little Genoese lad <t> as I was confident they would not be searched. The privateer was <a> quite small, hardly larger than one of our *North river* ferry boats – and had latine sails, Two small guns in the bow was all her military equipments. As for us we had not even a pistol on board. They were under french colours and hailing us, orderd the captain to come on board.

334. The paragraph to this point is a loose paraphrase of Swinburne, *Travels in the Two Sicilies,* I, 43.

He took the papers of the ship and went – After some time the boat returnd with the captain, accompanied by several of the privateers men, <and> one of whom ↑appeard to be an officer. He was↓ a tall ragged fellow with his shirt sleeves rolld up to his elbows displaying a most formidably muscular pair of arms. His crew would have shamed Falstaffs ragged regiment[335] in their habilliments – in their countenances the lines of villainy & rapacity were strongly marked. They were armd with rusty cutlasses & stillettos (a kind of dagger) stuck in their belts. The leader gave directions for shortening sail – and asked us several questions about where we were from & where bound – & what was the cargo &c These we answerd him by means of the Genoese captains & one of his own men who could talk a little English. He then demanded the passports & bills of health of the passengers, and told me I must go aboard of the privateer with the captain – as the commander of the privateer could talk french and wanted to make some enquiries for which purpose I could serve as interpreter. I accordingly prepared to go. the Genoese captain stopped me privately & with tears in his eyes begged me for heavens sake not to leave the ship as he believed they only intended to seperate us all that they might cut our throats the more readily. I represented to him the impolicy of contradicting their orders as we were in their power – besides that it was as easy for them to dispatch us on board the ship as it would be on board the privateer we having no arms. The poor man shook his head and said he hoped *the Virgin would protect* me. When we boarded the privateer I confess my heart felt heavy enough – a more villainous looking crew I never beheld. Their dark complexions, rough beards and fierce black eyes scowling under enormous bushy eye brows, w<as>ere enough to inspire distrust & apprehension. They were as rudely accoutred as their comerades that had boarded us – and like them were armed with cutlasses Stillettos & pistols. They seemed to regard us with a malignant smile as if triumphing over their prey and leaning on one anothers shoulders mutterd into each others ears looking at us all the while with a malacious half averted eye. The captain of the privateer read our passports &c &c and told us he only wanted to see if we had the regular bills of health adding some confused story of his being stationd there to watch that no vessels escaped from the Quarantine at Leghorn. After a while he ↑told↓ us we might return on board with which we cheerfully complied

335. Falstaff's description of it is in *1 Henry IV*, IV, ii, 11–47.

tho our pleasure was rather dampend when <he told us he s> we found that he retained all our papers. On arriving on board we understood that they had been rummaging the ship and had ordered the two anchors to be dropped. As soon as our sails were almost all in on a signal being given the privateer <g> fired a Gun gave three cheers and hoisted *English colours.* The captain that was on board of us turned round with a grin said we was a good prize and that they were in the English service. We told him to reccollect that we were Americans. He replied it was all one to him – every thing that came from Genoa was a good prize as the port was blockaded. We replied that he was mistaken, that there had been no English vessels off Genoa for some months and consequently they could not pretend but that the blockade had ceased. He said we would find the contrary when we arrived at Malta where he intended to carry us. They then commenced overhauling the ship in hopes of finding money. One of the first things they examined was my trunk and this the captain rummaged completely but without finding any thing that he cared for. He had one of his gang with him that understood english and they had nearly a couple of hours work in reading my papers as I had many letters from my friends & letters of introduction (my <lettl> letters of credit I had secured in my pocket) Among others they found two letters of introduction for Malta one to Sir [*blank*] Ball the Governor & another to a principal English merchant.[336] After reading these they treated me with much more respect than before. The captain told me I might put my clothes in the Trunk again and see that there was nothing missing – I bundled them in carelessly as I thought I should never wear them again – and locking the trunk offerd the key to the captain. He told me to keep it myself [–] if he wanted my <truk> trunk opened again he would apply to me. His companion was tired of reading my letters as they were cheifly introductory ones – he turnd to th<is>e other and told him it was unprofitable work for he could find nothing in them but reccommendations – – "Eh bien["] replied the captain "I believe we may as well leave this <gentl> persons things alone for the present[.] there [is] nothing to be got by searching them[.] *c'est un homme qui court ↑tout↓ le*

336. Sir Alexander John Ball (1757–1809), English rear-admiral, was governor of Malta from 1802 until his death. In his letter to William Irving, December 25, 1804–January 25, 1805, Irving called him "Sir Isaac Ball."

In 1809 there were forty English merchants in Valetta, the chief city of Malta (Edward Blaquière, *Letters from the Mediterranean,* London, 1813, II, 348).

monde.[”] (tis a man who is rambling all over the world) By this time the Myrmidons up on deck had lost all patience and came into the cabin with an evident impatience to be let loose to pillage. The captain gave them some order that I could not understand and immediately they went to work ransacking the whole vessel. They were extremely disappointed in finding there was so little cargo on board. The whole consisting in five or six pipes of Brandy some few reams of writing paper <&> a little verdigrease & two boxes of Quicksilver. (The vessel intends to take in a cargo of wines at Messina.)

The <Casks> boxes of Quicksilver they hoisted out of the Run in triumph thinking they containd money. They disregarded our assurances to the contrary and broke them open with the utmost eagerness but were extremely chagrind on the discovering their contents

In searching the trunks of the Genoese captains one of them stole a watch & some wearing apparel – and they took likewise some trifling articles from the sailors. After I had locked up my trunk I went up on deck and found the Genoese captain that I mentiond before – in a great alarm. He said the privateers men were drinking brandy and would get intoxicated and then he did not know what would become of us. He assured me that he was convinced that they did not intend to carry us to Malta nor did he think they had any commission but that they were a set of pirates merely intent upon plunder. I was of the same opinion for <amid> ↑amongst↓ all the crew I did not percieve a single englishman they consisting of Maltese Porteguese Ragusans, Italians &c. I was much diverted by a dialogue between one of our sailors and one of the ruffians that spoke english. The fellow asked the sailor why he looked so sulky at him – “I suppose” says he [“] you think I want to do you harm” [“]Oh no” replies Jack “I dont fear any such thing [–] you cant do *me* any harm if you would my honest friend [–] you can only take my life & that I dont care a chew of tobacco for” <Indeed> “I have no wish to take your life” says the other – [“]Oh ho – you havent – have you? Here Tom Jim” cries Jack calling his mess mates “just come & look what a moderate fellow here is – he dont wish to take my life – Smite my timbers if you ant the most moderate rogue that ever I met unhung.” “Indeed” answerd the other “Ive no enmity against you but I’d rather any harm should come to myself rather than you –” “I wish so <d>too” says Jack “with all my heart – however if gods willing I am content that you & your companions & captain may live all the days that the Gallows will spare you,” The peculiar drollery of the sailors manner gave the highest point to his discourse – he is the wag of the crew and could not restrain his Jokes even when surrounded by a <crew> gang of cut throats.

By this time the commander in chief had come off from the Island where I found there was a nest of these miscreants & that they had two or three vessels. Our papers had to undergo another examination but I could percieve that they were convinced it was not politic for them to detain us. They therefore told us that tho we was a *lawful prize* yet they out of favor would permit us to proceed – that they wished to behave *honorable* always and do as little injury as possible. They only desired that we would spare them a little provisions as they were entirely out. We of course had to comply with this *request* and they took about half of the provisions we had on board. We having laid in just sufficient for our passage from Genoa to Malta. They likewise took some articles of ship furniture &c and then gave us a *receipt* for the provisions ordering the english consul at Malta to pay for them! The common fellows of the crew were highly enraged at not being allowd to pillage – they declared that it was a good prize, and shewed the most ravenous disposition to plunder. At length about sun down they bid us *adieu* and to our great joy took their departure. What prevented them from pillaging I cannot imagine unless it was the fear that we would inform some of our American frigates & that one should be sent in pursuit of them to destroy their nest. Having a fair wind we set sail in hopes of leaving this retreat of pirates behind – but the wind soon fell and we were becalmed almost the whole night. We had considerable apprehension that some of the gang would come off in the night and pay us another visit. <and> I laid down in my clothes but my sleep was broken & disturbed with horrid dreams. The assassin like figures of the ruffians were continually before me & two or three times I started out of my birth with the idea that their stilletto's were raised against my bosom – Early this morning a fair wind sprung up and we had the satisfaction of leaving the island far behind us before sun rise. Had we been becalmd to day in the neighborhood – it is most likely we should have enjoyed their company again.[337]

This morning we passed Monte Christo[338] a small island or rather a

337. Irving briefly recounted the privateer episode in his Autobiographical Notes, January 15, 1843.

338. Isola di Montecristo.

high rock that rises abruptly out of the sea in a conical shape. It has a little herbage & shrubs in the crevices of the rocks & towards the summit which sustain <a> numbers of wild Goats. The people from Corsica often come here to hunt this animal.

December 31

We have had our <old> usual weather – head winds & calms for the last twenty four hours. <the> We have however, cleared the small islands that were so troublesome, <with> as we did not dare to carry sail at night. This part of the mediterranean is what was called *Etrurian* or *Tyrrhenian <Sea>* or *Tuscan Sea.* We have lost sight of the Corsican shore, which in fact we <were> are anxious to avoid, as the Genoese captains say it is infested with pirates, the inhibitants being rude and hardly civilized. A vessel that is becalmed in sight of the shore runs great risk of being visited by the fishermen who make no scruple of plundering where they can do it with a prospect of impunity.

January 1, 1805

For the first time in my life has a New Year opened upon me seperate from my family and friends. When I picture to myself the social festivity that reigns among you on this day, the cheerfulness the good humor & hospitality that prevails through all ranks – how do I sigh at being unable to participate in those enjoyments, and feel an unusual lonesomeness & depression of spirits. <It is perhaps a selfish> It is perhaps wrong to yield to such emotions. My friends are all enjoying themselves and I should be pleased with the idea. They are happy – and <do> surely I may flatter myself that in the midst of their hilarity they will bestow some thought on me, <and> wonder where I am wandering or in what part of the world I am spending this festive day. It passes ↑with me↓ in much the same manner as Christmas – writing & reading in the Cabin. We have commenced the Year however with a pleasant favorable wind and our ship sails gaily before it –

<Never have I passed this>

The weather continues remarkably mild. Tho it is now the middle of winter I frequently get out of bed in the middle of the night and with no other covering but my great coat – walk the deck for an hour or more without feeling in the least degree uncomfortable. We have no fire in the cabin nor have we felt any want of it.

Friday morning, January 4

For the last forty eight hours we have had fine <bree> favorable wind and spreading every sail have had a charming run. This morning a little after sunrise we came in sight of the Lipari Islands which now bear <ab> S. W. B. S. about 9 or ten leagues distant. Among the rest Strombolo[339] is distinctly visible tho' we cannot yet decern the smoke from its crater

7 Oclock in the evening

The day has been delightful and the breeze continues wafting us pleasantly towards the "Sicilian shores."[340] By degrees the Lipari Islands became more visible Alicur[341] was the first one we saw after which the other ones were soon in sight. They rise boldly out of the sea and to a considerable height. In the afternoon we could plainly see the smoke of Strombolo the crater being on the <S>N.W. side of the mountain.

Æolus has certainly given us a most gracious reception into his dominions[342] – <The fierce winds are chaind> the storms ↑are↓ pent up in their caverns and each unruly wind safe tied up in his respective leather bag, a pleasant breeze only is commissiond to conduct us safely thro his Empire and urge us to our destined port. The sun has descended in all the boasted splendors of an Italian sky – the horizon brilliantly transparent with just clouds enough to recieve his parting rays and enrich the prospect with a variety of colors.

The moon has <just> begun to acquire luster from his absence and being but two nights old sheds a pale <ray> ↓light↑ upon the waters <to use a pretty *della cruscan* phraze a '*silver shower* of radiance> –'[343] Now could any one wish a more delightful time to enter into the re-

339. Irving's spelling of Stromboli follows that of Patrick Brydone (see n. 345 below).

340. *The Æneid,* tr. John Dryden (1697), I, 49–50:

> Now scarce the Trojan fleet, with sails and oars,
> Had left behind the fair Sicilian shores.

341. Alicuri, or more commonly, Alicudi.

342. Æolus, ruler of the winds, lived on the floating island of Æolia, according to *The Odyssey,* X; the area has been identified with that of the Lipari, or Aeolian Islands.

343. A group of eighteenth-century English poets, most of whom lived in Florence, called themselves the "Della Cruscans," after the Accademia della Crusca, founded in Florence in the sixteenth century for the promotion of linguistic purity. Robert Merry, who adopted the pseudonym "Della Crusca," was the leader of the group. The phrase quoted by Irving seems to come from Merry's "The Adieu and

gions of Æolia? <is> ↑are↓[344] not the very weather & prospect <it-self> ↑themselves↓ enough to enliven the imagination without the idea that one is passing among the very haunts of fable and romantic fiction? Strombolo just begins to shew his fires. The explosions are sudden & <?sho?> of a short duration with an interval of from ten minutes to a half an hour. We are yet too distant for them to appear of much magnitude tho the light <appears> ↑is↓ very brilliant.

Brydone[345] mentions that when he saw the islands several of them emitted smoke particularly Volcano & Volcanello. That is no longer the case, & Strombolo is the only one that emits either smoke or flame. The Genoese captains inform me that in bad weather this volcano is particularly violent in its eruptions continually casting up stones &c with a great noise – and that it makes a <great> ↑loud↓ roaring when the south wind blows. It is a singular thing that this volcano should always <de> emit its flames &c in sudden bursts or flashes, one would concieve that <as> the <matter> inflammable matter <is> collected in its bowels would burn steadily or if it <is> really <of a> sufficiently combustible to take fire suddenly & flash, that it would all go off in one explosion like a quantity of gunpowder.

12 at night

We have now got to the southward of Strombolo so that his <Volcano> ↑crater↓ is no longer visible being situated on the NW side ↑& below the summit of the island.↓ The explosions of this island did not answer the expectations I had formed from the discriptions given by Brydone & other travellers,[346] either <They are not> in their magn<e>atude or the height to which they are thrown But they vary according to the weather, and are sometimes formidable indeed.

The island is high and <of> rocky and shaped something like a

---

Recall to Love," *The British Album* (London, 1790), I, 2:

> The pale-cheek'd Virgin of the night,
> That piercing thro' the leafy bow'r,
> Throws on the ground a silv'ry showr.

344. "are" is in pencil.

345. Patrick Brydone (1736–1818), Irish traveler and writer, is best known for his *Tour through Sicily and Malta* (London, 1773), which went through eight or nine editions during his lifetime. Irving is referring here to this work, I 27, 30.

346. *Ibid.*, 27–28. Swinburne refers to "the fiery operations" of Stromboli, the fire thrown up "from a huge orifice in its side," the "convulsions of this incessant projection of flames and other substances" (*Travels in the Two Sicilies*, II, 427).

wedge. Tho there is not much ground on it capable of cultivation yet it contains a number of Inhabitants, who <are r reside> chiefly reside in a small village on the lower part of the Island. The chief fruits of the island are grapes and those not in great quantities

The largest and most fertile of these islands is Lipara. <It produced> And here Virgil fixes the habitation of Æolus. His sway extended over all these islands which were called Æolia & feigned to be the empire of the winds. Both Virgil & Homer mention them more than once[.][347] the former if I reccollect right, in the first part of the Ænead represents <them> ↑the winds↓ as shut up in ↑their↓ caverns round which they roam in search of a vent, roaring & howling at their <conf> imprisonment. This fable is evidently founded on the internal noise of these <mountains> islands which antiently it is probable <contained> ↑had↓ each its proper crater. Homer <on> for his part ties the winds up in leather <?f?> bags or skins and ↑says that↓ when Ulysses visited <him> ↑Æolus↓ in his dominions, as a great favor ↑he↓ made him a present of them.[348] The curiosity of Ulysses companions, however, got the better of their prudence and they opened the bags to take a peep at their contents. The winds burst forth from their narrow prisons – a dreadful storm was the consequence and they paid for their temerity with their lives, being all shipwrecked & drowned except Ulysses who drifted thro' the Straights of Messina on a plank or mast. It was to these islands too, I believe, that Juno repaired to solicit Æolus for a storm that might destroy the fleet of Æneas – but happily the latter was protected from the effects of it by Venus.[349]

One of the Islands antiently called Hiera (at present Volcano) is also described by Virgil as one of Vulcans forges where he made the armour of Aeneas at the request of Venus. Here Virgil describes the employment of the Cyclops somewhat minutely as being engaged forming a thunderbolt for Jupiter. Volcano is said to have been the production of a violent convulsion of the earth in the time of the Roman Republic – indeed it is the opinion of many, and not without probability, that all these islands have been at first produced in a similar manner and afterwards encreased in size from the discharges of their own craters.[350]

347. *The Æneid,* I, 52–60; *The Odyssey,* X, 1 ff.

348. To this point in the paragraph Irving drew on Brydone, *A Tour through Sicily and Malta,* I, 35–36.

349. *The Æneid,* I, 49–345.

350. In the first three sentences of this paragraph Irving drew on Brydone, *A Tour through Sicily and Malta,* I, 37–38, including the quotation from *The Æneid,* VIII, 416–32.

These islands appertain to the King of Naples, to whom they yield a considerable revenue producing abundance of alum, nitre &c and excellent figs raisans – currants & other fruits. They are celebrated for producing the <delicate> rich sweet wine held in great estimation termed Malvasie.

January 5

At day break this morning we found ourselves within a few miles of the Straits of Messina and near to the Calabrian coast.[351] The Sun rise presented to us one of the most charming scenes I ever beheld. To our left extended the lofty Calabrian mountains their summits still partially envelloped in the mists of morning and the <clo> sun having just risen from behind them, breaking in full splendor from among the clouds. Behind us at a distance lay the Lipari islands and among them Strombolo vomiting up clouds of smoke. To our right Sicily rose gradually from the sea and swept up into verdant mountains. <?the?> skirted with delightful little plains in a high state of cultivation.

Immediately before us was the celebrated straight immortal in history & song. <and> The whole country arround was verdant and blooming as if in the midst of spring. Villages, seats and towers diversified the prospect forming a variety of picturesque objects. Our favorable breeze still continued and we glided on gently to the mouth of the strait. About a mile or perhaps a little more from the entrance of the strai<gh>t is situated *Scylla* the rock so celebrated in fable and <on> which both poets & historians were antiently so fond of clothing with imaginary terrors. It is at the foot of one of the high Calabrian mountains and advances boldly into the sea having at some distance (at least from the <situation> ↑points↓ from whence I beheld it) ↑something of↓ the appearance of a large square tower. On top of it is a small fortress and immediately behind it (tho on the same ridge) is built the town of <Syclla> Sciglio, which is the present name of the rock.

In front of the rock at its feet I could percieve two or more smaller ones which reared their heads high out of the water and appeared to be of a conical form. The whole is of a very picturesque form and would be a charming subject for the pencil.

351. In this sentence, in his description of the "dogs" of Scylla, comment on the smoothness of Charybdis, reference to the theory that Sicily and Calabria were once joined, explanation of the name of Pelorus, and descriptions of Calabria and Messina in this entry, Irving drew on Brydone, *A Tour through Sicily and Malta,* I, 38, 40, 41–43, 45, 49, 51–52, 78–79.

The fable[352] of this rock is, briefly, that Scylla daughter of Phorcus, concieved a violent passion for Glaucus one of the deities of the ocean; whether her affection was returned or not I cannot say – but Circe the enchantress who also loved Glaucus, became jealous of her (some say she intreated Circe to inspire Glaucus with a tendernes for her) and exerted her spells over the fountain in which scylla bathed so that when she next entered it she was changed into <an>a hideous monster, from her waist downwards like a dog. Struck with terror and dispair at her horrible metamorphosis the nymph threw herself into the sea where the poets say she remained the terror and peril of mariners, and surrounded by dogs who kept up an incessant howling and yelling. These dogs are doubtless the small rocks that I have mentioned as being at the foot of the large one, and their howling is the noise of the currents from the straights that breaks & dashes against their bases. The danger that the antients so often mention from Scylla was <doub> owing to the current setting upon it which might force the vessels thither – tho at present there appears to be no danger. *As to the redoubtable gulph or whirlpool of Charybdes we sailed thro the middle of it and so far from being swallowed up, I did not even feel any agitation of the vessel, it may be more formidable at particular times, but when we passed it it was <par> scarcely any thing more apparantly than a rippling of the sea.[353] Perhaps Jupiter shewed particularly favor to us as *whilome* he did to the celebrated ship of Jason which the poets[354] particularly mention, he sufferd to pass safely thro all the dangers of Scylla & Charybdes. The<s>re must have been most certainly, infinitely more danger attending those places antiently than at present, to occasion their being mentioned so repeatedly as being formidable & terrific. If, as many suppose, and I see no great reason to doubt, <the> Sicily & Calabria formerly joind and were seperated by a violent convulsion, undoubtedly the straits must have been far more narrow and the current more rapid.

* This is a mistake <I did> Charybdes is situated in quite a different place[355]

352. This account of Scylla is most fully given in Ovid, *Metamorphoses,* XIII, XIV. Irving, however, may have been using a secondary source which has not been identified.

353. The movement of Charybdis is also called a mere "rippling" in Swinburne, *Travels in the Two Sicilies,* II, 387.

354. Irving is apparently still relying on the reference to the *Argo* in *The Odyssey* as misrepresented by Swinburne (see n. 331 above).

355. Modern geographers identify Charybdis with the whirlpool Garafaro, outside the harbor of Messina, some ten miles from Scilla.

As to the Calabrian shore it is bold and mountanous so that the sea has not probably gained much on that side and it remains in the same state as it was immediately after the supposed convulsion. The Sicilian shore on the contrary which is lower, may have gradually yielded to the sea and the the straits widening the whirlpools & eddies that may have originally taken place from the current being rapid & confined, have by degrees subsided as the latter gaind space. Thus Charybdes has dwindled away and ceased to be an object of terror while Sicily from the stability of the shore, remains in its former state, but from the practability of the entrance, is no longer difficult to be avoided. <At present you can pass either side of> ↑To pass↓ Charybdes <whereas> ↑you was↓ formerly <you was> obliged to steer on the Calabrian side and consequently by Scylla towards which the current tended. This current ↑as it is termed↓ I believe is nothing more than a common tide. It runs northerly thro the straights for six hours & returns southerly for the same length of time and like other tides seems to be regulated by the moon.

Opposite to Scylla ↑on the Sicillian shore↓ is Cape [*blank*][356] <c>formerly termed Cape Pylorus ↑(or Pelorus.)↓ Some ascribe the origin of this name to <han>Pelorus Hannibals pilot whom he slew on suspicion of having wanted to betray him by bringing him to a place where there was no passage by which means he might be surrounded by his enemies; but on finding too late his error he appeased the manes of Pelores by erecting a statue or monument to his memory. By others it is said to be named after the pilot of Ulysses who was drowned here. At the point of the Cape is situated the Fanal or light house – a singular looking building and apparently old. The straights at this place is about a mile across but immediately widens. Before we entered we saw Strombolo make a <vast ex> great explosion infinitely superior to any that we saw last night. The smoke arose in a vast pillar to the clouds, and then spread in <grea> volumes around. This the Genoese captains told me was a sign that bad weather is at hand.

As we approached the enterance of the straights the prospect became more and more beautiful. Sicily presented a rich picture of cultivation & fertility and at a vast distance we could percieve Ætna rearing itself far above the other mountains – covered with snow and the summit shrouded in thick clouds. Calabria has likewise an appearance the most luxurient and picturesque. It is part of what was termed great Greece

356. The point is Capo di Faro.

and was antiently renowned for its abundance. <?ov?>But at present – it is over run with woods – its inhabitants miserable – oppressed, barbarous & indolent unwilling to cultivate the earth as they know its produce would be wrested from them and starve in a land that with a little industry & attention would flow with "milk & honey"[357]

> But what avails her unexhausted stores
> Her blooming mountains & her sunny shores
> With all the gifts that heaven & earth <bestow> impart
> The smiles of nature & the charms of art
> While proud oppression in her valleys reigns
> And tyranny usurps her happy plains.[358]

Advancing on our course we opened a hill that had <?f?> all along intercepted the view – and Messina its castles forts and harbor broke upon our <view> sight!

This only was wanting to compleat the beauty of the scene – of all cities I have ever seen this in my opinion is the most charming to approach. It is built at the foot of the mountains in a half moon round <the harbor> one side of the harbor facing the east and ↑some of↓ the houses gradually rising on the side of the mountain & <being of> shew to great advantage. The churches, palaces, towers &c <shew> appear one above the other and <?as?> many of them are handsome and of picturesque constructions. <They have a noble> On the summits of the heights around the city are situated forts, castles & convents and the <Key> ↑promontory or mole↓ in front of the harbor is fortified by a noble cidatel and several batteries.

If you can figure to yourself the city <thus> with its beauty of situation and picturesque architecture – its grand harbor – the straights that extend themselves before it and gradually widen into the ocean, speckled with numerous sails – the opposite Calabrian coast, boldly rising into mountains clothed with wood and their bases adorned with smiling <villages, cornfields>, ↑fields and↓ villages, &c &c If, I say, you can figure to your imagination any thing like the scene and over the whole cast the enlivening beams of the morning sun brightening every object and dancing on the tumulous waves of the ocean you may then have some idea of the enchanting prospect that presented itself

357. This phrase occurs several times in the King James translation of the Old Testament; see, for example, Exod. 3:8, 17; 13:5; Jer. 11:15; 32:22; Ezek. 20:6, 15.

358. Joseph Addison, "A Letter from Italy, to the Right Honourable Charles Lord Halifax" (1701), ll. 107–12. The punctuation here differs slightly from the original.

as our vessel "proudly riding oer her azure realm"[359] advanced to the city.

Never perhaps did nature assist more in forming a safe and beautiful harbor than at Messina.[360] A narrow slip of land runs out from the foot of the mountains at the <east>South end of the town, and making a curve, compleatly encloses the harbor like a huge basin, leaving only an enterance from the north <west>, between the end of this slip or promontory and the main land. This neck of land has very much the shape of a Sickle, which was observed antiently by the Greeks, who called the place by that name. <or> (Zancle or Sickle) In their fables they relate that the Sickle of Saturn (who when deposed by Jupiter, had fled into italy & taught agriculture) fell at this place and formed this singular promontory. It is well fortified by a strong cidatel & several batteries, tho at present they are not well garrisoned. The harbor is as <tranquil> safe as a mill pond. The middle of it is extremely deep and requires a great length of cable ↑to↓ <for> anchor<ing> but near the key and the other borders it shallows to a very commodious depth. As we knew we should be quarantined we went directly to the quarter allotted for that purpose, which is opposite the Lazarretto built on the promontory. After anchoring we went to the health office which is on the key <from seperated from the> and raild off with iron barrs. Here we made our report and had our papers examined after they had been well fumigated and roasted almost to cinders. The people in these countries carry their dread of the fever to the most rediculous lengths. They Quarantine vessels from every port though never so healthy – and though we came direct from Genoa where there has been no instance of the fever known – yet they use as much precaution with us and avoid us with equal care as if we had just left a city reeking with infection.

I had a hearty laugh at the apprehensions of one of the ↑men of↓ the health office<men>. A small window <of th> over the lower steps of the stoop was opened, and he was sent to the door to tell our captain that he must talk thro this window to the people within. The captain

359. Thomas Gray, "The Bard" (1757), II, 2, ll. 71–73:

> Fair laughs the Morn, and soft the Zephyr blows,
> While proudly riding o'er the azure realm
> In gallant trim the gilded Vessel goes.

360. Irving may have drawn in this description of Messina on Swinburne, *Travels in the Two Sicilies,* II, 397.

not understanding italian thought that he was told to <go> come in the house and was advancing up the stoop when the fellow half frightened to death sprung to the other end of it and hallood for him to keep back. The captain stopped short in astonishment. The fellow made several attempts to ↑pull↓ shut the iron wicket of the stoop but as the captain stood close by it, he was violently apprehensive and as often as his fingers almost reachd the door he started back again as if the <b> rails were red hot. At length he succeeded in jerking it shut and immediately run into the house trembling at the risk he had run of taking the fever from our <fat> ↑honest↓ captain who in circumference of body and rosyness of complexion seemed the picture of health itself.

We had afterwards to go in a body – sailors and passengers, to the Lazaretto to be examined. There we found the commandant of the Lazaretto and a <physca> physician or two. We had to stand at some distance and answer their enquiries, after which we were ordered to take off our cravats and open the collars of our shirts that the doctor might see our necks & breasts. <With this> It appears, the sage geniuses imagined that it was possible to perceive whether people had the infection lurking in their veins, by taking a hasty look at their necks & chests at ten or fifteen feet distance. We were then told to whack our arms together, like our labourers do on a cold day to warm <ourselves> ↑themselves↓[361] – after which we were dismissed as healthy men. Tomorrow they will let us know how long we are to be quarantined.

There are no American merchant vessels in this port but the one I came <it> in. This evening arrived the schooner Nautilus[362] from Syracuse, being one of the armed vessels that we have appointed to cruise in the Mediterranean. There are several english transports here procuring wine and other necessaries for Lord Nelsons fleet.[363]

January 6[364]

This morning we were again at the health office and the Questions repeated. On our return we spoke to the Nautilus and Capt. Strong found

361. "themselves" is first in pencil, then, over the penciling, in ink.

362. It was one of the vessels in Com. Edward Preble's squadron, sent to the Mediterranean in 1803 to continue the American operations begun two years earlier against the Barbary States in protest of their piracy.

363. Nelson had been in command of the British fleet in the Mediterranean since the outbreak of war between England and France in 1803.

364. Irving drew on this entry and the next two entries in his letter to William Irving, December 25, 1804–January 25, 1805.

an <old> acquaintance in the Lieutenant Mr Geo W Reed[365] of Philadephia. He afterwards came off to our ship and remaind at a little distance for some time. From him we learnd the particulars of the expedition against Tripoli,[366] of which I had heard very exagerated accounts at Genoa, <He also informs us that a number of gun boats are preparing here for another attack that they have in view next spring or summer! > ↑by all accounts it was a most daring or rather, desperate attack, the Americans having but one Frigate and six gun boats; it is no wonder therefore that they did not make much impression.↓

We were also visited by Mr. Broadbent[367] <an Eng> and the Captain[368] of the Nautilus. The former is an English merchant that does the chief of the American business here, <for> is agent for our ships and it is expected will be appointed consul. I had a letter of introduction to him from Mr Wollaston[369] of Genoa which I delivered.

He informed us that Genoa was again <declared> put under blockade last October and that we were fortunate in not meeting any english cruizers as they would certainly have carried us in to Malta they having lately served an American Brig in that manner. The captain of the schooner has very politely offered me a passage to Syracuse and if I please to Malta, he will sail in a day or two. If I can possibly get permission to quit the Quarantine I shall accept his offer.

Our Quarantine is now ascertained to be twenty one days, an extravagant time considering that we come from a healthy port, are all hearty and have scarcely any Cargo on board. But so it is – they have no conscience in this part of the world in regard to Quarantines and <think> never think of Quarantining less than a week or fortnight. Perhaps our time is <l> so long in consequence of having been boarded by the privateer as th<at>ose visits generally make a material difference. Those long Quarantines are a heavy tax upon com-

365. George Washington Reed (1780–1813), son of Joseph Reed of Revolutionary fame, entered the navy in 1799 and was commissioned a lieutenant in 1803 (William B. Reed, *Life and Correspondence of Joseph Reed,* Philadelphia, 1847, II, 230–38).

366. Com. Edward Preble made five attacks on Tripoli in August and September 1804, but failed to take the city.

367. John Broadbent (d. 1826) was appointed U. S. consul in Messina in 1805 and served in this office until his death (Despatches from U. S. Consuls, Messina, RG 59, NA).

368. John Herbert Dent (1782–1823) became midshipman in 1798, lieutenant in 1799, commander in 1804, and captain in 1811 (*Herringshaw's National Library of American Biography,* Chicago, 1909–14).

369. Frederic Hyde Wollaston, a native of England, was U. S. Consul in Genoa from 1799–1805 (Despatches from U. S. Consuls, Genoa, RG 59, NA).

merce particularly with the Americans who pay high wages to their seamen. It appears to me that they will occasion the American trade to the <Ame> Mediterranean greatly to decrease. At present the *mania* rages with uncommon fierceness and a vessel can hardly go out of a port and return the next day without being put on Quarantine.

I have amused myself part of the day with spying at the town with a very good telescope we have on board – but it is impossible to distinguish the streets accurately <to> or to see any of the houses to advantage.

Brydone[370] mentions a noble range of houses of uniform construction that extended for about a mile along the beautiful Quay of Messina. They were completely demolished by a tremenduous earth quake in [*blank*][371] and nothing but the fronts remain in ruins to testify their former beauty. Messina has suffered <several of> often from these awful visitations and there is not a year passes but some commotion of the earth more or less violent, is felt here. The day has been very fine, like one of our warm spring ones and indeed I found it uncomfortably warm to set in the sun.

This evening it has began to rain which verifies the prognostication of <bad> approaching bad weather made by the Genoese captains when they saw the violent explosion from Strombolo yesterday morning.

The <flags> colours of the ships of different nations which crowd the port make a gay appearance and as they are all more or less armed, we have a <continuous> popping of cannons at intervals all day long.

There is a *pretty* assortment of vessels with us in Quarantine. Our next door neighbor is a <Tunisian> ↑Venetian↓ and beyond him Greeks, Napolitans, Ragusans &c, &c are jumbled together and the <mixture> confusion of tongues & languages might rival the tower of Bable itself.

At the Lazaretto there is a large square surrounded by the Hospitals Ware house &c where we are allowed to walk, guards being kept there with bayonets fixed on the ends of sticks, to attend and take care that the crews of different vessels do not touch one another.

At this place I generally find a collection of curious uncouth figures with their national dresses. The present *"Cock of the Walk"* appears to be an old rich Greek with a great turban enormous trowsers or

370. *A Tour through Sicily and Malta,* I, 46.

371. The earthquake occurred in 1783.

breeches that tuck in at the knees and a pipe of two or three yards in length. He is generally attended by four long bearded Capuchins who are Quarantined with him and perhaps are his travelling companions At any rate they seem to pay him humble court, doubtless for the good of his soul and the edification of his pocket. They make a mighty handsome groupe as you may well suppose.

It is past twelve oclock & I am sleepy –

Good night

January 8

Tho' as yet but two or three days of Quarantine have as yet elapsed I already begin to be heartily tired of it, and to concieve it an intolerable species of imprisonment. We have been told repeatedly to take a guard on board, but the honest old captain who is <heartily> highly chagrined at the length of his Quarantine, refuses to trouble himself about them and says they may send their guards if they choose but he will not search for them. We consequently remain without any contrary to their regulations. For my part I find this mighty convenient as I range the harbor in our boat and hold frequent discourses with the officers of the Nautilus. The guards from shore stamp and swear and bawl after me incessantly, if they had not a great respect for the Americans here I expect I should be used like <those> other persons whom I see now and then driven back to their vessels. Indeed one of the boats did attempt a thing of the kind yesterday and gave us chase having a guard in it armed with a bayonet on the end of a stick. As we did not regard that kind of fire arms we laughed at him and advised him to keep his distance – he thought proper to take our advice as he saw four stout American sailors in our boat ready to *pat him on the head* with their long oars.

I have in consequence recieved two or three severe reprimands at the health office which I pretended not to understand and of course took no notice of, but I expect I shall be stopped soon by their firing at the boat from ↑one of↓ the batter<y>ies as they have threatned something of the kind.

To pass away time I have procured a book or two from the shore that treats of Sicily[372] – and am busily employed in translating them into english, this is very difficult as I am but little acquainted with the lan-

372. Among them was Giuseppe Buonfiglio Costanzo, *Prima* [*e Secunda*] *Parte dell'Historia Siciliana,* Venice, 1604 (Irving to William Irving, December 25, 1804–January 25, 1805).

guage but it is attended with three advantages as I find amusement in it, improve myself in italian and inform myself concerning this interesting Island

The captain, honest old soul, is continually lamenting his deplorable situation and exclaiming against the health office and government. I have detected the old gentleman in a great attachment to Methodism and a violent affection for Lunar observations. He has also an invincible propensity to *familiarize* names and Jack's & Jill's every body he speaks of. Our conversation therefore is whimsical enough and we alternately discuss the New testament and the nautical almanack and talk indiscriminately of *Joe* Pilmore, *Jack* Hamilton More, *Tom* Truxton,[373] *Kit* Columbus & *Jack* Wesley. Methodism and Lunar observations <al> preside by turns and you may judge how well calculated to shine at either.[374] The poor old gentleman thinks he is among a set of Barbarians who are *groping in ignorance* and "stumbling upon the dark mountains."[375] He groans whenever the bells ring for mass, abominats the herds of priests and monks that crowd this place, and has plainly demonstrated to me that the Roman church is the great beast with seven horns and the pope is no more and no less than the whore of Babylon.[376] Take him alltogether, he is a worthy soul with a kind heart and good disposition; he will sit for an hour or two and talk of his wife and children with so much honest pride and affection as shew he must be of a most amiable domestic character.

January 10

I fear I shall be disappointed in my hopes of <partin> departing in the Nautilus. Capt. Dent who commands her informs me that he expects

373. Joseph Pilmore (1739–1825), English clergyman, was converted by John Wesley at the age of sixteen, came to America in 1769 and was the first Methodist preacher there; subsequently he became an Episcopalian. John Hamilton Moore (d. 1807) was an English author, compiler, and teacher of navigation; he is best known for his *Practical Navigator and Seaman's New Daily Assistant* (London, 1772), which had gone through nineteen editions (with slightly varying titles) by 1814. Thomas Truxtun (1755–1822), American naval officer, sailed as a privateersman in the Revolution, as a commercial captain took the first Philadelphia ship to China in 1786, was awarded a medal for heroic action in the naval hostilities with France in 1798, and retired in 1801.

374. In this description of Strong, Irving drew on his letter to William Irving, December 25, 1804–January 25, 1805.

375. "Give glory to the Lord your God, before he cause darkness, and before your feet stumble upon the dark mountains . . ." (Jer. 13:16).

376. Rev. 13, 17.

orders to sail for Palermo in which case I cannot think of accompanying him as I being a *quarantined* person would subject his vessel to Quarantine in that port. Dent <is> appears to be a very clever gentlemanlike fellow. I have had several conversations with him and he has given me considerable information with respect to our Mediterranean affairs. We have several vessels at Syracuse, which <?I?> is their rendezvous.[377] I shall therefore perhaps find some acquaintances there. Our officers are generally very good looking fellows – their uniform has lately been altered and is very handsome & becoming.[378] Our Sailors are <gen> also superior in looks to any other except the English and our vessels are much admired. There are several gun boats preparing at this place for the projected attack on Tripoli; which most probably will take place in the latter part of the spring or commencement of the summer ensuing when the weather will have settled.[379]

January 15[380]

The weather has been variable since our arrival – frequent showers of rain have fallen, but not a day has passed that did not afford some hours of sunshine, and the air has been always temperate and agreeable. For two or three days past I could have worn light summer cloathing without any inconvenience. The evenings are uniformly delightful. <the moon is nearly full and shines with> It is really romantic to sit on deck and watch the gradual departure of day and the slow approach of night. It reallizes the descriptions that poets and writers of romance delight in <and I know not that the pictures want any thing to render them> and this, you know, is one of the countries where they love to place the scene of their fables. I have frequently sat for two or three hours and enjoyed the luxury of the prospect. The sun gradually declining behind the sicilian mountains amid a rich assemblage of clouds that render his

377. Syracuse was made the base of supplies for Preble's squadron partly because he anticipated fewer desertions there than at Gibraltar or Malta, where previous squadrons had been based and where deserters were able to take refuge under the British flag. See Gardner W. Allen, *Our Navy and the Barbary Corsairs* (Boston, 1905), pp. 159–60.

378. The uniform instructions order of August 27, 1802, was the first to provide for a distinctive dress for the Navy: a blue and gold uniform with decorations of gold lace (James C. Tily, *The Uniforms of the United States Navy*, New York, 1964, pp. 56, 60, 63).

379. Before the American forces could attack Tripoli again, peace was negotiated early in June.

380. This entry and Irving's letter to William Irving, December 25, 1804–January 25, 1805 (portions for January 14 and 15, 1805) are virtually the same.

exit more splendid – Their colours gradually deepening into a glowing crimson, then <p> changing into a purple and at last sinking into a modest grey. By this time the moon begins to shew her paler glories on the other side of the horison – breaking from behind the high mountains that form the Calabrian shore. By degrees she attains a commanding height, pours a full stream of radiance oer, the rapid and restless waters of the <streights> straits – & the more tranquil waters of this delightful harbor. Her "silver beams" brighten up the surrounding forts & castles – and the white buildings of Messina – and "sleep in gentle brilliance"[381] on its neighboring towers & convents. All is tranquility and repose except now and then the silence is interrupted by the sound of some vesper bell, the watch word of the Guards or the full chorus's from some of the ships in quarantine whose crews every evening chant a hymn to the Vergin. This music is simple solemn and affecting – and is peculiarly in unison with the scene. <Amid such> The other evening I was highly delighted when, after having sat on deck a long time indulging in those delicious reveries such scenes are calculated to inspire, I was aroused by a strain of soft Sicilian music that came from a distance and gradually swelled in the silence of the night – Where it came from I could not percieve. They sounds were so <sweet so clear> ↑soft↓ so sweet yet so clear & distinct in their modulations that they seemed almost æreal. By turns they swelled into a full body of harmony and then died away in liquid cadence. It seemed like <the> a choir of æreal spirits that were traversing the air – and being in the country of romance I was almost tempted to yield to its sway and indulge in the fancy that they were so. [382] <Not>

I fear I tire you with discriptions – I wish to make you partaker in all my pleasures, and those that are imparted to me by <the> surrounding scenery are generally the greatest. My feelings are very often as much influenced by the prospects that surround me as others are by the weather and a lovely landscape has always a most enlivening effect on my spirits.

381. This quotation, which has not been identified, possibly comes from the Della Cruscan School. In his letter to William Irving, December 25, 1804–January 25, 1805, it appears as "the moonlight . . . *sleeping in gentle radiance.*"

382. Possibly Irving was influenced in writing this paragraph by Brydone's account of "aerial" forms which he saw near this area of the Mediterranean in *A Tour through Sicily and Malta,* (I, 87, 88, 90). Apparently he saw the famous atmospheric phenomena known as the Fata Morgana. It is also described in Swinburne, *Travels in Two Sicilies,* I, 365–67.

There has some snow fallen on the tops of the mountains but it soon disappeared, nor was the cold felt in the lower places. The skirts of the mountains are green & flourishing and I observe the ground plowed and cultivated like in spring or summer. Fruit is exceeding cheap. For a basket of fine oranges figs raisins nuts &c I paid but a shilling sterling – and this too was at Quarantine where the prices of course are imposing. The Oranges are from Calabria – very large and delicious – for a dozen I paid about *seven* cents, and doubtless in the city they are cheaper

One of my amusements is sailing about the harbor for which purpose I have had the <yal> yaul fitted up with sails. We have now two guards aboard one of whom I am obliged always to take with me. He attempted several times to stop <f> me from sailing about for amusement, but finding his menaces were not understood nor regarded he has given the matter up. The poor guards were terribly alarmd they day before yesterday. I wished to get a letter to the post office by way of the Nautilus as the health office opens every letter that passes thro it. If however the Nautilus was observed to take a letter from us unsmoaked she would be Quarantined. I watchd therefore an opportunity when both the guards were on shore at the Lazzeretto to get two of the hands to row me to the schr. – I had not got far from the ship before <the> I was percieved from the shore and the guards set up a hideous bellowing. I pretended not to hear them and told the sailors to pull away, they gave me a close chase in the long boat so that I was unable to get my letter on board and had to surrender to them. They made a violent noise about it and told me that if I went ashore without them I would certainly <fe> be fined and thrown in prison and they would be hung – I laughed at the bug bears they were conjuring up and merely answered them with *bye & bye.* This is a cant word the sailors make use of towards the guards whenever they do not wish to obey their direction, or to understand them – and <they> it has become quite common among all the guards at the Lazaretto. They <do not> cannot concieve its signification as it is used in such opposite cases. Our poor guards have been so often worried with it that they are quite out of patience at the sound and swear that it is *a word of the Devil* (una parola del Diavolo)

There are a number of English transports in port procuring wine and other stores for Lord Nelsons fleet. An English frigate arrived also a few days ago from the fleet off Toulon. Every day there are more or less vessels entering the harbor or passing thro the strai<g>ts which gives an air of life and business to the scene. Among other arrivals is an English privateer that has been cruising and among other vessels captured the Brig Favorite of Philadelphia bound to Genoa and near to that port. They carried her <into> in to Malta where she is performing quarantine at present & her fate is not determined. This Privateer is riding Quarantine the next ship but one to us. She has a most delectable crew of Maltese italians &c &c and but two or three englishmen on board. Yesterday they had a high altercation at the Lazeretto several of the sailors having mutinied against the Lieutenant. The latter stripped and was for boxing the whole of them but that was what they were not accustomed to and one of them drew his knife and if he had not been prevented would have stabbed the Lieutenant. I am surprized the English are not more jealous of the dignity of their flag. At present it is assumed by all the pirates in the Mediterranean with impunity, and is the rallying standard for the vilest wretches in existence. Perhaps there is no flag in the world <at> under which greater enormities are committed.

The captain of the privateer, I believe, was afraid to trust himself any longer among such a gang of ruffians so he sent them all ashore this morning *bag and baggage* & I dont believe Noah's ark itself could have furnished a more motley debarkation.

This <morning> ↑day↓ we had to undergo another health office manouvre. A chafing dish with charcoal and a couple of paquets of drugs were sent on board. We were all ordered down into the hold the hatches nearly all closed. A fire made in the chaffing dish and the drugs thrown on which occasiond a thick smoke of a disagreeable smell. Here we were huddled round the infernal pot of *incense* like a group of conjurers inhaling the suffocating steams of a melange of vile drugs for a quarter of an hour after which we were permitted once more to emerge into the "cheerful day."[383]

This I find is a sage expedient of the Health Physician to know if any person on board has the fever lurking in his veins as this fumigation immediately makes it break out. In the afternoon we were ordered

383. Thomas Gray, "Elegy Written in a Country Church-Yard" (1751), ll. 85–88:

For who to dumb Forgetfulness a prey,
This pleasing anxious being e'er resign'd,
Left the warm precincts of the cheerful day,
Nor cast one longing, ling'ring look behind?

ashore at the lazerretto where the Doctor again took a look at our necks and bosoms. We have now about twelve days more of Quarantine to perform and must undergo a repetition of these *pleasant* operations, perhaps with a few variations for they seem to be as fond of trying experiments upon us, as the philosophical professors at college do upon unlucky rats that fall in their clutches.

January 23

This day we had another smoaking of the drugs of which *assafoetida* is one of the principal. We then underwent a third examination from the Doctor who dismissed us as being *incorrigibly healthy* in spight of all their operations. Tomorrow we are promised *pratique* or entry – as they intend to allow us <two or> one or two days of Grace.

[*facing back cover*]
Mrs. Johnson[384]

[*inside back cover*]
Ship Matilda, 27th. Decr.
opposite Corsica

Acheté en Bordeaux Juillet 1804
Prix 3 liv.[385]

384. "Mrs. Johnson" is written in brown or black ink. Probably Irving refers to the actress, Mrs. Elizabeth Johnston; see page 219, n. 164.

385. All the writing on the page and also a small drawing of a profile (Figure 4) are in brown or black ink. The French, which is written upside down at the bottom of the page, means "Bought in Bordeaux, July 1804. Price, 3 livres."

EUROPEAN JOURNAL, 1804–1805

Volume 2
Messina–Rome

The manuscript journal is in the Yale University Library. It consists of 140 pages, written in ink of several colors, of a limp vellum-covered booklet of 190 pages, measuring 6 x 8 inches. Pp. [2, 51–96, 143, 144, 190] are blank.

The color of ink changes a number of times in the manuscript. Brown ink was used for entries from January 24 through part of the entry for February 5; blue-black ink for the remainder of February 5 through part of the entry for February 11; brown ink for the remainder of the February 11 entry through the entry for March 15; blue-black ink for entries of March 17 to 22; and brown ink for entries for March 24 to April 13.

[*front cover*]
1804 & 1805[1]

[*p. [1]*]
January 1805[?][2]

Notes
of a Tour in Europe
in 1804–5.

Vol 2d.
From January 24th. to April 13th. 1805
containing
Route from Messina thro Sicily & to Rome
with residence at different places.

By Washington Irving
of Sunnyside

1. Written in brown or black ink.

2. About an inch at the top of p. [1] has been cut off, leaving after "January" only the bottom edge of what appears to be "1805." This date at the top of the page is in blue ink. The remainder of the page is written in brown ink, except "By Washington Irving of Sunnyside," which is written at the bottom of the page in pencil in another hand.

Messina, January 24, 1805

This morning we were released from Quarantine after performing the necessary ceremonies of giving our names, professions countries &c at the health office. I immediately went on board the Schooner Nautilus as she expected to sail for Syracuse <th> in the evening – waiting only for the arrival of some timber which she <was> ↑is↓ to carry to Syracuse to repair the mast of the ship President.

In the course of the day I was ashore and rambled thro the city in company with Captain Dent, with whom also I dined at Mr Broadbents,[3] <an>the English gentleman to whom I brought a letter of introduction. He acts as navy agent to the American<s> ↑navy↓ and is to be appointed American Consul for <of> the Island of Sicily. He is a gentleman of the most mild & amiable manners and universally known & beloved. I found at his table several Englishmen, among whom was a Mr Smith,[4] an english lawyer on his travels but who has lived with Broadbent for two or three years.

Messina at present, presents very little to the curious eye of the traveller either as to antiquities or public edifices. The dreadful Earthquake in 1783 has reduced many parts of it to heaps of ruins, and is descernable more or less in almost every street & square. The elegant row of buildings that extended for a mile and a quarter along the Quay in a uniform style of architecture, are completely demolished, not one of them remaining in any degree habitable.[5] When standing they must have given an air of much grandeur to the city and added greatly to the beauty of the harbor. Many of the <houses> churches and palaces are also shaken to the ground and in some of the streets the higher stories of the houses have given way and <the> since, they have been repaired and rendered into two stories. The earthquake has been most distructive in its effects near the water and its traces are fainter in the upper parts of the city. The inhabitants have scarcely yet got over its paralizing effects and still talk of it with emotions of horror. They are just beginning to build again, but do it slowly – seem to consult very

3. In 1805 Broadbent lived in a house in the "teatro maritimo," a row of palaces along the harbor; exchange rooms were opened in his house that year by a group of Messina merchants (Giuseppe Oliva, *Annali della Città di Messina,* Messina, 1893, VI, 26).

4. No record of Smith in Messina seems to exist, the municipal archives having been destroyed in a fire following the earthquake of 1908.

5. In this sentence Irving may have drawn on Patrick Brydone, *A Tour through Sicily and Malta* (London, 1773), I, 46.

little the elegancies of architecture and seldom build higher than two stories. Many, however, still reside in the suburbs & vicinities of the town where they fled in time of the alarm, and have fitted up the cottages into comfortable & even elegant appartments nor can any thing induce them to forsake them.

On the top of one of the hills behind the city is an old castle said to have been built by Prince [*blank*] of England in the time of the cruisades when he made a long sojourn at Messina.[6] I could not get <t> quite to the castle and had to content myself with a view of it from a road that runs along the hill a little below it. It is now in ruins. A tower still remaining in pretty good preservation. It is of a Gothic structure and has a picturesque appearance. On a <h> neighboring hill is the convent for the nobility the church of which has a handsome front an[d] a curious steeple of a spiral form.[7] A terrace in front of the church commands a fine view of the city, harbor, straits, &c.

Among the churches the cathederal[8] is the most remarkable. It is extremely Gothic – the roof inside of wood with large rafters crossing the church, gilt and painted with pictures of saints & angels. On the pavement of the church is drawn a meridian line on which the sun is cast thro a small hole in the roof and tells the time of the year month day &c.

The houses throughout Messina are generally of a very moderate height – built of <witish> whitish stone & plaistered. Iron raild balconies to the second story are universal. The walls of the houses along the Quay appear to have been very <po> injudiciously constructed of bricks & round stones promiscuously jumbled together and badly cemented[.] they were therefore poorly calculated to withstand the frequent & severe shocks of the earthquake. The whole city seems but the shadow of what it was before this tremendous event.

The historians of Messina bestow the highest degree of antiquity on its origin. By some it is ascribed to Shem the son of Noah, called by the

6. The fortification of Rocca Guelfonia or Matagrifone was built in part by Richard I (Richard Coeur de Lion) of England when he, together with Philip II of France, wintered at Messina in 1190–1191 en route to the Holy Land during the Third Crusade.

7. The church of San Gregorio, founded in 1542, and the adjoining convent on the Colle della Caperrina were destroyed in the earthquake of 1908.

8. The Cathedral or Matrice, begun in 1092 and consecrated in 1197, has been rebuilt many times after damage by earthquake or fire. The meridian line, the work of a native astronomer, Abáte D. Antonio Jaci, was completed in 1804.

Italians Cam – & sometimes Zoroaster for his having been inventor of Magic. Having espoused Rea <*illegible*> (antiently termed Cybele) in Italy he passd into Sicily & was so pleased with the situation of the Faro that he built a city there which was denominated Zancla from the curvature of its port resembling a sickle. After having experienced some misfortunes it was again rebuilt by Orion in the year of the world 4434 and 1755 years before the Christian æra – he also built a temple on Pelorus and dedicated to Neptune – from those & other renowned deeds both in arts & arms he was enumerated among the heros and placed among the Stars.[9]

Messina has gone thro a variety of scenes of trouble & warfare and is conspicuous in antient history. It was here that the cause of the first punic war originated owing to the contentions of the Romans & Carthagenians for this place so important to the security of Italy. When in the hands of the Romans it was called Mamertina from the Mamertines, people of Campania.[10]

<The short stay I>

January 29

The short stay I have made at Messina prevents my being more particular in describing <It> it, this I shall postpone till my return. My stay in it was rendered unpleasant by an unfortunate rencontre in the streets the other evening between one of the officers of the Nautilus & the mate of an English transport wherein the latter was killd.[11] This occasiond much stir among the english in Messina who insisted upon the Governor's[12] demanding the officer from the Capt of the schooner. Capt. Dent refused to deliver him up <and re> but gave his word of honor that he should be delivered up to the commodore at Syracuse. With this

9. In this paragraph Irving drew on Giuseppe Buonfiglio Costanzo, *Prima [e Secunda] Parte dell'Historia Siciliana* (Venice, 1604), pp. 9, 42, 43.

10. The substance of the last two sentences appears in Henry Swinburne, *Travels in the Two Sicilies* (London, 1783, 1785), II, 397–98.

11. On the evening of January 23, 1805, an English sailor was stabbed to death at the marina of Messina, and subsequently charges were brought by the British consul against acting Lieutenant Charles G. Ridgely. In April Commodore Samuel Barron released Ridgely, who was brought to trial by a Sicilian military court in Messina and acquitted. See Letters Received from Captains by the Secretary of the Navy, RG 45, NA (where Ridgely's middle initial appears as "L"). Irving gave a fuller account of this episode in his letter to William Irving, December 25, 1804–January 25, 1805. See also n. 17.

12. Cavaliere Giovanni Guillichini was governor of Messina at this time.

the Governor was contented, tho the english were strenuous that he should use forcible measures. There was consequently, a constraint thrown over our <mann> communications with each other that rendered our intimacies unpleasant.

I was introduced to the Governor the other morning by Capt Dent & Mr Broadbent and had a very polite reception. He conversed with me some minutes and was particular in his enqueries concerning Genoa and how the french comported themselves in respect to that city. He shruggd up his shoulders at my account and seemed to anticipate a <f> similar fate for Messina <w it> from his remarks.

This morning we set sail with a light breeze but was detaind off of the port for some time waiting for the English Schooner that had the timber on board. We bore round the promontory that forms the Harbor and saw Charybdis at a distance foaming & dashing in large breakers. This is no longer an object of terror to the mariners nor is there any necessity for ships to take much pains in avoiding it. In calm weather however they are often baffled and worried in it and the helm losing its power the ship turns round & round. I cannot percieve the iminent risk that mariners were said to <run> ↑undergo↓ of running on Scylla when they avoided Charybdis. Scylla is sheltered from Charybdis by a low sandy point of land & is ten miles at least, distant[.] it appears to me there is a mistake in the place that is at present shewn for Charybdis & that it must have laid in the mouth of the straits.

Charybdis is said to have been a rapacious woman who stole Herculus's oxen in revenge for which he plunged her into the sea.[13]

We had a fine view of the two coasts of Sicily & Calabria, rising into rocky mountains but skirted with towns & villages. O<n>f the <summits of> ↑latter↓ many were situated on the summits of pointed hills or rocks & over hung the sea[.] this is to secure them from the inroads of barbary corsairs who infest these coasts. On the Calabrian shore we saw Reggio or as it was antiently termd Rhegium, it was formerly a Roman colony and was ruined by Dionysius – the Tyrant of Syracuse

He <sent> commanded the people of Rhegium that they should send him one of their most beautiful and noble young women for a wife – out of derision or carelessness they sent him the daughter of a

13. In this sentence and in the account of Rhegium and Dionysius in the next paragraph Irving drew on Buonfiglio Costanzo, *Prima . . . Parte dell'Historia Siciliana*, pp. 3, 6.

slave in revenge of which <they> ↑he↓ laid their city in ruins. It is now a small town pleasantly situated <at> ↑on↓ the Sea coast, and was much damaged by the same earthquake that was so destructive to Messina. Towards sundown we had a distinct tho distant view of Mount Ætna. It is coverd with snow more than half way down so that I fear I shall find it difficult to ascend it. The crater is also visible and emits smoke but not in great quantities. The Breeze has freshned up and is ahead, the schooner however is a remarkable fine sailor, but has to shorten sail to keep with the English schooner in convoy.

January 30

<This> After a night of stiff gales we found ourselves this morning <close under> half way to syracuse but the English schooner not in sight. The captain <of our> supposing she had put back to Messina – put about immediately and run before the wind for that port. We passd thro Charybdis which made a heavy broken sea. After all that has been said & sung of this celebrated place it would make but a contemptible appearance aside of our pass called Hellgate[14] – and is nothing to compare to it either in real or apparent danger. We came to anchor ↑safe↓[15] in the harbor of Messina where we also found the English Schooner. The city was quite in a state of alarm. News had been brought that a large fleet had been seen off the straits – The inhabitants were in great consternation thinking it was either the french or English fleet coming to take possession of the place. We were told that many of the richer inhabitants were pushing off into the country of [to] conceal their money & valuables.

January 31

This morning a <ship or> two ↑ships↓ of the line were seen entering the straits. The whole town was instantly in an uproar – the Marino was crowded with spectators – couriers passing and repassing from the city to the Faro and troops marching about to man the forts. Several more ships made their appearance and it was ascertained to be the English fleet – in a short time Lord Nelsons ship the Victory hove into sight – they all advanced most majestically up the straits – the people

14. A narrow channel of the East River on the eastern side of New York City, long dangerous to ships because of its strong currents and rocks.

15. "safe" appears below "anchor," which is the last word in the last line on the manuscript page.

seemed to wait in fearful expectation. The fleet however soon relieved their apprehensions – They continued on without entering the harbor We immediately got<t> under way making a signal for the English schooner to do the same as we wished to have a good view of the fleet. The English schooner was a long time in coming out which gave us a fine opportunity by standing back again to examine the fleet. It consisted of eleven sail of the line three frigates & two Brigs all in prime order and most noble vessels. We had understood before we left Messina that Nelson was in search of the French fleet which had lately got out of Toulon.[16] The fleet continued in sight all day. It was very pleasing to observe with what promptness and dexterity the signals were made, answerd and obeyd. The fleet seemed as a body of men under perfect dicipline. Every ship <seem> appeard to know its station immediately and to change position agreeably to command with the utmost precision. Nelson has brought them to perfect dicipline – he has kept them at sea a long time with very little expence – They seldom having more than three sails set all the while they were off Toulon. He takes great pride in them and says there is not a vessel among them that he would wish out of the fleet. We had a fine sunset the sun declining gradually behind Mount Ætna and displaying with great force of shade & colour its gigantic outlines. In the evening the wind freshned and blew ahead, but in the night was very light & baffling.

February 1

This Morning we found ourselves in pretty much the same situation as last evening – The schooner that we have to convoy is a slow sailer and the captain appears fearful of carrying sail so that we frequently have to lay to for him and he operates as a continual clog on our vessel In the course of the day the wind freshned and blew very strong – the sea washd over us repeatedly – the other schooner could not stand it, but scud before it under bare poles, but fortunately it subsided and came about in the evening to the west so that we were once more enabled to continue on our course.

I found the society of the officers very agreeable – the wardroom

16. Nelson blockaded the French fleet in Toulon for twenty-two months until on January 18, 1805, the French escaped and fled to the West Indies. Nelson pursued them across the Atlantic and back but never overtook them. On this occasion he had with him eleven ships of the line and two frigates. See *The Dispatches and Letters of Vice Admiral Lord Viscount Nelson* (London, 1846), VI, 325, 333.

consisted of Lieuts Ried Ridgely & Cassin – Tootle the purser and Dr <Lopez> ↑Jaques.↓[17] good humor reignd among them and they had always a joke or a good story at hand to make the time pass away gaily.

February 2

This morning we had lost sight of the schooner and determined to take no more trouble about her but make the best of our way to Syracuse. We soon ran in sight of the city and about two o'clock anchord safe in the harbor. Here we found several of our ships that are sent out against Tripoli – viz the Frigates President – Essex, Constellation & Congress and the Brig Vixen.[18] The harbor is extensive and one of the safest in the world – it is sufficiently capacious to accommodate large fleets with convenience. Indeed if we may credit antient historians it has formerly containd immense ones. I was impatient to land and view the interior of a city once so celebrated for arts & arms – that gave birth to men so renownd as Heroes & Philosophers.

But heavens! what a change! Streets gloomy & ill built – and poverty filth and misery on every side. No appearance of trade or industry <all is> no countenance displaying the honest traits of ease & independence – all is servility indigence & discontent.[19]

Our vessels, however, have given a great change to the face of affairs at Syracuse. They [The] money they have circulated there has given <someth> comparatively an air of life to the place and even began to encourage a faint return of commerce. Formerly it was impossible for the traveller to find an inn to rest at <by> but now there are two established in the english style – The accommodations tolerable (tho for Sicily excellent) and the tables they keep are very plentifully supplied particularly at Smiths hotel.[20]

17. Charles Goodwin Ridgely (1784–1848), at this time acting lieutenant, entered the Navy as a midshipman in 1799, was officially appointed lieutenant February 2, 1807, commander July 24, 1813, and captain February 28, 1815; see also n. 11. John Cassin (d. 1822) was appointed lieutenant November 13, 1799, became commander April 2, 1806, and captain July 3, 1812. James Tootell (d. 1809) became purser May 5, 1803. Gershom R. Jacques became surgeon's mate May 21, 1800, was discharged August 4, 1801, under the Peace Establishment Act, reappointed February 18, 1802, became surgeon November 27, 1804, and was struck off Navy records April 25, 1808.

18. The *Vixen* was a schooner.

19. Syracuse made similar first impressions on Brydone, as he recorded in *A Tour through Sicily and Malta*, I, 265.

20. No record of either of these inns seems to exist in the archives of Syracuse,

They have the best company of singers for their opera[21] that is in Sicily, drawn thither by the liberality of the American officers who were in the habit of throwing money on the stage to any performer who pleased them. The first singer Cecilia,[22] is a <handsome> ↑pretty↓ little woman and has a delightful voice of great <softness> sweetness & strength. I am surprized she is not engaged on some of the large italian theatres. She is supported by Capt. D<ent> in a very handsome manner.

February 4

Yesterday I was introduced by Capt. Dent to the officers of our vessels. On board of the Essex I found Wm Amory[23] of Boston Lieut of Marines – well known throughout the United States for his wildness & eccentricity – Of an honest heart & good disposition but the most heedless mad cap genius that ever existed. <He has [*illegible*] out th> Nothing but a most excellent constitution has supported him thro the extravagancies and excesses he has continually committed – He is at present far more steady and very few that have gone thro such a round of dissapation can boast of a constitution so good as Amory's is at present.

On board the same ship I was introduced to Lieut Woolsey[24] of New York with whom I was very highly pleased – In the evening I went to a most miserable private masquerade. The room in which it was held seemd as if part of a stable – yet I was told there were sevral of the nobility of Syracuse present. A number of American officers were there – as usual in high glee & full of frolic.

This morning I walked out of town to visit the celebrated Ear of Dionysius the Tyrant.[25] I was accompanied by Dr Baker[26] of the Presi-

21. The Teatro di S. Lucia was opened and the Comica Compagnia Lombarda Colonnesi-Fontana was formed in the fall of 1803 (Serafino Privitera, *Storia di Siracusa Antica e Moderna,* Naples, 1878–1879, II, 302).

22. Cecilia Fontana Bertozzi. In November 1804 the commanders and senior officers of the American Squadron in Syracuse presented her with a pennant, which is preserved in the Biblioteca Arcivescovile, Syracuse.

23. William Amory (1774–1812), who served first as midshipman in the English navy, became second lieutenant in the U. S. marines July 25, 1798, first lieutenant November 10, 1799, and resigned at a date not officially recorded ("Memoir of the Family of Amory," *The New England Historical and Genealogical Register,* X, 1856, 64).

24. Melancthon Taylor Woolsey (1790–1838) entered the navy as a midshipman in 1800 and was appointed lieutenant in 1804 and captain in 1816.

dent Davis[27] a midshipman and Tootle purser of the Nautilus. The scenery in the neighborhood of Syracuse is very pleasing. <The country is low with mountains> After leaving the gates we ascended a little rising land and had a charming prospect. To our left the picturesque city of Syracuse – before us the beautiful harbor calm & unruffled like a vast mirror reflecting the frigates that lay at anchor in the midst of it and the small craft that were gliding on its surface – beyond a large tract of rich level country diversified by trees and plantations and <of the> clothed with the finest verdure – and to our right the Hybla mountains bounded the view. The face of the country the mildness & salubrity of the air reminded me of our fine days in the month of May <and the fields were> particularly when crossing the fields where I saw a variety of wild flowers in full blow. The approach to the ear of Dionysius is thro a vast quarrey,[28] <from> one of those from whence the stone for the Edifices of antient Syracuse was procured. It is a soft kind of <wit> white freestone that is very easily cut but hardens on exposure to the air – The bottom of this Quarrey is cultivated in many places and being entirely open overhead to the sun and shelterd on every side from the wind by high precipices it is very fertile.[29]

Travellers have generally been very careless in their account of the *Ear.* Some one originally started the observation that it was cut in the form of a human ear, and every one who has since given a discription of it ha<ve>s followed in the same track and made the same remark. *Brydone*[30] among the rest, joins in it. I am not however surprized at his falling in the error for I have generally found him more fanciful than

---

25. The Orecchio di Dionisio is a large grotto of unusual acoustic properties, in the shape – partly natural but to a great extent artificial – of an ear, located on the outskirts of Syracuse. According to legend it was excavated by Dionysius the Elder (*ca.* 430–367 B.C.) who became Tyrant of Syracuse in 406 B.C., for a prison, after a plan whereby a whisper uttered in it could be heard in a high chamber where he would station himself to listen to his prisoners.

26. William Baker became surgeon's mate April 2, 1804, and resigned October 1, 1805.

27. John Davis (d. 1809) became midshipman November 7, 1801, and was officially appointed lieutenant March 26, 1807.

28. Latomia del Paradiso ("Quarry of Paradise") is one of the five *latomie* or quarries which are peculiar to Syracuse. They originally yielded stones for its construction and were later used as burial places and prisons.

29. Irving's description echoes the description of the Latomia dei Cappuccini (though it is not named) in Brydone, *A Tour through Sicily and Malta,* I, 267.

30. *Ibid.,* p. 270.

correct and <general> more studious of turning a handsome period or giving <an>a pretty story when imparting accurate information respecting the places thro which he passd. Indeed he gives such a hurried – careless account of the very interesting curiosities in <the vic> & about Syracuse that I doubt much whether he saw one third of them.

The ear is a vast serpentine cavern something in the form of the letter <ƨ> – S reversed; <it is of about wid> its greatest width is at the bottom from whence it narrows with an inflection to the top – something like the external shape of an asses ear. < >[31] Its height is about eighty or ninety feet and its length about one hundred and twenty.[32] It is the same height and dimensions from the enterance to the extremity where it ends abruptly. <By this discription> The marks of the tools are still perfectly visible on the walls of the cavern – The rock is brought to a regular surface the whole extent without any projections or <recesses> ↑curvatures↓ as in the human ear. <In> about half way in the <cabin> cavern is a small square recess <of about ten or> or chamber cut in one side of the wall even with the ground.[33] And at the interior extremity there appears to be a small recess at the top but it is at present inaccess<a>ible. A poor man that lives in the neighborhood attended us with torches of straw by which we had a very good view of the interior part of the ear. Holes are discernable <in> ↑near↓ the interior end of the cave which are made in the wall at regular distances and ascend up in an inclined direction. They are about an inch in diameter. Some of the company were of opinion that they have formerly contributed to the support of a stairs or ladder but there is no visible place where a stairs could lead to – and the holes do not go above half the height of the cavern.

There are sevral parts of the ear in which the discharge of a pistol makes a prodigious report heightned by the echoes & reverberations of the cavern. One of the company had a fowling piece which he discharged and it made a noise ↑almost↓ equal to a discharge of artillery, though not so sharp a report. A pistol also produced a report similar to a volley of musquetry. The <pes> best place to stand to hear the echoes to advantage is in the mouth of the cavern. A piece of paper torn in this

31. The drawing is smudged.

32. The measurements commonly given are 75 by 213 feet.

33. In this sentence Irving may have drawn on Swinburne, *Travels in the Two Sicilies*, II, 341.

place makes an echo as if some person had struck the wall violently with a stick in the back of the cave.[34]

This singular cavern is called the ear of Dionysius from the purpose for which it is said to have been destined by that Tyrant. <Like most> Conscious of the disaffection of his subjects and the hatred and enmity his Tyrannical government had produced he became suspicious & distrustful <of> even of his courtiers that surrounded him. He is said to have had this cavern made for the confinement of those persons of whom he had the strongest suspicions. It was so constructed that any thing said in it, in ever so low a <mumur> murmur – would be conveyed to a small aperture that opened into a little chamber where he used to station himself & listen. This chamber is still shewn. It is on the outside of the ear just above the enterance and communicates with the interior. Some of the officers of our navy have been <down> in it last summer; they were lowerd down to it by ropes and mention that sounds are conveyed to it from the cavern with amazing distinctness. I wished very much to get to it and the man who attended us, brought me a cord for the purpose but my companions protested they would not assist in lowering me down and finally persuaded me that it was too hazardous as the cord was small & might be chafed thro in rubbing against the rock in which case I would run a risk of being dashd to peices. I therefore abandond the project for the present

There are a number of other excavations of great dimensions and singular form <o>in different parts of this Quarrey – Some are <employed> occupied by persons who manufacture saltpetre[35] – the neighboring earth being strongly impregnated with it. Their furnaces have renderd the caverns black and dismally gloomy and added to the squalid, sooty appearance of the inhabitants ↑& their furnaces & cauldrons blazing boiling & smoaking↓ would afford a poet a tolerable idea for a discription of the entrance to the infernal regions. In one part of the Quarrey and near the centre is a lofty fragment of rock completely insulated. On the top of it are the ruins of a small tower that most probably has been a watch tower or a look out – at present it is inaccessable but near it lie <a confused> vast masses of Rock in which are discernable the remains of a stairs cut in the stone which formerly led to this

34. Echoes produced by the tearing of a piece of paper and the discharge of a gun are referred to by Swinburne, *ibid.*

35. They are referred to by Swinburne, *ibid.*, p. 340.

tower, but has been over thrown & shatterd to pieces by an earthquake. <At a little distance from this quarrey is>

A little distance to the east of the ear are the remains of an antient theatre.[36] It is built on the side of a hill – the seats still remain in good preservation many of them being cut in the rock of which the hill is formed. This Theatre from its situation and <ston> construction was supposed to be Grecian which was confirmed by a Greek inscription on one of the stone seats now in possession of Landolini, the Kings antiquarian at Syracuse.[37]

Just above the theatre are several arches of an antient aqueduct[38] that formerly supplied the city of Syracuse with water. In [It] now furnishes a <mill> stream for a mill situated near the theatre, and runs with extreme rapidity & violence.

<In the afternoon>

February 5

This morning I went to see the caticombs[39] in company with Lieut Ried, Tootle & Baker In our walk we passed a place where has lately been dug up the ruins of a temple supposed to have been dedicated to Venus. Several columns were laying near the hole[.] they are of grey granite some plain doric and others fluted spirally. Here they have found <the> ↑a↓ beautiful statue of a Venus[40] and a small statue of coarse alabaster of Esculapius. The former wants the head and an arm but I have no doubt but that they would be found on a farther search. <It is> The figure stands in an inclined posture something like the

36. The Teatro Greco dates from about 475 B.C.

37. Saverio Landolina (1743–1813), Italian antiquarian, was famous particularly for his discovery of papyrus at the spring of Cyane near Syracuse and his production of paper from it according to the directions written out by Pliny. He was employed by Ferdinand (1751–1825), son of Charles III of Spain, who, on succeeding to his father's Italian realms in 1759, became Ferdinand IV of Naples and Ferdinand III of Sicily, and in 1816 became Ferdinand I of the Two Sicilies.

38. This and an aqueduct which skirted the north wall of the city supplied ancient Syracuse with water.

39. The principal ones excavated at that time, now called Catacómbe di S. Giovanni, date from the fourth century A.D.

40. The "Venus Anadyomene," a Roman adaptation of the second century A.D. of a Greek work of the third century B.C., and the statue of Asclepius (Latin: Aesculapius), of the late Greek period, were found in the ruins of an ancient bath in the Bonavia garden on January 7, 1804, by Saverio Landolina; both statues are now in the Museo Archeologico, Syracuse.

Venus of Medicis.[41] One hand is covering the left breast and the left hand <ho> grasps a fold of a robe that is round her feet and raised up to her middle. They are in possession of Landolini.

The<i> workmen have desisted from any further search as the antiquarian has no money to pay them! Th<is>e environs of th<is>e city are perfect mines of antiquities[.] every now and then some new objects <is> are[42] accidentally coming to light. unfortunately however very little encouragement is given to develope them. The King of Naples has <given> ↑allowed↓ 600 ounces[43] for the searching of antiquities in Sicily – two hundred for each division – a sum by no means adequate for a country that abounds with them, but in a <buied> buried state, requiring considerable expence to restore them to view. It has been expended some time since. To arrive at the catacombs we had to pass thro' a small <church of> chapel[44] of a Gothic appearance. Here we found a venerable Capuchin whose wrinkled front and white beard seemed to say that he should soon be an inhabitant of the silent abodes that he was going to shew us. He lighted two flambeaus one of which he gave to our guide to carry. We first were <shewn> led by him to a subterraneous chapel where was the sepulchre of some saint or another whose name we could not understand. This chapel we were told was one of the first that was erected in Sicily in the very early ages of Christianity – perhaps founded by St. Paul during his stay here on his voyage from Malta to Rome. The walls around were adorned with uncouth pictures of saints and angels that appeared as antique as the chapel itself.

We did not remain long in the chapel but ascending passed thro a small inclosure or yard from which we descended by a small entrance into the Catacombs.

These are astonishing excavations in the rock that extend to an unknown distance under ground. <We> They consist of vaulted passages that branch out into various directions – on each side you pass

41. The "Venus de' Medici" is in the Uffizi gallery, Florence.

42. "are" is written over "is" and "s" is added to "object."

43. An oncia, a Sicilian and Neapolitan coin, was worth about $2 at this time.

44. The church of S. Giovanni, founded in 1182, has been several times restored. The lower church contains the tomb of St. Marcian (d. *ca.* 225), first bishop of Syracuse. According to tradition, St. Paul preached on the site during the three days he spent in Syracuse en route from Melita (Malta) to Puteoli in 59 A.D. The frescoes are of the sixteenth century.

continually large recesses that contain places for the dead. Some of these are very large with sixty or seventy receptacles for bodies in a row. These we were told had been intended as family tombs. <of ?6th?>[45]

In different places are round halls about 18 or twenty feet in diameter gradually lessening to the top where there is a round hole ↑in each↓ that was perhaps formerly used as a ventillator tho now they are generally stoppd up. from these halls are four passages that lead in different directions till they come to other halls and then branch out again, forming a complete labarynth where without an experienced guide a stranger would be completely bewilderd and lost. No bones are to be found in the catacombs at present having no doubt long since mouldered to dust. The walls are damp and water filters thro them in many places. Our old Capuchin pointed out to us one passage that he said led to Catania (*only* 40 miles distant). <The way> This was discoverd he told us, <was> by a priest and two boys who undertook to explore it carrying a supply of provisions and torches. The priest and one boy died on the way and the survivor was almost sinking when he emerged into day at the foot of Mount Ætna! The old father's story <is un> holds good its ground notwithstanding all its improbability for no body has hardihood or inclination to put its veracity to the test of experiment. These extensive catacombs <she> are a proof of what amazing population the antient Syracuse must have been possessd.

From hence we crossed several fields to a convent of Capuchins[46] that stands near the sea coast pleasantly situated on an eminence. Belonging to this convent <are> ↑is↓ the garden of the Latom<c>ie, formed in the bottom of one of the immense quarries <from which the> of antient Syracuse. You go down a <flig> number of steps cut in the solid rock before you enter the garden which is about one hundred feet below the level ↑surface↓ of the ground. You then arrive at a perfect labyrinth of sweets. The garden is seperated into different parts by the rocks and you pass from one to another thro rude & immense arches formed by the falling of part of the rocks. Great masses of rocks stand in two or three places in the midst of the garden <?80 or 90?> eighty or 90 feet high, their tops over spread with rich foliage and picturesque trees. <The sides of the> The <rocks> sides of the rocks that surround the

45. A canceled "6th" appears at the margin in the manuscript, as though Irving started to begin the entry for the next day at this point.

46. It has been suppressed. The church, of the sixteenth century, stands on the edge of the Latomia dei Cappuccini, in his description of which Irving may have drawn on Brydone, *A Tour through Sicily and Malta,* I, 267.

garden rise perpendicular & even like walls, <th> running vines Indian fig myrtle & over hanging the precipices and growing in some places out of the fissures of the stone. Shelterd from every chilling blast <the garden> & open to the genial rays of the sun the garden is in perpetual bloom and the fruits arrive to great perfection. Oranges lemons figs &c &c are in profusion, the trees were loaded with the two former and I saw here the largest & finest citrons I have met with in Sicily. In short the garden if in ↑the↓ hands of a person of taste, could be made a perfect Eden. Abounding with the most romantic & picturesque scenery and capable <of the most luxurient fertility &> ↑of producing the most↓ luxurient fruits & flowers.

"Here kindly warmth their mounting juice ferments
To nobler tastes and more exalted scents
E'en the rough rocks with tender myrtle bloom
And trodden weeds send out a rich perfume."[47]

In two places in this antient quarry there are remains of caves that have been cut similar to the ear of Dionysius, but either the rocks have caved in or something else has intervened to prevent their being finished. In one part of the garden we were shewn the tomb of an American midshipman lately killd in a duel with one of his shipmates.[48] He was buried in a hole cut in the side of the rock and afterwards plasterd up. <with> An inscription in english is marked on the outside above which the good fathers have added a cross.

After having rambled for some time amid the picturesque scenes of this singular & delightful retreat we ascended to the convent. As one of the company was thirsty & expressd a wish for a draught of water they led us into the refectory and produced a small pitcher of wine making at the same time very strong exhortations to sobriety & temperance observing that a little wine was good but to drink much was both injurious & sinful. I do not know how far their advice would have been followed had not the execrable taste of the wine forced us to comply with it. It surely carried <its> persuasions to sobriety along with it My complaisance induced me to force down half a tumbler full – Lieut Ried however could not contain himself, but spit <it> out the first mouthful

47. Joseph Addison, "A Letter from Italy, to the Right Honourable Charles Lord Halifax," (1701), ll. 59–62.

48. W. R. Nicholson became a midshipman March 2, 1803, and last appeared on Navy records June 4, 1803 (his name is given in the corresponding entry in Irving's "Traveling Notes, 1804–1805").

making dreadful wry faces. I was affraid the good fathers would have been offended but they appeared to take it in good part, <at> on leaving them we gave them some money, for they always expect some solid reccompence for their civilities.[49]

February 6

This morning Lieut's Murray & Gardner <of the Ship Pres> & Capt Hall[50] of the ship president Capt Dent of the Nautilus & myself sat off to pay another visit to the Ear of Dionysius. We dispatched before hand a midshipman & four sailors with a spar and a couple of Halyards. On arriving there we went to the top of the precipice immediately over the mouth of the cave. Here we fastned ourselves <suc> to one of the Halyards and were lowered successively over the edge of the precipice (having previously disposed the spar along the edge of the rock so as to keep the halyard from chaffing) into a small hole over the enterance of the ear and about fifteen feet from the summit of the precipice. The persons lowered were Murray Hall the midshipman & myself the others swearing their [they] would not risk their necks to gratify their curiosity

This is the famous chamber of Dionysius into which it is said he used to go to listen to the discourse of the prisoners confined in the ear.

The cavern narrows as it approaches the top till it ends in a narrow channel that runs the whole extent and terminates in this small chamber. A passage from this hole or chambre appears to have been commenced to be cut to run into the interior of the rock but was never carried more than ten or fifteen feet. We then began to make experiments to prove if sound was communicated from below to this spot in any extraordinary degree. Gardner fired a pistol repeatedly but it did not appear to make a greater noise than when we were below in the mouth of the cavern. We then tried the conveyance of voices – in this we were more successful. One of the company stationd himself at the interior extremity of the ear and applying his mouth close to the wall spoke to me just above a

49. From the comma after "part" in this entry, the next three entries and part of the fourth are in blue-black ink.

50. Daniel Murray became a midshipman July 13, 1799, was officially appointed lieutenant January 26, 1807, and resigned October 29, 1811. John M. Gardner (d. 1815) became a midshipman May 1, 1799, was officially appointed lieutenant January 19, 1807, commander February 4, 1815. John Hall, of the Marine Corps, became first lieutenant August 2, 1798, captain December 1, 1801, major June 8, 1804, and was discharged April 18, 1817, under the Peace Establishment Act.

whisper. I was then stationd with my ear to the wall in the little chambre on high and about 250 feet distant and could hear him very distinctly. We conversed with one another in this manner for some time. He then moved to other parts of the cavern and I could hear him with equal facility his voice seeming to <come> be just behind me. When however he applied his mouth to the opposite side of the cave it was by no means so distinct. This is easily accounted for as one side of the channel is broken away at the mouth of the cavern which injures the conveyance of the <c>sound. After all, I doubt very much whether the cave was ever intended for the purposes ascribed to it. <There are it is true numerous places in the walls> The fact is, that when more than one person speaks at a time it creates such a confusion of sound between their voices & the echoes that it is impossible to distinguish what they say. This we tried repeatedly and found to be invariably the case.

It is true, there are numerous places cut in the wall that still remain, to which it is said the prisoners were fastned but the stone is of a soft nature and if the prisoners were not bound hand & feet they could easily break thro these *stone staples* with their chains. Is it not equally probable that they were places to fasten animals to: which might be reserved here for public games? The Kings antiquarian Landolini, also differs in opinion with the historians of the *Ear*. He thinks it has been intended by Dionysius as a place of torture and that the cries of the tortured encreased by the echoes would be so tremend<u>ous as to make a lively impression on the minds of the prisoners who were brought within hearing of them – and induce them fully to confess their crimes to escape similar sufferings. This however, is an extremely vague conjecture and does not satisfy me more than the <original> first one so the matter must still remain in doubt, <and it is of sig great> affording a charming scope for conjecture to the antiquarians & the curious.

In the afternoon we visited the cathederal formerly a temple of Minerva but now dedicated to St. Lucia.[51] Two rows of vast tuscan pillars[52] with their capitols & <col> cornice still remain and having been

51. The cathedral occupies the site and incorporates some of the structure of a temple of the Doric order, supposedly dedicated to Minerva, built in the sixth century B.C. The Christian church dates from the seventh century, and is dedicated to the Virgin Mary as Maria Theotokos; it was reconstructed between 1728 and 1754. S. Lucia (*ca.* 283–304) of Syracuse is the patron of the city. The first chapel on the right in the cathedral, built in the eighteenth century, is dedicated to her.

52. In the Tuscan order of architecture, a modification of the Doric developed in the sixteenth century, the columns are unfluted; those in the Syracuse cathedral are fluted.

duly purified are permitted to form a part of this most holy sanctuary. In the church they have several curiosities – viz an amber cup of beautiful workmanship. <the cover has> ↑the last supper is↓ carved on the cover in a space about the size of a dollar and the figures are all distinct & well formed. An antique sandal of leather & velvet, a beautiful alto relievo of the last supper on an alter in one of the side chapels[53] – a considerable number of precious reliques of saints consisting of bones &c &c among which is <t>a thigh bone of one of the disciples but I forget his name. By the way these disciples must have been an uncommon bony set of fellows. I have seen no less than five thigh bones of St. John the Baptist three arms of St. Stephen[54] and four jaw bones of St. Peter. As to the cross it is distributed all over the world and were its fragments collected together they might form a tolerably stought ship of the line. The grand curiosity of this cathederal however – is – a bomb shell! – "and thereby hangs a tale."[55]

During the seige of this city by the Spaniards while a number of pious people were assembled at their devotions in the church a large bomb shell fell thro the roof into the midst of them, you may suppose their horror & consternation at the sight of such a tremenduous visitor – just at this critical period an honest old woman present (who was undoubtedly gifted with second sight) saw the shade of <St> Lucia arise (a very pious young lady who had died some time before) run to the bomb shell, put out the fuze and thus rescue the congregation from the danger & distruction with which they were threatned. The consequences were <whagh> what might be expected from a grateful & enlightned people. The bomb shell has ever since been preserved as a sacred relique – <St.> Lucia was instantly *be sainted* – and declared the <patron> saint of the city and a day is set apart every year to celebrate her <?ca?> memory with religious processions & rejoicings.[56] <It is a pity

53. The chalice was a gift of Charles III, King of Naples and Sicily. It and presumably the sandal and the bones were in the treasury. The relief is in the Chapel of the Sacrament.

54. St. Stephen the Deacon (d. 33 A.D.) was the first Christian martyr.

55. The phrase occurs several times in Shakespeare: *As You Like It,* II, vii, 28; *The Merry Wives of Windsor,* I, iv, 159; *Othello,* III, i, 8; *The Taming of the Shrew,* IV, i, 60.

56. On May 30, 1735, a Spanish shell fell on the Castello Maniace and did not explode; it is preserved in the Chapel of St. Lucy in the Cathedral. See Privitera, *Storia di Siracusa Antica e Moderna,* II, 260. Irving is mistaken, however, in ascribing the canonization of St. Lucy to this event; she was martyred under Diocletian in 304 and her *Acta* were written before the sixth century.

they did> Such is the origin of <these> Catholic saints and it reminds one forcibly of the manner in which the gods & goddesses of the antients generally originated.

Another object that attracted my attention in Syracuse was the famous *fountain of Arethusa.* According to Ovid[57] this Arethusa was a nymph in Dianas train – Alpheus a hunter was deeply enamoured of her, <and> she however fled from him with disdain and Diana turned the Nymph into a fountain and Alpheus into a river. His love survived his metamorphosis and he mingled his waters with those of Arethusa. The antients firmly believed that th<is>e <waters> fountain was conducted by subterranean canals under the sea quite from Greece. They used to tell of <the> a cup won at the Olympic games that was thrown into the fountain of Arethusa <at> in Greece[58] and the dish of a traveller that fell in the same fountain, both of which were thrown out by the fountain Arethusa in Syracuse. They likewise pretended that the blood of the victims sacrificed at the fountain in Greece <surface> stained the waters in Syracuse. Priestcraft has been the same in all ages and scruples at no falsehood or contrivance to support its impositions.[59] Brydone mentions a spring of <salt> fresh water that boils up in the sea at some distance from Arethusa[60] which was probably the water of Alpheus that they pretended was in pursuit of Arethusa. I however neither saw this spring nor did any person in Syracuse know any thing about it. As to the fountain of Arethusa it issues out of a low subterraneous cavern in a considerable stream and running a little distance empties itself into the sea. Where it rises I could not learn, but a gentleman who resides quite the other side of the city assured me it ran under his house and several other of the inhabitants that lived nearer told me it likew<ys>ise passed under theirs.[61] The stream after its leaving the cabin is generally crowded by a great number of half naked <fem> nymphs busily employed in washing, and all the stones in the brook are nearly worn thro by the custom of beating their clothes on them. These females are seldom remarkable for beauty nor do I think the chaste diana would

57. Ovid, *Metamorphoses,* V, 409–641.

58. Irving should have written "the river Alpheus in Greece," whose partially underground course fostered the legend that it passed through the sea and rose as the fountain of Arethusa in Sicily.

59. In the last three sentences Irving seems to have drawn on Brydone, *A Tour through Sicily and Malta,* I, 277–79.

60. Brydone refers to the spring, the Occhio della Zilica, *ibid.*, p. 279.

61. There are many springs in this part of the island.

deem any of them worthy of <her so> being enrolled in her immaculate train.[62]

Syracuse <was> in the time of its highest splendor was considered as one of the wealthiest and most magnificent cities in the world. It was founded by Archias[63] a Corinthian and consisted of four parts or in a manner four cities connected together viz – Acradina, Tyche, Neapolis and Ortygia. The walls that surrounded the whole were twenty two miles in circumference. The buildings were superb – adorned with the most costly marbles – At present the only part of the mighty Syracuse that remains is the Island of Ortygia that stands like a gloomy monument to point out the situation of former grandeur and voluptuousness, to impress in a striking manner on the mind of the traveller how uncertain are our most flattring calculations.[64]

Syracuse that was once the pride and wonder of the antient world, that <seemed calculated> rejoicing in its strength seemed to bid difiance either to the open attacks of violence or the slow and secret operations of time, whose buildings vast and impregnable seemed as durable as the mountains themselves and to require equal force to over turn them – Syracuse – has gradually crumbled into dust – it has disappeared <enti> from the face of the earth and hardly a vestige is to be found of its former edifices.

"The cloud capt towers – the gorgeous palaces the solemn temples" are no more and "like the baseless fabric of a vision" have almost literally left "not a wreck behind!"[65]

The inhabitants of the modern city are as miserable as the place they inhabit. Among the nobility the slightest observer may <observe a>

62. Brydone makes the same comparison in *A Tour through Sicily and Malta,* I, 277.

63. Archias founded Syracuse in 734 B.C.

64. In this paragraph Irving seems to have drawn on two sources: Buonfiglio Costanzo, *Prima . . . Parte dell'Historia Siciliana,* p. 6; Brydone, *A Tour through Sicily and Malta,* I, 253, 266–67, 285 ff. Actually a fifth city or district, Epipolae, was embraced in the boundaries of ancient Syracuse, as noted by Costanzo, and by Swinburne, *Travels in the Two Sicilies,* II, 327.

65. Shakespeare, *The Tempest,* IV, i, 151–54, 156:

> And like the baseless fabric of this vision,
> The cloud-capp'd towers, the gorgeous palaces,
> The solemn temples . . . shall dissolve
> And . . .
> Leave not a rack behind.

remark a continual <contentintion> contention between ostentation & indigence. False pride & real meaness of spirit. The lower classes are miserably poor servile & dishonest & abominably filthy.

The officers of our ships are continually followed by a regiment of beggars as they walk the streets who will not put up with a refusal. When our vessels first rendevouzed at Syracuse it was dangerous for the Americans to walk the streets at night as they were frequently attacked – The Sicilians however soon found that they came off the worst in those encounters as the officers were generally well armed – at present they have sunk into complete awe & respect of the Americans and any one who talks english may walk the streets at any time of night in perfect security.

February 8

I strolled about the town this morning in company with Capt Hall – Wadsworth[66] Baker & Lieut Cargill,[67] in the course of our rambles we visited several convents, looking at their churches and endeavoring to get a sight of the nuns.

The first we entered was the convent of St Lucia – The church[68] is very great & prettily painted. At one end is a gallery for the nuns secured by a grating of Gilt iron. The nuns enter it by a door that opens from the convent. After having viewed the church sufficiently we returned to the parlour. Here visitors <related to the> who have relations in the convent may be permitted to talk to them thro double iron grates – but as we had no such pretence to plead we were not admitted to that indulgence. A curtain hung before the grating on the inside which excluded the view of the interior Some of the young nuns lifted it up to peep at us but on our advancing to speak to them, instantly let it drop and we could hear them tittering and laughing among themselves for some time now and then venturing another sly peep. At some of the other nunneries we were more fortunate – we were always readily admitted to a view of the churches and in one of them a novic<iate>e[69] happened to come into the gallery – As soon as she saw us she ran and

66. Charles Wadsworth (d. 1809) became purser May 28, 1798.

67. No officer of this name appears in Navy records. A Robert Cargill, however, is listed as Ordinary Seaman on the muster roll of the *Congress* for 1804–1805 (Rec. of the Dept. of the Navy, RG 45, NA).

68. It was built in the eleventh century on the spot where the saint is supposed to have been martyred.

69. The alteration is in pencil.

called several of her companions. We endeavored to converse with them but our ignorance of the language prevented us, We however kept up a kind of conversation by signs and Baker was making love to them at an extravagant rate. They seemed exceedingly delighted with our visit and laughd incessantly, kissing their hands to us most graciously. at two or three other convents we had an opportunity in like manner of conversing a little with the nuns many of whom were quite young with health beauty & innocence blooming in their countenances. The poor girls seemed all glad to see us and happy to converse a little with us.

February 10

This morning I was again rambling about among the convents in company with Lieut Morris[70] – & Dr Baker. As it was Sunday the nuns & novic<iates>es[71] had leave to walk on terraces on the tops of the convents. From hence they made signs to us as we passed waving their handkerchiefs &c. In one street we were between the wings of two convents which were low enough to see and hear the nuns very distinctly[.] here we remained above an hour, talking to them in broken italian. In one of them was a young novic<iate>e[72] that I think the most lovely girl that I have seen in Sicily. I am told she is absolutely resolved on taking the veil it being a matter of choice with her. This is not the case with all – many of them being compelled to it by their families. A nobleman here is seldom very rich and wishes to leave all his fortune with his title, of course if he has several daughters he cannot afford to portion them all[;] neither can he afford to support them should they remain unmarried[;] he is therefore obliged to put the younger ones in a convent. As the Sicilians are very apt to have numerous families the convents seldom want for new candidates. It is a painful sight to behold young <gir> females – endowed with all the graces of person and charms of countenance that can render a woman lovely with apparent sensibility of mind – sprightliness of manner & susceptibility of heart – shut up for-ever from the world – deprived of those enjoyments most grateful to her age and sex and doomed to a solitary cheerless life that presents <to the> nothing but an anticipation of the same tasteless monotony and gloomy employments.

In the evening I went to a masquerade at the theatre. An Italian mas-

70. Charles Morris (1784–1856) became midshipman July 1, 1799, was promoted in 1804 to lieutenant for his exploit in being first aboard the *Philadelphia* before Tripoli, but the action was not made official until January 28, 1807.

71. The alteration is in pencil.

72. The alteration is in pencil.

querade is one of the most stupid amusements I have ever seen. I have been at several & found them all the same. No attempt at supporting any particular character – The italians are content to dress in any grotesque unmeaning habit that can draw a momentary laugh – <Some> ↑a↓ tall strapping fellow in the dress of a woman [–] others as old men [–] others <as h> in a dress partly made up of the garments of a woman & the other of those of a man. Thus stupidly accoutred they stalk up & down the room without speaking a word to any body for fear of being recognized by their voices.

I had dressed myself in the character of an old physician which was the only dress I could procure & had a vast deal of amusement among the officers. I spoke to them in broken english mingling italian and french with it, so that they thought I was a Sicilian; as I knew many anecdotes of almost all of them I teazed them the whole evening till at length one of them discoverd me by my voice which I happened not to disguize at the moment.

February 11

About half after eight this morning I took leave of Syracuse with extreme regret. I had found so many of my fellow country men there, that it almost appeared to me as if I was again in America. Many of them, too, such noble hearted fellows and of such real merit as to excite my admiration & esteem while they secured my warmest friendship.

The party with which I set out consisted of Capt. Hall commander of marines on board the President – Wadsworth purser of the president and Wynn[73] purser of the Congress and a smart active ↑french↓ servant[74] who spoke the Sicilian very fluently.

Hall is a young fellow of Charlestown (S. C.) about twenty six years of age of a lively disposition and very agreeable manners; he will be my fellow traveller as far as Palermo as he is on an expedition to <find> collect a band of musicians for the ship and is determined to make the tour of all Sicily before he completes it. Wadsworth is about thirty – of <connet> Connecticut; a fine manly fellow with much of the peculiar humour of his country – As to Wynn he is a handsome young fellow about five & twenty full of spirits –[“]a fellow of infinite jest –”[75] that

73. Timothy Winn (d. 1836) appears as purser on the muster roll of the *Congress* for 1804–1805, having been received on board from the *Argus* (Rec. of the Dept. of the Navy, RG 45, NA). He seems not to have been officially appointed, however, until May 17, 1815.

74. The man’s name was Louis (see entry of February 19, 1805).

75. Shakespeare, *Hamlet*, V, i, 204.

can tell a *good story* sing a *good song* or say a *good thing*[76] equal to any man I ever saw. Wynn[77] and Wadsworth travelled in a Latiga;[78] a kind of carriage that resembles in some degree a Sedan chair excepting that it holds two persons face to face and is borne by two mules, one before the other behind. It is very easy – and well calculated for these rough roads. Hall & myself as likewise the Servant were on mules. The whole company was well armed with Swords & pistols having been cautioned to provide against attacks as Sicily is reputed to be full of Banditti. Our calvalcade made no mean appearance and we paraded out of Syracuse with great *éclat.* Our Equipage consisted of <7> 11 men & 7 Horses.[79]

I shall ever remember the delight I felt upon turning my back upon syracuse I had now reached to the extremity of my tour; it seemed as if my face was turned homewards and that every step brought me <neared> nearer to America.

For some distance after we left Syracuse the country was level and stoney[80] – away to our <right> ↑left↓ at a great distance we descried the Hybla mountains. After riding a little ways we passed a circular hole cut in the earth or rather rock that seemed to decend into a cavern of great magnitude – probably some branch of the catacombs. It is just aside of the road and must be highly dangerous to benighted travellers. The rocks and sides of hills in the neighborhood of Syracuse are strangely peirced into rocks & caverns many of which appear to be natural others the remains of antient Quarries. After riding some distance we had a fine view of Ætna at a vast distance – its summit covered with snow. <It appeared> The prospect reminded me of the scenery of a theatre – rows of olives planted each side of the road served for side scenes and beyond we peepd over the brow of a hill and beheld

76. Presumably the italicized words are a quotation, but their source has not been identified.

77. From this word on, this entry and those following through March 15 are in brown ink.

78. A *lettiga* was a kind of stretcher, originally used to carry the wounded in battle.

79. This sentence is crowded in at the end of the paragraph and runs over into the space between the lines of manuscript.

80. Presumably Irving and his party took the road to Catania leading north out of Syracuse across the site of Tyche to the Scala Greca, where it descends to the coast. The latter point commands a sweeping view of Etna and the sea. A short distance out of Syracuse this road passes the so-called Necropolis of Grotticelli, the site of many ancient tombs, including those alleged to be Archimedes' and Timoleon's; presumably the "hole" which Irving saw was in this neighborhood.

stretchd before us <the vast plains> a vast extent of level country from which rose the stupenduous Mount Ætna. Its immense form seemed almost shadowy from the effect of distance.

About noon we reached a convent of Capuchins[81] and as we had no prospect of finding as good a place again we determined to stop there and dine having taken care to provide ourselves with some excellent salt beef & pork from one of the ships – which was ready boiled. The old fathers received us with much humble civility and produced us a pitcher of very good white wine – which seemed to be the only article of luxury that the convent possessed for they were a very poor fraternity.

We were shewn into a dirty room in the convent <but clean> where we seated ourselves on rough benches around a <ditey> dirty table, but cleanliness did not seem to form any part of the good fathers creed. Having made a hearty meal we visited the chapel and different parts of the convent without finding any object worthy of attention excepting that one of the monks shewed us in his cell different articles in wax work of his manufacture <He they[82] was> ↑They were↓ executed with much skill and neatness – consisting of small figures – he had taught himself – and often beguiled his solitary hours by this employment – afterwards selling his productions at Catania. His choice of subjects shewed the melancholy turn of the monks thoughts – the one he was working on represented a corpse that was just becoming a prey to insects & loathsome reptiles.[83]

We quit the convent and remounted our mules in high spirits having dispatched a couple of pitchers of the good friars wine and a few glasses of their rosolia for which we gave them a liberal recompense.

The Scenery thro which we passed in the afternoon was of a more varied nature than that of the morning and in some places very beautiful. The road was nothing more than a mule path – winding along according to the nature of the ground sometimes climbing a hill and bordering along the edge of a precipice – from whence we had a view of a charming little valley of the richest fertility watered by a small stream.[84] The mules are noted for their sureness of foot and walk fearlessly – tho cautiously along the brink of precipices of the most dangerous kind.

81. Presumably in the vicinity of Priolo.

82. "they" is written over "he."

83. Irving drew on his visit with this monk when he described the creations of the monk in the convent near Vesuvius in "The Story of the Young Italian" in *Tales of a Traveller* (1824).

84. The Cantara River.

The Sicilians always hang bells to the necks of the mules as they say <they> ↑the animals↓ are fond of the sound of them and will always travel more cheerfully with them

The country around seemed but little cultivated and not very fertile – we passed ↑thro↓ no villages. In the afternoon we passed <the> in sight of Augusta which lay on the sea shore in a bay a considerable distance on our right. This is a small fortified city and contains from 8 to 10 thousand inhabitants

This is the Megara[85] of the antients, originally called Hybla and famous for the excellence of its Honey. There were three Hyblas[86] in Sicily – Hybla – major – minor & Parva – the latter is the one in question tho <bot> all three dispute the credit of having been the one <that> so celebrated for its honey – authors have been inclined to yield it to the latter <th> from its being in the neighborhood of the small river of which I spoke in the preceding page – antiently termed the Alabus and <which> whose <coasts> banks are ever coverd with flowers & odoriferous plants from whence to this day is procured the finest honey. Augusta has a small castle situated on a rock in the sea[87] which had a picturesque appearance from the place where we viewd it.

In the evening after sun down we arrived at a miserable village which our muleteers called (perhaps in derision) Poveretto del Mondo.[88] At any rate the name was characteristic of it for a more poverty struck place I never beheld. The inhabitants were ragged dirty and meagre and their habitations low <mis> wretched hovels. Yet our muleteers intended that we should stop here for the night. We refused and ordered them to proceed on to <Leontini> ↑Lentini↓ where we were sure of a tolerable inn & expected to meet with Mr Dyson[89] the American agent who had set off two or three days before us. The muleteers began to expostulate in the bawling vociferous manner of the Sicilians,

85. Megara Hyblaea is across the bay from Augusta. Buonfiglio Costanzo identifies the two in *Prima . . . Parte dell'Historia Siciliana,* pp. 20, 21.

86. The three Hyblas in Sicily are Hybla Major, also called Magna and Geleatis, on the site of the present Paternò; Hybla Minor or Parva or Megara Hyblaea, believed to be the source of the ancient Hyblaean honey; and Hybla Heraea on the site of the present Ragusa. Apparently Irving did not know that "parva" and "minor" have the same meaning.

87. Augusta has three forts on islets in the harbor: Garzia, Vittoria, and d'Avalos.

88. "Little Poverty of the World"; the village was probably Villasmundo.

89. George Dyson served as American naval agent at Syracuse from May 25, 1804, to about September 1807; he left Gibraltar on September 24, 1807 (Miscellaneous Letters Sent by the Secretary of the Navy, RG 45, NA).

representing the badness of the roads the danger of Banditti &c But we were immoveable in our resolution of proceeding – As for the badness of the roads, a bright moon light renderd us easy as to that – and in respect to Banditti – we were five of us – well armd and could give them a tolerable reception besides we scarcely imagined that we could run a greater hazard of having our throats cut on the road than in such a vilainous looking place as the village. We therefore obliged the muleteers, tho unwillingly, to proceed. We found, in truth, that they had not deceived us respecting the roads which were extremely stoney and rugged but the evening was bright and delightful and our mules found their way without stumbling. In two or three places the road wound thro hollows surrounded by precipices which were full of dark caverns. In many of these the peasants live who tend flocks of sheep or herds of cattle driving the animals into the caverns at night. These wild & solitary places seemed admirably calculated for the haunts of Banditti and having heard so much of the numerous bands that infest Sicily I almost expected sometimes to see a troop rush from on[e] of the caverns as we passd. Our march however was unmolested except now and then by a shepherds Dog who disturbed by the noise of our bells & the bawling of the muleteers sallied out with open mouth in defence of his masters property. At a late hour we arrived at Lentini where we found a tolerable Inn for Sicily tho it would have been considered execrable in any other country. We had a <late> supper which to our sharp stomachs seemed delicious The people furnished us with fowls &c which our Servant <(who> cooked very decently. In fact we found him a most useful fellow. He was half frenchman half Italian understood french italian – Sicilian & English and could turn his hand to any thing. We were furnished with clean beds and passd the night very comfortably congratulating ourselves continually at having escaped the filth & wretchedness of *Poveretto del Mondo.*

February 12

before setting off this morning we walked about the town which is but an indifferent place – tho *rich* in convents & churches.[90] This is said to be one of the most antient cities of Sicily and to have been originally

90. The churches of Lentini are the cathedral or Matrice (S. Alfio), S. Luca, the Chiesa della Fontana or dei Martiri, and the Chiesa della SS. Trinita. Most of them date from the eighteenth century, the town having been virtually destroyed in the earthquake of 1693.

inhabited by the Lestrigons[.][91] it still retains its antient name <Leon> tho slightly changed. (from Leontin<i>o to Lentini) Hercules is said to have given them a Lion for a Standard from whence probably is derived the name of the city. The Lestrigons and Cyclops were the original inhabitants of Sicily and represented as savages & cannibals – clothed in skins & living in caves of the mountains. <Me> All historians join in mentioning that the original people of Sicily lived in caves and probably the vast number of caves to be seen at this day throughout Sicily may have been their habitations. The poorer class of peasants in Sicily even at present abide frequently in holes in the <mountains> rocks which they fit up into rooms closing the entrances with rude mason work of stones & mud & leaving doors & windows, which have a singular appearance in the sides of the precipices.

In the morning we passed thro a series of delightful plains the soil of which appeared extremely fertile and was clothed with the freshest verdure. These were the antient Lestrigonian plains celebrated by the antients for their fertility; at a distance we saw Lake Beverio which fable relates to have been made by Hercules. It abounds with fish & wild fowl, among the former is a species of Eel highly esteemd by epicures. We passed over a hill on which <In> were some antient ruins[92] which we were told were the remains of an amphitheatre tho to me they had little the appearance of being so. I endeavored at a house hard by to get some information concerning them and the name of the city that must antiently have stood there – but these were questions which it could not be expected that <ignorant> Sicilian peasants should answer who seem to me to have few ideas that do not relate to their immediate interest or concerns.

At length we had a noble view of Catania from an eminence. Before us lay the great catanian plains specled with troops of cattle and watered by the wandering Giarretta.[93] (the antient Simetus) Beyond it was the beautiful city of Catania its fair walls reflected in the tranquil bosom of the vast bay <which spreads before it> ↑at the bottom of which it is

91. In his account of Lentini, the Laestrygones and other early inhabitants of Sicily, the Leontine plains and the legends about Hercules in this paragraph and the next Irving drew on Swinburne, *Travels in the two Sicilies,* II, 313, 315, and on Buonfiglio Costanzo, *Prima . . . Parte dell'Historia Siciliana,* p. 21, 46, 415.

92. They do not seem to have been noted by other travelers or by guide books to the region.

93. The Giarretta is formed by the union of the Simeto (anciently the Symaethus) and the Gornalunga rivers.

situated↓ – and behind it rose the mighty Ætna its sides streakd with black torrents of lava and its summit presenting a contrast of cheerless winter to the luxurient spring that smiled around its skirts. We arrived at <this> Catania about two oclock and put up at the hotel of the golden Lion.

The Streets of Catania had a lively appearance, <being> and gave an idea of the cities being populous. Handsome carriages with rich liveries are very common – but this is the case in <all> most Italian and Sicilian towns – every person who would aspire to gentility & fashion must keep a carriage. There is generally a *corso* in the vicinity of the town – or in default of it – a large Street within the town – where the fashionable world resort in the evening in their carriages and ↑ride↓[94] up & down in two lines saluting each other as they pass.

In Catania this takes place in the principal street[95] into which the windows of our Hotel look. They also drive round the square[96] in front of the Cathederal – When the carriages have driven three or four times about the Corso they generally draw out of the main stream and stand still surveying the other carriages as they pass by in review.

This appears to me a most insipid recreation and by no means comparable to a ramble in a public walk where one may meet & talk with ones friends – for here there is no such thing as conversation – every thing is carried on by pantomime and they can only salute <each other> ↑their friends↓ by a nod of the head or wave of the hand as they whirl past each other.

While at dinner we were waited on by the Chevalier Landolini[97] to whom we had brought Letters of introduction from his Brother who is antiquarian to the King of Naples at Syracuse.

The Chevalier is a Knight of Malta and related to some of the first families in Catania. He is a very lively agreeable little fellow of about 45 years of age and has politely offerd to be our cicerone in shewing us the curiosities of the place.

After dinner (the Chevalier having left us) we went to the cathederal

94. "ride" is in pencil.

95. The Corso; now Via Vittorio Emanuele.

96. The Piazza del Duomo.

97. Pietro Landolina, brother of Saverio (nn. 37 and 40), became a Knight of Malta in 1790. He received the title of Marchese di Trezzano and di Sant'Alfano, held many public offices in Sicily, and wrote many works. See G. B. Crollalanza, *Nobiliario Storico delle Famiglie Nobili e Notabili Italiane* (Pisa, 1885), pp. 7–8; *Memorie delle Famiglie Nobili* (Napoli, 1875), pp. 104–5.

which is dedicated to St. Agatha the Saint who has Catania under her peculiar protection.[98] As <it> ↑there↓ was a féte in honor of the Saint – the cathederal was to be superbly illuminated and the image of the Saint to be carried round in religious procession. It was dark when we enterd the church which we found lighted up by an immense number of [*illegible*] wax candles stuck around the cornices &c It was crowded by the populace repeating their prayers most vociferously. The Service was performing and the organ played one of those peices of church music in which the Italians so highly excel. After bustling about thro the crowd for a long time we at length found ourselves in front of the chapel of St. Agatha which is at the upper end of the church & seperated from the rest of it by a grate of gilt Iron. We were looking thro the grate when an old gentleman who was seated on the inside with two ladies – observing by our dress that we were strangers came and spoke to the guard who immediately opened the grate and desired us to walk in. We complied most cheerfully as we had been much incommoded by the crowd whose curiosity appeared to be highly excited by the uniform of my companions & our strange language. The old gentleman was extremely polite to us – shewing us the interior of the chapel. He introduced us to the Ladies – one of whom spoke french very fluently & I had a long conversation with her. From their manners and the profound respect shewn them we judged them to be people of distinction. <They>

<After remaining here a little w>

In about half an hour the procession commenced from the other side of the church. The priests bearing the bust of St. Agatha[99] under a crimson velvet canopy. They were surrounded by the throng <of> who were enthusiastic in their exclamations – Stretching their arms towards the image – throwing their hats into the air and making the most hideous uproar. It was brought into the chapel where we were standing – the folding doors of <the> which were immediately closed – the mob pressed against the bars – stretching their arms thro the grates and calling on their *Santissima, carissima, Santa Agatha.* (most <holl> holy and dear St Agatha). The bust was deposited in an inner part of the chapel where it is inclosed in a curious shrine representing a <sm>

98. The cathedral was founded in 1092 and has been rebuilt many times after damage by earthquakes. St. Agatha (d. *ca.* 250), a native of either Palermo or Catania, suffered martyrdom in Catania. Her festal day is February 5.

99. It was executed in 1376 by workmen in enamel at Limoges and by the goldsmith Giovanni di Bartolo of Siena. The skull of the saint is preserved inside.

Gothic building[100] – which contains also the heart of St Agatha – these valuable articles are secured by strong <Irond> Iron doors.

We were admitted into this *Sanctum Sanctorum* and allowed to examine the image as narrowly as we pleased – which considering its extraordinary sanctity and our being vile heretics was an unusual stretch of civility.

It is the figure of a good natured looking little woman and is covered over with precious stones to an immense amount so that we no longer wonderd at the care with which it was secured by bolts & bars

This St. Agatha is looked up to by the populace of Catania with peculiar reverence and devotion – for they consider her as their cheif safeguard against the tremenduous convulsions and flaming torrents of Ætna.

These people must certainly be of the most steadfast faith in matters of religion for tho St. Agatha has permitted their city to be repeatedly laid in ruins yet they still place as great confidence in her protection as ever. I was mentioning to a Sicilian servant at the Inn my opinion that St. Agatha was rather careless of her charge when in 1693[101] she sufferd a torrent of Lava to overwhelm the largest & finest part of Catania. He shook his head and said the saint was not to blame. The people of Catania had been very wicked and inattentive to their devotions when St. Agatha determined to give them a lesson she therefore permitted the Lava to over run *a part* of Catania, that the other part might see from what miseries she had preserved them & take warning accordingly. Such is the flimsy manner in which the priests impose upon the credulity of this superstitious people

NB. In this sanctum sanctorum I had my pocket picked.[102]

[*Forty-six blank pages intervene between the entry of February 12*

100. The reliquary of St. Agatha is a creation of gold of the fifteenth and sixteenth centuries, kept in a small chamber in the wall of the chapel. Irving is mistaken about its containing the saint's heart.

101. The eruption of Etna in 1693 was the most disastrous on record, destroying not only Catania but fifty other cities and towns in Sicily.

102. This sentence is in pencil. Among the contents of Irving's wallet stolen on this occasion was the handkerchief of a Genoese woman whom he admired. She was said to be an Italian named Bianca, who was married to a Frenchman and who subsequently sent Irving a lock of her hair (PMI, I, 196–98). Presumably this was the same woman whom Peter Irving called Madame la Fleche ("Peter Irving's Journal," ed. Leonard Beach, Theodore Hornberger, and Wyllis E. Wright, *Bulletin of the New York Public Library*, XLIV, 1940, 602).

and that of March 7, 1805, in the manuscript journal. The entries in Irving's notebook for this period (all in pencil) are interpolated here so that the sequence of his activities may be preserved. For the rest of these "Traveling Notes, 1804–1805" and a description of the manuscript, see page 514. In his letter to William Irving, April 4, 1805, Irving wrote that while in Naples (March 7–23, 1805), he was "busied in bringing up my journal in sicily," that is, presumably in writing the journal from the notes; but evidently he did not finish doing so. In giving a resumé of his Sicilian journey in this letter he drew on his journal.]

February 13

<13 Having been a little generous in our remun> Our arrival has got wind among the town world and we have been crouded this morning with amber merchants beggars &c An old monk brought us a present of some pickles & oranges for which of course we had to pay 5 times their value[.] in fact our room is in a continual croud and confusion. <After> breakfast the Chevalier Landolini arrivd and we went with him to see some vaults the decent to which is in front of the cathederal of St Agatha. These are remains of antient grecian baths.[103] They are arched and built of brick & lava and extend to a considerable distance[.] on some parts <of> where the walls were plaisterd are the traces of antient coarse reliefs of figures &c[.] in one place we were shewn <the> an aqueduct of limpid water that runs thro the vault having been constructed in modern times The vaults are <h> not as high as they formerly were being filld up in a great degree by earth They are extremely perfect and in several of the posts the holes are remaining for the admission of the pivots or hinges upon which the doors turned. These vaults extend under the Streets and we <could> heard the carriages rolling over our heads making a rumbling like thunder. In these places the vaults are <arched> secured by plaistering latterly. The walls in many places are extremely wet and the water dropping congeals below. From hence we went to a place where the Lava had overflowed the walls. We descended ↑in a large opening of the lava↓ by a stairs to the level of the ground <a lav> where there is an excellent spring of water. The lava here is about 80 feet deep. In another place we descended into another hole where we were pointed out the place to which the sea formerly flowd and a granite pillar to which they used to tie vessels <to> The sea is now driven back to a great distance by

103. They were called the Terme Achillee.

the lava. After examining these we went to the ruins of the antient theatre[104] This was <formerl> built in form of a half circle and must have been extremely magnificent – built of <th> Lava. Three ranges of seats, lobbies & stares still perfect – seats also remaining but <the> stripped of the marble that formerly coverd them. This Theatre was filled up with earth by an earthquake but the former prince of Biscaris[105] had it cleard out at a great expence. He found in it a great number of statues cornices medals & small figures &c which he placed in his museum. This theatre has been of a vast size and together with the extent & magnificence of the other ruins testifies that this has been a grand & important place formerly. We then repaired to the museum of the Prince of Biscaris where we were shown a number of antique statues with antique figures utensils &c &c in bronze – a handsome collection of minerals & stones Some old armor which we tried on <but> It had been richly gilt and ornamented There was also a lance without a point such as was formerly used in jousts. an enormous sword. <an> weapons <of> & fire arms of different ages & countries, monstrous bottles antique vases

At dinner we were attended by a band of musicians as Capt Hall is about engaging one for the ship. In fact we are crouded by every species of being as we have been a little free with our money – <which> just as we were finishing our dinner a woman enterd who juggled with cards &c We of course had to see her tricks. When walking the streets we have generally a dozen or two at our heels attracted by the sight of the regimentals.

In the evening went to the opera[106] where we met the Chevalier Landolini who carried us to two or three boxes & introduced us to the Princess [*blank*][107] and several <of> other ladies of nobility[.] they were very polite and I found several that could talk french. They were very particular in enquiring about America & <if> what language we spoke[.] they could hardly believe that we were the same as the english –

104. The Roman amphitheater, built on Greek foundations, dates from the first century B.C.

105. Ignazio Paternò Castello, Prince of Biscari (1719–1786), excavated most of the ruins at Catania. The Museo Biscari, comprising his collection of antiquities and natural history specimens, is now incorporated in the Museo Civico.

106. Presumably it was in the Teatro Massimo Bellini.

107. Probably she was the Princess Marianna Ramacca (see entries of February 18, 25, 1805).

February 14

This morning ↑we↓ visited the convent of <St. Lucia> [*blank*][.] here we were introduced to the abbess but she had taken care to send the handsome nuns out of sight. <She> The nuns asked for loaf sugar to make sweet things[.] they also asked if we had any seed of American flowers[.] we were sorry that we had none with us.

Visited the convent of Benedictines fine church of noble size.[108] elegant altars of the best marble several of the real verd antique – The convent of vast extent with a clipd garden the earth spread on the antient lava. After viewing the convent & garden we returned to church where we heard a piece of exquisite music on the finest organ in italy[109] – immitation of echo. visited an antient ampitheatre[110] under the ground [–] having been coverd by lava it is clearing out at present [–] chambers for wild beasts apertures for giving them food &c

We cant stop to purchase any thing but that we are surround[e]d by a croud who stare at us as if we had dropd from the cloud

In the afternoon we paid another visit to the convent of Benedictines to see their museum[111] This consists of a very handsome collection of antiques natural history &c but arranged in glass cases which are very dirty so that we could not examine them. The convent has likewise a large library[.][112] <this> ↑corridors↓ of the convent 700 feet long [–] fine view from cupolo – Lava runs round the city. In the evening to the masquerade at theatre – place small. We were in Dominos.[113] Went in Box of princess [*blank*][,][114] danced[,] saw a number of handsome faces

PS. This morning walking with Wadsworth early we were addressed by a child of about 1<0>2 Years old clothd in the tatterd garments of a student who gave us a very long detail in elegant italian of the distresses of his family &c &c & desired charity. We had heard before of this <chil> boy as being remarkably smart having taught himself to

108. The monastery of S. Nicolò or S. Benetto, one of the largest in Europe, was first built between 1558 and 1578; destroyed in the earthquake of 1693, it was rebuilt between 1693 and 1735. The adjoining church of S. Nicolò, the largest in Sicily, was built between 1693 and 1735.

109. The work of Donato del Piano, a Calabrian priest, it has 5 keyboards, 72 stops, and 2916 pipes.

110. It lies beneath the Piazza Stesicoro and is still largely unexcavated.

111. It is now part of the Museo Communale.

112. It is now part of the Biblioteca Civica, of which it comprised the original nucleus.

113. The term denotes both half-masks and loose cloaks worn as disguises; probably Irving's party wore half-masks.

114. Probably the Princess Ramacca (see entries of February 18, 25, 1805).

speak latin fluently &c and that his conversation was particularly correct We desired him to call at the Hotel when all of us would be together & might give him something handsome. He called accordingly when the officers had determined to take him [*entry left unfinished*]

February 15

This morning went with the Chevalier Landoline to see a Russian Painter[115] who has been <employed> taking views of Mount Ætna[.] we [he] shewed sevral very elegant sketches and drawing[s] of his of different parts of Sicily. Returnd to dine – we were immediately botherd by amber merchants &c. A monk brot us a present <from> of fruit and a little while after there came a large cake coverd with sugar from the convent of [*blank*][116]

After dinner we set out on mules to ascend part of Mount Ætna. We had been assured repeatedly that it was impossible to get to the summit but we were determined to see as much as we could. Chevalier Landoline accompanied us part of the way on an elegant horse. miserable roads over the lava <fields> ↑Port of Achilles↓[117] [–] vast floods of lava [–] surface uneven [–] in many places coverd with the richest soil & verdure & amazingly fertile [–] in others the soil was just beginning to form itself and presented a curious picture of trees growing out of black lava [–] pretty mountaineer girl. delightful view of catania – plains of catania & Syracuse & sea – riant landscape [–] villages built of Lava – <P.S. Port> but very miserable – Port of Ulysses pointed out to us – three rocks in the sea called Cyclops. they are the rocks the poets said the Cyclops threw after the ship of Ulysses.[118] <Beggar woman with two daughters demanded charity – one of the girls had a fine countenance which lookd lovely in spight of her rags & dirt>[.] arrived at the country house of our Landlord situated in the village of [*blank*][119]

115. Probably Feodor Michailowitsch Matwejeff, or Matveef (1758–1826).

116. Presumably it came from the convent he visited on February 14.

117. Presumably Irving should have written "Port of Ulysses." The Porto d-Ulisse, or the Bay of Lognina, is supposed to be that described in Virgil, *The Æneid,* III, 570.

118. Homer, *The Odyssey,* IX. There are seven islands altogether, three of which are much higher than the others.

119. The village was probably Mascalucia (see n. 120). The hotel Leone d'Oro was operated by the well-known Don Lorenzo Abbate, whose vulgar nickname was "Cacca Sangue" (Brian Hill, *Observations and Remarks in a Journay through Sicily and Calabria in the Year 1791,* London, 1792, p. 195).

Shortly after our arrival we went <to> with Landlord to the house of Don Luigi Antonio Vaspisardi[120] a [one] of the first personages in the village who has a conversazione at his house every evening. He speaks french so that I could converse freely with him. I found him very intelligent & agreeable & much of the gentleman In a little while a number more of the villagers droppd in so that we had a <?mu?> clever assemblage. The evening passd in singing music & dancing This is the way says don Luigi that we pass our time. We are removd from the great world surrounded by lava in the old habitations of the cyclops – we must therefore depend upon each other for pleasure & amusement & cultivate the utmost harmony – Don Luigi supped with us & I was continually delighted with the ingenious nature of his remarks.

February 16

This morning Don Luigi breakfasted with us after which we set forward to ascend higher up this mountain.

Miserable villages – beggar woman. Lava boils as it flows [–] last eruption from Mount Rosso [–] ascended the crater – minerals – ashes – lava 1 league & ½ [–] extensive prospect Sand extended to Adriatic[121] – superb prospect. Catania – plains with rivers winding thro it – Syracuse – Calabrian mountains coverd with snow. plain of sand. The summit does not make eruptions any more – coverd with clouds – cloudy day. Stones around the crater [–] side of crater broken for the escape of the lava [–] barren region destroyed by the eruption [–] crater of an old volcano about the time of J. C. [–] gatherd minerals &c [–] fired of[f] a Pistol to hear the echoes. descended rapidly – crossd the plain of sand to the convent of St Nichola d'Arena[122] formerly the habitation of the fathers of the benedictine convent of Catania. 300 years old. Old <priest> monk received us gave us good wine resembling muscat – birds in the convent – Cupid & Psyche[123] [–] gave us a small keg of wine. We had to give up ascending the mountain further as the

120. Don Luigi Antonio Rapisardi di S. Antonio (1767–1859) was born and died in Mascalucia. He had a doctor's degree in juridical science, held several high offices in the Kingdom of the Two Sicilies, was much concerned with music and literature, and numbered among his friends many Europeans. (Information furnished from the family archives by Baron Matteo Rapisardi di S. Antonio of Catania.)

121. Irving should have written "Ionian."

122. S. Nicola d'Arena was founded in 1156 by Simon, Count of Policastro, nephew of Roger I. The monastery was transferred to Catania in 1518.

123. Presumably a painting.

day was advanced and it threatned rain [–] we therefore descended. Snow falling on the summit – raind below [–] all the high parts of the mountain coverd with clouds – road thro the lava – Thought of my friends as I rode along – arrived at village & had hardly descended when all the folks flockd to dinner so that we had hardly time to get into another room to dress – Jovial time at dinner. Seated ourselves aside the girls & made love to them. The visitors eat ravenously & got half tipsey. brought in Rosolia which they seemd to relish mightily. Hot punch finishd the buisness – they were quite happy <&> noisy & loving. We adjourned to the house of Don Luigi where we had music & dancing the whole evening –

Set out this morning to return to Catania[.] Don Luigi calld to bid us farewell – Joannas[124] unlucky fall whereby secrets came to light – saw our mountain lasses at a window – rainy morning – arrived safe at Catania. Last sundays in carnival firing of guns. Masqued figures in the street. two old whimsical looking men in silk coats with books[,] one blank[,] which they shewd to people pretending to tell their fortune & while they were looking turnd <far> over a page & blew a quantity of flour in their faces – a sportsman who had a gun of reed filld with dust[.] he came behind people as they <st> lookd another way tapd them on the shoulder & when they turnd round blew the dust in their faces. <clowns> punchinellos with bladders on the end of sticks with which they floggd the multitude [–] a man in grotesque habit seated in a childs chair on wheels drawn by four Punchinellos – Group of Dancers &c In the evening at Opera – benefit of the prima donna who sent us tickets – The audience brilliant – a great number of handsome women

February 17

Walked about the city [–] large convents. Houses mostly new the old city having been destroyed by the eruptions of Etna. Streets long & straight & intersect each other at right angles. Numerous carriages of the nobility which drive backwards & forwards thro the principal streets in the evenings – number of men with swords carrying a man to prison. His brother pelted them with stones[.] he was chased by a man with a sword & pistol but who did not dare to approach him[.] he got safe to a church where of course he was protected – dastardly nature of a Sicilian mob.

124. Presumably a member of Abbate's household.

February 18

This morning visited the cabinet of natural history of Don Joseph Joanne[.][125] fine collection of Volcanic productions of Mount Etna – Vessuvius & the Lipari islands with a variety of other Sicilian productions. Visited the caffe & billiard room of the nobility, introduced by Landolini Recvd. an invitation to a ball & masque to be given this evening at the Hotel Di Ville[126] by the nobility –

In the evening at the masque – saloon large & crowded – great variety of masques – but poorly supported – number of handsome women – Had great attention shewd us – danced several times – Parted with regret from the cavaliers – Italian masquerades <are> stupid.

Letter given us by the Princess [*blank*] for her sister in Palermo. Women in Catania very lecherous – their intrigues [–] fond of strangers[.] amber found in great Quantities in a small river near to Catania[127]

February 19

Set out this morning on our rout to Palermo <in company with>[.] our retinue was Capt Hall his servt the muleteer & myself. rain<y> in abundance – Chevalier Landolini came to <accompany> bid us farewell and to accompany us on our rout for the day but was deterd by the rain [–] bid Honest Winn farewell – raind continually as we rode thro the Catanian plain <ocean> surf beating on the sea shore – had to stop at a house named a tavern to shelter from the severe rain – miserable hut old man & woman & several children huddled round a fire in the middle of the hut on the earth – with no other aperture for the smoke to escape but the door [–] vermin – hunger of the people [–] pretty girl but dirty & ragged [–] 3 miles to the next village – The people good humord but rude in their manners. Old woman enquired what could induce such gallant cavaliers to come to such a poor miserable country – went to the inn [–] eat chicken [–] comforted ourselves with rosolia [–] old man pounded salt with a stone on a dirty board. When rain held up a little we pushd forward till we came to a ferry over the river Barca[128] There our muleteer wished us to stop & pass the

125. Giuseppe Gioeni (1747–1822), Sicilian naturalist, was especially noted for his observations of Etna.

126. Presumably the Palazzo del Comune, or Municipio, built in 1741.

127. Presumably the letter was given Irving by the Princess Marianna Ramacca for the Princess Stephania Camporeale (see entry of February 25, 1805, n. 158).

The amber of the Simeto River has been famous since ancient times.

128. Probably the place was Barca di Giarretta.

night but there was but one house at the ferry & that was so miserable that we thought we could not fare worse farther on[?] We crossd the ferry and joggd along very sociably. The weather had held up & we were more chearful. Vast quantities of wild fowl[?] along the road but the people are starving amid the luxuries of life[.] about dark arrivd at what our guide called the village of Asfero[*][129] <which>[.] it consists of but three or four hovels & only one of them appeared to be inhabited[.] food too meagre to tarry[?] cooking the supper which consisted of cabbage & wine[?][.] had a fire made on the floor and changing our boots we felt more comfortable[.] no chimney for the smoke[.] attackd a bottle of brandy[.] Louis[130] and the capt first endeavord to pursuade the people to drink some[.] they tried it but could not relish it he laughd at them and tosted off a glass of it by way of bravado[.] poor Louis soon felt the effects of it. We had finished with it[?] and Louy was sick to his stomach[?][.] all at once his knife <dropd> ↑fell↓ forward[?] jaw droppd & he fell back pale as a corps large drops of cold sweat rolling off of his forehead. People had no place in their house for us to sleep as it consisted of but two miserable little rooms[.] they informed us that we might sleep in the chapel which was the other side of the road facing their house. We acceded to the proposition with pleasure as we were in hopes of finding less fleas there. Poor Louis who had by this time got over his sickness made a wry face at the idea of sleeping in the chapel[.] he said he had every possible respect for *Le bon dieu* but he should not wish him for a maitre de Hotel. We had a quantity of straw spread in one corner of the chapel on which we spread a matrass we had brought with us <we put our> We were furnished with a small lamp & a pot of oil and securing the door of the chapel with a bolt & a stake that we found within we coverd ourselves with a blanket & great coat with our port manteaus under our heads for pillow[s.] poor louis spread some straw along side of our mattrass and laying a mule cloth on it he <commande> desired Le bon dieu to entertain his visitors well[.] we had brought all our baggage into the chapel & put our swords & pistols under our heads. I never slept sounder in my life but poor louis complaind terribly in the morning that what between fleas & the furies of the rain he had not slept an hour the whole night.

[*] (18 miles from Catania)

129. Sferro.
130. Hall's servant.

February 20[131]

In the morning sat out at day break and continued along the plains country still level but mountains in the distance – beautiful sunrise. Ætna partially visible. The country rich soil – a fine loam but carelessly cultivated[.] people squalid & miserable. <Stones> Round stones in the plain such as were antiently used in battles <?cut?> thrown by ↑a↓ machine called *catapulta* – great number of wild pidgeons plover curlews snipe &c[.] <at> between 7 & 8 oclock arrived at the village monomente[132] 8 miles from Asfero. <ran> consists of ranges of low cabins – inn wretchd[.] they had never seen americans before

Sat out after breakfast in the rain[.] it however soon held up & the afternoon was delightful – rich soil – plains well cultivated no hedges fences or enclosures[.] people live in miserable straw hovels probably temporary. plow with wooden plows – vast flocks of sheep & horned cattle – Passd thro the celebrated vale of Enna where Prosperine was carried off by pluto. Here was antiently a city of the same name with a celebrated temple to Ceres.[133] Plain has flowers scatterd over it even at this time of year but must be infinitely so in spring. no trees to be seen in <this> our route. towns situated on Hills viz. St Phillipo d Arragone Assaro[134] &c. Mules bad continually stumbling – roads muddy.

Arrived at village of Quadarara[135] [–] a few wretched houses Inn without water & hardly any furniture[.] purchased fowls & set Louis to work to fricaasee them & make soup [–] comfortable supper. The landlord brought us a large mattrass Hall chose to sleep on it I examind it & found it so full of fleas that I preferd to spread his mattrass on six chairs & wrapping myself in [a] great coat slept on it with portmanteau & pistols under my head. Louis slept in an adjoining little chamber. I had scarcely got asleep when I was awoke by him calling in italian "whos there"[.] I asked him what was the matter and he said he heard some one at the door[.][136] I laid my hand on a pistol with a determina-

131. The date has been added by the editor for the convenience of the reader. There is no break in the manuscript at this point.

132. Catenanova, called in the dialect of the region Mulimenti (information furnished by Baron Giuseppe Rapisardi di Antonio of Florence).

133. Enna was founded by a colony of Syracusans in 664 B.C. A temple to Ceres, of whose worship this was the chief seat, was built in 480 B.C.

134. S. Filippo d'Agirò, now Agira; Assoro.

135. Calderari, which derives its name from the Italian word for coppersmith, *calderaio,* in the Sicilian dialect *quadarara* (information furnished by Baron Giuseppe Rapisardi di San Antonio of Florence).

136. Faint traces of words underneath the journal entries show about here. "Mascalucia" is the only distinguishable word.

tion to fire if the door opend. I heard nothing however & soon fell asleep when I was again awakned by Louis voice. He had heard another noise at the door and seizing his dirk he groped along to it and opened it when in bolted a poor dog who had probably been attracted by the smell of our supper I had a hearty laugh at Louis adventure. Slept soundly but Hall & Louis were kept awake half the night with the fleas. <Sat off>

February 22

Sat off at Sunrise [–] cold morning [–] slight shower – country mountainous – hedges of aloes & prickly pears [–] plantations of olives & almonds the latter in full bloom. Castrogovanne[137] on a hight mountain – <a> said to be a good town with a large castle & lake on top of a mountain. Ascended to the town of Calascebetta[138] built on a neighboring mountain – ↑It is a principality↓ difficult ascent, winding intricately among the defiles and often along the edges of immense precipices[.] road slippery [–] my horse stumbled sevral times in the most dangerous places – enterd the lower part of the town & rode along the brink of a precipice[.] caverns in the rock where people lived [–] miserable houses – <w> a variety of wretchedness. People stared at us with the most stupid surprize For a hotel they were a going to shew us over a jail – we got into a miserable chamber with a dirty wooden table a bench & two crazy chairs – Town was antiently built by Count Rugario who erected a strong castle here for the purpose of subduing the neighboring city of Castrogovanne[.] 15. churches – poor convent for women – 5000 inhabitants [–] fine prospect from the highest part of the town – cultivated hills around Valley of Enna [–] at a distance Ætna – shrouded in clouds – bay of Catania. The house where we breakfasted at was soon surrounded by beggars. Gave an old decrepid man the remains of our meal. He pocketed the cold fowl & drank nearly a bottle of wine at a draught. When we mounted our mules we were surrounded by ragged children begging – we had a number of coppers in our pockets and threw them among them[.] they fell to scrambling

137. Castrogiovanni was the name of Enna from 1087 to 1927. Its altitude is 3110 feet. The castle was built by Frederick II at the end of the thirteenth century. The lake to which Irving refers is presumably Lago di Pergusa, south of Enna, from the shores of which Pluto is said to have abducted Proserpine.

138. Calascibetta has an altitude of 2880 feet. The town was founded by the Saracens in 851 and was fortified by Roger II, first king of Sicily. The most notable churches in Calascibetta are the cathedral, or Matrice, dating from the fourteenth century, the Chiesa del Carmine, S. Antonio, and S. Pietro.

& in the mean time we got off. Road continually ascending & descending mountains – cold wind on the summits P.S. Shepherd boy on side of a hill near the valley of Enna playing on a reed – mountain at a distance with snow on the summit[.] crossed the river [*blank*][139] repeatedly. About ½ past three arrivd at the village of Alimina – it consists of miserable cabins with two or three convents & churches – it is a marquisite. <Hot> Inn more tolerable than any we have seen on our rout having several rooms – fat Landlady [–] filth of the streets – abject misery of the inhabitants We had but made 20 miles this day and there were still sevral hours of sun but our driver told us we must rest here[,] it was 18 miles to the next village and the roads were bad so that we would be unable to arrive there till long after dark The fellow seems a stupid animal and has delayd us greatly by his bad mules &c[.] he promised to procure an additional mule to morrow & to get us to termina[140] in the evening. Hall swore if he <das> decieved him in this assurance he would give him a sound drubbing. We were to have got to Palermo in two days & half and now we shall be near 5 days. Had comfortable bed without fleas and slept sound.

February 23

Sat off at day break. Muleteer had provided a horse in place of a mule that had tired yesterday – the Horse worse than the mule – Louis threatnd him with the bastinado. The roads mountainous & muddy [–] country solitary – hardly a hut to be seen & those that we did see were more miserable than the cabins of our savages [–] many of them caverns in the rocks. I had continual amusement with poor Louis & his horse. the animal always laggd behind and he abused him incessantly. The muleteer insisted it was a good mule and was a little boisterous till Louis pulld out a pistol & swore he would shoot him. The poor muleteer threw up his hands & started back in astonishment. Ah meo dio – <cried he vostre excellenza> meo dio cried he He took care afterwards to keep at a good distance from louis. We arrived about 12 oclock at Caltavuturo a small village – a Barony Here we were shewn to a wretched hotel. We immediately orderd the muleteer to get another horse – A few moments after Louis came up on foot – he had stuck in the mud – floggd the owner of the horse & walkd on foot. The poor muleteer had a crowd round him to whom he related his providential

139. There are several rivers on the route which Irving followed this day, the chief of which is the Salso between Calascibetta and Alimena.

140. Términi Imerese.

escape from a man whom he declard had intended to take away his life. As soon as Louis enterd the tavern he flogged the other muleteer and told him if he did not get a better animal and arrive at Termini that night he would give him a tremenduous bastinado. The threat had a good effect. we had an excellent horse and performed the rest of our days Journey with redoubled dispatch. Caltavuturo is situated in a picturesque manner on a mountain with rock towering over it on the summit of which are the ruins of an old castle.[141] On several rocks <around> at a distance are the ruins of other castles[.] rugged descent from the mountain [–] wild country [–] masses of Rock. Arrived on sea coast. Saw termini at a distance[.] road along sea coast. Arrived at termini after dark. Much fatigued [–] laid down & slept till supper. At supper we heard that there was to be a <masquerade> ↑ball↓ in the evening at a private house but that we would be readily admitted. A gentleman enterd our room in masque of a turke who offerd to introduce us there as he was an acquaintance.[142] Hall who is ever ready for a frolic urged me to go. I consented & in sport dressd myself in one of his uniform coats & passd for a captain. <Numerous> handsome house. numerous company – polite reception. There was a <figure dance> ↑ballet↓ of the wood cutters to commence the ball – Several of the company held up scenery. We had partners <?ala?> introduced to us[.] I danced with the daughter of the Baron Palmeria[143] the master of the house & afterwards with another lady of the town. They were all very attentive to us The master of the house regretted that we could not stay longer at Termini in which case he should have been happy to have shewn us every possible attention

Termin<y>i contains about 3000 Inhabitants – <it has> the politer part live in the upper part of the town (as it is built on the side of a hill) and have a very neat street there. I have no doubt that Termini is the antient Himera[144] celebrated for its mineral baths which still exist and are in high repute. They were said to be made by Minerva and are

141. The Calat, or fortress, of Abi Tur was built by the Saracens.

142. Reportedly he was a tutor in the household (PMI, I, 119–22).

143. Nicolò Palmieri di Micciché was the last descendant of the main line of the family in Sicily (information furnished by Don Santo Stefano Alberto Policastro, Prince of Manche-Normandia, historian, of Catania). Irving met a relative of his, a Mr. Dawson, in Paris in 1823 (see entry of August 19, 1823).

144. The site of Himera, founded by a colony of Zancleians in 648 B.C., is a few miles west of Termini; it was destroyed in 409 B.C. by Hannibal. The temple there, of which a few ruins survive, was sacred to Minerva. Termini, built in 407 B.C., was known as Thermae Himerenses, taking its name both from the thermo-mineral waters there and the neighborhood of Himera.

beneficial in a variety of diseases. The town is most delightfully situated commanding from its high parts a fine view of the Mediterranean and of the sicilian coasts.

February 24[145]

From Termin<y>i we parted about 8 oclock. The road was a very good turnpike and continued along the sea coast. The surrounding scenery <highly> very handsome. We passd thro the village of La Trabia[146] that has an extremely picturesque old castle in good preservation. Another village of St Michele[147] has also an old castle on the shore & antient gates. The country highly diversified by plantations. Noble pallaces villages &c. Road borderd on each side by aloes Indian Fig and sometimes rows of trees. Hail storm. noble bay of Palermo. Rather too large city has a beautiful appearance at a distance. Grotesque Palace with images of monsters[148] &c Supurb gardens along the road. Arrive in Palermo at 2 oclock. Dressd and calld on the American agent Mr. Gibbs to whom we had letters. found there Mr. Amory of Boston to whom I had a letter.[149] He is going thro Europe the same route with me, & we arranged to be travelling companions

After setting a while we sat off in Gibbs open carriage for the grand street[150] where as it is one of the three last days of carnival there are great diversions Carriages in two lines one each side of the street pass each other & pelt one another with sugar plumbs Carrs with grotesque figures with tin shields wage war on every carriage. One very handsome representing a mill & having a number of Ladies & gentlemen of the nobility in it We had provided a bag of sugar plumbs to defend ourselves but it soon <got> ↑was↓ expended and we had to procure two others We were completely pepperd. A tremenduous <hail> storm

145. The date has been added by the editor. There is no break in the manuscript at this point.

146. The castle in Trabia is the Castello Lanza, dating from the fifteenth century.

147. Ponte S. Michele has the Castello di Trabía, dating in its present form from 1509.

148. Probably the Villa Palagonia (see entry of March 3, 1805, n. 177).

149. Abram Gibbs was U. S. consul in Palermo from 1805 to 1816 (Despatches from U. S. Consuls, Palermo, RG 59, NA). Nathaniel Amory (b. 1777) was a merchant ("Memoir of the Family of Amory," *N. E. Hist and Gen. Reg.*, X, 64). A letter of his to his brother Jonathan, Jr., from Leghorn, May 7, 1805, refers to his period of quarantine at Palermo earlier that year (Massachusetts Historical Society).

150. The chief street in Palermo, extending from the Porto Nuova to the Porto Felice, was then called the Toledo (now Corso Vittorio Emmanuele).

of hail & rain at first interrupted the sport but as soon as it ceasd they commencd again with redoubled fury <streets> The balconies of the houses on each side of the street full to the very garret with spectators <wh> among whom were sevral of the handsomest women of Palermo – The street crowded by the rabble who eagerly scrambled for the sugar plumbs & bon-bons that were thrown. Vast number of carriages in Palermo. In the evening to the opera[151] – first actress good – after opera they removed the seats lowerd the stage & prepard for a masque[.] masquerade numerous but indifferent The only <two> good characters were a diogenes – four shepherdesses supported by some noble ladies and a <mov> *walking Vessuvius* that vomited flames & had red hot lava representd very ingeneously. Nobility supped in their boxes.

February 25[152]

This morning walked out with Amory & Hall to look at the city – four Principal streets meet at right angles & form a cross.[153] High houses with iron Balconies[.] visited the church of the [*blank*][154] convent. It is encrusted within from the floor to the cieling with marble worked in mosaic The workmanship is good but the tout ensemble in my opinion is too much overcharged and <shews more a ta> shews rather a taste for the minute than for the simple grandeur that I think is most appropriate for a church.

The street is crowded by people and carriages and you are continually jostled by one and <?near?> startled by the other. <for this purpose reason perhaps> The better order of people generally ride in their carriages and it is esteemed almost despicable to be seen walking <on foot>[155] The gentlemen to be sure sometime walk in the morning on the Marino which is a noble promenade along the sea shore in front of the city at least 100 yards wide[.] along the margin of the sea is a fine foot walk of flag stones about 10 or 12 feet wide.

As the us<ing>e of[156] ones limbs is determined here to be vulgar & plebian we resolved to set up our *equipage* also – We have hired a

151. The opera house, in the Reale Teatro di S. Cecilia, was built in 1692.

152. Irving misdates this entry "24," and from this day through March 3, his dates are a day behind the calendar.

153. The former Toledo (now Corso Vittorio Emmanuele) and the Via Macqueda intersect to form the Quattro Canti or Piazza Vigliena.

154. Probably it was the church of the monastery of S. Caterina, decorated with polychrome marble, built between 1566 and 1596.

155. The cancellation is in ink.

156. The "e" is written over the "i" and the "of" over the "ng."

handsome chariot at 2 Dollars a day for the time we shall stay here. This afternoon we made our *debut* in it on the Marino where we found <th> a grand display of the nobility in their carriages This being the fashionable resort in the afternoon to see & be seen. We saw very few handsome ladies. We were *honord* by a very polite bow twice from the Vice roy[157] as he rode by in his carriage – pS. he has 4 running footmen in uniform & four footmen behind the carriage.

We dind this day with Mr Gibbs where we found Amory and a Sicilian gentleman. After dinner we *drove* to the Princess Camporeale to whom we had brought letter from her sister the Princess Marianne Gramaca of Catania.[158] We found her seated in company with sevral other ladies who were playing backgammon & <?several?> 3 old gentlemen She is about 30[?] years old – 5 feet high and of a brown complexion. notwithstanding all th<ese>is she is extremely susceptible of the tender passion and it is said has 3 or 4 cicisbeos. She recd us very politely but we were a little embarrassd at finding that she did not speak french or english. She however understood french a little and we kept up a kind of limping conversation I speaking in french & she in italian. In a little while however one of the gentlemen joind us who talkd french fluently so that we made out to get along very cleverly <in the evening went to the opera. Sat in Paterre under the Gover Vice Roys box> In evening to the opera[.] sat on the Paterre under the Vice Roys box[.] between the acts I put on my hat when an old Gentleman crossd from the other side of the theatre & told me very politely that it was the custom to be uncoverd when the Vice Roy was in the house.

February 26[159]

This morning we rode round to the mole to look at Amorys brig – fine view of the harbor from the mole – extensive arsenals – prisons Galley slaves have a building on the Quay where they manufacture & vend difft. articles

When returning Amory told us of a very curious custom he was witness too when he was here 3 years ago. At the time of the passover they

157. Allesandro Filangieri (1741–1806), prince of Cutò, was Viceroy of Sicily at this time.

158. Presumably Irving refers to Stephania Beccadelli, Princess of Camporeale, and Marianna Beccadelli Branciforte, Princess Gravina di Ramacca (F. San Martino de Spucches, *La Storia dei Feudi e dei Titoli Nobiliari di Sicilia,* Palermo, 1924, II, 195).

159. Irving wrote "25."

perform the same ceremony mentiond in the bible as being done by the jews of <lettin> pardoning one condemnd to death. The malefactor was brought into a large hall which was crowded with spectators many of them of the first rank. Then one of the most illustrious noblemen washd his feet & kissd him, he was then – [*sentence and page unfinished*]

In the evening attended a party at Mr Gibbs where there were a number of the nobility assembled. We had a very pleasant dance. I danced with Lady Acton – the lady of General Acton[160] a charming woman – after the dance we went to the theatre[161] where was a masquerade We <arr> got there about one oclock at night & staid there about two hours but the masquerade was very different This was the last night of Carnival and they did not break up till day light

February 27[162]

<G<P>reat> number of churches and convents in Palermo. Convents of vast extent. Beggars extremely importunate. A very little sustenance is necessary for them in this mild climate – The streets of Palermo are narrow Houses not remarkable for external elegance

This evening we were introduced by Gibbs to the family of the Prince Belmonte.[163] He is a man of the first rate abillities & enjoys the particular confidence of the king. He will not accept any place in Government but bends his <mind> chief thoughts to the improvement of his estate. He is very engaging in his person & elegant in his manners The Princess is a charming woman of infinite <grace> ease & gracefulness and very affable. they both speak french perfectly. She resembles in person & even countenance Mrs J[164] of N York. We found with them the

160. Sir John Francis Edward Acton, sixth baronet (1736–1811), was long the favorite of Queen Maria Caroline of Naples and was prime minister from 1779 to 1804. His wife was the former Mary Anne Acton, daughter of his brother Joseph.

161. Presumably the Teatro S. Lucia.

162. Irving wrote "26."

163. Antonio Pignatelli, Prince of Belmonte (1763–1828?), was one of the chief advisers of Ferdinand IV, king of Naples, and held many important diplomatic assignments. His wife was Maria Giovanna Pignatelli Aragona Cortes (d. 1769) (Ms. XV E3, Michele Pastina, "Compendio Storico ed Albero Genealogico dell'Ecc. Casa de' Signori Duchi di Monteleone, a.c. 57, Biblioteca Nazionale, Naples; Leone Tettoni and F. Saladini, *Teatro Araldico*, Lodi, 1841–1848, VIII).

164. Mrs. Elizabeth Johnson, an English actress who made frequent appearances on the American stage (George C. D. Odell, *Annals of the New York Stage*, New York, 1927, I, 400, 459; Francis C. Wemyss, *Wemyss' Chronology of the American Stage from 1752 to 1852*, New York, copyright 1852, pp. 77–78). Irving depicted Mrs. Johnson in *Letters of Jonathan Oldstyle, Gent.* (1802).

Countess of ——— [165] Sister to the Princess and several gentlemen of the nobility. We were received very politely and after sitting there about an hour and half we went to a conversazione which is subscribed to by the nobility – number of Ladies one particularly handsome – They playd at Faro billiards cards &c – We suppd there and returnd home about 2 oclock in the morning leaving a number there still who effectually turn night into day.[166]

February 28[167]

Visited the Royal Palace[168] a building by no means handsome externally but possessd of a number of elegant appartments. Two or three rooms hung with superb tapestry representing in lively colours and with great spirit humor & character the history of Don Quixote[169] – Other apartments adornd with very good paintings of fabulous history.[170] fine view of the city from the cupulo of the palace which commands a direct view up & down ↑one of↓ the grand streets[.][171] in the evening we were again to the conversatione. the beautiful woman was there also and Hall is quite in love with her. One of the young noblemen got completely tipsey and amused us highly. He was continually applying to me to tell him how to speak several sentences in english and then would run to Gibbs & repeat them in the most whimsical manner.

March 1[172]

This day we determined to risque dignity & every thing & walk about town We accordingly paraded along the grand street, but found that a carriage was a safe retreat from beggars pimps &c by whom we were crowded. The grand streets <are all cannot> are narrow and the

165. Presumably Maria Costanza Pignatelli Aragona Cortes, who married Giuseppe Antonio Filangeri or Filingeri, Count of San Marco (Tettoni and Saladini, *Teatro Araldico,* VIII). Her name appears after 1812 in the *Almanacco della R. Casa e Corte* of Naples.

166. A leaf has been removed from the notebook at this point.

167. Irving wrote "27."

168. The Palazzo Reale, or dei Normanni, was first built by the Saracens in the ninth century, was added to by the Normans in the twelfth century, and since then has been extensively altered. Its most notable part is the Cappella Palatina, with mosaics of the twelfth century.

169. Presumably in the royal apartments.

170. Probably the frescoes in the Parliament Hall of the myth of Hercules by Velasquez.

171. Presumably the Toledo (now Corso Vittorio Emmanuele).

172. Irving wrote "28."

houses extremely high on each side – there are several large but no handsome squares that we saw in Palermo. On the whole we were much disappointed in this city which certainly does not possess many objects to attract the travellers attention. Syracuse is far more worthy of his notice. In the evening I embarked aboard a small vessel loadned with fruit bound to Naples. I parted with my fellow traveller Capt Hall with the sincerest regret. He had proved a most agreeable companion of an amiable disposition and gentlemanlike & honorable in every particular. He <returns> ↑departs↓ tomorrow by land for Syracuse.

The wind was fair & brisk and we scudded rapidly before it but never did I witness such a diplorable scene as took place in the little cabin. There were a number of passengers and we were crowded together higgledy piggledy. The captain who was very particular in his services to me – gave me his hammock. I wrappd myself in my great coat & threw myself in it. Sleep I could not for a long time for never did I behold such sea sickness[.] every heave of the vessel (which rolld & pitchd most dreadfully) occasiond a heave among my unfortunate fellow passengers. An old woman laid near me who I believe calld on every saint in the calendar. after every cascade she would call a new one. Oh bellissima madre di christi. Oh santissimo Francesco Oh bellissima Santa Rosalia oh mea carissima santissima Rosalia.[173]

The saints however manifested their assistance in no other manner than in helping her to discharge the contents of her stomach which I believe it took the whole night to do.

March 2[174]

At day break this morning I scrambled out of the cabin and seated myself on deck where tho exposed to the spray of the sea I thot myself better off than in the hole I had left. At sun rise the wind had veerd about westerly and the master of the vessel without any more ado put about & stood back for Palermo. He was afraid to beat lest he should encounter some barbary cruisers for these chaps never venture to cross <till> from palermo to naples unless the wind is directly fair –

About 2 oclock we arrived in the bay of Palermo but the wind would not permit us to regain the port We therefore had to stand round a point and anchor in a beautiful little bay about 10 miles to the eastward of

173. "Oh most beautiful mother of Christ. Oh most holy Francis. Oh most beautiful St. Rosalia. Oh my dearest most holy Rosalia." St. Rosalia (d. 1166?) is the patron saint of Palermo.

174. Irving wrote "Jany 1."

the city. Here we went ashore and found a miserable tavern where we got some bread & cheese to eat for I had not tasted a mouthful for upwards of 24 hours.

Wretched object of want & poverty in a woman in the meanest rags She was waiting in the tavern I gave her a loaf of bread which she devoured greedily – Had a supper of boild beans – fried fish and hard eggs – Sailors brought mattrasses ashore and spread them in one of the rooms. I laid down in my clothes coverd with my great coat & slept sound till early in the morning when I awoke almost devourd with fleas

March 3[175]

I got up and as soon as day light appeard took a walk on the sea shore – beautiful sun rise – country picturesque with old towers & convents along sea coast. two of my fellow passengers talk french & are very civil I have found that language truly universal and in whatever situation I am thrown I generally find some one or other who can speak it. This morning we walked to a village about a mile & half inland calld Castelazzo[176] (IE. useless castle) Here are the remains of an old castle built <long> before the invention of fire arms

The village is small situated <high> on an eminence & commands a handsome view. Here we purchased some eatables & returnd to our auberge. after dinner we walked to the village of Bagaria Beautiful village houses built by the prince. Here is the palace built by the Prince Palagonia that is adorned by statues of monsters & distorted human figures.[177] returned in evening to our hotel I spread my mattrass on chairs this night but notwithstanding was overrun by fleas

March 4[178]

We hoisted sail this morning & returnd to Palermo. <Hall> Hotel very lonesome [–] missd Hall exceedingly. passd the day chiefly at

175. Irving wrote "2 Jany" in a small hand between "fleas" and "I got up"; there is no break in the manuscript at this point.

176. Present-day spelling, Casteldaccia. The suffix "accio" means "inferior" or "bad." There is no castle at this village, but there is a medieval house at Altavilla Milicia, 2 kilometers distant (information furnished by Touring Club Italiano).

177. Bagaria, present-day spelling Bagheria, is noted for the villas built in its vicinity by several Sicilian nobles. The most famous is that built in 1715 by Ferdinando Francesco Gravino, Prince of Palagonia, which is ornamented by scores of sculptures of monstrous figures. It elicited comment from many travelers, including Goethe, who described it in his *Italienische Reise* (1816–1817).

178. Irving first wrote "3," then corrected it to "4."

Gibbses. Amory & myself talkd of going to Naples by the way of Calabria[.] thot of taking passage to Messina in an Imperial ship[179]

March 5

Wind still contrary – walkd about the Corso with Amory Gibbs &c As I sat down to dinner a sailor came to call me on board [–] wind had sprung up favorable & we sat sail

The breeze continued favorable all the night and the sea not being so rough as on our former *sortie* we had less of sea sickness among the passengers. The good old lady however who had invoked the saints so piously had thought proper to stay ashore and not tempt their goodness any more.

March 6

The wind shifted in the morning but still was sufficiently fair for us to lay our course. In the evening we came in sight of the island of Capre antiently Capraæ where Tiberius[180] lived for some time in the most extravagant luxuries – abandoning himself to the grossest debaucheries. <As soon about dusk> I had laid down on deck and fallen asleep & on waking after dark the first thing that struck my eyes was Mount Vessuvius afar off making a most luminous appearance. It has been in a state of eruption for several months. I could plainly perceive the red hot lava running out of one side of the crater and flashes at intervals from its mouth – I <continued> was up the greatest part of the night contemplating this interesting object

[*Journal entries resume with March 7*]

March 7

As soon as I had landed & arranged matters with the Health office I repaired to the Hotel del Sole, kept by Grandosh[181] and reputed to be the best in Naples. I found it deserving of the reputation it had acquired and after the vile inns of Sicily it appeard absolutely a palace. Having

179. Presumably Irving means a ship of the Austrian Empire.

180. The emperor Tiberius returned to Capri in 27.

181. The hotel, in the Largo del Castello, was operated by a Frenchman whose name was probably Graindorge; it is spelled by other travelers "Grandorge" and "Grandorges." His wife was English. See Henry Coxe, *A Picture of Italy* (2nd ed., London, 1818), p. 318; Henry Mathews, *The Diary of an Invalid* (Paris, 1825), p. 145; Augustus von Kotzebue, *Travels through Italy, in the Years 1804 and 1805* (London, 1806), III, 61.

changed my clothes (as much for cleanliness sake as to get rid of the multitudes of fleas that had either accompanied me from Sicily or joind me on board the vessel) I orderd one [of] the crazy vehicles that they use here as hacks something like our gigs, but clumsy & tottering. I then went round to deliver some of my letters. At the counting hous of Fredk. Degen & Co.[182] I found two letters for me from Storm inclosing one from America. Degen was not at home. With Messr. Valen Roath & Co.[183] I found several more from Storm, and with Messr. Falconet & Co.[184] I found two large pacquets from America[185] that had been forwarded by the way of Bordeaux. I posted therefore back to the hotel happy as a prince with my pockets crammed as full of letters as a post boys knapsack. To recieve a letter from my friends when so far removed from them is always an exquisite gratification, but to be thus overwhelmd with letters and all of them containing pleasing intelligence was almost too much for me –. I knew not where to begin[.] I broke open every letter one after another – endeavord to arrange them according to their dates[,] read half a dozen lines at the beginning of one, then half a dozen at the end of another and then half a dozen in the middle of a third and after all could not reccollect a word of what I had been reading, in short I was completely bewilderd and it was some time before I could collect myself and go on systematically – Before I had read half of them I was obliged to break off as I had engaged to dine with Valen Roath & Co. and it was already past the appointed hour. I found there several honest American captains and <one> ↑an american merchant↓[186] by the name of Pickman[187] who was particularly civil

182. Frederick Degan was for many years in business in Naples; he was U. S. Navy Agent there in 1804 and consul from 1805 to 1809. Irving called him a Swiss (see entry of March 10, 1805), but another source identifies him as Prussian. (Despatches from U. S. Consuls, Naples, RG 59, NA; see also RG 45.)

183. Vallin, Routh and Co. were chiefly importers of oil (information furnished by the Banco di Napoli).

184. John Lewis Theodore Depalizeux Falconnet, a Swiss, was a banker in London between 1790 and 1799, thereafter in Naples (*The Gentleman's Magazine*, LX, July 1790, 667; William Lowndes, *London Directory*, 1799; Mariana Starke, *Travels in Europe between the years 1824 and 1828*, London, 1828, p. 501).

185. The letters from America which Irving received at this time were five from his brother William, one from his brother John Treat, and one from Alexander Beebee (Irving to William Irving, April, 4, 12, 1805).

186. The alteration is in pencil.

187. Probably he was Dudley Leavitt Pickman (1779–1846), a native of Salem (*The Diary and Letters of Benjamin Pickman (1740–1819) of Salem, Massachusetts*, ed. George Francis Dow, Newport, R.I., 1928, pp. 30–31).

& agreeable. Mr Valentine ↑one↓ of the firm appears to be a very worthy clever fellow & was extremely polite. I escaped as soon as possible and hastned back to the hotel to finish the perusal of my letters. I seemed as if seated among my friends enjoying their conversation.

March 9

Since my arrival I have been generally at home engaged in writing – yesterday I calld at Degens & found Mr Schwartz[188] (one of the partners) at home. He is brother to Mr Schwartz of Marseilles from whom I recieved such friendly attentions. He was very polite to me and invited me to dine with him on Sunday.

From the window of my room I have a fine view of Mount Vessuvius situated on the opposite side of the bay. It has lately made a considerable eruption and still emits vast volumes of smoke and a large stream of lava. At night the latter is very visible and appears like a red hot flood streaming down the side of the crater – My window also commands a large square,[189] eternally filld with a variety of objects coach men soldeiers monks friars fishermen lazaroni – Fruit merchants macaroni merchts Pie merchants and every other kind of tag rag and bobtail beings. <Nearly in front> A little to the right I have a near and complete view of *Castel Nuovo.*[190] (the *New* Castle) Notwithstanding its name it is a very antient building having been begun by Charles of Anjou and is said to be one of the oldest fabricks in the city. It is of immense size a square form with enormous towers or bastions. It is to me an extremely interesting object and must have been a place of great strength & imposing majesty before the invention of fire arms.

March 10

This morning arrived the ship Jersey, Capt. Blagg[191] from New York, via Leghorn, I received on my arrival in Naples a letter from America that Capt. Blagg had very politely forwarded me from Leghorn. I went along side of her but did not dare to go on board as she is quarantined

188. John Anthony Schwartz, a native of Switzerland, was brought up in Boston, where he was for a time a partner of Charles F. Degan (possibly a relative of Frederick Degan) (Despatches of U. S. Consuls, Naples, RG 59, NA).

189. The Largo del Castello or Piazza del Castello Nuovo (now the Piazza del Municipio).

190. It was built between 1279 and 1282 by Pierre de Chaulnes for Charles I of Anjou, king of Naples and Sicily, and enlarged by later rulers of the city.

191. Newspaper references to him spell his name "Blagge."

for twenty eight days. There is passenger in her Mr Philips[192] of New York who is making the tour of Europe He intends returning the same route with myself and I expect we shall be fellow travellers.

The weather is very unsettled and variable raining the greatest part of the day. The months of February and March are generally extremely wet & dirty at Naples, but I am told that it is probable that the latter part of this month will be pleasant as February has been particularly stormy this year.

The population of Naples is very great for <the> its extent. The houses are high and many families live under the same roof. Like most places that I have seen in france and italy, the best appartments are frequently the most lofty I have paid visits to people of the first respectability where I have had to mount up several pairs of stairs <f> before I arrived at their appartments. Very little attention is paid here to the external beauty of the house – The palaces are vast but destitute of exterior elegance. The entrances, the Stairs & corridors are miserably filthy – the walls black with dirt & cobwebs & never cleand – The landing places recepticles for every nuisance[.] in short a stranger judging from these appearances would consider himself entering the abodes of idleness – filth and indigence

Sickning with disgust at the apparent misery of the place and the <noxio> vile exhalations that assault his nose <he ascends to the door> ↑as he travels up sevral tiresome flights of steps↓ expects on the opening the door to be usherd into the most cheerless and slovenly <abodes> ↑chambers↓ – what ↑is↓ his surprize to enter into splendid appartments adornd with superb furniture rich tapestry and a profusion of exquisite painting and gilding! The abodes of pomp and Luxury! Such however is <continually> ↑universally↓ the case and <the italians> it appears as if the italians designed to render internal Splendor & voluptuousness more striking from the contrast of external poverty.

In the afternoon I dined at Mr Degen's whom I found a very gentlemanlike agreeable man. He is a Swiss but speaks english extremely well. He acts as Navy agent to the United States. In the evening I went

192. The principal Philipses above the status of laborer in the New York city directories in these years were Henry W. and Lewis, merchants, and Thomas, druggist. The Philips who was on the *Jersey* was possibly the man whom J. C. Cabell, at the time traveling with Irving, noted as being at the Hotel de Suède in Paris in the fall of 1805. See Cabell's Journal [No. 8], "Paris – Winter – 1805–06," [p. 11] (Alderman Library, University of Virginia).

to an Oratorio at one the the Theatres.[193] This is the only <kind> ↑place↓ of public amusement that is open in Lent. The subject was David's conquest of Goliah. The part of david was performed by <one of those> a celebrated singer of the *artificial* order. I had imbibed a prejudice & contempt for those poor devils and had a strong presentiment that I should not be pleased with his singing I was however most agreeably disappointed and in fact was charmed with the melody of his voice. The first singer among the women is a cousin of <C>Mr Caffarena<'s>[194] of <Nap> Genoa who has given me a letter of introduction to her which I have not yet deliverd. She has a good voice and is rather handsome than otherwise tho rather masculine. The Scenery was excellent the dresses good[.] in short I was perfectly well satisfied with the whole performance.

To an English ear, the italian music at first is very strange – it needs a little custom ↑& habitude↓ to become fond of it but in a little time you get familiarized to its peculiarities and highly delighted with it At least this is the case with me and with many others with whom I have conversed respecting it. Unfortunately the Grand theatre of St Carlo[195] is closed at present by which means I lo<o>se sight of <one of> the <g> most immense and if I may credit the Neapolitans the most superb theatre in Europe. I have arrived at Naples at the most unfortunate season for amusements lent being a time of humiliation among all *good Catholics.*

March 11

This morning Mr Norbert Hadrava[196] calld and breakfasted with me. This is a German old gentleman who dined at Mr Degen's yesterday. After dinner he played on the piano forte several tunes of his own composition – <his>he is very excellent on that instrument and I praized highly both his music & performance. This pleased the old gentleman so much that he called on me this morning with three

193. There were six theaters in Naples at this time (Kotzebue, *Travels through Italy,* II, 181–97, 224–36). Probably Irving went on this occasion to either the dei Florentini, the only one giving dramas, or the del Fondo, next in size to the San Carlo.

194. "a" is extended over " 's."

195. The Teatro San Carlo, one of the largest opera houses in Europe, was built in 1737 by Giovanni Antonio Medrano for Charles III, king of Naples and Sicily, later king of Spain.

196. No record of this person seems to be preserved in the archives of Naples.

pieces of his composition – viz. Yankee Doodle and Hail Columbia with very fine variations & a little german air of great sweetness. He begged me to accept them as a testimony of regard and finding I played on the flute he told me he would bring me one or two more pieces adapted for that instrument. I was very well amused with the old gentleman who seems to be an original in his way.

At eleven O'Clock Mr Degen calld upon me and introduced me to Mr Cab<all>el of Virginia and Col Mercer,[197] two gentlemen who arrived here from Rome the day before yesterday. I had heard very favorable mention made of Mr Cab<ell>al before and found him a very agreeable young fellow. He is said to possess superior talents and an amiable disposition. The rest of the day I spent at home in reading & writing as the weather was very rainy. I find a vast difference between the climate of this place and that of Sicily for though we had <some> ↑two or three↓ rainy days during our route from Catania to Palermo yet the weather was generally fine while we staid in the latter city.

March 12

This morning I rode out in company with Mr Cab<ell>al and Col. John Mercer to look at the *Tomb of Virgil* and the *Grotto of Pausillipo.*[198] The ride is thro the fine suburbs of Chiaja and along the out-

197. Joseph Carrington Cabell (1778–1856) was trained as a lawyer but devoted himself principally to the improvement of agricultural conditions in Virginia. He was in Europe from February 1803 to March 1806, most of the time in France. Eight manuscript journals of his which cover this period are in the Alderman Library of the University of Virginia. Two of them represent the period of time he and Irving were companions, from March to June 1805: [No. 7], bearing the inscription "J. C. Cabell. Rome Winter of 1805," and [No. 8], bearing the inscription "Paris – Winter – 1805–06. J. C. Cabell." The only systematic entries, however, are those from May 4 to 24, 1805, which Cabell headed "From Milan to Paris"; the remainder of both journals consists of random jottings, lists of books, and addresses. For an account of the association of the two men at this time, see R. B. Davis, "Washington Irving and Joseph C. Cabell," *English Studies in Honor of James Southall Wilson* (University of Virginia Studies, IV, Charlottesville, 1951), pp. 1–22. In his letter to William Irving, April 4, 1805, Irving described Cabell as "the most estimable young man I have encountered in Europe." Irving also impressed Cabell, who wrote Fulwer Skipworth from Rome, April 9, 1805, that he stayed so long in Naples in order to have Irving's company (Manuscript Division, New York Public Library).

John Mercer (d. 1817) was a member of the Virginia legislature, 1797, 1816–1817, and on the U.S. Board of Commissioners for settling claims under the Louisiana Purchase (Davis, "Irving and Cabell," p. 8).

198. Posillipo. The ancient spelling was Pausilypon.

side of the walk of the same name a handsome promenade built along the shore commanding a fine view of the bay – it is a very fashionable resort and reminded me of our favorite walk *the Battery.*[199] After riding a small distance we visited the church of <Sa> S. Maria del Parto. Here is a very handsome monument of the Poet Sannazaro[200] who is said to be the founder of the building. On each side of the tomb are the statues of <Appol> Apollo and Minerva, to render them however, worthy inmates of a Christian church they have been new *baptized* and the names of David & Judith inscribed on their pedestal. There is a very good basso relievo of Neptune pan and other figures, they have however left them in full enjoyment of their old titles as I suppose they were at a loss what scripture worthy to make pan – his horns & goats feet being abominably in the way.

<Passing> Turning in another direction we stopped at the foot of the Hill of Pausillippo to visit the tomb of Virgil. To get to this celebrated spot<t> you have to ascend a tiresome zig zag road up the hill and then pass thro a vineyard after which you find yourself over the enterance of the Grotto of Pausillipo[.] you then descend a flight of steps cut in the rock and arrive on a kind of platform on which is erect<t>ed the tomb almost peeping over the brink of the tremenduous precipice. It is a small building of brick & plaster of <a> [*blank*][201] form vaulted within. <Its interior dimensions are about fifteen feet high twelve feet long and about ten feet wide>[202] It has several apertures to admit both air and light and there are a number of niches in the walls such as are frequently seen in antient tombs for the <recesses> ↑reception↓ of <?Tr?> urns. The sight of this tomb awakens the most lively sensations in the mind. We recall the bright genius – the immortal lays of that poet whose name is eternally implanted in every clime <we consider that> Those lays that are endeared to us by early

199. The park and promenade at the southern extremity of New York City.

200. Jacopo Sannazaro (1458–1530), Neapolitan poet and prose writer, was given a small estate on this site and after his villa was destroyed had the church erected in 1529; its name is derived from his poem "De partu Virginis." The monument to him was intended to recognize him as an imitator of Virgil; the bas relief is an allusion to his poem "Arcadia."

201. The canceled "a" is in blue-black ink. Possibly Irving intended to write "columbarium" in the blank, the structure being of this form. Virgil was buried at Naples but the precise spot is unknown. The tradition that it is in this grotto, near the site of his villa on the hill, dates from the early Renaissance.

202. "Fifteen," "twelve," and "about ten" are in blue-black ink and the passage is crossed out in blue-black ink.

acquaintance and that we have been accustomed almost from infancy to admire. We consider their author no longer enlivened by the rays of genius or the inspirations of poetry – The very dust we spurn with our feet may be some of his sacred ashes! On the top of the tomb a little soil has lodged and it is over run with grass weeds and shrubs.* A bay formerly spread its foliage over it but the enthusiastic hands of travellers have stripped it of <almost> all its honors and hardly a vestige of it remains. The old man that tends the place cut us large portions of what little remained. He told us that it was the custom of *every stranger* to take a piece – We therefore of course did not like to break in upon old established customs. From the hill on which you ascend to go to the tomb – you have charming view of a part of Naples – the Castle del Ovo[203] – Ætna in the distance with the beautiful villages that skirt it and various other objects that form the beauties of the East part of the Bay. Having descended from the Hill we rode thro the Grotto of Pausillippo. This is a famous pass cut thro the mountain or Promontory of that name.[204] It is <about> of different heights from twenty to forty feet, about twenty feet wide and about half a mile in length cut thro the rock which appears not to be of a very hard nature. The passage is paved with square pieces of (I believe) Lava. This work is ascribed to different hands, but I have most commonly heard it supposed to be done under the direction of Caligula. We rode thro it in the carriage. The only light it recieves is from the two entrances and from two holes cut thro the top in a slanting direction. In the middle the passage is quite gloomy and persons passing seemed like obscure shades flitting by. We did not proceed farther in our ride as it was late but returned home the same way. I dined in company with Cab<ell>al & Mercer and spent a very agreeable afternoon.

* There sleeps the Bard whose tuneful tongue
Pourd the full stream of mazy song
Young spring with tip of ruby here
Showers from her lap the blooming year.[205]

203. Castel dell'Ovo, a fortress founded in 1154, dates in its present form from 1532–1554; it is on an islet in the bay joined to the mainland of the Pizzofalcone by a causeway.

204. It is thought to have been built under Augustus.

205. The lines of poetry are in blue-black ink in a very small hand at the bottom of the page. Presumably they are not by Irving; their source has not been identified.

March 13

Mr <Valen> Pickman of Boston calld upon me this morning to visit the Convent of St Martino,[206] owned by a fraternity of Carthusians. It is situated immediately under the Castle of St Elmo[207] <and> on a hill that commands the whole city. We went in company with Mr Valen in his carriage. He is a rigid Catholic and on an intimate footing with the good fathers of the convent. To ascend to the convent we passd thro a considerable part of the city and suburbs. The latter is built on the ascent of the hills and full of convents which seem to engross all the situations in Naples that command fine prospects and have a free & pure circulation of air. As to the Convent of St Martino it has more the resemblance of a superb palace the abodes of luxury & magnificence than the melancholy retreats of prayer, fasting and mortification. We passd thro a large outer court (into which the door of the chapel[208] <entered> ↑opened↓), and proceed thro an interior one of handsomer architecture from whence we were admitted into the <interior> inside of the building. Here instead of gloomy corridors and dreary passages I was surprized and pleased to find <a> them handsomely ornamented – the walls perfectly white and clean and light admitted sufficiently to give an air of life to the building. The chapel is profusely ornamented by the richest marbles and paintings of the first masters – As the monks were engaged in their devotions we did not stay sufficiently long to examine it attentively. In the Sachristy are also some noble paintings and pannel work done by the hands of some former brother of the convent – representing landscapes and figures in mosaic work of indian cane.[209] The old <fri> monk that attended us told us a lamentable story how the king had stripped their treasury[210] some

206. S. Martino was begun in 1325 but entirely rebuilt in the seventeenth century; it is now a museum.

207. Castel Sant' Elmo, the fortress on Monte Calvario, was built between 1329 and 1343 and enlarged in the sixteenth and seventeenth centuries.

208. The church, whose main entrance from the court remains locked, is reached through the monastery court, a corridor, and the audience room and chapter house of the monastery. It is decorated with colored marbles, frescoes and oils by Giovanni Lanfranco, Guido Reni, José de Ribera, Giuseppe Cesari d'Arpino, Massimo Stanzoni, Giovanni Battista Caracciolo, and others.

209. The paintings are by d'Arpino, Stanzioni, and Caraveggio. The presses have tarsiawork and reliefs by the Capuchin Bonaventure Presti, who also did the marble mosaic pavement in the choir of the church.

210. The tesoro adjoins the sacristy.

years ago of <coin t> Gold & silver vases, Utensils, and votive offerings to a vast amount – "He has made us much poorer" <sayd ↑sa> said↓ the old man ["]without enriching himself." <?The p?> He left however, the *most valuable* part of their treasures behind consisting in a vast number of Bones belonging to every saint in the calender that are carefully preserved in glass cases. The king most probably thought they could not so easily be reduced to current coin as the gold & silver reliques. <?The remains?> From the chapel we passed thro several long corridors and at length entered into another court.[211] This was <infin> much larger than the two others we had seen and of great magnificence. It was a large square surrounded by a Piazza supported by pillars of white marble and paved with white & black marble. Around it were arranged the cloisters of the fathers each having his seperate little room. The centre was occupied by a flower garden on one side, and on the other the cemetry of the convent being a small place surrounded by a handsome marble ballustrade on the corners of which were marble sculls. From hence we were led to a small saloon[212] in one corner of the building that commanded the most exquisite view of the city & bay. From one window we beheld the <city> Town far below us spread before our eyes like a map. We could trace every street, and point out each public building or square. Beyond it the harbor crowded with vessels – The beautiful Bay calm and gentle with two majestic frigates at anchor in it and various fishing boats and small vessels with picturesque latine sails passing & repassing over it. The charming environs that extend along the foot of Mount <Ætna> ↑Vesuvius↓[213] – with the numerous beautiful villages – Portici Caserta Pompeii &c &c <The Mountain> Vessuvius vomiting forth smoke, a long line of which traced the course of the lava down the mountain. The fine bold coast beyond the mountain – The distant mountains of Calabria coverd with snow. The picturesque island of Capre before us and a number of other objects calculated to render the prospect truly sublime & beautiful The day was fine & warm, the streets of the city were swarming with people and the hum of their voices mingled with the rumbling of carriages, reached our ears in indistinct murmurs. From another window we had a delightful view of the suburbs of Ciaja[,] the promontory of Pausillipo with the mouth of its grotto &

211. Presumably the cloister.
212. Presumably the belvedere, at the south east corner of the cloister.
213. "Vesuvius" is in a slightly different script.

the tomb of Virgil, the island of Ischia and a partial glimpse of the classic coast of Baia. We left this enchanting spot with regret and <almost ret> repaired to the appartments of the superior. He does not inhabit them at present as they are undergoing repairs. They are worthy of the rest of the building and are adorned with fine paintings by the best masters. For my part I should think the portraits of lovely women, decked with all the charms of youthful beauty, such as they generally represent their female saints – are but ill calculated to repress the wandring desires of the good fathers who have <?st?> taken the vows of eternal chastity, and are rather apt to entice their thoughts to the contemplation of earthly charms than to the more ideal "beauty of holiness."[214] I was mentioning this one day to a good humord old friar who spoke french and was very communicative.

The old man smiled and shook his head – "different situations" said he "produce different modes of thinking in beholding these beautiful paintings <said he> You admire the charms <of> that are pourtrayd in a sensual light. You admire them as the attractions of a mere mortal. We on the contrary consider them in a more refined and spiritual sense. We behold in that charming countenance for instance all the endearing and enlivening effects of divine love. The joyful confidence in heavenly protection – the serene and tranquillizing effects of a good conscience and gentleness of heart diffusing the most <ben> divine and benignant expression over the countenance. No harsh <trate> trait, no passionate line – no wrinkle of care or sorrow is there visible – every thing announces a soul at peace with its maker and itself and enjoying a blissful fortaste of the delights of heaven!" The venerable father went on in this strain for some time – you may judge of his arguments by the specimen I have given but you should have seen the enthusiasm of his countenance the animated expression of his eye, to feel the force of his discourse. Sterne would have gloried in describing him.

Having examined the chief parts of the convent we bade the fathers adieu and departed fully convinced myself that however their *thoughts* might be directed heaven ward they at least had an *eye* to earthly comforts. This convent was formerly immensely rich. The King for some time exacted 50,000 Ducats[215] a year from them and at the same time they were dispensing about 30,000 more, yearly in charities. The King

214. This phrase appears several places in the King James translation of the Bible: I Chron. 16:29, 20:21; Ps. 29:2, 96.

215. A ducat was worth $1 or less in southern Italy at this time.

however <had now at> quite <driven> ruined them and even drove them away – but a series of misfortunes convinced him (as the good fathers say) that heaven was manifesting its wrath against him for his maltreatment of them. He therefore recalld them and reinstated them in their former habitation restoring <their> a great part of their riches.

They now consist of forty five in number and <by all appearance they> if we may judge from their looks their meagre diet does not disagree with them. They are restricted from the use of flesh, but they make out to live luxuriously on the diet that is allowed them as they are well experienced in the art of cooking it in every form. Their <relig> vows do not prevent their comforting themselves with *excellent wine.*

On our return we stopped at the ware house of a celebrated Distiller of perfumes & cordials. He furnishes Mr Valen with the latter & was consequently very polite. He shewed us his Laboratory where he is engaged at present making perfumes for the King of Russia.[216] There appeard to me a Sufficient quantity made to deluge the King's whole palace. Among other <fr> names that we saw on different perfumes were several french ones, <The> that seemed to endeavor to out do each other in extravagance. <On one wall ↑shelf↓ of a room> One shelf was completely filld with bottles of *milk of Cupid* and another with *milk of the Devil!* (lait du Diable) – NB. no *pidgeons milk.*[217]

Dined at Degen's in company with Mr Cabell Col. Mercer, Sir <Genv> Grenville Temple of Boston and a <Mr>Capt. Stopford[218] an English Gentleman and three or four others. Sir Grenville is very much of the Gentleman and very pleasing company. In the evening I was <to>at[219] a conversazione at Mr Falconnet's. Here I was introduced to Mrs Falconnet an American lady of boston. she left america when quite young for England where she was married to Mr Falcon-

216. Alexander I.

217. An imaginary article for which one may be sent on a fool's errand. From the dash on, the phrase is in blue ink.

218. Grenville Temple (1768–1829), ninth Baronet, was born on Noddle's Island, Boston harbor. After the Revolution he served as Consul General to the United States from Great Britain. See George Temple Chapman, *An Account of the Temple Family with Notes and Pedigree* (New York, 1871), p. 9; Temple Prime, *Some Account of the Temple Family* (New York, 1887), p. 28.

Probably Sir Robert Stopford (1768–1847), English naval officer, at this time captain of the *Spencer.*

219. "at" is in blue ink.

net – she is a Lady of very agreeable manners. The conver<z>sazione was attended by a number of handsome ladies of the nobility and gentlemen of rank among whom were the Russian & prussian ambassadors.[220] Several English men likewise were present, and Sir Grenville Temple. The conversazione was not so stupid as many that I have seen. Some set down to cards – others formed themselves in Groups & circles & chatted very sociably. French was the language chiefly spoken – english a little but I do not recollect to have heard a word of *italian* the whole evening – About eleven oclock the Company began to disappear and I vanished among the rest.

March 14

This morning I rode out in company with Mr Cabell & Col Mercer to view the environs of Naples on the Eastern side. The day was very Serene and beautiful and we had a variety of enchanting prospects of the Bay and city from various points of view. We rode thro the elegant villages of Portici and Resina and about Eleven Oclock arrived at the ruins of Pompeii, situated about thirteen miles from Naples.

It is needless to give a very particular account of this place as it has so frequently been described and the excavations[221] that are still carrying on there are so trifling as not to afford <scope for further discription> ↑additional matters of interest.↓

On entering the town we found ourselves in a large square court <218 Paces in diameter> with the pillars of a <Portico> ↑colonnade around it↓ still remaining[222] – composed of brick stuccoed and colored red. They are fluted very handsomely and the stucco is of great hardness and as smooth as polished marble. Around the court are small

220. Mrs. Falconnet was Ann Hunter Falconnet (bapt. 1766), a native of Newport, R.I.; she was taken in 1786 to Europe with her sisters by their mother in hopes of finding treatment for the impaired eyesight of one. Ann married in England in 1790. See Records of Trinity Church, Newport; George Champlin Mason, *Reminiscences of Newport* (Newport, 1884), p. 250; *The Gentleman's Magazine*, LX, July 1760, 667.

The Russian ambassador was André d'Italinski (1743–1827). Irving was apparently mistaken about the other ambassador, since Prussia had no representative at the Court of Naples at this time (information furnished by the Director, State Archives, Berlin).

221. The first explorations of Pompeii took place in 1748, but the systematic excavations were mostly made after 1860.

222. Irving and his party entered Pompeii by the Porta de Stabia. The colonnade was originally intended as a shelter for theater-goers, but was afterward turned into a barracks.

rooms of a uniform size and construction with doors opening into it. This is supposed to have been a barracks for soldiers – the walls were scrawled full of inscriptions names & figures, these were <cafe> carefully sawed out and carried to the museum at Portici.[223]

From hence we entered <the> a small theatre that had antiently been a coverd one <the> but the roof at present is wanting. It gives a complete idea of the form of a Roman theatre. The seat<es>s <the stage> are perfect – forming a semicircle and rising one above another to the top of the building

The space between the lower seats and the stage is paved with beautiful marbles, and in the pavement is infixed the following inscription in large bronze capitals

M – OCVLATIUS – M – F – VERVS II VIR – PRO – LVDIS[224]

The foundation of the stage still remains but the flooring or pavement is gone. <P>The proscenium is likewise perfect but stripped of its marble ornaments. The <po> entrances the corridors the retiring places of the actors in short every essential part of the theatre is perfect. At a little distance from this is another theatre of larger dimensions such as was usually open with awnings to shade & shelter the spectators. This is likewise in excellent preservation. All their ornaments statues &c &c are carried to the museum at Portici. From hence we were shewn to the temple of Isis. This like every other building has been stripped of its ornaments & furniture which are lodged in the museum. The form of the temple and an idea of its former state can notwithstanding, be accurately formed. Three altars for sacrafice still remain – The place where the priest retired to purify himself The kind of sanctum sanctorum where the statue of the goddess was placed and the Sachristan behind it. The walls were stuccoed and painted with figures flowers &c executed coarsely. Their stucco is generally fine and very hard & smooth. The colors of the paint are several of them extremely beautiful particularly the red.

In one part we <were shewn> passd thro a street paved with lava. <In the> On each side were raised footways – Traces were worn deep

223. The principal artifacts from Pompeii are now in the Museo Nazionale, Naples; a few are in the museum at Pompeii.

224. "Marcus Oculatius son of Marcus Verus duumvir instead of games." That is to say, Marcus Oculatius, a duumvir, furnished the pavement rather than the games he would otherwise, as an important magistrate, have been expected to provide. See August Mau, *Pompeii, Its Life and Art,* tr. Francis W. Kelsey (New York, 1907), p. 156.

in the carriage <road> way by the wheels of the carriages – The houses on each side were extremely small. The front <of> generally occupied by a shop. In some of those were large ↑earthen↓ pots fixed in a kind of counter. These we were told were supposed to be the shops of dealers in oil. Every considerable house has a court within around which are the chambers for sleeping &c. They commonly have had no other light but what was admitted from the door that opened into the court. The walls are universally stuccoed & ornamented with coarse paintings representing fabulous history – landscapes – fruits flowers grotesque figures &c &c In the centre of every court is a marble fountain. The streets are extremely <narrow> ↑small↓ and tho by the traces of the wheels <they> ↑the carriages↓ must have been narrow yet I hardly percieve how they managed to pass each other.

<The excavations>

After having viewed this part of the town sufficiently we crossed thro a vineyard that is over a large portion of the town still buried – to another <c>uncoverd place. Here is a street open that leads to the gate of the town.[225] The houses are <ranged> built on each side in the same style as the other. <We> One of them is the largest yet discoverd having three courts & a <va> number of appartments.[226] All the best paintings are removed. The stucco being sawed out and framed carefully for the museum. One of the houses here has a very significant but indelicate sign ↑in mezzo relievo↓ to designate the business carried on within.[227] Without the gate are tombs both public and private. The Terentian family have a large square one[.][228] around it are masks of red earthen ware with distorted countenances as if weeping on the inside of which they used antiently to put lights. At some distance from the town are the ruins of a country seat[.][229] it consists of two stories

225. The Via Consolare, leading to the Porta Ercolano.

226. Probably the House of Vestals, excavated in 1769, composed of several houses thrown together.

227. Presumably the phallus carved on a pilaster of the House or Inn of Albinus (Marien Vasi, *A New Picture of Naples and its Environs,* London, 1820, p. 297). Formerly considered a sign of a house of prostitution, it is now believed to be a charm against evil, such as were produced in an adjoining shop.

228. An unroofed enclosure with a door at one end, it was built in honor of Titus Terentius Felix the Elder, aedile, by his wife Fabia Sabina. Several cinerary urns belonging to other members of the household are also buried in the enclosure. See Mau, *Pompeii,* p. 413.

229. The excavation of the so-called Villa of Diomedes between 1771 and 1774 caused much excitement because of the eighteen human victims of the eruption discovered in the cellars. It received its name from the tomb of Marcus Arrius Diomedes facing it across the street. See *ibid.,* p. 356.

towards the road and three facing the garden. <Here> On the first story as you enter from the road is a large court with small appartments for warm and cold baths Above, are bed chambers. In a kind of cellar that runs round three sides of the garden, are several large earthen pots (or amphoræ) that <formerly> antiently contain[ed] wine. In this cellar were found the bones of several unfortunates that fled thither for shelter in the confusion and terror of the event. To give any farther discription of pompeii is useless for after all these discriptions can never impress on the mind of the reader a correct idea of the houses streets or temples that are the subject of them. <?Too?> It is a painful thing to see reliques of such <interesting> inestimable value to the learned & the curious, in the hands of a prince who has not spirit or inclination to <de> complete their developement. To say that the King of Naples is too poor to support the expence necessary is a very unsatisfactory & incorrect excuse. He has a number of Galley slaves at his command who must be supported and whose labors might as well be directed towards the excavations at pompeii as to any other of the trifling duties they are employed in. The Lazaroni of Naples that swarm to the number of *thirty thousand* might be hired for a trifling expence and would execute the business in a very little time. At present a few workmen are employed who go on slowly and lazily yet some new object of curiosity continually recompenses the toil.

From Pompeii we returned to Portici where we partook of a miserable dinner at a miserable hotel having neglected the usual precaution of visitors to these parts, to bring refreshments with them from Naples. After dinner about five o'clock we prepared to ascend the mountain.[230] We engaged mules and guides and a cicerone of the mountain who produced a paper from the English consul certifying his <abill> abilities & attentiveness.

We mounted slowly up the mountain <thro a> along a road that passed among the most fertile <fields> enclosures – every moment catching a glimpse of the lovely scenery below us and of the mountain above vomiting out volumes of smoke <and> that rolled heavily along the atmosphere. After attaining a considerable height the prospect that opened upon us was indescribably rich and variegated The skirts of the mountain adorned with the beautiful villages of Portici, resina &c The enchanting bay of Naples tranquil and serene, the small fishing boats apparently reposing on its bosom. <At a> On one side the

230. Vesuvius.

picturesque Island of Capre the antient seat of voluptuousness – on the other side the city of Naples proudly rising out of the waters with its antient castles and white palaces the abodes to where voluptuousness is in modern times transferred. Beyond the point of Pausillipo the Islands of Ischia & procida, and at a great distance the classic <shore> coast of Baia and the Elysian fields[231] of the antients. The sun was just setting – it was one of those serene, delicious evenings for which this place is so often remarked. The Sky was clear and transparent with two or three floating clouds tinged with those rich colours <of> which are so much admired in the paintings of Lorrain. The horizon was <illuminated with> glowing with <golden glories> the parting rays. Over the whole view – The Bay – The city the islands was diffused the most Luxurient tinges – every thing was softned – enriched & <heightned and> ↑blended↓ into a harmony with the rest – forming a <scene of nature> prospect the most <as> lovely I ever beheld.

We continued slowly ascending – continually casting our eyes behind us and watching the gradual<ly> decrease of light and the effect it had in varying the colors of the landscape.

<At> It was twilight when we arrived at the hermitage. This is a house situated on an eminence about a mile from the foot of the crater. <A> It is the universal custom of persons ascending the mountain to rest here both before and after visiting the crater. The hermit has always a reviving glass of *Lachryma Christi* (a wine so called that grows on the mountain) and some slight refreshments at hand for which he *charges* nothing – but *takes* whatever you choose to give by which means he generally gets about five times the worth of the articles furnished. He handed us a book in which visitors to the mountain always inscribed their names, & frequently made their remarks on the mountain & gave a brief account of their excursion. Many of these were highly amusing from their pompousness – romance or stupidity – They all however joind in praising the *venerable hermit* for his hospitality, tho as far as I can learn he never was a *loser* by it. After having sat here some time by a comfortable fire and warmd <ourselves> our interiors by two or three glasses of *Lachryma Christi* (which tho not the most *delicate* wine, possesses a comfortable spirit & strength) we remounted our mules and pushed forward for the crater. The moon had

231. This place has been identified with the flat, richly cultivated area in the middle of the peninsula bounding the Gulf of Pozzuoli on the west.

risen and was very bright. We had a charming moonlight view of the same scenery that had delighted us so much at sun set – The city of Naples was very distinct.

After riding for some distance over rugged lavas of which our cicerone gave us the dates & histories we arrived at the foot of the crater. Here we dismounted and leaving our mules with one of the guides we began to climb, with the assistance of our guides who told us to hold on by a belt that was slung over one shoulder. We ascended in an oblique direction directing our course towards the stream of Lava that was running down the side of the crater. After <several restings and> a most fatiguing walk we arrived at the tremenduous flood.

"But oh what muse – or in what power of song
Can trace the torrent as it burns <af> along!"[232]

This stream of lava has been running some time so that the borders of it are quite cold and in the centre only, it pours slowly along.

I have before told you in my account of Mount Ætna that lava does not run like <comm> melted minerals, with an even surface – <There are> As it consists of a great variety of substances many of them less susceptible of fusion than others there are always a great number of fragments of matter – stones &c on the top which are sometimes almost black <and> but generally red hot – add to this the prominencies of the lava as it floats along grow cold and the <red> liquid matter running over it, forms a continual <unevn> uneveness. When the lava is thoroughly cold it has the appearance frequently of masses of black rock of <a> most uncouth forms. We <mounded> mounted on the cold lava that borderd the stream and advancing to the latter I thrust a walking stick into <the> it. I found that at first it was requisite to push with a little force to make the stick penetrate but the farther it went in the easier it was which plainly shews that the lava was far more liquid below than on the surface. Indeed the lava we stood on tho cold on the surface was in a red hot state below as we could plainly percieve thro different fissures into which if we thrust a stick it immediately took fire – We could now plainly percieve the course of the lava which had merely run down the crater and collected in a small

232. William Cowper, "Heroism" (1782), ll. 19–20:

But oh! what muse and in what powers of song,
Can trace the torrent as it burns along.

valley, at the foot of it. Quitting this place we <asse> ascended along the edge of the lava to attain to the crater, but this was by far the most fatguing part of the excursion. The ascent was exceeding steep. The ashes so soft & loose that we slipped back two thirds of each step, and the eddies of wind frequently brought volumes of sulphurous smoke upon us <that> almost stifling.

Our throats were sore from inhaling it. On our way the guides pointed out to us a spot where the lava seemed to spume out of a hole – being conducted from the crater to that place in a kind of coverd aqueduct formed by the cold lava's being incrusted over it. A little higher up was a hole that vomited up smoke & sparks. The cicerone took us on the lava about twelve feet higher up than the hole and told us to regard it steadfastly till the wind blew the smoke another way. We did so – and saw the lava rushing along in it like a torrent, by the direction of it we found it passed under the very spot on which we stood, the lava having there coold & formed a kind of coverd way.

It even began to feel very hot to our feet and we evacuated the place with precipitation – The guides seemed diverted with our apprehensions being themselves habituated to the scene. About ten yards further up was a small eminence or hillock in the lava out of which sulphurous flames issued with a violent hissing noise. We were toiling up the crater <he> nearly in a paralel line with this object when the wind sat directly from it and overwhelmed us with dense torrents of the most noxious smoke. I endeavord to hold my breath as long as possible in hopes another flow of wind would carry it off but at length I was obliged to draw in my breath and inhale a draught of the poisonous vapour that almost overcame me. Fortunately for us the wind shifted as I sincerely believe that in a little time we should have shared the fate of pliny[233] & died the martyrs of imprudent curiosity. Col Mercer as soon as he saw the smoke coming turned about and made a precipitate retreat and did not make a second attempt to ascend the crater. <For Ca> As to Cabell & myself we were so exhausted & bewilderd that we could not stir from the spot but should have fallen a certain sacrifice.

As soon as the smoke changed we renewed our exertions having all the encitements of lively apprehension to spur us on. At length we arrived <to> ↑at↓[234] the crater and took a welcome resting spell on

233. The Roman naturalist Pliny the Elder died of asphyxiation in the vicinity of Vesuvius, where he had gone to investigate the eruption of 79.

234. "at" is in a slightly different script.

some rocks of cold lava. We then walked round the edge of the crater which is composed of ashes & cinders. The inside of the cup is filld with vast masses of lava that almost rise paralel to the brim but are cold & black. It appears that the lava had filld the crater before it burst thro the side and that the surface had <?bec?> grown cold. The lava running from beneath the crust by coverd canals and not making its appearance till one third of the way down the crater.

In one place tho at a distance from us we could hear the mountain bellow & roar at some apperture from whence it vomited pillars of smoke. In another part was a small conical eminence that lately threw out flames & red hot stones. We descended <from> into the crater and climbed up the rocks of lava. Our guide conducted us on a small plain and pointed out to us various spots from whence sparks & smoke issued – Our thoughts & observations however were soon called nearer home. <We hap> I felt the lava under my feet beginning to <scorch> be uncomfortably hot and casting my eyes around, <th> saw thro several fissures within two or three feet distance the lava red hot beneath & <The> smoke arising out of them[.] the steam or vapour that arose from the lava we stood on was extremely warm – Our guide thrust his stick into a hole about three feet off and drew it out in a flame. We soon discoverd that we stood on a mere crust of lava and that under us was a complete red hot lake[.] we <evacuated ?our?> decampd from the hazardous spot with all possible expedition fearing lest it might give way under our feet or some explosion of confined vapours break out around us. Of the former I believe there was no ground for apprehension as the crust is too strong to be affected by the weight of the largest sized man. Our cicerone who is long habituated to the mountain said he expected there would be an eruption in that spot in a few days as the confined matter must find vent. We descended <do> the steep crater with infinitely more celerity than we climbed up it and in a little while found ourselves comfortably seated by the Hermits fireside

Notwithstanding all our curiosity & interest we were happy to have finished our visit. To a person unaccustomed to seeing the mountain in its present state, there is so much awe & apprehension mingled with the pleasure he recieves at viewing the Tremenduous Scene that he is almost happy when the business is over. He fears continually that some new eruption may take place – some fresh explosion – that the earth may give way under his feet, in short a thousand things that the old acquaintances of the volcano smile at.

Having recruited our strength & spirits with a few glasses of the highly extolld Lachrimi Christi we took leave of the *venerable & hospitable hermit* – first asking him what we had to pay he appeard offended at the question and said his house was not an *inn* – We saw thro this affectation of delicacy and that he knew well that he stood a chance of getting far more from the generosity of visitors than he could have the countenance to demand – We gave him therefore a Dollar which was about three times the worth of what we had consumed at his house. He had no delicate scruples to prevent his taking it – but did not seem by his looks to be satisfied with the compensation. We left him perfectly disgusted with his hypocrisy. We arrived at Portici about midnight and after a slight supper hastned to enjoy <our>the repose <with no [*two unrecovered words*]> our weary limbs required.

March 15

After breakfast this morning we visited the remains of Herculaneum. All that is to be seen there at present is <the rem an amphi> a Theatre but completely coverd with ashes & tufa <and> over which there have since ran several streams of lava and on top of the whole the present village of Portici is built. All this has conspired to prevent <th> the prosecution of its developement – as it would require great labor & expence and endanger the present town. The Excavations[235] are all subterranean and you descend by staircases – having provided wax torches. They have cleared out sufficient to give a correct idea of the theatre. They had also opened several private houses in some of which were found the celebrated manuscripts[.][236] these houses have since been closed up and all further work at Herculaneum has ceased. The paintings &c that they found here were superior to those of pompeii – They also found a vast number of statues busts vases &c &c[.] among the <two> former are two fine Equestrian statues of the *Balbi*, father & son which are on the ground floor of the Palace at Portici.[237] There is nothing in the theatre at Herculaneum that particularly <requires>

235. The first and most profitable explorations of Herculaneum were made between 1738 and 1765, but the excavations were filled in and systematic work did not begin until 1927.

236. The papyri found in the Villa Suburbana dei Papiri in 1782 are mostly treatises on Epicurean philosophy, now in the Muzeo Nazionale, Naples.

237. Marcus Nonius Balbus the Elder and his son, the Younger, who was Praetor and Proconsul of Crete and Cyrene, were prominent citizens of Herculaneum; the statues are now in the Museo Nazionale, Naples. The Palazzo Reale at Portici was built in 1738 for Charles III (see n. 195).

invites discription. From hence we went to the museum, (Portici) having provided ourselves with a permission to visit it – which is granted by the King. The Museum however is stripped if its finest curiosities – They are all packed up in cases & sent over to Palermo where they remain invisible. This was to preserve them from the greedy hands of the french in case they should visit Naples. Enough of the curiosities are left notwithstanding, to interest the curious in a high degree. They consist of a great variety of [*smudged word or words*] antient utensils <o>for different purposes

Instruments of husbandry surgery – war &c &c a representation of an antient kitchen imitated from one discovered in Pompeii – with a great part of the furniture, tho the most valuable articles are at Palermo. Vessels in glass – Earthen ware <broz> bronze marble &c. Sewing Threa<t>d reduced to cinders[.] figs almonds nuts beans peas wheat &c burnt to coals but retaining their original form perfectly. Eggs (or rather the shells of eggs) nets locks latches bolts, weights – musical instruments lamps – styles & tablets &c &c &c &c &c &c &c

The floors of the museum are <pla> paved with beautiful mosiacs found in Herculaneum & pompeii. In the lower appartments are a vast variety of paintings that were painted on the stucco of the walls but have been carefully sawed out, backed with slate & framed. They represent various <landsc> scenes in History & mythology – landscapes <fruit> animals fruits & flowers, but in general coarsely executed. on dark grounds.

While examining the museum I was accosted by <M> The Revd Mr Heyter[238] an english gentleman of my acquaintance who is sent out by the prince of Wales for the purpose of unrolling the Herculaneum manuscripts. He has been some time engaged in this interesting undertaking and has unrolled a variety. He shewed me the process which is very ingenious – The work requires time & extreme caution as the rolls are burnt to <a> coals. He was busy at a Greek treatise of a logical nature – He endeavors to fill up the spaces wanting by studying the subject and discovering the words necessary to maintain the connection. Some of the writings are now in hands publishing by order of the King of Naples. They will only be parted with as presents but as the Prince of Wales will be furnished with a copy there is no doubt but

238. John Hayter (1756–1818) was employed by the Prince of Wales (later George IV) between 1800 and 1809 to unroll and decipher the Herculaneum papyri. Possibly Irving had met him in Palermo, where the papyri were when Hayter began work.

that he will freely communicate them to the world – <f>Four books of Epicurus have been completely unrolled & copied –

After having satisfied our curiosity at Portici we returned to Naples. In the afternoon I rode on the grand course <to the> towards <the> Portici in company with Mr Pickman in an open carriage of Mr Valens. This was friday afternoon which in Lent is always a time that the fashionables choose to resort to this place and display their carriages & finery. The course is long but was crowded with carriages – Some of the Equipages were superb and many of the ladies beautiful – I saw a duke there who possesses a "plentiful lack of understanding"[239] driving a phæton *twelve in hand*[.] the horses were all black & well matchd – He however was much troubled with his equipage & <was> ↑took↓ the whole afternoon to ride from one end of the course to the other interrupting the other carriages continually. Some of the younger part of the royal family were on the course. This parade of carriages is a favorite amusement with the Italians but I know of none so vain trifling & insipid.

March 17[240]

This day was devoted to an examination of the Environs to the westward of Naples. The day was remarkably fine and warm. Our company consisted of Col Mercer Mr Cabell Mr Pickman of Salem & myself. <To> After passing thro the Grotto of Pausillippo and riding along a level plain on the borders of the sea for some distance we came to the town of Puzzuoli. <This stands on a>

This town is built on a Peninsula which it entirely covers – having an extremely picturesque appearance. <and> Regarding it from a little distance to the Westward it put me very much in mind of the situation & appearance of Syracuse. This city contains about ten thousand inhabitants. It abounds with interesting antiquities among which are The temple of Jupiter Serapis,[241] of which the court only is uncovered. It is square and of uncommon size, for all the antient temples I have seen are generally small – but this is supposed to have been an egyptian

239. Probably Irving is misquoting Hamlet's words to Polonius: ". . . the satirical rogue says here that old men . . . have a plentiful lack of wit . . ." (Shakespeare, *Hamlet,* II, ii, 197–98, 201).

240. This, the entry for March 17, and the two following entries, for March 21 and March 22, are in blue-black ink.

241. The so-called Temple of Serapis has been identified as a markethall of the first century A.D.

temple. Around the court are cells or small rooms for the priests and baths. In the middle is a raised place of a circular form on which formerly stood the altar. The rings to which the victims were fastned still remain as also some large marble vessels or cisterns used in sacrifice. The roof was formerly supported by sixteen columns of African marble which are since removed to the Kings palace at Caserta. There are also the remains of an ampitheatre, in one part of which they shew you the appartments in which St. Januarius the patron Saint of Naples, was confined.[242]

To the city of Puzzuoli Sylla retired after his abdication of the consulship.[243]

Leaving Puzzuoli we continued our ride along the delightful coast of Baia; we passed the ruins of a Villa of Cicero's[244] – of which nothing at present remains but <the> vestiges of the foundation along the brow of <the> ↑a↓ Hill which shew it to have been of great extent. A little farther on we passed Mount Barbaro <of> antiently Mons Gaurus, the hill where grew the *falernian wine* so celebrated among the antients. This and most of the hills in the neighborhood are supposed to have been formerly volcanoes or of volcanic origin – A short distance farther on to our left we passed Monte Nuovo a handsome hill of considerable size (said to be 400 fathoms high and 3000 paces in circumference) which was thrown up in forty eight hours in the year 1538[245]

We stopped a few moments on the high bank that borders the lake of Avernus.

Riding some distance further we passed thro the Arco felice[246] – a high arch of brick said to be one of the <an> gates of the antient city of

242. The amphitheater was finished under Vespasian. St. Januarius (d. 304) was thrown to wild beasts and finally beheaded.

243. Sulla's retirement to Pozzuoli and death there are alluded to in John Moore, *A View of Society and Manners in Italy* (London, 1781), I, 298. Irving began to draw on this work in writing his journal about this time; see entry of April 2, 1805, and subsequent entries.

244. It was known as Villa Puteolana, after the ancient name of Pozzuoli, Puteoli. Cicero called it his *Academia,* in imitation of Plato, and here wrote his *Academicae Quaestiones* and *De Fato.*

245. Irving's account of Monte Nuovo, description of the view from the Arco Felice and of the Piscina Mirabilis, and references to Lake Fusaro and the Elysian Fields in this entry are drawn from Thomas Martyn, *The Gentleman's Guide in his Tour through Italy* (London, 1791), pp. 97, 294–96.

246. The Arco Felice spans a cutting made in Monte Grillo by the Emperor Domitian for a roadway.

Cuma[247] Here we got out of the carriage and ascended a high bank from whence we were shewn the mouldering remains of the castle & other buildings of Cuma on a distant eminence – and fa[r]ther off on the sea shore the ruins of Liturnum where Scipio Africanus retired and where it is generally reported, he was buried.[248] It would be fatiguing to particularize every object we examined in this interesting ride <as>& <they may readily> discriptions of them may be read in almost every account of Naples. I shall therefore briefly mention that we passed the <La> beautiful lake Fusaro – or as it is sometimes called *Lago della Colluccia.* The tomb of Caius Marius – The remains of antient Baia[249] consisting of ruined temples &c Here we took boat and glid<ing>ed rapidly along the beautiful bay. Below us we could see thro the clear waters, the foundations of antient palaces – formerly the abodes of the highest luxury & <vlup> voluptuousness – but long since passed away with the hands that erected them. After crossing a considerable part of the Bay we again landed and examined the *Piscina Mirabile* a vast subterranean reservoir of water into which you discend by forty steps[.] forty eight pillars support the roof – This is supposed to have been constructed by Agrippa to supply his fleet with water, it is one of those enormous works common to the antients who seem to have prided themselves on the *magnitude* of their undertakings

After observing a few more curiosities we were conducted to the top of a small stone cottage that stands nearly on the end of the Point – <for the purpose of shewi> where we were desired by our cicirone to regard the surrounding scenery. It was indeed incomparably beautiful. To our right at a small distance was the *Mare Morto* a delightful little lake that communicates with the sea[.] over this it was antiently pretended the bodies of the dead were carried from [*blank*] to the Elysian fields which lie between two gently rising hills[250] forming a charming valley

247. The remains of Cumae consist chiefly of an Acropolis perforated with many galleries, one of which is thought to be the grotto of the Cumaean Sibyl as described by Virgil, and a few scanty remains of temples.

248. The only ancient remain at Liternum is the Torre di Patria, said to have been built of the materials of the villa of Scipio Africanus Major, on the site of his tomb.

249. The ruin Irving mentions is no longer called the tomb of Marius. Chief ruins at Baia (ancient Baiae) are three large buildings from Roman times, called the Temples of Mercury, Venus, and Diana but evidently public baths.

250. Monte dei Salvatichi and Monte di Procida.

Beyond this scene of Poetic fiction & romance lay the islands of Ischia & Procida – directly before us the island of [*blank*] like all the others rising boldly out of the sea with the most picturesque contours. To the left the eye wanderd enraptured along the lovely coast of Baia, renderd highly classic by the Poet & the historian – to the beautifully situated town of Puzzuoli – <Above it> catching a glimpse of the solfateria part of the camps Phelegrei the scene of Jupiters conflict with the giants[251] – then descending again to the sea coast and having a distant view of part of the town of Portici and the other villages that skirt the feet of Vessuvius – The mountain itself casting up a fine column of white smo<k>ak which rising majestically to a certain height gradually expanded itself into the air. from hence glancing along the bold rocky coasts of Castello Mare Sorrentum[252] and at length settling upon the singularly handsome island of Capri. The Bay tranquil and speckled with feluccas & chebecks – not a cloud broke the serene face of the heavens excepting <a> one of a beautiful form and whiteness formed by the smoak of Vessuvius.

Having reposed ourselves for a long time admiring this enchanting prospect we returned to our boat and retracing part of our former way landed at a small tavern (at least it was honored by the inhabitants with that title) built on the Scite of antient Baia. Here we produced a stock of cold provisions we had brought with us and a couple of bottles of excellent <Wine> Bordeaux Wine – and ordering a table to be spread in the shade in front of the house we sat down to a repast which tho perhaps not quite so luxurious as many that were given on the same spot two thousand years ago – was at least <rell> relished with as keen appetites as any moderate Roman ever boasted. To give a classic zest to our entertainment our host produced a flask of *falernian wine*, made from the grapes of *Monte Barbaro* announcing its title with particular earnestness. We seized the famous liquor and immediately filld our glasses – but with all our respect to the antients and our high opinion of their Epicurism we were unrefined enough to prefer the real Bordeaux and dicided that either the antients were unacquainted

251. Solfatara is a semi-extinct volcano in the Phlegraean Fields, or Campi Flegrei ("burning fields"), a district west of Naples, from ancient times a scene of great volcanic activity, and the scene of many episodes in Homer and Virgil. Irving apparently took his references to Jupiter here and later in this entry from Moore, *A View of Society and Manners in Italy*, I, 297.

252. Castellammare and Sorrento. The words "castello mare Sorrentum" are in a smaller hand and appear to have been added later in space left for them.

with the superiority of foreign wines – or that they had a mode of manufacturing their wines that their degenerate successors have long since forgotten. Indeed the latter is most probably the case for they take very little pains with the preparing of their wine here, seldom caring to do any thing more than express the juice of the grape. Between the effects of the Falernian & the Bordeaux we became quite inspired – the dinner passed merrily off and we resumed our seats in the boat with renewed spirits. Passing the foundations of several antient villas in the sides of the hills that bordered the sea we at length landed at the steam baths of Nero. These are passages just wide enough for one person to go conveniently abreast cut into the sides of a rocky hill. <f>Far in the interior you descend gradually to a hot spring of salt water where an egg may be boiled in a few moments[.] the vapour that arises from this spring is very warm & humid and rolls <all> along the passages issuing out of the mouth like a thick smoak – You may here take a complete steam bath[.] the nearer you approach the spring the warmer it grows. I was quite down to the spring where it felt almost suffocating – it is advisable in th<i>ese visits to strip of[f] coat <wast> waistcoat and shirt and on coming out wipe your body dry and dress yourself immediately[.] otherwise you are <y> very apt to take cold. The sand on the sea shore is warm near the rocks that contain this spring – and on scratching up the sand a few inches the water that arises is tepid. On our return to town we stopped at Solfaterra. This is the old crater of a volcano nearly filld with earth and about <two mil> a mile one way and a third of a mile the other[253] It is part of the Campi Phelegrei where Jupiter is said to have overcame the giants (with his thunder bolts) that made war against heaven. It is a large plain and in several parts of it are holes from whence issue sulphureous steams & smoak with great violence – The earth is strongly impregnated with sulphur & alum and they make the latter in considerable quantities by gathering the earth and placing it round the smoaking apertures. On striking the ground with a large stone a hollow sound is heard and you feel a considerable vibration of the earth under your feet which indicate that there are large caverns underneath. We arrived in town about seven oclock, highly delighted with our excursion and the interesting antiquities and lively prospects that we had enjoyed.

253. "a mile . . . the other" is in a smaller hand and appears to have been added later in space left for it.

March 21

For the three last days I have been confined to my rooms by a violent cold which I caught in my face on the mountain and encreased in the Baths of Nero. My face has swelld exceedingly and been extremely painful. I have <a>however an excellent nurse in my Italian servant, who has attented me with the utmost faithfullness and attention – and by bathing my feet at night with warm water – drenching me with herb teas and sevral other expedients has put all the pain to flight and restored me to such a comfortable state that I hope to be able to resume my rambles tomorrow. During my confinement, however, I have not been deprived of all opportunity of observation. I have before mentiond that one of my windows overlooks a public square – this is a complete world in miniature

It is continually crowded and presents an infinite variety of objects & incidents. <At one time from my window this morning> I sat for some time at my window this morning amusing myself by noticing the motley crowd below me. At a little distance under my window was an old Calabrian peasant playing on the bag pipes to a numerous & respectable <and> group of amateurs.

His instrument resembled the Scotch bag pipes exceedingly except that the drone was still more inveterate. It sang in the nose most delectably and I make no doubt would have the same effect on a Scotchman as it is said his own country instrument has. <a>Some what farther off was a shew man who had collected another equally respectable audience whom he was entertaining with the humours of Signore Punchinello and his merry family exhibited in a small portable theatre. The company appeared to be highly diverted with the *original* wit of Mr Punch and exhibited such a whimsical distortion of countenances that one would have supposed they had been grinning for a wager. In another part of the square was a spectacle equally ludicrous, occasioned by the misfortunes of *un milord anglais.* This is a young English nobleman who <has> belongs to the <Engl> Navy and has come to Naples with the spirited determination of *astonishing the natives a few.*[254] In the progress of this laudeble design he has already accumulated disease upon disease and laid the foundation of premature old age and fruitless repentance. He has just run a narrow risk of breaking his

254. Presumably the italicized words are quoted, but their source has not been identified.

noble neck & putting a hasty stop to all his brilliant pursuits. He has hired a small one horsed carriage something like <our> ↑a↓ *sulky* which is very common in Naples & of ticklish constructure – in this he drove tandem about town with all the eclat of a Jehu,[255] but in turning a corner of the square *in style* a few moments ago he <unfortunately> run over an unfortunate little Jack ass laden with herbs – and had a hoist sulky & all. about 15 or 20 feet. His lordship fortunately escaped unhurt but the <whorses> horses who seemed to have imbibed his spirit for *dashing* careend two or three times about the square – bandying the unhappy sulky from side to side to its utter ruin & distruction and <too> to the great annoyance of sevral groups of Lazaroni who were quietly reposing in the dirt & basking themselves in the sun.

Just, opposite to my rooms on the other side of the square is a guard house,[256] and here a large body of soldiers were going thro their manuel exercise. The Neapolitan soldiery are fine looking men, particularly the kings guards. They want but good officers to make them fight well – from them my attention was called away to a regiment of volunteers in the service of "the Church militant here upon earth."[257] These were a number of sleek friars forming a religious procession and bearing a corpse to its long home – laid out in all the gaudy ornaments that the surviving relations could afford to lavish upon it.

Those are a few specimens of the infinite variety of objects continually before my eyes in this scene of noize & bustle – you may fill up the picture to suit your own fancy with groups of Lazaroni some gambling for coppers, others lounging in the sun – voituriers – Equipages of the nobility – monks – mountebanks – abbè's, Greeks sailors – priests – charlatans – fruit men – coblers in short every kind of outré character you can imagine – I have been in no city where the population is so crouded and the bustle so great as at Naples, and I shall be heartily glad to bid it adieu and repose myself in the silent retreats of Rome, whose deserted streets and solitary temples are best calculated to encourage reflection and collect the scatterd and perplexed ideas. In Naples a stranger is subjected to the most infamous extortions & im-

255. A reckless coachman. See II Kings 9:20: "The driving is like the driving of Jehu the son of Nimshi; for he driveth furiously."

256. It was in the Castel Nuovo.

257. "Let us pray for the whole state of Christ's Church militant here in earth" (The Order for the Administration of the Lord's Supper or Holy Communion, *The Book of Common Prayer*).

positions. There is no such thing as honesty remaining in the national character. The unwary traveller is surrounded by <t> a cloud of harpies that are continually preying on his purse and <dester> destroying all his peace & comfort by their incessant peculations. <The every thing is enormously dear> – Every Accomodation is enormously dear – every <curiosity place> curiosity that strangers are in the habit of visiting are extravagantly expensive – The antient temples – ruins &c are inclosed and guarded by crowds of insatiable leeches every one of whom must be satisfied if you wish to pursue your researches with comfort. Add to this the universal misery – poverty stupidity & abjectness of spirit that prevails among the people and I know of no further inducements that are necessary to <ind> influence a traveller in hastening to depart from among them. For my part I only wait for my face to get perfectly well when I shall bid adieu to Naples with pleasure. It is a place where all economy is set at defiance[.] expence accumulates on expence and every moment produces some new unexpected & unjust demand.

March 22

Having recoverd sufficiently to venture into the air – Mr Cabell & myself took a carriage & rode out to look at the *Lake of Agnano* & the *Grotto del Cane* or Dogs cave. (PS Mr Mercer who was one of our party in former excursions saild from Naples two days ago in an American ship for Marseilles). Agnano is a beautiful little lake about three miles in circumference and surrounded by gently rising hills coverd with verdure. It would be a lovely retreat in summer were it not that an unwholesome vapour aris<i>es from the lake at that season and renders it dangerous to reside <in>or sleep in its neighborhood. On arriving at the lake we were shewn in a small house on the borders, the Steam or sweating baths of St Germano. These are places where a hot sulphurous vapour issues out of the earth much in the manner of those at Solfaterra. Some of the baths are used for the rheumatism and others for different complaints. Leaving this we repaired to the Grotto del Cane so much spoken of by travellers. This is a small cave in the side of a hill about ten or twelve feet <long> in depth. A strong mephitic vapour arises from the ground <to the> which is obnoxious to animal life. The man who shews it enterd the cave without hesitation for the vapour is not sufficiently powerful to operate with any degree of force more than the height of a foot from the ground – He tried the experiment with lighted torches ↑the flame of↓ which as they approached the ground <were grew> grew fainter & fainter & were suddenly extinguished. Another experiment is also made upon dogs which being held with their heads near the ground fall <and> into violent convulsions and would soon expire were they not restored to the open air. They lie for some time as dead but gradually recover.[258] From this experiment the grotto has obtained its name, for, tho the fact is established beyond all doubt, and at the expence of the lives of hundreds of unfortunate dogs – yet every traveller that visits it must have the thing repeated and gratify a cruel and silly curiosity or rather whim, with the agonies of one of those faithful animals. The man had provided a dog to regale us with the sight of his tortures. The poor animal had already undergone the experiment four times for the amusement of former visitors – He appeared sensible of the horrid tortures to which they were dragging him and struggled violently to escape. We interfered and told the fellow that <?he?> we had no wish to see the experiment, as we were convinced that the same vapour that extinguished the torch would be equally noxious to the dog – The brute did not appear willing to pass over this part of the ceremony perhaps thinking we should deduct something from his usual fee, for the omission. We at length told him, if he was very anxious to remove all doubt from our mind about the <unwholes> fatal effects of the vapour he might hold his own head over it, but as sure as he put the dog's there we would not pay him a farthing. This last <arg> sentence had more effect upon him than all <the> our others and having no inclination to <trust his own> risque <his> either his life or his money he <ret g> consented to wave the experiment.

The population of Naples is computed to be between four & five hundred thousand. Of these a vast number are useless persons who <rarely render the> are a clog upon society without rendering any real services. <A> Noblemen priests monks, lawyers, fiddlers servants, shew men & Lazaroni form a great part of the population. Of lawyers there are said to be 10,000 of Lazaroni 30,000. The latter are a set of poor vagabonds who will work when employed in any trifling manner as running errands carrying burdens &c. If they cannot find work they will

258. Irving's paragraph to this point contains echoes of Martyn, *The Gentleman's Guide*, p. 291.

beg and if that dont succeed – steal a little. As soon as they have got enough to supply the emergencies of the day they are content and either bask in the sun or gamble for what few coppers they have remaining. As to lodgings very few of them have any other than the porticoes of churches or palaces – for the mildness of this climate allows them to sleep the greatest part of the year in the open air.

March 24[259]

This morning I sat off for Rome in company with Mr Cabell. We had taken our places in a voiture and <had for> ↑found in it a↓ fellow passenger a Piedmontese who speaks french fluently and is a very lively good humored amusing fellow. After leaving Naples we passed along a fine road thro a fertile plain The plain grew more interesting as we approached Capua – It was covered with wheat fields which being in a flourishing state, gave it the richest verdure – from the plain arose at a distance a range of beautiful hills behind which afar off were seen mountains covered with snow. These are spurs of the <range of> chain of mountains that run throughout Italy called the Appenines.

About <nine>ten oclock we entered *Capua* the city once so celebrated for its luxuries – by which the victorious Army of Hannibal was enervated and ruined. Its glory has long since passed away and it retains nothing of the antient city but the name. It is fortified in the modern manner and at the gates we had to deliver our passports to the guards. We had an uncomfortable proof that what ever luxuries Capua might once have boasted, it could no longer be reproached for them. In the wretched inn to which we were led we could scarcely find any thing to eat. The Inn keeper as usual asked us what we chose to have, but in a little time let us know that eggs <&> cheese ↑& bread↓ were all the eatables he could furnish us with, on these we made our breakfast, luckily having taken care to provide ourselves with a pot of butter at Naples <f> where we had been forewarned that we would not be able to find any on the rout.

After leaving Capua we found the road more diversified by hill & dale, and presenting the most lovely prospect of that gentle yet picturesque kind in which the pencil of Lorrain has so much excelld. Every thing was rich, luxurient & smiling at the reviving touch of

259. This entry and those through April 13, 1805, are in brown ink.

Spring. As it was Sunday we had an opportunity of seeing the peasants arrayed in their finest *Gala* suits. The same taste for shew & glitter that prevails among the higher classes of Neapolitans extends itself visibly to the lowest peasants In the former it evinces itself in Equipages decorated in the most gaudy manner, in Jewels ornaments & dress of the most splendid kind – in the latter in a humbler but no less <glaring> ↑striking↓ manner. They are fond of glaring colours in their habiliments such as scarlet purple green yellow &c The peasant women have boddices of scarlet cloth trimmed with broad edgings of tinsel, aprons of bright green cloth yellow petticoats scarlet shoes & their hair twisted with gay coloured ribbons – the other parts of their dress may <be> vary in their colours but the scarlet boddice <a>or Jacket is universal. The men are equally fine in their colours. <and They ?grease?> Their hats are high crownd & conical and they think themselves happy if they have a peacocks feather to stick in the hat band – if they cannot boast of this ornament, a bunch of glaring flowers, ribbons or cocks tails supplies the want of it.

<In the evening we arrived at St Agatha>

I forgot to mention that Capua is not supposed to stand on the same spot as the antient town but[260] is <removed> situated two miles distant.[261]

In the evening we arrived at <Capua> St. Agatha a small village where we put up for the night in an Inn difficient in almost every comfort or accommodation. But in Italy a traveller must make up his mind to suffer the disagreeable with patience, in the midst of a country calculated to form a paradise ant [and] to produce every luxury & comfort he must content himself with miserable fare and cheerless accomodations

March 25

We left St. Agatha before day break, and a little after sun rise arrived at the river Garegiliano antiently called the Liris. The scenery around here is very pleasing. The river runs thro a fine plain – from some part of it rise the hills that produced the Falernian wine famous among the *Bon Vivants* in antient times. On the opposite banks <are>

260. At this point a leaf has been removed from the notebook.

261. Irving may have drawn in this sentence on Moore, *A View of Society and Manners in Italy*, I, 116.

is a tower & some old buildings that have a picturesque appearance. We crossed over to these in a scow. Here was situated the antient town of Minturnum, of which there remains a few ruins the most conspicuous of which are an ampitheatre and an aqueduct.[262] <It was near this town in the marshes that> Marius[263] after his expulsion from Rome having been driven by bad weather to Circeii passed from thence in a boat to the mouth of the Liris (Garigliano) to a place where he expected to be safe. being however closely pursued he hid himself in the border of the river in the marshes where he was discovered by horsemen immersed to his chin in water. He was thence carried to Minturnum and condemned to suffer the sentence passed against him at Rome but was suffered afterwards to escape. This river was an antient boundary of *Latium.*

Our road from hence lay thro a most charming country ↑to *mola de gaieta*↓[264] where nature seems to have vied with art in forming the most delightful scenery – A fine bay extends itself to a great breadth, the shores diversified by gently sloping hills or <ap> abrupt bluffs – olive orchards – cornfields, vineyards were intermingled in "gay confusion"[265] while from the centre of the bay arose the town of Mola as if emerging from the sea which washd the foundations of its walls and on the farther promontory that formd the bay Gaieta with its towers & walls had the most picturesque appearance – The bay was serene and speckled with fishing boats – and a fleet of feluccas with Latine sails that were just sailing out of it added to the beauty of the scenery. The italian towns are admirably calculated to <have> embellish a landscape, the houses have generally flat roofs which form terraces for walking[.] this has a much finer effect than the sloping angular roof. They have generally some old castles towers & churches that are also

262. Presumably Irving refers to the town of Traetto (since 1890, Minturno), whose buildings date from the thirteenth century. The remains of ancient Minturnae here also include ruins of a theater.

263. The incident to which Irving refers occurred in 88 B.C., when Marius was seeking to escape from Sulla, who had taken Rome and ordered his death. In this passage Irving apparently drew on a printed account which has not been identified.

264. Mola di Gaeta, now Formia.

265. Addison, "A Letter from Italy," ll. 63–65, 67–68:

> Bear me, some god, to Baia's gentle seats.
> Or cover me in Umbria's green retreats;
> Where . . .
> Blossoms, and fruits, and flowers together rise,
> And the whole year in gay confusion lies.

interesting objects. These kind of roofs are particularly remarkable <to> in the southern parts of Italy and especially at Naples. When I looked down on that city from the Convent of St Martino every house had a flat appearance and I <could> observed that they had all terraces on the top paved or plaistered. This is necissary in so warm a climate where the population is so crowded, as by that means the family can enjoy exercise and air which they cannot <cof> comfortably in the streets.

There is no country where the prospects so much interest <as do> my mind and awaken such a variety of ideas as in Italy. Every mountain – every valley every plain tells some striking history. On casting my eyes around some majestic ruin carries my fancy back to the ages of Roman splendor. I am lost in astonishment at the magnificence of their works, at their sublime ideas of architecture and their enormous public undertakings. Some <of> sepuchral monument awakens in my mind the reccollection of a man famous for his virtues or detestable for his vices – in the midst of these reflections an old castle frowning on the brow of an eminence transports my imagination to the later days of chivalry & romance. I picture to myself issuing from the gateway the gallant knight that "never was ydrad"* I see his fair lady waving her handkerchef from the battlements and praying success may ever attend his arm. I see the <th> hospitable feast, the tilt the tournament and every other custom that distinguished that enthusiastic age when prowes was the effect of love and when gallantry & romance presided over every transaction. From these pleasing reveries my mind is recalled to the contemplation of present circumstances & objects. I behold misery indigence & ignorance on every side[.] beggary stares the traveller in the face and importunes him at every turn – He sees a perfect Canaan around him and <to> the inhabitants starving in the midst of it. He sees the arts languishing – neglected, the progress of knowledge impeded and man gradually returning to a state of brutality – The works of former ages – magnificent in their ruins – reproaching the nation with its degeneracy. The land <nearl> scarcely cultivated – The peasant tills it with a heavy brow satisfied if he can snatch from it a scanty sub-

* "None did he dread, but ever was y-drad"[266]
<But ever w>

266. "Nothing did he dread, but ever was ydrad" (Edmund Spenser, *The Faerie Queene,* I, i, 2). This line and the cancellation below it are in pencil.

sistance. Such are the baneful effects of despotic governments – of priest craft & superstition of personal oppresion and Slavery of thought.

Oh liberty thou goddess heavenly bright
Profuse of bliss & pregnant with delight
Eternal pleasures in thy presence reign
and smiling plenty leads thy wanton train
Thou makest the gloomy face of nature gay
Givst beauty to the sun & pleasure to the day[267]

Mola was antiently Formiæ built by the Listrigonians who were said to be cannibals[268] We breakfasted here at a dirty *caffé*. After breakfast we walked about the neighborhood to enjoy the beautiful scenery. The female peasantry in this part of italy have generally very good countenances, <they> we saw a number that were really <h> very handsome, having considerable of the antient style of countenance. They entwine their hair with ribbands and twist it in a coil on the back of the head. This has a very pretty effect and resembles strikingly the head dresses of the females in antique paintings & statues. Beyond Mola we passed some indistinct ruins on each side of the road. The banks descend from them with an easy slope to the sea covered with olives. Here it is <told> ↑said↓ that Cicero was murdered near one of his villas. To the left of the road a little further on we passed a <high> tower in ruins called <t>The *Tomb of Cicero.*[269]

The road continued to be excellent and we rode along very agreeably. <*unrecovered*> At Fondi our trunks were searched by the custom house officers and our passports examined. In the neighborhood of fondi is a cave where Sejanus concealed Tiberius.[270] Leaving Fondi we crossed the beautiful river of Fontana de Petrono which wanders thro a charming valley. Near here are the ruins of a castle from whence the Pirate Barbarossa carried off a princess of the house of Collonna.[271]

267. Addison, "A Letter from Italy," ll. 119–26.

268. In this reference to Formiae Irving drew on Pierre Jean Grosley, *New Observations on Italy and its Inhabitants,* tr. Thomas Nugent (London, 1769), II, 251.

269. According to Plutarch, Cicero was murdered while being carried by his servants from his Villa Formianum to the sea. The villa is said to be represented by ruins in the grounds of the present Villa Rubino. The so-called tomb marks the spot assigned by tradition to the murder.

270. Irving apparently copied this sentence verbatim, adding "of fondi," from Martyn, *The Gentleman's Guide,* p. 263. The reference is to the occasion on which Sejanus saved Tiberius' life when it was endangered by falling rock in the cave.

271. In 1534 Khair-ed-din-Barbarossa, most famous of the Barbarossa pirates, attempted to abduct the Countess Giulia Gonzago from the castle (located be-

<We> Towards evening we passed thro the barrier <that> on the frontiers of the Kingdom of Naples and entered the territories of *His holiness the Pope.*

We put up for the night at Terracina[272] a very fine town – at least the new part which is situated in a plain on the sea coast – The old town is on a hill[.] we walked into it to see the cathederal.[273] This is built on the remains of an old temple of Appollo of which the marble pillars of the portico remain – at one side of the portico is a large antique vase of granite which ↑one of↓ the popes has caused to be erected on a pedestal on which is an inscription that in that vase many christians had been tortured & <died> sacrificed by the *gentiles* to an *idol called Appollo.*[274] <At> Over the gate of the town in a kind of iron cage is the skull of a murderer who killd a rival in a fit of jealousy.[275] An inscription tells the nature of his crime. At Terracina we found the inn very good for an italian one.

March 26

We sat off before day break and after riding a short distance we arrived at the commencement of the Pontine marshes. The <old> road formerly went over the mountains & was very indifferent but the present pope has draind the marshes & made an excellent road on the remains of the old *Appian way.* The marshes are now cultivated in many places but they do not appear to be very fertile. they <yeld> yield pasturage to large herds of cattle. The promontory of Circeii is just beyond Terracina from whence it can be distinctly seen & also

tween Fondi and Fontana di Petronio) of her kinsman by marriage, Prospero Colonna, in order to present her to Soleiman II, but she escaped. In retaliation Barbarossa sacked the town and took many prisoners. The episode is referred to in Grosley, *New Observations on Italy,* II, 254.

272. Four of the stories in *Tales of a Traveller* (1824) are laid in this town or its neighborhood: "The Inn at Terracina," "The Adventure of the Little Antiquary," "The Adventure of the Popkins Family," and "The Story of the Young Englishman."

273. S. Cesario was built in the ninth century on the site of a temple of Roma and Augustus and rebuilt in the seventeenth century.

274. The inscription reads in part, "Vasca in cui da gentili furono tormentati, e scannati molti Christiani innanzi l'idolo di Apollo" ("Vase in which many Christians were tortured and mutilated by gentiles before the idol of Apollo"). The source given on the inscription is Dominicus Antonius Contatore, *De Historia Terracinensi* (Rome, 1706). (Information furnished by the Perfectoral Commissioner of Terracina.)

275. Irving referred to such a cage in "The Inn at Terracina."

from the marshes. It is a high rocky promontory. Here Homer[276] makes Ulysses & his companions to have been detained by Circe the enchantress who fell in love with the hero & turnd his companions into different animals Homer describes it as an island. It still retains the name of Circeii. There are several houses built on the road thro the marshes but the situation is unhealthy – in summer particularly there arises a vapour from the marshes that is extremely unwholesome and said to render it <dan> even dangerous to pass the night on them. At noon we arrived at the end of the marsh where there is a large convent and an inn[.][277] the latter however affords nothing to comfort the traveller and had we not provided a stock of provisions in the carriage we should have had but meagre fare. Just facing the convent <i>are several broken columns among which stands a Roman mile stone in good preservation with an inscription on it in which I plainly distinguished the name of Cæsar. At a little distance on the other side of the road is an obelisk that has fallen from its pedestal, on one side of it is the inscription "Nunc ager Pontinus" and on the other "Olim pontina palus."[278] We rode on thro a level country with the Appenines rising from the plain on our right, <their heights> with towns and villages scatterd on their sides

In the evening we arrived at Villetri a town situated on an eminence in ascending which we had an extensive view of the vast marshes and the sea beyond them, with the promontory of Circeii & the Appenines bordering the prospect on the other sides. Villetri prides itself upon being the native place of Augustus,[279] his portrait embellished the sign of the tavern where we put up. The women in this town wear large clumsy <stomachers> ↑stays↓ that project out before in a grotesque manner. <a> This was the antient capitol of the Volsques or Volscians.[280]

March 27

We left Velletri this morning in a heavy storm of rain; we passed thro the little town of Riccia founded by Archelous, siculus 500 years

276. *The Odyssey,* X.

277. The post house at Torre dei Tre Ponti, built by Pius VI, consisted of a convent of Capuchins and stables or barracks for soldiers (Louis Simond, *A Tour in Italy and Sicily,* London, 1828, p. 389).

278. "Now the Pontine pasture" . . . "Once the pontine marsh."

279. The family of the Emperor Augustus (born Caius Octavius) came from Velletri, but the tradition that it was his birthplace is no longer acccepted.

280. "or Volscians" is in pencil.

before the Trojan war and called Hermina[281] – from hence we proceeded to Albano. just before we enterd this town we passed to the right a high sepulchral monument originally adorned with five cones or pyramids three or four of which are still standing. This is said to be the *Tomb of the Curiatii.*[282] Albano was originally founded by Ascanius son of Æneas 40 years before the foundation of Rome:[283] it was afterwards destroyed by the Romans but rebuilt. From hence we had a view of the Campania of Rome which broke upon us as we descended one of the streets of Albano. The view is interesting in the highest degree both from its real beauty and the chain of ideas it awakens. That vast & beautiful tract of level country diversified by gentle ascents and declivities which produce the most beautiful waving lines – the verdure spread over it, the Sea bounding the prospect on one side and the snowy Appenines <of> ↑on↓ the other. In the midst the eye is attracted to the spot where

"– Rome her own sad sepulchre appears"[284]

Her swelling domes, her nodding towers rise majestically from the plain and appear like mighty monuments of former greatness.[285] The Campania as you ride along presents continually some broken pile, <some> ↑or↓[286] mouldering ruin of antient palaces and temples – Here where formerly was seen the gilded dome, the sumptuous edifice the crowded streets nothing is now to be distinguished but a few heaps of rubbish – vast fields neglected and uncultivated coverd with grass & weeds, silent desolate & forlorn.

The air of the Campania is counted so unwholesome now adays that no one will inhabit or cultivate it. About half after one oclock we enterd

281. In this sentence and that about the founding of Albano Irving apparently drew on a printed account which has not been identified. The account he gives of Ariccia is similar to that in several guide books; see, for example, J. Salmon, *An Historical Description of Ancient and Modern Rome* (London, 1800), II, 294.

282. According to legend, three brothers of the Roman family Horatii and the three of the Alban Curiatii fought to determine whether Rome or Alba was to exercise supremacy; the Horatii were the victors. The tomb is now thought to be Etruscan.

283. The city said to have been founded by Ascanius 400 years before Rome was Alba Longa (see entry of April 14, 1805, n. 12).

284. Alexander Pope, "Epistle V. to Mr. Addison" (1720), l. 2.

285. Irving apparently drew on his description of the Campagna in "The Painter's Adventure," *Tales of a Traveller.*

286. "or" is in pencil.

the city by the lateran gate.[287] The antient wall remaining perfect on this side – This is the antique part of the city and we made our way

"Mid fanes & wrecks & tumbling towers"[288]

to our hotel which is situated in the modern part. To describe the emotions of the mind and the crowd of ideas that arise on entering this ["]Misteress of the World" is impossible – all is confusion & agitation. The eye roves rapidly from side to side eager to grasp every object but continually diverted by some new scene. All is wonder, restlessness, unsatisfied curiosity, eagerness & impatience.

On arriving at the hotel we determined to rest ourselves for the day – collect our scatterd ideas and prepare to examine things deliberately & satisfactorily. We heard that there were three American Gentlemen in Rome on their travels Viz Mr Alston of Carolina Mr Wells of Boston and Mr Maxwell[.][289] as Mr Cabell was acquainted with two of them we calld on them. Mr Alston only was at home. He is a young gentleman of much taste & a good education. He has adopted the profession of Painter thro inclination & intends to remain in Rome two years to improve himself *in* the art.

March 28

This day we <em> busied ourselves in looking out for appartments but found it difficult to suit ourselves – Holy week is approaching at which time crowds of strangers resort to rome – and the appartments begin already to be occupied. We have got tolerable ones for the present in the House of Marguerita a french man.[290] Our rooms over look a

287. The Porta S. Giovanni.

288. "Mid' Fanes, and Wrecks, and tumbling tow'rs . . ." (James Ogilvie, "Ode to Time," III, 3, l. 4, *Poems on Several Subjects,* London, 1769, I, 89).

289. Washington Allston (1779–1843), American painter, had gone abroad in 1800 to study art. Irving described Allston's influence on him during their association in Rome in a letter to Evert Duyckinck written in 1854. See Evert Duyckinck, *Cyclopaedia of American Literature* (New York, 1855), II, 14–16.

"Wells" was Benjamin Welles (1781–1859), a Harvard classmate of Allston's (Obituary Notice, *The New England Historical and Genealogical Register,* XV, January 1861, 90). A letter written to him by Allston from Siena, December 29, 1804, is in the Massachusetts Historical Society.

Probably Maxwell was Joseph William Maxwell, an American who graduated in medicine from the University of Edinburgh in 1803 (Samuel Lewis, "List of the American Graduates in Medicine in the University of Edinburgh, From 1705 to 1866, with their Theses," *ibid.,* XLII, 1888, 163). Irving later referred to him as "Dr." (see entry of March 30, 1805 and subsequent entries).

290. His name was Margariti, according to Marianna Starke, *Letters from Italy* (London, 1800), II, 61.

garden & the house being situated on a hill we have the advantage of good air & a fine prospect of part of the city.

The greatest part of the day has been devoted to the examination of the Villa Borghese.[291] This is delightfully situated at a short distance from Rome. The grounds are well laid out & are very extensive. The <vill Ha> Palace is <bult> built with great <judg> taste and the ornaments distributed with <the most> judgement. Here <are> is a collection of the finest statues in Rome – The rooms are crowded with *chef d ouvres*

> In solemn silence a majestic band
> Heroes & gods & Roman consuls stand
> Stern tyrants whom their cruelties renown
> And Emperors in parian marble frown.
> While the bright dames to whom they humbly sued
> Still shew the charms that their proud hearts subdued.[292]

There are eight superb rooms on the ground floor ornamented in the richest manner – particularly a long gallery[.] the pavements and walls are of the most costly and beautiful marbles arranged with exquisite taste, different parts of the walls are embellished with fine mosaics.

<Of the crowd of fine specimens in sculpture I was most pleased with the following –>

<The celebrated fighting gladiator by Agasias the Ephesian[293] To?wh?>

<Several of the finest>

The examination of this palace employed us several hours nor did we then <take any> depart without the greatest reluctance; <nothi> It is a most interesting employment to wander among the busts and statues of those Emperors philosophers & heroes[294] of whom we have so often heard and read, to <behold their> examine their features and endeavor to find in them traces of the characters which historians have

291. The Villa Borghese (now the Villa Umberto I) dates from the seventeenth century. The collection Irving saw there consisted chiefly of antique sculpture found in excavations on the Borghese family's many properties; most of it was sold to Napoleon in 1809 and taken to Paris, never to be returned. See Dorothy Mackay Quynn, "The Art Confiscation of the Napoleonic Wars," *The American Historical Review,* L (1945), 445. The present collection was formed largely after that time.

292. Addison, "A Letter from Italy," ll. 87–92.

293. It is now called the "Borghese Gladiator" and is in the Louvre.

294. See Angelo Dalmazzoni, *The Antiquarian or the Guide for Foreigners to go the Rounds of the Antiquities of Rome* (Rome, 1803), pp. 257–61, for a list of the busts and statues in the collection at that time.

given them. As these busts are most of them antique they are supposed to be correct likenesses of the originals

From the <palace> villa we returnd to the city passing under the antient wall of Rome. On entering the gate on this side a charming city view presents itself – The grand square called Piazza del popolo[295] with a lofty egyptian <oblisk> obelisk in the middle with a beautiful fountain behind it. Two churches of fine architecture and three long and well built streets that diverge from the square & afford an admirable perspective. Rome abounds with noble fountains, by the hands of the best masters. The water is brought from great distances and gushes from various parts of the fountains in large stream[s] or cascades. The fountain in Piazza Navona[296] is boasted <a>of by the Romans as the most magnificent in the world. It <is>consists of a vast basin in the midst of which is a rock 41 feet high pierced thro on four sides. On the top an Egyptian obelisk of granite coverd with hyerogliphics[.] around the base of the rock are four colossal figures of marble representing four grand rivers viz the *Ganges Nile Danube* & *La plata.*

This <statue> ↑fountain↓ <a>has the most imposing and striking effect and cannot <help> but forcibly arrest the attention & admiration of the most indifferent passenger.

March 29

This morning we visited the Farnese Palace[297] one of the finest in <Naples>. ↑Rome↓[298] A <Stranger> Traveller however cannot but regard it with indignation when he learns that it is built with the spoils of the <Colisseum.> Colisæum. (Flavian Ampitheatre.)[299] The stones of that grand remain of antiquity have been taken to form several palaces & churches – Those walls at which the traveller would have gazed with wonder & delight whose very remnants are counted one of

295. The Piazza as it now appears was designed in 1814. The obelisk was brought from Heliopolis in 10 B.C. and placed in the Circus Maximus; it was moved to its present location in 1589 and now has four fountains with lions at the base. The two churches to which Irving refers are S. M. in Montesanto and S. M. dei Miracoli, between the three diverging streets, Via di Ripetta, Via del Corso, and Via del Babuino.

296. The Piazza Navona contains three fountains. The one in the center, to which Irving refers, is the Fontana dei Fiumi, built in 1651 by Bernini. The obelisk is supposed to have been made in Egypt by order of Domitian.

297. It was built in the sixteenth century for Cardinal Alessandro Farnese, partly with stones from the Colosseum and the theater of Marcellus.

298. "Rome" is in pencil.

299. The Colosseum was originally called the Amphitheatrum Flavium in honor of the family name of the emperors sponsoring its construction.

the greatest <wonders> ↑curiosities↓ of rome have been demolished to give rise to others <at> which he either passes by with neglect and inattention, or with emotions of contempt and anger at their founders. When we see the finest monuments of the arts suffering from the hands of the barberous & illiterate; destroyed by the indiscriminate <hands of> devastations of war or the blind fury of national revolutions we sigh at the irreperable loss that the world of Literature & science sustains but concieve <it the result of one> it one of those misfortunes naturally to be expected, at a time when <the> reason and reflection are silent, and from men whose ignorance prevents their beholding those monuments in their proper light. But when we see persons, who, by their eminence in society the wealth with which fortune has endowd them, and the education they have recieved, should be looked to as the *Patrons of the Arts,* when we see them ravaging the few reliques of antient taste & magnificence that the hand of time has spared, destroying the few sad remains of the Mistress of the World, to gratify <their> a selfish pride or mean cupidity, our <feelings are aroused and our> disdain & disgust are awakened to the <most> highest degree. <We regard I regard those> It is a depredation of the most flagrant kind on the property of the learned world – and one of the highest wrongs to the traveller. For my part I regard the <owners> ↑founders↓ of these palaces much in the same light as I would a gang of miscreants who had plunderd the tomb, and paraded about in the robes of the deceased.

The palace Farnese is inherited by the present King of Naples who has removed to that city[300] The fine statues it contained among which the Farnesian Hercules & Farnesian Bull[301] were the most celebrated. The palace has at present a melancholy & deserted appearance in the interior –

In the <vast por[?]> court is a large Sarcophagus found in the tomb of Cecilia Metella[302] which contained her ashes. The <chief objec> sole object worthy of attention in this palace at present is a Gallery painted in Fresco by Annibale Caracci 65 feet by 20.[303] The painting that most struck my fancy was a large piece representing Bacchus and

300. Ferdinand IV was a grandson of Isabella Farnese.

301. Both statues are now in the Museo Nazionale, Naples.

302. She was the daughter of Consul Quintus Caecilius Metellus and the wife of M. Licinius Crassus. The edifice, on the Appian Way, dates from the Augustan period.

303. Annibale Carracci (1560–1609) was a member of a famous family of Bolognese painters. "65" and "20" are in a slightly different script.

Ariadne drawn in chariots and attended by Bacchanalians fauns satyrs &c <These> Other fine paintings are Galatea & tritons – Aurora & Cephalus, Poliphemus <&> enticing Galatea by the music of a reed – Poliphemus hurling the rock at Acis – Jupiter receiving Juno into the nuptial couch, Diana & Endimion Hercules & Iole &c &c. These are all by Carraci & his scholars and are counted among his finest works. We remained here a long time contemplating them after which we went to the *Farnesina* – <this is> (or small farnese palace)[304]

Here in a gallery are fresco Paintings representing the Fable of Psyche – by the immortal Raphael & his scholars[305] – These paintings have been much injured by the gallery's having been formerly exposed to the air – They still however are capable of giving the highest delight. The two grand pieces are The <banquet> ↑assembly↓ of the Gods where Cupid & Venus are disputing before Jupiter and a Banquet scene of the gods on the marriage of Cupid & psyche. In another room the Fable of Galatea,[306] here is a collossal head sketched in one corner; It is said that Michelangelo[307] calling to see Raphael and finding the rooms vacant amused himself with sketching this head with a piece of charcoal, meaning it as a hint to Raphael that he was too minute in his works & that he should proceed on a larger scale. The sketch is admired <as>by connoisseurs as bold & masterly.

From hence we walked to the summit of Mount Janiculus. From hence we had a charming view of antient and modern rome – The tiber – The Campania – Frescati Tivoli – and the beautiful ampitheatre of mountains[308] that surround th<e>is vast plain. We counted in the city eight large domes of churches besides a great number of smaller ones – As to towers steeples – columns &c they are almost innumerable. The fine monuments of antiquity could most of them be distinguished <The Colisseum> On this mountain in the <chur> Church of St Pierre[309]

304. The Palazzo, or Villa, Farnesina, on the opposite side of the Tiber, was built between 1508 and 1511, and later acquired by Cardinal Alessandro Farnese.

305. The frescoes were designed by Raphael and executed by Giulio Romano, Francesco Penni, and others.

306. This painting was done almost entirely by Raphael.

307. There is no justification for this attribution.

308. The Alban Hills.

309. In this entry Irving may have begun to draw on a French guide book, but none has been identified. For about a month he used several French forms of proper names: "Pierre" (here), "Louis" (March 31), "Gregoire" and "Andre" (April 2), "Patricienne," "Antoine," and "Baptistiere" (April 4), "Palais" (April 8), the headings of his "Route from Rome to Bologna," "Plaisance" ("Journey from Bologna to Milan") and the canceled "Pl" [Plaisance] (April 28). According to his own ac-

in Montorio was formerly one of Raphaels finest paintings *the Transfiguration,*[310] it is now at Paris. On this mountain also is the <temple> ↑fountain↓ pauline[311] which draws its water from <a place> the Lake de Bracciano 35 miles from Rome and is one of the most abundant fountains in the city.

March 30

Visited the museum of the Vatican. Vast variety of statues busts vases urns &c antique – marbles of the Richest species fine mosaics To give even a catalogue would be tedious. The architecture is superb. There are two <?persons?> figures by Canova a sculptor living in rome who Seems to have caught the spirit of the antients – one of them is Perseus with the head of Medusa and the other a Boxer.[312] They promise to remain *chef d ouvres* in the art, and to be counted among the most excellent pieces – in a museum which boasts several of the finest works of the antients. Those grand statues that have been taken out of the Vatican by the french[313] are replaced by casts of Plaister of Paris. The examination of the museum employed us for the day.

In the morning we had delivered our letters to our banker Mr Torlona[314] – a pompous little man who however was very civil and offerd to introduce us to a conversazione of nobility tomorrow night and gave us a general invitation to conversaziones which are held twice a week at his house. We also presented <?an?> a letter of introduction from Mr Degen of Naples to the Baron Humbolt[315] minister for the

---

count in later years, he read in Italy the work of a French traveler who described the country with more excitement than he himself ever felt, only to discover that the man had never been there (Irving to Irving Grinnell, October 28, 1858).

310. The church, mentioned in the ninth century, was rebuilt in the fifteenth century. The painting was confiscated by order of Napoleon in 1797 and placed in the Vatican on its return to Rome in 1815.

311. The Fontana Paolo was built in 1612 for Paul V by Giovanni Fontana and Carlo Moderna.

312. Antonio Canova (1757–1822) was the leader of the neo-classical revival in sculpture. Two figures of boxers by him are in the Vatican, "Damosseno" and "Creugante."

313. Among the most notable works in the Vatican confiscated by the French were the "Apollo Belvedere" and the "Laocoön." In 1815, after negotiations in Paris by Canova, most of them were returned. See Quynn, "The Art Confiscations of the Napoleonic Wars," pp. 441–42, 453, 455–56.

314. Giovanni Torlonia (1755–1829) was one of the leading bankers in Rome.

315. Karl Wilhelm, Freiherr von Humboldt (1767–1835), a German statesman and philosopher, was Prussian minister at Rome from 1801 to 1808. His brother was Friedrich Heinrich Alexander, Freiherr von Humboldt (1769–1859), scientist,

Court of Prussia at Rome. He recieved us very politely and we passed half an hour with him in an agreeable & interesting manner. He is brother to the celebrated Humboldt who has made such an extensive tour in America – and informs us that he expects his brother in Rome in a few days when he will make us acquainted with him. The Baron is said to be a very literary man, and bears an amiable character in other respects.

The evening was spent with our fellow countrymen Mr Wells Mr Alston & Dr Maxwell.

March 31

We visited the Palace Ruspiliosi[316] where we saw the Exquisite Fresco of Guido representing <appol> Apollo in his chariot preceded by <Hes> Aurora & Hesper and surrounded by the hours. This is counted one of the finest paintings in the world. The other remarkable paintings in this Palace are Sampson pulling down the temple of the Philistines by Louis Carrach The Garden of Paradise by Dominican and The triumph of David Over Goliath by the same.[317]

From hence we went to the garden of Aldobrandin ↑Aldobrandini↓[.] in the Cassino we saw a small fresco found in the baths of Titus representing a marriage ceremony[318] This is the best antique painting I have seen and tho evidently <as>a sketch – <shews that> confirms the opinion disputed by some, that the antients had attaind to excellence with the pencil as well as with the chissel. There is a grace in the figures a propriety & simplicity in the drapery and a degree of judgement in the coloring & lights & shades that delighted me. From this garden we saw the tower from which <the> Nero the Tyrant gratified his savage disposition with the contemplation of Rome in flames.[319] The tower is

---

explorer, and natural philosopher, who was on an expedition to South and Central America from 1779 to 1804.

316. The Palazzo Rospigliosi was built in 1603 for Cardinal Scipio Borghese.

317. Lodovico Carracci (1555–1619) was a member of a famous family of Bolognese painters. Domenichino (Domenico Zampieri) (1581–1641) was one of Carracci's best pupils. The first painting by Domenichino to which Irving refers is usually called the "Fall of Adam."

318. The Villa Aldobrandini was built in the sixteenth century and later acquired by Clement VIII (Ippolito Aldobrandini). The "Nozze Aldobrandine," discovered in 1605, was kept at this time in a garden of the villa; it is now in the Vatican.

319. Nero surveyed the burning of Rome in 64 from one of the towers in the Gardens of Maecenas. For a time, however, the tower where he watched was said to be the Torre delle Milizie or Torre di Neroni, to which Irving apparently refers;

of brick and <has been> forms at present part of a nunnery. We repassed from hence along the Quirinal hill, <now mon> by the popes palace,[320] where it is called Monte Cavallo from two collossal statues standing by horses which it is supposed they antiently held by the bridle. These are the productions of Phidias & Praxiteles two famous Grecian artists.[321] Monte Cavallo is said to enjoy the best air of any situation in Rome. We proceeded along the Strada Pia that runs along the top of the Quirinal hill – from one place we had a fine view – the street was intersected by another at right angles[322] – in one direction we looked away to the Pincian hill where the view was terminated by a grand egyptian obelisk – in another to Monte Cavallo where we beheld the fine collosal statues standing each side of another Egyptian obelisk[323] – In the third direction the view terminated with the superb church of St Mary Magiore[324] having an egyptian obelisk in front – and the fourth was closed by <the> one of the gates of antient Rome.[325] We went out at this gate and visited the Villa Albano.[326] This is of elegant architecture enriched with superb marbles & mosaics and crowded with antique statues Busts, urns, sarcophagus's &c., But boasts

---

it is located behind the church of S. Caterina in Magnanapoli and the adjoining convent of Dominican nuns.

320. The Palazzo del Quirinale, built between the sixteenth and the eighteenth centuries, was taken from the papal government in 1870 and is now the residence of the president of the Italian republic.

321. The statues, which represent Castor and Pollux, are Roman copies of Greek originals of the fourth or fifth century B.C., found in the Baths of Constantine and moved to the Piazza del Quirinale by order of Sixtus V, who erroneously ascribed them to Phidias and Praxiteles. At one time the figures were thought to be horse-tamers, and the name of Monte Cavallo was consequently applied to the Piazza.

322. The Via del Quirinale (formerly Strada Pia) meets the Via Quattro Fontane at right angles.

323. The first obelisk on the Pincian Hill, in the Piazza della Trinita, is a Roman imitation of the one in the Piazza del Popolo. That in the Piazza del Quirinale is one of two obelisks thought to have been brought from Egypt about the time of Domitian, moved to its present location in 1782.

324. S. M. Maggiore, one of the four patriarchal basilicas of Rome, was established, according to tradition, in the fourth century. It was rebuilt in the fifth, enlarged in the twelfth and thirteenth, and finished in the eighteenth century. The obelisk behind the church was brought from Egypt with that in the Piazza del Quirinale, moved to its present location in 1588.

325. The Porta Pia was built in 1561 by Michelangelo.

326. The Villa Albani (now the Villa Torlonia) was built in 1760 for Cardinal Alessandro Albani, who formed there a valuable collection of antique sculpture under the supervision of J. J. Winckelmann. Most of it was confiscated by the French in 1797 and never returned.

of no *chef d'ouvre,* tho a profusion of the richest marbles &c very finely disposed –

In the <evening> afternoon we had Sigr. Carrachiolo[327] a painter of landscape of much merit to dine with us and in the evening were visited by Mr Alston, The society of the latter is peculiarly agreeable.

April 1

Visited the church of the Capuchins,[328] where is seen in one of the chapels the ↑arch↓ angel <Gabriel> ↑St. Michael↓ with satan under his feet by Guido – A fine attitude and beautiful colouring. Saul restored to sight – Pietro de Cortona[329] *Church of Ste Maria della Vittoria.* – architecture good, the inside by Bernini – Overcharged with ornaments

Most remarkable thing in the church is a group by Bernini representing St. Teresa dying an angel aiming a dart at her.[330]

<Bernini Palace>

Barberini Palace[331] – an immense building by Bernini said to contain four thousand rooms in it – which I very much doubt – The most striking object in this palace is the <Hall> cieling of the Hall which is near 50 feet high and painted in fresco by Pieto da Cortona supposed to be his masterpiece.[332] The subjects are various and intended to be complimentary to the Barberini family.[333]

There is an immense collection of paintings and antique statues in

327. "Carrachiolo" is in lighter ink. Presumably the man was L. Caracciolo, remembered chiefly as an engraver of the works of Claude Lorrain. He probably came at the invitation of J. C. Cabell, who met him in Lyons in October 1803 and visited him in Rome. See Cabell, "1802–3 Journal No 2," October 23, 1803 [p. 58]; Journal [No. 5], "Notes of a Journey to Italy – In the Winter of 1804–5"; and Journal [No. 7], "Rome Winter of 1805," *passim.*

328. S. M. della Concezione, familiarly known as the church of the Capuchins, was founded in 1624 by Cardinal Antonio Barnerini, a member of the Capuchin order.

329. Pietro Berrettini (1596–1669) was called da Cortona after his birthplace.

330. The church was built in 1605 by Carlo Maderna, who made the interior one of the most complete examples of baroque decoration in Rome. The statue to which Irving refers by Bernini, one of the leading practitioners of this style, is commonly called "St. Teresa in Ecstasy."

331. It was begun in 1624 by Maderna and finished in 1640 by Bernini for Urban VIII (Maffeo Barberini).

332. To this point in the paragraph, in his titles of the paintings in the Barberini Palace, and in his descriptions of the Capitoline Hill, ruins in the Forum, ancient arches, and the Colosseum in this entry Irving drew on Martyn, *The Gentleman's Guide,* pp. 141–45, 195–97, 218–19.

333. The frescoes are allegorical representations of events in the history of the Barberini family.

this building – Many of the best of the former have been sold and among the latter there were none that particularly delighted me. The fact is I begin to be sati<e>ated with antique statues, and no longer feel interested by them unless they have something more than antiquity to reccommend them.

Among the pictures I was most pleased with the famous Magdalene by Guido, there is a particular stile & position of the countenance in which it appears to me this painted [painter] delighted The count<i>enance mild and <?helpless?> gentle, the eyes cast up to heaven with an exprission of languor – of grief – of devotion, rapture &c that gives an indescribable interest in it – as Stern observes an expression the very reverse of "fat contented ignorance looking downward on the earth."[334]

A young man cheated by gamesters, by Mich:angelo, de Carravagio – Joseph & potiphars wife by Carlo Cignani[335]

A saint or cardinal[336] – (I forget his name) by Guido – this figure struck me forcibly, the head is admirable and answerd exactly to my idea of Sterns monk at Calais.

After leaving the Palace I rambled about the antient part of the city examining antique buildings

Capitol[337] – is on an eminence to which you ascend in front by <a>an <vast flight of steps> ↑easy kind of stairs↓. at the top of the stairs on each side are colossal figures standing by Horses <the> called Castor and Pollux, there are likewise two trophies in marble said to be those of Marius. The Building of the Capitol is a centre and two wings, <of> stuccoed in front and of fine architecture <the centre> The centre is the Palace of the Senator of rome – <To> the right wing

334. The monk at Calais described by Laurence Sterne in *A Sentimental Journey through France and Italy* is said to have "one of those heads which Guido has often painted – mild, pale – penetrating, free from all commonplace ideas of fat contented ignorance looking downwards upon the earth – it look'd forwards; but look'd, as if it look'd at something beyond this world." *The Works of Laurence Sterne* (Oxford, 1926–27; Shakespeare Head Press Ed.), IV, 4–5.

335. Carlo Cignani (1628–1719) was a painter of the Bolognese school.

336. Presumably Guido Reni's portrait of St. Andrew Corsini (1302–1373).

337. The modern piazza on the Capitoline Hill and the stairs leading up to it were designed by Michelangelo, begun in the middle of the sixteenth and completed in the seventeenth century. The three buildings on top of the hill, also designed by Michelangelo, are the Palazzo Senatorio in the middle, the Palazzo del Museo Capitolino on the left, and the Palazzo dei Conservatori on the right. The statues at the top are late Roman works. The trophies, erroneously associated with Marius, date from 70–80.

is the museum of the Capitol and the left the Palace of the Conservator – In the area before these buildings is <an>a noble Equestrian Statue of Marcus Aurelius of Corinthian brass – said by many connoisseurs to be the finest <antiqu> Equestrian statue that remains from antiquity. I had not time to day to examine the museum & gallery of paintings but proceeded to take a peep at the *Tarpeian Rock.* This was an abrupt precipice in which the <hill> Capitoline hill terminated on one side and from which they used to thro[w] prisoners. The ground at the foot of this rock has been raised considerably (perhaps between 20 & 30 feet) by rubbish, it still however is a dangerous hight for a man to fall from, by the measurement of some it is near 60 feet perpendicular.[338]

In the Campo Vacchino[339] (antiently the Grand Forum) are a great number of interesting objects viz[340]

Temple of *Jupiter Tonnant* – Three columns with frieze & cornice all of beautiful workmanship – <half> the shafts of the columns are half buried – built by Augustus.

Temple of Concord – eight columns of granite of difft sizes.

Temple of Antoninus & Faustina. 10 columns of numi*dian* marble – fine workmanship –

Temple of Romulus & Remus now the church of St Cosmo & Damiano. Porphyry pillars at the door, door of Bronze – entabliture &c

Temple of Peace, Three vast arches remaining which shew what an immense & magnificent building this originally was. <By> The largest temple in rome –

Three columns of temple of Jupiter Stator – capitals of these columns the richest in Rome, the columns said to be a model of the Corinthian order.[341]

338. This paragraph contains echoes of Martyn, *The Gentleman's Guide,* pp. 195–97.

339. Irving should have written "Vaccino."

340. In the remainder of this entry Irving drew heavily on Martyn, *The Gentleman's Guide,* pp. 141–45.

341. What was formerly identified as the Temple of Jupiter Tonans ("the Thunderer") is now identified as the Temple of Vespasian, begun shortly after his death in 79 by Titus and finished by Domitian. No trace remains of the Temple of Jupiter Tonans built by Augustus on the Capitoline Hill. The Temple of Concord, built about 7 B.C. by Tiberius, was a reconstruction of an earlier sanctuary. The Temple of Antoninus and Faustina was built by the Emperor Antoninus Pius in honor of his wife Faustina the elder. The so-called Temple of Romulus (the infant son of Maxentius), a fourth-century structure, forms the vestibule to the church of SS. Cosma and Damiano, built in the sixth century and rebuilt in 1632. The Temple

<Oft the Triumphal Arches [*unrecovered*]>

Triumphal arches – Arch of Constantine – of Entire marble – part of it which was stollen from an arch of Trajan is of beautiful workmanship – The part worked in Constantines time is vastly inferior & is pointed out as an instance how the arts had diclined – beautiful Columns of *Jaune Antique* (antique yellow) marble.

Arch of Titus, built when he returned from the conquest of Jerusalem – the finest in point of architecture of any in rome – excellent reliefs of Titus & Vespasian carrying in triumph the spoils of the temple at Jerusalem – among which are the Golden Candlestick & the tables of shew bread[.] Composite order was first used in Rome in this arch.

Arch of Septimus Severus of saline marble[.] for a long time it had <nearly> been buried for half its height in the ground but the earth has been cleared away around it by the present pope – and the arch surrounded with a wall.[342]

Colisæum or *Flavian Ampitheatre* it derived the first name from a vast collossal statue of Nero in the character of Apollo 60 feet high that was found in the centre of it.[343]

It was begun by Flavi<a>us Vespasian after his triumph over the Jews. finished by Titus – Area is an oval 620 feet by 513 – 164 feet 3½ inches high – Circumference on the outside is 1741 feet. said to be buried 25 feet in the ground.

Built of blocks of Travertine stone. Much of it has been demolished as I have already observed to build palaces but it is still magisti<el>c

---

of Peace, built by Vespasian to commemmorate his capture of Jerusalem in 71, was not preserved into modern times; the structure to which Irving refers is the ruined Basilica of Constantine or Maxentius, dating from the fourth century, which stands on approximately the site of the Temple of Peace and which was at one time popularly identified with it. The Temple of Jupiter Stator ("the Stayer of Flight") was not preserved into modern times; the structure to which Irving refers is the ruined Temple of Castor and Pollux, built in 484 B.C. by the dictator Aulus Postumius, which early in the nineteenth century was often called the Temple of Jupiter Stator.

342. The Arch of Constantine was built in 315 by the senate in honor of his victory over Maxentius in 312. The Arch of Titus was built in 81 by Domitian in honor of the victories of Titus and Vespasian over the Jews. The Arch of Septimus Severus was built in 203 in honor of the tenth anniversary of the accession to the office of emperor of L. Septimius Severus.

343. A bronze figure of Nero as the sun god, 120 feet high, made by the Greek Zendorus for Nero's house, was moved to a spot near the Colosseum and later destroyed. Most authorities now think the name Colosseum is derived from the great size of the amphitheater (now estimated to seat 50,000) rather than from the statue.

& striking – said to have antiently held near <8>90,000 spectators. This <is the most> is one of the most interesting objects in antient Rome.

A variety of other antiquities occupied the rest of the day but the detail of them is fatiguing & uninteresting –

April 2

Went this morning to the church of [*blank*] to hear some sacred music vocal & instrumental – music tolerable – good picture on the cieling of the sachristy of the Virgin & a monk.

Church of St Pietro in Vinculo[344] – sublime statue of Moses by Michael Angelo, extolled by artists as the finest modern production of the art, and by some even preferred to the antient's.

Church of St. Martino,[345] decorated within with the richest marbles, superb altar – landscapes by Gaspard Poussin. Below the church are <the> part of the warm baths of Titus.[346] Arched and of vast solidity being in a state of perfect strength

From hence was an enterance into the Catacombs which [h]as been closed up, as two monks of the convent of St Martino, were lost in their labarinths.

Church of St Gregoire situated without the town on the Coelian Hill commanding a fine view of The Colisæum, temple of the Sun, Palace of Cæsar[347] &c In <this> one part of this building <is>are two fine fresco's by Guido & Domeniquin; The flagellation of St. Andre by the latter and the same saint going to be crucified by the former. They are

344. S. Pietro in Vincoli was founded according to tradition in 442 as a shrine for the chains of St. Peter; it was restored in 1475.

345. S. Martino ai Monti was built in 500, rebuilt in 1650. Its tribune, high altar, tabernacle, and crypt are all by Pietro da Cortona. The "landscapes" are frescoes of the Roman Campagna by the French painter Gaspard Poussin (1613–1675).

346. The Baths of Titus adjoined the more extensive Baths of Trajan; Irving is referring to the remains of the latter, which were for a time erroneously identified as the Baths of Titus.

347. S. Gregorio Magno, on the Caelian Hill, was originally built in 575 by St. Gregory the Great and dedicated to St. Andrew; a new church was built in the eighth century and dedicated to the founder; it was restored in the seventeenth century. Nothing remains of the Temple of the Sun, built by Augustus in 273; Irving is referring to ruins on the Quirinal Hill of what is now thought to be the Temple of Serapis, which were formerly identified as the Temple of the Sun. The ruins of the several residences of the Roman emperors from Augustus on, repeatedly rebuilt on the Palatine Hill, are called the Palace of Caesar.

much damaged by the humidity of the walls but retain enough of their original beauty to render them objects of admiration.

From hence we returned into the city by a road that passed between the Palace of Cæsar and the place of the Circus Maximus[348] having on one side of us the Capitoline and at a distance on the other side the Aventine hills.

Temple of Fortuna Virilis now a church of Armenians – columns ionic of stone stuccoed and masoned half in the wall – opposite to this is

Pilates Palace vulgarly so called – the intention of it not known, but supposed to be a building erected in later times with the spoils of other <bu> edifices.

Temple of Vesta, a beautiful little temple of a circular form converted into the church of Madonna del sole; surrounded by 20 columns of the Corinthian order.

Cloaca Maxima one of the Sewers of antient Rome. <was> a vast drain 14 feet high & as many wide built of <travetine stone and> great stones by Tarquinus priscus. It ran under a great part of the city and emptied itself into the Tiber.

Temple of Ianus, in reality supposed to be an exchange or market place – Built of Greek marble, with four fronts and pierced with four arches.[349]

Pont Palatin (nowadays Ponte Rotto – broken bridge) one of the most antient bridges of Rome. It was commenced by M Fulvius and finished by Scipio Africanus & L Mummius when <?cons?> censors. It has been <swept> – broken down three times by the swelling of the Tiber and

348. The Circus Maximus, largest of the Roman circuses, according to tradition was originated by the Tarquins but in its present form dates from the second century B.C.; it was several times altered and enlarged.

349. The Temple of Fortuna Virilis, built about the end of the third century B.C., is now thought to be the Temple of the Mater Matuta; it was converted into a church as S.M. Egizaca in 872 and given to the Armenian Catholics in 1570, but it is no longer used as a church. The building formerly called the Casa di Pilato (because it formed one of the stations of the cross in passion plays) is now called the Casa di Crescenzio or di Cola di Rienzo. The Temple of Vesta is so called because its form resembles that of the Temple of Vesta in the Forum but it is probably the Temple of Portunus; it is no longer used as a church. The Cloaca Maxima was constructed in the sixth century B.C., but its roof dates from the second century B.C. The Arch of Janus Quadrifons was built either as a shelter or an exchange for cattle dealers in the third or fourth century, mostly from ancient fragments; the niches were intended to hold statues.

In his description of the first four of these structures Irving drew on Martyn, *The Gentleman's Guide,* pp. 156–57, 160.

is now in ruins. It was likewise called the Senatorial bridge because the Senators passed over it when they went to consult the books of the Sybills which were conserved at Mount Janiculum. There are fine views from here up and down the tiber – with two other bridges and a few reliques of the Sublican bridge where Horatius Cocles defended the city singly against a host of Enemies.[350]

Temple of Iuno – Temple of Pallas – Nerva[351] &c Visited the Capitol & examined part of the fine gallery of paintings

In the evening went to a Conversazione at the Marquis of Torlona's – great number of the nobility there, and foreigners of distinction, particularly two Russian Princes – Assembly most deplorably stupid[.] hardly a handsome woman there[.] the company sat down almost universally to cards and we left them at an early hour. It is a just remark of a traveller in italy (I believe Dr Moore) that <at the conv> ↑<an>↓ an italian conversazione is a place where people meet to do any thing else but converse[352] – I have however been to several where they have been more rational.

April 3

This morning visited the Borghese palace[353] in company with Mr Alston, here are a great variety of fine paintings –

350. The bridge variously called Palatino, Aemilio, Senatorio, and Rotto is said to have been begun in 181 B.C. and finished in 143 B.C. The prophetic books about Rome's destiny, said to have been sold to Tarquinius Priscus by the Cumean Sibyl, were originally kept in the Temple of Jupiter on the Capitoline Hill; they seem never to have been kept on the Janiculum. Presumably the "two" other bridges to which Irving refers are the Ponte Fabrico and the Ponte di San Bartolomeo or Cestio (considered as one) and the Ponte Sisto. The Pons Sublicius, scene of the legendary defense of the city by Horatius Cocles in the sixth century B.C., was the first across the Tiber; the remains to which Irving refers no longer exist.

In this paragraph Irving apparently drew on a printed account which has not been identified, possibly a French guide book (see entry of March 29, n. 309).

351. The Temple of Juno Regina, of which nothing remains, was built about the same time and near the Temple of Jupiter Stator (see entry of April 1, 1805, n. 341). The Forum of Nerva, or Forum Transitorius, was begun by Domitian and completed in 97 by the Emperor M. Cocceius Nerva. In the middle stood the Temple of Minerva, of which only the base remains.

352. "I do not know what more can be said of these assemblies; only it may be necessary to prevent mistakes, to add, that a conversazine is a place where there is no conversation" (Moore, *A View of Society and Manners in Italy*, I, 385).

353. The Borghese Palace was begun in 1590 and completed about 1610. A list of the paintings in it when Irving visited it is contained in Dalmazzoni, *The Antiquarian or the Guide for Foreigners*, pp. 272–74. They were removed to the Villa Borghese in 1891 (see n. 291).

Afterwards went to the Mausoleum of Augustus.[354] This was a vast building and has been converted into a circus in which in summer the people of rome are entertained with the humane spectacles of bull baits. There is a remarkable echo in this circus and two persons applying their ears to the wall on opposite sides may converse with each other in whispers very distinctly.

Visited the working rooms of Canova. This man is the first <am> sculptor among the moderns and has produced several works that have established his fame. I saw at his rooms a group of Cupid and Psyche lately finished which I think surpasses any group I have ever seen for sweetness of workmanship and expression. He is busied at present about the statues of the Bonaparte family – that of the Emperor is to be a colossal one and naked in the style of the antients. I saw the casts of two statues of the mother and sister of Bonaparte which are very fine. He is likewise busied finishing a colossal statue of the present king of Naples in the <cla> dress of an antient warrior.[355] This is a most bitter satire on the poor King – he might as well have represented him in the character of Solomon. The statue is soon to be transported to naples and I doubt not will be regarded with many a sly grin & waggish remark.

In the evening we <walked> rambled out at the gate *del popolo* into the country – we pursued a bye road that winding a little brought us to the summit of a small hill in the rear of a neat villa. From hence we had a view of one part of Rome thro which the Tiber rolls its yellow turbid stream. The church of St. Peters was seen to remarkable advantage The buildings <that inter> between us seeming to sink to yield us a complete view of that magnificent Edifice –

The scene was <mel> of that kind calculated to produce the most melancholy yet pleasing sensations – Before us was expanded the interesting spot

> "where Romes proud genius reard her awful brow"[356]

354. It was built in 28 B.C. as a tomb for Augustus and the principal members of his family. Despoiled for building material during the Middle Ages, it was transformed in 1780 into an ampitheater for various entertainments and in the nineteenth century into a concert hall.

355. Canova's "Cupid and Psyche" is now in the Louvre. His statues of Napoleon, Letizia (Ramolino) Bonaparte (1750–1836), Pauline Bonaparte (1780–1825), and Ferdinand IV are respectively in the Palazzo di Brera, Milan, the Fondazione Querini Stampalia, Venice, the Villa Borghese, Rome, and the Museo Nazionale, Naples.

356. This quotation and the seven lines of poetry quoted later in this entry are,

<The> That imperious city that once gave laws to nations and proudly assumed the title of *Mistress of the World* – into whose walls were borne in triumph the spoils of Empires and whose warriors led captive at their chariot wheels the most potent kings of the earth. <That city> How have the mighty fallen![357] <Superstition like a baneful blast has passed over the> sunk from her former greatness into a state of ignorance & poverty – Rome presents at present, a complete contrast to what she was. A government that no longer commands respect out of its own territories – whose chief has in fact to undertake a long and degrading journey to gratify the pride and ostentation of a <?fo?> distant Tyrant – The soldiery of Rome – once the terror of the world, now the most contemptible beings that ever took up arms – composed of the refuse of society – The nobility that antiently vied with one another to acquire the public confidence and the applause of the nation by their merits and services – now content if they can gain an empty name by the splendor of their Palaces and the magnificence of their equipages – the people at large once manly, noble and independent in their manners now grovelling servile, superstitious – cringing to their priests and tamely submitting to the most glaring impositions. The arts languishing – in fact the whole nation struggling in the last stages of a national decline. Such were my reflections as I cast my eye over the city – <Her>The proudly swelling domes of its churches seemed to me but as so many monuments of the triumph of superstition & ignorance and the mingled sound of its bells, as the funeral knell of genius and liberty.

"I see the columnd arches fail
And structures hoar the boast of years –
Where Romes proud genius reard her awful brow,
Sad monument! Ambition near
Rolls on the dust & pours a tear –
Pale honour drops the flutering plume
And conquest weeps oer Cæsars tomb"

The scenery around seemd to correspond in affording melancholy impression – <The> Hills covered with the picturesque but <gl> mournful italian pine – groves of cypress – among which <can> were

---

with slightly different punctuation and capitalization, from James Ogilvie, "Ode to Time," III 2, ll. 3, 4, 7–11, *Poems on Several Subjects* (London, 1769), I, 89.

357. " . . . how are the mighty fallen!"; "How are the mighty fallen in the midst of the battle!" (II Samuel 1:19, 25).

seen in partial glimpses, The temples & statues that decorated the gardens of different villas – they <seemed> reminded me of the simple yet elegant fanes of ancient Rome – and resembled faint efforts to imitate her glories. The whole prospect was mellowed by the <sof> sober tint of evening and before we left the spot twilight had already began to orshadow the scene.

April 4

Hired an open carriage & visited

Temple of Pudiciti patricienne – (now the church of St Mary)[358] antiently none but maried women of Rome could enter this temple – remains are 8 columns of Grecian marble of Corinthian order – within the church – bocca della verita (mouth of truth) is a <large round> flat piece of marble, round, having on it eyes, nose and an open mouth, in the latter it is pretended by antiquarians that antiently they put the hand in taking an oath, and if they purgured themselves they would not be able to draw it forth again. An expedient no doubt highly convenient to perjurers.

Pyramid of Caius Cestus[359] this is a quadrangular pyramid in the style of the celebrated ones of Egypt – it is 113 feet high and 89 feet wide. It was erected to contain the ashes of Caius Cestus in compliance with his last testement, as is understood by an inscription on the pyramid. It is coverd by <pie> square pieces of white marble <a foot ?t?> of a foot in thickness – completely blackned by age. I was not able to enter the edifice because of a ditch of water that surrounded it. Within there is a sepulchral chamber the walls coverd with hard stucco and painted in different compartments with figures of women vases &c much damaged by time – The building is a picturesque object and different from all the other antient monuments. In front of it there is a large field in which they bury foreigners who are not of the Catholic religion.[360] Here are the tombs of persons of different nations – English Russians Germans &c – and among others I saw the monument of my

358. S. M. in Cosmedin was built in the sixth century, enlarged in the eighth, restored in the twelfth and again in the nineteenth century. It occupies the site of a Roman temple, according to one theory that of the so-called Temple Pudicita Patricia, but more probably that of Hercules built by Pompey.

359. Caius Cestius (d. 43 B.C.) was praetor, people's tribune, and member of the college of the Septemviri Epulones, in charge of sacred banquets.

360. It was first called the Cimitero Acottolico or Cimitero degli Acottolici al Testaccio, now commonly "The Protestant Cemetery."

fair countrywoman Mrs McEvers wife of <J>Mr James McEvers[361] of New York. She died in the flower of youth aged but 18 years. – This is a solemn – melancholy place – Scarce a traveller resorts here but he reads the epitaph of a fellow countryman, who wandring in search of health had at length escaped from his load of miseries & infirmities. He drops the tear or heaves the ready sigh to his memory, for, when so far removed from his native shores he looks upon every fellow countryman as of the same family.

In the neighborhood of this monument they point out a considerable hill[362] formed by pot sherds which by a particular law the potters were obliged to carry & deposit there. At present there are wine vaults in the hill which are said to be peculiarly excellent.

Went out at the <Port of St> *Gate of St Paul*[363] built by Bellisarius whose wall extends along this part of the city. Rode along the banks of the tiber for some distance – beautiful scenery – arrived at the

Church of St Paul without the wall[364] – This church is chiefly remarkable for the ranges of superb columns in the interior. <These columns are of the> There are 120 columns of which the most precious are 24 formed <of> each of a single piece of marble of a most beautiful kind called *pavonezetto*[.] they are of the Corinthian order – fluted – 36 feet high & 11 in circumference – each as I before remarkd of an entire piece of marble. The altars are ornamented by pillars of Porphyre – The church is paved with fragments of marbles containing old inscriptions &c. under the grand alter they tell you is preserved the body of the apostle paul I was happy to find his bones at length collected together for I had found them in my travells <sact> scatterd <all over the> throught all the convents & churches I had visited.

Church of St Sebastian without the walls – The <grand treasure & curiosit> object *most worthy* of the attention of the traveller in this

361. Ruth Brick Hunter McEvers (1784–1803), who was traveling for her health, died at Velletri. Her husband was James McEvers, a New York City merchant (typescript notes on the Bayard-McEvers families, New York Historical Society).

362. Monte Testaccio.

363. The Porta S. Paolo and the adjoining wall were built by Aurelian in the third century, but much of the construction was restored by the Byzantine general Belisarius (*ca.* 505–565).

364. S. Paolo fuori le Mura is one of the four patriarchal basilicas of Rome. The first church was built by Constantine to replace an oratory on the site of St. Paul's tomb. The second was begun in 386 and enlarged and embellished several times until it was the most splendid in Rome; it was destroyed by fire in 1823.

church is a stone on which our Saviour left the prints of his feet when he appeared once to St Peter – the prints to be sure are very visible and every toe is there, but the *artist* has not succeeded in representing the true print of a foot – after this if the Traveller chuses he may look at a very well executed statue of St Sebastian by Antoine Giorgetti after the model of Bernini[365]

From this church you descend into the catacombs. My curiosity was soon satisfied with them[.] they were low and half full of dirt. The bones remain in many of the nitches. They are said to extend in different directions for the distance of six miles.

Here many christians took refuge in the early ages of Christianity. They are not to be compared <wth> with the catacombs of Naples or Syracuse.

Tomb of Cecilia Metella of a spherical form 89[366] feet in diameter – well preserved and one of the most beautiful monuments of antient rome. faced with great blocks of travertine stone. The sarcophagus which containd the ashes of Cecilia Metella has been transported to the court of the Farnese Palace. By an antient inscription on the monument we are told that Cecilia Metella was the daughter of Q Creticus & wife of Crassus. – The walls are of an astonishing thickness and there is a small conical chamber open at the top, within <o>in which over the door was fixed in the wall the sarcophagus.

A short distance from this tomb is the *Circus of Caraccalla* – if you stand by the tomb <and> facing towards the circus & shout you hear two echoes extremely distinct. The Circus of Caracalla is long and <proportion> narrow in proportion (1524 feet by 395) having been destined for the racing with chariots

Fountain of the Nymph Egeria, a kind of grotto in the side of a hill of arched mason work This was the favorite retreat of Numa Pompilius to enjoy the coolness of the grotto and the delightful groves by which it was surrounded – The water is pure and limpid – The

365. S. Sebastiano, one of the seven pilgrim churches of Rome, was built in the first half of the fourth century and rebuilt in 1612. Originally dedicated to the apostles Peter and Paul because it was built over the cemetery where their bodies were temporarily interred, it was named after the ninth century for St. Sebastian, who was martyred in 288 and buried here. The stone to which Irving refers is in the first chapel on the right. Antonio Giorgetti (d. 1670), Italian sculptor, belonged to the school of Bernini. The catacombs of S. Sebastian are the only ones in Rome which have always been accessible and have consequently been badly despoiled.

366. The structure is 65 feet in diameter (see entry of March 29, 1805, n. 302).

grotto highly picturesque – The statue is much mutilated I however on the first glance percieved that the cumbent statue of the nymph as it is generally called was nothing more or less than the strapping *carcass of a man* – such are the errors into which these antiquarians are forever running.[367]

Temple of Bacchus nowadays changed into the church of St Urbain – a small square building in a field on the hill in which the <fount> Grotto of Egeria is erected[368]

Baths of Caracalla, immense ruins – antiently of the most surprizing magnificence. In these baths were found the famous Farnese hercules and the Farnese Bull.[369]

Church of St John & Baptistere of Constantine a small church containing the superb font where <it> the Emperor Constantine was baptized[370]

Church of St. John de Lateran,[371] founded by Constantine abounds in rich marbles and very good bas reliefs paintings &c[.] one of the altars

367. The Circus of Caracalla is now identified as the Circus of Maxentius, built in 309 by that emperor in honor of his son Romulus. What was formerly identified as the Fountain of the Nymph Egeria is now thought to be a nymphaeum of the villa of Herodes Atticus, Greek rhetorician of the second century. The Fountain of Egeria, it is now believed, was near the present Villa Celimontana or Mattei inside the city. Numa Pompilius (715–675 B.C.), second legendary king of Rome, had as his consort and adviser the water goddess Egeria. The statue presumably represents a river and thus suggests that the grotto was sacred to a male divinity.

368. What was formerly identified as the Temple of Bacchus is now thought to have been a temple forming part of the villa of Herodes Atticus. It was converted into a church as S. Urbano in the seventh or eighth century, and restored in 1634.

369. These baths were begun during the reign of Caracalla and finished under Alexander Severus. They were damaged by the Goths in the sixth century.

370. The Battistero di S. Giovanni, or S. Giovanni in Fonte, was built in 324, restored in the fifth and ninth centuries. It was not, as legend has it, the scene of Constantine's baptism.

371. St. John Lateran, the cathedral of Rome, dates from the fourth century, but has several times been damaged and restored, and entirely rebuilt in the fourteenth and seventeenth centuries. The altar of the Holy Sacrament is by Pietro Paolo Olivieri; the origin of the columns is uncertain. The temple of Jupiter of the Capitol, mentioned by Irving as the source of the columns, was begun by the Tarquins on the Capitoline Hill and dedicated in 509 B.C., on the site of the present Palazzo Caffarelli; it was three times destroyed and rebuilt, and its gilding was repeatedly plundered. The Cappella Corsini was built in the eighteenth century.

The Scala Santa, consisting of twenty-eight marble steps, is said to have been brought from Jerusalem by St. Helena. The portico was built from a design by Domenico Fontana in 1589. The chapel at the head of the staircase, the Sancta Sanctorum, was built in 1278 as a private chapel for the popes. The painting, on wood, is behind the altar.

has a fine front and architrave supported by four fluted columns all of bronze gilt. These were taken from the temple of Jupiter of the Capitol – by some they are said to be the same which Augustus had made after the battle of Actium out of the prows of Egyptian vessels[.] others say that they were part of the spoils which Vespasian brought from the temple of Jerusalem. In this church is the chapel of the Corsini family the most magnificent in rome.

The Holy Stair case, This antiently appertained to the palace of Pilate and was transported from Jerusalem to Rome. Having been mounted several times by our Saviour it is regarded as a thing highly sacred. It is conserved in a handsome building where there is a portico and different entrances with five stairs[.] the middle one is the holy one. It is continually crowded by devotees who crawl up it on their knees muttering their ave marias and kissing every step. The steps are of white marble, but the crowd is continually so numerous that they had nearly kissd & rubbed them thro, till one of the popes caused each of them to be covered with a piece of wood.

<As I had no intent of>

I went to the head of the staircase by means of one of the other stairs up which people are permitted to walk. Here we were shewn <the> a chapel in which an image of our Saviour is conserved <carved by> commenced by St Luke & finished by angels[.] it is safely locked up and not permitted to be seen by profane eyes but I am told it is much the same in point of workmanship as the Virgin at Loretto by the same artist. Here we were also shewn a bronze door from Pilates palace.

Temple of Minerva Medica, the ruins of a beautiful rotundo, situated in a vineyard into which we were admitted by a very pretty peasant girl – In this vineyard also is the subterraneous sepulchre of the Arruntii a Roman family – It has several inscriptions and <cinerary> cinérare pots in it & is decorated by pretty bas reliefs in stucco.[372]

Baths of Diocletian – the ruins of another of those immense edifices that exhibit the magnificence & ostentation of the antients.[373]

372. These ruins are now thought to be those of the nymphaeum in the gardens of Licinius built about 260. The name comes from a statue of Minerva found there, which probably occupied one of the niches in the wall. Behind the Temple of Minerva two columbaria were discovered in 1736, one of which was constructed in the year 6 by L. Arruntius, consul.

373. These baths were the largest in Rome, built in 305–306. Parts of the ruins were converted by Michelangelo to a church and a monastery, now the Museo Nazionale Romano and the Museo delle Terme.

There were several other things that I saw which are not worthy of notice – having nothing to reccommend them but their antiquity.

In the evening we visited the Prussian Minister Baron Humbolt. We found there Madam de Stol the celebrated authoress of Delphine[374] &c. She is a woman of great strength of mind & understanding by all accounts – We were in company with her but a few minutes – The minister was engaged to escort her to a conversazione at the Marquis Torlonias – We then went to a private concert at Mr Irvine's,[375] a Scotch gentleman who is settled in rome. Mr I was sick but we were introduced to his lady who is an italian woman but speaks good English – She is very handsome & of pleasing manners. The concert was extremely agreeable

April 5

Visited the Pantheon.[376] This is the most perfect and beautiful remain of antiquity in Rome The outside is stripped of the incrustation of marble that antiently ornamented it, but the inside is still superb and used as a church. The inside is 143½ feet in circumference forming an exact circle; the whole is extremely well lighted by a circular hole in the center of the dome which is 25 feet diameter – th<is>e dome is supposed to have been antiently covered with plates of silver or bronze. Around the interior are a number of recesses at equal distances ornamented with superb pillars of yellow antique, pavonezetto and other <?f?> beautiful marbles – The pavement consists of the same. This building was erected by Marcus Agrippus and dedicated to Jupiter the Avenger.

From the Pantheon I went to the church of St Peters[377] and passed

374. Madame de Staël's *Delphine* was published in 1802.

375. James Irvine had traveled in America (Irvine to E. Weeks, February 17, 1821; E. Weeks to Rufus King, November 30, 1823, in Despatches from U. S. Consuls, Rome, NA, RG 59).

376. The present building is a reconstruction by Hadrian after 126 of that built by Agrippa in 27 to commemorate his victory at Actium; it was consecrated as a Christian church in 609. In his description of it (except for the last sentence) Irving seems to have drawn on Martyn, *The Gentleman's Guide,* pp. 155–56.

377. The patriarchal basilica of St. Peter was founded by Constantine on the site of an oratory over the tomb of St. Peter. The present building was begun in 1506 by Bramante, worked on by several other architects, most notably Michelangelo, and consecrated in 1626. The loggia or loggie (gallery of thirteen bays) and the adjoining four stanze or rooms, decorated by Raphael, and the Sistine Chapel, painted by Michelangelo and other artists (but not Raphael), are all in the Vatican Palace adjoining the church.

some time in the lodges & chambers of Raphael and the Sixtine Chapel, admiring the chef d'ouvres of that inimitable painter. I then walked about in the church which for magnificence and profusion of costly marbles &c &c leaves every church I have seen far behind – discription would in vain endeavor to give an idea of its splendor.

Mounted up into the cupolo of the church and from thence into the ball – which is large enough to contain twenty men. Went outside and climed up an iron ladder that goes over part of the steeple & the outside of the ball and is affixed to the cross The latter is <in> very large & of bronze. The height is fearful and tremend<u>ous[378] and I clung to the cross as firmly as the strictest Catholic as a slip would precipitate me to an immense distance from hence the view was superb – I was as if on a point and could command an uninterrupted view on every side, no <intervening> object intervening to intercept it. The city laid below me like a map and I could trace <all> both the antient & modern parts – The winding of the tiber, the bridges, churches, temples, walls, ampitheatre &c. The Campania, the ampitheatre of hills that surround it, the Appenines to the left and the Mediterranean to the right After contemplating this sublime view for some time I decended from my hazardous situation, into the church. When I regaind the street and looked back I was astonished to see how small those objects appeared to me which when near were so immense. The ball appeared inconsiderable and the cross quite diminutive. That part of it to which I had clung with my arms thrown round it appeared as if it might almost be grasped with the hand and I suppose a man in that situation would appear like a mere pigmy, not discernable unless to an eye particularly attentive.

April 6

Revisited the Farnesina where are the paintings in fresco by Raphæl & his scholars representing the story of Physche &c

Afterwards visited a manufactory of paper where we were shewn the whole process of making it.

April 7

I sat out this morning to visit the village of Frescati, 12 Miles from Rome. I had commissioned our valet de place to procure a carriage and he engaged a crazy vehicle called a calesso something like our

378. The "u" is canceled in pencil.

chairs only higher & more ticklish – It was drawn by one horse and unfortunately the driver had put to it one of his youngest and most headstrong animals – The consequence was that we had scarcely got four miles from Rome before he began to shew his unruly disposition. He would stop suddenly, paw the ground, rear, kick up and go any way but the right one. These delays became so frequent and <grew> the horse grew so unruly that I was obliged to leave the carriage and walk thro the mud to Grotta Ferrata about 4 miles distant. I had told Joseph, the valet de place, not to pay the fellow a farthing as I thought he deserved to be punished for imposing such a mischevious animal on me. Joseph, however, who is as great a rogue as the driver, and no doubt a particular friend of his, paid him a dollar in direct contradiction to my orders. I severely repremanded him for it but he excused himself by saying that he was affraid if he had not have given the fellow something he would *stilletto* him at night. On then, we trudged and at length reached Grotta Ferrata.

This is a small village pretended to be built upon the scite of Cicero's villa.[379] There is nothing to see here but some fine fresco paintings by Dominiquin in the monastary of the Monks of St Basile.[380] These are very excellent <partiqu> particularly one where St. Barthelemi Nileo is represented opening the mouth of a dumb child. Over the altar is an oil painting by Annibal Carrache. This <village> convent is of a picturesque construction having been fortified formerly. From hence we proceeded along a fine avenue of stately trees from whence ↑I had↓ numerous <fine views> beautiful prospects of the Campania, Rome &c. This avenue led to the Villa Bracciano[381] – here is a <vaul> cieling painted <in> by domeniquin representing Aurora Cynthia &c. there are several other paintings in this villa, of merit. From hence the road winds along a hollow to the village of Frescati. The views as you pass

379. The site of Cicero's villa Tusculanum (where he wrote the *Tusculanes Disputationes*), near the ancient Tusculum, is in dispute. The ruins of the town are halfway between Grottaferrata and Frascati, east of both and about a mile and a half from each.

380. The monastery of S. Basilio was founded in 1004; the attached church of S. Maria, consecrated in 1025 and rebuilt in 1754, contains the pictures. The fresco by Domenichino, in the chapel of S. Nilo, shows a demonic boy cured by prayers of St. Nilus the Younger. The painting of the Virgin and Child with SS. Nilus and Bartholomew is in the style of the Carracci.

381. The villa was built at the end of the sixteenth century and is now known as the Villa Grazioli. The work by Domenchino to which Irving refers is a fresco allegorically representing sunrise, the midday sun, and sunset.

along are very picturesque and rich. <villas> Gardens, groves, thro the intervals of which are seen the white walls of villas or the antient towers of a church or monestary, groups of trees &c cover the gentle descent of the hills which sweep down into the vast plain of the campania, in which at a distance rome majestically rears her domes & towers. The lanscapes clothed in the gay colours & luxurient verdure of spring present the most enchanting scenery to the eye.

Frascati is situated on the side of a hill and enjoys fine air and an extensive and superb propect The whole Campania & surrounding country lying open to it.[382] There are situated a number of villas of the Roman nobility among which <are> the Villa Aldobrandini[383] is the most worthy of attention at present. It is seated above the village and enjoys all the advantages of air & prospect – <It at> It is particularly remarkable for the variety of its cascades, fountains, Jet d'eaus & other water works – there are several statues with instruments that play tunes by machinery set in motion by the water. In this villa are <Having seen the rest> likewise several frescos by the celebrated Domeniquin. At Frescati are seen the ruins of the antient city of Tusculum[384] and some remains that are commonly called the grotto's of Cicero.

At Frescati I endeavored to get a carriage to take me to town. The scoundrels thought that they had me in their power and that I would be obliged to take a carriage at their own price[.] they therefore charged me most exhorbitantly. Joseph seconded them in their charges and assured me that I would not be able to get <them> ↑one↓ cheaper. I had already been pretty well convinced of this fellows dishonesty and saw clearly that it was a combination to cheat me out of several dollars, I determined for once to disappoint them and to punish Mr Joseph I therefore told them that they would find I was not in their power as completely as they thought, I had a pair of legs sufficiently strong to carry me to rome and that I would rather walk three times the distance than submit to their impositions. I accordingly sat off and orderd Joseph

382. A reference to this prospect occurs in "The Little Antiquary" in *Tales of a Traveller.*

383. It was built between 1598 and 1603 by Giacomo della Porta for Cardinal Pietro Aldobrandini.

384. Tusculum (see n. 379) was presumably an Etruscan town, destroyed by the Romans in 1191. The ruins comprise, besides the so-called villa of Cicero, an amphitheater, a forum, and a theater. Three of the stories in *Tales of a Traveller* are laid on this site or in its neighborhood: "The Painter's Adventure," "The Story of the Bandit Chieftan," and "The Story of the Young Robber."

to accompany me. The fellows then wanted to bargain with me at a lower price but I had determined to disappoint them and walked on without paying any attention to their talk. The distance was twelve miles and poor Joseph was heartily fatigued before we got to Rome where we arrived in three hours. I then told him to be careful what kind of a horse he got me another time and how he countenanced the impositions of every vagabond.

In the evening we accompanied the Baron de Humboldt to the conversazione of the Marquis. [*blank*][385] Minister imperial at the Court of Rome. Here we found a crowded assembly that filld four rooms, consisting of the first nobility of Rome and several foreigners of distinction. The company was very brilliant, as usual they mingled together for an hour or so, conversing together till the assembly was formed when the greatest part set down to cards – Whist & Faro are the favorite Games.

I <sh>have <d> remarked the truth of an observation of Dr Moore's that "a stranger will form no high idea of the beauty of the Roman women from the specimens he sees in the fashionable circles; but he will be often struck with the fine character of countenance he sees in the streets; and percieve a resemblance between living features and those of the antique busts & statues"[386] There are in fact very few handsome countenances in proportion among the ↑female↓ nobility but I have seen many among the lowest classes, even the rugged peasantry that have great sweetness and <even> intelligence of expression.

In the conversaziones of Rome great style is observed. Servants are stationed in the several rooms thro which you pass and your name is announced in a loud voice from one to another. Whenever we were usherd into any of them we could <hav> hear *gli cavalieri Amer<a>icani* bawled from one servant to another thro a long suite of apartments. There is likewise a custom observed among the servants here that I have witnessed no where else and which appears exceeding mean. Whenever you attend a conversazione or even pass a social evening at any fashionable house the next morning a servant is at your door regularly for a *buono mano*[387] – this has invariably been the case

385. Johann Emanuel Josepf, Graf Khevenhüller (1751–1847), member of a distinguished Austrian family, was the minister of the Holy Roman Empire in Rome at this time.

386. Irving's quotation varies only slightly from his source, Moore, *A View of Society and Manners in Italy*, II, 64, 66–67.

387. Irving referred to this custom of asking for a tip also in his letter to William Irving, April 4, 1805.

wherever we have visited in rome though perhaps we did not stay in the house but a quarter of an hour.

April 8

Visited the Palais Pamfili or Doria[388] where there is a superb gallery of Paintings particularly landscapes. Many of these are by Gaspard and Nicholas Poussin and there are several by the inimitable Claude Lorraine particularly two large ones which are counted two of his best productions.

In the evening we went to a private concert given by the Countess Carodoro[.][389] here we found the same crowd of nobility that flock to all the conversaziones. The company were chiefly in black which is the fashionable dress in holy Week. The Countess sang a long piece <with> in a superior stile. Her voice is strong clear & sweet.

April 9

Villa Ludovisi[390] – collection of antient Busts & statues – Papirus who pretends to reveal the secret of the senate to his mother – very excellent – It is the work of Menelaus of Greece. – <Phetus> ↑Pætus↓[391] & Arria – the latter dying the former stabbing himself. Pluto & prosperpine by Bernini –

Noble fresco of Aurora by Guerchin de cento.[392] Painting by the same author representing fame.

April 10

Museum of the Capitol – Vast variety of Busts statues sarcophagus's &c. The finest have been transported to Paris and casts of Plaister

388. The Palazzo Doria, dating from 1435, was reconstructed by the Doria-Pamphili family in the seventeenth century. Adjoining it is the Galleria Doria Pamphili. The paintings are probably Lorrain's "Mill" and "Temple of Apollo."

389. Probably the Countess Carradori. For one branch of the family, see Vittorio Spreti, *Enciclopedia Storico Nobiliare Italiana* (Milan, 1932).

390. The Villa Ludovisi, built in the seventeenth century, was razed in the nineteenth century when the Via Veneto was constructed. Most of the statuary in it, including the first two pieces Irving refers to, are now in the Museo Nazionale Romano. The first of the two is now called "Electra and Orestes," by Menelaos. The second is now described as a Gaul slaying himself after slaying his wife, copied from bronze figures on the citadel of Pergamum in the second century B.C. Bernini's "Rape of Prosperpine" is now in the Villa Borghese.

391. "Phetus" is canceled and "Pætus" written above in pencil.

392. Giovanni Francesco Barbieri, called Gercino (1591–1666), born at Cento, belonged to the Bolognese school. Both paintings by him are on the ceiling of the Casino dell' Aurora, belonging formerly to the Villa Ludovisi.

<sup> substituted[.] what highly interested me were antient busts of Philosophers, historians poets emperors &c – as we may suppose many of them to be faithful likenesses.

In the evening we were to a private conversazione at the Baron DeHumboldts. The assembly was more rational than any I have seen in Rome, it was small and the people seemed as if they really met to converse together.

NB. This was the first day of the three which are particularly celebrated in holy week.[393] We attended <th> in the afternoon at the chapel in the Popes Palace at *Monte Cavallo* where the *Miserere* was sung by a number of voices among which were several very fine *artificial* ones. The Miserere is a most solemn affecting piece of music representing the passion & suffering of our Saviour. To heighten the melancholy effect most of the candles were put out and the chapel made <a> gloomy and obscure.

April 11

This morning we went to St Peters to see a continuance of the ceremonies of Holy Week. They commenced in the Sixtine chapel where grand mass was celebrated – The chapel was filld with the nobility & foreigners. From thence there was a grand procession to the pauline chapel[394] – of cardinals – Bishops prelates &c &c with wax tapers – among which strutted the cardinal who acted in place of the pope – A silk canopy was held over his head <incense> & <were> Vases of burning incense were carried around him – The cardinal as I said strutted in the midst his eyes cast to the ground, affecting humility but at the same time swelling with vanity and pride.

Afterwards there was a procession to another chapel where amongst other ceremonies the cardinal washed <and> the feet of twelve monks clad in robs of white woolen representing the twelve apostles – after he had washed and kissd the feet of each of them he gave them a bunch of white flowers and they in return kissd his hand – Never did I see such an ostentatious piece of humility

They then in another chapel celebrated the last supper the twelve

393. Irving drew briefly on this entry and the next in his description of the Holy Week ceremonies he attended, in his letter to William Irving, April 12, 1805.

394. The Cappella Paolina, in the Vatican Palace, was built in 1540 by Antonio da Sangallo the Younger for Paul III as was also the Sala Regia through which the Capella is reached from the Sistine Chapel.

monks again representing the apostles. This solemn farce may have a serious effect on the minds of Catholics but I could see the smile of contempt & dirision on the faces of most of the foreigners and even some of the apostles seemed highly amused with the ceremony of having their feet washed – but still more so at the entertaining ceremony of the <dinner> supper.

In the evening the Miserere was again sung in the Sixtine chapel after which the company adjourned to the grand church in the centre of which was suspended a Grand cross illuminated with a great number of lamps. This had a noble effect on the surrounding arcades, aisles and recesses throwing a large mass of light that produced exquisite light & shade. Here the fashionable world resorted in crowds as to a promenade walking round & round, bowing smiling & talking to each other.

April 13

This morning we revisited the Moses of Michael Angelo – The whole town was busy firing off pistols squibs & crackers[.] we were at a loss to understand the meaning of it till we were told it was in commemoration of the resurrection of our saviour!

Paid a <final>farewell visit to the antient forum and the antiquities – went thro Cæsars palace and into the baths of Livia[395] – beautiful arabesques and fresco ornaments on the walls most of them Gilt

The ruins of Caesars palace have a very picturesque appearance – Noble view of the city and country around. Beautiful simplicity that characterized the antient architecture ornaments implements &c. The views in italy rendered peculiarly interesting by mouldering columns – temples &c Trees of a rich and luxurient appearance – herbage – bushes &c very beautiful.

This morning I recieved a visit from the Chevalier Giustiniani[396] to whom I had brought a letter from lady Shaftesbury and had not delivered it till yesterday.

[*inside back cover*]

Caradoro[397]

395. These ruins, on the Palatine Hill, are called the House of Livia, who was the wife of Augustus, but are thought to be the remains of his house.

396. The Giustiniani family has so many branches that it does not seem possible to identify this individual.

397. "Caradoro" is written in brown or black ink. See entry for April 8, 1805, for a reference to "the Countess Carodoro."

[*back cover*][398]
D[*illegible*]
Roma Triumphans[399]

The
The D
Villefr[anche]

398. Besides the random words and letters, this page shows sketches of two owls and the profile of a man (Figure 5); all are in brown or black ink.
399. "Rome Triumphant."

EUROPEAN JOURNAL, 1804–1805

Volume 3
Rome–Zurich

The manuscript journal is in the Manuscript Division of the New York Public Library, No. 3A of the Washington Irving Papers. It consists of 171 pages, written in ink, of a limp vellum-covered notebook of 186 pages, measuring 7½ x 5⅝ inches. Pp. [2, 60, 62, 88–93, 181–86] are blank. On the spine is written "1805." Inside the front cover is pasted a label that reads "In memory of Gordon Lester Ford, presented to the New York Public Library by his son-in-law and daughter, Roswell Skeel, Jr. Emily Ellsworth Ford Skeel."

All the writing except the entries for April 19 and 21, May 2 (except the postscript), and the column "Remarques" in "Route from Rome to Bologna . . ." is in brown ink; the rest is in gray ink.

[*front cover*]

1805.
April 14 to May 15

[*inside front cover*]

Washington Irving

[*p. [1]*]

Notes
of a Tour in Europe

Vol 3.
From April 14th. to May 15th. 1805
containing
a journey from Rome to Zurich
in Switzerland.

Route from Rome to Bologna[1] by the way of Loretto <&> Ancona Rimini &c[.] NB. The figures in the first column denote the nights of the month and the places where I lodged –[2]

La Nuit du mois	Postes d'Italie		Nom's des postes.	Remarques –
1805	1		Prima Porta	
April.		¾ qu[?arters?].	Borgettaccio[3]	
		¾	Castel nuovo	
	1	–	Rignano	
14.	1	–	Civita castellana	– Inn indifft.
	4	½		
		¾	Borghetto	
		¾	Otricoli	
	1	–	Narni	
15.	1	–	Terni	Inn good
	3	½		
	1	–	Strettura	
	1	–	Spoleti	Angel – decent
	1	–	Vene	
16.	1		Foligno	indifferent – post[4]
	4			
	1	–	Case Nuove	

1. Irving intended traveling north from Rome by way of Florence, but altered his route, he said in later years, because a malignant fever was prevalent in Tuscany and a cordon of troops had been drawn around the region (Irving to Sarah Paris Storrow, October 27, 1856). In his expense accounts he allowed for a vetturino from Rome to Florence ("Traveling Notes, 1804," inside front cover, p. 459). Apparently he wrote William Irving that he and Cabell timed their journey so as to arrive in Paris for the lectures on botany at the Jardin des Plantes which began in May. In reply William wrote on July 8, 1805, scolding him for traveling too hastily through Italy, seeing neither Florence nor Venice (STW, I, 65–66).

2. The French headings for the rest of this entry suggest that Irving was using a French guide book but none has been identified (see also entry of March 29, n. 309). The column headed "Remarques" is in gray ink.

3. Now Malborghetto. In his names of posts, Irving misspelled Borghettaccio, Spoleto, Serravalle, Valcimara, Loreto, Camerano, and S. Niccolo.

4. All inns in this entry which Irving calls "Post" were presumably called La Posta.

La Nuit du mois	Postes d'Italie		Nom's des postes.	Remarques –
	1	–	Serra valle	
	1		Trave	
17.	1		Valcimarra	post – solitary & poor
	4			
	1		Tolentino	
	1		Macerata	
	1	–	Sambuchetto	
18.	1		Loretto	tolerable post
	4	–		
April	1	–	Camurano	
	1	–	Ancona	good inn – dear
	1		Case Bruciate	
19.	1	–	Sinigaglia	– excellent inn – post
	4			
	1	–	Marotto	
	1	–	Fano	
	1		Pesaro	Post – excellent
20	1	–	Cattolica	wretched inn – dirty – unaird & extortionate
	4			
	1	½	Rimini	
	1		Savignano	
	1		Cesena	
21	1	½	Forli	Post. an excellent inn
	5			
	1		Faenza	
	1		Imola	
	1	¼	St. Nicolo	

La Nuit du mois	Postes d'Italie		Nom's des postes.	Remarques –
22	1	¼	Bologna	Pellegrino an excellent inn & reasonable – good attendance
	4	½		

April 14, 1805

This morning I left Rome in company with Mr Cabell,[5] on our Route for Paris. We had hired a voiture to take us to Bologna by the way of Loretto and Ancona for which we paid 15 louis.[6] The driver was to find us supper & beds on the road as also for a servant[7] <whom> who had been travelling with Wells Alston & Maxwell, and whom we had agreed to take with us as far as Bologna. He is a flemmand speaks several languages and is highly reccommended to us for his faithfulness, honesty and good disposition. We left Rome at the Porta <?Vigne?> ↑Angelica↓[8] near to the church of St Peters at <of> which majestic building we took a farewell look as we quit the city. We rode for some distance along the silent diserted Campania – formerly so celebrated, now <an>a barren unwholesome waste – this <n>seeming neglect I am universally assured is owing to the unhealtheness of the air on the Campania – particularly in summer. Various reasons are given to account for this bad quality in the atmosphere. Some ascribe it to the vast quantity of vegitable matter that putrifies annually – others to the humidity of the ground &c &c. Dr T.[9] of Naples expresses it as his

5. In his letter to Fulwer Skipworth, April 9, 1805, Cabell said he had intended to resume traveling "a few days" after he and Irving reached Rome on March 27, but that when Irving promised to accompany him to Paris, he deferred his departure "two weeks" (Manuscript Division, New York Public Library). Apparently they remained together another week in Rome in order to see some of the Holy Week ceremonies (STW, I, 65).

6. A louis was worth about $1.15 according to Irvings' expense accounts.

7. John Josse Vandermoere of Brussels (Irving to Elias Hicks, May 4–June 19, 1805; see also entry of May 25, 1805).

8. The Porta Angelica was built in 1563 by Pius IV on the south side of what is now the Piazza Risorgimento; it is no longer standing. In the manuscript "Vigne" is in lighter ink.

9. Presumably he was Dr. Thomson, or Tompson, a physician, whom J. C. Cabell knew. Cabell had a letter of introduction to him as "Thomson" and referred to him as "Thompson" several times in the journal he kept in Rome. See Journal [No. 5], "Notes of a Journay to Italy – In the Winter of 1804–5," [p. 149]; Journal [No. 7],

opinion that it arises from the want of cultivation and thinks that were the Campania immediately peopled and the whole population employd in tilling and sowing the soil, that tho the first generation might be unhealthy and die the second would be as hearty as people in other cultivated plains of Italy.* We rode for some distance along the Tiber and passed by the bridge termed antiently the Milvian but now adays Ponte Molle – it was near this bridge that Constantine defeated the Emperor Maxentius.[10] We then ascended some hills that gradually arise from the plain being the first swellings of the appenines which we could see at a distance coverd with snow. From the brow of the hill I took a last look at Rome, whose swelling domes and stately buildings have a magnificient appearance from every point of view. shortly after we passed a tomb <to> a little on one side of our road to the left called The tomb of Nero.[11] It is of a small size and very plain.

The Road for most of the day lay thro th<is>e uncultivated wastes of the Campania, <within> whose gently swelling <contours form> knolls form beautiful waving lines – covered with the finest carpet of verdure. The plain bounded by the snowy Appenines or the picturesque blue mountains of *Alba longa.*[12] We had laid in a stock of provisions to be independent in some degree of the miserable inns on the road and at 12 oclock made a luxurious repast <heigh> renderd doubly so by keen appetites and enlivened by the enjoyment of a continual change of scenery as we rode along. This country thro which we passed is <Sabin> the antient Sabina from whence came the Sabine women. In the afternoon it rained very briskly. We rode thro Rignano a small

* a comfortable encouragement to the First settlers.[13]

"Rome Winter of 1805," [pp. 166–67] (Alderman Library, University of Virginia). Others attributed the unhealthiness of the Campagna to depopulation; see, for example, Jean Pierre Grosley, *New Observations on Italy and its Inhabitants,* tr. Thomas Nugent (London, 1769), I, 367–71.

10. The Pons Milvius, originally built in 109 B.C., has been several times destroyed and rebuilt. The name was corrupted and vulgarized to Ponte Milvio, and Molle, during the middle ages. Constantine defeated Maxentius about four miles from the bridge in 312.

11. The tomb of P. Vibius Marianus, procurator of Sardinia and prefect of the Second Italian Legion, dates from the end of the second century and was commonly called the Tomb of Nero.

12. This city, extending in a long line up the slopes of Mons Albanus on the west side of Lacus Albanus, is said to have been the oldest of the Latin cities. From it the Alban Hills take their name. Castel Gandolfo now occupies the site.

13. This note is in pencil.

town with antient walls and towers and of a very picturesque appearance about the environs. It possesses an aqueduct by no means inconsiderable[14]

In the evening we arrived at Citta Castellana the last town in Sabina. It is situated on a hill in a position well calculated for defence. By some this is said to be the antient city of Fescenium whence the Romans got the idea of Fescennine verses, of a ludicrous nature and much admired by the vulgar – Others say it is the Veii that was so celebrated in the early times of the republic. Historians relate an annecdote of Camillus when beseiging this town that does him much honor. A schoolmaster who had the children of the principal people entrusted to his charge basely betrayed his trust, inviegled them out of the<ir> city & carried them to the camp of Camillus expecting to be highly rewarded by him for so important a service. That celebrated General struck with indignation at so flagrant a piece of treason, orderd the hands of the schoolmaster to be tied behind him and delivered him to his own scholars to whip him back into the city. Touched by such generous conduct the town no longer held out but surrenderd more to his generosity than his arms.[15]

We found the inn (tho <tol> quite tolerable for the generality on this road) like most others in italy – large and cheerless. The evening was chilly and there was no fireplace in our room. A fire however was made in a large hall – hung round with old pictures – comfortless as the hall of an antient castle. Supper was soon brought on and revived us and a flask of cheerful Ovietto wine put us quite in good humor. This is a pleasant light white wine made in these parts, which we drank continually at Rome[.] it reminds me very much of good New York cider. This day we have made 38 miles which considering the time we set out is very well[.] we have an honest worthy old fellow for a muleteer who seems highly disposed to render us comfortable & satisfied.

14. The aqueduct is presumably that built by Paul III near Nepi.

15. Civita Castellana, on the site of ancient Falerii, was one of the twelve cities of the Etruscan Confederation. Fescennium was a town of the Falisci in Etruria; its site has not been identified. In writing the sentence about it and the next, Irving drew on Grosley, *New Observations on Italy,* I, 373. Veii was one of the twelve cities of the Etruscan Confederation, situated at the confluence of the two streams which form the river Valchetta, about twelve miles from Rome. The story about M. Furius Camillus (d. 365 B.C.), Roman general and dictator, and Veii is told by Livy in his *History of Rome,* V, 27, but Irving probably derived it from the recapitulation in John Moore, *A View of Society and Manners in Italy* (London, 1781), I. 377.

April 15

We resumed our route this morning at an early hour. The day was more settled and fair than the preceding and enabled us to enjoy the beauty of the country to a high degree. Sometime after sunrise we descended into a charming valley where we crossed <an> a bridge of three arches built over the Tiber in the time of Augustus.[16] We then ascended some of those low mountains called the spurs or branches of the Appenines – After riding for some time thro a succession of wild scenery we came in sight of Narni. We approached to this place by a road cut along the face of a mountain. <below> Opposite to us were other mountains covered with ever green trees to the very summit, which gave them an exceeding rich appearance. Far below us in a narrow bed straightned by the feet of the <?to?> two mountains – the Nar[17] foamed along <contrast> its white waters offering a striking contrast to the deep green in which the mountains are cloathed. The waters of the Nar have a whitish appearance either from the clay or chalk with which they are discolored. The Town of Narni is celebrated for having given birth to Nerva one of the few good emperors that Rome has boasted. It stands high up, on the side of the mountain, the Nar roaring along below it, and a little above it are the remains of an old castle – the whole is picturesque in a high degree. This place was antiently spoken of as being difficult of access. <From h>Here are the remains of a bridge of Augustus thrown over the river at this place – formed of large blocks of marble – We did not see it.[18]

After riding for a short distance we discended into the beautiful and fertile valley between Narni & Terni; about two oclock we arrived at the latter town.

Here we hired a calash to take us to the Cascade of Terni[19] about five miles distance For this we agreed to give two dollars and four

16. The Ponte Felice was built by Augustus over the Tiber near Borghetto and was restored in 1589.

17. Now the Nera.

18. The Roman town was Narnia. Nerva's birth here is mentioned in Moore, *A View of Society and Manners in Italy,* I, 376, and Grosley, *New Observations on Italy,* I, 372, where he is complimented. The castle was La Rocca, built in 1370 and modified in the fifteenth century. The bridge was Ponte d'Augusto. In describing it Irving drew on Thomas Martyn, *The Gentleman's Guide in his Tour through Italy* (London, 1791), p. 129.

19. The Cascata delle Marmore was created by channels cut to prevent the Velino's overflowing its banks by throwing it over a precipice into the Nar; the first channel was cut in 271 B.C., a second in 1400, and a third in 1785.

pauls[20] *buono mano* to the postillion. The vehicle was awkward enough when we came to examine it, but there was no alternative except we chose to go in a clumsy four wheeld carriage & pay double. They endeavored to fix a shabby cicerone upon us but we refused him having been warned to do so by our travelling books. The road after passing for some distance thro the valley, ascended in a serpentine manner one of the high mountains of the appenines. The ascent was tremenduous, cut along the face of the rocks by which it was overhung on the one side while on the other we pe[e]rd over precipices of an alarming height. The views <of t> from the mountain were of the most picturesque & charming kind. We overlooked the extensive valley between Terni and Narni – covered with the richest verdue adorned with vineyards <&> olive orchards – and groves of trees. The Nar "tumultuous in its course"[21] wandering thro it. The mountains around bold, high and variegated – some clothed in rich evergreen trees to the very summit, others arid and softned by partial patches of vegitation. The valley of Terni was celebrated among the antients for its fertility and the richness of the soil. The meadows according to pliny were mowed four times a year.[22] It is <one of the fine> the commencement of Umbria one of the antient divisions of Italy – Addison speaks of it in a beautiful manner

> – <cover me in> Umbria's <blest> ↑green↓ retreats
> Where western gales eternally reside
> And all the seasons lavish all their pride
> Blossoms & fruits & flow'rs <promiscuous> ↑together↓ rise
> And the whole year in gay confusion lies.[23]

Before we arrived at the falls we had quite an assortment of cicerones. In spight of our expressd determination to take no person in that capacity a ragged fellow had followed us from Terni <from> ↑for↓ the purpose. It had amused us to notice the manner in which he contrived

20. A paul was worth about 10¢ according to Irving's expense account.

21. Joseph Addison, "A Letter from Italy, to the Right Honourable Charles, Lord Halifax" (1701), ll. 17, 19:

> How am I pleased . . .
> To view the Nar, tumultuous in his course.

22. Presumably the allusion is to Pliny the Elder, but this sentence and the preceding one are paraphrases of Martyn, *The Gentleman's Guide,* p. 129.

23. Addison, "A Letter from Italy," ll. 64–68. The alterations in the quotations are in darker ink.

to ingratiate himself and how by degrees <he> at length he managed to mount behind the calash and introduce himself We determind to pay him for his ingenuity but he was not content with his own success – As we were passing along he beconed to a friend of his who was working by the way side, to join him. This manouvre did not escape our notice – The other abandond his work and followd us attended by a boy.

The calash stopped within about two hundred yards of the fall not being able to proceed further. Here we took our ragged cicerone to serve us as a guide[.] his companion was for going along but we stopped him & demanded what capacity he acted in. He replied that he was *custode della caduta* (keeper of the falls!) We could not but laugh heartily at this flagrant piece of imposition, To pretend to be keeper of a cascade that was open to every ones view. but such are the eternal impostions of this country. We orderd the fellow away and went with the ragged cicerone whom we had brought from Terni.

The falls are extremely picturesque & <beautiful> wild. The River Velino comes roaring and foaming along thro narrow passes among the heights of the Appenines – over hung with rocks and tufts of beautiful trees. It rushes to the brink of a precipice over which it precipitates itself for a great height on the rocks below down which it dashes and bellows in a foaming torrent forming several more leaps till it mingles with the Rapid waters of the Nar and rolles along boiling & roaring thro the narrow valley. The first pitch is extremely bold and beautiful.[24] Such extravagant and contradictory estimates have been said of it that I am affraid to mention my opinion but I do not think at farthest it is above 200 feet perhaps not above 180. The waters have a beautiful appearance as they fall – feathery like snow and the whole may be compared to a vast *avalanche*. The spray mounts up in a mist as high as the top of the fall. The whole cascade taking in the subsequent descent & pitches till its junction with the Nar is computed to be <600>700 feet tho I think this very far beyond the truth. The cascade may be viewn from different <?posts?> points that are very fine on one of which is erected a small brick belvedere This commands a noble view of the

24. The river falls in three leaps of about 65, 330, and 195 feet respectively; it is the second to which Irving is referring. Several estimates from 100 feet to 800 feet are cited in Martyn, *The Gentleman's Guide,* p. 128. The actual height of the falls is about 650 feet.

fall – of the Appenines in the neighborhood clothed in trees and of the small valley thro which the Narr wanders before its junction with the Velino. In this house we found seated our *custode della caduta* who renewed his application for a buono mano. He followed us to the calash importuning us the whole way. The cicerone & Postillion seemed to second his demand We feared to be too strenuous in a refusal apprehending that we might get in a dispute which in such a solitary place and amongst such unprincipled vagabonds might have been attended with disagreeable, perhaps dangerous consequences – especially as we had neglected to bring our pistols with us from the inn which <we> are always productive of respect. We determined therefore to give the fellow three pauls and diduct it from the sum of six pauls which we had designd to give the cicerone; <but> we were the more pleased in doing this as it was a kind of punishment for the fraud of the latter. The fellow accepted it and parted quite contented. On setting off in our calash we had nearly met with a disagreeable accident[.] one of the horses was young and kicked & reard up just before we arrived at the dangerous parts of the road[.] we luckily jumped out safe & succeeded in stopping him. After coaxing him some time we remounted and set forward at a round rate the postillion galloping carelessly <along> with the ticklish machine <near the> along the brink of tremenduous precipices – such is the force of habit – We returnd safe to Terni enjoying a lovely sunset. P. S. This town is remarkable for being the native place of Tacitus the historian.[25]

April 16

We left <Spolleto> Terni as usual at an early hour this morning. For a long way our road wound along the deep gullies and defiles of the Appenines which began to assume more majestic and imposing heights. They rose on each side of us, in awful <majesti> grandeur, covered with evergreens & oaks. the scenery was wild and solitary, but now & then a hamlet occurring to interrupt the loneliness – or the white towers of a convent half concealed in the mountain foliage. Continuing in this manner for some time we at length came to where the road ascends the mountain. This pass is called *Il somma* being the

25. The birthplace of Tacitus is in dispute. It is given as Narnia in Moore, *A View of Society and Manners in Italy,* I, 371, and in Grosley, *New Observations on Italy,* I, 372; in Grosley Narnia is said to be "remarkable" for nothing else.

highest on the Mediterranean side. To facilitate the passage of carriages they furnish oxen at the foot of the mountain. These are very fine in this part of the country – of a silver grey color, as are all the cattle in the neighborhood

The route over the mountain presents nothing remarkable[.] the views are all confined to the neighboring eminences. We descended by degrees and riding some distance Spoletto broke upon us in an handsome manner.

This town is situated on the swell of a hill which gives it a striking appearance. On the summit of the hill is an old castle with square towers built by Theodoric[.][26] just below the castle an aqueduct is thrown across a deep gully and communicates with a neighboring mountain.[27] This mountain is singularly beautiful. It is very steep[,] covered with a continued forest to the very summit, composed of ever green trees some of which are higher than the others which serves to break the uniformity – This however is done in a superior manner by the white walls and turrets of convents of which there are a considerable number half buried in the woods and forming a striking contrast by their white walls to the deep green of the forests. It has been a rainy morning <at>& at the time of our enterance in Spoletto it pourd in torrents. This is a very neat pretty town, the streets well paved and an air of comfort industry and content among the inhabitants. The inn (sign of the angel) is very decent and one of the best <of> on the route but the attendants seemed sulky. After breakfast, the weather having held up, we walked out to look at the curiosities of the town. In the upper part we passed thro a gate on which is a latin inscription mentioning that Hannibal was repulsed from that gate by the inhabitants after the battle of Thrasymenes[.] it is thence called *Porta fuga* (gate of flight).[28] from below the castle we had a near view of the aqueduct said to be Roman but evidently of Gothic architecture and very ugly in its kind

From hence the prospect is superb. The weather had held up and

26. La Rocca was founded in pre-Roman times, rebuilt by Theodoric the Great (*ca.* 454–526), king of the Ostrogoths, and again in 1355–1367.

27. Ponte delle Torri, dating from the fourteenth century, was probably built on Roman foundations. It connects the town of Spoleto with Monte Luco.

28. At Lacus Trasimenus (Lago Trasimeno or Lake Tresimene) Hannibal defeated the Romans under T. Quinctius Flaminius in 217 B.C. The Porta della Fuga was built in the twelfth and thirteenth centuries.

the sun broke out as if to give us a fair view of as lovely a valley as ever it shone upon. The valley of Foligno is of great extent, laid out in beautiful enclosures, olive plantations vineyards &c. vast pastures & meadows, waterd by the "smooth Clitumnus."[29] In various places are scatterd white towns & villages – some peeping out of groves and woods of olives, others boldly rising to sight on the tops of small hills, and others adorning the sides of the Appenines that surround this enchanting Canaan. The antients ↑Romans↓ were extravagant in their praizes of th<i>ese lovely regions[30] – They <spok> speak in high terms of the salubrity of the air, always fanned by gentle Zephyrs – of the richness and fertility of the soil, watered by the gently gliding streams of the Clitumnus. Their grand victims of sacrifice were always chosen from among the herds that were raised here. The cattle are generally of a silvery grey or white which the antients supposed was owing to their drinking the white chalky waters of the Clitumnus. We were interrupted in our contemplation of this interesting & classic scene by the appearance of an approaching shower which made us hasten back to the inn. The country people are enjoying the Easter hollidays and dressed in their finest cloathing which is to a stranger highly grotesque consisting as usual among the italians – of the gayest colours they can find. I have been much pleased with a trifling mark of taste & fancy in the men both in these parts & between Rome & Naples – it is, the custom of sticking a bunch of gay flowers in their hats. I think a notion of this kind is <seldom> never seen among low brutish people, and argues a certain degree of sentiment. I was amused by the sight of a custom observed <in> among the boys in New York of cracking boild eggs with one another at Easter. Here it is done by men as well as boys. The people of Spoletto are comfortably clad, and what is uncommon we were not accosted by a single beggar.

From hence we continued along this delicious valley. Near the picturesque town of Trevi which is situated on a hill we passed the source of the Clitumnus and a little farther on we stopped to examine a small

29. Addison, "A Letter from Italy," ll. 17, 20:

> How am I pleased . . .
> [To] trace the smooth Clitumnus to his source.

30. In writing this and the next three sentences Irving apparently drew on Grosley, *New Observations on Italy,* I, 361.

antique temple erected to the god of that name.[31] It stands to the left of the road as you go towards Foligni and the face of it is towards the valley. It is in excellent preservation – of the Corinthian order and of exquisite architecture. It has been duly purified and turned into a christian chapel but fortunately the alteration has not affected its external appearance and it stands I think one of the most beautiful monuments of antiquity I have ever beheld. The situation too is so charming. Just below it glides along the tranquil current of the Clitumnus – clear & limpid not having as yet assumed the whitish dirty color that afterwards distinguishs it – and beyond is spread the lovely valley of which I have already spoke. We remained here a long time before we could tear ourselves away from so interesting a spot. The afternoon was a continuation of the April weather we have experienced for these two or three days. showers & sunshine alternately succeed each other – yet the atmosphere is delightfully mild & salubrious and well deserves the character it has acquired. The intervals of sun shine too seemed more pleasant by the effect of contrast. The sun breaking from among the clouds often threw partial gleams of light on the white towers of a village or convent half embowerd among the woods of the Appenines – and sometimes formed a beautiful rain bow in the valley. The fertility of the country is remarkable & the mountains are often coverd half way up with olive trees of an amazing size.

A little before sundown we arrived at the Town of Foligny. This is a very <th> industrious, thriving place – The streets regular decently built & well paved – The people have a comfortable appearance and there are no beggars in the place – in fact how should they be otherwise than comfortable surrounded by such a paradise. In the evening we went out to take a walk around the city – We found a cicerone ready at the door; these fellows are always on the look out in these small towns tho there is seldom anything worth seeing. As he was a decent looking fellow, however, we determined to indulge him. He took us to a place where they hold the horse races in time of carnival. This is constructed on a kind of terrace without the town. All along the side of the course is a range of brick seats or lodges numberd, which are owned by particular persons – The whole has a handsome

31. The church of S. Salvatore, constructed of materials of ancient tombs not earlier than the fourth century, was once thought to be the temple of Clitumnus mentioned by Pliny the Younger in his *Letters,* VIII, 8.

appearance. From hence we had another fine view of the valley The sun had long since set, yet the air was serene & delicious and the sound of a convent bell from among the heights of the appenines seemed in unison with the scene. There was formerly a fine picture by Raphael in this town but it has been transported to paris by the french.[32] Foligni has an excellent manufactory of wax tapers &c which it sends to Rome florence &c. It has also manufactories of good paper.

April 17

We left Foligni early in the morning and soon began to ascend among the Appenines. The road was very steep and winding, and in a little while we lost sight of the delightful <fall> valley we had left. Oxen are furnished to assist in drawing carriages up this formidable ascent. After a considerable time spent in toiling along the mountains often on the edge of vast precipices we at length attained the highest part of the road and began gradually to descend. About 12. oclock we passed thro Serravalle a small village situated in a narrow pass between two mountains and formerly fortified strongly but the old walls & towers are now in ruins. We were the whole day winding among the heights amid the most wild and romantic scenery – now passing along <a> narrow defiles almost closed up by tremenduous mountains and now opening upon pleasant little valleys enlivened by cultivation

Sometimes on the brow of an apparently inaccessable mountain stood the ruind towers of an old castle that recalled past days of feudal force to mind – in other places small towns situated on eminences had a picturesque effect

In general however, the scenery was wild & solitary – few marks of cultivation, and but now and then a few miserable cabins of goat herds The mountains themselves afforded a variety of tones of colours not unpleasing. Some times of a <red> dull red colour from the nature of the soil, at other times of a grey tint and coverd in many places with ever green shrubs & some of them were clothed to the summit with different species of ever green trees <an> with now and then clumps of oaks & chestnuts intermingled. <H>Flocks of white goats browzing on their sides had a picturesque appearance and often those animals

32. The "Madonna di Foligno," originally in the church of the convent of S. Anna, was confiscated by order of Napoleon in 1797 and transferred to the Vatican in 1815.

strayed to the very brinks of fearful precipices & cropd the bushes that over hung their sides.

In the deep defile of the mountain, that we pursued, a foaming torrent[33] roard along that gradually encreased by the junction of different mountain streams until it became quite considerable and added highly to the wildness of the scenery. We remarked that the air was much colder at these heights than in the valleys we had left. It rained part of the time and we observed that on the summits of mountains a little higher than where we were, there <rain was> fell snow instead of rain. The clouds rolling in heavy masses among the mountains sometimes shrouding a great part of them from our view had a striking effect.

In the afternoon we passed a rude Gibbet erected along side of the road. Here our voiturier told us that about three years before a daring robbery had been committed by a gang of villains on a Spanish princess whom they plunderd of money to a large amount.[34] The whole country turned out in pursuit of them, they were taken – four of the most culpable <executed> ↑hung↓ and quartered and the rest sentenced to the galleys for life. The voiturier pointed out to us where the limbs of the former were still hanging on trees by the road side. Indeed the place – as well as many other parts of the road which we had passed this day seemed well calculated for robberies – being enclosed by mountains – lonesome & without any habitation near. – – In the evening we put up at the post calld Valcimarra. This is a solitary house situated among the Appenines – The people however are very civil and have given a better supper than we expected. Our old voiturier who is a *thirsty soul* and generally finishes a bottle or more with his meals, came to us after supper ↑half *mellow*↓ to give us a long account of the history of the robbery above mentioned. The old fellow sat himself quietly by the fire and with his eyes half shut entered into a most lamentable detail. To this he added several other similar stories for the truth of which he appeald every now and then to a servant girl who was present – she supported him with additional circumstances to render the histories more terriffic. Among others she told us a tedious story about an old castle that we had passed in the afternoon that stood on the high brow of a precipice – this she assured us had been haunted

33. The Chienti.

34. Irving made the robbery of a Spanish princess at an inn in the Apennines an episode in "The Belated Travellers" in *Tales of a Traveller* (1824).

by devils (diavolini) ever since a murder had been committed there and how an old villager in the neighborhood had been terribly allarmed by an apparition there one night as he was returning home – which he frightened away by calling on our Lady of Loretto[35] – I asked her how the apparition looked – and she answerd – exactly like a *great goat.* I told her we had seen whole troops of those kind of apparitions on the sides of the mountains. The solitary wildness of these mountains and the universal bigotry of the inhabitants to all the miracles & fables of the Romish religion are sufficient to encourage such silly superstition.

April 18

We resumed our route this morning before day break as we wished to arrive at Loretto at an early hour of the evening. The moon was just setting behind some of the mountains and threw an uncertain light on different p<oin>arts of the <mou> narrow valley.

The air was pure and cool and the <utmost> silence <prevaild> and repose of the scene was only broken by the dashing of a stream that we had traced all the day before, down the defile thro which we passd. We wrapped ourselves up in our great coats and seating ourselves in the carriage began slowly to descend the mountains. After some time the day began to dawn – The atmosphere was uncommonly pure and transparent varied by several floating clouds that assumed a variety of fugitive tints as the light encreased – by degrees the horison became more and more illuminated – Already the snowy heights of the loftiest mountains were brightening with the rays of the sun which began to gild the grey summits of the lower mountains[.] at length the sun broke from behind a mountain and poured a rich gleam of radiance on <every part> ↑the lower parts↓ of the landscape. Having accomplished the most difficult part of our decent the road became more level – A beautiful valley[36] opened upon us of the most pleasing verdure – thro which the torrent we had followd from the mountains – swelld by additional streams – wanderd in ↑a↓ gentle current – seeming to have changed with the Scenery from wildness & confusion, to tranquility & repose. <The valley was> Near the commencement of the

35. This name designates the Virgin Mary as the center of the cult at Loreto. According to legend, her house at Nazareth was carried by angels in the thirteenth century to a laurel grove in Italy; the settlement that sprang up around it took the name Loreto from the grove and was given municipal status by Sixtus V in 1586.

36. The valley of the Chienti.

valley stands the <village of> Town of Tollentino neat and clean – here we stopped and took coffee at a very decent coffee house. From hence we continued along this charming valley <amidst> which offerd an agreeable contrast to the wild appenines we had left. The valley was surrounded by gently sloping hills sevral of them crownd with villages & towns. At a distance the Appenines appeard behind rearing their snowy summits above the hills. The weather was so delicious that we got out of the carriage & walked which we could do without loss of time, from the slow pace of the mules. I dont know that I ever saw a finer spring day – there was that pureness, that mildness & elasticity in the air for which this delightful climate is celebrated – The blossoms and flowers of the fields diffused a most exquisite fragrance. The country people were busily employed working in their fields – they were well clad and appeared to be cheerful & contented singing as they worked – The women worked in the fields in common with the men I have read a remark of some author who says it is a sure sign of laziness in the men when the women do hard manuel labor. We passed thro a variety of such charming scenery watered by the wandering stream from the Appenines – after riding by the town of Macerata (the capital of the marquisate of Ancona beautifully situated on a hill) we cross a long wooden bridge over the river[37] and stopped the other side to refresh the mules at an inn close by the ruins of Recina a colony built by Pertinax but ruined by the Goths.[38] The chief of these ruins now remaining are part of the walls of a small ampitheatre. This building was very small and bespeaks the colony to have been but thinly populated. After remaining here two hours we again set out – we could not get the old voiturier to part before – he had drank his two bottles of wine for dinner & was as happy as a prince singing the whole way. The same kind of gentle scenery surrounded us as before – beautiful vallies – waterd by small rivers – <gent> Hills gradually swelling in wa<y>ving lines – towns & villages on the points of rocky heights and the snowy Appenines closing the distance. At one place we passed where an itinerant musician was seated at the door of a cottage with all the inhabitants gatherd around them whom he

37. The Potenza.

38. Helvia Ricina was built by Publius Helvius Pertinax (126–193), Roman emperor (193) and ruined by the Goths in the fifth century; the ruins also include part of a bridge. In his sentence Irving may have drawn on Grosley, *New Observations on Italy*, I, 357.

was entertaining with an old ballad accompanied by a guitar which he held in his hands. At another place our carriage was beset by a crowd of children who demanded charity singing long doleful ditties at the same time. The salubrity ↑of the air↓ of these enchanting vallies is doubly grateful after descending from the chilly appenines.

From Recanati a small town we had the first view of the Adriatic and the steeple & dome of Loretto on a distant eminence. We arrived there about five oclock.

This town so celebrated for containing the holy house where our Saviour was born; is small containing about 6500 inhabitants and is not remarkable f<i>or any fine buildings. It is situated on a hill at some distance from the sea. We had hardly got in the inn before we were asked if we would wish to see the *Santa Casa* and finding the church would shortly shut up for the night we consented to take the servant of the hotel by way of a cicerone. The chief street of the place thro which we passd is full of small shops where they sell rosarys crosses medals &c and we were continually accosted from them to know if we wished to buy any thing.[39]

The grand church that encloses the Santa Casa has been described by almost every traveller and after all there is nothing about it worthy of much approbation – The front is in that bad taste that characterizes most of the facades of the italian churches. There are three grand doors of bronze with small compartments decorated with very good mezzo relievo's representing various parts of scripture history. In the different chapels within the church are excellent copies from the paintings of celebrated masters – worked in mosaic but so well that at a little distance they have all the effect and appearance of an oil painting. The holy house is closed up in a superb case of white marble with bronze doors which were shut at the time of our visit but will be open tomorrow morning. In the marble pavement around this case is worn in deep grooves by the crowds who crawl round it on their hands &

39. The "Santa Casa" (house of the Virgin Mary) is enclosed in the Chiesa or Santuario della Santa Casa. The church was begun in 1468, continued 1479–1486, completed in 1500 by the erection of a dome, and added to by various artists up to the eighteenth century. The façade was built between 1570 and 1587 under Sixtus V, whose statue stands at the top of the steps. The bronze doors, made between 1590 and 1610, have scenes from the Old and New Testaments and are the work of several artists. The mosaics in the chapels include those of St. Francis by Domenichino and the archangel Michael by Guido Reni. The marble casing was designed in 1510 and is ornamented by reliefs and statues by various artists. Irving's description of Loreto contains echoes of Martyn, *The Gentleman's Guide,* p. 122.

knees. The bronze doors of this case are likewise ornamented with reliefs in one of which representing the scourging of Jesus Christ, his figure is half kissed away by the lips of the superstitious crowds. The marble casing is decorated with rich reliefs statues &c in the greatest profusion – it is an admirable piece of workmanship. It stands in the middle of the church in the center of the cross formed by the church. The architecture is by Bramante[40]

April 19

At an early hour of the morning we visited the church of the *Santa Casa.* The doors of the church were open and we found numbers within kneeling around the holy house outside of which a priest was performing mass. The doors that open into the holy house were likewise open and we walked in *sans ceremonie.* This celebrated building is said to be 31 feet 9 inches long and 13 feet 3 inches broad & 18 feet 9 inches high[,] the ceiling arched.[41] It consists of but one room. The walls are of brick with the remains of plaister in some places. At the upper end is the Sanctuary as it is calld which was formerly seperated from the rest of the room by a grating of silver. This however was carried off by the french[42] and a common one of wood & iron substituted. Within the sanctuary in a small nitche is placed the statue of the Virgin with the infant Jesus in her arms. This is said to be the workmanship of St Luke, it however does but little credit to his skill as a sculptor and had he not succeeded better as an evangelist he had made but little <impression ↑figure↓ upon the w> figure in the world. The image is very small and quite black, they pretend that it is made of the cedar of Lebanon.[43] <It is clothed in a stiff frock that formerly coverd with precious stones> It was formerly coverd with a robe coverd with precious stones, the french however were ungallant enough to strip her of her finery and less costly cloathing has been substituted. In the sanctuary is preserved the holy porringer in which the pap of our saviour was prepared. The pilgrims always take care to trail their

40. "The . . . Bramante" is in lighter ink.

41. These dimensions are given by Martyn, *The Gentleman's Guide,* p. 123. Accounts vary slightly.

42. The plunder of Loreto occurred in 1797 when Napoleon's forces took the Papal States.

43. In this sentence, for his list of the products of Ancona and Senigallia, and his description of the Senigallia fair, Irving apparently drew on Martyn, *The Gentleman's Guide,* pp. 121, 123.

rosaries about in this vessel, which gives them superior efficacy. As the priests were performing mass we could not get a sight of this inestimable relique.

At the lower end of the house facing the Virgin is the window thro which the angel entered at the annunciation

The fortunes of this sacred edifice have experienced a sad vicissitude within a few years. On the threatned approach of the French to Loretto the countless treasures of the holy house were removed to Rome where they have ever since remained (unless His holiness the pope may have disposed of them in some other manner)[44] The riches of the chapel afforded noble spoils to the conquerors. They stripped it of gold jewels lamps & every thing that was valuable. Even the diminutive statues of the Virgin & our Saviour were included in the spoils and carried to Paris. The good lady however made so poor a figure beside the Venus De Medicis[45] that the frequenters of the Louvre soon got out of conceit of her and sent her back to the pope at Rome who re-envoyed her to Loretto. They have endeavored to supply the place of the former riches by inferior representatives. The vast number of golden & silver lamps that were hung up in the holy chapel are succeeded by brass ones – the angels of gold that attended around the Virgin bearing wax tapers are replaced by wooden ones gilt. In short the house presents but a feeble shadow of its former magnificence. A few votive offerings[46] of silver hearts legs &c are hung up about the sanctuary but those invaluable presents that were formerly made by different potentates have long since ceased. <to> There were a number of poor people inside the holy house on their knees attending mass and would at particular part of the ceremony beat their breasts with great earnestness, on leaving the room they kissd the walls, crossd themselves several times and bowed towards the Virgin. The absurd story of the transportation of this building from Nazareth by angels

44. Most of the Loreto treasury was paid the French by Pius VI to fulfill the stipulations of the Treaty of Tolentino in 1797, but subsequent gifts formed a new one.

45. The "Venus de' Medici" was among the Italian works of art removed to Paris by the French in 1797. In his Autobiographical Notes, January 10, 1843, Irving recorded meeting in northern Italy a New Englander who had come abroad for the sole purpose of seeing this statue, passed it without recognizing it, and upon having it pointed out expressed his disappointment by saying, "Hell."

46. The Spanish princess in Irving's "The Belated Travellers" in *Tales of a Traveller* (1824) makes a pilgrimage to Loreto and contributes votive offerings to the treasury of the Santa Casa.

is well known and is one of the greatest triumphs over human credulity that ever priestcraft atchieved.

We left the church disgusted with the climax of superstition we had witnessed and repaired to our voiture. Just as we were entering the carriage our attention was arrested by a troop of pilgrims male & female returning from the *Santa Casa*[.] they had performed their pilgrimage and were now on the way home. they had their hats in their hands decorated with a small silver image set round with flowers – in the other hand was their pilgrims staff and they were chanting the litany of the Virgin – their music was extremely simple yet not unpleasing and the novelty of the circumstance contributed to render it more satisfactory.

From Loretto we rode about fifteen miles along a road rather hilly and uneven, to Ancona. The scenery was very fine. On one side <plesant> pleasant valleys varied by gentle hills and at a distance the snowy Appenines exalting their picturesque summits half shrouded in the clouds – on the other side was the Adriatic – ruffled by a gentle zephyr and specled with numerous little boats & latine vessels.

About ten oclock we arrived at Ancona. This is a small city beautifully situated on the slope of a hill[47] and making a noble appearance at a little distance. We approached it by a handsome quay built along the sea. The town is one of the most bu<i>sy places in the popes dominions[.] it has considerable commerce and is very populous for the size. The streets seemed thronged – every body was in motion and the town seemed full of *trade stench & filth.* Such an air of thrift & industry however was enlivening after having been in the idle stagnant towns of the interior. The grand articles of export are wool silk & grain.

There are here an excellent Lazerretto and mole built by one of the <moles> Popes.[48] A mole of white marble was built here by <Augustus> ↑Nerva↓ who erected in the middle of it a triumphal arch,[49] also of white marble which still remains in surprizing fine preservation – probably kept fresh & clean by the spray of the sea.

It is of the Corinthian order and the architecture is very fine. I saw a number of greek taylors here there appearing to be considerable trade

47. Ancona is situated between Monte Astagno and Monte Guasco.

48. Clement XII (Lorenzo Corsini) (1652–1740) became pope in 1730. The lazaretto was built in 1733.

49. The Arco di Traiano was built in 115 by Apollodorus of Damascus in honor of Trajan's development of the port.

with that nation. There were also many Galley slaves at work in the harbor who appeared to be tolerably well contented – singing as they labored. From Ancona we continued along the shore of the Adriatic close to the sea to Signigalia. This coast is rather lonely there being few other houses on it except <fishing huts.> fishermens huts. The people are fearful of the turks who sometimes land here and carry off families even out of the towns. They sometimes plunder the carriages of travellers as they ride along the shore & <?are ha?>even make the passengers captive. This road is <sid> said to be somewhat unsafe on that account as well as that there have been instances known of the trunks being cut off from behind carriages. These circumstances determind us not to venture on the road after dark and we put up at Sinigalia at a good hour. This is one of the handsomest towns I have seen in italy of its size. It is built extremely neatly & regularly of grey brick and there is an air of cleanliness and comfort about the houses extremely pleasing. The streets are broad <&> straight <& the> & clean & the houses high. At one place a river[50] runs thro the town. It is faced with stonework on each side so as to form a kind of canal for the vessels. The houses that face it are built on arcades and make a very respectable appearance. Upon the whole we were quite charmed with the place. It seemed to combine uncommon advantages & beauties for a town of such small population (containing but [*blank*]).[51] Above all we put up at a very good inn and had an excellent supper which put us in the best of humours.

Senegalia appears to be chiefly of modern construction; the houses have generally the <appear> looks of being built in the course of the last century – Its trade consists in corn hemp & silk – A considerable fair is held here in July.[52]

April 20

Leaving Senegallia at the usual hour we rode along the coast of the Adriatic to Fano. About two miles distance from the city between it &

50. The Misa.

51. The population of Senigállia in 1805 was about 19,000 (information furnished by the Ufficiale d'Anagrafe Delegato, Senigállia). The town was so often devastated by fires and fighting during the middle ages that it presents a relatively modern appearance.

52. The Senigállia fair, held between July 20 and August 8, was founded in the thirteenth century and survived until the close of the nineteenth century. A detailed account of it is given in Grosley, *New Observations on Italy,* I, 159–64.

Segnigallia we passd over the Metro (antiently Metaurus) famous from the Defeat ↑& death↓ of Asdrubal by the Romans which took place on its banks.[53] The River like all the others that I have seen in Italy is yellow & turbid.

At Fano we stopped to breakfast. This is a neat, busy town and possesses several decent Streets. The chief object of curiosity is an arch of Triumph of Augustus,[54] built of white marble but considerably injured.

The conduct of our voiturier at this place fully convinced us of the truth of what we had often been told, that there is no confidence to be placed in any of his profession in Italy. – He had rested outside of the gates and had been making a great noise because we remained some time in the city – tho we had stipulated that we were to stop at every place worth seeing – he had at length sent our servant in search of us. This however was but trifling; but during our absence he had agreed with two officers, to take them up in front of the carriage though we had hired the whole carriage for ourselves and expressly refused the evening before to take any person into it. As the old driver had discovered himself to be mulish in the extreme we did not think it <woth> worth while to dispute with him, particularly as he was a Neapolitan and spoke the italian so execrably that I could not understand him without difficulty

Like the generality of travellers we sufferd ourselves to be imposed on rather than enter into a disagreeable altercation. These fellows know this well and never fail to take advantage of strangers that do not speak their language. Another imposition that we have sufferd <fr> in this route is from the man who furnished us with the carriage. He was to have given us a new voiture that had taken Mr Cabell & Mercer to Naples and three horses – instead of which he sent us a crazy old vehicle & three mules – As we were on the point of starting we did not care to be delayd but have repented ever since our consenting to <use> travel in such a machine. It lets in the rain & wind in different parts is ill hung and every way uncomfortable.

From Fano we continued on to Pezaro thro which we passd without

53. Hasdrubal (d. 207 B.C.), Carthaginian general, was killed at the Metaurus, now the Metauro, in 207 B.C. as he was attempting to join forces with his brother Hannibal. The last part of Irving's sentence is a paraphrase of Martyn, *The Gentleman's Guide,* p. 12.

54. In the fourth century an attic was added and the arch dedicated to Constantine.

stopping. This is another thriving little sea port, and has a bu<i>sy yet neat appearance. Lucian Bonaparte[55] resides here at present having quit the italian republic on ↑hearing↓ the news that his brother the Emperor intended visiting it. Pezaro was famous formerly for the court of the Duchy of Urbino which was reconed the standard of Taste, elegance and courtesy in Italy.[56]

From this town we passed on to La Catolica – Before we arrived there we were stopped at a custom house on the road – the last one in the popes territories, we were sufferd however to proceed on giving a buono mano of three pauls. We had neglected to have our trunks sealed at Rome and were consequently annoyed by the custom houses at different places on the route. They likewise demanded our passports at most of the towns but very often content themselves with asking the name of one of us – and where we are from &c. The sight of our passports written in french with the signature of the french secretary at Rome seems to awe them into respect for they have the greatest fear of the french.

At La Catalica we entered the Italian Republic, or as we were told by the custom house officers The *Kingdom of Italy* having lately been so denominated by the Emperor of the French. There our trunks were searched, but on feeing the officers they did it but slightly and disturbed our clothes very little. They then sealed them up at our request which will protect us from any farther visitation till we get to Bologna.

La Catalica is a miserable little village consisting of a few houses, yet here our voturier put up for the night tho it was but little more than three oclock in the afternoon. Whatever we could say to the contrary had no effect – <our> He pretended that his mules were tired and that they must have rest & feed[.] in short he seemed determined to revenge himself on us for having made him wait in the morning at Fano. We were obliged therefore to content ourselves in an uncomfortable inn, where the cheerless accommodations were aggravated by sulky attendants. We were shewn to a dirty room on the walls of which – over the fire place, we found written with a pencil "La plus chere et plus mauvaise auberge du Monde, faitez la prix avant de

55. Lucien Bonaparte (1775–1840) had angered his brother by marrying against his wishes and lived during this period in Rome.

56. From 1512 to 1631 Pesaro was the seat of the Della Rovere family, dukes of Urbino, whose court is described by Castiglione in *Il Libro del Cortegiano* (1528). It is referred to as an "elegant court" in Martyn, *The Gentleman's Guide,* p. 120.

manger" (The dearest & most miserable Inn in the world [–] settle the price before you eat.)

The scenery thro which we passed this day was by no means equal to that of the preceding part of our Journey, tho some part of it was pleasing – <It lay generally> Our route lay generally along the coast and sometimes on the heavy gravel of the shore. Just before we arrived at La Catolica we <passed> enjoyed a very handsome prospect – A fine castle lay to our left on the summit of a green and picturesque hill.[57] The battlements of the castle and a strong wall belonging to it flanked by towns surrounding the summit of the hill gave it a commanding appearance. The hill swept down into an extensive and charming valley coverd with cornfields & vineyards. At a distance extended the chain of Appenines that assumed tints of the purest blue & purple.

I have observed that this side of Italy is peculiarly devoted to the culture of grain – Tho even in the corn fields rows of mulberries & vines are planted. <The>

The peasantry of Italy as I have already observed are generally <g>of good countenances particularly the females, in fact <there is> I have never seen so much real beauty among peasant girls and females of the lower class as in Italy.

April 21

We departed from La Cattolica at day break and about nine oclock arrived at Rimini. We entered the town thro a Triumphal arch built of white marble in honor of Augustus. It is of the Corinthian order of architecture. <We> After breakfasting at Rimini we resumed our route. The other antiquities of this place are a pedestal in the market place on which they pretend Julius Cæsar stood & harangued his soldiers – and a noble bridge of three arches over which we passed on quitting the city. It was built of white marble under Augustus and is in an excellent state of preservation.[58]

57. Probably La Rocca in the walled town of Gradara, built in the thirteenth century by Sigismondo Malatesta, enlarged and restored by Giovanni Sforza in 1494. It is the supposed scene of the tragedy of Paolo and Francesca da Rimini.

58. The Arco d'Augusto was built about 27 B.C. in gratitude for Augustus' restoration of the Via Flaminia. The pedestal was built in the thirteenth century in what is now the Piazza Tre Martiti, to mark the spot where, according to Lucan, *Pharsalia,* I, 236, 299–351, Caesar addressed his soldiers in the forum of Ariminum, the ancient city on the site of Rimini, after crossing the Rubicon. In his description

Between Rimini & Cesena our voiturier stopped at the little town of Lex, to feed his mules. This gave us an opportunity of taking a good view of the famous Rubicon which passes just without the city. There is a bridge built over it, apparantly on the arches of an antique one – it consists of three arches.[59] The river itself is inconsiderable and might be passed without notice, tho it is not destitute of beauties; the banks are shaded by poplars and willows and above the bridge there are several gently swelling hills, well cultivated that form very pleasing scenery.

The remarkable anecdote that gave celebrity to this river is well known. Caesar when about to return to rome in contradiction to the will of the senate – paused on the margin of this river which <bounded> founded the boundary between italy & the Cisalpine Gaul "If I do not pass this River" said he "I am ruined – if I do pass it to what woes will Rome be exposed."[60]

This River that makes so great a figure in history is nothing more than a muddy stream that we would hardly dignify with the name of a brook in America. Indeed I have been exceedingly disappointed in the classic streams of Italy that have been so often sung by the poets; I have found them generally yellow dirty & <shallow> turbid and the nymphs must surely have been mere drabs that inhabited them.

From Lex we rode thro Cesena a <?f?> considerable town to Forli where we put up for the night. The number of carriages with livery servants which we saw in and about this town bespeak it a place of some consequence & politeness, we also understood at the inn that there was to be an opera this evening but our fatigue prevented our going to it. We however are happy to find ourselves once more in a country where rational amusements are tolerated. There are a number

---

of it Irving drew on Martyn, *The Gentleman's Guide*, p. 115. The Ponte d'Augusto, or Ponte di Tiberio, across the Marécchia, was begun during the last year of Augustus' life and was finished by Tiberius in 21.

59. Presumably by "Lex" Irving refers to the present Sant' Archangelo di Romagna. The Ponte Consolare there, dating from 186 B.C., was destroyed in World War II. The identification of the Rubicon, the ancient boundary between Rome and Cisalpine Gaul, has often been disputed. The tradition, sanctioned by an ecclesiastical court at Rome in 1756, that it was the modern Uso, prevailed through the nineteenth century. In 1933 Mussolini identified it with the Fiumicino, slightly north of the Uso, and named that river the Rubicon.

60. The chief authorities for Caesar's hesitation at the Rubicon are Suetonius, Plutarch, and Lucan, who record that he had a vision of Rome in distress but do not ascribe these words to him. Irving may have been drawing on a printed account which has not been identified.

of french soldiers <bill> in the town many of whom we saw about the streets as we entered.

Our road to day quit the Adriatic coast at Rimini. The country appear[s] very level – almost a continual plain with the chain of Appenines far to our left. The soil is tolerable and sowed with grain – in the fields mulberry trees are planted in rows and the vines hang in festoons from one tree to another.

This was Sunday and the country people were dressd out in all their finery. As in the other parts of Italy they seemed very fond of gay colours tho here a bright yellow is the most fashionable. Their dress is very awkward. They wear stays and a number of petticoats <that make them> & their shoes are high heeld & very coarse so that the whole gives them a most clumsy appearance. The men <in this part of> follow the general <Italian> custom among the italian peasantry of wearing gay flowers in their hats. They likewise almost universally wear a large blue cloak that envelopes every part of them except their eyes & nose.

April 22

On leaving Forli this morning we found the road throngd with french soldiers who are on their way to Casteglione to form a camp for the purpose of celebrating the approaching coronation of Bonaparte as King of Lombardy.[61] Each man had his knapsack on his back, his gun on his shoulder and a loaf of brown bread slung on one side and was trudging along thro mud and mire with all the cheerfulness & flow of spirits of a Frenchman. They were mostly young men fresh & healthy.

At Imola we stopped to breakfast. <th> At the caffé we found an old gentleman holding forth to a knot of *Quid nuncs* with a newspaper in one hand and his snuff box in the other. We soon found him to be the politician of the coffee house <to> whom all the others regarded as an oracle. He was a meagre old gentleman with "overwhelming brows"[62] renderd so by continually poring over the newspapers. His long nose had been moulded into a narrow form near the top by the spectacles

61. Probably the soldiers were going to Castiglione delle Stiviere. Napoleon crowned himself King of Italy in Milan Cathedral on May 26, 1805.

62. Shakespeare, *Romeo and Juliet,* V, i, 37–39:

> I do remember an apothecary,
> And hereabouts he dwells, which late I noted
> In tatter'd weeds, with overwhelming brows.

that almost constantly bestraddled it and was plentifully bedaubed with snuff, that article so indispensible to a politician.

He soon made himself acquainted with us and after enquiring the news &c entered into a long discussion of the situations of the different powers – their vast preparations both by sea & land – all which sa<d>id he with a sagacious nod & wink – convinces me that we are about to have *a peace!* The old man seemed to exult in this profound conclusion – and to congratulate himself on his great foresight & calculations – I've always said so in *this very* place said he turning round to his companions as if to appeal to them for the truth of what he said –

"Missieurs" – added he, with a mighty wise misterious look, holding his snuff box in one hand and laying the forefinger of the other aside of his nose to give importance to his observations. "Messieurs – Je suis un homme d'observation – Je lis. Je pense. Je fais mes reflections – <mais> Je ne dis rien – mais – nous verrons – nous verrons – soyez vous sure nous sommes pres a la paix."[63] At the conclusion of the sentince the old man saluted his nose with a powerful pinch of snuff and turned round in triumph to his admiring circle of diciples. Almost every little caffé has its politician of this kind, who directs their opinions and is the sage of the circle. Just before we were quit the caffe the old gentleman drew us on one side and informed us as a *great secret* that for his part he had discoverd to his own satisfaction the designs of the great preperations of the French which were no more nor less than an expedition against *the Grand Turk!*

After leaving Imola we rode along a fine even road thro a beautiful level country. It is almost a continued plain to Bologna excepting that a range of gently waving hills extend to the left and beyond them the blue shadowy chain of Appenines <The country plain>

This level country would become tiresome to the eye was it not beautifully diversified by different species of cultivation – by gentle streams that wander thro it, <wil> shaded by poplars & willows – by flourishing hedges of white thorn &c <that have a beau> By stately oaks <and> elms and poplars that border the road throughout – and a variety of similar pleasing objects. The country <was> produces <a> great <de> quantities of wheat which was in a state of forwardness and renderd the fields beautifully verdant – <th> The salubrity of the atmosphere, loaded with the fragrance of the blossoms

63. "Gentlemen, I am a man of observation. I read; I think; I make my reflections. I say nothing. But we shall see, we shall see. You may be sure we are close to peace."

of the trees and the flowers that were scattered over the fields, was truly d<i>elicious. Every Zephyr <seemed> wafted the most exquisite perfumes. As we approachd Bologna the scenery became still more interesting – the Hills were laid out in gardens – ornamented with superb villas – neat cassino's and picturesque convents – The whole scenery was of that gentle tranquil kind that is calculated to <awaken> sooth & delight – and the <rich rays of> sun gradually verging towards the horison, threw a mellow harmonising glow over it that rendered it a perfect fairy land. No harsh or wild object intruded itself to destroy the gentle character of the landscape – The Appenines were softned by the distance and formed a shadowy line in the horison of the softest purple – The hills <were> that borderd the plain were smooth and waving – diversified by groves of poplars – elms or melancholy cypress – and generally above the <th> tops of the latter were seen the white walls of a convent. The rivers were smooth and winding – and gave life & spirit to the landscape – without producing wildness.

We arrived at Bologna about sun down, and put up at the <Hotel> Albergo del Pelegrino, glad <Thus> to be emancipated from the miserable carriage in which we had been jolted along for nine days successively.

Thus have we accomplished one of the most beautiful routes of Italy. Umbria so celebrated for its charms has even exceeded my expectations. The chain of lovely valleys among the Appenines – of Terni – Foligni &c waterd by poetic streams, the wild, romantic passes thro the Appenines – the gentle scenery of the Adriatic coast that succeeds – all combine to form a variety the most interesting imaginable. Italy is well deserving the character it has acquired of being the Garden of Europe – and of being likewise <a nest of> the abode of poverty, villainy – filth & extortion. A Traveller pays dearly for th<is>e <enjoyments> ↑intellectual↓ pleasures it furnishes, by suffering from bad accomodations in dirty inns – from the impositions of inn keepers servants &c – from wretched carriages, roguish drivers, corrupt custom house officers in short a combination of rogues of every class. He is under the disagreeable necessity of bargaining for every meal before he eats it or else paying the most extravagant price – and of entering into an agreement in writing with the voiturier before he takes his carriage – in which he specifies where he is to stop at, and every minute arrangement on the route. None of these voiturini are to be depended on – our own case is a proof that the most seemingly honest of them will decieve.

<This evening>

NB. I forgot to observe in the course of the preceding notes, that at Cesena we quit the antient Umbria and entered into what was called Cisalpine Gaul. The Rubicon formed the line between them

This evening I went to the opera. The theater[64] is large and elegant – the scenery magnificent and well executed. There was some very fine music and a pleasing ballet of Rinaldo in the Garden of Armida – from Ariosto.[65]

April 23

This morning our <vot> voiturino called to settle with us – We called in a servant of the hotel who spoke french and got him to serve as interpreter for us. We then gave the <vot> voiturino a severe reprimand for his conduct on the route – in which he had behaved sevral times very impertinently and obstinately. Had broken my portmanteau <and> tho I had desired him several times to alter the position of the trunks to prevent such an accident – Had given us an infamous carriage & three mules tho we had agreed for a new one & three horses – had taken up two officers in front of the carriage tho we had expressly hired it for ourselves & had committed several <of> other <pieces> faults equally flagrant We therefore had resolved not to give him the four Dollars *buono mano* which we had promised in case we were well served.

The fellow made a violent noise and blustering and at length was insolent enough to give Mr C the lie – in consequence of which he was immediately bundled out of the Room neck & heels. We sent hi<m>s money after him by a servant, but he refused to take it without the buono mano & went off swearing he would find <some wha> some way to make us pay it. We apprehended he would go to the police and occasion us some trouble so we resolved to be before hand with him. Mr C. called on a banker of his acquaintance a Mr Morelli,[66] stated the case to him and desired him to accompany him to the office of Police. They accordingly went together – the office was not open, and while they were waiting in the antechamber who should enter but our worthy voiturino himself. He appeared a little startled at find-

64. The Teatro Comunale was built between 1756 and 1763 by Antonio Bibiena.

65. Possibly *Armide et Renaud* by the seventeenth-century Italian Luigi Rossi (William C. Smith, comp., *The Italian Opera and Contemporary Ballet in London 1789–1820,* London, 1955, p. 82). Ariosto's *Orlando Furioso* (1516, 1532) contains a Rinaldo. Rinaldo and the sorceress Armida, however, are characters in Tasso's *Gerusalemme Liberata* (1581).

66. No record of this person seems to be preserved in the archives of Bologna.

ing Mr C beforehand with him and began to talk to him but Mr C. ordred him off. The officer of police was extremely polite – after Mr C had represented the case the officer calld in the voiturino heard his story gave him a severe reprimand and orderd him to take the pay we offerd him and go about his business. The fellow complied tho most ungraciously. To shew the magistrate that it was not for the sake of the four dollars that we contended Mr C gave them to Mr Morelli to be put in the poor box in his neighborhood. We have every reason to be highly satisfied with the politeness of the magistrate – and were every traveller to <be equally> pursue this line of conduct in respect to these voiturini it would have a great effect in putting a stop to the notorious knavery of that class of people in Italy. Our old voiturier seemed quite astonished & confounded at our out manouvering him – He had grown grey in iniquity and having taken in so many older heads in his time he had no expectation of meeting with such a rebuff from (as he thought) two raw, inexperienced youths. Travellers are very often apt to comply with the demands of these fellows rather than have any difficulty with the police which they think will be attended with trouble, loss of time & expence – and they fear after all that the police will decide in favor of their countryman the voiturier. Our case is an example to the contrary where <the> justice was executed in a manner the most exemplary & expeditious that a traveller could desire.

We have had a number of offers this day of carriages for Milan from which we have selected one. The carriage is new & excellent & three good mules. We have seen the mules on the road between Rome & Bologna and were well satisfied. The owner of the carriage is a respectable looking man apparantly worthy of confidence – The driver whom he intends giving us bears a <go> character of civility honesty & attentiveness – Our servant knows him and assures us we may depend on him. We have agreed to give him eight Louis' for which we are to have the carriage to ourselves, and a repast per day for each of us with accomodations at night. If we are well served we have promised a liberal *buono mano* the great *primum mobile* of the italians.

This morning we presented our letters of credit to our Banker Mr [*blank*]

I also presented a letter of introduction to Mr Thomas Massa from his brother in law Mr Morelia[?] of Genoa.[67] My reception was extremely polite. He is a banker and a dealer in Drugs.

67. Massa was presumably Tommaso Massa. The "Massa fratelli" were in business

After dinner we walked out of the city to a convent[68] of monks situated on a beautiful hill. From hence there is a fine view of Bologna and of the vast extent of country around. This is all an immense plain and would produce a tiresome sameness were it not happily diversified by a variety of different tints and colors. The fruit trees with which the country is coverd afford a great diversity of coloring especially at this season when many of them are in blossom. The seats – cassinos – <?v?> chateaus convents villages &c scatterd over the plains also add greatly to their beauty. The prospect as far as the eye can reach is a perfect level – except on the side where we were. On this side it is true there is a chain of lovely hills which I have mentiond in my account of our approach to the city – and this convent is situated on the summit of one of them.

Here is a circular court[69] on the walls of which are some fine paintings by Guido Reni – Louis Carrachi &c but so much injured by the weather that they are hardly discernable. Many of them are likewise wantonly injured. Amongst others there is a fine head of a man in one of Carrachi's pictures – a painter was copying it, but after various attempts he found it impossible to copy the fine eye in the original till in a fit of chagrin he siezed his knife and absolutely <picked it out> scraped it out of the wall distroying an object which it was impossible for his weak genius even to imitate.

The church of the convent was neat & had some good oil copies of the original frescos of the Hall.[70] – – –

April 24

This morning we visited the Zampieri palace.[71] The collection of paintings belonging to this palace tho not so large as many that I

several years later as commissioners, with a bank at their place of residence, Via Pietrafitta 621 (Salvatore Muzzi, comp., *Nuova Guida di Bologna con Pianta,* Bologna, 1857, p. 67). "Morelia" was possibly a Morello, the name of a Genoese family (*Almanacco del Ducato di Genova,* Genoa, 1822).

68. S. Michele in Bosco, dating from 1437, was suppressed in 1797; it is now occupied by a hospital.

69. The circular portico of the cloister contains remains of frescoes by Lodovico Carracci and his pupils from the history of SS. Benedict, Cecilia, Tiburtius and Valeriana.

70. The church was built between 1494 and 1510. The "Hall" was presumably the corridor, 427 feet long, containing the chambers of the monks.

71. It was built at the end of the sixteenth century and was long celebrated for the collection of paintings it contained. Most of them are now in the Pinocateca di Brera, Milan.

have seen, is one of the most excellent in Italy. There is more choice & selection displayed than in the generality of Galleries – which fatigue the visitor by crowds of copies and paintings by inferior hands. Several of the pictures in this Gallery are esteemed as chef–d'ouvres in the art. Among those that most pleased me were three ceilings painted in Fresco, one by Lodovico Carraci representing Hercules & Jupiter.[72] another by Annibale Carraci – the subject Virtue opening the heavens to Hercules – a third Hercules suffocating Antæus by Guerchino (very fine. great strength activity and muscular expression in the hercules). A Titan under a rock hiding himself from the thunderbolts of Jupiter – a noble fresco by Annibale Carraci cupids dancing round a tree with the rape of Proserpine – a sweet picture by Albani.[73] The cupids well formed and beautifully colored the landscape exquisite. St Peter weeping and St Paul comforting him – by Guido. This pleased me as much as any painting that I have seen from that master. <The>Fine heads attitudes coloring &c. The dismission of Hagar by Guerchino – a charming painting – The countenance of Hagar is well designed – it has an expression of great greif & emotion without destroying the beauty of the face – Sarah has her back turned to the spectator and a part of her face is in profile. There is much grace and dignity in her figure, but the face of Hagar delighted me. A cieling by Agostino Carrachi – subject Hercules relieving Atlas <from> by supporting the heavens. These are a few that struck me the most tho there are many others of the highest excellence.

Bologna was ever famous for cultivating the sciences.[74] It boasts the most antient university in Europe, this is now adays removed from its old building to the *Institute*.[75] This is an institution that does

72. In his descriptive titles of the works he especially admired (except the Guido and the Agostino Carracci) Irving seems to have drawn on Martyn, *The Gentleman's Guide*, pp. 110–12.

73. Irving is referring to two paintings on copper by Francesco Albani (1578–1660), Bolognese painter.

74. Irving's sentence is a partial quotation from Martyn, *The Gentleman's Guide*, p. 105.

75. The University of Bologna, founded in 1119 by Irnerius, a teacher of law, is the second oldest university in Europe. It first occupied the Archiginnasio, built in 1562, which now houses the municipal library. In 1803 it moved into the sixteenth-century Palazzo Cellesi (now Pozzi) which already housed the Instituto delle Scienze di Bologna, founded in the seventeenth century. Its library was much enriched in the eighteenth century by the efforts of Benedict XIV and Cardinal P. M. Monti.

honor to the city. It is a grand academy for the arts and sciences. There is a room for antiquities and casts of celebrated statues very well furnished, another for chemical apparatus – another for Dioptrics – three others for experimental philosophy and physical apparatus Six rooms for natural history which are well filld and classically arranged – but above all the anatomy room is most deserving of attention. Here are several representations of the human body in different states so as to <represent> display the veins arteries – muscles &c &c and also detachd members of the body – all worked in wax with astonishing nature and precision Besides these advantages the institute likewise has an excellent Library <with> of books in different languages – manuscripts – maps prints & drawings – and an academy of drawing & painting, where they design from casts & living models. Lectures are given here by eminent professors in the sciences and the greatest care is taken to render the institution as perfect as possible.

I was all over the building this morning which like all other academies palaces and public edifices in Italy is open to the inspection of the strangers. Indeed they take a pride in displaying this monument of their science. The different apparatus are kept in the finest order, and well arranged. In one room a professor was lecturing on natural history. In the library was another with a number of students at different desks studying. From the observatory on top of the building there is a fine view of Bologna and the <be> lovely country around it. –

<We> Next to Rome Bologna most claims the attention of the painter.[76] It is famous for giving birth to the Carrachi's, those men to whom the art owes so much. who restored painting from the depraved languishing state in which they found it in 1580 – and revived the grandeur simplicity and vigour of the old school. Lewis (or Lodovico) Carrachi was the first that commenced this grand undertaking – he was originally a Taylor, but the bent of his genius soon shewed itself – he drew his brothers Annibale & Agostino into his scheme. They opened their school & had for pupils <some> ↑men↓ that have since turned out worthy of the first rank as painters ↑viz↓ Guido Albano Guerchino Domenichino – & a number of others <the> less celebrated but each possessing a high degree of merit. The palaces churches & public edifices are filld with paintings in oil and fresco, by these eminent masters. Even the Madonnas &c that are painted <on the

76. This sentence contains echoes of Martyn, *The Gentleman's Guide,* p. 95, and of Moore, *A View of Society and Manners in Italy,* I, 310.

houses> in different parts of the streets are many of them worthy of attention.

<The school of C>

The style of the Carrachi is distinguished by its grace ease & freedom and for strength vigour & energy. <They> It became deservedly celebrated in Italy, and there is not a gallery of any consequence in the country but <what> boasts some of its productions[77] – The finest that I have seen out of <rome> ↑Bologna↓ are I think the frescos that ornament the <hall> saloon of the Farnese palace at Rome. We have visited several of the churches in this city which are full of them.

Bologna is very deficient in point of architecture, few handsome buildings are to be seen. The fronts of the houses are built upon arcades. (like our <feder> City Hall in New York)[78] This mode gives it a singular rather than an handsome appearance, as the arcades are very irregular, each house varying in the height or size of that belonging to it, and very little attention being paid either to the proportions or order of architecture. They are however extremely convenient to the foot passengers – as they are sheltered from the rain, well paved and secure from carriages & horses. In such a country as italy it may be doubted whether such a mode of building is advisable – Among a revengeful people who seek satisfaction with the stilletto – these dark arcades afford the best of opportunities at night to <lurk> lie in wait and wreak their vengeance <i>on an unsuspecting adversary. This barberous custom however, is losing ground very fast in italy and is only known now & then among the lower classes. The wearing of the stilletto is prohibited – tho they are still born[e] about privately by many, and I have even seen them openly exposed for sale in the shops. The French have contributed greatly to this change whereever they have established their authority in Italy

The roads are less subject to robberies and murders, tho I saw two crosses by the road side between Rimini & Bologna which I was told were signs that murders had been committed on those spots. We

77. In his account of the Carracci Irving drew on Grosley, *New Observations on Italy,* I, 134.

78. The building to which Irving refers was built in 1699–1700 to house the Assembly and Council and became the official residence of the Mayor in 1740; it was remodeled in 1788 as Federal Hall for the U.S. Congress by Pierre C. L'Enfant and used by that body until 1800. See Isaac Newton Phelps, *The Iconography of Manhattan Island, 1498–1909* (New York, 1915–1928), VI, 538–39.

were generally advised not to travel after dark, particularly along the coast of the Adriatic, where, besides the risque from banditti, there have been instances of travellers having been carried off with their baggage by Turks who landed from their boats. In Rimini they still speak with emotion of a body of turks that landed there last summer – enterd the town and carried off several families!

This evening we went to the theatre again[.] the same opera was performing – and Mr Cabell reccollected having seen it performed when he<e> was here before – about two months and an half ago[79] – It is the custom in Italy to continue the same opera for one two & three months[.] the italians go every night – are every night re-delighted and at the end of each song roar out bravo – bravissimo as if in an agony of delight. In the ballets they seem most delighted with the buffa Dancers. These are muscular fellows who whirl round, jump up with their heels as high as their heads and <?c?> perform a variety of the most *outré* feats of activity. They are likewise accompanied in their dancing by women who spring up with wonderful agility – till their scanty clothing of fine muslim <app> flies up about their ears an[d] then the old italians roar out with rapture – bravo – bravissimo – ecco la (see there).

The theatre of Bologna is very large with five rows of boxes – the stage is capacious and well furnished – next to Bordeaux it is the handsomest theatre I have seen in <It> Europe.

The Bolognese manufacture silks of various kinds – velvets – crapes – paper &c <beside> ↑Their↓ hams & sausages are well known by epicures. They export flax hemp honey & wax.[80] There is a great show of life and bustle in the streets which gives it an air of liveliness in spight of its gloomy architecture and heavy arcades. The people, from their intercourse with the french seem to have imbibed something of their disposition and manners and to <have> possess considerable vivacity.

79. Cabell was in Bologna January 26–31, 1805, and recorded in his journal that he attended the opera and the theater (where he saw a "tragedy"), but did not give the name of either performance (Journal, [No. 5], "Notes of a Journey to Italy – In the Winter of 1804–5").

80. These export items are listed in Martyn, *The Gentleman's Guide*, p. 113, and most of them also in Moore, *A View of Society and Manners in Italy*, I, 276–77, and Grosley, *New Observations on Italy*, I, 127.

The Italians generally are grave and even pensive. There is a sincerity and sentiment about them that we do not often find in the french They appear to be warmer in their attachments and more sensible to lasting impressions. A Frenchman is all life, gaiety & spirit – his feelings are acute and ↑as↓ easily ↑<as>↓ wounded <but> as delighted yet they do not retain long any sentiment either of anger or pleasure. Though <his courage is> no one is more sensible of an insult or more prompt to resent it – yet he is easily pacified the least concession restores him to good humour.

He is ever ready to render you any service that does not materially incommode himself. No one can exceed him in politeness or an attention to those little civilities and good offices that render the intercourse of man & man agreeable – no one can out do him in proffers of friendship & services – yet these ↑last↓ are mere matters of form and mean no more than the generality of people do when they subscribe their letter to a stranger with* "Your obedient humble servant." perhaps the next time the french man meets you he hardly knows you. An Italian on the contrary tho perhaps not so ardent in his professions of friendship nor particularly in his attention to the minutae of politeness, <is> feels more what he expresses – he conceives an attachment more easily nor is it so easily effaced. His resentments are deep and lasting. ↑He is↓ susceptible to tender impressions and a high degree of sentiment is observable in all his connections.

Before leaving Bologna I should not forget to note down a fine <fountain ↑statue↓ that stands on> statue that ornaments <the> a fountain in the square of St Petronius[81] – it represents Neptune holding his trident in one hand and extending the other in <a com> an attitude of command. The statue is of bronze by John of Bologna and is a noble piece of workmanship. The figure is majestic imposing & severe.

To the west of the city is a singular portico of arcades that extends from the city to the church of St Luca situated on a hill about three

* This same remark I have since found in the works of Dr Moore[82]

81. The square is now the Piazza Vittorio Emmanuele. The fountain was designed by Tommaso Laureti in 1564.

82. Moore, *A View of Society and Manners in Italy,* I, 68–69; see also pp. 59–60, 80–85.

miles distant.[83] This coverd way is built for the accomodation of a religious procession that once a year bear a picture of the Virgin (said to be painted by St Luke) in solemn ceremony thro the streets of Bologna and afterwards return it to its sanctuary in the church. We were advised to walk out to the church and look at the painting – but the poor specimen we had seen at Loretto of St Lukes skill in the sister art, made us unwilling to give much credit to his talents in the art of painting.[84] Indeed we were told that the picture had nothing but the sanctity of the painter to reccommend it.

There are two remarkable towers in Bologna built of Brick. One called the Asinelli tower was erected in 1109 – it is 327¼ feet high – square and narrow. It leans three feet and an half and has a threatening appearance. There are stairs within by which one may mount up to the top from whence there is a fine view of the city and the country around. Close to this tower is another one of the same form tho not so high. It is called the Garisenda tower. It is about 140 feet high and leans about 8 feet 9 inches out of the perpendicular so that it appears ready to fall every moment. These inclinations in the towers were no doubt owing to one side of the foundation having sunk. <They are> Such towers were frequently erected in Tuscany & Lombardy, in the dark ages, and were intended as family cidatels and watch towers.[85]

April 25

We found some difficulty today in getting our passports signed by the police authorizing us to proceed to Milan. In consequence of the approaching coronation of Bonaparte as Emperor of Lombardy orders have been issued enjoining the greatest strictness in respect

83. The pilgrimage church of Madonna di S. Luca, on Monte della Guardia, built by Fancesco Dotti between 1723 and 1757, was so-called from an ancient painting it contained of the Virgin, ascribed to St. Luke and brought from Constantinople in 1160. The hill is reached by an arcade two miles long consisting of 665 arches with numerous chapels, built between 1674 and 1739.

84. Much the same thing about the painting at Spoleto ascribed to St. Luke is said in Moore, *A View of Society and Manners in Italy,* I, 370.

85. The Torre degli Asinelli was built by Gherardo degli Asinelli beside the ancestral castle; its height is commonly given as 320 feet. The Torre Garisenda was built by Filippo and Ottone Garisenda in 1110; it is about 160 feet high and is said to lean 10 inches. Martyn gives the date of the Torre degli Asinelli, the dimensions of both towers, and the historical explanation of such towers in *The Gentleman's Guide,* pp. 112–13.

to passports. <and> Even the inhabitants of the other italian cities find it difficult to obtain permission to <pro> go to Milan. We applied to our Banker and to Mr Morelli for assistance and in consequence of their representations and of our passports being perfectly *in regle* we were granted the liberty of proceeding. The approaching coronation seems to create much agitation among the italians, but they seem to keep their sentiments to themselves so that I <could> ↑can↓ not learn satisfactorily in what light they view it. Certainly nothing can be better for their country than for the Emperor to unite & consolidate the number of petty states into which this country has been split up; into one grand government that shall give strength and importance to the whole.

This city is long and narrow – about five miles in circuit and extremely populous containing about 60,000 inhabitants.[86] It is as I have before observed – situated in one of the most luxurient plains in the world that furnishes it with a great variety of excellent fruit

Journey from Bologna to Milan
April 26th. 1805.
By the way of Modena Plaisance[87] Lodi &c

Nights of the month	Italian posts	Names of Posts	Observations
	1 ½	Samoggia	Pass the river <Rem> ↑Reno↓ on a bridge
	1 ½	Modena	excellent hotel – ↑post↓ pass the Panaro – bridge
	1	Rubbiera[88]	pass the Secchio – bridge
26th.	1	Reggio	Inn good.
	5		
	1	St. Ilario <Pof>	Pass – River lenza – bridge

86. Martyn, gives these figures in *The Gentleman's Guide,* p. 95.

87. The French form of Piacenza (see "Route from Rome to Bologna . . . ," page 294, n. 2).

88. In his list of posts, Irving misspelled Rubiera and in his observations, the river Enza.

Nights of the month	Italian posts	Names of Posts	Observations
	1	Parma	Hotel de france[89] – good.
	1	Castel Guelfo	
	1	Borgo St. Donnino	
27th.	1	Fiorenzolo –	Inn tolerable people very civil – sign of the white cross
	5		
	2	<Pl>Piacenza	Pass on Po on a stage built on barks
	2	Zorlesco	
28th.	1	Lodi	I Tre Re (three Kings) an excellent Inn.
	5		
	1 ¼	Marignano	Pass the Lambro – bridge – beautiful scenery –
29th.	1 ¼	Milan	Hotel Royal. poor – de Citta[90] better
	2 ½		

April 26

About five oclock this morning we left Bologna and set out for Milan. The day has been very fine – and having an excellent carriage & mules and one of the best roads in Italy we have came on very pleasantly. The road lay thro the vast plain that extends quite to Turin. It is perfectly level, but as I have before remarked – beautifully varied by different species of cultivation – by a diversity of trees – The stately oak, the slender poplar, the Elm, the cypress the mulberry &c – by noble fields of wheat – rich <pas> meadows – waterd by frequent streams that empty themselves into the Po. To the left is still seen the long chain of Appenines – crowned with snow and forming beautifully waving lines in the distance. The wheat is planted in long beds

89. Irving should have written "di Francia."
90. Irving should have written "Della Citta."

about three feet wide with deep furrows between to carry off the water. At equal distances in the wheat fields are planted rows of Elms or mulberries – A vine is placed by each tree which runs up it and from thence shoots forth its branches – these are attached to the end of the branches of the vine that grows on the next tree – and they are brought down in the middle by a weight so as to form a perfect festoon. This is an economic scheme to save room – but I doubt whether the shade of the vines does not impoverish the grain. They must have a beautiful appearance in summer when in full verdure.

About 10 oclock we stopped at Modena to breakfast. This is a neat little <town> city said to contain about 23000 inhabitants[91] – like Bologna it is built upon arcades but here they are not so gloomy. After breakfast we took a cicerone and walked out to see the town. He first took us to a square Gothic tower to see the *Secchia* or Bucket – a trophy of a victory gained by the Modenese over the Bolognese <in> ↑within↓ the very walls of Bologna – This has been celebrated by the poet Tassoni born in this place – and is regarded by the Modenese as <i>an invaluable relique.[92]

It is suspended by an Iron chain from the vault of a gloomy room in the tower, <which is secured by several> to attain which you have to pass thro *five* strong doors the inner one of *Iron* – this extreme precaution was taken lest the Bolognese should attempt to carry off this taunting monument of their dishonor – great parade was made in shewing it to us. Our <valet de pl> cicerone went for the man appointed <to keep the key> to shew it. He came with a large bunch of keys and a wax taper. The door of the tower was unlocked – our cicerone was obliged to remain without – We mounted two or three narrow flights of steps and then four doors more were unlocked before we gained access to the chamber that contains this inestimable curiosity. Cabell who did not know its history – had his expectations highly raised by such extreme precautions, but when he enterd the chamber and found the mighty treasure was nothing but an old wooden bucket

91. In his figure for Modena's population, his description of the *secchia* and the cathedral in Modena, and the last two paragraphs of this entry Irving drew on Martyn, *The Gentleman's Guide,* pp. 90, 91, 93.

92. The bucket, which was carried off in 1325 at the battle of Rapolino, is in the Torre Ghirlandina, the detached campanile of the cathedral, which was built between 1100 and 1319. Alessandro Tassoni (1565–1635) wrote the mock epic *La Secchia Rapita* in 1614; it was published in 1622.

with iron hoops, he burst into an hearty fit of laughter. The man who was shewing it to us seemed quite affronted at this apparent ridicule and would hardly answer any questions we asked.

From thence we entered the cathedral <an>a heavy Gothic building – here are one or two tolerable paintings an assumption that possesses handsome coloring & figures[93] – They were fitting up the church against the arrival of the pope – The approach of his holiness seems to create a great degree of preparation in the towns & villages – Every little place seems to possess the same desire to distinguish itself and to think as much of its insignificant churches & ornaments as even the magnificent city of Rome itself – Each one is ambitious of applause and of obtaining the pontific smile of approbation – This emulation seems even to extend still lower and I remarked at one part of the road today an old woman briskly employed in cleaning up an earthen image of the Virgin & our Saviour that decorated a nitch on the outside of her house, in hopes it might attract the notice of his holiness as he passed.

We were thro the Ducal palace, formerly possessd of a noble collection of paintings, but the finest were formerly selected for the King of Poland[94] and the remaining pieces of merit have been carried away by the French. Some cielings in Fresco by Franceschini and Tintoretto are the best things that remain.

In this palace there is a noble lib<e>rary[95] open to the public and containing an excellent and numerous collection of books in every <library> ↑language↓[96] – that are handsomely arranged and fill several rooms.

Passing thro the same kind of scenery as in the morning we arrived at an early hour at Reggio. We were several times stopped during the day <to> by the officers of police and custom at the different towns thro which we passd. the former were satisfied with an examination of <the> our passports – to the others we <?ma?> displayed the cer-

93. The cathedral was built between 1099 and 1184. The "assumption" is probably the Madonna in clouds, with SS. Jerome, Sebastian, and John the Baptist, by Dosso Dossi.

94. The Palazzo Ducale was begun in 1635 by Bartolomeo Avanzini for Duke Francesco I. Augustus III (1696–1763) of Poland was sold in 1744 a hundred of the best paintings in the collection (information furnished by the superintendent of the Galleries of the Province of Modena and Reggio Emilia). The episode is referred to in Martyn, *The Gentleman's Guide,* p. 92.

95. The Biblioteca Estense was brought from Ferrara in 1598.

96. "language" is in pencil.

tificate of our trunks having been seald up at St Cattolica – and tho we had since broken the seals & opened them a paul or two generally blinded the custom house officers to that circumstance.

The road we have come on today as well as a part of the road before our arrival at Bologna is formed on the antient Æmilian way.

Reggio is a decent little town of about 17,000 inhabitants – the houses like many other towns in these parts – are built upon arches. There are a few good paintings in the <pl> churches – (unless they have been latterly taken away by the french) They have also a theatre.[97]

The celebrated Ariosto one of the finest Italian poets was <fr> born in this place in 1474.

April 27

On Quitting Reggio this morning early we found a large body of French troops leaving it also on their way to Castel<l>eone[98] where they are to form a grand camp (as we are told) to be reviewd by the Emperor – They went by a different road from the one we took – and they made an interesting and martial appearance as they filed off at a distance their arms glistening thro the trees.

Our road this day – lay thro the same kind of level fertile country as yesterday. <?f?> distributed in <?small?> ↑fruitful↓ cornfields vineyards and luxurient pastures that produce the famous parmesan cheese. The cattle are large and in fine condition.

About 10 oclock we arrived at the city of Parma. This city is populous and seems to have some trade – this opinion may have been occasiond by the concourse of people we found there on entering – it happening to be market day. The town possesses between 30 & 40,000 Inhabitants. There is <no> ↑scarcely any↓ good architecture in the place.

In the cathederal[99] (which is a very gothic building) is a famous painting of Corregio in the dome representing the Assumption of the Virgin. It is so much damaged that the figures can hardly be distinguished[100] – Taking them in their best state those paintings in domes

97. The chief churches in Reggio are the church of Madonna dell Ghiara, with frescoes by Luca Ferrari, Lionello Spada, and others of the Bolognese school; and S. Prospero, with frescoes by Camillo Procaccini. The Teatro di Cittadella there was built in 1740 (information furnished by the mayor of Reggio).

98. Probably Castiglione delle Stiviere.

99. It was begun in 1058 and completed in the thirteenth century.

100. To this point in the paragraph Irving seems to have drawn on Martyn, *The Gentleman's Guide*, pp. 87–88.

seldom shew to much advantage and fatigue a person very much in looking at them – I perfectly agree with my fellow country man Allston who says that a man who will paint in a dome does not deserve a spectator to his performances.

In the right side of the cross there are some fine paintings on the cieling <by th> which represent the prophets and sybills[101] – We had picked up a ragged cicerone who seemed to know very little about his business, he ascribed every painting we admired to Corregio – and he did the same with the sybills & Prophets – They indeed appeared to be in his style and pleased us exceedingly.

In the church of St. Giovanni Evangelista <there> we were shewn another cupolo by Corregio, but the cupolo was so dark that we could not dicern the painting.[102]

In the Ducal palace[103] is a fine Library – an academy for young painters and sculptors and a large theatre, for some time past sufferd to <la> go to ruin – formerly celebrated for its size and for the distinctness with which voices could be heard throughout it.

At Parma there is a printer of the name Bordiani who has acquired a great character as being the first in his profession We stopped at his Book store and were shewn several <suburpt> superb works of his printing the Tipe & execution beautiful – I purchased of him a petrarch for a very reasonable price.[104]

After leaving Parma we crossed the river Taro – broad & shallow except in one part where we were ferried over on a platform placed on two barques. When we passed thro the other divisions of the river, which were very shallow – our Carriage was beset by a herd of sturdy fellows one of whom flounderd ahead – another took hold of the foremost mule and the rest to the number of *seven* hung on the carriage holding by the wheels – traces &c As soon as we arrived on terra

101. They are the work of Girolamo Bedoli Mazzola.

102. The church was begun in 1510 and its façade added in 1604. The frescoes in the dome by Correggio represent Christ in glory surrounded by apostles and angels.

103. The Palazzo Farnese or della Pilotta was partially built for the Farnese family 1583–1602 but never completed.

104. Giambattista Bodoni (1740–1813), Italian printer and type designer was one of the originators of "modern" type; he designed the type face named for him about 1798. The Bodoni Petrarch which Irving bought was probably *Rime di Francesco Petrarca,* ed. G. J. Dionesi (Parma, 1799), 2 vols., 8° (there was also a folio edition). He paid $2 for it (see his expense account for this date in his "Traveling Notes, 1804–1805").

ferma they all advanced in a crowd soliciting a buono mano <and> for the many perils and dangers they had encounterd in *guiding* us over (tho we could have found the way very easily ourselves) & in short we had to pay them to get rid of them. At a little distance from the river we passed Castel Guelpho that gave name to the party of the Guelphs.[105] It is an interesting looking old castle with square towers and stands near the road. In the afternoon we met a Pilgrim with his staff – bare legged – on his way to Loretto. A little after sun down we arrived at the small village of Firenzolo where we put up. The Inn is tolerable <but> the attendants civil and good natured. We were fortunate enough to arrive rather early for shortly after the inn was crouded with new comers who found great difficulty in finding beds.

April 28

We left Fiorenzolo this morning about sun rise, having been cautioned by Mr Morelli of <Mil> Bologna not to travel in these parts in the dark. Indeed we had heard from others as well as from him that the country as you approach Milan is very much infested by robbers, particularly after leaving Lodi. Between that place and Milan it is dangerous to travel either before sun rise or after dark, and very often at midday as at that time the peasantry are not in the fields, but at home eating dinner, which affords a good opportunity for the Robbers. Mr Morrelli had been robbed himself, <in these> near Milan last summer. We had sufficient proof that his information was well grounded, for between Fiorenzola and Piacenza we passed several crosses ↑(in three places)↓ naild to trees near which travellers had been robbed & murdered. One of the crosses appeared quite new. In one place five crosses were naild on one tree, in another place two.

The scenery was the same as yesterday except that to the right we saw the chain of Alps coverd with snow, that run along the borders of Switzerland & the Tyrol. They had a beautiful appearance reflecting the rays of the morning sun. The weather was serene and delicious. We arrived at <Pla> Piacenza about nine oclock.

This city is situated <of> on the Po <whch> which is navigable only for shallow barks. It is a place of considerable extent but very

105. The castle was built for the Ghibelline Orlando Pallavicino as Torre d'Orlando, but captured in 1407 and renamed by the Guelph Ottone Terzi of Parma. Irving's sentence is a partial quotation from Martyn, *The Gentleman's Guide*, p. 90.

deficient in respect to architecture. There is one street[106] in the west part of the city that is handsome on account of its width and straightness tho <there is nothing> the buildings are not remarkable excepting the façade of the church of St Agostino,[107] which is a chaste Ionic by Vignola.

In the grande Piazza (place) there are two noble equestrian statues in bronze of Allessandro 1. and his son Ranuccio Farnese.[108] The horses are very spirited and the figures commanding – they are said to be the work of Giovanni Bologna. In rear of these statues is the Palazzo Publico[109] – a curious Gothic Edifice of Brick & stone.[110] Here there w<ere>as a great croud of Peasantry assembled in their Sunday finery – listening to the humours of a mountebank – a species of exhibition mightily relished by the Italians. There are some good paintings in the churches by the school of Carraci. In the cathederal the cupola and choir are by Guerchino – In the choir we were shewn two fine paintings by Landi an artist now living in Rome.[111] One represents the burial of the Virgin – Her body is exquisitely graceful and well formed – the drapery disposed with vast taste and the expression of death in her countenance striking[.] the other figures around are very excellent but I disliked in <one> an angel, above the disposition of one of the legs which is thrown up in an awkward position. The fellow Picture represents the apostles gatherd at the tomb and two angels dropping flowers on it. The forms of the angels are highly beautiful and their coloring is so soft and aerial as almost to seem to melt into the surrounding air.

In St. Madonna della Campagna[112] are also some good paintings

Near Piacenza on the banks of the Trebia a small River that empties

106. Via Giuseppe Taverna.

107. S. Agostino was built by Giacomo Barozzi, called Vignola (1507–1573).

108. The Piazza dei Cavalli derives its name from the statues of Alessandro I Farnese (1545–1592), duke of Parma, and his son Ranuccio I (1569–1622), who was his successor to the dukedom. The statues were designed 1620–1625 by Francesco Mochi (a pupil of Giovanni da Bologna).

109. Built in 1281 and after, it is now the Palazzo del Comune.

110. This paragraph to this point contains echoes of Martyn, *The Gentleman's Guide*, pp. 86–87.

111. The cathedral was built between 1122 and 1233. The frescoes in the dome are of prophets and sibyls by Guercino and Pier Francesco Morazzone. Those in and around the choir are by Camillo Procaccini and Lodovico Carracci. Gaspare Landi (1756–1830), a native of Piacenza, was associated with the Academy of St. Luke in Rome from 1802 to 1820.

112. S. M., or Madonna, di Campagna was built about 1525 by Alessio Tramello. It was decorated chiefly by Giovanni Antonio de' Sacchi, called da Pordenone. A list of the chief works in it is in Martyn, *The Gentleman's Guide*, p. 86.

into the Po – the Roman army under the consul Simpronius was entirely defeated by Hannibal[113] – A body of ten thousand of the Roman troops broke thro the Carthagenian army and got safe to <Pl> Piacenza

After leaving the city we crossd the Po on a kind of Platform built on two barks. the river appears shallow and is muddy.

In the afternoon we passed several rice plantations which are laid completely under water by means of canals. Indeed the whole country is irrigated, so that it can be plentifully waterd any time of the year – this renders the pastures exceeding luxurient The hay is said to be cut four & five times a year. The cattle are superb and the cheese and butter excellent, being the best of Parmesan – (this part of the country is near to Lodi.) <Indeed> The whole of Lombardy is famous for its fertile plains. This afternoon we passed some more crosses that told of the fate of some unforunate travellers and are uncomfortable objects to the passenger. We had fine weather the whole day, and the country glowed with all the charms of spring. We were saluted with the continual song of the Goldfinch and nightingale with which birds the country abounds. As it was sunday the country people were shewing off in all their finery and displayed the same fondness for gay colors that I have observed in all the other parts of Italy.

Before sun down we arrived in the little town of Lodi. This place is pretty well fortified. We entered by a handsome new gate of the Doric order.[114] There are two french regiments quarterd in the town which give it an air of great life. The people appeared to have caught the french manners – We found them seated without the doors – the middling classes well dressd – the girls particularly habited in the french fashion a *la greque*, which set of[f] their natural charms to great advantage. I remarked that there was <much> a greater proportion of the women handsome, than in the generality of towns.

After we had taken our Room at the hotel (I tre Re) and arranged matters for dinner we walked out to see the famous bridge of Lodi. We went out of the <city> town at the Porta Nuova from whence there is a lovely view of the Plain of Lombardy beautifully diversified by groves pastures cornfields &[c] and the prospect terminated by the long chain of Alps coverd with eternal snow. The Bridge of Lodi is of

113. In 218 B.C. Hannibal defeated the combined forces of the consuls Tiberius Sempronius Longus (d. 210 B.C.) and P. Cornelius Scipio (d. 211 B.C.?) at this point. His defeat by "the consul Sempronius" is referred to in Grosley, *New Observations on Italy*, I, 99.

114. It was built in 1782 and torn down in 1912.

wood built on Piers and about 180 or 200 yards over. It is celebrated by one of the most brilliant <moments of> actions of Bonaparte; The marks of the cannon balls in the walls of the houses are still visible and shew how hot must have been the fire of the austrians along the bridge on which Bonaparte had the intrepidity to expose himself.[115]

Lodi is a neat little town of about 12 or 14,000 Inhabitants – The cheese of Lodi is the best of Parmesan.[116]

April 29

We did not leave Lodi till after sunrise having been particularly cautiond about the road between it and Milan as being very much infested by robbers – <The> Last evening we saw three brought into the town by a Gen d'armes, we could not learn the particulars of their crime. We had not rode far from the town before we passd a cross on a tree that appeared to have lately been placed there The road however was <full> renderd perfectly safe at the time we passd – by the number of peasants going to their labor in the fields. The morning was extremely beautiful <and the fertile plains interspersed with canals and borderd by the Grison Alps> and our ride very pleasing – the country around much the same as yesterday – fertile plains intersected by canals – The banks of which were coverd with poplars willows and ash trees – The prospect bounded on one side by the <?blu?> Appenines softened by the distance into the softest tints – and on the other side by the bold craggy summits of the Grison Alps – coverd with snow and brightening in the sunbeams. Our road (as it had been throughout Lombardy) – was borderd by fine trees – the poplar – oak, ash Elm &c. About nine oclock we arrived at Milan and put up at the *Albergo Reale* (Royal hotel).

April 30

Milan is an extensive town and very populous – (said to be above 6 miles in circumference & to contain about 140,000 Inhabitants)[117] The

115. On May 10, 1796, Napoleon's forces crossed the bridge over the Adda River at Lodi under heavy artillery fire and thus secured Lombardy for the French. The battle, in which Napoleon took a personal part, was the first in which his courage as well as his strategy was proven. See William M. Sloane, *The Life of Napoleon Bonaparte* (New York, 1912), I, 359–62.

116. In this paragraph Irving seems to have drawn on Martyn, *The Gentleman's Guide*, p. 84.

117. In his figures for Milan's area and population and his description of the cathedral there (including its dimensions) Irving drew on Martyn, *The Gentleman's Guide*, pp. 69, 70.

streets are crowded by people who seem all busy – This together with the vast number of shops give it an air of great business. It appears to <be co> be by no means deficient in manufactures particularly in gold ↑& silver↓ work – such as gold & silver laces, embroideries – tinsel – gold & silver thread – <It> also silk handkerchiefs – stockings – gloves – raw silk &c &c

It is a kind of deposit for the merchandize that passes between Italy France Switzerland & part of Germany – and the goods passing thro the hands of the Milanese enrich them very much by commissions.

The streets are not by any means handsome* nor does the city possess any squares of importance excepting the one in front of *the cath<e>deral*[118] – This is a singular building of vast size which has been building about *four hundred years* and is yet unfinished. Those who commenced it sat out on a scheme of grandeur and expence that they could not complete and their successors have contented themselves rather with repairing what was already built than compleating the edifice. Workmen are constantly employed on it, but as fast as they build up one part another gives way so that like the web of penelope the work does not seem to be nearer to completion at the end of the year than it was at the begining – every high wind or storm of rain or snow topples down some spire or turret or image.

<The> As far as it is completed it affords a beautiful specimen of the Gothic style but strangely mingled in some parts with other styles of architecture. The whole outside of the church is covered with fine Carrara marble excepting the front, part of which still remains rough brick work.

The profusion of statues, reliefs and other carved ornaments with which the outside is decorated is astonishing – (addison reccons within & without 11,000 statues in which compalation he must have included the figures in the reliefs)[119]

The grand steeple is very high and of superb Gothic architecture (180 feet high) all of white marble. This church was begun in 1386 and

* Excepting a fine broad street that leads to the gate of Rome.[120]

118. The alteration is in pencil. The church, one of the largest and most ornate in Italy, was begun about 1386, dedicated to Maria Nascenti in 1567, but not completed until 1813.

119. Addison's estimate is contained in his *Remarks on Several Parts of Italy* (London, 1705), p. 28, but Irving is taking it from Martyn, *The Gentleman's Guide*, p. 70.

120. Corso di Porta Romana.

is <next to> after St Peters at Rome the largest church in Italy.[*] From the profusion of marble & carvings with which it is loaded it has already cost more than St Peters tho the latter is finished. I endeavored, but in vain, to gain a sight of the inside of this church – a vast number of workmen are busied in fitting it up for the approaching coronation and they do not permit any person to enter it except those concernd in the work.

May 1

The city of Milan bears more the appearance of a french town than any other that I have seen in Italy. There is a bustle and vivacity in the looks and motions of the inhabitants that is not <f>often found among the Italians. They have assumed considerable of the french character from their frequent intercourse with that nation.

Two theatres are established in Milan and both enjoy the smiles of the public. The Grand theatre[121] is very large has five rows of Boxes and will contain four thousand people with great ease – perhaps many more. The boxes are all taken by private families or persons, for the season. This is the custom throughout Italy, <where> every genteel family must have its particular box where they recieve company of an evening and in carnival time sup and play cards. <These boxes> To render the boxes commodious for these purposes they are seperated from each other by partitions – and such as choose, have curtains which they can let down in front and entirely exclude themselves from the view of the theatre. In Milan every box has its silk curtain and as the colour <of these> is dictated merely by the fancy of the proprietor[.] the audience part of the Grand theatre <has> puts one in mind of a harlequin Jacket. The stage is very large and well lighted and the scenery really superb – They <b> performed a very pretty ballet in

[*] Size of the cathedral – 180 feet high 249½ long 148½ broad.[122]

121. This is the famous La Scala opera house, one of the largest theaters in Europe; built by Giuseppe Piermarini, 1776–1778, its seating capacity when Irving visited it was 3600.

122. These dimensions are given Martyn, *The Gentleman's Guide,* p. 70. The building is commonly said to be 486 feet long, 268 feet wide at the transept, and 151 feet high in the nave.

To carry out what appears to have been Irving's intention the editor has added a bracketed star to Irving's text and note. Irving wrote the note on the size of the cathedral at the bottom of the page, cutting it off from the text with a broken line to indicate it was a note but apparently forgetting to add the stars.

which there were several changes of scenery, all of them magnificent – one of them represented a Tournament; the dresses were appropriate and beautiful. The italians are remarkable for their taste and skill in scenery – their architectural scenery surpasses any I have seen in france for richness & elegance. They do not shift their *flat* ↑scenes↓ like with us – in two divisions from top to bottom, and shoved off at the sides – but hoist it up and lower it down from above – This way I think is preferable, as it prevents the scenery from being soild & dirtied in putting it on and off of the frames and in shoving it along. It must be noticed however that the italians when they hoist the scenery do not roll it up, but let it hang completely spread – rolling would crack & ruin it. The <house> audience part of the house recieves no light but the reflection from the stage – Any persons who choose may have lights in their boxes. This makes the stage show off to far more advantage, and the eyes of the spectator are not distressed by a variety of cross lights and glaring objects in the audience part of the house. In france they suffer the house to be illuminated by one chandalier hung up in the centre.

I reccollect our ladies in New York complained sadly that the theatre was badly lighted, tho they had the light from the stage; a large chandalier hung up in the centre and smaller ones hung in different parts, and yet the ↑audience part of the↓ theatre is not above a third as large as the grand theatre of Milan. An Italian entering in our theatre would be astonished to see such a glare of light and would immediately exclaim that <the effect> all the splendors of the stage would shew to no advantage but the eye be confused by a variety of lamps and chandaliers.

I observed that french refinement had <prefa> prevailed in the Grand theatre in silencing the clamorous disagreeable mode the italians have of expressing approbation. The audience to be sure clapped their hands extravagantly but our ears were not stunned by the bawling and even yelling of bravo bravissimo, ecco la &c. Applause is not in Italy confined to the honest vulgar – the boxes join in the acclamations and are equally warm in applauding their favorite songs or performers.

There is no people that enjoy music with such *gusto* as the Italians. It has in fact become almost as necessary to them as food – The lowest peasant is as much an amateur as the nobleman – tho his taste may not be as refined. <The former nobleman> The delicate ear of the latter must be regaled by the high wrought and <exquisitely> exquisite music of the opera, while the former is delighted by the inferior efforts of itinerant musicians – or perhaps the simple notes of his reed as he tends his herds. I have seen small bands of these wandring musicians in every <town> ↑city↓ of Italy thro which I have passed. They generally consist of four or five men and women who play on different instruments and it is very rarely that I have seen more than one person in the whole band who was not blind. This one serves for the guide and conducts his companions <topp> opposite to some hotel where there are a number of strangers. Here they station themselves and begin their concert vocal & instrumental with a noise and fury that sets reflection and study at defiance, so that the unfortunate travellers thus assailed have to raise the siege by throwing a little money amongst the beseigers.

At the opera you <im> can tell when a favorite piece of music is to be sung by the universal kind of hiss throughout the house commanding silence – The singer commences – the whole house is as silent as the tomb. they seem to drink in the "concord of sweet sounds"[123] with breathless extacy – very often on an inflexion of voice or <turn> a fine turn executed with peculiar sweetness you hear indistinct murmurs of approbation & enjoyment that seem to escape from <different> the audience unconsciously – At length the singer arrives at a part of the tune that is particularly <exquisite> ↑high wrought↓ – she exerts all the powers of her voice, warbles <in> ↑with↓ the most exquisite modulations – shuts her eyes and calls forth <the most> her most latent powers of melody till she at length settles on one note – prolongs it with the sweetest trills as if unwilling to descend from the exalted regions to which her voice has attaind[.] <till at length> ↑at last↓ when her breath is almost spent she falls into the final note <with all the> and ends her strain with a full body of sound The audience that had remained all the while in a state of breathless rapture – that had hardly stirred a muscle for fear of losing a single delicate inflection of her voice – now give full vent to their feelings and the house resounds with almost frantic exclamations of *bravo bravissimo.*

When I first attended an Italian opera I considerd all this as redicu-

123. Shakespeare, *The Merchant of Venice,* V, i, 83–85:

> The man that hath no music in himself,
> Nor is not mov'd with concord of sweet sounds,
> Is fit for treasons, stratagems, and spoils.

lous affectation. I allowed the italians the highest musical disposition but thought they carried their applause <to a> beyond their real approbation. In a little while however, by frequenting the opera's and accustoming myself to the novelty of their music I began to find a fondness for it stealing on myself and I now hurry to an opera with as much eagerness as an italian and listen with a delight to the music that affords me a full idea of what must be their enjoyment whose chief passion is for harmony. Many illiberal strictures have been made on Italian music by the English – but I believe they have chiefly been the productions of men who would not suffer themselves to get recconciled to the difference between ↑the↓ italian and English style – for the least attention to it – were they real amateurs, would shew them the superiority of the former.

I have found the Americans and english travellers in italy with whom I have conversed – generally exclaiming against the stupidity & absurdity of an Italian opera – If they expect to find as much attention paid to the <language> dialogue as in the english opera they will be disappointed – the italians do not attempt it, the music is their principal object & the dialogue is merely a vehicle to convey it. A traveller therefore when he goes to an opera must consider himself merely as going to a concert where he is to enjoy sound and not sense. Beside were the dialogue ever so good there is not one american or Englishman in ten that knows the language sufficiently to enjoy it. For my part, when I attend an opera, if the music & singing <is> ↑are↓ good I am perfectly contented and if I can make out any thing of the plot so as to be interested by it – or if I am amused by the grace or humor of any of the performers I consider it as so much into the bargain.

Beside the Grand theatre there is a smaller one[124] built since Tho small in comparison with the Grand theatre it is capable of containing a large audience. The inside is handsome and the curtains of the boxes uniform – of green silk, which gives it a neat appearance – the stage is well lighted and the scenery & dresses very rich.

<Besides these there are numerous places of amusement for the>

<The pit, like the grand theatre>

The pit (or paterre) is furnished with neat chairs <of yellow stuff> coverd with yellow worsted and stuffd so as to be very commodious to the audience. The price of admission to the theatres is thirty sous which

124. Presumably the Canobbiana, of the same shape as La Scala, built in 1779.

will admit you into any part of the house – Those who take boxes by the season have also to pay this price of admission each night.

Besides these fashionable resorts there are numerous places of amusement for the poorer classes who cannot afford the expence of the grand theatres; and for the honest mob there is always a variety of entertainments going on in the grand square.[125]

We amused ourselves with walking there yesterday after dinner – At one end of the square a juggler had drawn around him a numerous rabble whom he was entertaining with the trick of shaking eggs out of an apparently empty bag – the fellow went thro a variety of deceptions with admirable dexterity and tho I watched him for some moments with the strictest attention I could not detect <him in> one of them – The honest multitude took no pains to discover his impositions – contenting themselves with the old conclusion that he dealt with the devil. Not far from him another Juggler had attracted an audience equally numerous and respectable – he had displayed a great variety of apparatus which were arranged on the ground – and was <displaying> ↑performing↓[126] a number of feats of dexterity in balancing swords platters tables &c In another place punch & his family <who> were holding forth from a little portable theatre and in a fifth a sturdy fellow was exhibiting his agility & graces on a little horse which he had learned a number of tricks & manouvres. These humble candidates for the favors of the multitide have no price for their performances but throw themselves upon the generosity of their audience who reccompence them with a few sous for their strenuous efforts to please. Some of these fellows are not deficient in humor & eloquence and I have heard them hold forth to the mob for <a> some time with an energy and <volubilbly> volubility that generally succeeded in drawing the pence from the pockets of their hearers.

I went yesterday thro two galleries of paintings – the first belonging to the Archbishop – few good paintings in it. Two small ones particularly pleased me – one was David with the head of Goliath – the other Judith cutting off the head of Holifernes both by Guerchino.[127]

125. Piazza del Duomo.

126. "performing" is in pencil.

127. The gallery was that in the Palazzo Arcivescovile. A list of the paintings there in the period when Irving visited it is in Martyn, *The Gentleman's Guide*, pp. 74–75. The painting of Judith and Holofernes is now attributed to Artemio Gentileschi (1590–*ca.* 1642).

Figure 1. Man in long coat and hat, mentioned on page 3.

Figure 2. Two men, tree, and profile, mentioned on page 32, somewhat reduced.

Figure 3. Waterfront scene, mentioned on page 32, somewhat reduced.

Figure 4. Small profile, mentioned on page 171, n. 385.

Figure 5. Two owls and profile of a man, mentioned on page 292, n. 398.

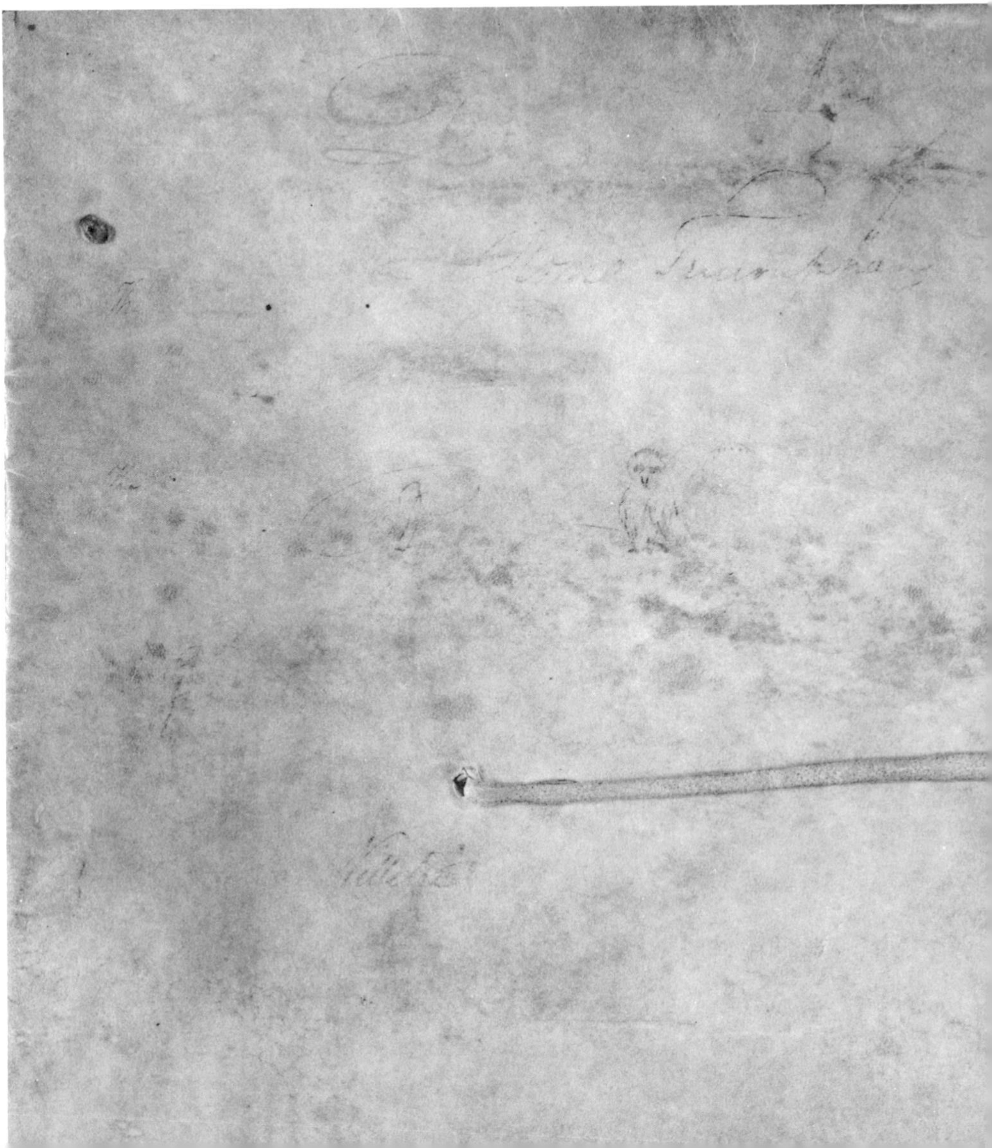

Figure 6. Boat and shoreline, mentioned on page 348, n. 132.

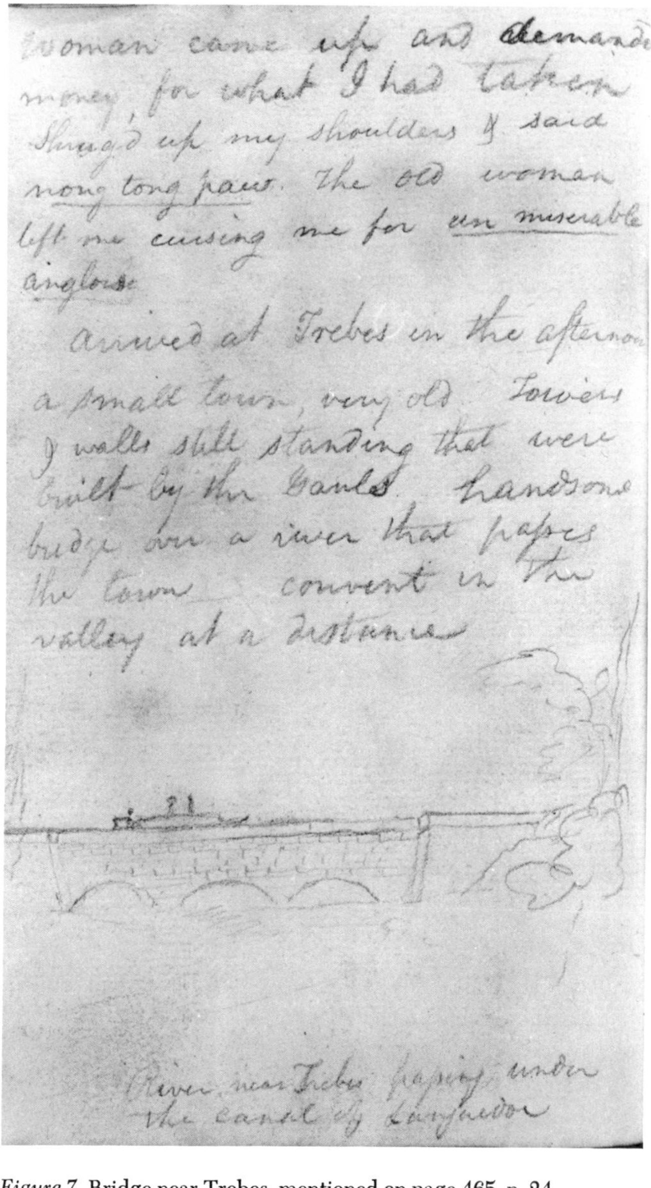

woman came up and demanded
money for what I had taken
Shrug'd up my shoulders & said
nong tong paw. The old woman
left me cursing me for un miserable
anglaise

arrived at Trebes in the afternoon
a small town, very old Towers
& walls still standing that were
built by the Gauls. handsome
bridge over a river that passes
the town convent in the
valley at a distance

River near Trebes passing under
the canal of Languedoc

Figure 7. Bridge near Trebes, mentioned on page 465, n. 24.

Figure 8. Castle with caption "Trebes," mentioned on page 496.

Figures 9, 10. Church or convent, mentioned on page 496.

Figure 11. Walled tower, mentioned on page 497.

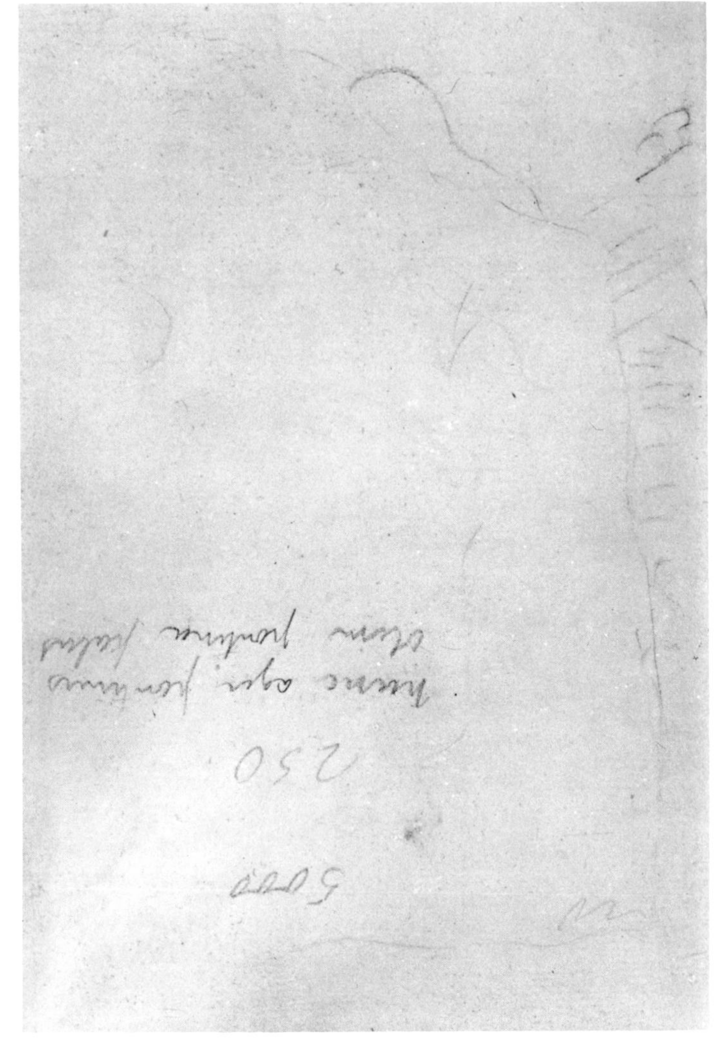

Figure 12. Unfinished Ear of Dionysius, mentioned on page 535.

Figure 13. Ear of Dionysius, mentioned on page 535.

Figure 14. Head of a soldier, mentioned on page 546.

Figure 15. Building and bridge, mentioned on page 547.

Figure 16. Building, mentioned on page 548.

Figure 17. Seaport with caption "Scylla," mentioned on page 548.

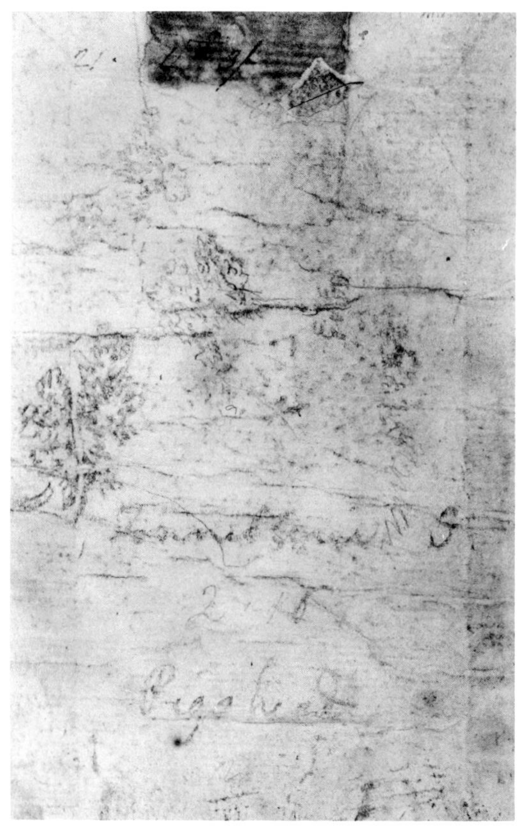

Figure 18. Sketch of trees, mentioned on page 558.

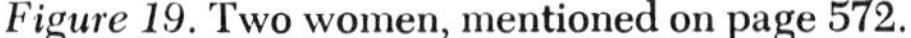

Figure 19. Two women, mentioned on page 572.

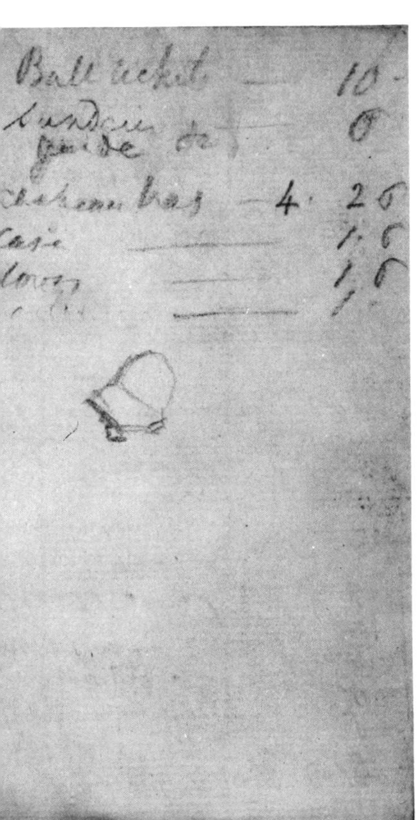

Figure 20. Small profile, mentioned on page 576, n. 110.

Figure 22. Woman in a chair, mentioned on page 582.

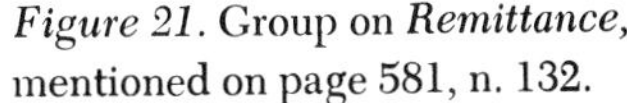

Figure 21. Group on *Remittance*, mentioned on page 581, n. 132.

Figure 23. Landscape, mentioned on page 582.

Figure 24. Half-reclining figure, mentioned on page 583.

Figure 25. Soldier with a sword, mentioned on page 583.

Figure 26. Group with a flag, mentioned on page 583.

Figure 27. Old man with a parrot, mentioned on page 583.

Figure 28. Man seated shaving, mentioned on page 583.

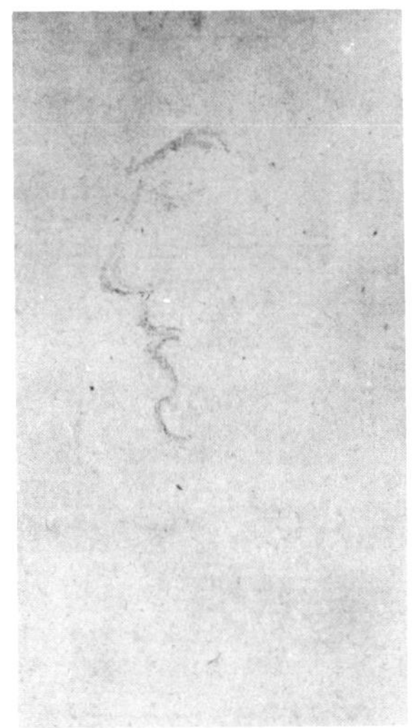

Figure 29. Profile, mentioned on page 583.

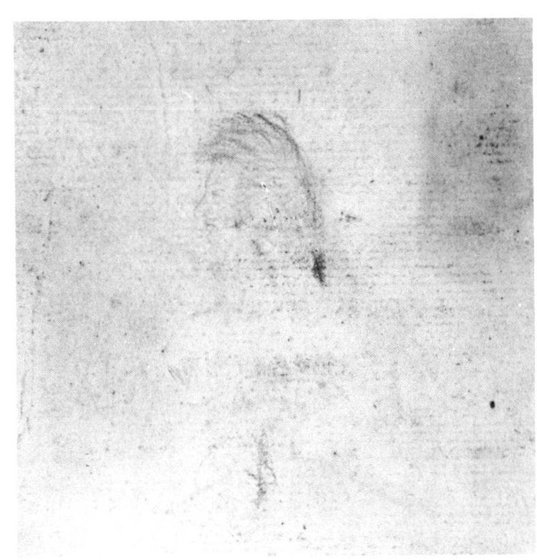

Figure 30. Small profile, mentioned on page 584.

Figure 31. Man with high coat collar, mentioned on page 584.

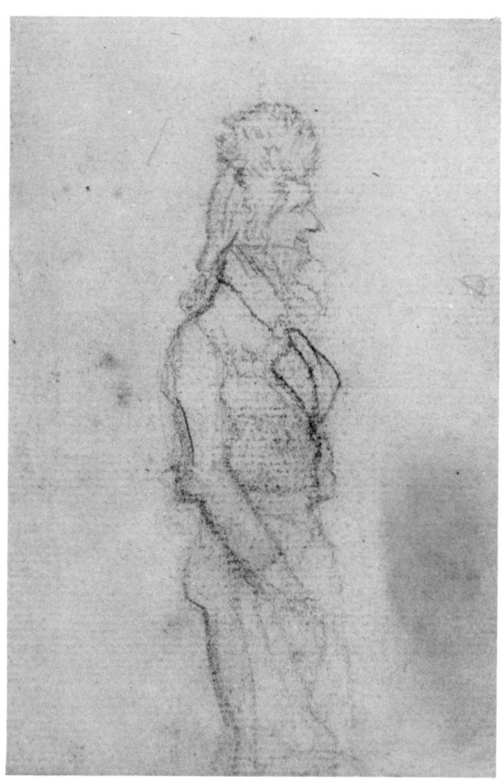

Figure 32. Side view of man in peruke, mentioned on page 584.

Figure 33. Side view of man in coat and hat, mentioned on page 584.

Figure 34. Back view of man captioned "since then im doomd," mentioned on page 584.

Figure 35. Seated man in broad-brimmed hat, mentioned on page 584.

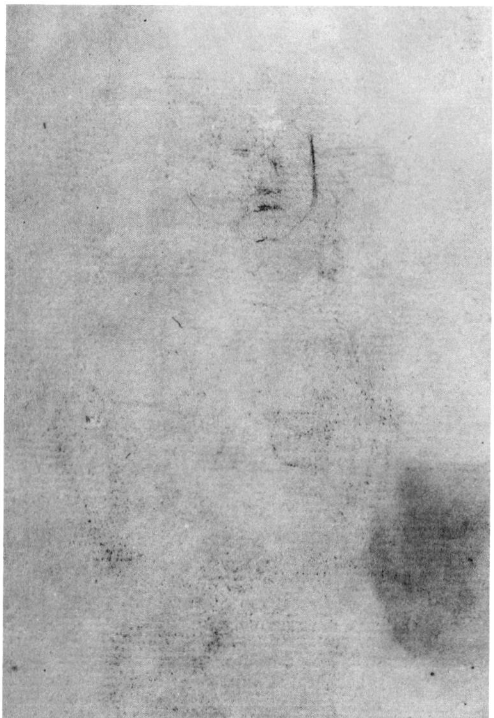

Figure 36. Partial sketch of face, mentioned on page 584.

Figure 37. Back view of standing man in broad-brimmed hat, mentioned on page 585.

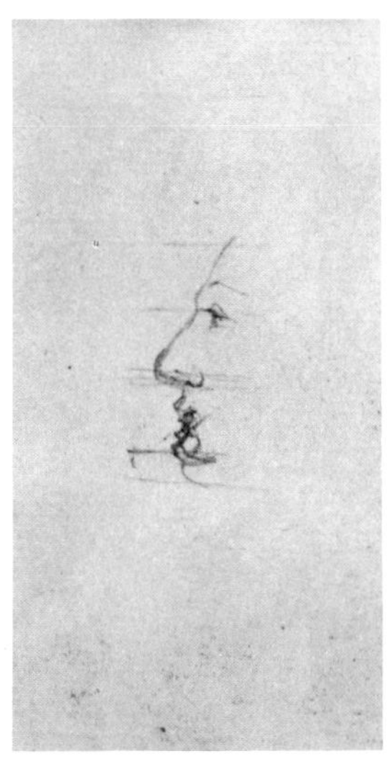

Figure 38. Profile, mentioned on page 585.

Figure 39. Three small profiles, mentioned on page 585.

Figure 40. Back views of two men, mentioned on page 585.

Figure 41. Side view of soldier with sword, mentioned on page 585.

Figure 42. Man in full-skirted coat, mentioned on page 585.

Figure 43. Side view of man in cocked hat, mentioned on page 585.

Figure 44. Side view of man in cocked hat with long sword, mentioned on page 585.

Figure 45. Side view of woman standing, mentioned on page 585.

Saturday ~~August~~ July 31st 1803.

I sailed from New York for Albany in company [w]ith Mr & Mrs Hoffman. Mr & Mrs Ludlow Ogden [M]iss Eliza Ogden, Miss Ann Hoffman Mr Brandram [&] Mr Reedy ^& Stephen Van Rensselaer^. We sat off about 3 o'clock in the [a]fter noon and came to anchor in the evening [a]t the enterance of the highlands.

Sunday Aug 1.

~~We~~ Went ashore with Mr Ogden & Mr Brandram [f]or Milk. we found a Mean house with a [l]azy looking fellow seated in the fireplace.

While the woman of the house was ~~getting the~~ [m]ilking the cows we were entertaind by some [c]urious enquiries & speculation of Brandram (who [w]as lately from england.) He declared the man [l]ived in "luxury & disapation" having nothing to do [ex]cept to work a little on his farm. That he [ha]d good Milk to drink and rye bread to eat [a]t the same time Brandram wished he had a [l]ittle of wine from on board the sloop that he [m]ight cool it in a neighboring spring

6. Opening page of the New York Journal, 1803. MS journal page [5], slightly reduced; s 3–4.

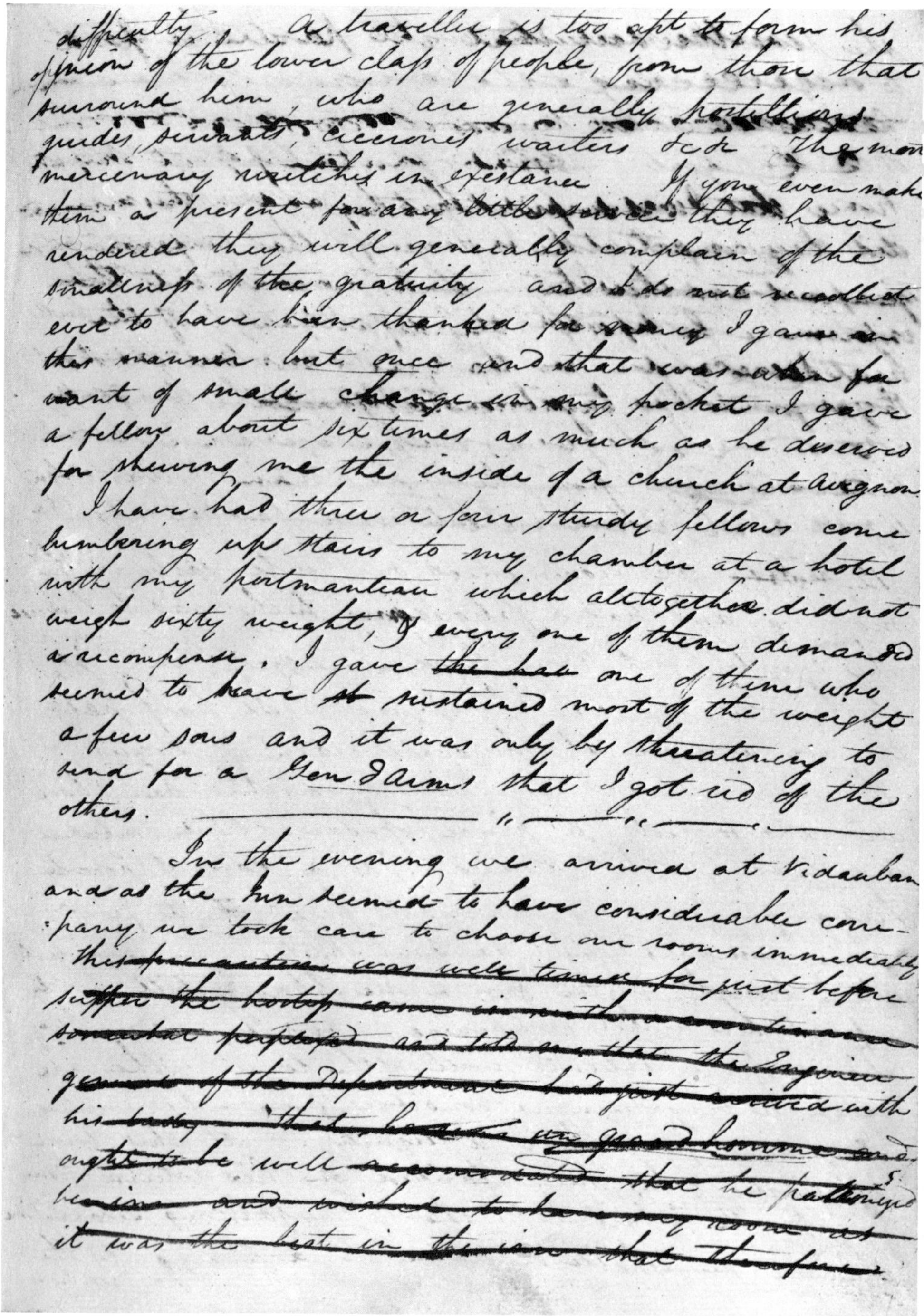

difficulty. A traveller is too apt to form his opinion of the lower class of people, from those that surround him, who are generally postillions guides, servants, cicerones waiters &c &c the most mercenary wretches in existance If you ever make them a present for any little service they have rendered they will generally complain of the smallness of the gratuity and I do not recollect ever to have been thanked for money I gave in that manner but once and that was when for want of small change in my pocket I gave a fellow about six times as much as he deserved for shewing me the inside of a church at Avignon

I have had three or four sturdy fellows come lumbering up stairs to my chamber at a hotel with my portmanteau which altogether did not weigh sixty weight, & every one of them demanded a recompense. I gave ~~the bea~~ one of them who seemed to have ~~it~~ sustained most of the weight a few sous and it was only by threatening to send for a Gen d'Arms that I got rid of the others. ——— " ——— " ———

In the evening we arrived at Vidauban and as the Inn seemed to have considerable company we took care to choose our rooms immediately ~~this precaution was well timed for~~ just before ~~supper the booby came in with a countenance somewhat perplexed and told us that the Engineer general of the Department had just arrived with his lady, that he was in good humour and ought to be well accommodated that he patronized the inn and wished to have my room as it was the best in the inn that the fire~~

Figure 47. Canceled incident of the French engineer, in European Journal, 1804–1805, Volume 1. MS journal page [91], slightly reduced; text pages 88–89.

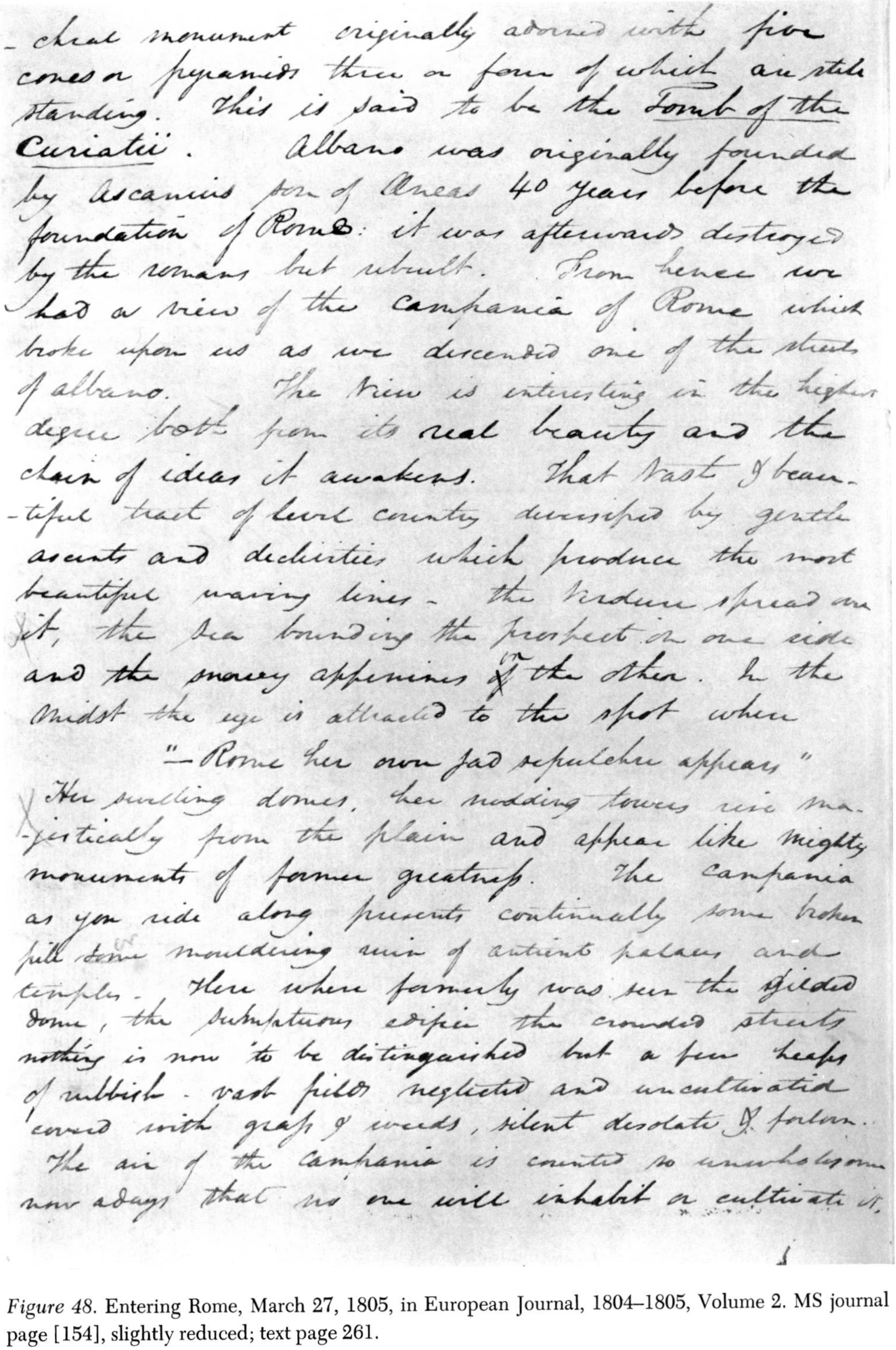

-chral monument originally adorned with five cones or pyramids three or four of which are still standing. This is said to be the Tomb of the Curiatii. Albano was originally founded by Ascanius son of Aneas 40 years before the foundation of Rome: it was afterwards destroyed by the romans but rebuilt. From hence we had a view of the Campania of Rome which broke upon us as we descended one of the streets of albano. The view is interesting in the highest degree both from its real beauty and the chain of ideas it awakens. That vast & beau-tiful tract of level country diversified by gentle ascents and declivities which produce the most beautiful waving lines - the verdure spread over it, the sea bounding the prospect on one side and the snowy appenines on the other. In the midst the eye is attracted to the spot where

"—Rome her own sad sepulchre appears"

Her swelling domes, her nodding towers rise ma-jestically from the plain and appear like mighty monuments of former greatness. The Campania as you ride along presents continually some broken pill or mouldering ruin of antient palaces and temples. Here where formerly was seen the gilded dome, the sumptuous edifice the crowded streets nothing is now to be distinguished but a few heaps of rubbish - vast fields neglected and uncultivated covered with grass & weeds, silent desolate & forlorn. The air of the campania is counted so unwholesome now adays that no one will inhabit or cultivate it.

Figure 48. Entering Rome, March 27, 1805, in European Journal, 1804–1805, Volume 2. MS journal page [154], slightly reduced; text page 261.

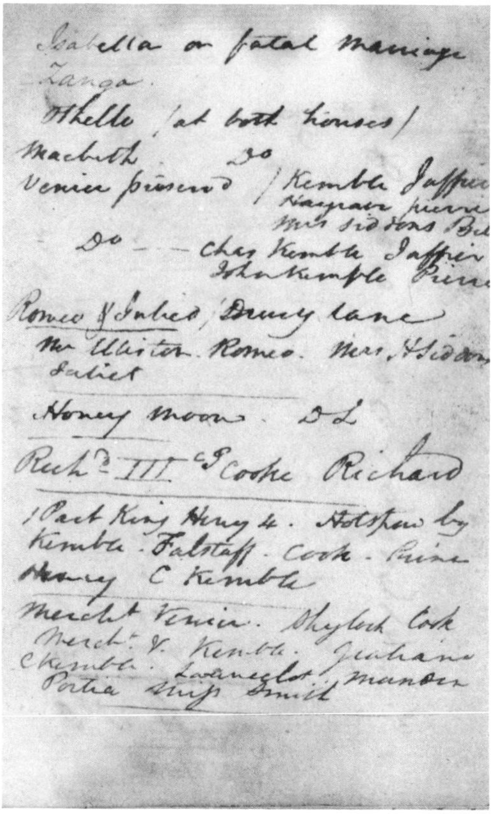
Isabella or fatal marriage
Zanga
Othello (at both houses)
Macbeth Do
Venice preserved / Kemble Jaffier
Hargrave Pierre
Mrs Siddons Bel
Do --- Chas Kemble Jaffier
John Kemble Pierre
Romeo & Juliet, Drury lane
Mr Elliston Romeo. Mrs. H Siddons
Juliet
Honey moon. D L
Richd III. Cooke Richard
1 Part King Henry 4. Hotspur by
Kemble. Falstaff. Cook. Prince
Henry C Kemble
Mercht Venice. Shylock Cook
Mercht V. Kemble. Gratiano
C Kemble. Lorenzo, manner
Portia Miss Smith

Figure 49. Notes on plays, London, 1805, in Miscellaneous Notes, 1805–1806. MS notebook page [19]; text pages 564–66.

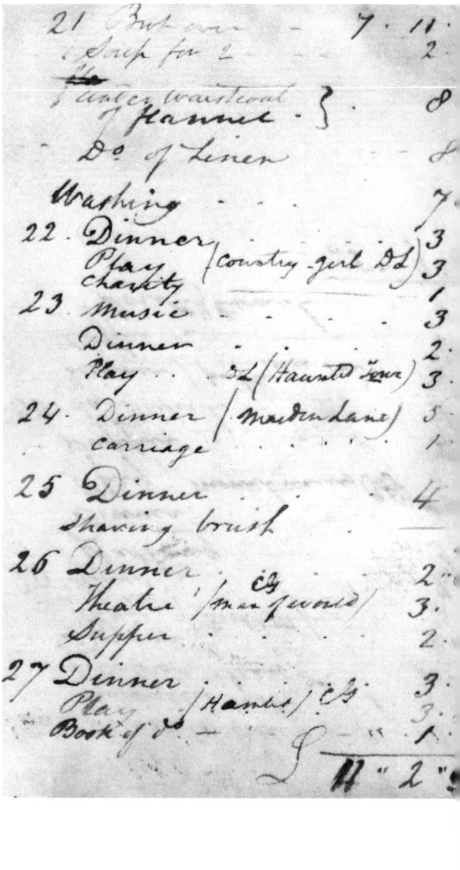
21 Boot ... 7 . 11
Soup for 2 ... 2
Under waistcoat of flannel } . 8
Do of Linen 8
Washing . . . 7
22. Dinner 3
Play (country girl DL) 3
charity 1
23 Music 3
Dinner . . 2
Play . DL (Haunted Tower) 3
24. Dinner (Maiden Lane) 5
carriage . . . 1
25 Dinner . . 4
Shaving brush
26 Dinner 2
Theatre CG 3
Supper . . . 2
27 Dinner 3
Play (Hamlet) CG 3
Book of do — 1
£ 11 " 2

Figure 50. Page of expenses, London, December 1805, in Miscellaneous Notes, 1805–1806. MS notebook page [27]; text pages 570–71.

In the other[128] is a fine portrait of Laura celebrated by the sonnets of Petrarch. The countenance is of a singular character – and what I should rather consider fine & dignified than beautiful. It is said to be a faithful resemblance.

I had forgotten to mention that in the Archbishops palace we were shewn a painting by St Luke which completely established the poor opinion we had contained of the talents of that primitive painter.

This morning I visited the famous Ambrosian Library. I was disappointed in my expectations of finding a vast collection of Book[s;] this library appears to me most deserving of attention for a great number of manuscripts. In the academy of this liberary amongst an odd jumble of statues torso's busts – sea shells &c is preserved the skeleton of a celebrated beauty of Milan who on her death bed desired that her body might be dissected and her skeleton exposed a lesson to the vanity of her sex.[129]

I was yesterday morning introduced by C—— to the Abbé Amoretti Librarian of this institution.[130] He is an agreeable friendly old Gentleman of a philosophical disposition He entertained us with several pieces of information respecting the sciences and shewed us an experiment he had made with much success <upon> with a piece of whale bone upon different <sub> metals & substances.

Milan contains several churches[131] <of> possessing some pieces of painting and sculpture worthy the attention of the traveller but we were so fatigued <by> in body and our imaginations so much satiated with the profusion of masterpieces we had seen that we could not prevail upon ourselves to visit any of them – The mind gets satisfied with any enjoyment, <it cannot be> the highest productions of the arts will cloy

128. Probably Irving is referring to the collection of the Duke of Lodi in the Palazzo Melzi (J. B. Carta de Modène, comp., *Nouvelle Description de la Ville de Milan*, Milano, 1819, p. 53). J. C. Cabell recorded visiting in Milan "A private collection of paintings in the House of an Italian Count" which included a portrait of Laura (Journal, [No. 5], "Notes of a Journey to Italy – In the Winter of 1804–5").

129. The Biblioteca Ambrosiana, founded in 1618 by Cardinal Federico Borromeo, Archbishop of Milan, is housed in the Palazzo dell' Ambrosiana. The skeleton, which Irving does not indicate that he saw, seems to have been fictitious. It was referred to by several travelers, among them Grosley, in *New Observations on Italy*, II, 445.

130. Carlo Amoretti (1741–1816), Italian naturalist and geographer, was resident scholar in the library from 1797 until his death.

131. The most notable is S. M. delle Grazie; the rectory of the Dominican priory adjoining it contains Leonardo da Vinci's "Last Supper."

by too great profusion and like the body – the mind <bust> must repose at intervals to acquire a new appetite. <We> I have been kept in constant employment and my mental powers in continual exercise since my arrival at Naples by a succession of fine paintings statues buildings & curiosities and I have hardly room left for another picture or bust.[132]

May 2

We parted from Milan at an early hour this morning on the route for Mount St Goatherd. We had engaged the same carriage and mules that had brought us from Bologna to take us to Sesto on Lago Maggiore – the voiturier having acquitted himself much to our satisfaction. We agreed to give him three Louis to take us to Sesto – an extravagant price as the distance was but a days ride but we could not find any others more reasonable.

The country thro which we passed was a continuation of the vast plain of Lombardy, but less interesting than those parts of it we had already seen – In many places the soil appeared poor and sandy and the road was generally indifferent – The country was still diversified by canals and rows of fine trees planted along their margins and along the hedges. <Among> The latter <the> resounded with the sweet notes of the nightingale the Goldfinch and other birds and now and then the sky lark mounting to the heavens pourd forth a rich strain of melody that was distinctly audible long after his little body was invisible.

In the afternoon the scenery became suddenly more interesting – The plain was varied <by> and broken into hill and dale, and in a little while Lago Maggiore ↑(or Locarno)↓[133] broke upon our view presenting an assemblage of the most pleasing objects.

A beautiful sheet of water surrounded by verdant hills covered with Groves cornfields & pastures – The banks of the lake ornamented by cottages <surrounded by> ↑embowered in↓[134] tall trees – and its glassy bosom specled with the white sails of the small boats that glided along its surface <jast> just at the <entrance> ↑end↓ of the lake where it vented itself into the Tesino[135] – the white houses of Sesto seemed to

132. The next six manuscript pages are blank; the seventh contains a sketch of a boat and shore line (Figure 6).

133. "or Locarno" is in brown ink. The northern end of Lago Maggiore is sometimes called Lago Locarno.

134. "embowered in" is in pencil.

135. The Ticino.

rise out of the water – The river Tesino <wanderd> ↑ran↓ for a short distance in a beautiful broad stream among gently swelling hills and at length winding among them was lost to the sight – On those hills in many places were seen <the> small groups of houses forming picturesque little villages and here and there the white spires of a convent peeped over the tops of the trees in which the main body of the Edifice was shrouded. This enchanting scene was closed by the lofty alps whose bleak summits clothed in eternal snow formed a dreary chilling contrast to the smiling luxurient scenery below.

We entered the little village of Sesto with a numerous retinue <at> running after our carriage – more respectable for their number than their appearance. They consisted of boatmen who were all clamorous in reccommending their different barks to transport us across the lake. This village tho it makes a pretty appearance from a distance is like all Italian country places an abominably dirty place within. We found a tolerable inn and were shewn to a neat room the different windows of which command lovely views of the lake and the adjacent scenery. Here we summoned the master of the Hotel and got him to procure us a bark to take us to Magadino – a small town the other end of the lake – the time requisite for making the voyage is two days and we agreed to give two Louis d'or's for the vessel – hands & all. They attempted to exact much more but we had fortunately been advertized of the customary price at Milan and soon brought them to our terms.

After dinner we took a walk along the borders of the river In the course of our ramble we fell in company with a simple good humord country lad who spoke a little french and entertained us highly by the naiveté of his remarks. He was asking us about the approaching coronation and on our telling him it would be a fortunate thing for his country "Croyez vous donc messieurs said he – ils viendront plus des voyagers à notre lac"[136] (I should have observed before that he was a boatman but this question fully shews that). <A convent bell> ↑We heard just then↓ the sound of a Bell from a convent situated on a hill the other side of the lake which was ringing for vespers. You have a great number of monks and priests in your village no doubt said I. "Pas beaucoup monsieur" said he "mais pourtant nous en avons assez – Je n'aime pas les pretres"[137]

136. "Do you think then gentlemen . . . that more voyagers will come to our lake?"

137. "Not many, sir, . . . but nevertheless we have enough of them. I do not like the priests."

Comment – replied I, is it possible you do not love those men who are always praying for your good – ["]En verité <messes> monsieur – said he – ils sont bien pour les priers – mais parblieu – ils sont assez bien pour les manger & l'amour – cest impossible de gardir un poulet ou une Jolie femme dans la village pour ces gens la." – <Ils sont les hommes qui prient plus a la [*unrecovered*] que la [*unrecovered*]>[138]

P.S. In the course of our route this afternoon we overtook a little fellow of about 12 years old trudging along under the weight of a large knapsack. His <sturdy> "shining face"[139] and sturdy looks pleased us highly. I asked him where he was from – he told me that he was a chimney sweeper and was travelling from Milan to his native village on the banks of the Locarno – he had been three days on the road & had still 50 miles to go – We gave him 20 sous which procured us a thousand thanks and our honest driver gave him a seat in front of the carriage as far as Sesto.

May 3[140]

After breakfast this morning we embarked on the lake. Our bark was small coverd with a linen awning and rowed by four stout men. The morning was over cast but the weather mild and pleasant and the <scenery> ↑country↓ so beautiful that we did not feel the need of sunshine to enliven us. We gently moved along thro a succession of romantic scenery – on our right the shore of the lake was level to a considerable extent, forming beautiful meadows in which grazed flocks of sheep & cattle – on the other side the coast was more abrupt and coverd with verdure – the trees and shrubbery extending to the waters edge – before us at a distance <?lay?> the two noble promontories of Anghiera & Arona boldly advanced into the lake, the former

138. "What! . . . " "To be sure, Sir, . . . They are good for prayers, but zounds, they are quite good for food and love. It is impossible to keep a chicken or a pretty girl in the village on account of these people." <They are men who pray more for the [*unrecovered*] than the [*unrecovered*]>

139. Shakespeare, *As You Like It,* II, vii, 145–47:

> And then the whining school-boy, with his satchel,
> And shining morning face, creeping like snail
> Unwillingly to school.

140. Irving drew on this and on the next two entries, often verbatim, in his letter to Elias Hicks, May 4–June 19, 1805.

surmounted by a picturesque castle[141] – the latter adorned by a village whose white buildings had a handsome effect in the prospect – The surrounding country as it receded grew more mountainous and the snowy alps closed the interesting scene.

About nine Oclock we landed at the village of Arona – with an intention of visiting the celebrated statue of St. Carlo Borromeo while the boatmen took their breakfast. This statue is on the top of a high hill that rises from the lake – We found the walk to it long and fatiguing. St. Carlo was a nephew to Pope Pius the <sixth> fourth and born near Arona – In consequence of his charity and good works he acquired the highest esteem of his country men – he was cardinal & archbishop of Milan. This statue is immensely large – *sixty feet* high and made entirely of Bronze brought from Milan in pieces. It is more remarkable for its size than for either grace or beauty for the cardinals habit in which it is clothed effectually prevents either. One hand is extended partly and under the other is a large book.[142] The statue stands on a proportionable pedestal of Granite and the whole is erected on a mound of earth to which you ascend by an avenue of handsome horse chestnuts. It has been said by some that this statue is as high as the famous Colossus of Rhodes[143] – I forget the proportions of the latter but from the observations I have heard concerning it St. Carlo must yeild the palm to his more antient rival. The Saint was surrounded by flights of little birds – some of whom had made their nests in his ears and eyelids and others in the hems of his garments – probably thinking <the person of the Saint would be sacred from the attempts of> their nests would be protected from violation by the sanctity of the places where they were built. At any rate their height placed them far above the reach of the most aspiring urchin

From the hill on which the statue stands is one of the most lovely views imaginable The eye embraces a great extent of the lake winding among the mountains – in some places <s>ruffled by gentle Zephyrs –

141. La Rocca, the castle at Angera, was founded by the Torriani family in the twelfth century, passed to the Visconti in 1314, and to the Borromei in 1449.

142. S. Carlo Borromeo (1538–1584), archbishop of Milan, canonized in 1610, was born in the castle of Arona. The statue of him, erected in 1697, is 75 feet high on a 40-foot pedestal. The head, hands, and feet are bronze, the robe of wrought copper. In his description of the statue Irving drew on William Coxe, *Travels in Switzerland, and in the Country of the Grissons* (London, 1789), III, 327. J. C. Cabell also cites this work in his journal entries made in Switzerland (Journal [No. 7], "Rome Winter of 1805," May 4–24, *passim*).

143. The Colossus of Rhodes was about 120 feet high.

in others smooth and tranquil reflecting the cottages groves and churches that ornamented its borders or the white sails of the little barks that seemed to repose upon its surface.

The mountains presented a variety of character – Some rough and craggy rose abruptly from the waters edge and were lost in the lowering clouds that rolled half way down their <sterile> sides – others rose in gentle gradations clothed with trees – among which the white walls of villages and the towers of chapels and convents were partially seen among the envelloping foliage – The first species were rocky and barren – the latter cultivated and fruitful and skirted with luxurient plains varied by delightful groves & meadows. At the feet of some of the mountains small villages seemed to project into the <sea> ↑lake↓, which was speckled by their fishing boats – Opposite to us was the romantic promontory of Anghiera crowned by its castle[144] which with a small village below it, <were> ↑was↓ reflected in the tranquil bosom of the lake. We could not quit this charming spot without lingering some time to enjoy its delights so sending ↑back↓ the boatman who accompanied us, to the village to tell his companions when they had finished their breakfasts to come for us to the foot of the mountain – we threw ourselves on the grass and determined to enjoy the prospect at leisure. The air was pure and salubrious – and <The> perfumed by the fragrance of numerous flowers that were sprinkled over the Mountains. The repose of the scene was only interrupted by the chirp of the swallow as he skimd over the tranquil lake below us and dipd his wings in its glassy surface – the full melody of the nightingale the Robin & the lark, or the distant song of the peasants at work in a field on a neighboring hill. Such scenes are <most> ↑best↓ calculated to soothe the mind into the most pleasing state of tranquility and even voluptuousness. Such a situation Ogilvie must have had in his minds eye <when he> in the following verse

On the airy mount reclined
What wishes sooth the musing mind
How soft the velvet lap of spring
How sweet the Zephyrs violet wing.[145]

144. To this point in the sentence Irving drew on Coxe, *Travels in Switzerland,* III, 314–15.

145. James Ogilvie, "Ode to Evening," ll. 103–6, *Poems on Several Subjects* (London, 1769), I, 101. Irving's punctuation and capitalization differ slightly from Ogilvie's. The quotation and the sentence preceding it are in a smaller hand, apparently added later.

After reembarking we continued our voyage along the lake skirting its borders – now passing by a neat village that rose out of the water and now gliding along the base of a mountain whose summit seemed almost lost in the clouds. Towards the afternoon the weather <seemed> ↑began↓ to break away – the clouds rolled to the snowy heights of the Alps which they completely envelloped and the sun breaking out from among them enlivened the enchanting scenery – chequering the lake and the mountains with broad masses of light and shade. <About two oclock we> After sailing some time we opened a promontory that had hitherto intercepted the view – and the famous Borromean (or as they have been termed enchanted) Islands[146] broke upon our sight. <The appearance of> These little islands – covered with groves of Laurel – oranges and lemon – ornamented with palaces and all the decorations art can bestow – rising out of the bosom of the lake and surrounded by stupenduous rocky mountains – crowned with snow and broken <ito> into cliffs & precipices – produce an assemblage of romantic and truly enchanting scenery that baffles all the powers of description. Isola Bella (I.E. beautiful Island) in particular has the most delicious appearance at a distance – it is exceedingly small not above a third of a mile in circuit – but laid out into a complete garden decorated by a superb palace[147] – Its groves, its orangeries – terraces – towers and bowers of Lemon & other evergreens make it at a little distance answer in a striking manner the discriptions of Fairy abodes given by the poets and where [were] not the days of Romance at an end I should certainly have concluded it was some elysian isle formed among the silver waves of the lake by the wand of an Enchantress. Numerous Travellers have united in extolling it in their works Among others Keysler very quaintly compares it to "a pyramid of sweetmeats, ornamented with green festoons and flowers."[148] On approaching near to it the illusion disappated and its charms in a great measure vanished. The Works of art became too visible and we were disappointed in finding it laid out in the pre-

146. The Isole dei Pescatori, Bella, Madre, and S. Giovanni are called "enchanted" in Coxe, *Travels in Switzerland,* III, 312.

147. The island was barren and had only a few buildings until 1650, when Count Vitaliano Borromeo and his brother Cardinal Gilberto Borromeo built the palace (which was never finished) and laid out the garden, which is in ten terraces and contains statues, vases, and fountains.

148. Isola Bella and Isola Madre are called "two pyramids of sweet-meats" in John George Keysler, *Travels through Germany, Bohemia, Hungary, Switzerland, Italy, and Lorrain* (London, 1760; 3rd ed.), I, 374, but Irving is quoting from Coxe, *Travels in Switzerland,* III, 312.

posterous style of clippd walks artificially formd trees and all the formalities of stone terraces – statues and dutch flower beds. We were all thro the Palace which is immensely large and magnificent. The grand saloon which was intended to be <very> vast & superb is not finished nor is there any likely hood that it ever will be The palace commands equisite views of the lake – many of its windows & balconies overhang the waters. We were all thro the garden – which is built upon arches. <the> and part of it usurped from the lake – the soil is artificial brought from the neighboring shores. From the grand Terrace in the garden which is raised to a considerable height you have a noble view of the delicious scenery by which you are surrounded. In the neighborhood of this Island are two others one called Isola Madre on which is likewise a palace – and the other island is exceeding small coverd completely by a small village of fishermens huts with a church in the midst.[149] These Islands are owned by the Borromean family who own likewise a great extent of country bordering on the lake and are extremely wealthy. One of the family is the ornamenter of Isola bella. In the palace we were shewn a considerable collection of paintings some of which were very good The lower story of the building is laid out in the style of grottos inlaid with pebbles shells &c.

We had engaged a dinner at the hotel (del Delphino) but while we were dining it clouded up and began to rain violently so we determined to remain here all night particularly as the inn has very good rooms.

The Inn keeper wished to be extortionate and we found written on the walls with a lead pencil – "In this house deduct one quarter of the bill – C. C. Aug 3d. 1802." We however adopted a better plan into which we have been driven by the knavery of the Italian <au> Inn keepers of making our bargain before we eat any thing This is done by all Italian travellers and we have found it very advisible. In this case as in many others it succeeded completely and we were accomodated at a reasonable rate. Our Flemish servant John has proved himself an excellent fellow at making a bargain so we generally set him to arranging matters with the Inn keepers and we find that he most commonly brings us off at a much cheaper rate than we could ourselves.

NB. I should have observed that we passed several places today where laborers were at work forming a new road nearly complete that

149. The Palazzo Borromeo on Isola Madre was built in the seventeenth century. The "other island" is presumably Isola dei Pescatori, which belongs to the fishermen. Isola S. Giovanni is near the opposite shore.

is to cross the Simplon, one of the chief passes into Switzerland – this road runs along the borders of the lake and will be very pleasant & commodious. They were blowing rocks with Gunpowder and the explosions sounded like the reports of cannon – thundering among the echoes of the mountains. – <Opposite to> From Isola Bella we had a distant view of one of the Granite quarries on the side of a mountain which furnishes the great quantities of that stone which <is>are used in Milan.

We remarked in the course<d> of the day considerable variations in the atmosphere – In the ↑early part of the↓ morning it was mild and pleasant; afterwards it became quite chilly occasiond by the cool breezes from the snowy mountains – In the afternoon the weather again resumed its mildness The mountainous nature of this country must occasion great fickleness in the climate.

May 4

The rain that commenced yesterday afternoon continued all night and fell in great quantities this morning. We accordingly thought of staying all day on the island in hopes the next day might bring fairer weather. We had <previously> agreed with the man who hired us the boat, that we should remain at Isola Bella in <th> case the weather was bad, but as we knew that in such cases the boatmen generally expected a buono mano we sent John to sound them. He returned with word that they demanded four crowns buono mano in case they stayed – vexd at the extortion of the scoundrels we told John to offer them two dollars but if they refused to take it – to tell them we were ready to depart as soon as we had breakfasted

The fellows would not agree to it, expecting that we would comply with their demand rather than set out in the rain – We had determined however to shew them otherwise, and as soon as we had breakfasted we calld them up in the room and again offerd them the two dollars[.] on their refusing to take that sum we orderd them to carry our trunks to the boat – they lingerd about in hopes that we would give up – but seeing us put on our boots & coats they had a kind of consultation and offerd to accede to our price We had now resolved <th> not to indulge them, <and> having observed that the covering of the boat was good and effectually kept out the rain – We told them it was then too late to talk – that they should have agreed to our offer at first & that now nothing was left for them to do but shoulder the trunks & march – This they did with a bad grace – grumbling all the way and I could hear one reproaching the others as they went down stairs for not closing with our offer at first. It is one of the travellers chief grievances in this country and one that almost overbalances his pleasures – that he has to quarrel and dispute with every inn keeper, voiturier – boatman servant &c whom<e> he employs unless he is of a disposition to suffer himself quietly to be imposed upon. In no other country perhaps is there a more universal combination to cheat and fleece the unfortunate traveller – and he is surrounded from the moment he sets his foot in the country to the times he leaves it by a crowd of rogues of every discription who are on the continual look out to defraud him and play into each others hands with the most consummate dexterity.

The morning was wet and gloomy – the mountains were completely veild by the mists & <fogs> rain<s>. We saild close along the shore of Isola Madre – This Island is less beautiful at a distance than Isola Bella but is far more interesting on a nearer approach. The west end in particular – is very picturesque – Nature is not tortured as in the other Island, but is left more to her own caprice – The trees are large and of handsome forms and combined with the rocky shore and two or three stone buildings on it of an <fr> appropriate form – present a complete picture. Opposite to this Island is the village of Palanza which has a very pretty appearance situated on the border of the lake.

About ten oclock we stopped at the village of Intra a league from Isola Bella. While the Boatmen were breakfasting we went with a letter of introduction from the Abbé Amoretti of Milan to Sigr. Cæsare Imperatore[150] an inhabitant of the village. We found him an honest civil old Gentleman who cheerfully complied with the request containd in the Abbés letter – which was that he should give us letters for Magad<o>ino & Bellanzon<e>a[151] which would facilitate our getting horses in those places to cross Mount St Goatherd. The old gentleman advised us to remain in Intra all day as the inn was decent and if we went on we should not only encounter bad weather all day but be obliged to remain in Magadone to night where there was no tolerable

150. In the entry for May 4, 1805, in his journal J. C. Cabell also spoke of the letter of introduction from Amoretti, spelled Imperatore's first name "Cesari," and recorded: "Mr. Imperatore who was an unlettered man, had heard of the death of Genl. Hamilton" (Journal [No. 7], "Rome Winter of 1805"). Irving's and Cabell's journal entries between May 4 and May 24, 1805 contain several parallels.

151. Bellinzona. The alteration is in lighter ink.

inn – whereas by setting out at an early hour tomorrow morning we should arrive at Bellenzon<e>a[152] in the evening & the next morning could set out on our route over the mountain. We determined to take his advice – and on sounding the boatmen we found them willing to accede instantly to our proposal – fearing to provoke us by any hesitation, to another departure.

In the afternoon the weather cleared up and we rambled about the delightful environs of the village and along the borders of the Lake. The village is situated in a lovely little valley at the feet of high mountains, one of which slopes up gradually – its side is finely cultivated and sprinkled with cottages churches & convents. Along the valley run several streams on each side of the town – A stone bridge thrown over one with a white church at its extremity is a picturesque object in the landscape. farther on at some distance is a bold promontary on a low part of which rises a singular tower and on the extremity of the promontary is erected a small temple[153]

The mountains around the lake are of a variety of forms bold & romantic & in some parts remind me of the fine scenery of the Hudson. There are certain views of this lake that brought strongly to my mind the character of the mountanous part of Lake Champlain in the state of New York.

Tho the Inn (Lion d'or) is very neat and promised well yet we were furnished with an extremely scanty dinner and the dishes so miserably cooked that we could hardly eat them – Every thing was dressd with a profusion of oil. After some time we found out the occasion of this melancholy lack of provisions. John came in full of news – "there was to be a grand feast the next day at the hotel in honor of St. Joseph[154] and there were above fifty or sixty persons to set down to dinner – All the *prog*" John said "was engaged to gratify the greedy stomachs of the fathers who were determined at this feast to shew their zeal for the saint to the utmost of the powers.["] We could not learn any thing of this saint except that he was patron of the village – and if we might judge by this honorary festival – a great patron of good eating & drinking.

Thermometer at night stood at 55 Deg.[155]

152. The alteration is in lighter ink.

153. See entry of May 5, 1805, n. 157.

154. Presumably the Feast of the Solemnity of St. Joseph the Patriarch, which takes place on the third Wednesday after Easter.

155. This sentence is in lighter ink, as is the next entry.

May 5

This morning was clear and cloudless and we were enlivened with the anticipation of a pleasant voyage over the remainder of the beautiful Lake of Locarno. On settling the bill with the Inn keeper we had another specimen of Italian extortion. We had sent John yesterday as usual to make a bargain with the master of the Inn before we enterd his house – The latter declined making a bargain or naming any price saying that he would charge according to what we eat – another person who stood by assured John that the Inn keeper was very honest & might be depended on – John brought us his report accordingly and gave such a favorable <custom> account of the Inn keeper that we determined to trust him and for once depart from our customary rules – We were deservedly punished for our confiding to the honesty of an Italian Inn keeper after repeated experience that no trust is to be reposed <o>in their moderation. The fellow had the conscience to charge for dinner bed & breakfast for us & our servant 29 livres of Milan[156] tho we had eaten hardly any thing – It was too late to remonstrate with him so we paid him the money with several hearty <express fo> expressions of contempt for his extortion & dishonesty.

The weather was mild and pleasant – About seven oclock the Thermometer stood at 60 Deg. <There was> The wind was a head which rendered our progress more slow – but we kept along the borders of the lake w[h]ere it was not very strong[.] about a mile from Intra we passed the promontory on which stood the little temple which I mentiond yesterday – This is an elegant little rotunda of the Tuscan order built of white granite supported on eight pillars Within it on a pedestal stands the statue of St Francesco of white marble. It was a good thought to put a saint within as <he>it renders it sacred from the abuses of the Peasantry. The whole was erected by a Marquis of Milan[157] and as far as we could learn, thro mere fancy, as he has no dwelling near the spot. It is a charming object in the landscape.

I remarked that as we advanced towards the northern end of the lake

156. A livre of Milan was worth about 14¢ according to Irving's expense accounts.

157. In 1798 the Marchese Cacciapiatti of Novara, then in the Duchy of Milan, built a villa on a promontory south of Intra known as "St. Francis' Headland," near what was from the fifteenth century to the Napoleonic Wars a Franciscan convent. Probably the structure to which Irving refers was a chapel of the villa. The villa is still standing but any such chapel seems to have been destroyed in 1855 when a public road was cut through the garden (information furnished by the Touring Club Italiano, Milan).

the mountains encreased in size – They were green round the base and many of them cultivated about the skirts – but the vegetation gradually disappeared towards the higher parts of the mountains and their summits were arid & sterile – <many> ↑some↓ of them however were more fertile than the rest & <specled> ↑speckled↓ with cottages and convents – which had usurped patches of land half way up their sides. The mountains were generally of Granite & large masses of different colors had <f> seperated from the heights and lay scatered about the shore.

The Lake makes frequent bays – its shores are undulating and it varies continually in width from one & a half to three or four miles. As we kept close along the western shore we had a <continu> constant variety of prospect every moment opening some new point and catching a Glimpse of a church or convent situated on some picturesque <bluff> height – a small village or hamlet of fishermens huts on the <beach> border of the lake with their boats drawn up on the shore or some other object that served to give variety & life to the scenery. About ten Oclock the boatmen rowed into a beautiful cove to rest there till the wind subsided – which by this time had encreased very considerably. Here we encountered a Swiss botanist* who with his servant was making the tour of the Italian alpes. He entered into conversation with us very sociably and gave us several interesting particulars concerning Switzerland. He is of Bex not far from the Lake of Geneva. When the wind seemed to have subsided we <g> again set out[.] the Swiss Botanist discharged the boat in which he had come and joined us in ours. – As the wind still blew strong <the men> two of the men walked along the beach & drew the boat by a rope the other two remaining on board to row. We walked a great part of the way along the shore – climbing the rocks, and passing thro the vineyards <?till a?> The banks were sprinkled with flowers and coverd in some places with Thyme which diffused the most delightful fragrance. By the time we reached the little village of Canova[158] the men were quite fatigued and we <continued> ↑consented↓ to rest there. While we were down on the shore there came

* Mr Schleicher[159] of Bex – Canton de Vaud – he is really a German.

158. Cánnero.

159. J. C. Schleicher was the author of *Catalogus Planatarum in Helvetia Cis- et Transalpina Sponte Nascentium* . . . (Bex, 1800?), which had several later editions. In the entry of May 5, 1805, in his journal J. C. Cabell recorded that he and Schleicher exchanged addresses "with a promise of mutually sending each other plants from our respective countries" (Journal [No. 7], "Rome Winter of 1805").

down a procession of the children of the village one of whom (a pretty little girl, bore a branch of a tree decorated with ribbands of different gay colors – They begged some charity for masses to be said for <a> poor people and when we had given them a few sous they all joined in a short song of the *complimentary kind* and then marched off highly satisfied.

We <after> din<ing>ed in an indifferent inn kept by an honest old couple <we> who were extremely reasonable in their charges which I remark as an uncommon incident in this country. The people that we saw in this village seemed to differ from the generality of Italians in their looks and to have something of the Swiss countenance.

At this village the Botanist parted from us being impatient to proceed – He sat out on foot for Locarno leaving his servant in the boat with his baggage.

After dinner we insisted on proceeding as the Lake appeard quite calm. The boatmen endeavord to prevail upon us to stay saying that there was too much wind and that tho it was calm in the bay where we were yet <y> we would find it very rough in the narrow gorge of the mountains thro which we had to pass. We however were inflexible having been told at Milan not to trust to them as they were apt to detain travellers in little villages where they were in concern [?concert?] with the Inn keeper.

They resumed their oars very unwillingly and we proceeded very smoothly. The side of the mountain above Canova is curiously dotted with little huts in which the country people reside when at work in the fields. About a mile & half from the village we passed the old castle[160] of Canova founded on a rock in the middle of the lake. it entirely covers the rock and the waves wash the bases of its walls. During the time the Spanish held this country this was a formidable castle and ↑as↓ our boatmen told us it was <then> inhabited by robbers who used to commit depredations on the barks that passed, and on the neighboring country the situation of the castle rendering it particularly inaccessible – This building is at present uninhabited. It is strikingly romantic and accords with the wild picturesque scenery around – As the lake still continued calm we began to reprimand the boatmen for the difficulty they had made about parting – they still adhered to their

160. There are two ruined castles, the Castelli di Cánnero, on islets near the shore. In the fifteenth century they harbored five Mazzarda brothers, notorious brigands.

original assurance that we would find there was too much wind – and we began to be quite angry at their obstinacy

I've no kind of patience said C—— with such impertinent scoundrels that will persist in a falsehood – "Sacre Dieu – cried the Swiss servant Ils devront etre tou<s>tes perdu"[161]

The poor devils were in a fair way to be condemned hung & d—d in the bargain when the turning of a point threw us point blank in face of the wind and soon convinced us there was more truth in their assertions than we had been willing to allow. We however held our tongues ashamed to tell them to turn back tho we percieved that in persisting to advance we would be inevitably drenchd. After two or three hearty splashings from the <?sea?> waves that dashd over us we <ho> came in sight of the village of Canobia. To get to it we had to double a point so rather than incur another cold bath we got the boatmen to put us ashore and we walked to the village while they followd in the boat. The rogues seemed highly pleased at our misfortunes and I suspect that we owe two or three drenchings to their manouvres turning the broadside of the boat to the waves. <In> The village of Canobia is considerably large – neat and <well sit> handsomely situated the houses of stone plaisterd & whitewashed We found here a tolerable inn and felicitated ourselves at having reached here in preference to staying at the little hamlet of Canova.

May 6

(6th Therm: this morning 56 Deg.)

The wind that prevented our progress last night had considerably subsided this morning and we prepared to resume our boat. On set<l>tling the bill with our host we found him quite reasonable – We remarked the same change in countenance that we had observed yesterday in the inhabitants of Canova – the people begin to assume the Swiss features and the honesty that characterizes that nation.

From Canobia to Magadino the distance is twelve miles. The lake makes a bend among the mountains, which <he> at this end rise to a great height and are crownd with snow. They generally decend steep to the edge of the water, their skirts cultivated and diversified by villages – and the sides clothed with trees. The snow on the <tops>

161. "Holy God . . . they must all be ruined." The correction is in darker ink.

heights <sup> thawing, supplied numerous streams that dashd down the precipices and had a very picturesque appearance.

The bases of the mountains were cultivated with wheat, vineyards & mulberry trees.

After we had been some time on our way the wind subsided – the lake became perfectly tranquil and beautifully reflected on its glassy bosom the vast mountains that environd it, and the groves the hamlets & villages that decorated its borders. Before our arrival at Magadino we passed the town of Locarno situated on the west side of the Lake. This place formerly stood on the margin of the <water> lake but the mountain torrents have gradually formed a soil beyond it and at present it stands a quarter of a mile back from the shore. This <village> ↑town↓ gave name to the Lake which is indifferently <termed> called Lago Maggiore or Lago di Locarno. The town of Magadino has sufferd the same fate as Locarno, a space of ground having been formed between it and the Lake by the torrents which wash down soil from the mountains. At the water side are a few houses where they receive and store the merchandize <brought> that is to be forwarded either on the Lake or to Bellinzone. Here is also a custom house & health office. We had brought letters to the principals of these <where> houses – from our Banker of Milan & in consequence were very politely treated. They had our passports ↑& bills of health↓ countersignd, and our trunks sufferd to pass without opening. They likewise endeavored to get us horses for Bellizone a <vill> town about three leagues distant where we intended taking mules to cross the mountain. Unfortunately however they could find but one old horse in the place so we were obliged to put up with him – We <L>left John behind to come on with the baggage in a cart – and sat off in high glee with our <old charger> old steed. The road lay through the lower part of the Levantine Valley which <in this we were> is extremely beautiful, <shaded by chestnuts & wall nut trees> laid out in rich pastures and fertile fields of wheat & Indian corn – <T>Waterd by the Tesino and shaded by groups of poplars wallnuts chestnut & mulberry trees. The valley is quite level between Magadino & Bellenzino and bounded by vast mountains crowned with snow. The peasantry had very much the Swiss air, were generally tall and stout and very civil in their behaviour always making a bow or moving the hat as we passd. We managed pretty tolerably with our single horse riding by turns and sometimes riding both at once. <The> I should have observed that at Magadone we entered in the Swiss territories tho properly speaking we do not enter Switzerland till on the summit of Mount St. Goatherd – This territory on the Italian side of the Alps was gained from the Milanese by the Swiss in the fourteenth century partly by conquest & partly by treaty.[162] The town of Bellinzone is situated on the level of the valley in a delightful spot – On two hills <are> stand two old castles overlooking the town and high up on a point of the mountain to the East of the town another one square with one tower[163] <the whole have> they have the most picturesque appearance and accord with the antient walls & battlements of the town. At the Gate we were addressd by two french <guards> ↑soldiers↓ in a very polite manner who asked us if we were members of the *grand council*[.] on our answering in the negative they said we must go before the police with our passports – that measure being observed towards all strangers. One of them accompanied us. He was a very civil, honest looking fellow and on his saying he was a Swiss I was immediately prepossessd in his favor. He told us the government was very strict at present in respect to strangers and examined their passports particularly – He told us that he had been in the service a great while, had seen many hard battles and was in the famous Expedition to Egypt – <I told him> You have then seen some glorious battles said I – ["]Ah Monsieur said he, there is very little glory for a poor common soldier – We fight hard and support all the danger & fatigues of the battle, but are never mentiond except as killd or wounded and then generally in hundreds. For my part I have my share of the fortunes of war <sad> added he pointing to his leg which was lame & swelld." He had recieved a wound there in Egypt and it had never been perfectly heald but had latterly swelld very much[.] he comforted himself however with the good consequences it had produced of procuring him a congé and leave to return to his family He said he had a brother who kept an hotel at Lyons who would be glad to receive him into his house – We were highly pleased with the poor fellows frankness and gave him a piece of money for which he was ex-

162. Throughout the fifteenth century the Swiss Confederation made forays south of the Alps and in 1440 secured cession of the Valle Leventina from the Duke of Milan. Between 1500 and 1512 they also acquired the territory of the Canton of Ticino, the Val d'Ossola, and the Valtellina. Irving apparently got his information from Coxe, *Travels in Switzerland,* III, 315–17.

163. The Castelli Svitto or di Montebello and Corbario on the east, and Grandé or San Michele on the west were built in 1445 by Filippo Maria Visconti, Duke of Milan.

tremely thankful. Having arranged our affairs with the officers of Police who were very polite, we searched out the inn. We had brought letters to the Inn keeper who was <exces of> consequently very attentive to us and has procured us <mules> ↑horses↓ to cross the mountains at a rate far more reasonable than we had expected to pay. In fact we seem to have got among another set of beings[164] and begin to look around us once more with confidence – <our> I should never have believed that I could have left Italy with so much delight, but we had really been so continually cheated and imposed upon throughout the whole of our Journey that we were happy to turn our backs upon that country this morning – with all its charms, and felt no regret at the thoughts that there was no prospect of our ever reviewing its delightful scenery.

The Levantine Valley is about 8 Leagues long and extremely narrow – It is very populous,[165] but the villages are commonly built <at>on the bases of the mountains to preserve them from the inundations that sometimes take place in this valley, especially in the low, flat parts. <of the valley.>

Thermometer this Evening – 5<6>7 Deg.

May 7

Bellinzona was formerly one of the Swiss Bailliwicks but since the augmentation of the cantons from the number of 13 to 17 it <has> forms a part of the canton of Tecino (or in English Tesino.)[166] We sat off at half past six this morning on horseback, having engaged three horses for ourselves & servant & one for our baggage – <to> paying at the rate of two Louis d ors a horse from Bellinzone to <Alf> Altorf situated on the other side of the mountain. <The valley> Our road lay along the eastern side of the valley <amid> and commanded the most delicious views. <of>

The rich meadows of the valley were studded with innumerable wild flowers of the most beautiful forms & colors. The chest nut wall nut

164. Irving's opinion of Swiss character in this entry and subsequent ones is expressed also in his letters to William Irving, May 31, 1805, and to Alexander Beebee, August 3, 1805.

165. Irving took his facts about the valley to this point from Coxe, *Travels in Switzerland,* III, 314.

166. By the Swiss constitution of 1803 six cantons were added to the thirteen which had formerly composed the Confederation.

Poplar willow &c planted sometimes in masses – sometimes in rows & avenues diversified the scene – forming frequently a continued bower thro which the road passed and overhanging the waters of the Tesino – The valley was enclosed on each side by vast mountains which bounded the view in every direction. <The gradati> It was curious to notice on their sides the gradations from luxurient spring to sterile <b> cheerless winter – rising from the fertile bosom of the valley their bases were well cultivated and clothed with majestic trees in full foliage – as the mountain ascended the cultivated patches disappeared – the trees lost their verdure – they became diminutive & naked – large masses of grey rock projected from among them [–] higher up, the trees entirely ceased – rugged cliffs barren and precipitious succeeded and the whole was crowned by snowy peaks glistening with the sunbeams. Down the gullies rolled foaming torrents, formed by the dessolution of the snow – dashing from rock to rock forming streaks of white foam amid the dark foliage of the <trees> forests and hurrying with noisy turbulence to the Tesino. The road frequently passed under vast masses of rock and mountains almost perpendicular – the sides fringed with trees or broken in cliffs and precipices among which the goats heedlessly skipped from rock to rock – sometimes regarding us over the edge of an impending crag and fearlessly cropping the moss or bushes that hung on its edge.

As our <mules> horses went at a slow pace – continually on a walk, I frequently dismounted and suffering them to proceed – rambled among the rocks – lingering on the banks of the Tesino in spots that commanded views particularly beautiful and sublime. I was seated on a fragment of rock enjoying one of those scenes when a number of Swiss peasants of both sexes passed by with their knapsacks on their backs as if on a Journey – They saluted me in the civil frank manner of the country and I got up and joined them. I found them like all the swiss that I had seen – <?f?> unreserved and ready to converse. They told me they were returning from Milan to their homes in the valley – they had been three days on their Journey and should arrive at their village in about five hours – One of them a young fellow of about twenty asked me several questions about America – he said he should like to go there, but it was too far – he would not be able to return often and see his relations and native place. He said he had several cousins who had gone from home and done well in different parts of france italy – holland & germany. they were all chocolate makers – In every part of the world said he smiling – you find swiss chocolate makers. A moment after he broke out in the liveliest expressions of exultation – "Ecco lo signor" (<said he> cried he "nostre montagna – Oh che bella veduta – Ecco lo Signor – quella grande montagna tutt<o>a[167] copert<o>a di neve – Oh che bella veduta[″] (– "Look there Sir – theres our mountain – Oh what a charming sight – Look there sir that great mountain all coverd with snow – oh the charming <shight> sight –")

He pointed out to me a distant snowy mountain <under> at the foot of which w<as>ere[168] *their* valley and *their* cottages – one of the finest vallies & mountains, he said – in the world. I was extremely pleased at this <me> testimony of that love for their native place so <?no?> predominant in the bosoms of the Swiss. It has been frequently remarked <and in those> among the soldiery of this nation when employed in other countries – In France and holland they will not permit the music of the swiss regiments to play a certain <favr> favorite air of their country – as it recals their native mountains & cottages to mind where they had so often heard it in their youth and renders them sad & melancholy.

The valley has a gradual ascent and <?decr?> grows more narrow – straightned by the Immense mountains – The <?mark?> cultivation ceases except in <?seve?> a few places where there are scanty patches of meadow land. The mountains become more wild <either> ascending into lofty peaks – bristled with pine or broken into vast impending precipices <↑of↓ rocks piled on rocks> from the threatening sides of which – g<ian>reat blocks of granite have detached themselves and tumbled in huge fragments into the valley. The river became more turbulent & impetuous – We saw in several places peasants angling among the rapids for trout. The cottages & villages were very poor and bespoke the sterility of the surrounding country. We passed numerous crosses of that kind which we had remarked along the road in the plains of Lombardy which marked the place of an assassination – We supposed these to be erected for the same purpose and began to doubt the many assurances we had recieved of the Swiss roads being entirely secure from robberies. The wild solitary nature of the scenery seemed peculiarly favorable to the robber – We passed long defiles <where> without seeing any human habitation excepting the miserable huts of goatherds perched up

167. "a" is written over "o" in darker ink.
168. "ere" is in pencil.

among the cliffs <at>& <the> here & there a convent built on high bluffs of the mountains.

About the middle of the day we arrived at the little village of Giornico. This is an assemblage of miserable cottages – some of them are built of wood The Inn was indifferent and the dinner they furnished, very poor[.] we had however acquired a keen appetite from the pure air of the mountains and did <ful> ample justice to their fare. After dinner our Landlady and her two daughters entered the room – The names of the latter they told us were Marianne and Rosa – They appeared to have all the frankness and goodness of heart that distinguish<ed> the Swiss. There was a simplicity and good humor in the manners of the girls that highly delighted me and reminded me of the country girls of America. Rosa the youngest was a delicate pretty girl. The old lady had an ease in her manners that I did not expect to find in such a situation & C. made a just remark, that with a fashionable education and seated in a drawing room she would have been deemed an elegant woman. They entered into conversation with us very freely and in a few moments we were as sociable as if we <?t?> were old acquaintances. The old Lady had <a swell> one of those swellings in the throat that are so frequent in mountainous countries and which are ascribed by some to the drinking of snow water. (they are called in Switzerland *Goitures*) We enquired of her concerning it. She said it did not proceed from Snow-Water for she drank nothing but milk & wine – She ascribed it to child bearing – "Alors said Cabell, il ne faut pas faire les petites" – "Ah Monsieur["] replied she smiling "quand on est mar<ie>rié[169] <y> vous savez bien on est obligé de faire les petites *par force*" <"et alors["] rejoind C—— laughing "viennent les Goitures – (*en bas*) *par force*" "Ah mon dieu" said Marianne Je ne me marierai jamai[s] pour cela.">[170] <We> The good folks were highly delighted with our sociability and wished us to stay there all night – they would then they said – have all the young people of the village and make up a dance – Our time and arrangements however would not permit us to profit by their good will[;] otherwise we should have been much pleased to remain and witness the manners of the peasantry in their moments of gaiety and amusement. We shook hands with them

169. "rie" is written over "ie" in darker ink.

170. "Then . . . it is not necessary to have children." "Ah, sir, . . . when one is married you well know one is obliged to have children *perforce.*" And then . . . come goiters – (*below*) *perforce.*" "O heavens, . . . I shall never marry because of that."

in the most friendly manner at parting – and as I mounted my horse Marianne called to me from the window <to> not to forget to stop there if ever I pass that way again. <"Et certainement said I et alors Marianne je vous trouverai <avec un grande>[171] mariee avec un grande goiture["] – "Ah jamais jamais["] said she earnestly>[172]

After leaving Giornico the valley ascended more rapidly and decreased in width till it became a mere gorge, scatterd with vast fragments of Rock, with the Tesino, now a narrow torrent – soaring and foaming thro them. This river forms innumerable picturesque cascades and turbulent rapids – the road often wound along the edge of precipices that overhung the torrent and was in many places built up with rough stones covered with earth, <a narrow ?vall?> where the precipices were broken & uneven; <in It also pass> in several places also we pass over bridges of a single arch, boldly thrown from rock to rock, while below the river thunderd <along dashing from> thro the narrow passes of the cliffs <and> ↑dashing↓ over immense blocks of Granite. We frequently descended from our horses and walked where the road was threatening or the scenery very beautiful. In the middle part of the day we found the weather extremely warm, partly owing to the constant exercise we underwent. Toward evening we passed thro a defile that was truly sublime & even Terrific. The mountains seemed to have been rent asunder by some violent commotion – being almost perpendicular, for the distance of perhaps an hundred yards. The distance between them was not more than thirty yards in many places. Thro this, the Tesino rushed in a foaming torrent dashing from rock to rock & forming repeated falls. <accompanied with> The road wound close along the face of one of the perpendicular mountains. In many places <the> it was built up with stones, & in others cut into the side of the mountain with rocks overhanging it just leaving a sufficient space for a a man on horseback to pass under them

The Eye in glancing upwards could only view the heavens in a perpendicular direction, between impending cliffs of a vast height fringed with pines and bushes that shot from their fissures & margins. The gloom

171. This cancelation is made by a single straight line, presumably by Irving at the time of the entry; the rest of the passage is canceled by heavier, zigzag lines, obliterating more letters, made probably at a later date and possibly by someone other than Irving.

172. "And certainly . . . and then, Marianne, I shall find you <with a great> married with a great goiter." "Ah, never, never . . . ."

of the <defeel> defile, the threatening aspect of the enclosing mountains and the awful noise of the torrent, had an effect the most impressive and sublime on my imagination.

About dusk we passed a neat white house where we paid a kind of toll. Here the valley widened and was laid out in meadow land – the river was more tranquil and <there> wanderd gently thro the verdant fields, the whole forming a pleasing contrast to the wildness and sterility of the mountains. Here we came in sight of the snowy summit of St Goatherd which still seemed a considerable distance a head of us. The Evening was serene and calm, the day was gradually disappearing and the moon began to acquire an influence over the landscape. The solitude <↑& silence↓ of the scenery was> and silence of the scene was only interrupted by the noise of torrents, tumbling down the <mountains> ↑precipices↓ or the sound of the vesper bells from different convents & village churches situated among the mountains. The distant sound of the latter floating <al> across the valley and falling in melancholy tones upon the ear, seemed in perfect consonance with the sublime and solemn scenery around us. – The moon shone very bright and amply recompensed us for the want of day light. – <The> We continued riding for some time after night had set in – One time along a precipice with the river rolling along below us while on the otherside vast rocks impended over our heads and forests of Pine <cast a dark shado a> threw the road into complete shadow. – At another time we passed thro a defile of the mountain where the perpendicular precipices scarce left room for the river and the road to pass and which was entirely shrouded from the moon beams. We did not feel perfectly at our ease in these gloomy places – the numerous crosses we had passed during the day recurred to our memories and these wild terrific solitudes seemed well calculated for the haunts of robbers and assassins.

The air became quite cold before we arrived at our place of destination, yet the atmosphere was bracing and enlivening. <The summit of Mount St Goatherd became The effect of the moon beams on the mountains was truly beautiful, and the snowy summit of a distant one, that glistened in> The frozen summit of a distant snowy mountain glistening in the <sun>moon beams had a fine effect. About nine oclock we reached Airolo where we intended passing the night. This village is commonly said to stand at the foot of Mount St Goatherd, tho properly speaking it stands at that part of the mountain, where the snowy summit takes a rapid rise – in fact we have been ascending the greatest part of the day up the mountain tho the ascent was more gradual than that which rises from Airolo.

The Inn was comfortable and cleanly built of wood – the chambers of pannel work with low ceilings also of wood. We were recieved in an open friendly manner by the people of the inn and shewed into a room where the family generally sat, which was warmed by a large granite stove. The Landlady was a worthy old lady <that had a> ↑of great↓ respectability of appearance. Her son a young man of about 27 waited on us & was very attentive – yet there was a dignity and independence in their manners that I have never before seen among the servile officious Inn keepers of Europe. They seemed to have the spirit of liberty within them <and to> that placed them above the grovelling abjectness of mind that <stoops to> bows before superior wealth. The young man shewed a degree of intelligence & information that surprised me and confirmed what I had heard & read of the information among the swiss – He <talked> conversed the whole evening with us concerning the politics of Europe & America – His observations were extremely just and shewed much reflection & decernment – the whole of his conversation was open manly & candid. He expressed his dislike to the french without reserve – they had invaded the liberties and happiness of his country, they had plunderd the inhabitants, burned their houses and committed every enormity – the brave Swiss had attempted in vain to defend their homes & liberties, and had <fall> been sacrificed either by the open force or the secret machinations of their enemies. The crosses that we had passed during the day were most of them erected on the spots where these martyrs to freedom had been slain and what we had taken for the signs of robbery and murder were really the simple yet glorious monuments of many a gallant Swiss who had fallen in the last struggles for liberty. We were assured that the roads were perfectly safe from depredations and (as we had often been told before) a man might travel thro the country with his purse open in his hand in perfect safety.

The young man told us that avalanches were very frequent in the higher passes of the mountains, and that the best time to cross it is in the morning before the sun has had sufficient time to soften the snow & <detatch> detach it from the rocks. – These avalanches are vast masses of snow that form themselves by degrees against the sides of the mountains and in the rifts of the peaks. The frequent snow storms of winter encrease them continually and the cold freezes and binds them to the rock. In the spring <when the sun is & com> and at the commencement of the summer when the sun is powerful, they thaw & soften – their hold on the rocks is loosened – <and> they at last <detatch> detach themselves and bearing with them rocks & trees, thunder down a frightful ruin into the valley. Hapless is any object that encounters their tremenduous progress. Hamlets – cottages – peasants – travellers are swept away and buried in the snow. These avalanches as I before observed happen commonly in the middle part of the day or in the afternoon after the sun has operated for some time on the surface of the snow. The passage of St Goatherd is likewise dangerous in rainy weather as the rain very frequently loosens vast masses of rock from the impending cliffs, which are precipitated into the road and frequently kill the passengers.

May 8

At half after five this morning the Thermometer placed in the open air stood at 36 Deg. The morning was clear and cool and we prepared to set off that we might cross the mountain at an early hour.

Our worthy old Landlady was already up, while we were taking a dish of excellent coffee she related to us various particulars of their sufferings during the time the french were ravaging their country. They had been dispersed in every direction. Her son <was engaged with the enemy> was engaged in the scanty but intrepid ranks of his brave fellow countrymen – gallantly attempting to defend their rights & Liberties against an overwhelming foe; he narrowly escaped with his life. The old lady in company with her mother in law were at one time obliged to take refuge in an hamlet in the higher part of the mountains – and had to wade thro dreary valleys to their waists in snow. At length they were advised to change their residence as it was well known that her husband was not well disposed towards the prevailing powers – "He was a freeman" said the old lady with spirit "and he had a right to think as he pleased." They had then removed to Lugano where they remained several months till the fate of their unfortunate country was ascertained and affairs a little tranquilized. At present she said – the french had left them – "they have taken all that we had and have no farther inducement to stay in a country they have impoverished – They say they have given us liberty, but alas! it is liberty *in chains*!"

I could not enough admire the unconquerable spirit of these people – <they> instead of a conquerd nation they have the dignity the manners the independence of freemen. Continually since I have been in Switzerland have I been struck with the similarity in sentiment and manners between the Swiss and the Americans – It is impossible this nation can <eve> always be kept under. the love of liberty burns too strongly in their bosoms.

On settling accounts at this inn I could hardly prevail on the old lady to fix any price, and the one she did fix was so moderate <that> considering the sterility of the surrounding country and the excellent accomodations we had enjoyed – that had I have dared to have done it I should have given far more than her demand.

From Airolo we began to ascend the snowy regions of the mountain. The snow was frozen and hard and the horses slipped so frequently that we preferred to dismount and walk. The persons who procured us horses at Bellinzona had not been particular in having them rough shod – a precaution absolutely necessary in crossing the mountain – We were extremely embarrassed in consequence. the horses were continually slipping & stumbling and at length the one that carried our trunks fell down and could not rise again till all the baggage was taken off

Three peasants that were passing by at that time offerd their services to lead our horses up the mountain, which spared us a great deal of fatigue & embarrassment as they understood the mode of managing the animals. The road ascended in a Zig Zag direction and was exceeding steep. In spight of the cold and the fields of snow around us we were extremely warm with exercise and found our surtouts so oppressive that we had to pull them off and carry them on our arms. After toiling for a long time up the steep ascents we passed thro a narrow valley of the most desolate aspect. It was enclosed by high points of the mountains covered with snow except in some places where the naked rock <broke thro the> projected in frightful masses thro the surface The defile was rendered still more dreary by the wind whistling thro the cliffs & the mournful sound of a stream that ran thro the centre often passing under the snow for a considerable distance. The road is marked at regular distances by posts to guide the traveller when the track has been coverd by a storm of snow. This valley seems very dangerous on account of avalanches and we saw many places where torrents of snow had rushd down lately from the cliffs.

About eight oclock we arrived at what was formerly called the

Hospice.[173] <Here> This was originally inhabited by Capuchin friars, who administered to the wants of strangers; explored the mountain after storms, to search for any unfortunate traveller that <was> had sufferd from the cold or snow. They were accompanied by dogs in these excursions – which displayed great sagacity in finding persons buried in the snow. A hospital was erected adjoining to their habitation where the sufferers were treated with attention & humanity by the benevolent fathers. At the time that the french <carried fr> brought the blessings of liberty into this country the poor friars were driven from their habitations which were burnt down. What became of them I do not know except that I reccollect to have seen one in America some years ago. *

<The house> A house is erected on the ruins of their mansion, and serves as an inn – Here the Passports of travellers are examined & signed. This dwelling stands at the enterance into the small valley that forms the summit of the <valley> mountain. There are irregular peaks that surround it and enclose the view but those are only to be attained by clambering from rock to rock <thro> & over masses of Ice & snow. In the summer time there are two or three small lakes in this valley but at present they are covered and the road crosses them. No place can be more dreary and even horriffic than this valley – Not the least symptoms of vegetation is to be seen all is dismal silent & desolate except <when> ↑that↓ the silence is sometimes interrupted by the hollow murmurs of the wind <as> among the cliffs or the roaring of a torrent. The peasants who had been so servicible to us in our ascent, had walked on a head without expecting any reccompense – Surprised at such disinterestedness of conduct which I had so long been unaccustomed to I hastened after them and accosting a woman who had led my horse I put a piece of money in her hand. The honest soul seemed quite surprised – she insisted on returning it, and it was with great difficulty I could prevail on her to retain it. What a striking

* At 8 oclock at the hospice Therm: stood at 38 Deg[.] there must have been an incorrectness in it from the effects of agitation in travelling

173. First built in the fourteenth century, it was from 1683 to the end of the sixteenth century in charge of Capuchins from Milan. The buildings were destroyed by the French in 1799–1800, but were later rebuilt.

difference between the conduct of this woman and that of the greedy extortionate inhabitants of Italy whose services are always interested and who are never satisfied with the reward you give them <tho> however liberal it may be. The poor woman when she found I would not recieve it back <gav> made me a thousand acknowledgements and insisted on attending us <as far> down the mountain as far as her village that she might render us every service in her power. The descent was steep & hazardous, but we arrived without Accident, in the Valley of Urseren.

This valley is situated in the high parts of the mountain and in summer is extremely verdant, <tho> but it has not yet thrown of[f] entirely its winter dress. It possesses excellent pasturage and produces cheese & butter. We passed thro the little village of Hôpital[174] the houses of wood with glazed windows remarkably clean – We then traversed <the greatest part> part of the valley and stopped at the village of Andermatt. This stands at the foot of one of the mountains – A wood of pines above the town serves to protect it from the avalanches, <and> these trees are held sacred from the axe; I have been told it is death to fell one of them. The Inn at this village was neat & comfortable – the cleanliness of the Swiss is particularly agreeable after coming out of Italy. We found the family seated at dinner and they reminded me exceedingly of the families I have seen of substantial farmers in America. The children were well clad & healthy and the eldest daughter a very pretty smart looking girl. We dined here and were <attended> waited on by one of the sons of our Landlord – a young fellow of about nineteen, manly civil & intelligent. Like all the Swiss that I have seen he entered in to conversation without reserve, was <id> independent in his remarks and frank in expressing his sentiments. He <made> shewed the same indignation against the french that we had found universally prevalent. They had stripped his country fetterd the nation and oppressd them till there was nothing left to gratify their cupidity "Servile wretches" said he indignantly "that pretended to the name of freemen – they once fought for *Liberty* they now fight for an Emperor!"

The Valley of Urseren is about nine miles long. The river Reuss which takes its rise on the St Goatherd – runs through it.

About a quarter of a mile from Andermat we passed thro the Hole

174. Now Hospenthal.

of Uri (Trou d'Uri)[175] Here the mountains barely afford room for the reuss to rush along – The road is perforated thro the solid rock for the distance of eighty paces. This subterraneous passage is very humid and continually dropping water. Immediately after passing thro this we arrived at the tremenduous Devils bridge (Teufels-bruck)[176] This is a <bold> bridge of a single arch boldly thrown across a vast abyss and resting on opposite rocks. The Reuss thundering down precipices and over vast blocks of granite rushes under it with <tremendu> astonishing turbulence & impetuosity – the spray of the cataract mounting high up in the air and often falling on the bridge in a drizzling shower – the <dangerous> descent to this bridge from the side of Urseren – is very hazardous – the pavement of the road when we passd was partly coverd with snow – wet & slippery – We did not venture on horseback. The wildness of the surrounding scenery – rocks piled on rocks – mountains of granite – perpendicular often overhanging – without a single tree or bush to enliven them – the roaring cataract, the light bridge in a manner suspended in the air far above the torrent all combined to compleat a scene sublime & terriffic. The bridge itself is not so much an object of curiosity – it is not above forty feet in length – but it forms a striking object in the stupenduous scenery. The peasantry have forgotten the name of the architect, and without giving themselves any farther trouble, ascribe the whole work to the Devil – for they think no other workman would hazard himself so far as to build a bridge in such a terrible situation.

<The scenery>

About this place we entered the canton of Uri.* The scenery now assumed the most savage & dreary aspect. The mountains, bare rugged, without tree or verdure, often impending over the road and threatening to overwhelm the traveller with rocks & avalanches. The Reuss roared thro the middle of the valley – forming repeated cascades. The road was built along the edge of precipices that over hung the river, and we frequently looked down a fearful distance to the torrent below us. Very often in these dangerous passes we met mules laden with merchandize crossing the mountain and it was with difficulty

* Here the Valley of Schœlennen commences

175. The French name of Urner Loch. The tunnel was first cut in 1707.

176. The Teufelsbrücke is described in similar terms in Coxe, *Travels in Switzerland,* I, 313.

we could pass them without jostling. The torrents from the mountains were not so frequent as on the italian side of St Goatherd but we passed several places where avalanches had swept down the gullies of the mountains and carried ↑away↓ rocks & trees in their course. After passing thro a variety of scenery <?st?> such as I have already attempted to discribe – we <reg> arrived at the more fertile parts of the valley and in the evening we had a most delightful view of the country as it approached the Lake of Lucerne – The Reuss lately turbulent wanderd in gentle mazes thro the richest meadows – its waters beautifully borderd by willows. We rode for some distance <tho> by moon light and about nine oclock arrived the town of Altorf.

May 9

The <town> ↑village↓ of Altorf is a melancholy monument of the misfortunes of War, <It was> ↑having been↓ burnt down by the french. <and> The walls of the old houses are still standing and have a dessolate appearance. About five years ago the inhabitants began to rebuild their village and it is rapidly rising out of its ashes – like the Phoenix, with superior beauty A very neat church[177] is erected, the inside finished with taste & simplicity and ornamented with a Pulpit of beautiful stucco. The houses are of stone plaisterd & white-washd which gives them an exceeding neat appearance.

We are lodged at the Hotel of the Black lion, the accomodations and table are excellent and we could not be better attended, We are waited on by the hostess herself, a neat little woman, of uncommon information and intelligence. She seems perfectly well versed in the history politics & government of her country and has given us a variety of very interesting information

In the principal street of the village is the place where the gallant William Tell shot the arrow from off the head of his child. The spot where he stood is marked by a fountain ornamented with a statue of Tell and his child The former with his cross bow the latter with the apple – The statue is of common stone. At the distance of about ninety yards from this spot is another fountain which marks the spot where the child is said to have stood. I was astonished at the distance and hardly thought it possible that he could have hit so small a mark with an arrow so far off – But our Landlady told us that she had frequently

177. Built between 1801 and 1810.

seen shots equally good with the cross bow. In the village also is a small chapel on which is painted the transaction. The countenance of Tell's statue <possesses> expresses all the resolute manliness of a freeman.[178]

The cross bow was still in use in Switzerland till of late years. The young men of Altorf were accustomed to shoot once a week at a mark. At the time of the distruction of Altorf the cross bows shared the fate of the village & were consumed. Since that time they have not been resumed – The people have not regained their former gaiety Their former amusements are neglected and the nation seems to brood over its wrongs.

I have already mentioned the love of the Swiss for their native homes. Our Landlady gave us some instances of it – She told us that they had employed as a servant a mountainier who had all his life time been engaged in tending cattle on his native mountain. In a little while he began to shew discontent & uneasiness – The sight of a cow a goat or a sheep affected him strongly and even frequently melted him into tears, recalling to his mind the flocks & herds he had left behind, <and the> but the little air I have before mentioned – which is sung by the mountainiers as they tend their cattle, <had so> completely overpowered him; he pined away for some time melancholy & homesick till at length he took a sudden resolution – asked his dismissal & hurried back with delight to his native Alps preferring the inhospitable regions and scanty fare of the mountains to all the pleasures & comforts of the valley. How beautifully has Goldsmith discribed this *amor patriae* of the Swiss

Dear is that shed to which his soul conforms
And dear that hill that lifts him to the storms
And as a child, when scaring sounds molest
Clings close & closer to the mothers breast

178. William Tell, the traditional hero of Switzerland, is credited with being chiefly responsible for the formation of the Swiss Confederation and the expulsion of the Austrian rulers early in the fourteenth century, though both of these events actually required a much longer time, and now he is thought to have been legendary. The statue of him to which Irving refers was executed in 1785 to replace an older one; it is now on the fountain at Bürglen (information furnished by the Archivist of Zurich). The chapel to which Irving refers, presumably that in the adjoining village of Bürglen marking the alleged spot of Tell's birthplace, was built in 1522 and decorated with paintings of his exploits.

Irving drew on this paragraph, including the quotation, in his letter to Alexander Beebee, August 3, 1805.

So the loud torrent, & the whirlwinds roar
But bind him to his native mountains more.[179]

From a small convent of Capuchins[180] situated upon the side of the mountain that rises from the town we had a charming view of Altorf the beautiful valley in which it stands and a part of the lake of Lucerne The honest fathers <are> have nearly finished their house which was burnt down by the french. We were shewn every part of it by a fat jolly member of the fraternity who seemed to thrive amazingly considering the slender diet of his order.

In the neighborhood of Altorf a small plain on the top of the mountains was pointed out to us as being the <?road?> scene of a battle between the Austrians and french in which the former were defeated.

Our landladys house was turned quite into an hospital by the wounded – she said the austrians <lay> when wounded were quiet and dejected – the french on the contrary, tho wounded perhaps in both legs and unable to stand, still retained their gaiety and amused themselves with singing and playing on the flute and one officer who was wounded in the head and could not turn himself in bed was so full of his jokes and witticisms that she could not stay in the room with him.

There are no longer any french to be found in these parts – they did not harmonize well with the <simple> honest independent Swiss. The local government of this canton has not sufferd any change <fy> from the french, <a> nor do the people pay any thing except a regular sum exacted by the government of the canton to pay off the requisition made in time of the war.[181]

May 10

<It had been> The weather which had gradually clouded over produced yesterday a violent storm of wind and rain so that we rejoiced in having made our journey across the mountain in two days – Three days is the time generally allowd and we had blamed our muleteer for hurrying us across in two which obliged us to rise early and remain out after dark.

179. Oliver Goldsmith, *The Traveller* (1764), II, 203–8. Line 204 should read "hill which lifts." Irving took the quotation (but not the error) from Coxe, *Travels in Switzerland,* I, 285.

180. Founded in 1581, it is the oldest in Switzerland.

181. This paragraph is in a slightly different hand, apparently added later.

It is a singular fact mentiond to us by our Landlady that when the weather is very fine the other side of the mountain it is stormy on this – and vice versa. She has even known the season on the Swiss side to be exceeding wet; constant rains prevailing while on the Italian side they have been suffering <with drout> for want of rain. The wind in this valley blows only in two directions – north & south. The latter which crosses the mountain is exceeding hot in summer & even in winter produces a mildness in the atmosphere – It is strange that it should retain, the heat it acquires in Italy, after passing such high snowy mountains. The snow does not lay generally on the alps in summer but only on the loftiest mountains. <We were surprized at an effect> In passing the mountain and after our arrival in Altorf, we felt a great flushing and burning in the face – Our countenances were flushd and red as if violently sunburnt, and to day the skin of Mr C——s face begins to rub off in a light scruff – this we were told was from the reflection of the sun from the snow which had very frequently such an effect on travellers passing the mountain who were unaccustomed to the changes from verdent vallies to dazzling plains of snow. Even the peasants sometimes use precautions to prevent themselves from being sun burnt & they also cover the eyes of their oxen when passing the mountain – lest they should be injured by the glare – this latter circumstance I observed in descending the mountain.

This morning the storm had ceased – the clouds were breaking away and the weather was cool & windy – Thermometer at 6 oclock stood at 41 deg. The snow had fallen plentifully on the mountains and even extended down their sides almost to the valley – feathering the trees in a very beautiful manner. Being assured we might safely venture on the lake, we sat off from Altorf about ten oclock. Our Landlord and his wife attended us in the street to the little waggon we had engaged to carry ourselves & trunks to the borders of the lake – We parted more like old friends then like Inn keepers & their guests. What a <difference from> ↑contrast to↓ the Inn Keepers of Italy with whom the stranger is in a constant state of hostility regarding them as knaves continually on the look out to defraud him. The distance from Altorf to the lake is about a mile <Here> At the landing place stands the little village of Fluellen that has a very picturesque appearance situated on the borders of the lake. We readily found a bark to take us to Altorf and had again a strong contrast between this country & Italy. In the latter when entering the village of Sesto on lake Maggiore we were thronged with raggamuffins all eager for us to engage their boat – They were exhorbitant in their demands seeing that we were foreigners and made no scruple to demand twice as much as they really took. Here on the contrary the prices are fixed by government and the rates posted up in the hotel. No waterman came running after us troubling us with their importunities We enquired for a bark & waterman and were supplied with them instantly without any noise.

We embarked on the lake about half past eleven. This is often called tho improperly the Lake of Lucerne. Its real name is the Lake of the four cantons[182] from its being enclosed by the four cantons of Uri, Schweitz, Lucerne and Unterwalden. It consists of three branches or compartments which are distinguished by the names of the Lakes of Uri – Schweitz & Lucerne. The part we first traversed was the lake of Uri. The awful sublimity of the scenery on this peice of water, defies discription – neither the pen nor pencil could do it justice and the painter must be mortified among these scenes with the conviction of the insufficiency of his art to scan the grandest works of nature. Stupenduous mountains rising perpendicular from the lake or often over hanging its transparent waters in vast masses – sometimes rising in a steep ascent clothed with forests of pine and beech whose dark & lively greens were beautifully intermingled – often presenting the appearance of having been split & rent by violent convulsions – in other places the mountains in a manner piled on one another rising in fantastic peaks clothed in snow – Such was the nature of the surrounding scenery. The abrupt elevation of the mountains from the water rendered landing impracticable except in five or six places.

This branch of the grand lake is about nine miles in length and about from one to two & a half miles in breadth It is exceeding deep – and cannot be sounded in the middle – We coasted along on the western side of it keeping close in shore to avoid the wind which was a head <The fri> Frequently we passed along the bases of mountains that ran perpendicularly to an astonishing height – On looking up we saw the <mo> brinks of the precipices fringed with pine which appeared like diminutive bushes – often vast masses of rock impended over our heads in the most threatening <posture> positions. There was a

182. Irving wrote a poem on the Vierwaldstättersee which was copied by J. C. Cabell into his journal; it has been printed in R. B. Davis, "Washington Irving and Joseph C. Cabell," *English Studies in Honor of James Southall Wilson* (University of Virginia Studies, IV, Charlottesville, 1951), pp. 12–13.

majesty a sublimity – and if I may so term it a severity in the grandeur of the scenery that inspired awe & enthusiasm. After rowing some distance we landed at a small chapel[183] sacred to the gallant Tell on the very spot where he is said to have sprung ashore and escaped from the boat in which the <bailiff> Tyrannical Bailiff was <conf> conveying him a prisoner to <Kussnaht> Kussnacht. The chapel is situated on a little promontory of rocks – A beautiful wood of Beech & pine overhangs it and the mountain rises in a steep ascent clothed with forests. The scene is strikingly romantic. The chapel is open in front, <do> and <the inside ↑walls↓ are painted cors> on the inside of the walls are painted coarsely in fresco the history of Tell. Our waterman <shewed> expatiated with honest pride, on the story and virtues of their brave countryman but unfortunately for us their detail was all in german. Never perhaps was the memory of a man more cherished & <ad> revered by his fellow countrymen than that of Tell is by the Swiss. His Image his history is <culti> erected & painted in every town and the peasants with an honest pride glory <in him as their> in relating to travellers his history.

On the opposite side of the lake at some distance we passed the village of Gruti near which it is said <the three> Werner <the>a[184] Staufach of Schweitz – Walter Furst of Uri & Arnold de Melchthal of Unterwalden, the three heroes of Switzerland, took the oath of fidelity to each other when in 1308 they <conceed<it>ed>[185] ↑concerted↓[186] the revolution that was to restore liberty to their country.[187]

<In a little while we>

On the western side in a beautiful bay lies the village of Brunnen. The mountains here form a romantic valley finely cultivated – behind which rises a mountain crowned with snow and shooting up into wild & fantastic peaks. Sailing round a beautiful bluff adorned with an overhanging wood of beech & pine we entered into the middle branch termed the lake of Schweitz. Here the scenery takes a new character – The beautiful is mingled with the Sublime – The mountains were

183. It is called Tell's Chapel, located at Tell's Platte. In his description of it Irving drew on Coxe, *Travels in Switzerland,* I, 275, 276.

184. The alteration is in pencil.

185. "ed" is written over "it" in pencil.

186. "concerted" is in pencil.

187. Apparently Irving took the account of von Stauffacher, Fürst, and von Melchthal from Coxe, *Travels in Switzerland,* I, 291, 297.

frequently clothed to the summit with the richest foliage – Sometimes they gave place to beautiful little valleys at their base speckled with neat cottages half embowerd in trees. at the western extremity of the lake the eye rested with delight on a romantic valley – diversified by verdant hills and bounded by stupenduous mountains crowned with snow – The austerity that characterizes the sublime scenery of the lake of Uri was here softned by the forests of bay and pine that feathered the mountains and over hung the lake. About <the middle> two o'clock we stopped at the village of Gerisau[188] for the boatmen to dine.

This little place was formerly a Republick – and the smallest one in Europe. Its territory was about a league in breadth and two in length. It contained about 1200 inhabitants about 300 of whom were capable of bearing arms. It was composed of a small burgh and several scatterd <villages> houses It had its council of nine persons – Its court of high Justice of 27 Judges – its general assembly of Burgesses and its militia! This republic in miniature could only be approached by water excep[t]ing by a small and difficult path over the mountains. Since the alteration in the Swiss cantons it has been incorporated in that of Schweitz. The village[189] is most romantically situated on the border of the lake in a small valley at the foot of the stupenduous Mount Rigi. It has several very neat houses of stone white-washed and a pretty looking church with a spire – The whole has an air of the greatest cleanliness and makes a most picturesque appearance at a little distance. We rambled thro the village and into the church yard. The graves were marked with ↑small↓ crosses of carved wood – many of them gilt and ornamented with little pictures of saints and sometimes coarse minatures apparently of the deceased. Among these humble monuments of departed friends there were some that peculiarly interested and affected us. On several of the crosses were hung wreaths of flowers and others were planted on the graves These are simple testimonials of affection that speak to the heart and awaken our tenderest feelings sooner than all the parade of marble monuments which merely excite our admiration at the skill of the architect or the sculptor.

188. Gersau was an independent state from 1390 to 1817. In his next three sentences about it Irving apparently drew on Coxe, *Travels in Switzerland,* I, 286–87.

189. Irving drew on the rest of this paragraph in a letter to a brother, November 1805, and described the churchyard at Gersau in "Rural Funerals" in *The Sketch Book* (1819–1820).

After refreshing ourselves with a bowl of rich milk & bread we left the little village of Gersau impressed with the kindest opinions of its inhabitants. We continued for some time further along the lake of Schweitz <al> skirting the base of the snow topt Rigi. Our boatmen were exceeding merry joking with the peasants and goatherds that were employed on the shore. There is a simplicity & goodness of heart in this people that delights me. Poor old honesty – expelled from all the splendid courts & refined *conversaziones* of Europe, has taken refuge in the wild mountains of Switzerland <and seems to be kindly cherished by> and reigns undisturbed in the hearts of its worthy inhabitants

The lake of Schweitz runs nearly in an east & west direction[.] it is surrounded on <the northern> ↑one↓ side by the canton of Schweitz and on the other by that of Unterwalden.

Passing thro a narrow straight of about a mile in width we entered into the Lake of Lucerne. Here the grand lake puts on a third variation. Throwing off[190] completely <her> its rude features it assumes a character the most mild and gentle. <Waving hills> swelling hills gently waving valleys – promontories of a moderate elevation covered with tufted groves – the whole interspersed with wood and vale, village and cottage formed a scene on which the eye reposed with delight after having been for a long time accustomed to the vast and sublime objects of nature. On one side of this lake however, there are still some remains of the romantic scenery thro which we had passed. The mountains are bold and craggy of great elevation & well clothed with trees[.] among the rest Mount pilate boldly rises its lofty head coverd with snow and piercing the clouds. These form a striking contrast to the tranquil beauties of the opposite side of the lake. In traversing this charming piece of water we enjoyed the mild glories of a setting sun, beautifully illuminating the landscape the whole of which was accurately reflected in the glassy bosom of the lake. The town of Lucerne is situated at the extremity of the lake and rises from its waters in the most picturesque manner We arrived there about seven oclock and put up at the *Cheval blanc* an excellent hotel.

On paying off our boatmen we gave them a trifling gratuity <for> by way of a *buono mano* as the italians term it. The sun was small and an italian according to invariable custom would have murmured at it and endeavord to extort more, as if it was a matter of right instead of

190. The second "f" is in pencil.

generosity. These good souls however were amazingly thankful and expressed their gratitude in numerous awkward scrapes & bows and simple grins. Such trifling incidents would not be worthy of remark except as they serve to display the character of the people – In every country extortion & cupidity are most apt to <display> evince themselves in persons of this class who have to deal mostly with strangers.

May 11

Lucerne – the capital of the canton of the same name is one of the largest towns of Switzerland. It is well built containing several very neat houses – the streets are kept clean and the outside of the houses are plaistered & whitewashd. The situation is delightful on the borders of the most beautiful lake in Switzerland – divided by the transparant stream of the Reuss surrounded by picturesque hills covered with tufted groves of Beech & pine – <and> commanding an extensive view of the lake and its romantic borders and the sublime scenery of the Alps. The population is between five and six thousand. The commerce and manufactures are not very considerable. The forwarding of merchandize to & from the lake for Italy – france &c gives business to a number of its inhabitants.

This morning we were to see the greatest curiosity of the town, which is <accla> highly worthy of the travellers observation. This is a plan of Switzerland by General Pfeiffer.[191] Here is represented *in relief* <on a table> the exact face of the country for the space of 60 square leagues comprising portions of the cantons of Zurich Zug Lucerne – Berne, Uri, Schweitz & Unterwalden Every Lake, river, torrent, mountain hill valley town village, cottage road & even path is marked with astonishing accuracy & proportion. The roads are <m> denoted by threads of flax – the rivers by threads of silver and the torrents & cascades by chains of silver thread. The whole is formed of a composition of wax, pitch, clay &c spread on wood and shaped into the proper forms. It is then tinged with different colors so as to give every mountain, valley rock & wood its true character – The highest mountains are not above 10 inches above the level of the plan & one inch answers to about 900 <in hei> feet in height. The work is strong and firm – the man that shewed it to us had a long stick to point out different objects and

191. François Louis Pfyffer (d. 1802), a native of Lucerne, became lieutenant-general in the French service and retired to Lucerne in 1768.

he often knocked it against the little villages & churches with a force that I thought would have laid them in ruins, but they were not injured. They are formed I believe of little flat bits of iron painted. The size of this plan is about 20½ feet by 12 french measure, it consists of between one and two hundred compartments which may be easily taken apart. The correctness of this singular kind of map is really surprizing – We traced without hesitation the <?hol?> whole of our route after we had passed the St. Goatherd. Genl. Pfeiffer was busied for twenty years in the completion of this work. during that time he traversed almost every mountain & valley of Switzerland taking plans & forming models on the spot. During the prosecution of his undertaking he was twice arrested as a spy and often subjected to the suspicions & jealousy of the peasants who did not wish their mountains to be well known, looking upon them, with justice, as the bulwarks of their liberty; and the strong holds of their country. ↑For this reason↓ Mr Coxe[192] says <that> the General was frequently obliged to work by moon light. His work is an admirable monument of persevering patience and mechanical <genius> talents, but it would be an undertaking too minute and confined for a man of <genius> elevated genius & capacious mind.

We also visited a curious gallery of paintings finished within a few years representing the dresses of the peasantry in the different cantons. It is an entertaining collection and among the different *costumes* are many highly grotesque & absurd. Short petticoats seem to be universal among the <peasant> female peasantry of Switzerland – generally shewing their legs nearly up to the knees Their dresses <of> are of cloth of gay colors decorated with different ornaments – the whole is very expensive and costs more than three simples dresses of the french fashion – of course they cannot afford to wear their finest cloaths except on Sundays, and one suit must last a long time – Their hats are commonly of straw with broad brims & low crowns decorated with ribbands & artificial flowers and stuck <at> a little on one side of the head so as to give ↑them↓ a smart coquetish look. In the canton of <under> Unterwalden the women wear small three cornerd or cockd hats and the men commonly wear hats of straw – a whimsical exchange – it is fortunate the women have not asumed the breeches also. We were shewn this collection by a pretty little woman the daughter of the

192. Irving's description of Pfyffer's experiences contains echoes of Coxe's description in *Travels in Switzerland,* I, 255.

Painter.[193] She said her father had often met with embarrassments in the pursuit of his work. He always drew both countenances figures & dress from living objects and it was very difficult sometimes to prevail upon the peasants to suffer him to take their likeness – they did not understand the meaning of it and were apprehensive of some ill design He had often to reward them handsomely and even that could not always prevail upon them. Two or three times he had to take to his heels when their distrust and anger were excited.

In the cathederal <of?th?> we were shewn a very large organ of fine tones. The pipes are immense and the sound of it makes the whole building vibrate. They boast here that it is the largest in Europe – <of the> truth of that I cannot dispute not having seen the grand<est> organ<s> of Haerlem but the organ of Catania far surpasses this in my estimation for sweetness of tone.[194]

There are three long wooden bridges[195] in Lucerne that pass along a corner of the lake and over the river Reuss – They are covered with a roof and open at the sides – commanding beautiful views of the lake. These are the promenades of the town & may be frequented in wet as well as dry weather. They are decorated with indifferent paintings representing the numerous battles of the Swiss – the history of William Tell and the dance of Death. This last is a curious collection of paintings that ornament the smallest bridge. They represent persons of different ranks & in different occupations arrested suddenly by death – <Some times he is in the> Death is as usual represented as a skeleton but often

193. The collection, consisting of 132 portraits, is the work of Joseph Reinhardt (1749–1829), Swiss portrait and historical painter and designer of costumes. His daughter Clara made over a hundred drawings of costumes between 1795 and 1818; her collection is now the property of the Kunstgesellshaft, Lucerne.

194. The Hof-Kirche zu St. Leodegar, said to have been founded in the seventh century, was rebuilt after a fire in 1633, but its towers of 1506 and 1515 were retained. The organ was built in 1650 by Hans Geisler of Salsburg, and reconstructed in the seventeenth century. Irving may have compared it to the organ at Haarlem, long considered the largest and most powerful in the world, because J. C. Cabell, who saw it in the spring of 1804, compared the two in his Journal [No. 7], "Rome Winter of 1805," May 10, 1805.

195. Kapell-Brücke, dating from 1333, has 112 paintings by Hans Wugmann and his son Hans Ulrich (fl. 1600) of lives of the patron saints of Lucerne and of Swiss history. The Spreuer-Brücke (*ca.*1569) has seventeenth-century paintings of the Dance of Death by Caspar Meglinger and others. The Hof-Brücke, on the site of the present Schweizerhofquai, was built between 1252 and 1288 and demolished in the nineteenth century; it was ornamented by paintings of Old and New Testament subjects.

in ludicrous dresses & attitudes. At one time he has jumpd up behind a poor fellow on horseback at another he is strutting along with a lantern lighting a fat alderman into a bog.

We walked in the morning to a kind of belvidere on a fine hill[196] to the west of the town. The ascent to it is by rude stone steps and passes thro beautiful groves of beech & pine. <On>From an eminence on a green platform shaded by noble trees the eye commands one of the finest views in the world and <I thing the> I think, superior to any I had ever seen before. <To the right extends the The awful th> The sublime the picturesque the gentle & luxurient are mingled in an uncommon manner. Stupenduous mountains of barren rock covered with the dreary habilliments of winter are contrasted by gentle hills and dales clothed with verdant groves, blooming orchards, rich <meadous> meadows and all the gay charms of an advanced spring. The lake is a most interesting object in the landscape giving life to the whole – reflecting in its placid bosom the varied scenery that surrounds it – and specled in different places by the little boats that glide along its surface.

The Lake of the four Cantons is about nine leagues in length. The waters are very transparent. <and> It abounds in fish particularly excellent trout of a great size. I was surprized to see numbers of wild ducks sporting <to> in the water near to the shore without appearing to be in any wise alarmed by the noise – <on> ↑or↓ the sight of the inhabitants. I was told afterward that there is an old law <exint> existing which prevents the killing of any waterfowl on the lake within a certain distance of the town. The poor birds seem to know this priviledge and sport about within those limits without any apprehension. This is an instance how tame, wild fowl will grow when unmolested

May 12

This morning we witnessed a parade of a small body of volunteer militia belonging to Lucerne. It did not consist of more than one hundred and twenty or thirty men. Their uniform was Grey turnd up with green, blue pantaloons & green plumes in their hats – as many of them were of the best families of Lucerne, they were extremely well clad and accoutred. They went thro their manual with a correctness and precision that I have never before seen in volunteer troops. This parade

196. Probably the Gütsch.

takes place every Sunday morning and they have frequently private exercises on week days. No troops ever gave more general satisfaction by their evolutions which is not very singular when we consider that the spectators were composed of their relations & friends. <The Each> ↑Each↓ old lad<ies>y looked with fond exultation on her darling son as he boldly strutted along under his musket – and the lovesick damsel eyed him, arrayed in all the auxiliary charms of warlike accoutrements – with a secret palpitation and delight.

The square[197] where the troops paraded was crowded by the inhabitants of the town and the peasantry of the surrounding country. The latter were equipped in <?al?> their *gala* finery and displayed all the colors of the rainbow. Never perhaps was the human form more disguized or a taste for personal decoration more burlesqued than by the Swiss peasantry. They wear large stomachers plentifully decorated with glaring ribbands – long waists – several petticoats <that> of cloth that strut out as stiff as an half opened umbrella but so short that they scarsely descend below the knee and very frequently reveal the *garter!* Their hair is nicely combed and plaited in two tails that descend almost to their heels. on the very <summit> top of the head is stuck a large flat straw hat with a crown about half an inch high garnished with bunches of the <the> brightest colored ribbands. This hat stands as horizontal as a platter except when a puff of wind blows up one side or other – one hand therefore of the wearer must be constantly employed in guarding the arrangement and equilibrium of this favorite but troublesome piece of finery.

There is a great equanimity in the dispositions of the Swiss and a tranquility in their manners both when engaged in affairs of business & pleasure They do not appear to have the extravagant vivacity and gay flow of spirits of the french, nor the warm passions and sentimental gravity of the italians <Their seriousness> neither <have they the> is their seriousness the effect of sluggishness of idea or mercenary calculations as with the dutch – or of the proud reserve of the german or Englishman. It is the result of calm reflection, of a mind naturally strong and accustomed to think for itself. They partake in the amusements of the moment with great cheerfulness but are not liable to be hurried away by them into the commission of any folly or excess. To a stranger they are easy of access open in their manners remarkably frank and candid in their conversation and independent in their observations.

197. Probably the Schwanen-Platz, the chief square.

A frenchman is apt to turn everything into a jest or bon *mot* – An italian always agrees to the truth of what you say resigning his real opinion out of politeness – An Englishman hears you with impatience when you contradict him, and opposes you with positiveness and obstinacy – The Swiss on the contrary listens to you with attention – weighs the justice of your remarks and the truth of your arguments and makes his reply accordingly with manly politeness and freedom. The innate honesty of the Swiss renders him unsuspicious of others and he enters into conversation with a stranger and expresses to him his opinion without any hesitation – This we have repeatedly had occasion to remark <since> in our short sojourn in this country.

We walked out of town this afternoon to see <the> a number of the citizens shoot at a mark. They had excellent rifle guns of a large bore with triggers formed of a piece of wire and so delicately set as to go off on the slightest touch. With these they fired at arms length and we saw them frequently put a bullet in a small mark at the distance of *two hundred yards.* Here we fell into conversation with a Swiss gentleman who had all that polite sociability I have above mentioned. He informed us that the Swiss marksmen are extremely sure with those rifle peices killing a man with the greatest ease at the distance of three and four hundred yards. Armed with these and posted in the awful defiles of their native mountains they are really formidable – The history of Switzerland abounds with instances of scanty handsfulls of Swiss withstanding powerful armies of their enemies. This gentleman seemed to take a delight in recounting the martial deeds of his country men <among others he told of us of> and of the resolute struggles of the democratic cantons in defence of their liberties. He likewise informed us that there had been a desperate engagement between the french & austrians in the tremenduous pass of the Devils Bridge in which the former were defeated – He mentiond in strong terms the present poverty of Switzerland – stripped repeatedly by the french – "However" said he, "we must do them the justice to say they robbed us in a very civil manner." ["]There are two ways to plunder a man – the one with grossness & barbaraty – the other with politeness and good humour – the french adopted the latter and plunderd us <wi>very genteely *with their hats in their hands*!" He also mentioned that the plan of General Pfeiffer had been of injury to his country – as the french <were able to aq> acquired a complete knowledge of the paths and defiles of the mountains from it. I expressed my surprize that a nation so jealous of its liberties as the Swiss should have permitted in the first instance so particular a plan to be made of their mountains which were in a manner their bulwarks & strongholds, a general might as well permit a plan to be taken of <the> an important fortress committed to his charge – He did not make any satisfactory answer to this. He mentioned to us of several small lakes on the tops of the mountains that were frozen nearly all the year yet abounded in fish – We asked them how the fishes did to subsist in such a frozen place – "<oh [*two words erased*]> ↑Ma foi↓!" said he. "*ces gens la* sont accoutomé au froid . . *comme nous autres* –["][198] We laughed heartily at the whimsical mention of the fish which reminded us of a french postillion who in <an>a violent fit of swearing at his horse was at a loss for a name bad enough for him and exclaimed – sacre – sacre – sacre *poisson*![199]

On parting with this gentleman he made us a very friendly offer of his services to shew us the <city> ↑town↓ and accompany us to those spots in the neighborhood that commanded the finest prospects, but as we had resolved to part tomorrow morning from Lucerne we were unable to profit by his politeness.

May 13

It was our intention to have performed the journey <to>from <Z>Lucerne to Zurich <pa> by the way of Kussnacht and the lake of Zug in which case we should have *went* ↑gone↓[200] part of the way by water & part on foot. In consequence of this arrangement we sent our trunks to our Banker to be forwarded to Basle <and waited all yesterday> Rainy weather detained us however, all yesterday <and becoming fear> and seeing this morning that threatening clouds still hung about the horison; we changed our minds hired a carriage and sending for our Trunks, set off by land.

The face of this part of Switzerland is of a character totally opposite <th> to that which distinguishes it in the parts thro which we had passed. The stupenduous Mountain crowned with snow and <fif> lifting its bleak head into the clouds – its rugged sides broken <with>

198. "My faith, . . . these fellows are accustomed to cold . . . like the rest of us." Cabell recorded the same remark by the Swiss in his Journal [No. 7], "Rome Winter of 1805," May 12, 1805.

199. "Cursed, cursed, cursed *fish*."

200. "went" is underlined and "gone" is written in pencil.

into impending rocks and fearful precipices down which roared the foaming torrent – the dreary vallies & defiles strewed with <the> immense ruins of the over hanging cliffs – resounding with rivers that swelld by the mountain torrents thunderd <thro their rocky channels> along their rocky beds in repeated falls & cataracts – These sublime features that mark the Alpine parts of Switzerland had abruptly ceased and given place to others of the gentle tranquil kind. The eye now wandered over vallies of luxurient fertility. Covered with flowery meadows, waving fields of wheat, orchards in full bloom & groves of the richest foliage neat white cottages enlivened the scenery and the lively waters of the Reuss, winding thro the centre of the valley often half concealed by overhanging woods and glistening thro their branches, gave animation to the whole. The valleys were surrounded <g> by gentle undulating hills highly cultivated and often clothed with groves & woods of the oak the beech the pine & the fir whose varied & contrasting foliage had a rich & picturesque appearance. The country was universally blooming under the genial influence of spring and the notes of a thousand birds resounded on every side. The mind participated in the striking change of scenery – and the enthusiasm and awe inspired by the sublime horrors of the Alps, here subsided into tranquil delight & placid admiration

The peasantry are <well> decently and comfortably clad and there is an appearance of neatness and comfort in their houses – their countenances beam with honesty & contentment.

The road passed sometimes <?at?> thro lovely vallies at other times along the sides of hills that commanded extensive prospects – and several times thro small woods of pine beech & oak. The country is laid out in small fields enclosed sometimes with hedges but more frequently with wooden fences similar to our post & rail fences in America – indeed the face of the country often reminded me of American scenery – perhaps owing in some degree to the frequency of wooden <?cottages?> farm houses & barns. The generality of the bridges that I have seen in Switzerland are of wood, coverd with roofs and wooden sides with windows & open spaces to give light – This precaution <preserves> keeps the bridge dry and prevents its decaying so soon as it otherwise would.

About two oclock we stopped at the village of [*blank*][201] This is the

201. Presumably Horgen.

first village in the canton of Zurich – <Here we quit the country of> Here we first entered into <the> a protestant country – the <Lutheran> ↑reformed↓ doctrine being universal in this canton. The village church, neat & plain offerd a striking contrast to the ostentatious splendors of those churches we had hitherto been accustomed to behold. We here regaled ourselves with a repast of bread & milk. The milk in this country of luxurient pasturage, is uncommonly rich & delicious. At this village we had[202] to take two horses more to our carriage to assist in drawing it up some high hills in the neighborhood – The afternoon was very rainy. <which was> In the evening we came in sight of the lake of Zurich and the town situated on its borders surrounded by lovely scenery. The obscurity of the weather prevented our enjoying this delightful prospect to advantage – We continued riding for some distance along the brow of a high hill catching frequent views of the magnificent scene below us till at length we descended into the valley and about dusk arrived at our inn. We had some difficulty in procuring an appartment as the <in>[203] Inn was crowded, however after a short parley they accomodated us with a large handsome chamber that over hangs the lake and commands a superb prospect.

The country thro which we passd <presented> is fertile in grain wine, wood & pasturage According to Coxe "the proportion of grain to the other productions of the earth will appear from the following calculation – there are 217.424 acres laid out in grain, 14.466 in vines 94.553 in meadows 42.549 in pasturage and 103.772 in forest. Sufficient corn is not produced in the canton for its own consumption – the deficiency is supplied from Suabia It consumes the greatest part of its own wine The canton contained in 1784 – 174.572 souls at least 2/3 of the inhabitants derive their livelihood by spinning thread & silk & making linen for the manufactures of the town of Zurich vide Cox. Vol I Let. VIII[204]

To prevent a scarcity of Bread a public granary is established by the government and in seasons of scarcity it is sold at a more reasonable rate than in the market. It may be questiond whether these public granaries which form a species of Monopoly, are truly equitable & politic.

202. At this point in the manuscript the word "In" appears as if Irving had intended to start a new paragraph but had changed his mind and continued with the paragraph he had already begun.

203. "Inn" is in pencil.

204. This paragraph is a close paraphrase of Coxe, *Travels in Switzerland,* I, 67–68.

In a time of scarcity when the price of provisions and consequently of every thing else rises, it is hard upon the farmer that his produce should be undersold and himself be obliged to vend his grain at the common price when the different necessaries that he stands in need of have encreased perhaps double in their price. <do not such> Do not such circumstances tend to discourage the cultivation of Grain? The rights and interests of the farmer should ever be among the first objects of governmental protection – On <g>agriculture such <a nation> a country <of> as Switzerland cheifly depends.

May 15

Rainy weather confined us to the house for the most part of yesterday but to day the clouds <ar>have broken away and the weather is fair & warm. This is <said ?here?> said to be an extremely late rainy spring – the face of the country, however, is beautiful and every thing seems to be in a state of great forwardness.

Zurich is situated at the <?le?> extremity of the Lake and seems almost to be built in the waters. The Lake here empties itself by the river Limmat, which runs in a broad transparent stream thro the centre of the town. Several wooden bridges are thrown across it supported on strong stone piers capable of withstanding the force & rapidity of the river.

In the environs are several delightful public walks shaded by stately trees – One is on the top of the ramparts[205] commanding an extensive view of the Lake and its enchanting shores – Another is laid out in a beautiful lawn at the place where the Limmat is joined by the Sihl[206] – The union of these waters is singular – The Limmat is pure & transparent, the Sihl turbid and muddy – both are in rapid in their courses, yet after their junction they <hurry> ↑flow swiftly↓ along for three leagues before their waters <unite> mingle with each other. In <an>one of the public walks ↑just at the junction of the above rivers↓ is erected a monument to the memory of Solomon Gessner the celebrated author of the Death of Abel and of a number of Idyls that bespeak a mind replete with pure sentiments & elegant ideas[207] He was one of the number of celebrated <pers> men that Zurich has produced. The <tow> monu-

205. Possibly Irving is referring to the Hohe Promenade, but all the ramparts of the city had promenades.

206. The Platz Promenade.

207. Salomon Gessner (1730–1788), Swiss writer, painter, and etcher, created a rococo literary vogue with his pastoral prose *Idyllen* (1756–1772) and poem *Der Tod Abels* (1758). The monument to him in the Platz Promenade was erected in 1793 by Jean François Doret.

ment is of black marble surmounted by an urn of white marble – on one side of the monument is a medallion of the head of Gessner – and below it a large square <bass> mezzo relief representing a scene from one of his idyls – both the medallion & relief are of white marble and carved at Rome by some skillful artist – on the opposite side of the monument is <?inscribed? a german> a German inscription in Gilt letters – The whole monument is simple and elegant. It is surrounded by a grove of pine and willow that diffuse a melancholy & appropriate shade.

<A Tomb is also in pre>

A monument is also preparing <for> in memory of Lavater[208] the celebrated Physiognomist, who was likewise a native of this place. The death of this amiable man has been differently related – the following was told us by an inhabitant of Zurich.[209] At the time that the French were in possession of the town an affray happened <near the house> in the street between an inhabitant and a Swiss soldier in the french service – the noise attracted the attention of Mr Lavater whose house was in the neighborhood – with that active benevolence that distinguished th<is>at estimable man he hastened to seperate the contending parties, when, without any known provocation the Swiss soldier leveled his musket and shot him thro the body. He recoverd partly from the immediate effects of this wound and was able to receive & entertain his friends with his usual aimability and spirits – but the fatal stroke was given to his constitution and after lingering about a year, he expired, exciting to the last a universal sentiment of love and admiration. His funeral was followed by an immense concourse of persons of every rank and age among whom were a great number of French officers, every one seemed anxious to pay the last sad honors to a man they loved so well; the people of Zurich still speak of him in the most affectionate terms. As an instance of his generous disposition it is mentiond that tho repeatedly urged he would never reveal the name of the man who shot him – He solely exculpated the french from the charge

208. The monument of Lavater executed in 1802/3 by Heinrich Dennecker was then in the Stadtbibliothek; it is now in the Zentralbibliothek.

209. Probably he was a Mr. Escher, brother of a naturalist to whom J. C. Cabell had a letter of introduction. Cabell's account of Lavater's death is substantially the same as Irving's. Cabell called on Lavater's son, to whom he had a letter of introduction from Henry Fuseli. See Journal [No. 7], "Rome Winter of 1805," May 14, 1805.

of having caused his death and declared that the deed was done by a Swiss but nothing could prevail upon him to expose the wretched culprit.

Zurich has little architectural beauty to boast[;] its houses are more designed for comfort than for elegance. The rooms <of the> are profusely lighted; very often the whole front of the room is almost a continued window. The cielings are extremely low. They have few fire places. The rooms are generally warmed by immense stoves of earthen ware or porcelaine – The mouths of these open into another room where they put in the wood and it requires a brisk fire and some time to heat them. The night that we arrived in Zurich was very cool and we were shewn into a large uncomfortable room furnished with a stove of this kind – We ordered a fire to be made in it which was immediately done – but was so slow in heating the stove that after we had been above two hours in the room & supped C—— found it so cold that he had to go to bed – in the night it had become warm and heated the room to such a degree that he had to throw off most of the covers & could hardly sleep. These kind of stoves must consume a great quantity of wood and it is surprizing that the Swiss do not adopt some more economical and more convenient mode.

At the town house on the side fronting the River Stimat[210] there is a mineral spring which furnishes two constant spouts of water. The water tastes slightly of sulphur, it is much used by the inhabitants to drink, and is even brought to table.

The lake furnishes very fine fish, we had <this> yesterday at dinner a piece of a trout that when alive our Landlord told us weighed twenty weight. He tells us that the salmon <in the> mount the rivers to the lakes to spawn, they do not however make any stay in the Lake of Zurich but pass directly thro it to the lake of Wallenstadt, nor are they <?even?> ever caught in the <fl> former.

In the course of our walks to day we passed by the orphan house[211] an institution deserving of the highest encomiums both for its charitable intentions and the able manner in which it is conducted. It is situated in a most healthy position on a beautiful green eminence at the foot of

210. Limmat.

211. The orphanage, the Waifenhaus, was built between 1765 and 1771; it now houses some of the municipal offices.

which flows the rapid Limat. The children are well educated fed & clothed. We saw one of them walking in front of the house; he was dressed in blue and had a very smart appearance. Besides this there "is an alms house for poor Burghers – an hospital for incurables, and a foundation for the poor which puts out children as apprentices and distributes money clothes & books to poor persons in the town & canton" vide Cox. I. Let 9.[212]

This afternoon I rambled about the delicious environs of this town. From a cottage situated on a knoll on the west side of the lake[213] I had one of the finest views possible of the surrounding scenery. At a distance below us was the lake perfectly calm – like a broad mirror reflecting the variegated prospect. The Banks rise gradually in gentle hills, enriched with meadows, clothed with orchards and flourishing woods and spotted with villages Farm houses seats & cottages. The Western bank is backed by a long bold ridge in many places almost perpendicular with rich forests clambering up its rugged sides. <To the left at the extremity of the lake in a> At a great distance the stupenduous mountains of Glaris & Schwartz reared their fantastic heads above the clouds and sublimely terminated the prospect, offering the contrast of bleak winter to the luxurient charms of spring. The rays of the declining sun slanting along the hills, gilding their tufted tops lighting up the spires of the village churches – & the white walls of the cottages and resting in bright refulgence on the snowy summits of the alps – heightned the richness of the enchanting landscape.

It was pleasing to see in the clear bosom of the lake the quivering reflections of the village steeples on the cottages that graced its borders – In another direction from this eminence I had an excellent view of the town of Zurich rising from the edge of the lake, encompassed with verdant hills & lawns and brightening in the rays of the setting sun.

212. This paragraph is a close paraphrase of Coxe, *Travels in Switzerland,* I, 83–84. The alms house was probably the Pfrundhaus St. Jakob; the hospital for incurables was the Spital; the foundation for the poor was the Almosenamt, located in the convent of the friars of St. Augustine (information furnished by the State Archivist, Zurich).

213. Presumably Irving is referring to the Katze, where a bastion was built in the seventeenth century.

[*inside back cover*]

Short is our span, then why engage
In schemes for which man's transient age
  Was ne'er by fate design'd?
Why slight the gifts of natures hand?
What wandrer from his native land
  E'er left himself behind?

The restless thought & way ward will
And discontent attend him still
  Nor quit him while he lives
At sea, care follows in the wind;
At Land, it mounts the pad behind,
  Or with the post boy drives

Altorf 10th. May.

[*back cover*]

Eliza
Eliza
Eliza[214]

214. Probably the woman of this name, apparently English, who was a fellow-passenger of Irving's on the *Remittance* from London to New York in 1806 (see "Miscellaneous Notes, 1805–1806," pages 580–82; see also a third appearance of that name in those Notes, page 562).

EUROPEAN JOURNAL, 1804–1805

Volume 4
Zurich–London

The manuscript journal is in the Manuscript Division of the New York Public Library, No. 4 in the Seligman Collection. It consists of 94 pages, written in brown ink, of a stiff vellum-covered booklet of 102 pages, measuring 8 x 6⅝ inches. Pp. [2, 12–14, 37–40] are blank. Inside the front cover appears the bookplate of Robert Hoe.

[*front cover*]
1805[1]

[*inside front cover*]
Washington Irving

[*p. [1]*]

Purchased at Zurich
Price 1½ livres

Notes
of a Tour in Europe
in 1804–5.

Vol 4th.
Containing Route from Zurich to Paris
& from Paris to London.
from May 17th. to Octr. 8th. 1805.

May 17, 1805

We left Zurich <this> ↑yesterday↓ morning between 7 & 8 oclock in a carriage which we had hired to take us to Basle.

The weather was extremely pleasant and the day clear. We rode

1. Besides this date, in brown ink like the rest of this journal, there is on the front cover, as there is on the back cover, a great deal of writing in pencil, none of which on the front cover is legible.

thro a succession of beautiful scenes of the fertile, gentle kind, richly wooded hills and luxurient valleys watered by the lively current of the Reuss; <about the middle of the> till we arrived at the town of Baden. The environs of this town are very picturesque – on a hill that overlooks it are the ruins of an old castle originally built by the Romans,[2] but it has passed thro so many hands and <stood> ↑seen↓ so many disasters that it can scarcely be said to whom the architecture may be ascribed

Baden is celebrated for its warm baths which are resorted to for the Rheumatism Gout &c Our Landlord told us that there were sometimes one thousand visitants at a time at the springs – they lodge in several hotels built in the neighborhood of the baths and there are frequently an hundred persons in a house. As at all other watering places many flock there for fashion or pleasure. They have balls very often when there is much company. We were a little surprized on being told that many take these warm baths for *nervous* complaints. The patients bathe twice a day & remain a long time in the water. We <did not remaind any> ↑stopped↓ but a few minutes at Baden and rode from thence to Brugg (or Bruk) a small town situated upon the Aar near its confluence with the Reuss and the Limmat. Finding there was a *table d'Hôte* (an ordinary) in the inn we agreed to dine <the> at it as those are excellent places to <join> encounter people of different countries & to see variety of character. A table d'hôte a packet boat & a stage coach are similar in one respect that <you> they banish all disagreeable restraint & ceremony and you may address yourself to the company and begin a conversation with any stranger you find next you without danger of being thought impertinent. The acquaintances formed in this manner are frequently the most agreeable & sincere – they are voluntary on both sides and not the reluctant connections formed in consequence of letters of introduction or other obligatory causes.

We found at the Table several Swiss of respectable appearance among whom were two or three officers. Tho a little reserved at first yet the frank sociability of the Swiss character soon predominated and we were in a few minutes on the most intimate footing. Four of the company I found, were also on the way from Zurich to Basle having set out a little before us. One of them was a fat rosy faced old Gentleman, a merchant of Geneva. His countenance expanded with good humor

2. Presumably the castle Stein zu Baden, destroyed in 1415 and again in 1712. Baden was known to the Romans as Thermae Helveticae.

and he had an archness in his eye that gave additional force to the jokes he frequently utterd. After some conversation we found him to be a warm republican and a man of sound understanding & correct principles. Another of this party was minister of a protestant village between Zurich & Schauffhousen. He appeared to be a man of great enthusiasm & sensibility and passionately fond of the fine arts. He was going to Basle to see some paintings of Holbeins & other celebrated masters[3] – Of the other two – one was an engraver of Basle[4] and the other a gentleman of Lucerne. As soon as they found out that we were americans they evinced the same curiosity concerning our country that I have generally experienced among the men of sense that I have talked with in Europe. It is flattering to an American to perceive, how rapidly his country is encreasing in importance and exciting the attention and admiration of the old world. While Europe is wasting its strength in perpetual commotions, the United States, blest with profound peace and an excellent government, is gaining daily accesses of wealth & power and rising by tranquil yet rapid degrees to take the ↑most↓ conspicuous seat among the nations.

After dinner we parted with an agreement to sup together at the place where we should put up. We had a charming view in the course of one afternoons ride – from the summit of a hill over a beautiful valley enlivened by the meandrings of the Aar. Upon the banks of that river <wh> stood the small village of Schintznach noted for its tepid mineral waters.[5] The valley was surrounded by hills coverd <by> with long tracts of finely variegated forests, and the prospect was terminated by the snowy Alps now fading in the distance.

A variety of other scenes of equal beauty presented themselves continually. The villages in this part of the country were poor and ill built – And the cross erected in different parts of the road shewed us that we were again in the regions of popish influence. Early in the evening we arrived at our inn in the small village of Stein and a little while after we were joined by the gentlemen whom we had met at dinner. Our inn was delightfully situated on the banks of the rhine just where it made a

3. The Kunstmuseum of Basel is noted for its collections of Hans Holbein the Younger and Conrad Witz.

4. Possibly he was Johann Rudolf Huber (1766–1806), etcher. Both the Huber and the Falkeisin families, members of which Irving met in Basel, were noted for their artists working in metal.

5. In this sentence Irving apparently drew on William Coxe, *Travels in Switzerland, and in the Country of the Grissons* (London, 1789), I, 135.

large bend. Higher up on the opposite banks of the river stood the larger village of Stein,[6] which together with a fine bridge that crossd the Rhine in front of it – formed picturesque objects. The eye stretched over an extensive tract of rich low country – that swelld in beautifully waving lines enriched with tufted groves and noble forests and bounded by gentle hills of the most picturesque contours. The sun set was extremely rich and diffused a mellow golden gleam over the landscape that softned the whole into the sweetest harmony. At one time the sun half shrouded among clouds shot forth slanting gleams of radiance that lighted up one part of the landscape gilding the village spires and tipping the foliage of the woods while the other parts were thrown in shade – The effect was singular and highly picturesque. It was such an evening as is frequently seen in the gentle paintings of Lorrain. I was detained on the banks of the river till long after sunset by the beauty of the scenery and was just returning to the inn when I was arrested by the sound of a vesper bell from a convent[7] <situated> belonging to the village of Stein situated – as I before mentiond – at some distance on the borders of the river. Shortly after, the nuns commenced to sing the evening service. The strain was simple and solemn – often dying away upon the ear and then swelling again in a full body of sound – every now and then I could distinguish the deep sonorous voices of the monks who assisted in the service. The river favored the conveyance of the sound, and the strains floated down the stream very clear and distinct. The nature of the music – the time the place – joined to the solemn tones of the bell that sounded at intervals all combined to produce an effect on the imagination indescribably impressive – It <is> was one of those scenes that may really be termed *romantic.* I was told afterwards that this was a convent of nuns of the best families.

At supper our company was encreased by the addition of a gentleman <who had just arrived> with his wife & sister who had just arrived – He was a young merchant of Frankfort, very polite & agreeable and the ladies were both handsome and interesting. The supper time passed away extremely pleasantly – The conversation turned on the scenery of Switzerland – the manners & the government & then on

6. The town across the Rhine from Stein is Säckingen, where there is a bridge. Possibly Irving was confused by the name of Hauerstein, on the opposite side but to the east.

7. Presumably the abbey for women at Säckingen, founded in the sixth century by St. Fridolin, abolished in 1806.

different circumstances relative to America concerning which they seemed to have much curiosity

This morning (17th) after an early breakfast we resumed our carriage. <and> Our road part of the morning lay along the banks of the Rhine. This is a noble stream of water that runs very rapidly – it is of a sea green colour. The banks are beautifully clothed with thick bushes & trees that over hang the river and frequently dip their foliage in its waves – The surrounding scenery is extremely rich & variegated. At Rheinfelden we crossed a long wooden bridge over the river which was here extremely rapid – the town the bridge and a rock on which the bridge rests – crowned with ruins – are a most picturesque combination of objects. <To> At length we came in sight of the city of Basle delightfully situated on the banks of the Rhine in the midst of a rich low country. It has a beautiful appearance from a distance – We arrived there about twelve oclock – crossing the river over a noble wooden bridge of 600 feet in lingth. The inn w[h]ere we have put up is the Three Kings – the accommodations & table excellent.

This afternoon we were to see a <g> collection of prints belonging to Messr. Falkeisen & Huber[8] who <als> deal in paintings and engravings. We were treated extremely politely – shewn a great number of Swiss & italian views and a small gallery of paintings among which were several of merit. Mr Falkeisen also promised to call upon us tomorrow morning to accompany us to the collection of Mr. Birmann[9] another artist of Basle – <at Mr Bir> at Mr F's we met Mr Rheinhardt author of the cabinet of Swiss costumes that we visited at Lucerne – He appeared to be a little man of great vivacity and passionately attached to his profession.

I was delighted to find a <great> number of Swiss families (to the amount of 150 persons) on the point of embarking <on the Rhine> for America where they intend forming a settlement. Boats are prepared that are to take them down the Rhine to Rotterdam where they will embark in a vessel for Baltimore We talked with one of the directors of the expedition a Mr. F. R. Hassler[10] of Arau who speaks English –

8. Possibly they were Theodore Falkeisin (1768–1814), copperworker, and John Friedrich Huber (1766–1832), medallion worker and stamp cutter, who went into trade in works of art in 1805.

9. Peter Birmann (1758–1844) was a landscape painter and art dealer.

10. Ferdinand Rudolph Hassler (1770–1843), Swiss geodesist and mathematician, a native of Aarau, emigrated in 1805 to the United States with his family and

appears to be a man of abilities and extremely well informed respecting our country. He told us they were not as yet exactly fixed as to the place of settlement their thoughts seem to incline either towards the back part of Virginia – the state of Kentucky or of Tenesee

May 18

We went this morning in company with Mr Falkeisen to view the collection of Mr Birmann.[11] The latter received us very politely and shewed us a very neat collection among which were – a Landscape by Lorraine taken from nature in the environs of Rome – a head by Reubens another by Holbein several peices by Breugel and several other paintings of considerable merit. Mr B also shewed us some very excellent drawings of his own from scenes in Italy & Switzerland. The obliging and agreeable manners of the proprietor <made> heightned the pleasure we experienced in <witnessing> examining his cabinet. He has had a number of his views engraved. I have continually found among the artists in Europe more sincerity and disinterested politeness than among any other class of people with whom I have been acquainted. Mr Falkeisen is an instance of this. We had called upon him, absolute strangers, with no other object than to gratify ourselves by looking at his collection; <and> We let him know that we did not intend to purchase any thing – yet he took as much trouble in shewing us the curiosities of Basle as if we had been particularly reccommended to him. He procured us an opportunity of visiting the Liberary of Basle[12]

This contains a small collections of Books among which are several editions antient and rare and consequently valuable among book worms. Among others we were shewn one of the works of Erasmus which

---

about one hundred others, intending to establish a colony in the South. They landed at Philadelphia, but finding the project entailed too many difficulties, he abandoned it there. See Florian Cajori, *The Chequered Career of Ferdinand Rudolph Hassler* (Boston, copyright 1929).

11. In 1803 Birmann's firm was liquidated. Some of the works in it went eventually to the Kunstmuseum in Basel, but none of these mentioned by Irving is there (information furnished by the Curator of the Museum).

12. The Library of the University of Basel. Among its collections was the so-called Amerbach-Kabinett (now part of the Kunstmuseum), an art collection containing chiefly paintings and drawings by the Holbeins and other Swiss and German artists of the sixteenth century. Presumably the altar piece by Holbein to which Irving refers is the so-called "Passionstaffel," a panel on which are represented eight scenes of the Passion of Christ (information furnished by the Curator, Kunstmuseum, Basel.)

he had presented to Holbein and the other had ornamented it with numerous appropriate figures drawn on the margin with a pen many of them possessing much merit. Another book was shewn us as a great curiosity – it was a common prayer book in German and we were told to find out wherein the curiosity of it consisted – We searched for some time in vain, till at length we were told by the librarian with a kind of triumph that the whole book was written with a pen but so closely in imitation of printing that the deception could not be perceived. It had employed the writer several months – <a great deal of time thrown away.>

In the liberary are several peices of Holbein who was a native of Basle – among which is his famous altar peice on wood but I was chiefly pleased with a Last supper by the same painter in which the figure of Judas is particularly conspicuous & well characterized.

In the evening we were visited by Mr. Hassler and his Wife[13] a lady of pleasing manners and genteel appearance. She seemed to look forward to her voyage with anxiety mingled with apprehension and was particular in her enquiries respecting america. She is of English extraction and speaks the language extremely well. She told me that many of the poor Swiss that are about embarking are very heavy hearted as the time approaches to depart – The people in this place & in fact most of those who stay behind represent their projected expedition in the most fearful points of view. She told me that when they were about quitting the village where they resided the street was thronged with their neighbors & acquaintances who stretched out their hands after them with their eyes streaming with tears <as if their fellow countrymen> considering them as if departing for another world full of dangers and troubles.

We had an instance of the sentiments of the common people of Basle in respect to this expedition from a smart lad of about 19 who waited upon us at table today. C asked him carelessly if he did not wish to go to America also – He replied no – that he would rather remain where he was. He said people seemed to think that money was scatterd about the fields and highways in America but they would soon find out their mistake and that they would have to work as hard as in Europe. Why said C. have not several Swiss written back from America favorable accounts of this situation – ["]Ah – replied he thats nothing – when

13. Marianne Gaillard (1772–1858), of Bern (Cajori, *The Career of Hassler,* pp. 138–39).

they write bad – government in America *open the letters & stop them* so that we may not hear anything disadvantageous of the country." What – said C. Do you think our Govt. is like your suspicious detestable governments in Europe Why should Govt. trouble itself whether the Swiss emigrate to America or no – "<Oh> Why replied the Lad – We know very well that you have wars with the indians and you want people to *assist you in carrying them on*![”]

We could not but laugh heartily at these absurdities tho we felt provoked at the authors of them who are doubtless employed by government to stop the torrent of <pop> emigration.

May 19

This morning at an early hour we departed from Basle in the Dilligence for Paris Our fellow Passengers were a French merchant of Lyons who was merely going with us as far as Belfort – and a pretty looking girl <on> going on a visit to her friends at Mullhausen. We stopped at Bourg Libre on entering france, and here the Dilligence was changed – Custom house officers attended to search our Trunks – they were very polite merely opening the trunks for form sake – a *buono mano* of course. Here we entered the Department of the *Haut Rhine* formerly *Alsace*. The country was level and cultivated with grain and very clear of woods[;] this gave it a naked appearance very uninteresting after having passd thro the bold & variegated scenes of Switzerland. As I had no prospects therefore to engage my attention I soon fell asleep – Honest John followed my example – The <french> merchant of Lyons was outside of the carriage in the cabriolet and C—— found himself seated in a manner alone aside of the pretty french girl – According to the *custom of the country*[14] he began making love to her but in the midst of his courtship I awoke. <I held my> I kept my eyes shut for some time listening to his fine speeches to which the damsel <seemed to> pretended to turn a cold ear[.] at length my disposition to laugh became so strong that I had to awake completely and interrupt one of the most amiable conversations that ever took place in a Dilligence. C—— tried in vain to induce me to sleep again We had much entertainment in conversing with the girl about Basle & Mullhausen

14. In the play of this name by John Fletcher and Philip Massinger (1619–1622), Count Clodio, the Italian governor, tries unsuccessfully to have a girl according to the "custom of the country," which allows him to spend the bridal night with every bride.

(the latter her native place)[.] in her replies there [was] a degree of simplicity & naivete that charmed us. She seemed to partake both of the Swiss & french character. About 10 oclock we arrived at Mullhausen and here we had to part with our pretty fellow passenger.

Mullhausen is a thriving industrious little town & possesses considerable manufactures particularly calicoe & painted muslins. We walked about it in company with the Lyons merchant. He conversed very much about America and its flourishing situation – the rapidity with which it was encreasing in wealth & importance – about the policy of our government to preserve peace with all nations as by that means we were daily accumulating strength & power. But he said he did not think we would be able to remain at peace – There was such a thing as *jealousy* among nations – we were <viewe> regarded with a jealous eye by European powers. "They beheld the young Eagle rising in the west and daily encreasing in vigor"[15] We told him that as long as we acted with amity & justice towards other nations, we hoped we should be able to <?resid?> remain in perfect peace – He shook his head and said there were a thousand ways of provoking a war and that the Old European powers were so well versed in them that they would never be at a loss for an excuse whenever they felt themselves in a condition to engage with us.

While I was at Dinner the Landlord (who is very wealthy) gave me the name of <a> ↑his↓ brother who had departed some years before for America and had engaged in trade with the Indians. He had written <repated pep> repeatedly to him <?fore?> for two or three years back but his letters had been returned with the information that his brother had changed his residence. He begged me if I ever rencontred his brother, to beg him to write to his friends in Europe – but at the same time he expressed his belief that his brother was ["]*killd & eaten*" by the savages. What frightful ideas some of the ignorant people in Europe have of America – They think that whoever goes there runs the narrowest risk<s> of his life either from the *yellow fever* or the *Savages.* I am convinced that these ideas are produced by the false representations of scoundrels who are employed by <goven> the governments to <?p?> discourage emigration.

In the afternoon the country was more pleasing – We had several beautiful distant views of a <finel> country finely variegated with hills & vales <?groves? and> wood & water and at a great distance we

15. Presumably the quotation is from the Lyons merchant.

saw the lofty summit of the Wetterhorn, coverd with eternal snow and tinged with a lovely rose colour. The country resounded with the notes of the skylark <?great?> ↑& we saw great↓ numbers of th<at>ese birds mounting up in the air & pouring out a strain of the richest melody. At one place we passed by where all the village was assembled on a green. The young men were <either> in groups chatting & laughing <– or engaged in a [*unrecovered*] the young girls ?th?> the girls had formed a ring and were dancing to their own songs and the old people were seated under some trees enjoying the scene in the highest degree. This <was> would have been sufficient to have convinced us (had we been ignorant of it) that we were entering in the gay country of France

In the evening we arrived at Belfort <and found> where all the world seemed to be on the move thronging the promenades. This is an old town – walled – and on a high rocky eminence that overlooks the town stands the old ciditel – the whole is very picturesque. The principal church in the town has a neat façade of the doric order.[16]

In the evening we were <?convering?> conversing again with the Lyons merchant concerning america; he was very <anxious to> inquisitive about our manners – and of course about our women. We assured him that they did not come short of the european ladies in respect to personal charms – and that they were remarkable for their affectionate fidelity to their husbands – This last eulogium produced a true Frenchmans remark – "Mon dieu" said he "*c'est un pays malheureux pour les garçons.*" "Certainement" said C—— "<if> il faut se marrier la"[17]

This day is the anniversary of my departure from America.

May 20

We parted from Belfort early in the morning The Lyons Merchant had left us and his place was supplied by a young frenchman who by his behaviour induced me to suppose that he had never been in a carriage before. He was in continual apprehension that the Dilligence would overset, and at every jolt sprung from one side to the other with the agility of a monkey. Whenever the carriage stopped at a village

16. The citadel was built by the Marquis de Vauban in the seventeenth century when he fortified the town. The church of St. Christophe was built between 1729 and 1750.

17. "Heavens, . . . that's an unhappy country for young men." "Certainly, . . . it is necessary to marry there."

he had a long story to tell the people at the inns of the many narrow risks he had run of having his neck broke. <This> We were now passing thro what was formerly called Franche Comfété, at present the department of the *Haut Saone.* The country was varied by gentle hills, but the soil appeared to be extremely poor.

We stopped to change horses at a village where several houses had been burnt down about 2 years before. The people still used this desaster as a pretext for demanding charity, and the carriage was surrounded by beggars. <They> From long practice they had reduced their petition almost to a kind of song, and as an inducement to our liberality, promised to pray for the *confirmation of our healths.* This was almost as whimsical as an old beggar who assaild us yesterday, and not having ingenuity enough to invent a speech of his own, endeavored to move our compassion by repeating the *lords prayer three times.*

We dined at the small village of Lure. The Prefet accompanied by several officers was going out a hunting and the whole village resounded with the noise of the hounds the horns & the huntsmen. We were told that the neighboring forests were infested by wolves and that they were well stocked with game. The Game laws have been <revised for these> [revised] ↑about↓ six months ago, and no one is permitted to shoot or fish without a license – the game of course has become latterly much more numerous.

At Lure we took up a frenchman and his daughter the latter a smart little child of about seven years of age, she had the manners and conversation of a woman. Her father appeared to be a man of very little information – he was however, very curious about the United States – *Were they near Asia?* I told him no – "Alors" said he "ils sont tout pre<d>s de l'afrique" – "Mon <Monsieur> pardon monsieur point de toute" – "Diable comme je me trompe – ils sont dans la voisinage d'Europe – " I had again to inform him he was mistaken – "F——tre["] replied he "est il possible – ou sont ils donc Monsieur?"[18] To put an end to his enquiries I told him they were between Africa & Europe – and with this information he seemed perfectly content. He could not however for the whole afternoon get it out of his head that we were Africans and on my noticing several objects that we passed he asked me if we

18. "Then . . . they are quite near Africa." "My <sir> pardon, sir, not at all." "The devil, how mistaken I am! They are in the neighborhood of Europe. . . . The deuce [*foutre*] . . . is it possible? Where are they then, sir?"

had the same in Africa – He demanded likewise if it was not *diablement* hot in our country, and whether we agreed pretty well with our *neighbors* the *Turks.*

The country thro which we rode in the afternoon was arid & sterile except in one place where we passed thro a fine oak forest. There were a few vineyards with very small vines – The weather was extremely warm. The peasants that passed us appeared a gay contented set almost always with a smile on their countenances.

In the evening we arrived at the neat and extensive village of *Vesoul.* The buildings were very decent, of stone – and the whole village had an extremely flourishing appearance. Here we observed the french character diffused throughout the place – all was stir and life. The shops tastily arranged – the busy occupations of the day being over the inhabitants were dressd clean and neat – seated outside of their doors, or flocking to the promenade. All this gives an air of the most pleasing gaiety to a french village. No nation seems to enjoy their hours of recreation better than the french. While about their occupations, they move with cheerfulness and allacrity – every thing is executed with dispatch dexterity and grace – the moment their work is over – they <whip> ↑put↓ on their fine clothes – powder their heads and away to the promenade all life and good humour. They are remarkable for their attention to personal cleanliness and their [there] is a propreté in the dress and appearance of the <commonest> ↑<most> most common↓ servant girl that is extremely attractive. I have seen a pretty *Grisette* who had put on her short gown and petticoat – her red apron and large cap in so *piquante* a manner as to attract the attention from a belle decorated in all the finery of the last fashion. None can equal the french women for displaying what charms they have, to the greatest advantage – it seems to be their chief study.

In the church we saw a tolerable groupe representing the death of our Saviour – in Terra cotta – The façade of the church <was> ↑is↓ neat. There is a handsome promenade in the neighborhood[19]

May 21

Left Vesoul at 3 'OClock in the morning – The frenchman and his daughter had left the dilligence and we had in his place an old musician

19. Presumably Irving refers to the sixteenth-century polychrome group of the dead Christ and several saints in the chapel of the Saint Sépulchre in the church of St. Georges, built in the seventeenth century. The Allées Neuves, northeast of the city, were laid out between 1770 and 1775.

of Besançon. The country was <low &> level & uninteresting – the soil arid and sterile – Such scenery is particularly fatiguing after coming out of the rich and varied cantons of Switzerland. The weather was extremely warm and we passed a most uncomfortable morning This was heightned by the bad arrangement of the dilligence in respect to meal times – We had eat no breakfast and rode till near two oclock before the dilligence stopped for us to dine. The place where we stopped was the small & miserable village of *Combeau fontaine* and the inn reminded us of the cheerless *albergo's* of Italy. The dinner was such as might be expected We were however cheerd with a bottle of Burgundy that soon put us into good humour with every thing around us, and before we departed, we cordially agreed that tho the dinner was villainous, yet it was as good as the people could furnish, and tho the house was wretched and dirty, yet the hostess was a mighty civil good sort of an old lady. This town <was> is situated in what was formerly calld Burgundy – and we passd thro a corner of that province. After dinner we sat out, quite fresh. We soon entered into the District of the *Haute marne* formerly part of Champaine. The old musician had been in a small *cabaret* (inferior kind of tavern) in the village and regaled himself with a cheerful glass, he was quite merry & talkative and afforded us high amusement. His remarks were odd & laughable and he appeard by no means defficient in understanding and shrewdness. By his looks he seemed to be rather fond of his bottle, which opinion was confirmed by his subsequent conversation. He said he had once entertained thoughts of going to america with several of his fellow countrymen of the same craft as himself but *le diablement long voyage par mer*[20] had always deterrd him – Est ce que vous craignez le mer donc said I – "Ma foi oui monsieur" – "vous n'etes pas donc <un> fils de Neptune" – Au contraire monsieur, je suis <*un des*> *fils de Bacchus*! ["][21] – We laughed heartily at this honest avowal. He lamented exceedingly the war said he had fine times formerly at Geneva when there were generally a number of English there. He loved the English – they were *des bonnes enfants* who loved *horses women & wine* and scatterd their money about *si jolliment* – *Then* he had plenty of custom – but at present one must go on ones knees in france to gain a miserable crown. Provisions, to be sure, were cheap enough, but money

20. "The devilish long voyage by sea."

21. "Are you then afraid of the sea?" "My faith, yes, sir." "You are not then a son of Neptune?" "On the contrary, sir, I am one of the sons of Bacchus!"

was extremely scarce. He gave us a number of entertaining annecdotes about Besançon his native town, from some of which it appeard that the ladies of that place were not the most virtuous in the world. The Marshall of the District was importuned to build a hospital to contain such unfortunate women as were diseased – "In that case," said the marshall "we may as well <b> erect a wall that shall encompass *the whole city*." While we were talking a procession of peasant women passed by headed by a priest bearing a cross and praying. This was intended, to induce *le bon dieu* not to rain on their land. The old musician regarded the procession with the utmost contempt <– ma> "Regardez la" – said he "ma foi on doit etre bête comme les francois pour faire un sottise comme ça"[22] The old fellow seemed to be quite loose in his religious sentiments; he told us of some dry arguments he had had with the *curé* of their village – in one of which he demanded why our saviour had not sent his deciples among the savages in America – the priest was mute – ["]Ah je sçai pour quoi monsieur le curé –" said old orpheus "il sçavoit bien que le diable avait besoin <pour> ↑de↓[23] quelques gens <a> pour nettoyer sa cuisine et il lui lessait ces malhereuse sauvages la."[24]

In the evening we arrived at Langre[25] which is handsomely situated on a hill enjoying an extensive prospect. This is said to be the highest town in france. Four rivers take their rise near it – viz the Saone, the Seine, the Meuse and the Marne. The houses are built of good stone and the town has a flourishing appearance – it possesses manufactories of cutlery. As soon as we entered the inn we were addressed by a smart young barber who with all the politeness of a frenchman craved *the honor* of shaving us We declined his services, but he persisted in his solicitations so earnestly yet politely that I at length told him that after I had returned from taking a walk, he should shave me. He stepped back a couple of paces with an affectation of the highest surprize – "Mon cher monsieur comme vous vous trompez – toujours faitez le barb primierment et *alors* pour la promenade" ("My dear sir how you are mistaken – always shave *first* – and *then* for <the> a walk – " In short we found he had always a reason or argument at hand so that we were

22. "Look there . . . . My faith, one must be a fool like the French to do a foolish thing like that."

23. "de" is in lighter ink.

24. "Ah, I know why, sir priest . . . . He well knew that the devil had need for a few folk to clean his kitchen and he left the unhappy savages for him there!"

25. Langres is situated on a plateau rising to 1550 feet.

at last obliged to set down and let him shave us, telling him that we only did it, to have the pleasure of being shaved by a master of the art – "Certainement messieurs" said he with a gay bow of acknowledgement "ça fait une difference voyez vous."[26] I have often remarked this peculiar faculty of persuasion and insinuation that prevails among the french artists & trades people – their gaiety and goodhumour, free from all impertinence continually engages you to employ them or to purchase their articles of merchandize.

At the Table d'hote where we supped we found several frenchmen & one Swiss. The conversation turned on America, our flattering prospects – our peace and tranquility &c One of the frenchmen with many sagacious nods & knowing looks said he knew very well what were the politics of America – that we were deeper than people were generally aware of – that we were all peace and friendship at present but were only waiting to become more strong, when we intended to drive all the *europeans out of America!* He was well convinced of this – he had long observed the course of politics – He had been a subscriber to a *paris paper* for some years (that any person should pretend to discover american politics from a french gazette – the most contemptible of all publications). The rest of the country [company] opposed him with warmth – For us we did not take the pains to combat such absurd assertions – What strange Ignorance prevails in Europe with respect to the United States – P.S. The inn was very good

May 22

We departed at our usual hour this morning, and had to ride a long distance, to Chaumont, before we could get any coffee. This is the most miserable, uninteresting journey that I have made in france – The country level, arid and unpleasing to the eye – the road dusty & hilly and it is but here and there in particular villages that the traveller can meet with comfortable refreshments. We had nine horses to the dilligence this morning on account of the uneveness of the road, and even then the clumsy vehicle moved at a very slow rate. We encounterd two or three processions of peasants bearing crosses & chanting – France seems to be rapidly resuming its former superstitions. Chaumont is an old town surrounded by venerable walls that are of no use at present. Five rows of trees were planted around it which give it a very handsome appearance. We took coffee here at an indifferent inn and it re-

26. "Certainly, gentlemen . . . that makes a difference, you see."

quired some time and several demands & directions before we could get all our breakfast arranged. They did not understand the *mystery of* bread & butter with coffee as the french eat nothing with it but dry bread. The servant girl began to loose patience and look sour. <I ha [*illegible*]> I had learnt, however, the way to deal with the french, "Ah mon dieu" said I "quel malheur pour une *jolie fille* d'etre si sombre" the compliment immediately produced a smile "Voila donc" cried C—— "comme ses *beaux yeux* eclairent!"[27] The girl immediately became all gaiety & goodhumour and waited upon us the whole of our breakfast with the greatest cheerfulness. How easy is any little pique or ill-humour of the french appeased – their resentments never endure for any length of time. A pretty speech, a well timed joke or *bon mot* or a neatly turned compliment delights them and they resume their gaiety & good humour in a moment.

The country thro which we passed the remainder of the day was the same as that I have already described – red, arid & <unf> uninteresting. Sewed with oats, rye and a little wheat but no vineyards That part of Champaine that produces the famous wine lay a great distance to the <sou>North. In the afternoon we stopped at a small village and had a most delicious draught of milk. <This is a beverage highly refreshing to the traveller, cooling and nourishing>. In the course of our days ride we had crossed several times the River Aube – a handsome stream of water. In the evening we arrived at the village of *Bar sur Aube* and put up at an indifferent inn.

The environs of this village are very pleasant possessing a fine promenade shaded with majestic Elms. There is hardly a town or village in france that has not its public *promenade.* An evenings walk seems to be absolutely necessary to the frenchman, and he always likes to see a numerous company around him. For this reason he prefers a walk in the neighborhood of the town where there [is] a throng of company tho at the same time he is almost choaked with dust – To a solitary ramble thro *silent groves* or *peaceful vales.* In the former instance he <draws> enjoys at the same time his love of *motion* and his love of *bustle and show;* but in the latter he would be left to draw his amusement from himself and his own reflections, – which is not his *forte.*

We have remarked the great number of beautiful children that we have seen on this route – the towns and villages seem to swarm with

27. "O heavens, . . . what a pity for a pretty girl to be so sad. See there now, how those beautiful eyes shine!"

them, and the rising generation has a most promising appearance. They are healthy, active and handsome. This is one of the beneficial effects ascribed by many to the revolution. <The people fared better> The land being devided among the people, instead of being monopolized by individuals, was better cultivated. The people consequently became more prosperous, fared better, had more to eat, and (a natural consequence) begat more children. It has been an observation of long standing among natural philosophers, that the circumstances of the parents have generally an influence on the looks of their children. When they are oppressd, wretched, starving in a manner, their offspring are commonly ill favourd & Squalid but when the mind and bodies of the parents are easy & comfortable their children generally speaking are healthy and handsome. There are bounds to every rule – and this certainly does not always apply to the children of such wealthy persons as have consulted their appetites rather than their health and whose bodies have been ennervated by luxury and indulgence – extremes commonly approach each other and the children of the wealthy and luxurient <more frequently> are often as far from the standard of beauty as those of the indigent and wretched.

At the Table d'hôte this evening among several other frenchmen, was a young officer. He took the lead in the conversation and was the foremost man in the company – this behaviour I have generally observed <among y> from ↑young↓ officers of the army under this military government. They feel their power and importance – and bluster and swear and strut about the hotels to the admiration of the Landlord and the *garçons.* Their stories are most generally concerning themselves and told with a self sufficient air truly *Gascon.* This young fellow gave us a variety of annecdotes concerning himself some of which were told with humor and were not deficient in amusement. It appears to me however, that, in talking the design of a frenchman is not so much to entertain others as to amuse himself. <The> He is satisfying what in him may almost be termed *an appetite* – An englishman is naturally taciturn, talking seems to be a labor to him and he will seldom take the trouble to bestow it on any person unnecesssarily for whom he has not some kind of esteem or affection – otherwise it is sheer necessity that forces him to open his mouth – he wishes to acquire information – and he knows that he must in a manner purchase it by exchanging his own ideas for those of others. A frenchman on the contrary delights to talk – he cares very little whether you give him any ideas either valuable or amusing in return; he is pleased with his own remarks and laughs at his own jokes & witticisms more heartily than he would at those of another. He commonly opens his mouth the moment an idea imperfectly presents itself and before <he has> it is well develloped to himself – the idea forms itself as he forms his sentence. The french have a vivacity of imagination a quickness of thought that frequently dazzles & delights – but they do not generally appear to reflect deeply. It is very rare to see a frenchman so absorbed in thought as to be abstracted from every thing around him – his eye fixed on a particular spot, <and> rapt up in that *absence* so common among the english & americans – They remark this in strangers immediately – and frequently when in company with french I have fallen into one of these kind of reveries – they have tapped me on the shoulder rallied me on my gravity and told me that I ought to be <fl>*toujours gaie* – <"Par bliu> "Par bleu" said an old frenchman one day "comme ces anglaises sont pensives – ils pensent et ils pensent – mais ils ne <jamais> disent <de> ↑jamais à↓ ce qu'ils pensent" ("s' blood how thoughtful these english are – they think – and they think – but they never tell what they think about)

May 23

We were awakened this morning at about half past one o'clock, with the intelligence that the dilligence was ready to start. We had slept but about a couple of hours <and those> ↑which↓ did but serve to tantalize us. Such, however, are the inconveniences that attend travelling in a french dilligence. The travellers comfort is the least article of consideration To add to our disagreeables – the weather had changed remarkably in the night and was quite cold. Some time after day break we stopped in a small village and took coffee – here our company was reinforced by a frenchman of Troyes who appeared to be very intelligent and gave us considerable information concerning the country. He told us that tho the land was apparently poor and sterile yet it produced very well. The crops to be sure were not so abundant as in other parts of France but, then, they never fail – the land also is more easily worked.

I have remarked in those parts of france thro which I have travelled that there are very few farm houses in the country – there are, however, many more at present than before the revolution – the land is as I before mentiond, more in the hands of the common people. The peasants most commonly live in the villages & towns. In this part of France there are <f> very few hedges or other boundaries to the farms. The country is very bare of trees in consequence of the universal use of it for fuel. The country notwithstanding abounds in some places with coal but the french have an inveterate prejudice against it. We were also told that <govt> government imposes discouraging constraints on the use of it.

Immediately after the revolution the property of the deceased parent was divided equally among his children – but within 18 months this law has been altered and the parent is allowed to give some of his children *double* the portion of the others. The Game laws have been latterly revived and game begins to encrease – We saw pa<r>tridges repeatedly feeding very tranquilly in the adjacent fields.

The peasants live on Bread wine, salt pork, milk garden stuff and sometimes fowls &c[.] they eat three times aday generally – but at particular seasons four times. They live <in g> very well and have generally plenty to eat. The country this morning presented some pleasing scenes. The Seine wandering among groves and verdant fields – with sometimes a village on its banks. <The> Waving fields of rye – oats and wheat – and thriving orchards. Th<e>is part of the country produces abundance of fine fruit.

About the middle of the day we arrived at Troyes an old town containing about 30,000 inhabitants. It is ill built ugly and irregular. The houses commonly of frame work filled up with brick plaister & rubbish The cathederal and other churches are in the Gothic style.[28] We entered the town with a prodigious noise, the postillions cracking their whips incessantly according to custom – what the use or meaning of this custom is I have not ↑yet↓ learnt Moore <humouros> humorously and perhaps justly ascribes it to that *love of racket which every frenchman sucks in with his mothers milk.*[29] The french – certainly appear to enjoy themselves most when in the midst of noise *clatter & hubbub.*

At Troyes we experienced a degree of insolence from the hostess of

28. The church of St. Pierre et St. Paul was begun in 1208 and finished in 1638. The other most notable gothic church in Troyes is St. Urbain, built between 1262 and 1286; most of the others are late Gothic.

29. John Moore, *A View of Society and Manners in France, Switzerland, and Germany* (London, 1780), II, 30–31. Irving purchased a copy of this work in Milan on April 30, 1805 for 10 livres (see the expense account in the "Traveling Notes, 1804–1805" for this date).

the hotel [*blank*] that I have never witnessed before in the good humoured country of France.

As the dilligence was to stop in the town for about two hours we asked at the hotel to be shewn to the sitting room. I orderd a bouillon for myself Cabell not having an appetite would not take any thing – he was fatigued and unwell and there being a couple of beds in the room he threw himself on one of them to take a little repose. He had hardly lain down ten minutes before the landlady – a young woman – happening to come to the door saw him and immediately flew into a violent passion. It appeared that these were beds merely placed there for show and she considerd it a heenious crime for a person who had not *calld for any thing* to tumble one of her beds of state. She snatchd the pillow from under poor C——s head before he was well awake and began abusing him with the utmost volubility. He immediately quit the house with expressions of the utmost comtempt – as soon as I had finished my *bouillon* I paid for it and then threw down three or four livres for the use of the bed telling her she had dearly earned them by her insolence – she coulord up very highly and began to apologize, saying that had she have concieved "that monsieur was *un homme comme il faut*["] – [30] but I cut her short telling her it was her duty to be civil to travellers of every discription – that we were not accustomed to see such brutality and meanness among the french but that from her behaviour I did not believe she was *of that nation* –" This last remark seemd to touch her pride as I expected it would – but I did not wait to hear any apologies or remonstrances.

At Troyes we took up two more passengers a man & woman. The latter had a little ugly pug dog which she was continually carressing and talking to in the most affectionate manner. These insignificant little whelps are great favorites with the french ladies – and they pet them and feed them up with delicacies as if they were children – what a contemptible figure does one of these <littl> contemptible useless little animals make <along side> ↑aside↓ of a large noble mastiff an animal whose services & fidelity render him deserving of favor. It is with disgust I see a fine woman wasting her time and lavishing her caresses on an ugly little cur, when perhaps many a worthy fellow of spirit & talents may <sue &> languish in vain for a smile.

Some of the scenery thro which we passed <this> ↑in the↓ after-

30. "A man of gentility."

noon had a pleasing appearance. The fields looked verdant and refreshing – the Seine stealing thro beautiful groves and its silver waves glistening thro their branches had a lively & picturesque effect.

In the latter part of the afternoon we began to ride on the *Pavé* – this name is given in france to paved roads of which there are a great number that diverge from Paris in every direction like rays from a centre. As far as the pavement extends the roads are bordered by fine elms which give a grateful shade to the traveller at the same time that they are amusing to the eye.

In the evening we stopped at an inn in the village of *Nagent sur S<a>eine* where we partook of an excellent supper and found the old landlady particularly attentive and civil. After supper we resumed our seats in the dilligence being doomed to ride all night a measure always observed by the Dilligence the night before they arrive at Paris. Much to my comfort however – the old frenchwoman and her little whelp had quit the carriage. The night was cold and windy and I anticipated a night of sufferance – happily however I soon fell asleep and did not awake again till morning. An old lady in the carriage kept watch the whole night being in great <24th.>[31] apprehensions of Robbers because she reccollected the story of a robbery and murder that had been committed on that road *before the revolution.*

May 24

Shortly after day break we took a comfortable dish of coffee at Nanges and returned to the carriage. The country became more interesting – The handsome seats and chateaus <shew> evinced our approach to the capital. The Dilligence stopped at the Post house of Grosbois about *eleven* oclock for us *to dine* but we were so impatient to get to paris that we merely took a *bouillon.* In the neighborhood we were shewn the chateau formerly belonging to Genl. Moreau[32] in which he was arrested, the building being invested at night by 200

31. "24th." appears to have been written first on the page about here and then the sentence written over it as if Irving had changed his mind about the length of the entry for the twenty-third.

32. Jean Victor Marie Moreau (1783–1813), French general, defeated the Austrians at Hohenlinden in 1800. Having fallen out with Napoleon over personal matters, he became implicated in the 1803 conspiracy against Napoleon. He was arrested in 1804 at the seventeenth-century Chateau de Gros-Bois, tried, and exiled for life.

soldiers – The Edifice is old fashiond and built of brick, its surrounding domains are extensive & delightful. Moreau was obliged to sell this property to defray the expences of his LawSuit. A frenchman our fellow traveller, eulogized the general very highly – he said he was beloved by all france even by the *Emperor himself!!*

After riding for some distance further we at length came in sight of *Paris* the *Seat of Empire,* and, as some frenchmen modestly say, the *Modern Mistress of the World.*

The distant view of Paris is very fine – situated in a beautiful and extensive valley or rather plain enlivened by the wandring Seine. To us it was a most interesting sight – and like mariners after a long voyage we haild with joy our haven of repose. We entered by the Fauxbourg St. Antoine and were soon in the midst of noise bustle and confusion.

[*A leaf has been removed from the journal at this point and four blank pages intervene between the entry for May 24 and the next, that for September 22, 1805. The notes Irving kept from May 24 through June 19, 1805, are interpolated here so that the sequence of his activities may be preserved.*

This manuscript is in the Berg Collection of the New York Public Library. It consists of 5 leaves (9 pages) measuring 4½ × 7 inches, written in black ink (now faded to brown), apparently torn out of a blankbook. Page [10] is blank.][33]

May 24

Arrived in Paris this afternoon <?at?> Extortionate charge at Diligence office for our Trunks [*blank*] livres for bringing three Small Trunks from Basle. Clerk attempted to cheat us out of 18 livres – N.B. Our old conductor had whisperd to him "ils sont deux messieurs qui voyagent avec leur Domestique"[34] this occasiond an immediate rise in the price, Cabell overhead the old rogue – Put up at Hotel de Richelieu Rue de la loi.[35] After dinner rencontre Maxwell in the street was surprized to see him – he was very sociable. & goodhumoured[.]

33. A few Paris addresses and French phrases appear in the "Traveling Notes, 1804," and "Miscellaneous Notes, 1805–1806"; see pp. 459, 511–13, 564, 585–86.

34. "They are two gentlemen who are traveling with their servant."

35. Now the Rue de Richelieu.

told me how he & Wells had come on from Naples in the military courier having left their old carriage at Naples – the old machine cost them 80 crowns from Rome to Naples C & myself made the same Journey for 12 crowns[36] – They had been only 15 days coming from Rome – eating in the carriage and travelling several nights successively

We walked together on the Boulevards – Full of company gaily dressd[.] from thence we went to the Palais royal[37] Met there Mr Wells & a Mr Gibbs[38] an American gentleman of handsome property & a mineralogist.

The garden was throngd with the frail nymphs that wander about it. One of them joind us & we had a long walk & talk with her. a very pretty little girl with a peculiar archness of countenance her conversation was lively and even witty and her manners easy and exceedingly polite – What singular beings these french women are!

May 25

This morning calld on Messrs Rougemont & Scherer[39] my bankers – disappointed at finding no letters there from my friends. Rougemont a mighty busy important polite little fellow. Had a levee of Taylors. shirt makers – bootmakers &c to rig me out *a la mode de Paris* – John Josse Vandermoere[40] prime minister – Mr Wells & Mr Maxwell calld on me and left their cards this morning. Singular conduct of these young men – When in Rome the[y][41] never returned a visit we made

36. Apparently a crown was worth about 83¢ according to Irving's expense accounts. He paid $10 for a seat in the voiture from Naples to Rome (see his expense account, March 24–27, 1805, "Traveling Notes, 1804–1805").

37. The palace proper, built by Jacques Lemercier (1629–1634) for Cardinal Richelieu, was until the Revolution the residence of the royal family; most of it was altered or rebuilt in the nineteenth century. The name also designates the buildings, galleries, and gardens surrounding it; in the early nineteenth century these areas contained shops, eating places, a theater, and gambling tables.

38. George Gibbs (1776–1833) was a Rhode Island merchant and a patron of science.

39. "Rougemont" was also called "Rougemont de Lowenberg" (William Lee, *A Yankee Jeffersonian*, ed. Mary Lee Mann, Cambridge, Mass., 1958, pp. 69, 98). A few years later he and Sherer separated (*Almanac de 25,000 Adresses de Paris, pour l'Année 1817,* Paris, 1817).

40. He was the Belgian servant who had been traveling with Irving and J. C. Cabell since they left Rome (see entry of April 14, 1805).

41. The incomplete words in this paragraph and the next are the result of torn places in the manuscript.

them and we never saw each other except in accidental rencontres in the street &c Mr Cabell & Col Mercer also calld – they are both lodged at Mr McClures.[42] Col M. was obliged to perform a Quarantine of 30 days at Marseilles passing from Napl[es] having been boarded by an english privat[eer.] I had forwarned him at Naples of the necess[ity] of performing quarantine at Marseilles <My> Dined at a small Table d'Hote kept in the Hotel [–] its more like a family din[ner] My Landlord sits down at table with hi[s] sister an old lady – and his neice & cous[in] two pretty girls and very agreable –

Old Lady has an old cat with a fami[ly] of Kittens of whom she is extremely fo[nd] – kisses them and makes as much of the[m] as if they were her children – Fre[nch] women remarkably fond of domestic animals

In the evening went to the Theatre Montansier[43] in the Palais Royal. This is a little theatre much frequented by the frail fair ones – Acting humorous & rather gross. Scenery tolerable – house crowded. After theatre took a stroll in the garden of Palais Royal – Accosted by a *fille de Joi* who begged me to purchase a bo↑u↓quet[44] for her – I saw it was a meer scheme of the poor girls to get a few sous to buy herself some bread for the next day <she having had no custom that night>[45] – it was evident she & the old woman who sold boquets acted in concert. I pitied her and paid double price for the bo↑u↓quet.[46] The poor creature kissd me thankd me a dozen times & wanted me to go home with her

My head is as yet completely confused with the noise & bustle of paris –

42. William Maclure (1763–1840), Scotch geologist who became a naturalized American, was in France to settle spoliation claims. At this time he lived at Rue des Brodeurs, No. 20 (J. C. Cabell, Journal [No. 8], "Paris – Winter – 1805–6," [p. 11]). Irving expressed admiration for Maclure in his letter to William Irving, May 31, 1805.

43. The theater in the Palais Royal was named for the celebrated directress Marguerite Brunet (1730–1820), called La Montansier, who acquired it in 1790 and enlarged it the next year. For a description of the productions, see Claude François Xavier Mercier, *Manuel du Voyageur a Paris* (Paris, 1801), p. 61. The play produced on May 25, 1805, was *Tout de Monde a Tort* (Charles Beaumont Wicks, comp., *The Parisian Stage . . . Part I, 1800–1815,* University of Alabama, 1950, p. 72).

44. "u" is in pencil.

45. The cancelation is in pencil.

46. "u" is in pencil.

May 28

Mr Cabell calld on me <and> this morning. Accompanied him to Mr McClures to whom I was introduced – found there Col Mercer & ↑was↓ overjoyd to find a number of [A]merican[47] newspapers. Mercer <?C?> joked me about my going to Theatre Montansier before any of the other theatres – it being the most disreputable theatre in the city Told him I had caught paris by the Tail. Mr Mc Clure lives in <Rue des ?Bour?> Rue des Brodeurs[48] – the other side of the paris – cross the [*blank*][49] bridge to go there Superb view up & down the Seine from this bridge – iron bridge – pont neuf (or *new bridge* tho one of the *oldest* in paris)[50] other remarkable places that I saw. Palace of Tuileries. Garden of D[itt]o Place concord[,] Boulevards[,] Louvre[51] &c[.] dined at Mr McClures – observations at dinner – Mr McC said he had observed that there was as it were a line running from [*two half lines blank*] like the line of vine countries and that all to the south were generally catholic & to the north Protestants. Mr Cabell has no opinion of southern climates – thinks the further we go south the more abject & degraded we find the people – a remark that I have found true as far as my experience extends. The greatest improvements in arts & sciences originate in northern countries.

Elective govts. most calculated to render nation great – France owes

47. This word and the four incomplete words in the next paragraph are the result of torn places in the manuscript.

48. Now Rue Vaneau.

49. Probably the Pont Royal, built between 1685 and 1689, the most direct route from Irving's hotel to Maclure's residence.

50. The iron bridge was presumably the Pont des Arts, just completed, for foot passengers only. The Pont Neuf was begun in 1578 and finished under Henry IV.

51. The palace of the Tuileries was begun in 1564 for Catherine de Medicis by Philibert Delorme, continued by several architects through the seventeenth century. It was burned during the Revolution. The garden of the Tuileries, laid out by André Le Nôtre in 1684, was a fashionable promenade until the Revolution and is maintained by the government as a public garden. The Place de la Concorde was laid out by Louis XV; it received its present name in 1795. The boulevards of Paris, forming roughly three circles round the city, consist of the Boulevards Interieurs, around the old town; the Boulevards Éxterieurs, which formed the limits of the city to 1860; and the Boulevards d'Enceinte, around the old fortifications. The Louvre, originally a fortress built about 1204 by Philip Augustus, was rebuilt as a Renaissance palace by Francis I and succeeding monarchs and finished in the nineteenth century. It first housed an art collection when the Musée de la République was opened there in 1793.

her power t[o *blank*][52] years of elective government in which time the men of abilities rose to the top & managed affairs – <Those> It is the number of those men that still rem[ain] in office that gives the french govt. its present vigor. Crowned heads make a most contemptible appearance[.] at present Bonaparte is the most brilliant and rea[lly] intelligent – next to him is the Emperor of Rus[sia] who is assisted by able counsellors.

Mr McC thinks that wine will thrive in America – he even thinks that when labor becomes cheap and we divert our thots from grain we will even exceed Europe in the quality of our wines – The wine countries of Europe are in such a state of ignorance & superstition that they are not capable of improving the qualities of their vines by experiments as would be the case in the enlightened enterprizing country of America. Thinks that if our Fox grape had the french grape ingrafted on it it would do very well We have a winter grape likewise small and full of seed – A mode might be observed with it as is made use of in wine countries. The peasant cuts the vine close leaving but three or four sprouts[;] all the juice consequently which would go to invigorate the profusion of stem and branches is carried into the bunches of grapes and increases their size. In the evening I went to the Opera (or Imperial Academie of Musick) opera <Turkish Caravan of Cairo with the ballet of Telemachus in the island of Calypso> ↑opera Alceste ballet Acis & galatea↓[53] Musick superb Dancing exquisitely fine – one beautiful dancer in whirling round wisked up he[r] thin pettcoat very high – two old frenchmen in front of me seemed to take fire & be in an extacy at it. One kissing his fingers (*ala francais*) exclaimed Ah [*erasure*] est belle [*erasure*] est charmante.[54]

52. Presumably the person whose opinion Irving recorded was referring to the French Constitution of 1791, which provided for elections to both religious and secular offices.

53. The Académie Impériale de Musique or Académie Royale de Musique, also called the Opéra, was built in 1793. The opera Irving heard was *La Caravane du Caire* (1783), by André Ernest Modeste Grétry. The ballet was *Telemaque dans l'Île de Calypso* (1790), music by Miller, choreography by Pierre Gabriel Gardel (Theodore de Lajarte, comp., *Bibliothèque Musicale du Théâtre de l'Opéra,* Paris, 1878, I, 366–67). "Alceste" was possibly either that by Jean Baptiste Lully (1674), long a favorite in Paris, or that by Christoph Willibald Gluck (1766). *Acis et Galathée* (1805) had music by Darondeau and Gianella, choreography by F. A. Duport (*ibid.*, II, 38).

54. "[She] is beautiful, [she] is charming."

May 29

Got my protection from the Police – In the evening to the Theatre Francaise – Tragedy of the Templers – Talma – La Fond & Mademoselle <?Armand?> Georges[55] – Talma fine figure – great powers – I do not admire french style of acting.

May 30

Recd. letters from my friends Took a bath this morning at bathing house erected in a boat on the Seine – luxurient baths – french very fond of the bath – french woman very attentive to the cleanliness of their persons. purchd carricatures on English manners – of n[?o?] [*page torn*] point – french poor for caricatures.

May 31

Tended lectures on botany[56] Evening – Opera – <Alceste Cupid & psyche Acis & Galatea>. Bards[57] – music subli[me] [*page torn*] costume & scenery fine & appropriate

June 1

Dined at Grevens[58] with Maxwell – elegant restaurateur [–] 200

55. The Théâtre Français was built between 1786 and 1790 by Victor Louis; closed during the Revolution, it was revived by Napoleon in 1803. *Les Templiers* (1805) by François Juste Marie Raynouard, opened on May 14 and became a great success. Talma played the role of Marigny fils, La Fon that of Philippe le Bel, and Mlle. Georges that of Jeanne de Navarre (Herbert F. Collins, *Talma,* New York, 1964, pp. 167–69). Mlle. Anne-Aimée Armand (1774–1846) was a distinguished French singer. Marguerite-Josephine Weimer (1787–1867), known as Mlle. Georges, was a French tragedienne, one of the most famous actresses of her time.

56. The free lectures were delivered at 7 A.M. on Mondays, Fridays and Saturdays by René Louiche Desfontaines (1750–1833), French botanist (J. C. Cabell, Journal [No. 7], "Rome Winter of 1805," p. [179]). In his letter to William Irving of May 31, 1805, Irving said that he attended in order to improve his French, adding that he intended to engage a French master soon. For his notes in connection with his study of botany, see the "Miscellaneous Notes, 1805–1806," pp. 1207–16. For this study he purchased (August 21?) a "Botanical Dictionary" (STW, I, 395). Toward the end of the summer he paid for two months' tuition in French (PMI, I, 150). He recorded both these expenditures in his notebook for May 19–October 1805 (unlocated).

57. "Cupid & psyche" was probably the ballet *Psyché* (1790), music by Miller, choreography by Pierre Gardel (Lajarte, *Bibliothèque Musicale,* I, 369). "Bards" was *Ossian, ou les Bardes* (1804), music by J. F. LeSueur, words by Dercy and J. M. Deschamps (*ibid.,* II, 34–35).

58. Possibly Grévins, a Parisian family name of that time (Mercier, *Manuel du Voyageur,* p. 70).

Dishes. Went to theatre <Montansier full of Girls of pleasure> Vaudiville [–] little bourgeoises[59] – Saw Mercer there

June 2

Walking in the Garden of the Tuilleries encounterd young french officer with whom I had travelled in dilligence last summer from Bordeaux to Toulouse. He had passed all the winter at his mothers in Languedoc & had come to Paris in hopes of getting a commission to *go over to England* in the flotilla. Warm in praise of the Emperor – said the army universally loved him & would carry him even on their hands. In the evening to the opera. Ballet Cupid & Psyche Very fine tho not very superior to that at Marseilles – except some of the dancers finer.

June 4

Left Hotel de Richelieu and took room the other side of the Seine Hotel d'angleterre rue du Colombier Fauxbourg St Martin[60] at 60 Livres pr month[.] room pleasantly situated on ground floor well furnishd <with a cabinet> &c. looks out on a handsome little garden. Hotel genteel & extensive – In the neighborhood of Vanderlyn.[61]

June 5

Strolld to palais Royal to dine – took the first restaurateurs that offerd – <the> (les deux freres – two brothers) give dinners wine &c for 40 sous ahead – ps. the meats are what are left from grand restautateurs & servd up again

59. The Théâtre du Vaudeville was established in 1791 in the Rue de Chartres; forced to abandon political pieces, it developed a repertoire of small comic episodes in which an illustrious person became involved in a series of misadventures. By "little bourgeoises" Irving probably refers to one of the theater's performances.

60. This street, now Rue Jacob, is in the Faubourg St. Germain. About this time J. C. Cabell left Paris for Clermont; he returned in October after Irving had departed for London (Cabell, Journal [No. 6], "Paris to Clermont 1805").

61. John Vanderlyn (1775?–1852), American portrait and historical painter lived in Paris for several periods; in the spring of 1804 he lived at the "Hotel de Marigne [Marigny?]" (Cabell, Journal No. 3, "Trip from Montpellier to Paris Spring of 1804. From Paris through Holland," [p. 148]). In his letter to Peter Irving, July 15, 1805, Irving asked his brother to notify the American Academy of Fine Arts, for which Vanderlyn was to collect casts and other items, that his financial position was precarious. In August Vanderlyn drew Irving's portrait in crayon, for which he was paid in cash on August 12 (PMI, I, 151). Irving recorded the transaction in his notebook for May 19–October 1805 (unlocated). The portrait is now in the possession of Miss Jane VanWart, Rottingdean, Sussex. An engraving of the drawing is reproduced as the frontispiece of this volume.

June 6

<Went> dined with Vanderlyn at a Swiss restaurateur in Louvre – cheap [–] in evening went to little theatre of Jeunes Artistes[62] – <po> garden des Capuchins [–] boys acting plays – sing the fine airs that are produced at <fo> the great theatres.

June 7

Dined with Carter[63] at restaurater [–] 3 livre 5 sous –

June 8[64]

Went with Vanderlyn to theatre of Port St Martin[65] – built in 30 days in time of revolution [–] intended for an opera – Superb theater.

June 9

Theatre Vaudeville – pretty little theatre

June 10

Theatre de gaiety – acted an oriental piece called the Pied de Nez – (↑the↓ noze a foot long)[66] – – Good scenery & machinery

June 11

Theatre Vaudiville

June 13

Went to a 15 sous ball in Palais Royal with Vanderlyn – crowded with filles de joies.

62. The Théâtre des Jeunes Artistes, in the Boulevard St. Martin, was opened in 1795; its title came from the fact that it had two troups of adolescent and child actors. Irving may have been confusing it with the Théâtre des Jeunes Comédiens (see entry of June 16, 1805).

63. Probably he was the Carter whom J. C. Cabell knew in Paris, living at this time at Rue du Théâtre Français No 6 (Cabell, Journal [No. 7], "Rome Winter of 1805," [p. 195]; Journal [No. 8], "Paris – Winter – 1805 – 6," [p. 20]). He may have been a William Carter of Virginia who later owned a sketch by John Vanderlyn of the garden of his house in Rome (William Dunlap, *History of the Rise and Progress of the Arts of Design in the United States,* New York, 1834, II, 35).

64. An "8" in another hand appears before Irving's "8."

65. The Théâtre de la Port Saint Martin, in the Boulevard St. Martin, was built by Nicolas Lenoir in 1781 in 56 days for the production of opera.

66. The Théâtre de la Gaité, in the Boulevard du Temple, originated in 1759. The play was *Felime et Tangut, ou le Pied de Nez,* by P. Villiers and H. Pessey ([Paul Lacroix], *Bibliotheque Dramatique de feu M. de Soleinne,* Paris, 1843–1845, III, 220).

June 14

Dined at Beauvilliers[67] for about 10 livres – Superb restaurateurs – in evening went to Opera Saw Oedipe and <Tel> Achelle[68]

June 15

Theatre Montansier

June 16

Theatre Jeunes Comediens – garden des Capuchins[69]

June 17

Theatre Montansier

June 18

Theatre de la imperatrice[70]

June 19

Theatre des jeunes Artists. Boulevard [–] good scenery and machines

[*The journal entries begin again with the following entry for September* 22.]

September 22

After <two> four months residence in Paris[71] I left it this morning in the Dilligence for Bruxelles in company with Mr Thomas Massie of Virginia and Mr John Gorham[72] of Boston. We sat off about half after

67. Located in the Rue de la Loi, it had the reputation at this time of being the best of the Paris restaurants (see, for example, Francis W. Blagdon, *Paris as It Was and It Is,* London, 1803, in which the menu is printed on pp. 444–52).

68. Presumably *Œdipe* by Voltaire, one of the operas for which Talma was famous, and the ballet *Achille à Scyros* (1804), music by M. L. C. Z. S. Cherubini, choreography by Pierre Gardel (Lajarte, *Bibliotheque Musicale,* II, 36).

69. The Théâtre des Jeunes Comédiens was opened in 1805 on the Boulevard des Capuchins; its performers were students who played comedy, vaudeville, and comic opera.

70. Built in 1782 by Charles de Wailly and J. M. Peyre in the form of a classical temple on the Place de l'Odeon, it was first known as Théâtre Français.

71. On September 20, two days before he left, Irving recorded in his notebook, May 19–October 1805 (unlocated): "Paid for ten dinners, Hotel d'Avrance, 50 livres" (quoted in PMI, I, 151).

72. Thomas Massie (1783–1864), physician and politician of Virginia, was studying in Europe in 1805 (*Encyclopedia of Virginia Biography,* New York, 1915,

five in the morning. At day break the weather was quite over cast and we anticipated bad weather as it was about the time for the Equinox. It however turned <t> out to be a very favorable day for travelling

Early in the morning we passed thro the plain of Montmorency and saw to our right the little village of that name – <the> celebrated for having been the favorite residence of Rousseau[73] It is situated in a small valley formed by the gentle inclinations of surrounding hills and the <village> is beautifully embowered in trees. <Here were the delightful haunts of that celebrated author where he composed those works that were to delight astonish & instruct mankind.>

About half after nine we stopped at a mean inn in the little village of Louvres where we partook of a miserable breakfast renderd doubly insufferable from having just quitted the luxuries of Paris. Our <com> fellow passengers consisted of two fat old ladies another somewhat younger but nearly equal in size and two young men of Geneva who were going to Embden. After leaving Louvres we continued riding thro a country level and not very interesting excepting here and there a tufted knoll of beautiful trees or a village peeping thro fine groves afforded a pleasing diversity in the landscape. The country about here is chiefly cultivated with grain – the harvest was scarcely gathered owing to the unusual coolness & backwardness of the Summer. At a little village where we stopped to change horses the carriage door was surrounded by the girls of the village with plates of peaches grapes &c[;] as several of them were very pretty we could not refuse to purchase some of their merchandize altho the price was dear enough. We dined at the town of *Pont Ste Maxence* so-called from the fine stone bridge over the <seine> ↑Aisne↓[74] which it possesses.

Here we had a dinner plentiful enough but vilely cooked; grease seemed to be the grand ingredient in the sauces. This was but cheerless fare to palates spoiled by the cooks of Paris; luckily however, we had keen appetites and did ample justice to the greazy dishes of our host.

II, 201). John Gorham (d. 1829) received a B.A. from Harvard in 1801 and a B.M. from Harvard Medical School in 1804; he was in Europe from 1804 for several years, part of the time studying in Edinburgh. A letter by Gorham to Leverett Salstonstall, dated London, October 22, 1805, describes his journey from Paris to London but does not mention his traveling companions (Massachusetts Historical Society).

73. Rousseau lived in Montmorency from April 1756 to the winter of 1757/58; here he wrote *Julie, ou la Nouvelle Héloise.*

74. The bridge was built between 1774 and 1785 by Jean Rodolphe Perronet.

It is the custom of the dilligence (the reason of which I cannot learn) to <ride> travel all the last night in going to Paris and the first night on quitting it. Our fate therefore was to <sl> pass this night in the carriage For myself, I felt perfectly contented having secured a snug corner, but my unfortunate fellow traveller Massie was continually bewailing his fate being placed between the two fat old Ladies – <where he> Old Falstaffs smothering in the basket of dirty clothes was <an> enviable compared to his – He declared he was *"melting hot – hissing hot."*[75] At one oclock at night we stopped to *sup* at the little village of *Roye.* We were ushered in to a miserable inn and sat down to a supper that might have served as a counterpart to our dinner excepting that the table was scanty as well as indifferent. <An> A poullet that I suppose had figured on the table for a longer space of time than ever it did in the farm yard, a tureen of villainous soup maigre – and two or three sour tarts made up the show. To console us however we found that the two fat old ladies were to quit the dilligence here to the great relief of Massie, who diclared he should otherwise have been melted to a mere shadow before morning. Having paid three livres each for our wretched supper & sulky attendance we resumed our seats in the dilligence and continued travelling all night.

September 23[76]

The morning was <very> charming – the landscape gentle and rich – long <sloping and> sloping lawns & beautifully waving swells tufted with noble groves and strips of wood land – The slanting beams of the rising sun stealing over the broad scenery – forming fine masses of light & shade and brightening up the spires of village churches <half> embowerd among the trees. The air was pure & salubrious, and the weather peculiarly agreeable for travelling. About nine oclock we arrived at *Peronne La pucelle* (the maiden) so called from its having never been taken tho several times besieged particularly by the Austrians in the time of Louis 14 and by the revolutionists during the french revolution. Its walls and gate bear the marks of innumerable shot. The town has a very picturesque appearance on approaching it

75. Falstaff said he was "glowing hot . . . hissing hot" when thrown into the Thames in the basket of dirty linen in which he had escaped from Mistress Ford's husband (Shakespeare, *The Merry Wives of Windsor,* III, v).

76. There is no break in the manuscript at this point except for a parenthetical "23d."

It is completely surrounded by water & morasses and the old walls and towers are shrowded with trees. We stopped at a kind of caffé to breakfast and while it was preparing Massie & myself took a walk about the town. It is <an ugly> a dull looking ugly built place the houses old and dirty. From the walls we had a very fine prospect of the surrounding country. The walls are of Brick and do not appear capable of withstanding a long siege – Nature however has done more than art towards rendering this place impregnable [–] it is as I before observed surrounded with water and the inhabitants can <indu> inundate the neighborhood whenever they choose –

We returned to our caffé where we partook of a very good breakfast served up with cheerfulness and attention. An old woman servant was boasting to us of the dignity of the town which she said well deserved the name of Maiden having never yielded either to force or stratigem, but the honest old Soul was quite vexed when we told her that from what we saw of the Maiden ↑town↓ <she> ↑it↓ was too ugly & old to merit any great pains and we supposed the beseigers were of the same opinion – The old woman seemd quite concerned for the honor of her native place.

Leaving Peronne we rode thro the same kind of country – level but pleasing – like most parts of france the fields are not divided by either hedges or ditches and I cannot concieve how the people avoid encroaching upon each others land – Such an arrangement would occasion perpetual law suits in America. There are no farm houses to be seen in france[;] the peasantry always reside in villages where the houses are as crowded together, as high, as dirty, and the streets as narrow and filthy as in the mean parts of their cities. They go out to their fields at regular times of the year either to plow – to sow or reap and <after> between those times perhaps they do not visit them atall. What a difference between them and the American farmers whose pride & delight is to be continually watching the progress of their crops patroling their farms & seeing that every thing is in order. P.S. This is the department de la Somme formerly part of Picardie.[77]

At Peronne we had left the third fat woman and now we had nobody in the carriage with us but the two swiss. They were very agreeable, one of them in particular could talk tolerable good english and was a lively facetious fellow.

We passed thro two or three mean villages – some of them with mud

77. "P.S. . . . Picardie." is in a smaller hand.

walls but the better sort of Brick, all covered with thatch. They were but one story high in general – and being more scatterd than usual and surrounded with fine trees they had a more rural appearance than french villages in general.

The road from Paris to Bruxelles is paved throughout – this makes it unpleasant to the traveller from the noise & jarring of the carriage which it occasions, but it favors expedition, the road being equally good in the worst weather – the pavé is only in the center of the road – in fine weather the carriages can <ride> pass on each side of it on the ground. The pave between Paris & Bruxelles is excellent being kept in constant repair, of which indeed it is continually in need. We dined at Cambray a strongly fortified place once taken by the Duke of Marlborough[78] The town is old but *clean*[;] the latter character is common to the towns in flanders. It contains 13,000 inhabitants and manufactures Linen cambreck, lace &c but since the war <the> business has greatly diminished and the town appears solitary and lifeless. We dined at the *Hotel du grand Canard* where we had a bad dinner tho' they had plenty of excellent provisions in the house – The passangers in the dilligence, however, are badly treated in france.

I do not reccollect in any part of france thro which I have travelled, to have been so much importuned by beggars as on this road The carriage door was surrounded by them whenever we stopped – This notwithstanding is one of the most fertile parts of France. In the Evening we arrived at Valenciennes but unfortunately too late to see the fortifications which are very strong. This place was taken by the Austrians during the revolutionary war after a furious siege[79] – sixty thousand men are said to have fallen before the walls. We could percieve as we entered the town the ruins of <def> several houses that have not been repaired. The town bears strong marks of the siege also in its walls. It is a silent dull place without any business at present.

At supper a man of about thirty came and seated himself at one end of the table and began to knock & bawl for the waiter most vociferously; he then turnd round & informed us that he had just supped but had a mind to take a little wine and ran on with <conside> great volubility giving an account of himself – How he was taking the mineral waters

78. In 1711 the 1st Duke of Marlborough took Bouchain, a town in the neighborhood of Cambrai (Winston S. Churchill, *Marlborough his Life and Times*, London, 1955, II, 856).

79. On July 28, 1793.

at Aix la Chapelle and came often to see his acquaintances at Valenciennes. We hardly took any notice of him or his conversation, <except that he was> and thought him a strangely impertinent fellow – <On>After getting a bottle of wine and joking with the waiter who seemed to be a great friend of his he again addressed us and hearing <I was of> us mention New York he asked me if I was of that city. On my answering in the affirmative he demanded how Mr Daniel Ludlow[80] was – with whom he said he <was> had connections – He said he had been in America, was very intimate with General Hamilton with whom he had frequently dined – Judge Pendleton, Brockholst Livingston General Jackson &c were all his particular friends – and he had corresponded with several of them.[81] I observed that as he had been so much in America he ought to speak english very well – <but> he said he could merely <st> understand a word or two. From his manners & appearance I was induced to believe that he had figured in America in quality of *Valet de Chambre,* <to> Gorham was still more uncharitable and <th> concluded that he was a *Spy* of the police, which opinion I was inclined to adopt myself particularly as I afterwards learned that he spoke the English language very fluently. He said his name was Charles Heems. When we had done supper we rose and left him without ceremony as he had made a very unfavorable impression upon all of us.

September 24

We rose at three oclock <in the m> and continued thro the same low rich scenery that characterizes the Netherlands. We passed several places where they were cutting their hemp – the flax was already cut. The villages thro which we rode were of brick thatched – and <made> were extremely picturesque being shaded by fine groves. The houses looked clean within – the glass windows well washed and the kitchen furniture ranged on dressers was as bright as the good woman could make it. The peasantry have a healthy sturdy look; quite different from

80. Daniel Ludlow (1750–1814) was a New York merchant and banker.

81. Alexander Hamilton (1757–1804) was the first of the major generals named by John Adams in 1798 at the will of Washington (Broadus Mitchell, *Alexander Hamilton, the National Adventure,* New York, 1962, II, 423–53). Edmund Pendleton (1721–1803), Virginia jurist, was prominent in pre-revolutionary activities. Henry Brockholst Livingston (1757–1823), New York jurist, was a member of the U. S. Supreme Court from 1806 until his death. Andrew Jackson was at this time major general of the Tennessee Militia.

the peasantry of the *wine provinces*, their skin is fair their complexions fresh & their eyes blue. The dutch character begins to appear, each peasant whether at work or idle has his pipe in his mouth.

The weather was the same as on the preceding days – cool & pleasant with now & then a slight shower. We soon enterd in the department of Gemappe formerly part of the [*blank*] of Hainaut.[82] We passed by the place where was fought the famous Battle of Gemappe – where Dumorier defeated the Austrians.[83] We saw the hill from which he drove them – a few of the fortifications were still visible – sixty thousand men are said to have fallen in that battle. The country <around> in these parts is beautiful – which ever way we turned our eyes we saw villages peeping from among the groves. The soil appears to be extremely rich – fine lawns and meadows well stockd with cattle. It is that kind of scenery which is always seen in the productions of the Flemish painters.

We arrived to breakfast at Mons. This is a large <walled> town the walls of which are in a very ruinous condition.[84] As I am not however a great connoisseur in fortifications and do not contemplate them with the eye of an Engineer, an old ruind wall with crumbling towers pleases my eye more than <the> when in all the strength and regularity of perfect repair. I look chiefly with an eye to the *picturesque*. The town of Mons is extremely clean. The houses are built many of them in the Dutch fashion and the Dutch and french character, (tho so very opposite in their natures) seem to be considerably mingled in this place. The houses are very clean, built of Brick & painted. The <sp> shops are arranged with great neatness and the whole town has an air of cleanliness comfort and prosperity which I have seldom seen in any french town. The Hotel was excellent and for the first time since we left Paris we made a comfortable meal. The floor was sanded an article of cleanliness that I had never before seen in Europe[85]

After leaving the town we had a very fine view of it from about a half miles distance. The country encreases in beauty – The fields are hedged – and we begin to see farm houses of a thriving & comfortable appearance. (The first time I have seen them in Europe) Large kitchen gardens well

82. Jemappes is in the province of Hainault.

83. Charles Francois Dumouriez (1739–1823) the French general, defeated the Austrians at Jemappes on November 6, 1792.

84. Mons was fortified in the fourteenth century.

85. "The floor . . . Europe" is in a slightly smaller hand, crowded between two lines in the manuscript.

stockd with vegetables, testify that the peasantry live well – I experienced that pleasure or rather that comfortable sensation which every traveller who has any sensibility must feel – on passing thro a flourishing country where the inhabitants appear to be easy an[d] happy around him. We passed in the road two carts filld with coal each drawn by two *stout dogs* and a *horse!* <A singular>

The Scenery th<o>ro which we passed the rest of the day was much as I have described except that it seemed to grow more beautiful – long swelling hills and gentle valleys tufted with groves among which were scatterd villages & neat white cottages – The soil in many places is improved with plaister of paris – The farmers appear to take more care of their land than in old France[.] I saw many large orchards – and at a distance fine tracts of woodland. The cottages were all extremely clean – built of Brick & thatched. In one part of the road we were followd a long ways by little children singing & tumbling head over heels by way of soliciting charity[.] one of them was a very pretty little girl. I gave her a small piece of silver and the poor little creature seemed to be in raptures.

The road was borderd by noble trees as in fact it is almost the whole way from Paris We stopped to dine at a small village at a hotel called *La pomme d'or* (the golden apple) where we had a most infamous dinner. My fellow travellers were so full of their jokes upon the name of the inn & the fare it afforded that the Landlady got completely out of temper. I have remarkd that the <Digl> Dilligences of france generally put up at very inferior inns – The traveller if he wishes to dine well should always go to some other hotel in the town.

After passing by several fine country seats we arrived after dark at Brussels and put up at the Hotel de Flanders an excellent inn situated in one of the finest parts of the town

September 25

Bruxelles (or in English, Brussells) is the chief town of the department of the *Dyle* and was formerly Capitol of Brabant.[86] It contains about eighty thousand inhabitants; its manufactures are of those kinds common to the Netherlands – Linen cambreck &c and particularly Lace which is highly esteemed.

86. Brussels was the seat of the Duchy of Brabant until it was annexed by the House of Burgundy in 1430.

The upper part of Bruxelles, which is built on a hill <and is sh> is extremely beautiful. It is the residence of the Beau monde and the buildings are large & elegant built of a whitish stone that retains its color well and is peculiarly fine for building. The Hotel where we put up is situated on the *place royal*,[87] which is one of the handsomest squares that I have seen in Europe The <centertre> centre of the principal side is dignified by the noble façade of a church,[88] in the composite order. The houses that form the rest of the Square are spacious and uniform of simple and excellent architecture; several of them are hotels, the rest are the houses of individuals, but they all have the appearance of palaces. <From ↑On↓ one side of this square you are> From one side of this Square you pass by a short but noble street, into the Park.[89] Here we took a stroll this morning. It is laid out with admirable taste, and tho much smaller yet I think it superior by far <to th> even to the boasted Tuilleries of Paris. The walks are spacious well gravelled and ornamented with statues busts &c <Bet> But what I chiefly admired was, that from what ever <spot> centeral spot you turned your eyes, either a magnificent edifice or an extensive and beautiful view presented itself. In one part of the Park a little portion of ground is laid out as a place of recreation – Here there is a fine saloon for refreshments – several billiard rooms – Different kinds of amusements as swings – flying horses &c &c At the latter some ladies and Gentlemen were diverting themselves, we were very liberal in our praises of the beauty of a fine girl in the company when to our astonishment we heard them speak english, and our valet de place told us that they were some Irish emigrants who resided at Bruxelles[.] fortunately we had said nothing with which the ladies could possibly be displeased. It was delightful once more to hear my native language spoken by a pretty girl.

After amusing ourselves sufficiently in the Park we went to the *Ecole Centrale* in the antient palace of the court. Here is to be seen a <?caf?> cabinet of Physic & natural history – a Botanic Garden – a Liberary and a gallery of paintings. We only visited the Latter which contains several paintings by Vandyck – Rubens & his scholars &c and a painting by

87. The Place Royale was laid out by Barnabé Guimard in 1777.

88. St. Jacques sur Caudenberg, the church of an Augustine abbey, was rebuilt between 1776 and 1785; the portico is of the Corinthian order.

89. The Rue Royale leads from the Place Royale to the Park, which was laid out in its present form after 1774.

Raphael in his second manner, which possesses much merit, particularly the figure of two children in the bottom of the picture.[90]

We afterwards walked to the Square [*blank*] no less worthy of attention than the *place Royal* tho in a completely different style. The architecture that surrounds it is chiefly gothic – One side is occupied by the *Hotel de Ville* an immense Gothic pile with a lofty steeple; <this edifice is> <an> a fine specimen of that species of architecture Opposite to it is another large public building <of> in the same style and probably built about the same time.[91]

The lower part of Bruxelles is far inferior to that which I have already discribed – The streets where business is stirring – are muddy and as there are no side walks the foot passenger is as badly off as in paris. The houses are built very much in the dutch style and are remarkably clean – the windows well washed – the floors sanded and in the shops – the scales measures &c highly polished. <an> The lower class speak the Flemish language, but among the better educated & polite the French is universal. The Houses <are> in the lower parts are of Brick generally but painted or whitewashed so as to have a cleanly appearance. A small river which runs thro Brussels furnishes water for a canal[92] by which they have communication with Antwerp and different parts of Holland. There is a very fine view from a bridge that crosses this canal at the [*blank*] end of the town. On one side you have the little port of Bruxelles crowded with <small> canal vessels some of which are of a very respectable size, tho all of the clumsy dutch form – beyond you over look part of the city and catch a glimpse of its principal build-

90. L'Ancienne Cour was the residence of the Austrian stadtholders of the Netherlands after 1731. The paintings by Vandyke and Rubens which Irving refers to are presumably now in the Palais des Beaux Arts. The "Raphael" is presumably a copy of that artist's painting in the Louvre of the Virgin, Jesus, and St. John called "La Bella Giardiniera"; it has since been lost (information furnished by the Conservator, Musées Royale des Beaux-Arts de Belgique, Brusells).

91. The square to which Irving refers was the Grand Place, one of the best preserved medieval squares in Europe, almost entirely destroyed by the army of Louis XIV; most of its facades date from 1696–1700. The Hotel de Ville was begun in 1401 and finished in 1454; the back dates from the eighteenth century, the original having been destroyed by the French in 1695. Opposite it is the Maison du Roi or Broodhuis, formerly the seat of the government, built between 1514 and 1525.

92. The Senne feeds the Willebroek canal. Since there were several bridges across the canal at the northwest corner of the city, it does not seem possible to identify the one on which Irving stood.

ings – on the other side you have before you a long stretch of the canal and its verdant banks enrichd with walks of stately trees – and <your eye wa> you have a partial view of the rich environs of Bruxelles. After having made a tour of the finest parts of the city we returned along the ramparts to our hotel. The walls are old and of no further service excepting as they form a delightful promanade that formerly extended round the city. The french however, when they took Bruxelles,[93] demolished part of the Ramparts and cut down many of the trees. The inhabitants alarmed for their b[e]loved walkes made such representations as put a stop to their violactions [violations]. Our old *valet deplace* expatiated upon these outrages with particular earnestness. I soon found that the french were no favorites with him. He told me that they had experienced wretched times but that matters were now assuming a happier appearance. We passed one place where they were about erecting an arch in honor of the Emperor.[94]

Bruxelles has lost much of its stir and vivacity since the war. It once possessd a great number of opulent families – In fact at present the fashionable world is numerous <tho mostl ?I did?> in general they are <y> at present in the country at their seats. It still retains <that> to a great degree that Luxury & show that ever attends a court. The ladies dress very much & have handsome equipages – and the number of elegant private houses is surprizing. The women are handsome and I am told very amiable & agreeable.

One thing that should be remarked of Bruxelles is that there are no beggars to be seen in the streets – an uncommon thing in Europe! This is owing to an excellent establishment where the poor who cannot find employment else where are obliged to work, and are regularly fed & paid for their labor.[95] They work in Linens stuffs &c but generally the articles are of the coarse & common kinds, as it is not to be expected that in establishments of the kind – fine manufactures would be as carefully finished as in private manufactories.

93. In 1794.

94. It was built, presumably for the entrance of Napoleon as First Consul into Brussels July 21, 1803 at the end of l'Allée Verte, with inscriptions glorifying him; it is no longer standing (Alexander Henne and Alphonse Wauters, *Histoire de la Ville de Bruxelles,* Brussels, 1845, II, 471).

95. Presumably it was under the auspices of the board for the administration of all charitable institutions in the city (information furnished by the archivist of Brussels).

They have here also <an> the (*Grand Hospice Civil* (or) grande civil hospital)[96] where they recieve sick of every discription even from prisons. Women <who> are recieved likewise for lying in. The declarations that they make on entering the hospital are sealed up and they are put in private appartments where none but their attendants are permitted to enter. Those who would wish for accommodations superior to those generally given <h> at the hospital, may have them by paying a certain price.

In the evening we went to the Theatre,[97] where we were lucky enough to be seated near the stage. <This is a t> The theatre is tolerably large but very indifferent within <and> being badly painted. The actors are but <?fa?> tolerable. Among the actrices we were peculiarly charmed with the figure and countinance of a young woman whom I think the handsomest that I have seen on any french stage. The <h> audience was very scanty and reminded me of the <th> empty houses I have often seen at the New York Theatre.

September 26

This morning I rode out with Mr Gorham to view the Chateau Lacken[98] which is <pripar> preparing as a country residence for the Emperor whenever he should deign to honor Brussels with his presence. The ride was charming our road lying thro a series of beautiful scenes passing by neat country seats & elegant chateaus. The chateau of the Emperor is situated on a hill commanding a wide and <beautiful> lovely prospect. The Edifice itself is large and magnificent of the <Doric> ↑Ionic↓ order and well proportiond – We were much chagrind <and> at not being able to gain admission into the interieur – It was undergoing <rep> alterations and we were told no visitors would be admitted till they were finished. <We therefore pro> This superb building was purchased during the war by a Doctor who got it from its original proprietor for an inconsiderable sum He was about pulling it down to sell the stone by which merely – he would have made a great profit, when luckily the Emperor or some of his family saw it and purchased it.

96. Established in 1783 as l'Hôpital Royal in the suppressed convent of St. Pierre by the government, it was named Grand Hospice Civil after the French took over the country in 1794 (Henne and Wauters, *Histoire de Bruxelles,* III, 431).

97. The Théâtre Royal du Parc was built in 1782.

98. The royal chateau at Laeken was built between 1782 and 1784; from 1802 to 1814 it was in the possession of Napoleon.

As we found it impossible to see the inside we proceeded farther on to a small chateau situated on a higher Eminence.[99] This is a small edifice of the Ionic order built with great purity of taste. The inside is laid out with equal elegance in the antique style – One of the chambers was painted in imitation of Gothic architecture – but the others were generally either Grecian or Egyptian

A small corridor was artfully contrived to have an appearance of considerable length[;] this was done by diminishing the heigth and breadth of the passage as it approached one end.

The view from the front <rom> rooms was Exquisite. The eye wanderd over a fine open country that surrounds Bruxelles and which presents a picture of the most luxurient fertility. <Fine> Long level lawns fringed with beautiful trees – gentle hills that extended along in waving lines – crowned with groves – and sweeping gently down into the vallies. Villages rearing their spires from among rich bowers – and in the center of the Landscape the charming city of Bruxelles <lifting> ↑with↓ its gothic towers – as if domineering over the surrounding scenery. The day tho fair & pleasant was rather hazy – This however did but serve to soften the landscape throwing a kind of transparent <viel> veil over the distant objects and enriching the long tracts of woodland with a tint of purple.

It was with great regret we quit this delightful retreat and departed from the little villa which seemed to be particularly adapted for classic retirement. It is the sweetest copy of the antique style that I have seen since I left Italy.

September 27

We left Bruxelles at ten oclock last evening in the Dilligence for Liege – intending from thence to take a boat if possible, for Maestricht. The dilligence had three seats and held nine persons – it was completely crowded and we passed a most uncomfortable night.

About nine oclock we stopped at a small town to breakfast; the inn was not of the most elegant order, but the dutch neatness and cleanliness that was observable throughout rendered us perfectly satisfied. Here we were relieved from two or three of our fellow passengers, which put us more at our ease in the dilligence. The country thro which we passed in the course of the day was not peculiarly interesting – It

99. The Chateau Belvedere was built in 1788 for the Vicomte Edouard de Walckiers; it is now a royal residence.

was low & rather uniform, tho here and there presenting a picturesque scene. It bore marks, however, of great industry and patient labour. In some fields which we passd the peasants were turning the whole surface with spades to the depth of a foot & a quarter, or half, so as to produce in a manner a new soil.

After leaving the small town of Tirlemont we saw three large mounds of earth, which one of our fellow passengers (a gentleman of Malines) informed us were the tombs of Roman generals who accompanied Cæsar in his conquest of Belgia[100] They <we>are of that kind which the roman soldiers formed by each casting his shield full of earth on the corpse of <t>h<e>is ↑p↓ General. Medals coins, sepulchral lamps &c have been found in them. We saw three or four others in the course of the day near the village of Tongres,[101] near which also were the remains of Roman fortifications <(I.e. a Roman> (supposed to have been a Roman Camp)

The peasantry of Brabant have extremely the dutch or rather German look; The french character begins completely to disappear. They are sturdily built, with an honest simple countenance – good humored & tranquil. The fat conductor of our dilligence exclaimed violently against the french, "they had spoiled all the people of Bruxelles <and> particularly the ladies, nothing but *french frippery & nonsense* was to be seen or heard, and even the <?peol? of peasantry> country people began to talk that silly language, – for his part he thought the german language much more <f mus> *fine & musical.*"

The towns thro which we rode tho not distinguishd by any fine architecture were generally very neat; the houses often but two stor<y>ies high, inhabited probably by but one family – this has a great effect in rendering them more clean, whereas in french country <houses> ↑towns↓ the houses are several stories high, crowded with families, and extremely filthy.

In the course of our ride the Malines gentleman, who appeared to be a man of information, pointed us out the spot where was fought a severe battle between the French & Austrians in the third year of the Republic, in which the Austrians were defeated.[102] A little village in the neighborhood <bear> still bears traces of the battle. The church has

100. Irving should have written "Belgica" or "Belgium."

101. The French form of Tongeren. The Roman settlement was Aduatuca Tungrorum.

102. Presumably the battle on the plain of Neerwinden, near the village of Esemael, where on March 18, 1793, the French were defeated by the Austrians.

the marks of several cannon balls in the steeple and the walls of private houses are disfigured in the same manner. What unhappy scenes have been witnessed in these low countries. <Contin> Repeatedly the seat of war between other nations, overran by armies; the unfortunate inhabitants driven from their humble cottages, their little possessions laid waste, the hard earnd produce of their industry snatchd from them without the least hopes of retribution. Families scatterd and impoverished, and obliged to fly to strangers for shelter. It is strange however, that these repeated calamities have not been able to damp the persevering industry of the peasantry. The father still goes on improving his possessions and laboriously adding to those stores which he has no certainty his children will ever enjoy.

We stopped to dine at St Rond[103] a small town built of Brick like most of the towns in the Netherlands. Unfortunately for our keen stomachs it was friday (*meagre* day) and no meat was to be had <as the> Stock fish figured the most conspicuously on the table among two or three plates of little river fish, We however prevaild upon the good landlady to broil us a chicken, tho I believe she looked upon us as infidels for making such a request.

At St Rond we with much difficulty procured us carriages to take us to Maestricht, as we found it would be making a large <turn> ↑angle↓ to go to Liege. We were joind in the proposal by the gentleman of Malines who was going to <Mastrich> Maestricht to see his relations. We were obliged to take two carriages, one for our baggage, the other for ourselves, they were a kind of cabriolets, with four seats very ill contrived and inconvenient With these we pushed on thro one of the vilest roads that I have seen in Europe – (having quit the Pavé at St Rond) The road was deep and broken and we walked a great part of the way. In spight of all our exertions we did not arrive at Maestricht till after <the> dark and were highly embarrassed at finding the gates shut. After knocking and bawling for a long time we at length obtained audience of a centinel who after long solicitation consented to let us in on our promising to give him *trink gelt.* (drink money) While he was gone to search the key an *Inspecteur des* <connuf> *contributions* arrived with some papers and an order to be admitted, the <s>centinel returnd and began to make some more difficulties about admitting us when the Inspector shewed his orders, orderd that the gate should be opened and we enterd carriages & all as his *suite.*

103. St. Trond.

September 28

We put up last evening at the Hotel du Levrier a neat inn, the table good and attendance civil and active. We were joined at Breakfast by our fellow traveller of Malines, a very worthy agreeable fellow, who joins the french gaiety and politeness to the German sincerity. We were much amused by his conversation with our Landlady, a smart handsome woman of about thirty who has already had eight children. She is a merry good humord soul and possessd of much wit & repartee. After breakfast we walked out to look at the town accompanied by our attentive fellow traveller. It is a neat, clean place, built in a mixture of the french & dutch styles and contains about 15,000 inhabitants. It has an air of industry and comfort and no beggars are to be seen in the streets. From the Bridge that crosses the Meuse there are charming views up & down the river, commanding parts of the fine adjacent country. This town has been the subject of repeated seiges and the walls bear marks of shot received in them during a seige in the time of the Revolution. After returning from our walk we took leave of our agreeable fellow traveller who was going into the country to visit his <acq> relations. We were much indebted to him for the civilities he had shewn us both in accompanying us about the town and in procuring us a carriage to take us off tomorrow. I have never yet travelled in a public carriage in Europe without meeting with some person who was attentive and polite. We then went to the prefecture to have our passports examined – here it was our misfortune to undergo the insolence of office from a German police officer who had all his national pride, joined to <the> a most di<e>spicable meaness & littleness of soul. He had desired us to be seated in the private office where he was writing when my fellow traveller Massie, from the fatigues of travelling and a natural carelessness of manners had the presumption <of> to stretch himself <in the car> without considering the august personage who was present. The narrow pride of the secretary took the alarm; he mutterd some indistinct censures to M on the impoliteness of his manners and his want of respect, and not receiving an apology (in consequence of not being understood) he begged us to retire into the outer room. My surprize at such unexpected and insolent treatment renderd me unable to express myself in french, <and> I immediately left the house returnd to our lodgings and wrote a severe letter to the secretary – My companions enterd soon after with the passports and on their advice I concluded it best to take no notice of the affair. The fellow had it in his power to embarrass us exceedingly if he should choose to do it, and I had already experienced what it is to be in the hands of the french police.

With what rapture do I look in such moments to my native country. There no petty tyrant clad in a little brief authority dares insult the stranger with impunity. The friendless traveller is not arraignd and examined at each town like an enemy and made to suffer the insults of upstart puppies. Happy country, with what rapture shall I once more breath your free & independant air.

About mid day we sat out to visit the Quarry of St Pierre.[104] This consists of vast excavations in the interior of a high hill adjacent to the city – some of which excavations are said to run the distance of two & three leagues. We were provided with two guides & torches and enterd the caverns <at a hole> at a kind of vaulted passage in the side of the hill about half a mile from the town – After pursuing the vaulted passage about 100 yards we came to where the excavations were made in the solid rock – These were in many places very lofty and wide and branching into inumerable passages so that a person not extremely well accustomed to the place would soon be lost. Accidents of the kind have happened it is said more than once. We were shewn a place where a boy (whose candle had burnt out) in wandering in the dark fell down a high precipice – it was three days before he was discovered and he died in two days after having been extracted. The stone is chiefly cut out of here during the winter, in summer the workmen are employed in the city. The stone is of that <wite> whitish kind used in building at Paris Bourdeaux &c. It is soft and easily cut at first but after being exposed some time to the air becomes harder and blackens. In one place we saw the bones of a french officer who was distroyed by a small magazine of powders having taken fire in one corner of the quarry.

The walls are covered with names of the visitors who are anxious that their names should survive their memories. Among others we saw the names of several princes – their ambition seems to have been but humble and I heartily pity them if their names are not more honorably recorded The name of the notorious *Major Semple*[105] figured in several

104. Petersburg is a hill on the outskirts of Maastricht which is honeycombed by sandstone quarries.

105. James George Semple, alias Semple-Lisle (b. 1759), English adventurer, also passed under several other names. He served in the British army in America in 1776.

parts of the caverns. Our old conductor who has galanted strangers thro these subterraneous passages for a score & half of years gave us a bit of red chalk and scraped a place for us to write our names. We did not choose to displease the old man as he seemed to consider it a thing indispensible, but not being ambitious of immortality we scribbled fictitious names and the old gentleman was highly satisfied.

In one place a branch of the caverns was filld up with rubbish[;] this our conductor told us was from the springing of a mine by the french to distroy a fort situated on the hill over head and that 600 men were killed by the explosion. After wandering for about <three q> an hour through the most intricate passages we at length emerged into the cheerful light of day[106] having <travelled> ↑walkd↓ undeground about a half a league. <On> The <fre> change on leaving the caverns was delightful – We came out of an aperture in a small hollow of the mountain – The day was clear & beautiful – below us flowed the gentle waters of the Meuse beyond an open and variegated country, and at a distance the <picturesque town> town of Maestricht brightening in the landscape. Just above us on a knoll of the mountain was an antient ruined castle[107] that was a picturesque and interesting object. What cried I is wanting here to furnish an english book maker with the subject for a romance – Here <is a ?fan?> ↑are↓ immense subteraneous passages – a skeleton & an old castle. Nothing is wanting replied Gorham but a proper hero & heroine – and as we are in a country formerly held by the Dutch they ought properly to be of that nation What say you to the beautiful Polly Van Higginbottom confined in that old tower waving her white pocket handkerchief out of the window while below the gentle yet gallant Mynheer Van Snickensnacken of Amsterdam is smoking his pipe & mounting the Meuse in a Track scuyt[108] to rescue his love from the power of the tyrannical Von Sloppenhausen."

We had a charming walk to town ↑in the course of which we passd↓ thro an old convent of monks, tho at present employed as a private house. From a balcony of this convent there is a beautiful view of the

106. Cf. "the warm precincts of the cheerful day," from Thomas Gray, "Elegy Written in a Country Churchyard" (1751), l. 87, partly quoted in the entry of January 15, 1805.

107. The castle Lichtenberg dates from the thirteenth century and has a superstructure built in the fifteenth and sixteenth centuries.

108. A treckscuyt is a covered boat for goods and passengers used on Dutch and Flemish canals.

Meuse running below, at the foot of sevral intervening green terraces – and the gentle scenery that surrounds Mæstricht.

September 29

At half after five this morning we left Maestricht in a Dilligence for Bois le duc.[109] The carriage was an awkward two wheeld machine drawn by three horses, we had agreed last evening to hire the whole of it for ten crowns, but it seems Mynheer the driver thought proper to break the engagement in order to accomodate one of his fellow townsmen. Our fellow passenger was an uncouth looking old Dutchman who was going to Amsterdam A handkerchief cramd with Bread & cheese & boild eggs – and a pipe seemed to comprise his travelling equipments. The cheese had a most powerful odour and if we might judge from the smell & blackness the pipe had decended to him from his ancestors. According to Dutch fashion he made no hesitation of smoaking in the carriage and soon envelloped us in a most villainous fog. In this manner we rode the whole morning – seated in an ill hung uneasy carriage, jolted part of the way over a broken worn out pavé and thro the most cheerless barren tract of country that I have seen in Europe – It presented nothing but a wide waste of sandy soil coverd with a scanty vegitation, but with scarcely a tree or bush throughout and no house to be seen except now and then where there happend to be a small spot of tolerable land. We stopped to dine at a little hamlet consisting of about eight or ten houses. The Inn was simple and the furniture common but very clean. The tea service – the glasses & china rangd out on the <d>chest of drawers & mantle peice, the well sanded floor, the decent clean old fashiond look of the Landlady and her dutch language reminded me forceably of some of our dutch country inns in the state of New York. We had a very comfortable & plentiful dinner and were surprized when we were told that the bill was only *three livres* for the whole.

After riding some distance further <our> we had to stop at two different custom houses as this was the frontier of France. They let us pass however without scrutiny and shortly after we enterd the line of *Holland.* The pavé instantly changed for the better and we rode the rest of the day on an excellent road. The country still continued barren and cheerless – an unprofitable waste. The people whom we saw were completely dutch – smoaking their pipes with all the tranquility &

109. The French form of 'S Hertogenbosch or 'S Bosch.

vacuum that appertains to the national character. After dark we put up at the village of Helmont – The Landlord alone speaks french <th> and it is singular & embarrassing to find myself once more among people to whom I cannot make myself understood.

September 30

We were awakened <at> <an> before day break this morning to resume our places in the carriage in order to arrive at Bois le duc in time for the Packet. The scenery was nearly as uninteresting as that of yesterday, except that we passed thro two or three neat villages and once or twice past snug country houses surrounded by hedges & wet ditches which seemed to bespeak the unsociable inhospitable dispositions of the proprietors

About eight o'clock we arrived in Bois le duc a large town, extremely clean & neat tho built in the old fashioned dutch taste.

After leaving france the dutch women (I.E. the common sort) have a most grotesque appearance. Tho nature has been niggardly enough towards them in respect to personal charms, yet they have recourse to <nature> ↑dress↓ to make <themselves> ↑their figures↓ still more uncouth, and load <their> themselves with stays & petticoats till they have no longer either "shape or comeliness."[110]

We stopped to breakfast at the Golden Lion where we were extremely well served and attended; we had hardly time to eat our breakfasts when we had to hurry off to the Packet which was about departing. We found that it was bound to Delft instead of Rotterdam, but learning that Delft was but three leagues <farther off of> distant from the Latter place we immediately embarked.

The boat was of the clumsy dutch make, but remarkably clean, <every> the sides, timber heads &c &c being all finely painted & varnished – The rudder decorated with an awkwardly carved female head bedizzind off with all the finery that a dutch imagination could conceive, and over the stern waved a long flag <of the> painted with flowers of the gaudiest colours. These boats have ↑commonly three or four↓ very neat cabins furnished with cushions and a kind of steerage forward for passengers who wish to go cheap. We found several Dutch gentlemen and ladies aboard – the <latter> ↑former↓[111] as usual *smoaking their pipes.* We were drawn along a canal by horses till we

110. Cf. ". . . he hath no form nor comeliness" (Isa. 53:2).
111. "former" is in darker ink.

entered in the Meuse,[112] when we hoisted sail and descended with fair wind & tide. The surrounding country was level and offerd nothing of the picturesque – vast meadows stocked with noble cattle extended themselves on every side. The constant humidity of the country renders the verdure of its pasturages perpetual.

In the same cabin with us, was an open worthy looking old gentleman who <talk> spoke french and was very polite in acting as our interpreter. Hearing us talk english, he thought we were of that nation. "I love the english" said the old gentleman laying his hand on his heart with peculiar warmth – "they are an honest <peopl>Nation" He said he had been very unfortunate, reduced <f> by the revolution from a state of opulence, <to> almost to penury. He had commanded a ship ↑once↓ <under the> but the <present> new government had dismissed him from command. I thought the latter circumstance seemed to touch the worthy old gentleman more than the loss of his fortune.

In the afternoon we lost our wind and the tide turning we had to stop for two hours opposite the large town of Dort. As soon as the tide made in our favor we proceeded <and> on to Delfshaven, a small town about half a league from Rotterdam Here we would gladly have landed altho it was two oclock in the morning – but we could not make the boatmen understand us. I walked up to the small quarter deck of the boat where two or three dutchmen were seated aside of the ladies. I addressd one of them <(an old> in french and asked him if <th> he would have the goodness to interpret for us to the boatman The old gentleman drew his pipe out of his mouth stared me in the face wiffd out a cloud of tobacco smoak drawld out ik canniet [kan niet] Engels[?] zeggen[113] and replac<d>ing his pipe again took no more notice of me. A young dutch beau was seated between two of the ladies – in such a situation one would think that if he had any politeness it would be shewn – he however heard me make the request – saw my embarrassment yet never made an offer of his services altho I had heard him talking french very fluently about half an hour before – how different would have been the behaviour of a frenchman in the same circumstances. As we could not get on shore we had to make ourselves contented and proceed to Delft. We soon entered the canal that leads to that town, and were again drawn by one horse. Along the banks of the Canal we saw several Dutch country seats, more remarkable for their clean *snug*

112. In Dutch, the Maas.
113. "I cannot understand English." The sentence is in pencil.

appearance than for the beauty of their architecture The trees, hedges &c were all clipped and trimd into a *regular* appearance. little tea houses were built in several places over the water edge – Here Mynheer smoaks his pipe in the afternoon and dozes over his favorite canal whose muddy sluggish waters resemble his own stagnant ideas. In one of these little pavillions <I observed amongst a variety> which was very elegantly furnished I observed a *long handled brush* hung against the wall in a most conspicuous situation. This appears to be one of the most estimated articles of a dutch housewifes furniture. We stopped at the suburbs of Delft, and finding that a Track schuyt would set off for Rotterdam in half an hour we had not time to enter the town, but <merely> hurried to an inn to breakfast. On entering I found that there was nobody could speak a word of French or English – A servant girl shewed me to a room and brought me a *pipe* that being the first thing a dutch man thinks of on entering a tavern After some difficulty I made her understand that we wanted something to eat – but the girl seemed still much astonished at my refusing a pipe.

After a hasty breakfast we embarked on board a Track scuyt for Rotterdam – These boats are long and flat – and coverd almost the whole length with a stout roof and sides. The interior is divided into two compartments – the one forward is cheap and dedicated to humble passengers. As the chamber aft was envelloped in a cloud of Tobacco smoak we preferred sitting on the roof which is flat – We returned a great <distance> part of the way by the same <?calal?> canal along which we had passed early in the morning – It is in many places higher than the surrounding country – which could be inundated at pleasure – This is the grand safeguard of Holland – and renders her almost impregnable by land. About ten oclock we arrived at Rotterdam. The first thing that strikes a stranger upon entering this town (or in fact any other place in holland) is the extreme cleanliness of the houses. Th<is>e rage for cleaning & scowring amounts almost to a folly in Holland – you are incommoded by it perpetually. We ran several risks of being drenched <fr> by servant maids who were washing windows which to all appearance were not in the least soiled or dusty. The climate and situation of holland renders this cleanliness necessary – otherwise from the humidity of the air & the dampness of the soil they would be subjected to intermittants & overrun with vermin. What originally arose from necessity has gradually become a habit and has so strongly engrafted itself in the dutch character that tho removed to a country and climate completely different, it will still prevail for several generations – We have proofs sufficient of the truth of this in America.

The canals which pass thro the principal streets of Rotterdam give great beauty to the city. <Thy> They are many of them 90 feet wide, on each side are <walks> pavements of from 20 to 30 feet wide planted with rows of noble trees which render them agreeable promenades. The communication from side to side is preserved by large draw bridges which are placed where the large streets intersect each other. By means of these canals large ships can be brought into the very centre of the town. The buildings along some of these canals are very handsome – The dutch have adopted a better taste in building and no longer erect houses with the Gable ends towards the street. There is an Elegant row along the fine Quay that fronts the River called the Bomb quay[114] – The houses are of Brick, three & four stories high and shaded with large trees.

In walking the streets you are perpetually regaled by volumes of tobacco smoke – every mouth is furnished with a pipe – even the porter that trundled along our trunks in a wheel barrow could not proceed till he had light his pipe.

October 2

A Dutch town soon becomes fatiguing to a traveller, particularly after having visited the gayer cities of Europe. There is a sameness in the houses – streets, people, manners &c that in a little time satiates curiosity. We had heard there was a dutch theatre[115] at Rotterdam and had anticipated the infinite gratification we should experience in seeing Mynheer acting the lover and dissolving in the tender excess of sentiment, or expiring in all the bathos of Tragedy – unfortunately however, the theatre was closed.

Our first care on arriving was to search for a vessel that intended parting for England – We soon found a neat packet that sails tomorrow under prussian colours clearing out *for Embden.* This is a kind of pretence tho well known to the french agent here, who participates in the profits. We have procured our passports and had them countersignd

114. The Boompjes.

115. The Schouwburg in the Coolsingel was founded in 1774 (G. van Bevn, *Geschiedkundige beschrijving der stad Rotterdam en beknopt oversigt van het hoogheemraadschap van Schieland,* Rotterdam, 1832, pt. 1, p. 185).

by the french authorities, the wind is fresh & fair so that every thing promises a fine passage. <Tomorrow>

The price in these packets is six guineas[116] a head[;] the passanger finds his own provisions.

We were much pleased at encountering today the two swiss who had been our fellow passengers from Paris to Brussels – and still more so when we found that they were to cross the channel in the same vessel.

October 3

This morning we sent our trunks aboard and put ourselves in compleat sailing trim The vessel however, was detaind for several hours for want of the written *permit* of the French General without which no vessel can leave Rotterdam. In fact he acts in direct violation of a french ordonnance in permitting vessels to pass to England, but as he gets a guinea of the passage monney of each passenger he <comprom> suffers his official honour & vigilance to slumber.

We had given up all hopes of sailing this day and had gone after dinner to take <an> a social glass of excellent old port with our consul Lawson Alexander, Esqr.[117] when we were disturbed from the first bottle by orders to repair on board. Before we could arrive at the Quay the vessel was already underway and we had to take boat & follow her some distance down the Meuse.

The packet resembles very much both in appearance and accomodation <an>a handsome Albany sloop, she is an excellent sailor, and the Captain ([*blank*]) a rough good hearted man and very active in his profession.

October 4

We came to anchor last night off Mass sluys[118] where we continued this morning till we were visited by the officers of the Guard ship &c –

116. A guinea was worth about $5.04 at this time.

117. Alexander was acting agent for the consulate at Rotterdam in 1801 and acting consul from 1802 to 1807. He was commissioned Commercial Agent there on December 21, 1803 (Despatches from U. S. Consuls, Rotterdam, 1801–07; Alexander to Secretary of State James Madison, July 1, 1807, Letters of Application and Recommendation during the Administration of Thomas Jefferson, 1801–09; Madison to Alexander, July 13, 1807, Domestic Letters, XV, Records of the Department of State, RG 59, NA).

118. Maasluis.

our passports examined, & the customary fee (or bribe) received – after which we weighed anchor about nine oclock and stood down the Meuse with a fair wind We passed [*blank*] and the Brill[119] having grounded once, about an hour on a sand bank – At length we got safely to sea and soon lost sight of the continent. We have 2<2>3 passengers aboard who are distributed in the cabin & forecastle, which latter is fitted up very neatly. They consist of English Germans Swiss & a Sicilian[120] a very good humord amusing fellow – The wind is brisk and we scud before it – The passengers for the most part sick, and groaning for a sight of Land once more.

It is amusing to see the sudden change in the behaviour of passengers going to sea[.] while in the river, the whole vessel resounded with chat & laughter Some were eating most heartily and all were in high spirits [–] as soon as we got out to see, a solemn silence reignd throughout, except now and then interrupted by the violent retchings of some unfortunate devils who were offering to Neptune over the sides of the vessel – Every one wore a long rueful phiz – and the very name of provisions was held in detestation – Massie & myself not being troubled with sea sickness felt a sharp appetite, but on producing a ham & fowls – our fellow passengers seemed to regard us as perfect cannibals.

One of the most provoking circumstances attending sea sickness, is, that tho one of the most deadly sensations in the world yet it seldom excites any sympathy – your companions rather jest and make merry at your sufferings than attempt to solace them.

October 5[121]

This morning on going up on Deck I had the first sight of *Old England* – We were opposite Margate and not above three miles from shore. The vessel had been standing off and on all night and was now coasting along with a fine wind. The sunrise was beautiful, the atmosphere pure and serene, <the> and I could scarcely believe it was the Island of smoak & fog that I saw before me –[122]

We passed the long range of Shetland hills – then the Nore opposite

119. In Dutch, Brielle.

120. Probably Giuseppe Emanuele Ortolani (see entry of October 7 and n. 124).

121. Irving misdated this entry and the next. Here he wrote "4."

122. A leaf, apparently written upon, has been removed from the notebook at this point. The words "and I . . . before me" and "We passed . . . hills" are crowded between lines of the manuscript.

to which lay a number of merchant ships & frigates, and with a pleasant breeze we proceeded gently up the Thames. On each side the country was pleasing and presented that scene of industrious cultivation that characterizes England. The fields ↑were↓ divided by hedges <and> along which were planted fine trees that varied & enrichd the landscape. Neat villages were frequently seen that had a flourishing & comfortable appearance.

The sight of English villages imparts to me a degree of pleasure that I never experienced in beholding those of France & Italy. I form to myself pictures of rural happiness – of comfort – plenty – simple manners yet a degree of social intercourse & society that <imparts> partakes in a certain measure of the manners of the cities. In french & italian villages on the contrary I saw nothing <fut> but poverty, dirt and slovenliness. The inhabitants seemed to have no idea of the elegancies of life nor of polite society. The cause of this difference may be ascribed to the custom in England of people of fashion's living on their estates – and that people of easy circumstances frequently reside in the villages and carry thither the manners of polishd society.

In the evening we arrived at Gravesend <opposite to which> and cast anchor opposite the town. Here we were visited by the officers of the custom house & alien office and were told that we must remain on board till passports arrived for us from the Alien office at London Unfortunately this is Saturday – tomorrow the offices will be shut at London so that no application can be made till monday.

The country round gravesend is gentle and rich – and at sunset the prospect was beautiful, the sky<e> would not have discredited the boasted climate of Italy and <It> the moonlight ↑evening↓ that succeeded was heavenly.

October 6[123]

We have passed this day on board tantalized with the view of the shore where we are not allowed to land. To soften our situation however – we have charming weather and having amusing company on board we contrive to pass away the time as tolerably as could be expected. <This> We have had a fine sirloin of Roast beef from shore accompanied by a few bottles of London porter, <and having> which seemed to be wonderfully well relished to several passengers from the

123. Irving wrote "5."

continent who had never before tasted these english luxuries In the evening we dispatched an Express to London to procure our passports as early tomorrow as possible.

October 7

We waited all yesterday in vain for the arrival of the Express and it was not till late at night that we gave over all expectation of him.

It is singular that the police is not better arranged in such a port as Gravesend where passengers are continually arriving from the continent. Surely the <grand> alien office at London might find some officers worthy of descretionary powers to reside at Gravesend. In france where the police is far more strict and jealous towards strangers, a <neutral person> subject of a neutral power would never be detaind several days at any port, before he procured permission to Land. Passengers from England to Holland are only detaind two or three hours. This unreasonable detention of strangers at Gravesend – so far from <resulting from> ↑proving↓ the strictness and circumspection of the English police only convinces me that it is stupidly and clumsily arranged. In whatever port a branch of the Alien office was established it ought to have officers capable of judging from the passports vouchers and declarations of strangers whither or no they were admissible in the country. Whereas the Alien office at Gravesend can do nothing without previously consulting that of London, and receiving an order from it to permit such & such persons to Land.

This morning an order arrived at ½ past Ten o'clock for the landing of all my fellow passengers excepting the Sicilian, a young prussian & myself. This <was>is singular – The same express that carried the letters of Mr Massie & Gorham carried a letter also f<or>rom Mr Ortolani (the Sicilian)[124] and one from myself to our Minister Mr Monroe to whom I was the bearer of Dispatches from our Minister in Paris.[125] In consequence they have all departed and Ortolani and myself have the cabin to ourselves. The day is overcast and hazy – and yields a specimen of the weather I am to experience throughout the winter – What a contrast to the Sweet climate of Sicily, <where I

124. Probably "Mr. Ortolani" was Giuseppe Emanuele Ortolani, a lawyer, apparently of Palermo. He was the author of, among other works, *Sur le Dernier Revolution de France* (London, 1805).

125. James Monroe was then ambassador to England. General John Armstrong (1758–1843), Revolutionary army officer, formerly a member of the U. S. Senate, and later Secretary of War, was ambassador to France at this time.

passd the bitter[?] months of last year> I look back to her <myrtle groves> "orange groves & myrtle bowers"[126] with regret.

October 8

After between three and four days of tedious delay my passport at length arrived this morning in company with one for my fellow passenger the prussian – (Mr Ortolani did not recieve any tho he had written to his minister on the subject). After having had our baggage slightly examined on board of a cutter stationd at Gravesend for the purpose we went on shore, where I found at the White hart Tavern a letter from Mr Munroe waiting for me, which explained the occasion of the delay in my passport – The rascally express whom we had sent to London had taken no further pains with my letter to our minister than to <give> put it in the post office at London, in consequence of which it did not arrive to hand till the day after. The fellow instead of returning to us with an account of his success, went to the Alien office <aft> at Gravesend got them to advance his pay of a Guinea & half, and then industriously kept himself out of our sight. In landing we had to suffer the usual impositions incident to such situations – boatmen, porters, waiters &c all put in their claims and tried to pluck as many feathers from us as possible We orderd a post chaise, and having arranged our affairs with the alien office (in regard to procuring a passport for London) we set off for the capitol as expeditiously as possible. In places <such><lik> like Gravesend where the traveller is thrown upon the mercy of tavern keepers porters &c he must expect every kind of extortion – they well know it is necessity not choice that places you in their power, and that, let them treat you as they please, in case you pass that way again you are obliged to pass thro their hands whether you will or no. I find it is generally in vain to remonstrate in such circumstances – the <trave poor traveller> unfortunate traveller cannot contend against a combination of scoundrels when he has no body to second him – I therefore endeavor to make as expeditious & honorable retreat is [as] possible – pay the scoundrels their demands, and endeavor to get out of their clutches as soon as possible. It is the duty of every person to resist imposition & roguery – it is manly – it is honorable to do so – but th<eir>ere are circumstances where resistance is vain, is impossible – The traveller when in haste to proceed – or when overcome with

126. This quotation has not been identified.

lassitude & fatigue – prefers rather to suffer in his purse than to engage in altercations that would retard him in his progress or harrass his languid spirits.

Our ride from Gravesend to London[127] (22 miles[)] was very agreeable altho the day was overcast. The country presented a smiling picture of successful industry – <of> every spot of ground was highly cultivated – The fields seperated by excellent hedges – <in wh> along which were planted fine trees that heightned the verdant appearance of the scenery – Snug farm houses flourishing villages – healthful peasantry – testified the prosperity of the inhabitants – We rode continually within sight of the Thames whose gentle stream wanderd among the most rich and gentle scenery – The road was crowded with private and public carriages – the latter surprized me by their excellence after having been accustomed to the awkward uncouth <vehicles of> Dilligences of France[128]

[*following page blank*]

October ?[129]

Though myself surrounded by haughty english thot I would repel their pride by tenfold[,] <and was> gatherd my forces within[,] stood ready for all events and was perhaps the proudest spirited fellow in London the whole afternoon – (I had expected to be delighted on finding myself in England that my heart would expand[,] my feelings all fly out to hail my kinsmen[.] quite otherwise – except during my ride from Gravesend to London I have found my heart has closed up – all the social feelings have retired within me – I look about me with distrust If I wish to know the direction of <the> a street I first examine the phisiognomy of my neighbor and when I have selected I make my enquiry with caution – like a wary fencer standing on my gard for fear of insult – In no other country have I felt any thing like this On

127. In London Irving put up first at the New York Coffee House, then at the Royal Exchange, and soon afterward took rooms at 35 Norfolk Street, in the Strand (Irving to William Irving, October 26–29, 1805).

128. A leaf has been removed from the notebook at this point.

129. This entry is in pencil and begins on the last page of the blankbook and reads upside down from back to front of the volume. The dateline has been added by the editor. Irving drew on it in his letter to William Irving, October 26–29, 1805.

arriving in paris I felt all confidence affability the gay goodhumord air of those around me – Their eternal politeness & civility put me perfectly at ease. I even delighted in making enquiries of them[,] <to hear their> witness the prettiness and pattient politeness of their replies. I felt perfectly safe from impertinence and the argus pride which is ever on the watch lest personal dignity should be <insulted> violated – Seemed to slumber during my whole stay in paris. In London I have <all my force in preparation – every> summond all my forces to their fate and under the cloak of politeness am as completely armed as ever was the mysterious hero of a tragedy. I feel like one of our savages when visiting a strange tribe. He courts their friendship tho he <distrusts their> eyes them with <cauti> distrust[;] he holds out the calumet of peace but grasps his tomahawk in the other hand ready to defend himself

These are my sensations <when I> in respect to the common intercourse with man and man[;] as to my personal safty they are quite different In england I feel myself a man – in france I was a cypher – a worm that might have been crushd <without> with impunity – where <death wou> fate would have caused no enquiry. Here the rights of individuals are so clearly ascertaind that I <can> am perfectly shelterd from oppression or worry. I no longer feel myself in the power of a dispotic government to whom the will is Law[;] I am in a country where I may make my complaint even against the poten[t]ate himself

You will wish to know my impressions[.] I have given you them as they arose[.] if <yo>they should surprize you – reccollect that I may be mistaken my taste alterd by french acting and wants habituated as is always necessary. The first scenes were between Villainy & Candor by brunton & C Kemble – They appeard to me void of fire – soul animation – moving puppets – no grace of position – their dialogue mere prosing – I feard my taste changed and vitiated by france. Mrs Siddons made her appearance and I was at peace with myself – What a wonderful woman. Her looks her voice her gestures astonishd me – She penetrated in an instant to my heart – She froze it and melted it by turns[.] a glance of her eye – A start an exclamation thrilld thro every nerve of my body – Mrs Siddons reminds me very much of her sister Mrs <Siddons> ↑Whitlock↓ [–] their figures are similar tho that of Mrs S is superior [–] their countenances even have some resembl[ance.] Mrs S has a noble voice rich full and capable of great modulation [–] her gestures & position are admirable [–] Her dialogue accent animated & powerful[130]

The great Kemble[131] – I almost fear to say it – but I am only <tel> discribing first sensations – the great Kemble miserably disappointed me. <He has a noble fervor an excellent counten> He delighted me in many instances by the judgment & correctness he displayed – but he did not reach my heart – my head approved but my heart did not suscribe to his power. His ↑?posing?↓ appeared to me completely studied & artificial – I could percieve no fault in his conception or execution of the character but I never lost sight of Kemble throughout. I may compare it to a painting by a correct painter – the picture is a true copy of nature – We behold in it truth of drawing – correctness in filling up but then the picture is hard & cold It wants warmth animation life to give it interest.

Kemble is graceful in his movements & gestures correct in his dialogue – his countenance as I before said is fine but his voice is very bad. It is shrill harsh and ↑nasal↓ <?sounds the t?> has not that rich sonorous fullness requisit to tragedy. It is deficient in the deep bass tones. We hear at best vague sounds. I had not sufft opportunity to judge. I was far off – The character was not sufficiently calculated to display his skils – At all events it is my firm opinion that one must become accustomed to Kemble in order to perceive his excellences and Ill not say another word to you about him till I have seen him several times

130. The play was presumably *The Fair Penitent* (1703) by Nicholas Rowe. By "villainy" and "candor" Irving apparently meant the villain Lothario and the hero Altamont, who appear early in the play. John Brunton (1775–1849), actor and theatrical manager, was a member of a well-known theatrical family from Norwich (W. Davenport Adams, ed., *A Dictionary of the Drama*, Philadelphia, 1904; John Parker, ed., *Who's Who in the Theatre*, 11th ed., London, 1952, p. 1549); he played the role of Altamont in the performance of *The Fair Penitent* at Covent Garden, October 22, 1805 (Playbill, Theatre Collection, Harvard College Library). Charles Kemble (1775–1854), fourth and youngest son of Roger Kemble, was noted for his talent in comedy. Sarah Kemble Siddons (1755–1831), the best-known of Roger Kemble's children and the most celebrated actress of her day, played the role of Calista. Elizabeth Kemble Whitlock (1761–1836), daughter of Roger Kemble, married the actor Charles E. Whitlock and went with him to America; after his death there she returned to the English stage.

131. John Philip Kemble (1751–1823), eldest son and second child of Roger Kemble, was best known in heroic roles.

[*back cover*]

I walked out . . . look for Lodgings . . . Norfolk & arrived . . . with the . . . who told them we were[132]

[*During the rest of his European trip Irving apparently kept only a very scanty record of his activities. He remained in London until January 17, 1806, and sailed for America from Gravesend the next day. He recorded his expenses from October 7, 1805, to January 3, 1806; the chief events of the days from January 17 to 28, 1806, on which date the vessel on which he was traveling was at the Downs, and of an undated day later in the voyage; and a few addresses and names of current plays in London. For these entries, made in the "Miscellaneous Notes, 1805–1806," see pages 564 ff.*]

132. Like the front cover, the back cover is filled with writing in pencil, of which only these few words on the back are decipherable. The words would indicate that this writing was done in England soon after Irving's arrival in October 1805.

TRAVELING NOTES, 1804

Bordeaux–Genoa

The manuscript notebook is in the Manuscript Division of the New York Public Library, No. 2 in the Seligman Collection. It consists of 157 pages written in pencil and black and brown ink of a paper-covered booklet of 186 pages, measuring 5⅝ × 3⅜ inches. Pp. [135–39, 141, 144–65, 167] are blank.

[*front cover*]
1804[1]

[*inside front cover*][2]
<August for 3 m. 1513>
from 2 August to 1 Dec. 1513

deja at times
bientot [*illegible*]
aussitot immediately at once[?]
tantot sometimes – soon
égalment equally
[*unrecovered line*]
alors then in that case
sort fate charm &c
pourvu provided[3]
chapeau bras 32 Pauls[4]
Blk silk Breeches at rome 55 pauls
Mosaics 3. – 48 Pauls
voiturino from rome to florence[5]

1. Written in black ink.
2. All writing inside the front cover is in pencil, with "August for . . . 1 Dec. 1513" across the top of the page. Possibly 1513 represents a sum in livres.
3. "deja . . . provided" is written sideways on the upper half of the page.
4. A paul ("paolo") was a small silver coin worth about ten cents.
5. Irving did not take this route: see "Route from Rome . . . ," pp. 294–96.

to Milan 10 sequins[6]
<from> 15

25.6[7]

4.4
2.10
12.2
3.3
3.7

[*p. 1*][8]

from Bordx to Toulouse	107
to Carcassona	66
to Montpellier	38.16
	211.16
to Avignon	38
5 days at Nismes	30
To Vaucluse	24
from Avignon to Marseills	73
	37<5>6.16
30 days at Marseilles	
Hotel expences	260
From Naples to Rome	23. ↑ducats↓ 62 ↑gr↓[9]
Voiturino from Rome to florence	10 sequins
12 days at florence	
to Bologna	
My total expences from <Mar> Bordeaux to Marseilles includg my stays at towns or on the road & every expence[10]	258.9 ↑Livres↓ about ↑$↓49.20

6. According to the exchange rate at this time, a sequin was worth about $2.25.
7. Presumably a total of 25 livres and 6 sous. All these figures are written upside down at the bottom of the page.
8. This page is in ink written over pencil except for "to Bologna," which is in pencil.
9. According to the exchange rate at this time, a ducat was worth about 80 cents and a grano about .8 of a cent.

[*p.* 2][11]
at Paris ↑May↓ 28 ↑to↓ June 20 591
between 1&2 hund for clothes
Lodging at 4 livs pr month
Hotel Cerutti same street

From Bordeaux to Marseilles
by land 85¾ Posts 538 miles
From ditto to Toulouse
32¼ Posts 193½ m.
From Toulouse to Bezieres
22 P. 132 miles
From Bezieres to Montpellier
9 P. 54 miles

[*p.* 3][12]

Chancellor of Bordeaux	Hair chestnut, eye brows do., Eyes Grey, nose long, mouth middling, chin large, forehead middling, face oblong. 5.7 Inches height
police at Bordx.	Hair & eye brows chestnut, eyes blue, nose middling, mouth middling chin round, forehead high, face oval.
cr. surety Marseilles	Hair chestnut, eye brows black, eyes chestnut, nose aquiline, mouth small, chin round, forehead common face oval. Hiegh<t 2> 5 feet – 2 inches 1 line ↑French measure↓
passpt. Marseilles	Hair chestnut, eye brows, dark, forehead high, eyes grey, noze large, mouth middling, face long, chin turned, height 70 centimetres
consul at Genoa	5 feet 7 or 8 inches high (Am measure) Hair chestnut, eye brows black) forehead middling eyes grey, nose rather long mouth middling chin round, visage oval figure slim

10. "113.27 ↑gr↓ " appears in faint writing at the bottom of the page. Irving may have written it on this page before the other material.

11. This page is in pencil.

12. This page is in ink. The sideheads read up and down the page in the manuscript.

August 5, 1804

Castres, Suppd tolerable in[n] Supper 3 liv, bad wine – dear <the people>

August 6

Langon[,] arrivd at 3 P M. Bad inn[,] did not take any thing – Crossd ferry. ferryman tried to make us pay – N B. the Dilligence pays all ferriage

Passd thro a town at day break, ↑(Caudrot)<St Macaire>↓[13] nobody stirring – ruind castle ↑St Macaire↓ very picturesque from the first gleams of morning & the river washing its base

La reole[,] poor inn – coffee bad 15 sous – Town formerly defended by walls & towers old look. – Ancient church Manufactory of combs & cutlery

Marmand, Church[14] turnd into a <Sta> Hay Loft – Women with handkerchiefs on their heads of a particular form Peasants with caps like Scotch Bonnets.

Tonneins[.] Manufactories of Tabac[.] purchased fruit &c[.] <spin> quilting girls fine view of Aigullon chateau &c latter partly demolished.

Indian corn, Postillions cruel to the horses. Rivers turbid from the rain, Country fresh & verdant from the same cause Men & Women Threshing out of doors. Girls retain the same dress as their grandmothers. very sociable Porte St Marie. Funeral ceremony[,] fine view from the outside of the town, road passes under the castle of [*blank*] [,] river below the road.[15]

Agen – 9 oclock[.] large town manufactures of silk & woolen – Supper & bed. 3.10[.] servant 10 s.

August 7

Croquelardit[.] Small town old church[16] with images of earthern ware Miserable inn coffee 10s Superb prospect <after> winding up the

13. "(Caudrot)" and "St. Macaire" are in ink, as is also "St. Macaire" in the next line.

14. The Chapelle des Annonciattes, called the Chapelle de la Misericorde since 1836.

15. Presumably the castle was the Chateau Clermont-Dessous, dating from the Middle Ages, above the Garonne River road.

16. Possibly St. Christophe.

hills Castle on an eminence on the right Beautiful vally with the Garonne beneath[,] peasant girls on asses Vineyards cottages chateaus villages &c Scenery from the hights grand & extensive. view of Moissac when winding down the mountain <pla> town considerable built of Brick – Towers & fortifications ruinous Singular church[17] Stores for grain

handsome cross of Gilt iron surmounted by a *cock rampant*[.] neat pedestal of carved Brick[,] ruins of a Brick bridge[,] view of the river highly picturesque – Ferry viaur R.[18] Castel Sarassin – Wine cheap Liquor 12 Sous. Plains of Languedoc Postillions 2 liv

Arrivd at Tolouse in the evening – <7>8 oclock

August 8

at Toulouse. Town Built of Brick not so handsome as Bordeaux Large cathederal[19] of Brick with high tower. Capitoul handsome[,] fine Bridge over the Garonne[,]esplenade beautiful – charming walks. Anciently a capitol of the Visigoths[.] Young french officer very polite in showing me the town[.] people speak Patois

Theatre poor[.] you go to it thro a convent. Old scenery poorly lighted –

August 9

Took passage on board a post boat on the canal of Languedoc charge for one day from Toulouse to Castelnaudrey – 12 leagues is 42 sous. A great number of passengers of all discriptions. Old woman running after the boat with cot on her shoulder Barge men joking her. The canal serpentine, the banks adornd with rows of elms & poplars – goldfinches singing continually The plain thro which the canal goes very fruitful villages castles &c Stopped to dine at an Auberge Dinner 45 sous. fine view from the canal of towns castles &c Situated on hills

The plains produce great quantity of indian corn. An Italian soldier on board who had servd at St Domingo[20] had been wounded in the right arm & was returning to his native place. Frequent locks in the

17. Probably St. Pierre, dating from the twelfth century, with a fortified belfry porch.

18. The river was actually the Tarn.

19. St. Etienne was built between the eleventh and the seventeenth centuries.

20. Probably he had served with the French troops sent by Napoleon to Saint Domingue, now Haiti, in 1802 to restore French rule.

canal. The Baggage was now & then shifted into a post boat waiting above the canal. Two very pretty french girls aboard lately from a boarding school.

The Boat large with a cabin almost its whole length. Boat drawn by horses. In the evening at <n>9 oclock arrivd at Castel naudray – small disagreeable. Inn Poor of the Gold Lion – hotel de notre dame good. 2 churches.[21]

August 10[22]

Hay driver with cockd hat & Josephs coat of divers colours – rainy w[e]ather Women up to their middles in water at the edge of the canal washing – keep a continual noise with their battons like a number of boatbuilders – great number of windmills

PS. Little Doctor in the same boat with me. Yesterday was very galant to the two french girls. Had a world of compliments to make them when they left the boat to go to their homes kept the boat waiting by his talk One of the girls was going off when he seized her by the gown She caught hold of his hat & it came off with his brutus wig[23] in it Girl threw the wig in the canal a laughable object the Dr baldheaded fishing for his wig –

This day he resumed his galantry on a young woman in the boat

Soldier aboard rec<l>ounting the circumstances of a murder lately committed. All the passengers attending to him with open mouths & ears

Canal in some places higher than the adjacent country Numbers of beggars at every auberge Beggars in france are very cunning in posting themselves wherever they thing [think] money will be changed – At the places in the theatres where you buy your ticket the moment you get your change a beggar or two stands ready with his hat to recieve the sous you get among the change Afternoon The country grows more picturesque – Mountains in the distance melting into the softest blue. The plain narrower and varied by small hills – A beautiful river wanders thro it ↑with willow banks.↓ Pass round a bluff of land on the summit of which is an old castle

21. St. Jean Baptiste dates from the third century, but has been much restored. St. Michael was built in the fourteenth century.

22. The dateline has been added by the editor. The day of the month appears at this point but there is no other break in the manuscript.

23. A wig of rough-cropped hair. The *OED* gives 1851 as the date this word first appeared in print.

Houses all built of stone which is very plenty in this part of the country.

Fields generally <div> seperated by ditches in this part of the country – The Hedges which are general in other parts of France give the country a fine verdant appearance quite opposite to the ragged look of our worm & log fences All this day <the locks have been descending> We *descended* by the <looks> locks

Young midshipman on board who had also came by the same Dilligence with <us>me from near Bordeaux. He <was la had come> ↑is lately↓ from Brest and is travelling to Toulon where he has a Brother in law. he is very curious in enquiring about America, has a high opinion of it and says he intends to visit it as soon as there is peace.

Passed by where they were building a new canal to make a circuit by the way of Carcassone & return to the main one.

The river that I mentiond above passes thro the canal & is let out into the vally the other side. Handsome Stone bridges that it passes under.

Several places to let out the superfluity of water caused by the river. Some of the Peasants dark complexioned with black hair – look considerably like indians.

The river after crossing the canal winds beautifully thro the valley on the other side Mountains in the distance very rocky – Wherever there is soil they are well cultivated No forests in this part of the country – the land completely sowd with grain &c. <few> Saw few vineyards since I left <Tolouse> Toulouse

Rain on the mountains <two> one or two miles off – A large castle on the brow of a <pre> Steep rocky highland, <half> nearly lost in the mist – Cloud seems to touch the castle

A small river passes *under* the canal. Walked along the bank & gatherd figs An old woman came up and <as>demanded money for what I had taken Shrug'd up my shoulders & said *nong tong paw.* The old woman left me cursing me for *un miserable anglois*

Arrived at Trebes in the afternoon a small town, very old Towers & walls still standing that were built by the Gauls[,] handsome bridge over a river that passes the town Convent in the valley at a distance[24]

beautiful sunset at Trebes Sun casting a yellow gleam on the old

24. On the remaining half of the manuscript page is a sketch of a bridge captioned "River near Trebes passing under the canal of Languedoc" (Figure 7).

Towers and sparkling in the river that runs thro the valley Charming sky Clouds of varied tints – delightful & pleasant. took a walk round the walls Miserable auberge very dirty troubled with fleas at night[.] high scene between the Doctor and a servant girl at supper

August 11

Beautiful morning fine highland scenery, Mountains barren, coverd with scanty herbage <fields of Buckwheat in the valley> Dined at Auberge at Dinner Met with an <Gentleman> American Gentleman & his wife of Boston who had lately come round by the way of Lyons from Paris They were going by the canal to Toulouse & from thence to Bagneres. It is impossible to describe the pleasing sensations on meeting with fellow country men so far from home & so unexpectedly. Time passed <?agr?> very agreeably at dinner. The lady was handsome and very agreeable – parted with regret A frenchman aboard is very anxious to know the reason why I am so silent. ["]Vous pensez toujour tojour – said he <may> mais vous ne parlez jamais –"[25]

Afternoon. Country more level. Beautiful appearance of the Distant Scenery. <The hills of the> Small castle on a hill in the foreground beautiful plain behind with a river winding thro it view terminated by highland of the softest tinges passed by a small town situated on the banks of the canal. Number of women washing clothes in the canal – Great scarcity of petticoats among them One petticoat seemed to have been divided among two or three of them – <P>

Olive trees began to appear

<Put up for the>

Arrivd before sun down at an auberge ↑at <D> Somail↓ where we put up for the night. Auberge poor tho very large. Took a walk with the Doctor & the midshipman in an adjoining garden. The owner of the garden was very polite took him for the landlord of the auberge & desired some grapes of him for supper he gave us several fine bunches & some excellent figs Found out afterwards that we were mistaken and that he was a private person who lived in the neighborhood.

Lovely sun set. The sun sinking behind distant hills with the mildest glory One of those beautiful evening skies common in the south of france The Hills of different tinges of blue & purple and the softest and richest <hues lights> colours in the valleys.

<Inn poor>

25. "You think always, always, . . . but you never speak."

August 12

Sat off from Someil at Day break At eight oclock left the Boat in company with the Dr & the midshipman & got two peasants to guide us to a neighboring town and shew us to a house where we might get coffee. Town[26] very old Walls ruinous – Curious gate that had formerly had a Draw bridge. the public house miserable & had nothing to give us wanderd about the streets enquiring for bread found a Baker at work in his shop & had to wait half an hour till <the brea> some bread he had just put in the oven was baked [–] grotesque looks of some of the peasant women short & thick with red petticoats and black wool hats with round crowns & enormous brims. returned to the boat & made a hearty breakfast on bread wine & Grapes <passed thro> The Boat passed thro the *Montagne percée* This is a most singular piece of workmanship. The canal is cut thro the Body of a hill of solid Rock, the passage is arched over head and is [*blank*] long and [*blank*] high.[27] The horses go over the top of the hill & the padrone & his assistant get out <and> on a narrow foot way that runs along one side of the passage – and drag the boat <after them> along. Sufficient light is admitted at each extremity to see quite plain in the interior –

Canal <passes along muc> much higher than the adjacent country and overlooks the valleys

View of Beziers from the canal at a distance very handsome The town situated on a hill that commands the plain large ancient church ↑& convent↓ particularly conspicuous. The plain beneath the town fine cultivated in vinyards & plantations of olives Wall around the town appears in good state Approach the town over a handsome bridge of several arches over a river that runs at the foot of the hill. Zig zag road up the face of the hill to one of the gates of the town. Grand prospect from the hight over the plain The valley presenting the richest assemblage of vineyards olive plantations &c &c with a fine river winding thro. High mountains in the distance[.] at the foot of the hill The river passes by in a beautiful sheet of water The bridge of stone crossing it and the suburbs of the town on the banks

The Doctor agreed with a Frenchman <for the f> to carry me & the midshipman to Montpelier in a Berlin[.] he also settled for us with the boat men for the portage of our Trunks from Toulouse. I pretended

26. Probably Mirepeisset.

27. In his journal entry of August 14, 1804, Irving gave its length as 480 feet. It is about 12½ feet high.

that I could not speak a word of French & turnd them all over to the Doctor to settle for me. <The Doctor> of course I escaped much quarrelling and as the Dr was an old traveller he saved us from imposition The Owner of the Berlin demanded 18 livres a piece to carry us to Montpelier but the Dr made him take exactly half the money.

Laughable scene between the Dr & <the> a woman who brot our Trunks on a cart from the canal & who wanted to get more than her due. The dr completely outtalked her & <when> threw down the money he thought proper to give telling her if she did not think proper to take it she might let it lie[.] he then walked away leaving the poor woman almost choked with rage & swearing that if that little man had not talked so much she would have had twice the money

The Doctor took a place in the Berlin also to go to Adge

Afternoon. Berlin old & dirty drawn by two mules instead of three as the fellow had stipulated. Went on a walk the whole way

<Beziers>

Pezenas pleasant little town[,] handsome walk outside the walls

August 13

Beautiful morning Grand view of the Mediterranean from an eminence. Smooth & tranquil. <Adge> ↑Meze↓ a small town beautifully situated on the sea side. ↑it is a↓ Fishing town. Left the little Doctor here who intended taking a fishing boat to go to Cette.[28] He has proved a most singular & amusing character Had a great quantity of talk considerable information and the art of making himself acquainted with any body in five minutes. He has a great flow of spirits & is very fond of quizzing – continually passing himself off on the peasants for a variety of characters. Sometimes a German sometimes a Swede now a Turk and <for> now a Dutchman With a Shoemaker he passed himself off for a Tanner with a farmer for a wine merchant with others for a captain in the American army & with officers for a secretary to the American minister at paris who was travelling with Dispatches to Commodore Preble in the Meditterranean – He was of course extremely amusing & I was sorry when he left us.

Travelled for the morning within sight of the Mediteranean. The sea serene & unruffled with fishing boats employed in various directions. Stopped at Gigean to feed the mules A small old town

28. This word is written over another proper name, not legible. The present-day spelling is Sète.

PS. Yesterday we began to see mulberry trees a sign that we were entering a silk country

Road continues to command the beautiful plains of Languedoc. Cultivated with vinyards grain & <pla> fields of olives & almond trees

In the afternoon at 5 oclock arrived at Montpellier. handsome town – environs particularly Fountains in the city decorated with statues &c walls out of repair but handsome. Tower with trees on top Superb public walk raised above the valley with stone ballustrade around it ↑called la place de peyrou↓. Temple in the middle[,] fish pond &c Grand aqueduct resembling two bridges one on top of the other crossing the plain from a neighboring hill to supply the city with water. Fine view from the walk before mentioned The vally interspersed with country seats &c view on one side terminated by mountains on the other by the Medditeranean[.] on a clear day you can see from this place the Alps on one side & the Pyrenees on the other each at a vast Distance

Theater a handsome building of stone The inside finished with much taste & nearly about the size of our theater in New York[.] Music of the opera excellent[.] some of the singers have good voices. Their gestures &c too extravagant for my taste Scenery but tolerable

August 14

Young midshipman took the dilligence this morning early for Avignon on his way to Toulon.

Walked about the Town in the morning – Weather very warm – Not the right time of the year to benefit by Montpelier <?First?> Took a walk to[29] on the grand esplanade near the aqueduct. The Temple very cool from <the> a fountain in the middle of it. The temple is of the Corinthian order, built of white stone Aqueduct <built> of same stone has about 50 grand arches[.] the upper part has nearly three times the number of smaller arches.

Evening at theatre Melodrames fine combat with sabres. Crown of laurel thrown to one of the actresses at the conclusion of the peice a custom frequent in france[.] returned to the hotel & was surprized to find the little doctor there[.] he had dispatched his business at Cette & is going to Nice

NB Hotel du Midi an excellent inn. Charges 6 liv. 10 sous pr day[.] if you take coffee & milk for breakfast you pay extra.

29. Irving apparently forgot to cancel "to."

August 15

Interior of Montpellier disagreeable. Streets narrow & dirty. very dusty. Weather warm at present. The Doctor introduced me to Mr Walsh a gentleman <who acts here as American consul> ↑of this city↓. Met with the most open & hospitable reception Walsh insisted on our dining with him to day – He is originally an Irishman but naturallized[,] is a fine clever hearty fellow Sent his young man with us to shew us the town

Passed a most agreeable afternoon with Walsh. A fine free hearted fellow gave us a letter of reccommendation to Nismes. This day was the fete of the Assumption. Celebrated in the churches of the town Law does not allow of public processions where there are protestants in the place as is the case of Montpellier[.] dance of men & women in the street in the evening. They were a company of Bakers. the men dressed in Pink jackets white <pa>vests & pantaloons a sash round their waists & cocked hats with bunches of different colored feathers. The Girls in yellow boddices & white petticoats, little yellow hats stuck on one side of their heads

Climate of Montpellier changed considerably of late years. Spring & summer very variable. extremely hot all the while I was there The autumn is the best season.

Doctor engaged a voiture to take us to Nismes.

More pretty faces in proportion among the girls of Montpellier than of any place I have seen in France.

Population about 30,000.

August 16

Sat off early in the morning for Nismes. Pretty actress in the voiture. <Mett> Met four conscripts in chains guarded by two soldiers on horseback going to join the army These are young men who are made soldiers *per force* & as they are often reluctant to leave their native homes & the scenes & friends of their infancy they are carried in chains & imprisoned in the principal towns to prevent their escaping

Arrived at Lunel to dinner, a clean little town famous for its white wines. Two postillions quarrelling which is the greatest rogue One charges the other with stealing from the travellers who charges him in turn with stealing from his master & travellers too

A Fair at Nismes. Large square crowded with the Peasantry and their different merchandizes. puppet shews &c The whole town was

<ris> resounding with the squeaking of little trumpets, the shrill sound of childrens whistles & the clack of the french women who were decked off in awkward finery & throngd every public walk. It was the fair of St Roque.

Ampitheatre 67 <feet> ↑toises 3 feet↓ one way 52 ↑5 feet↓ the other 66 feet high* <on the outside two orders Tuscan & doric each of 60 arcades>. 4 Gates open into the arena. Much defaced. Blackened by fire – it was filld with faggots by Charles Martel & set on fire to destroy it as it served as a fortress to the Saracens

Supposed to have been built in the time of Adrian or Antoninus Pius. Said to be large enough to hold 17000 people The inside is crowd[e]d with shabby houses, and the ↑lower↓ arcades on the outside are masoned up & turnd into Botiques & dram shops – Built of whitish stones Some historians make Nismes 580 years older than rome A colony was settled here by Marcus Agrippa son inlaw of Augustus

<Temple of Diana Squa oblong & in good preservation>

Greatest part without cement the stones 18 feet long.

In the evening while at supper Three officers of the Police with a file of Soldiers entered <our> the appartment & demanded to examine our Passports. A young man in the room was very impertinent to the officers & was threatened with arrest

Singular trial of three girls for murder

Maison Quarrée 82 feet long 35 broad 37 high. Adorned with columns of the Corinthian order extremely beautiful as is likewise the cornice Door formerly was the only place that admitted the light, windows have since been made in the walls but very small <The tem> Supposed to be a temple erected in honor of Caius & Lucius Caesar grandsons of Augustus The building is in excellent preservation and is a noble specimen of architecture. It is spoken of with enthusiasm by french artists

Temple of Diana is near the Fountain and in ruins It is generally cal[l]ed by the above name tho disputed by many writers who pronounce it a temple where they sacrificed to the infernal deities. trunks of statues in the interior & fragments of marble pillars. Several other antiquities of less note as The *Tower* magne[,] mosaics, a roman gate &c

Fountain of Nismes & the adjoining gardens & works superb. built of hewn stone decorated with marble statues &c

* It is of the tuscan irregular approaching the doric.

Manufactories of Nismes silks, silk stockings & woolen goods. Handsome walks. houses tolerably built but the town very dusty. The dust is light & the least wind carries it thro the streets in clouds

Hotel DeLouvre is said to be the best inn[.] I found it very dirty, and was much troubled with fleas and bugs. very noisy. My chamber was over the yard & I was continually disturbed in the night by dogs horses carriages & french <ostlers who are the> postillions who are dreadfully noisy beings

In one of the public walks is the lower half of a statue of Liberty[30]

August 19

This morning Dr Henory left me to return to Montpellier & from thence to Cette where he intends to try to find ↑a↓ ship for Nice He was too unwell to go on any farther by land

Yesterday evening I was thro the circus, a shabby looking genius who lives in the place, acting as cicerone A number of rows of seats still remain, they are enormous stone – oblong. in the walls I saw many stones about 18 feet in length & immensely thick[.] it is impossible to conceive how they were raised & placed in their present places. There is no cement in the walls except what has been put in modern times to sustain the fabric from giving way. The Pavement of the corridors is of small <octang> sexangular stones of different colours. The cicerone offerd me a number of coins which he said he had found in the building & asked 10 sous apeice for them

Avignon[31]

↑19↓ left Nismes in a Dilligence for Avignon <at>Near La Foux country began to change & to become mountanous. Beautiful situation of La Foux on the banks of the Gard. Highland scenery around. Road winds among rocky Precipices as it approaches the river from <an opening> La foux is on the opposite shore. Beautiful ride among the mountains after leaving La foux. The view when descending from the mountains to Villeneuve & Avignon almost surpasses discription – <The> Villeneuve at your feet the grand convent of Chartreuse <in the> on an eminence commanding the town with a gleam of sun shine

30. Presumably it was erected during the period of the Revolution. No such statue is now standing and no reference to one seems to be recorded (information furnished by the Director, Archives of the Department of Gard).

31. "Avignon" stands alone on the manuscript page in large letters.

breaking thro the clouds and resting on its battlements of yellow stone. at a little distance the antient towers of Avignon are seen to rise[.] they are both seated in a vast & inchanting valley The rhone passes rapidly by them and wanders thro it <f> seen from the height for many miles. the Scene terminated by ridges of mountains some in shade and others lighted up with the rays of the setting sun.

Ludicrous appearance of the Peasant women with broad brimd black wool hats with very small crowns & about an inch of the brim turned up all round.

Two French gentlemen that came in the dilligence were very attentive to me. Enquired particularly about America of which they seemed to be extremely ignorant. One wanted to know if I was not affraid to pass the sea – at another time he asked me <if I was not affr> how I had courage enough to leave my country to travel in a distant one without knowing the language of it. He said he should be affraid to go to America without understanding english. I told him the Americans were a strange set of fellows that run about all parts of the world without caring to learn the language before hand

August 20

Walked about the town early in the morning. Several well built Streets. An eminence in one part of the town on which stands the chateau, the finest old castle I have seen in france[.] on one side of it was the church de Notre dame[.] I ascended to it by <some> two flights of stairs of stone in front of the hill. In the portico of this church I saw the faint remains of a painting of much celebrity. It is a warrior mounted on horseback striking his lance into a dragon. Near him is a lady kneeling in an attitude of supplication. This latter is said to be a likeness of the Fair Laura, immortalized by Petrarch. The interior of the church is superbly ornamented with sculpture & formerly was highly adornd with paintings But the revolution has made dreadful havoc in it, destroyed the paintings and shatterd the exquisite carvings and reliefs in many places. Fragments of statues &c are strewd about the floor, they are now busy repairing it. What has irritated me most is, the intelligence that the church of the cordeliers which contained the tomb of Laura is totally demolished & nothing of the tomb to be seen. There was in the same church the tomb of the brave chevalier Crillon.[32]

32. Louis des Balbes de Berton de Crillon (*ca.* 1541–1615), French general, distinguished himself at the battle of Lepanto and, under Henry IV, at Ivry and the seige of Paris.

Gendarmerie. fine horses[,] barberous way of chastizing one by throwing large stones at him.

Charming walk shaded with trees around the city outside of the walls & part of the way along the Banks of the Rhone Walls tolerably perfect, flanked with square towers. Grand view from the esplanade above the chateau. The whole plain to a vast extent lies before you, and has the most luxurient appearance – vineyards cornfield, olives &c The Rhone winds thro in a serpentine course forming beautiful islands. The other side of the Rhone are the picturesque towers of The Chartreuse & Villeneuve. <You look> ↑I looked↓ over a small rampart <and see at a great> built on top of this rocky precipice & <see>saw far below <you> ↑me↓ the boatmen &c on the shore, in groups joking & amusing themselves tho their <voics> voices were very indistinctly heard. The ruins of an old bridge with an antique tower on it added another picturesque object to the scene. The time was shortly after sunrise. Every thing seemed fresh an[d] blooming[.] the air was refreshing and mild and seemed to waft health on every breeze. Never did a landscape have such a tranquillizing & happy effect on me as this. I sat down on a stone contemplated the scene around me and thought of my friends far distant for <an> hours together. Never do I see any beautiful view but it unaccountably calls to my reccollection my family and friends. But in the whole course of my tour thus far I have never thought of them with such tranquil unpainful reccollections as <when> at this time.

The churches in Avignon have undergone <mis> cruel treatment. Some very fine ones have been changed into stables salt petre works &c. Several however are undergoing reparations but it is impossible for them to replace the fine gothic workmanship that they have marrd.

This city had sufferd two or three times from the overflowing of the Rhone & <in> on one house in nearly the center of the town I saw an inscription that in fifty five the water had come to that place

Hotel dela Palais Royal is tolerable

Avignon was called by Rabelais Le Isle de Sonnante from the continual ringing of Bells in it. There are a vast number of churches still remaining tho as I have remarked many are in ruins & almost all the bells have been melted into coin

20th left avignon in the evening in a voiture & rode all night. A fine moonlight. the country lookd tranquil & delightful We rode round part of the walls of the city with the Rhone on our left glittering with the moon beams[.] after riding for two or three hours the country grew uninteresting. I endeavored to get a little sleep but the carriage was ill contrived & uneasy so that in the morning[33] my head was quite sore & sweld in lumps where I had leand against the carriage

I had formd a high opinion of the beautiful scenery of *Provence* but was disappointed in <this> my expectations The country thro which we travelled was generally sterile & unpicturesque. at midday we stopped to dine at *Aix*. This was formerly a Parliament town & the capitol of Provence. It is situated in a valley & walled but the walls are ruinous The streets are well paved & clean & the city has several handsome public walks. <Ro> Vestiges of Roman Baths were discoverd the beginning of the last century & new baths built upon them. They are resorted to by persons afflicted with gout gravel scurvy consumption &c. I had not time to look about at the place as we sat off again immediately after dinner[.] in the evening we arrived at Marseilles.[34]

September 7

I have been much pleasd with my stay at Marseilles. the city is very handsome & I have found some Americans here whose company has tended to make the time pass agreeably. Mr Appleton a young Gentleman of Boston who <has> is here with a ship in Quality of Supercargo, has pleased me particularly from his amiable manners. I have received the most polite attentions from Mr Schwartz in consequence of letters from his partner in New York Mr Abm. Ogden[35][.] I shall leave here tomorrow in company with Dr Henory who arrived here a few days after me *by land* having been unable to get a passage from Cette by water. The police have kept me dancing attendance on them for three days for my passport.

Yesterday arrived the Brig Hatty in 60 days from New York. I went out in a boat with three or four Americans to meet her in the Bay before she came to quarentine but I was much disappointed to find out she had neither papers nor letters on board.

33. I.e., the morning of August 21.

34. "in the . . . Marseilles." are the only words on p. [54]. Below them is a large "X", crossing out the remainder of the page.

35. Presumably Abraham Ogden, Jr. (1775–1846), a brother of T. L. Ogden (William Ogden Wheeler, *The Ogden Family in America*, Philadelphia, 1907, p. 190). Probably he is the man of the same name listed as a merchant in the New York city directories from 1807/08 to 1846/47.

PS When I first arrived I put up at the Grand Hotel des Ambassadors (chez Everard)[36] but was advised to change my lodgings for the *Hotel Franklin* where the Americans generally reside[.] I was much pleased with the change, the Hotel des Ambassadors being noisy & extortionate & the *Hotel Franklin* is kept by a very worthy old lady who endeavors to render the residence of her boarders as agreeable as possible The rooms in her house are very handsomely furnished.

September 8

I shall set off from this tomorrow, the passport not having been given to me soon en<g>ough to go before

<Oreal>

from <?Jacquil?>Marseilles to	Post	leagues
Tourves		10
Brignolles	1½	3
Flassans	1½	3
Luc	1	2
Vidauban	1½	3
Muy	1½	3
Frejus	2	4
Lestrelles	2	4
Cannes	3	6
Antibes	2	4
NICE	4	8

Between Vidauban & Frejus Figs 9 livres pr cwt 10 livres if they pack them up.

Grapes 10 sous pr cwt 120 ↑lb↓[.] 2 sous & ½ pr Pot of wine[.] A pot holds near 3 bottles[.] pine planks 4 ft pr 9 inch 20 sous pr doz – not quite ½ inch thick

September 10

Left Marseilles at 4 oclock this morning. passed thro a country hilly & sterile but cultivated by the aid of manure, some scenes were very picturesque. Rode thro the town of Oreal. This was two or three years since a town of robbers The Fauxbourgs robbd the richer part of the

36. M. Evrard was a hotel proprietor in Marseilles and director of the diligence from Marseilles to Avignon (information furnished by the Director, Archives of the Department of the Bouches du Rhône).

city & committed depredations on every traveller so that the road was almost abandond. In consequence of severe laws & punishments they were suppressd

Dined a[t] Jacquil, another town of robbers formerly Inn dirty & miserable After dinner we ascended among the mountains, the road was a cross road to avoid an elbow made by Toulon. We had to walk a great part of the way it was so rocky & rugged. No houses to be seen & no cultivation[.] this part of the road was particularly infested with robbers a year or 18 months since They would make their appearance in large troops & completely strip the travellers. Tho gulotind by a dozen at a time it was with great difficulty they were suppressd.

Slept at *Tourves.* An infamous inn. town very dirty. <At>Near the town passed the Ruins of a noble chateau formerly belonging to the Baron – gulotined in the revolution – at supper had spoons with coats of arms engraved on them, probably the spoils of some chateau

The towns in this part are loathsome from the quantity of manure collected in piles to fertilize the adjacent country.

September 11

Sat out at 4 oclock Morning very foggy. Stopped at Brignolles to breakfast Inn dirty as usual. <I>On this road you are generally waited upon by servant girls very dirty & often very insolent. The people of the inns are boorish & noisy. At this Inn they at first said they had nothing to give us for breakfast but veal just killd We made out however to get eggs cheese bread figs grapes &c & breakfasted very comfortably. Wine is so plenty in this part of the country that they sell it at *one sous* a bottle. It is generally however new and harsh. The country thro which we passed this morning was very fertile. In one place I saw this years *fourth* crop of oats in great forwardness.

In the afternoon we passed several places where they were gathering the vintage They do not however make it such a season of Jollity & rejoicing as in other parts of France The peasants throughout the South of france particularly in Provence have a Stupidity & heaviness of looks & manners that I had not expected to find in a nation so celebrated for gaiety. Slept at Vidauban a small town. Inn so so. They wanted me to give up my room to the chief Engineer ↑of the Department↓ & his lady who had just arrived. They told me he was a grand man and ought to be well accomodated and that[37] he wished to have my room as he had

37. From "and that" to "retain my," filling one page of manuscript, the writing has been erased or rubbed until it is almost illegible.

slept in it before & liked it the best in the house. I told the woman that I should not give my room up for all the engineers in the kingdom That I was an American gentleman a character [?as good as?] if not superior or more so as any engineer [?in France?] That <if> I was however [not un]willing to give a part of my room [and even part] of my bed to the [?engineer's?] lady but as [?to her husband?] I begged to be excused. The hostess retired muttering something I could not understand, but I heard no more from the grand man & was sufferd to retain my chamber without molestation.

September 12

Sat out early in the morning & had a fatiguing ride among the mountains. Country not very productive. Figs in vast abundance At half past ten arrived at *Frejus*. ruins of a Roman ampitheatre without the village. remains of roman wall round the village[.] roman aqueduct

In our mornings ride we had a distant view of the road winding up the mountains which we were to mount in the afternoon[.] it had no very inviting look being very steep and high The mountains about here are part of the chain of Alps & are called the Alps Maritime They are however of an inconsiderable height compared to the Alps of the interior. *Frejus* was formerly a place of some trade and importance but it is now in decay & ruinous.

It was here that Bonaparte & his *suite* landed when he returned from Egypt. He staid but till his baggage was brought ashore & post horses procured & then sat out direct for paris. The Laws ordain that any person <f> coming from the Levant & not performing Quarentine shall suffer death. Bonaparte landed in spite of this law.

After dining at Frejus we rode some distance within sight of the Medditeranean & then began to ascend the Mountain of *Estrelles*. This mountain is said to be 8 miles over. The road is very steep & winding. After ascending some distance we got out to walk. As the road wound up the heights we every now & then caught a view of the sea calm & beautiful. On its banks rose the steeples of Frejus & on the other side a wide valley <spread> variegated with <variety of> cultivation

In one place we passed two old women who had been on a pilgrimage to a hermitage among the mountains and were returning to their native homes in Italy near Milan I was surprized to see two such ancient infirm beings undertaking such a long & toilsome Journy

The Sunset was lovely shedding its last beams on the highest points of the mountains while the lower ones were melting in rich colors. The

<air was> evening was serene & delightful the air pure and invigorating and loaded with perfumes from the variety of aromatic shrubs & herbs that grew upon the mountains. <After sundown> The road had passed the highest part of the mountain & having descended a little continued winding along among the heights often on the brink of vast precipices. At last about dusk we arrived at a <soli> House where the driver told us we were to put up for the night as the next town was a considerable distance off and <it was> the road thro the mountains too dangerous to think of passing it in the night. I did not like the looks of the house <sol>large & solitary & embowerd in thick trees. <The inside was miserable The room>

I should have mentioned before that the passengers in the carriage were Dr Henory & myself and an<d> <Ital an> Italian lady the wife of a French officer Her husband had been taken by the English & she had set out from <the> Cape Francois[38] to get to her native home in Italy. From the Cape she got to Charlestown & from there to Bordeaux. Young & artless she had been continually imposed upon in the road. At Aix she was brought to bed of her first child <and> ↑which↓ was <now> at the time we travelled with her about a month old. I could not but feel the greatest pity for a young creature so artless & unprotected. She said she had been cheated & treated with slight with neglect & insult upon the road. She had met with no person who treated her with such respect and attention as we did and she said it seemd as if she was *in heaven.*

<On entering the Inn I mentioned we dis>

Before the Inn door were some rough looking fellows seated on a bench drinking wine. I did not at all like their looks On entering we enquired for a room for the lady & rooms for ourselves. The hostess, a sulky <lo>Creature took a candle & shewd us up stairs to one wing of the house where there were two rooms one with three beds & the other with two. The rooms were miserably dirty – no glass in the windows and but one crazy chair in each which was all the furniture they containd. This was a cheerless uncomfortable prospect for weary travellers and we asked if she had any better bed chambers She said no these were all she had in the house that were *furnished.* We were therefore obliged to be content and giving the room with two beds, which seemed the best, to the officers lady we took the other. After a miserable supper we retired to our chamber and having Secured the

38. Cap Français, original name of the city of Cap Haitien, Haiti. Presumably the young woman found her way to Charleston, S.C., and thence to Bordeaux.

door endeavored to get such repose as the hardness of the bed & the fleas & bugs would permit. I own I did not feel well at ease. The wild & solitary situation of the house and the rough look of the people were enough to awaken disagreeable sensations particularly as I knew that about 18 months or two years since these roads were very much infested with Robbers. However in spight of all these disagreeables I soon fell asleep & awoke in the morning without having been either *robbd or murderd.*

September 13

We sat out at break of day and continued wind[ing] among the wild & romantic mountain scenery, now and then catching a glimpse of a distant valley. The mountains <were>are covered with Pines Laurels Box myrtle cypress tamarisc &c and with a variety of <sweet> aromatic herbs & shrubs as Hysop thyme Lavender &c &c. <At last we descended into the valleys and> At last we came again in sight of the Mediterranean and after dificult & rugged descents we gained the valleys and approached the sea. Having passed thro the little village of Cannes we continued riding along the sea shore having on the other side <pla> vineyards & plantations of figs & olives & behind them the Alps rising in <majes> in magestic grandeur. We stopped to dine at Antibes a small sea port well fortified & garrisoned. We dined at a table d Hote in company with several French officers who were very polite. After <a continuation of the same> dinner we sat off again & passed St Laurent a little village formerly the frontier town of France where they used to examine the trunks of passengers but at present the line is extended. We crossd the *Var* on a long wooden bridge & in the evening arrived at Nice

The whole journey from Marseilles to this place had infinitely <dis>& agreeably disappointed me as I had expected a <hot> journey thro a sultry barren country On the contrary the road passed thro scenes fruitful picturesque & romantic – The country (except among the mountains.) was generally well cultivated and the profusion of grapes & figs along the road afforded <contin> luxurient regales.

Nice is a sea port that contains between twenty & thirty thousand inhabitants It formerly belonged to Italy but is now a part of France & is the capital of the Department of the Maritime Alps.

September 14

This morning I waited upon the police to obtain a passport for Genoa, & was referred to the Prefet. <we>I went to see him in company with Dr Henory & found the Secretary General in th<is>e office. He wrote a permission on the Drs passport immediately, but on seeing mine he declared it was impossible for him to grant me permission to depart as my paspt was special & put me under the surveillance of the police. Dr Henory endeavored to represent my case in such a manner as would induce him to give me a passport, but he assurd us that tho he felt for my situation yet it was completely out of his power till a better passport or an order from the Grand Judge arrived authorizing my departure or that I was reclaimed by one of our consuls. He told me he would relieve me from the rigid surveillance of the police which otherwise would have obliged me to present myself every day at the office of the municipality For this purpose he gave me an attestation of my having left my passport with him and of my being <at> allowed the liberty of the city. He also promised to write to the Com: General of Marseilles enclosing my passport and requiring another that would permit me to depart. As this was as much as I could expect from him I thanked him for his politeness & took my leave. I immediately wrote to Mr Schwarts of Marseilles to represent my case to the <gne> Commissary General & endeavor to satisfy him of the ident[it]y of my citizenship.

September 15

This day I wrote to Mr Cathalin & Mr Lee our consuls at Marseilles and Bordeaux mentioning my situation and requesting them to use their influence with the police or if there was no other way – to reclaim me as an American citizen. I have also wrote to T H Storm at Genoa which letter will be delivered to him by Dr Henory and I expect they will both exert themselves to get the consul of that place to reclaim me. After dinner being unwell I retired to my room & laid down I had not been asleep long before I was awakened by the noise of some persons entering my chamber & was surprized to see an officer of the police accompanied by the Dr The Doctor told me the officer had come to request my papers which must be carried before the Mayor[.] he told me that as I was unwell he would attend for me. I accordingly gave my papers & they went away together. About <h>a quarter of an hour afterwards the Dr came back humming a tune in a most furious manner.

he entered my chamber & throwing himself into a chair began to vent his spleen in a profusion of maledictions. He told me some scoundrel of a spy had been & denounced me as an Englishman which occasioned their demanding my papers. He wished me however to go with him to the mayors office, as the adjunct of the mayor spoke english and was prejudiced in my favor from the Doctors representation. I accordingly changed my dress and accompanied him. I experienced a very polite reception The adjunct assured me he felt sorry for my situation and if it had been any wise in his power he would have suffered me to proceed immediately but that they were responsible to superior authority and dared not act contrary to the directions of my passport. He assured me I should not be again molested in their city but should remain perfectly tranquil and as soon as it was in their power they would facilitate my departure with pleasure. I expressed my sense of the polite treatment I had recieved from the police of Nice and assured him however hard my case was I was perfectly convinced of their Justice and indulgence How long I shall remain here heaven knows but it is certain the hours will drag heavily. I am entirely among strangers hardly speaking their language. I brought on no letters to this place except one to a french Mercht. and they are of all beings the most inhospitable to an American except when they expect some advantage in return. Dr Henory goes tomorrow and however I might wish his agreeable company to relieve my lonesomeness, it is my interest to have him go as on his & Storms exertions at Genoa I chiefly depend for my liberation.

September 16

The Feluca in which Dr H is to depart does not go till to morrow so <I may notch> like Sternes prisoner[39] I may notch down another day <at> of <the> imprisonment.

We are Stared at as we walk the streets the same as turks would be in New York. As the place is small they immediately know a stranger & by our air they percieve we are foreigners. Passing by the post office & talking in our own language we were overheard by a little humpbackd centinel with a gun twice as long as himself who was in company

39. The prisoner in the chapter "The Captive" in Laurence Sterne's *A Sentimental Journey through France and Italy* (1768) is described as having a "little calendar of small sticks . . . at the head [of his bed], notch'd all over with the dismal days and nights he had pass'd there" (*The Works of Laurence Sterne*, Oxford, 1926–27, Shakespeare Head Press Ed., IV, 93).

with one or two of his comrades "God dam dem" cried the little vagabond "dese english dey spik english.["]

September 17

This morning Dr Henory sat off in a Felucca for Genoa Tho sorry to part with a man who had proved himself so much my friend and who was such amusing company yet I could not but rejoice on one account as it would probably facilitate my departure as I depend chiefly on exertions from Genoa – I returned to the Hotel solitary & down hearted enough but <partly> by walking, reading studying french &c I contrived to pass away the day till it grew dark & then crept to my bed & tried to get asleep as soon as possible

September 18

Passed much the same. The <day> clouds that were thick yesterday & threatned rain have dispersed. Had strawberries at dinner I believe they are gatherd in the mountains. Chestnuts here are enormously large & very excellent. In the evening I took a walk in the country. Weather delightful. They are drying figs throughout. Walked thro walks & groves of oranges They are green at present.

September 19

A ditto of the preceding day – Amused myself with writing letters to New York tho I do not know when I shall have an opportunity to forward them. <Read in> In the evening took a walk in the country with ↑one of↓ the sons of the maitre d hotel for a guide He carried me to a country seat the owner of which was very polite & hospitable shewd me his garden &c & insisted on my entering the house & refreshing myself with wine, sweet biscuit & fruit.

September 20

Read in this mornings papers that the yellow fever was in New York. It has made me low spirited all day as it is out of my power to recieve letters in Nice my letters being forwarded to Italy.

September 21

This afternoon I recieved a letter from Mr Schwarts of Marseilles informing me he had recd. my letter from this place & had immediately waited on the Com. Genl That the latter had desired that our consul might wait upon him in his official capacity which had been done and he had no doubt the proper papers giving me liberty to proceed would be forwarded by the first post. I returnd him a letter of thanks for his very friendly behavour in this affair.

September 22

This morning I received a letter from Dr Henory dated the 20th. at Monaco a little town about 3 leagues from here[.] they had been obliged to put in there the first day on account of the rolling of the sea & had been detained there ever since, suffering from bad inns & extortionate inn keepers. These felluca men are the veriest cowards that ever venturd on salt water & are affraid of the least swell of the sea.

Waited on the Secretary genl this morning[.] he had not yet recd. any letter from the Com. Genl of Marseilles & promised to send me word the moment he recd. one Amused myself with writing letters part of the day & in the evening took a charming walk in the country & visited some of the Gardens

September 23

This day according to the new French calender is the first of Vendémiaire the first day of the 13 Year of the *Republick.* it was usherd in by the firing of cannon. <& th> The shops generally were shut & the people kept it as a holiday as we do the 4 July. In the evening one of the public walks was illuminated by pots of turpentine or some similar combustible placed on posts at some distance from each other[.] the soldiers & peasantry were dancing.

September 24

Amused myself as usual with writing reading &c At Dinner met with a french officer & his wife an Italian lady very handsome. Walked round the town & on the public walks with her in the evening <& p> she was very agreeable & the time passed pleasantly – This was post day but I have recieved no letter nor passport from Marseilles.

September 25

The air fresh & rather too cool this morning. The Equinox is gathering & the clouds begin to threaten

September 26

Recieved two pacquets this morning from the post office one from my indefatigable friend Dr Henory dated Genoa where he arrived 23. He had spared no pains in getting my reclamation from our consul, & with the assistance of H Storm procured it <&> inclosed it in the letter & sent it off immediately. the Pacquet also inclosd a letter from H Storm written with all that warmth & openess of Heart that distinguishes him & urging me to lose no time in hasting to him[.] Dr Henry writes that Storm has behaved with the utmost zeal and friendship in my cause I receved the reclamation with rapture. The other pacquet was from our consul Cathalan at Marseilles inclosing a letter in my behalf to the prefet of this place

---

After dancing attendance all day at length in the afternoon I was enabled to have my papers read – Answer – That I must wait four or five days till they recieve a reply from the Com Gen of Marseilles to a letter that has been written him – This is the infamous manner in which I am trifled with by these scoundrels – but I am in their power & *patience par* force must be my motto.

September 27

Called on Monsr Guide a principal merchant of Nice, to whom I had brought a letter of introduction. I told him my situation & shewed him the reclamation & the <letter> protection I had brought from America. He desired me to leave them with him & he would call on the prefet (with whom he was personally acquainted) either to day or tomorrow

In the evening I went to the theatre – a shabby little place. I was however pretty well pleased and laughed heartily at the personation of a Gascon by one of the actors. An actress performd several characters in one piece of a country girl, poissard[40] &c &c & acquitted herself very cleverly

September 29

I have not heard nor seen any thing of Mr Guide since – The time has <dra> crept on slowly. I have read out all my english books & bought yesterday a supply of french one's to pass away the time.

<cal>

– calld on Mr G—— this morning – he had seen the Secy particular – and the answer was I must rest here till my passport with which I travelled from <Mar> Bordeaux to Marseilles was procured from the

40. "A low, vulgar woman," "a fishwife."

latter place – that then it would be sent on to Paris to the Grand Judge and submitted to his descision – if he decided in my favor a <pas> permission would be sent me to depart – if otherwise – heaven knows what I must do or where Ill go.

Thus am I amused with false promises and banterd about like a child, and now after all I am to rest perhaps a month on an uncertainty[.] I have written to Genoa an acct. of my situation but I cannot expect any more assistance from there than what has already been given me.

September 30

This morning there arrived here a body of chasseurs between 12 & 15 hundred on their route to Naples. I was setting at my window reading when I heard the sound of the drum at a distance The window looks toward the country & road on the Marseilles side so that I had a fine <view> opportunity to view their approach. By degrees the <drums> sound of the drums grew louder till they ceased & the music of the regt. began – it swelld louder & louder as they approachd till I could distinguish a fine martial air. An angle in the road presented the troops to my view their arms gleaming in the sun and having a galant & warlike splendor. They continued in a long train marching on the road the other side of the Paglion (river) <all the> & their crossing of the bridge was highly picturesque They appeard fatigued with marching & coverd with dust –

October 2

Nothing new has occurd to alter my prospects or enliven my situation. The <Equizoctial> Equinoctial storm that has been long gathering has began to day. It is called here the Rain of St Michael[41] & generally lasts two or three weeks – a dreary prospect, for even if I recieve a passport I fear it will be impossible to find a fellucca that will venture the voyage to Genoa during the prevalence of the storm – The falls are generally very rainy here.

October 4

The rain has cleared away & the weather is again charming This slight rain I expect is but an *avant courier* of the Equinox. Yesterday & to day dined in company with two Polonese noblemen brothers – The

41. The feast day of St. Michael is September 29.

Counts [*blank*] They were very agreeable had travelled considerably – had been four months in England & understood a little of the language – they intend parting tomorrow for Genoa by land & expressd much regret that it was not in my power to accompany them.

October 5

This morning early I sat out with one of the sons of my landlord to visit Ville Franche a small town about a league & half from Nice on the sea shore. The morning was fresh & delightful. We ascended the mountains to the east of Nice and from th<eir>e <sum> eminence to which we arrived we had a charming view of Nice & the adjacent country. The sides of the mountain were highly cultivated & swept down into the delightful valley of Nice – <enriched with> which is a complete garden – the olives oranges & citron trees ever green afford a most refreshing regale to the eye. the white country seats & cassinos interspersed amidst the deep green of the surrounding groves have a very pleasing effect. The ampitheatre of hills cultivated in gardens to the very summit appeared from the height from which we surveyed them to be almost level with the valley and the Alps bounding the view in the distance were brightend by the ruddy beams of morning – The town of Nice & its port were far below us beyond <this> it the Medditerranean spread its unruffled bosom & <Ant>at a distance the small town of Antibes & its fortifications were plainly visible. To our left – and in a manner in the foreground of the picture the mountain ascended <into> to a rocky height on which was seated the castle of Nice. This is called the Monte Albano

While we were enjoying this expansive & delightful view we were overtaken by the Polonese noblemen who were on the<y>ir way to genoa. They were mounted on mules with their servant & a guide. We <contin> proceeded together for some time till their road took a different direction when after mutual adieus we parted but I could see them <for> now & then for a long time afterwards as their road wound among the heights of the mountain.

We afterwards discended to Ville franche which is most romantically situated <at the> in a small hollow at the foot of the mountain & partly built on the ascent of one of them Here is a chateau in which the criminals – vagabonds &c of Nice are confined[.] there is also an excellent & deep port defended by a mole On a point that runs out far into the sea is the Finale or light house of Nice – From Ville franche we returned to Nice by sea in a small boat – the sail was enchanting from the fineness of the weather & the calmness of the ocean.

October 8

Received a letter this day from Wm. Lee Esqr our consul<a> at Bordeaux in answer to one that I wrote the 15th of Sept. he mentions that he had applied to the Com: Gen. of Police to rectify my passport but had not yet recieved an answer. he had also written to our minister at Paris requesting him to interest himself in my favor. He advises me if I meet with *great detention* to write to our minister myself – this letter does not appear to yeild much ground of rejoicing – <I>

I got acquainted with a young italian physician who lodges at the same hotel with me. He is a young man of much taste. Well acquaintd with his native authors & such English ones as have been translated. He is likewise a good musician He introduced me to a young french physician of Nice who speaks English is a great amateur of natural history & has travled considerably to form a collection of Plants insects &c. The latter shewed me his botanical garden &c The day passed quite agreeably in consequence of having a little agreeable company.

October 9

This day in company with the Italian & the french Physician I sat out to visit some roman ruins situated among the mountains at some distance from Nice The road as it ascended the defiles of the mountain commanded enchanting views of the valley – with Nice at some distance & beyond it the Medditerranean

The ruins consisted of an Ampitheater <much> & a temple of diana[.] of the former some arcades remained in a ruinous condition. but the space of the arena was still distinct. It was converted into a little plantation of olive trees <at> which seemed to say that the savage contests & battles that had once been celebrated there had given place to peace & tranquility The temple of diana <was> is conv[e]rted into a habitation of Peasants so that its original appearance is much altered – Both buildings are of small square stones like the ampitheatre of Bordeaux and like that intermingled at certain distances with layers of broad thin bricks. This has been the sc<ene>ite of a roman town <an> but from the <size> ↑smallness↓ of the ampitheatre the place could not have been considerable. The situation is highly romantic & picturesque

The french physician was so much interested in <the> Mrs Radcliffes Romance of the Italian – translated in french[42] which I had lent him that he read it all the road & had nearly broken his head against several walls & trees which he encountered.

October 10

Received letters today from H Storm, Genoa & Dr Ellison of Bordeaux. They had both did every thing in their power to release me[.] Storm has written to the Am: Minister at Paris & to the consul at Marseilles By the same post I received a letter from Robt L Livingston Esq Son of the minister mentioning that they had recd a letter in my favor from Mr Lee & had immediately sent a passport to the Grand Judge for his signature & that it would come on either by the same or the next courier. He mentioned having recd. a letter <f>in my favor from Mr C—— of N York which I had sent on from Bordeaux & <expressd his> that he had expected to see me at Paris. The letter was very polite & the information it contained highly *satisfactory* as it gave me a prospect of soon receiving a passport.

October 14

Two couriers have arrived since I recieved the letter from Mr Livingston but no passport has come to hand. This morning I went to the cathederal to see mass performed in presence of the Prefet & other authorities & the soldiers of the garrison. The cathederal is handsome in the interior – decorated with reliefs &c[.] the paintings of value have been removed & inferior ones substituted. The music of the regiment played at different times during the Service. At a certain signal of the drum all the soldiery presented arms, knelt down & *prayed*[.] at another signal after the space of a moment they rose up again. <This> ↑It↓ is something of a novelty to me to <see prayers so> see soldiers pray by the word of command

In the evening I recieved a visit from Mr Lowel an American Gentleman who arrived last evening on his route to Italy. I accompanied him to his lodgings & was introduced to his wife & sister. They part tomorrow morning for Turin.

The sight of a fellow countryman in this corner of France was cheering & grateful.

42. *L'Italien ou le Confessional des Pénitents Noirs,* tr. André Morellet (4 vols. Paris, 1798). Apparently Irving purchased it in Nice on September 28, 1804; see his expense account for that date in "Traveling Notes, 1804."

October 15

After all my trouble, my letters solicitations &c &c &c my <letters> business has been effected from a quarter that I least expected it. My honest Swiss landlord had many times expressd how much he felt for my situation and wished me several times to let him go to the Secretary General (who he assured me was *un brave homme*) & intercede for me As I never had any idea that his influence would be of any avail I constantly declined it. Yesterday – however the worthy soul when he saw my disappointment at not recieving a passport by the courier, could contain himself no longer but sat off unknown to me and visited the Sec Genl. he represented my situation as forc[e]ably as possible & the Sec: promised to speak to the Prefet in my favor[.] to day he told me what he had done & begged me to go with him to the Sec Genl. To please him I consented though without expectation of recieving any benefit. What was my surprise then when the sec: told my landlord that he had spoke to the prefet in my favor & that I might go to genoa as soon as I pleased leaving my papers with the municipality of Nice and giving my parole d honor that I would rest there under the surveillance of the french authorities till a decision was obtained from Paris. Honest Laurent (my landlord) was more delighted if possible than myself and presented a striking <pict> instance of disinterestedness & worth of heart <seld> very rare in his profession in France

October 16

By the courier of to day I recieved the long wished for passport from Paris accompanied by a Letter from R L L[43] who has behaved very politely[.] I immediately <who> went to see the Sec Genl. he thought I had come after the promised permission & was just commencing an evasion when I drew out of my pocket my passport & handed it to him. This put the matter quite in a new light. The proper signatures were made & all the ceremonies arranged at the commune – health office &c & in the evening I found myself completely in train to part with a felucca that sails tomorrow morning[.] at the beaureau de commune I found a young german who sails in the same felucca & talks english perfectly.

October 17

Sat sail early in the morning. I was in company with seven others

43. Robert L. Livingston.

from the same hotel They were french officers very polite & gentleman-like & in our party was included the young german – One of the officers was appointed cashier of the party. We found three other passengers in the felucca.

The weather was delightful we <coastted> coasted along partly rowing & partly sailing but always keeping near the land for fear of the little privateers that infest the coast. The shore was a continual succession of mountains rocky & barren but the lower parts cultivated with olives oranges &c & skirted with villages all which had a most picturesque appearance from the water. The officers were several of them sadly sea sick. Passed by Monaco a small town situated on a rock that projects into the Sea. It has a romantic appearance –

in the evening arrived at St Remo, in the Genoese territories. Town situated on the side of a hill and appears very handsome from the water. Streets narrow but generally clean. We had difficulty to find accommodations as a number of troops on their way to Genoa had filld the town. Landlord of the Inn seemed not very anxious to receive us Said he had but one bed. He thot the officers wanted to be billeted on him[.] when they told him they intended to pay like other travellers he soon reccollected three or four beds – We made out therefore to find lodgings the officers sleeping two in a bed and a small mattrass being given to me.

Took a walk about the town to see it. The streets as we ascended into the higher parts of the city narrow (perhaps 5.6 8 feet wide) winding & often *vaulted,* passing under houses. They were also very steep & intricate, and so dark that you could hardly see your way. Many of the lower parts of the houses never enjoy more than a feeble twilight. On the highest part of the city is a handsome building but whether a convent or seminary I could not learn From here there is a very handsome view of the surrounding hills cultivated with vines olives oranges &c & interspersed with handsome white cassinos & country seats. The town swept down before us to the sea which spread its expansive bosom in the distance. The town is extremely well peopled[.] there are two or three convents for men & women & several churches. In the latter there was immediately to be seen a striking contrast with those of france[,] being in good state and undamaged by the fury of revolutionary mobs. The statues pictures &c in excellent preservation. After a supper of good fish &c we retired to our *hard* beds & *endeavored* to sleep.

October 18

Early in the morning set sail again. Morning very clear & fine. The Island of *Corsica* visible opposite St Remo <several of the high> a chain of heights being very distinct Sun rising out of the sea Passed the prettily situated villages of Larma – Santa La Riva – St Stephano and came in sight of Port Maurice when the wind turned a head & so violently that we had to put back to St Stephano[.] here we had much difficulty to get ashore by reason of the surf. The Felucca was then drawn up on the sand. As we could no<f>t find any accommodations in the village we sat off & walked for Port Maurice about 3 leagues distant. The sun was very hot & as <the> we had to walk in the middle of the day we found it very <hot> uncomfortable. The road was the one that leads from Nice to Genoa & only practicable for mules & asses & I hardly see how those animals get along. The road is very stoney & rugged – cut along the face of the mountains & often along the edge of precipices sometimes ascending like stairs. Before we had walked half way to Port Maurice the wind sprung up very favorable for Genoa & had we been aboard we might have made half our distance. Port Maurice is handsomely situated on a hill. Our auberge was on the level sea coast & we were too fatigued to ascend & view the town. This town & Oneiglia another little place about a mile distant furnish the best oil of the rivage & have considerable trade. We found miserable accommodations

October 19

Our vessel having arrivd last evening we sat sail at an early hour. We continued coasting along <in sig the> within a mile or so of the shore. The land is the whole distance a continual mountain of rock but cultivated with surprizing industry with olives <villages> oranges &c so that it has the appearance of a continual garden The villages convents &c are white & have a beautiful appearance among the green of the trees

This chain of mountains is a part of the Grand chain of the Appenines that run thro Italy

Passed [*remainder of page blank*]

In the afternoon at 5 oclock the Padrone would have put in at Noli but a little breeze springing up we insisted on his continuing on to Savona about 3 or 4 leagues further[.] the breeze soon died away and the men had to take to their oars. The evening that succeeded was calm & serene and a beautiful moonlight[.] as we saild along the shore we could distinctly see the white villages churches &c and <of> now and then the vesper bell of <a> ↑some↓ convent situated on the side of the mountain, would break the repose of the scene. I observed a religious respect among the sailors that I had looked for in vain in France. When they heard the bells they generally puld off their caps made a sign of the cross & repeated their prayers About half past seven oclock we <came> arrived at Savona and entered the port which is defended by a mole battery &c &c <Wh> We found every thing silent and on hailing the shore were informed that the gates were shut and that we could not be admitted The officers made a great noise about the matter – there had a northerly wind sprung up which made it quite cold and we had not eat any thing since morning but a little dry bread[.] our altercations appeared to be of no avail and I was preparing a place to sleep on board the boat. We had however among the company a french commissary – he demanded to be allowed to land mentioned his rank &c and after much dispute & nearly an hours waiting in the cold we were suffered to land. Savona is a large town well fortified – there is an Excellent college there for the education of youth[.] the harbor is said to be capable of recieving large ships but I saw nothing there but small craft[.] the situation is extremely pleasant <a> Here we again found a difficulty in procuring beds and I was content to sleep on a straw one.

October 20

We parted from Savona at day light and had Genoa plainly in view. We passed several small villages <Anbissolla> Albisolla which contains a magnificent pallace – Sestri di ponente – Novi – voltri &c and among others Cocorato famous for being the birth place of Christopher Colombus – it is handsomely situated on the shore with hills rising gradually behind it and in the rear of them the high rocky mountains About half after one oclock we arrived at Genoa[.] I put up at the Hotel di torri and as soon as I could dress myself I visited my friend T H S[44] It is impossible to express my joy to see an old & particular friend so far from home and after having been so long among strangers

October 25

I have been so continually engaged with S—— that I have scarce

44. T. H. Storm.

had time to look about We have rambled about the city to look at the churches palaces &c. but have had so much to talk about that <we> I have not had time to examine any thing particularly

Among other palaces we visited that of the illustrious Doria[.] it offers a melancholy picture of magnificence in decay & the seats of wealth & luxury deserted. It was plundered by the french when they conquerd genoa – dismantled of its fine pictures &c. The long suits of rooms silent – deserted & spoild of their furniture where once the brilliant assembly the grotesque masquerade or luxurious banquets were celebrated had a dreary appearance. The rich tapestry hung neglected & fading on the walls & the admirable frescos were ruined by damps. This is the oldest palace in Genoa.

On entering this celebrated city is [I] was lost in admiration & surprize so different was it from all the other cities I had seen & so far did it pass them in magnificence The splendor of its palaces and the many grand specimens of architecture with which it abounds have justly acquired for it the name of *Genoa the Superb*. The streets are very narrow which prevents you from viewing the palaces to advantage. Many of the inferior streets are not above six or seven feet wide. The principle streets called *Strada Nuovo* & *Strada Balbi* or as the English call them *The Streets of palaces* are narrow but well paved. They present a continual succession of magnificent palaces adorned with marbles – painted in frescos with historic mythologic or fancy peices & often richly decorated with sculpture. There are not in the whole world two other streets <of> to equal these in <↑the↓ continual succ> uniform splendor of Edifices. The churches astonished me with their magnificence – Sculpture pictures frescos &c were lavishd to decorate them – I had not had much opportunity to witness the grandeur of the Catholic churches in France as there they are almost all ruined – I am told that I shall see churches far more superb before I leave Italy – The armory that once contained several suits <&>of ancent armor & antient implements of war, was also plundered by the French. Several of the Helmets serve the tailors at present as chafing dishes to heat their irons. I have seen them repeatedly converted in this manner in the streets of Genoa.

The Genoese women are generally well made and handsome. I have seen several of them extremely so. They are infinitely superior to the french women for personal beauty They are amorous & very fond of intrigue. The streets swarm with beggars – monks &c The other evening

<26th.>[45] I was to the theatre. This building is poorly contrived[–] it is very high which is extremely unfavorable to the voices of the actors. All the Boxes are hired out by the year and <y> if you do not know any of the owners of them you go into a part of the house like the Pit in our theatre w[h]ere are rows of benches with backs to them You can go with the same ticket to every part of the house. The scenery was good. The operas appear to me the most miserable sing song affairs that ever were exhibited on a stage. The[y] in a manner chant every word. Some of the music of course is excellent but the dialogue must be miserable. The chief drollery of the place lay in the grimaces of one of the comic performers who was endowed with a whimsical phyz and twisted it into all the unnatural ludicrous <grima> forms he could devise accompaning his hideous faces with distortions of body equally monstrous. This which would have been hissed as an insult to the understanding of the audience in america – was here loudly applauded

October 26

Yesterday morning sat off with S—— and Mr Caff<i>arena an englishman who lives with him as clerk – to *Sestri* a country place about 6 miles from Genoa on the banks of the mediterranean where the fashionable people of Genoa have country seats <(ps fashion> (<PS>NB the fashionable world at present is generally in the country) We intended to visit a palace & some gardens. The ride was enchanting along the shore of the mediterranean We passed thro St Pietra d'Arena one of the magnificent suburbs of Genoa – Arrived at Sestri we discharged the voiture & <deci> resolved before we visited the garden to call on Mrs. Bird an English lady & wife to <the former> Bird who was formerly English consul at Genoa – We were very politely received and I was introduced to Mrs Bird & her daughters the oldest of whom was a tall beautiful girl & immediately put me in mind of M—— of New York There was also there Mrs Walsh an english lady & three or four fine girls her daughters. We prevailed upon the young ladies to go with us to see a neighboring garden accompanied by Mrs Walsh – After rambling about the garden which was beautiful & laid out in the English taste – we returned to Mrs Birds to dine. The dinner

45. "26th" appears to have been written first on the page about here and then the sentence written over it as if Irving had changed his mind about the length of the entry for the twenty-fifth.

<time> not being ready we were delightfully entertained by Music by Miss Bird & the other girls who played on the Harpsicord & sung charmingly The dinner hour passed merrily away[.] we were all in high spirits & pleased with one another. After Dinner we danced to the Harpsichord & it was late in the evening before S—— & myself reccollected that we were engaged at Lady Shaftsburys[.] we sat off for town but it was so late that the carriage gate was shut so that we would be obliged to walk near a mile and as it was raining very hard we stopped in at the theatre of St Pietra d'Arena till the rain subsided. The th[e]atre was small & the stage scenery & performers miserable. After resting there an hour we again set off and stumbling in mud holes &c we made out to reach home in time for bed

Friday, November 5

Time has passd rapidly & pleasantly with me in Genoa from the agreeable acquaintances I have formed. I was introduced by Storm to Lord Shaftesbury and his family who are detained here prisoners of war. His lordship is one of the richest earls of Great Britain having an income of 40,000 £ Sterling. He had a fall sometime since from his horse <which g> and recieved a violent blow on the head which has not to this day acquired its former steadiness but seems sometimes half flighty. Lady Shafestbury is a charming affable woman & <has once been> still bears the remains of much beauty They have one child – a daughter Lady barbara ashley Cooper a very pretty girl of fifteen & exceeding lively. I have also been introduced to some of the first nobility of Genoa but I cannot say that generally I admire them. They seem to me a spiritless stupid set of beings tho this may be the effect of the depressed situation to which they are reduced by French tyranny and the disasterous situation of Genoa.

[*the following 5 pages, pp. [135–39], blank*]

[*p. [140] shows page-size drawing of a castle, with "Trebes" written above (Figure 8)*]

[*p. [141] blank*]

[*pp. [142–43] show drawings of a church or convent (Figures 9, 10)*] *[pp. [144–65] blank]*

[p. [166] shows page-size drawing of a walled tower (Figure 11)]

[p. [167] blank]

[p. [168] blank except for lines as if for expense account]

[Irving's expense accounts on the following pages begin on p. [184] and read upside down from back to front in the notebook, ending on p. [169]. For the convenience of the reader the editor has here arranged the accounts in normal chronological order.][46]

Bordeaux June 30th.

		Livres	Sous	$
30	Gloves		30	31
	Theatre	4		76
July				
<1> 1	Pd in advance for 4 July dinner	30		5.65
	Syrop & water	L	12	12
2	Shoes	7		1.44
	Coach	2		39[47]
	Protection	10 .	10	2
3	Tailors	5 .	5	1
	Silk stockings	9		1.<78>68
	Board & lodggs 2 nights 1 day	L 24 .	10	4.72
	Theatre	<3>3 .	10	66
4	Porter	1	<2>10	30
5	Caffe de la Comedie[48]		25	25

46. The writing is in brown ink unless otherwise noted.

47. In this column the figures "39," "<78>," "66," "56," "51," "1.12," and "1" are in pencil. Starting with the figure "64" the entire column is in pencil, and, unless otherwise noted, the last column in the rest of the expense account is entirely in pencil.

48. Possibly the tavern, of doubtful reputation, in part of the amphitheater.

xx 7	Sall de Gaiete[49]		25	25
10	Blank Book	3 ↑liv↓		56
11	Theatre Francaise	1	10	30
12	Franconi[50]	2	10	51
14	Rabais Garden[51]	6		1.12
x 15	Voiture	5		1
	Museum		15	15
17	Garden	3	10	64
	Shoes	6		1.12
20	Dentist	12		2.25
x 22	Paper		20	20
23	boat	1	10	30
		144 li	12 so	$27.52
				68

	Amt. brot over		
		144.12	27 5<2>3
July			
24	Hat	24	4.50
x 25	Clothes (linen)	102	20.38
x 29	Seamstress	6	1.12
	Laundress	20	<4>3.76
31	French master	24	4.50
	Taylor	241	45.20
		561.12	106.9<8>9
	1 months Board & Lodg 8 Louis		36
		561.12	1<3>42.99
		192	
	total Livres	753 12	
	errors in calculatn[52]		60
			143.59

49. The Théâtre de la Gaité.

50. The Franconi Circus, located between Rue Charles Marionneau and Rue Segalier, was under the management of M. Segalier (information furnished by the Director, Archives of the Department of Gironde). Presumably it was an enterprise of Antoine Franconi (1738–1836), an Italian by birth, who was the most celebrated circus rider of his day; he presented entertainments for years in Lyons and Bordeaux.

August[53]

		liv	
1	Travelling cap	3	58
2	postage	6.10	1.20
	Caffe & stampd pass	19	19[54]
3	Shoes	9	1.68
	Mem. Book	1.<3>10	31
4	Passport to Marseilles	3.–	56
	<Seat in dilligence to Tolouse>	<60>	<11.25>[55]
	Charity	1.5	25
x 5	Board & lodgg	24 livres	4.50
	Porter, servts &c	12 ↑liv.↓	2.25
		61.4	

From Bordx to Toulouse

	Seat in dilligence <60>	60	11.25
5	Castres, Suppr <3 liv>	3	56
6	La Reole breakfast <15>	15	15
	Tonniens fruit <5>	5	5
6 & 7	Agen, Sup. & bed	3 10	67
	Servt	10	10
	Castel Sarrasin Bread wine &c.	12	12
	For my Trunk from Bordx	↑liv↓ 5.–liv[56]	95
8	Porter	10 sous	10
	Postillions on the road about	1.10	30
	Guide	3.–	56
		78.12	26.58[57]

51. The garden at Chateau Raba, belonging to Gabriel Salomon Henriques (see journal entry of July 14, 1804).

52. "errors in calculatn" is in pencil.

53. The ink in this entry is written over pencil. The heading "liv." is in pencil only.

54. Both "19's" on this line are in black ink.

55. The cancellation and the numeral "25" immediately below are in ink.

56. "liv" is in pencil, as is also "sous" in the line below.

57. Presumably Irving added the 25 cents of the canceled $11.25 in the entry of the 4th; the total should be $26.33.

	August		
	Amt brot over		
		78.12	26 58
	at Toulouse		
8	Post Book	3 ↑liv↓	<4> 56
	Theatre	3 10	66
9	Boardg 1½ ↑day↓	9	1 68
	from Toulouse to Montpellier[58]		
	Fare to Castel naudy.	2.2	40
	Paid boy for bring trunk.	1.15	33
	Postillion & fruit woman	7 sous	7
	Dinner.	2.5	45
	Servt. & Postillion.	6	6
10	Sup. & bed at Castel naudary	3.10	66
	Servt	10	10
	Post Boat to Trebes	2.2	40
	Dinner at auberge	2.10	45
11	Sup & bed at Trebes	3	5<1>6
	Servt	5	5
	Bread	3	3
	Post boat for the day	2.2	40
	Dinner	2.5	45
x 12	Sup. & bed at an auberge	3.–	56
	Post boat to Beziers	1.8	28
		1<0>21.12	34.73

	August		
By	Amt brot over	1<0>21.12	34.73
12	Bread	<3> 3 ↑sous↓	3
	pd for Trunk from Toulouse	liv. 6	1.12
	Dinner at Beziers	3.	56
	Servt	5 ↑sous↓	5[59]

58. "Montpellier" shows traces of pencil, but the line is in ink.
59. "5" is in ink.

13	Sup & bed at Pezenas	3.10	66
	Servt	5	5
	Meze. breakfast	1 –	20
	Montpellier[60]		
	Voiture from <Meze> ↑Beziers↓	9	1.68
	Porter[61]	15	15
	Theatre	3.6	62
14	ditto	2.6	44
16	Hotel expences	20.10	3.78
	Laundress	1.10	30
	Saloon on esplanade	15	15
	Voiture to Nismes	6	1.12
	Serv't & porter	1 7	27
	Eggs &c at Lunel	16	16
	Servt	4	4
		182.4	46.11

August. Amt brot over

		182.<livres> 4	46.11
16	Porter at Nismes	7	7
	trifling expences	12	12
17	Caffé	8	8
	Notice Sur. Antq. Nismes[62]	4.10	66
	Livre de Petrarch & Laura[63]	1.10	30
	Music man	6	6
18	Caffé	9	9
	Pd. for a letter to Bordeaux	2.2	40

60. In the margin between "Meze" and "Montpellier" Irving drew a slanting line in ink.

61. In the margin beside "Porter" and "Theatre" Irving wrote in pencil "from Toulouse 51 8," apparently meaning "51 livres, 8 sous."

62. See journal entry of August 17, 1804, n. 117.

63. No work by this title has been identified; if Irving quoted it correctly, it may have been a cover title.

	Board & lodg at 6 ↑L↓. 10 ↑s↓ a day	16.10	
	Laundress	10	10
x 19	Caffé	12.	12
	Servt.	1	20
	Porter	6	6
	Dilligence to Avignon	12	2.25
	At Avignon		
20	Cicerone at Eglise de Notre dame de dom	3	55
	Caffé	10	10
	Pd in advance for voiture to Marseilles	15	3.80
	Porterage	6	6
	Hotel 1 day & supper	10	1.90
	Porterage	1	20
	Servant	14	14
		253.16	57 37

	August		
	Amt brot. <over>[64]	<192.16>↑253.16↓	57.37
21	Dinner at Aix	3	56
	Servt.	.7	7
	Postillion & servt.	1.6[65]	26
	At Marseilles		
22	Protection from amer: consul	21	4—
	Theatre	3.12	68[66]
23	Boardg at Everhards 1. Sup. bed & breakfast	9	1.66
24	Carte de Sureté	— 15	<25>15
25	Laundress	2.18	54
x			

64. Apparently when Irving canceled "192.16" he also canceled "over" by mistake.

65. In the margin opposite this line Irving wrote "258.9."

66. "68" is in red pencil.

26	Sundries	1.6	26
2<8>9	Theatre & caffe	3.	56
		300	6<5> 6.11
	Boardg & lodg for 9 days at the Franklin hotel at about 8.10 pr. day[67]	76.10	14.36
			80.47
		376.10	
		61.4	
	Livres	437.14	

The remainder of my bill for 19 days board is charged in the next month[68]

	September		
1	Garters (elastic)	1.10	30
x 2	Ticket for balloon	1.10	30
6	Blank passport	1	20
	Sundries	5	95
7	Silk stockings 1 pr at 12 ↑liv↓ & 2 pr at 13 ↑liv↓	38	7.—
	Laundress	6	1.12
	Shoes 2 pr	12	2.25
	Theatre	3.12	68
	Sundries	3	56
x 9	remainder of my Bill at Hotel for 19 days including trifles lent &c	90.10	18.50
10	Servants	6	1.12
	Dinner at <Oreal> ↑Jacquel↓	3	56
11	Sup & bed at Tourves	3	56
	Breakfast at Brignolles	1 10	30
12	Sup & bed at Vidauban	3	56

67. Under the ink, pencil reads as follows: "Boardg 8 days at about 8 pr day."
68. This sentence is in pencil.

	Servt	4	4
	Dinner at Frejus	2 10	50
	Servt	2	2
		<187.16>181.8	35.52
			6[69]
	September		
	Brot over <187.16>[70]	181.8	35.52
13	Sup & bed at auberge on the mountain	3 ..	56
	Servt	.. .3	3
	Dinner at Antibes	3. —	56
	Caffé[71]	.. 7	7
14	Caffé at Nice	.. 19	19
	Voiture from Marseilles to Nice ↑liv↓	48 ..	9.—
	Gratuity to Driver	3. ..	56
x 16	Caffé	.. 15	15
		249.0[72]	46.64
17	Caffé	.. 14	14
18	Do	.. 16	16
19	do	.. 16	16
20	Do	.. 16	16
21	Do.	.. 16	16
"	Purchased a small leather Portmanteau	9.—	1.<6>72
"	Postage of a letter from Marseilles	.. 8	8
22	Caffé	.. 16	16
	lead pencil	.. 10	10

69. This "6" and the canceled sum in the left-hand column are in pencil.
70. The canceled sum is in pencil.
71. In the left margin below "Caffé" Irving made two short parallel lines in ink as if to mark his position.
72. This total was arrived at by counting the canceled amount brought over; it should be 240 livres, 12 sous. These figures are in pencil. The last two amounts in the column ("16" and "8") above the total show pencil under the ink.

x 23	Caffé	16	16
	letter paper	8	8
	Livres	256. 8	49.72
	carried over		
	September		
	Amt. brot over	256.8	49.72
24	Caffé	16	16
25	ditto	16	16
26	ditto	16	16
27	ditto	16	16
	Writing paper	10	10
	Almanack	3	3
	Theatre &c	3.—	58
28	Caffé	16	16
	Bookseller for L'It——n[73]	5.	95
29	Caffé	12	12
x 30	ditto	16	16
	Theatre &c	2.10	48
		272.19	52 94
	Boardg 17 days at 4.10 pr day	76.10	13.60
	trifling expences omitted[74]	12.	2.30
		361.9	68.84

	October	1804	
Nice			
1	Caffé	16	16
2	do	16	16
<13>	Theatre	1.10	30

73. Presumably the French edition of Mrs. Radcliffe's *Italian;* see journal entry of October 9, 1804.

74. This item is in pencil under the ink.

3	Caffé	16—	16
	Theatre &c	2 ..	40
4	Caffé &c	1.—	20
	Theatre	1.10	30
5	Boat from Villefranche to Nice	1.10	30
	Caffé	16	16
6	Caffé	16	16
x 7	Caffé &c	1.	20
	Theatre	1.10	30
8	Caffé	16	16
9	Caffé &c	1—	20
10	ditto &c	1.—	20
	Postage of Letters	3.5	63
	Theatre	1.10	30
11	Caffe	16	16
	Theatre &c	2	38
12	Caffe &c	1.—	20
	Purchased Morses Geography[75]	3	57
13	Caffe	16	16
x 14	do &c	1	20
15	do &c	1.	20
16	do	16	16
		31.19	6.32

	October[76]	1804	
	Amt brot: over	31..19	6..32
16	Postage of a Letter from Paris containing my passport	3.13	
	<Perquisite> Gratuity to an officer of Police	1.10	

75. The famous geography of Jedediah Morse (1761–1826) was first published as *The American Geography* in 1789; later editions bore the title *The American Universal Geography*. There were seven American and almost as many European editions.

76. From "October" through "14 last month" the writing is in blue ink. The remainder of the page is in brown ink.

	Beaureau de Santé	1.—	
	Laundress for since 14 last month	11	
	Remainder of Bill at Hotel since 13th Sept	178.10	
	Postage of Letters	4.14	
	Degrasseur[77] &c	3	
	Servants	15	
		250 6	
17	Caffé	12	
	Maletot[78]	7	
	Supper at St Remo	2.10	
18	Breakfast &c	18	
	Pd. boy for carrying Pmanteau 2 leagues	1.10	
	Sup at Port Maurice	2.10	
19	bed & breakfast	1.12	
	trifles	10	

October

	Amt brot over	260.15	
20	Sup & bed at Savona	2.10	
	Chocolate at do	9	
	Fruit &c	16	
	Passage in felucca from Nice to Genoa	13. 7	
	Gratuity to men for carrying me ashore at St Stephano	15	
	Provisions in the boat	5.15	
	Gratuity to sailors	1.5	
		285 12	54.50

77. "Dry cleaner."
78. "Tax."

at Genoa		money of Genoa	
20	Porter	1 5	
30	Mending boots	8.<8>	
31	Hotel expences 11 days viz room at 4 liv pr d. 2 dinners 12 liv wine 8 Valet deplace 8	72	
		80.15 of Genoa	12.50
			$67
	Postage of a paquet of Letters from Bordeaux	24.–	3.40
			$70.40

November

Genoa		Money of Genoa
1	Shoes	4.10
3	Lottery	4
5	Shoemaker	4
6	Cloth for pantaloons	36
x		
10	Hair dresser	2
14	Gloves	1
x		
16	White Jean for 2 waistcoats	11
	Breast pin	4
	Theatre	1
	Silk for black Breeches	27
	Expences at Sestri at different times	20
20	Mending boots	.. 14
	½ doz cambrick frills for shirts	13.7

	Cloth for a Grey Frock purchd. the beginning of the month at ↑liv↓ 10.10 pr palm[79]	105	
	blk florentine for breeches purchd. at same time 54 ↑sous↓ a palm	27.9	
24	Gloves	1.4	
30	Bill at Hotel 30 days Lodging Room 4 liv pr day	120	
	Police ticket	1	
		383.4	51.30

December

3	Great Coat cloth at 6 liv pr palm 17 palms Silk Serge at 30 ↑sous↓ pr plm 5 palms ¾ palm Silk Velvet 4 ↑liv↓ 1 doz buttons 2 . Making 12 .	127.2
5	Taylors bill for making frock pantaloons &c mentiond in last month 30 livres deducted for a drab frock which he spoild in cleaning	21.6
8	Leather suspenders	4
	Gloves	1.4
	hair dresser	2 —

79. Presumably a palm in this use was approximately seven or eight inches.

	Chapeau bras	24 ..
	breast pin	2.
	Money spent at Sestri &c	24
12	Theatre &c	2.10
	Shoes purchd. the 4 or 5th	5 –
15	Kerseymere Gaitres	13
20	Shoes	5
	Sestri	7
	Theatre	1 10
	Postage of letter from Bordeaux	8
	Mendg boots & shoes	4
		L 251.12

December contind.

	Am brot over	251.12
20	Dictionary of 3 langu. 3 vol	12.
	Blank books	2.4
	Lead pencils	2
	Padlock for small portmanteau	1.10
	Bill at Hotel for Room &c 4 liv pr day 20 days	80.–
	Washing – 2 months	48
	Exchge. commissions for 7720 Liv Genoa on marseilles	38 12
	Servant	8 –
	Shoeblack	1
	Porter	1.10
	Boatmen	1.10[80]

80. The "10" is in pencil. Possibly Irving did not count it in when adding up the column. If it is counted, the total figure should be "479.18."

21	Boatmen	2	
	Theatre	1	
22	Boatmen	2	
	Theatre	1	
	Cheated out of <10>	10	
23	Pd. Domenico	16[81]	
		479.8	73 50

Sketch of my rout[82]

From Bordeaux to Toulouse	34	
from do. to Beziers	22¼	
Montpellier	9¼	
Nismes	6½	
Avignon	5½	
Aix	9½	
Marseilles	4–	
from do. to Tourves by a crossroad	5–	
Nice	20	
	116	Posts
	2	
	232	leagues
	3	
	696	miles

Quennedy Palais royal
takes likeness By Stenograph[83]

81. This line is in blue ink.

82. Items on this page, p. [185], and the next are presented in normal order. "Sketch . . . 696 miles" is written right side up on the page.

83. Probably the Quenedy, "physionatrace," whose address a few years later was Rue Neuve des Petits Champs 15 (Francesco Piranese, *La Pariséum ou Tableau Actual de Paris,* 2nd ed., Paris, 1809, p. 171). This sentence is in pencil and right side up on the page.

Pr Cash from New York	94$
Recd from Bosc[84] & co	– 250
	344

6 | 120
20[85]

Hotel des freres Maiçones[86]
rue de Grenelle St
Honore Recommended[?]
by M. Martel[87]

<Co> carao[?][88]

[*inside back cover*][89]
Storm 10.10

Dominicho del Amore[90]
minature painter a Rome

84. Jean Jacques Bosc (1757–1840), head of the Bordeaux banking firm of J. J. Bosc et Cie., was a member of the chamber of commerce in the city in 1823 and deputy of the Département of the Gironde, 1831–1833 (Édouard Féret, *Statistique générale, Topographique, Scientifique, Administrative, Industrielle, Commerciale, Agricole, Historique, Archeologique et Biographique du Départment de la Gironde,* Bordeaux, 1889, III, 85).

85. "Pr Cash . . . 20" is written in pencil upside down on the page.

86. This page is in pencil, erased except for the last word. Possibly the name is "Maçons." A person of this name was operating a few years later a "bureau des delegues des entrepreneurs" in the Rue de la Mortellerie 151 (*Almanac de 25,000 Adresses de Paris, pour l'année 1817,* Paris, 1817).

87. Three Martels were listed as residents of Paris a few years later (*ibid.*).

88. This word is upside down on the page. Possibly it represents a false start (the first two letters are lighter than the rest) and the first two syllables of the word "Caradoro" (see journal entry of April 8, 1805, n. 389). Underneath is part of an expense account, apparently between Bordeaux and Touslouse, erased.

89. All writing except the first four lines is upside down inside the cover. "Storm 10.10" is in ink; "Recd . . . $155" is in ink over pencil; all other writing on the page is in pencil.

90. Domenico del Amore (fl. 1800), miniature painter, is known only for a signed portrait of a child, exhibited at an exposition of miniatures in Berlin in 1906.

Juam Padrone[91]

30 –
21

Recd. Aug 1
of Mr J & J Bosc Livres 1312. 10

$250

Recd. Decr. 9 of
De la rue freres[92] Liv. 1000 of Genoa

$155

Hotel de Luxembourg[93] St [*illegible*] ↑<St[*illegible*]>↓
pres la que Augustins
Boston[94] rue Vivienne

[*back cover*]
1804[95]

91. Possibly the name of the padrone of the vessel on which Irving sailed from Genoa to Messina.

92. The De la Rue Fratelli were bankers in Genoa a few years later (*Almanacco del Ducato di Genova per l'Anno Bisestile 1828,* Genoa, 1827, p. 111).

93. The Hôtel du Luxembourg was in the Rue de la Harpe, which is crossed by the Rue St. Severin and is near the Quai des Augustins.

94. The Hôtel Boston.

95. "1804" is written in black ink. Below it is a red seal with the initials "W.I."

TRAVELING NOTES, 1804–1805

Genoa–Lucerne

The manuscript notebook is in the Manuscript Division of the New York Public Library, No. 3 in the Seligman Collection. It consists of 155 pages, written mostly in pencil, of a parchment-bound booklet of 190 pages, measuring 5⅝ x 3⅞ inches. Pp. [42, 93, 121, 123, 128, 132–35, 137, 139, 141, 144–47, 149, 154–59, 164–70, 174–78] are blank.

[*front cover*][1]

1805
Travelling Notes

17.10
12.14
3.16[?]

2/5.7
2.14
5.7 [?]
16[?]
4.16

[*inside front cover*]
Due Mr C[abell] from me 4 liv[2]
Due Mr C ½ livres
for carriage to Sesto[?]

Sferro[3]
Monomente
22 miles
Catenanuova

1. All the writing on the front cover is in ink. The figures are upside down on the lower half of the cover.
2. This line is in ink, upside down. The other writing on the page is in pencil.
3. "Sferro . . . Naples" is written sideways on the page.

Maria Console[4]
<St>
Le Chapel de
St Savorina
a Naples

[*p. [1]*]
December 23, 1804

Saild at 1 oclock from Genoa with a fine wind in the ship Matilda[.] Matthew Strong of Phila bound for Messina in Sicily. This morning Storm bid me farewell – <a heavy parting>

January 3

Came in sight of Stromboli & other Lipari Islands. Stromboli at night made frequent explosions

January 4

<Sail> Bearing up to the mouth of the straight. Famous Rock of Scylla & its town on the left on the Calabrian coast Glorious sun rise – sun rises over the Calabrian mountains. Rich clouds[.] the coast of Sicily low & beautiful – verdant at this season. Mountains inland Aetna at a distance coverd with snow Summit in clouds. Stromboli makes a great explosion[,] smoke rising in a vast column to the clouds[.] Genoese Capt says it is a sign that bad weather is at hand. Scylla rather a rocky bluff – & by no means so dreadful as the poets represent it. <Think> I was mistaken – Scylla is situated below the bluff and at a distance appears something like a square tower[.] at the foot of it are some smaller rocks. country lovely & green like spring time & well cultivated – houses picturesque[.] Cape Pelorus has a fine level plain raisd above the sea

Messina opens beautifully round an eminence

Mountains back of Messina very picturesque. The Calabrian particularly so and not Alpine but long & level on the top cloathed with brush all green <& al> Approach to Messina beautiful – Harbor fine & safe

Had to go to the health office. Fellow affraid of the fat little captain

4. "Maria consul." Possibly Irving intended to write "Maria consola" ("Mary consoles").

5. La Capella S. Severino is in the church of SS. Severino e Sosio, which was built in 1490.

<for fea> lest he had the fever – his whimsical behavior – returnd aboard – Old Greek and three <Monk> Capuchins – We had to go to Lazaretto to be examined. Made us open our necks & breasts & whack our arms – Had some fruit refreshing after salt meat

January 11

At Quarantine for 21 days. Capuchin monks at the health office who had been on a pilgrimage to Jerusalem to see the tomb of our Savior – Said they had made many converts – Escaped from the guards & endeavord to get a letter on board the Nautilus[.] disappointed, the guard gave me close chace. Had the boat rigd for sailing – Charybdis facing the city the other side of the promontory. Storm, snow on top of the mountains but mild in the low places. Beautiful nights. Fruit exceeding cheap & very good – bawling of the guards[.] English privateer with crew of Maltese &c. One of the ruffians regretted that they had not encounterd us before we got in the harbor. Bye & bye a cant word among the sailors & guards. Ringing of bells perpetual. Convents are in great numbers & priests in <ignorance> regiments. The Key is a fashionable walk. The Nautilus sixty fathoms from shore & in 50 fathoms water – water extremely clear & fish plenty.

January 14

Sailed about in the harbor & viewed an English Frigate that had just come in Numbers of English vessels in the port. Constant arrival of Ships Brigs &c. Confusion at the Lazaretto among the crew of an English privateer in Quarantine. Men fighting & mutinous against the Lieut. One drew his knife on him[.] they were composed of Maltese &c The capt sent them all ashore.

January 15

We were obliged this morning to descend passengers & crew into the hold to have the hatches laid down and a fire made with charcoal in a chafing dish on which were th[r]own certain drugs which raised a thick smoak of a disagreeable smell[.] here we had to stay a quarter of an hour

This <was> ↑is↓ a measure observed towards all the ships twice during Quarantine if they have any <f>yellow fever lurking in their veins this drives it out.

In the afternoon we were ordrd ashore at the lazerretto where we again had our necks & bosoms examind by the Doctor –

January 24

Admitted to Pratique & went on board the Nautilus

January 29

Set sail for Syracuse in company with English schoonr – Wind came ahead & blew hard

January 30

Put back to Messina. News had been brot to Messina that <the english> a fleet had been seen off the Straits[.] the people were all alarmd supposing it to be the french or English come to take possessn of the place.

January 31

This morning a ship or two of the line was seen entering the harbor The whole town was in an uproar. The Quay lined with spectators couriers passing & repassing More ships made their appearance & it was ascertaind to be the english Fleet. Lord Nelsons ship hove in sight. The forts were mand & the people seemed to wait in fearful expectation The fleet however passed by the harbor & continued thro the Straits making a noble appearance.

We got under way making a signal for the English schooner to do the same & stood out of the harbor.

The English Schooner was some time in getting under way which gave us a fine opportunity of examining the fleet. It consisted of 11 sail of the line three frigates & two Brigs. They appear to be in search of the French fleet which has lately got out of Toulon & it is expected have gone round the other side of Sicily. The Fleet continued in sight all day and we were much amused by observing their signals & evolutions. In the evening it freshned & blew strong ahead but in the course of the night baffled very much.

Fine sunset. sun sinking behind mount Ætna

February 1

This morning we found ourselves much in the same place as last evening The Schooner that we have to convoy is a poor sailor & the captain appears to be <a poor jud> affraid to carry sail so that we have frequently to lay to for him and he operates as a complete clog on our vessel.

This day we had very strong gales that washd over us repeatedly. The other schooner scud before them with almost bare poles but fortunately the wind subsided & came about in the evening to the west so that we were again enabled to continue on our course.

Society of the officers very agreeable – ward room extremely lively.

February 2

Arrived in Syracuse about 2 oclock[.] beautiful harbor – country more level. Names of officers on board of the Nautilus 1 Lieut G W Ried – 2d. Ridgely – Master – Cassin [–] Purser Tootle [–] Dr Jaques –

Syracuse miserable & dirty Two hotels at present in the english style. Rehearsal at the opera – number of american officers ashore support the opera.

February 3

Went on board the Frigate President & was introduced to Capt Cox.[6] Fine ship but out of repair.

Ship Essex also – Capt Barron[7] – found there Amory of Boston[,] Woolsey of New York – miserable masquerade at night. saw there Thorne[8] of New York.

February 4

Went to see the Ear of Dionisyus in company with Tootle[,] Davis a midship of Presd.[,] Baker a Doctor

Beautiful scenery in the neighborhood of the city. Situation of the old city – immense excavations in the rock. Ear serpentine in form of an <s> S <and> by no means resembles a human ear. height the same to the extremity – narrows to the top where there is a channel about [*blank*] that runs the whole length & communicates with a chamber at the top. Shape like the external form of an asses ear holes in the rock to which prisoners were fastend. Square chamber in the rock – chamber also aloft at the interior extremity[.] musket &

6. George Cox was appointed lieutenant June 15, 1799, commander May 27, 1804, and resigned April 8, 1808.

7. James Barron (1769–1851), entered the Navy as a lieutenant in 1798, was made captain in 1799, and commodore in 1807. In that year he was courtmartialed for neglect of duty and suspended for five years. Reinstated in 1821, he retired in 1848.

8. Probably Jonathan Thorn, who became a midshipman April 28, 1800, was officially appointed lieutenant February 16, 1807, and was furloughed May 18, 1810.

pistol reports very loud – paper torn makes likewise a great noise. voices are distinctly heard – Peasants bring torches of straw. various other appartments caverns & recesses in the rocks in some of which they make salt petre. A tower standing on a high peice of rock – various vast fragments lying around that have formerly had a stairs cut in them have been tumbled down by an earth quake. Subterraneous garden – Amphitheater[,] aqueduct[,] water turns a mill with exceeding violence.

In the afternoon whent down a hole in the middle of the street in Syracuse near the hotel – hole round – about 15 feet deep with niches to descend[.] you then go along about 10 feet & come to a precipice down[9] which you look into a chamber about 15 ft square narrowing to the top and 40 or 50 feet high. <As we> by the light of our flambeau we could distinguish another passage opposite us similar to the one by which we entered. As we had no cord sufficiently strong we did not venture to descend. This excavation was accidently discovered about 3 weeks since by <a w> an ass falling with his hind feet into it.

three officers of our navy have been down in it to the bottom of the chamber but could not find that it extended any farther except in one direction which terminated very soon. It is conjectured by some to have been a granary – by others a place of confinement Whatever it was intended for it appears not to have been finished. At some distance from the hole on the surface of the ground are similar ones which have not been uncovered – perhaps these have antiently been dungeons under some building

Visited the fountain of Arethusa – does not appear to me to spring up all of a sudden as Brydone[10] says but to be conducted thro subterraneous passages for some distance under the earth

February 5

Sat off to visit the Caticombs &c in compy with Lieut Ried. Tootle and Baker. in our way we passd a place where they have lately dug up the ruins of a temple &c. Several of the columns lie near the hole. They are of grey granite some plain doric & others fluted spirally. Here they have dug up a beautiful torso of a Venus <It> & a small statue of Esculapius. The former wants the head & an arm, but I have no doubt that they would be found upon a little more search. They have desisted

9. "dow" is at the end of one line and "n" at the beginning of the next.
10. Patrick Brydone, *A Tour through Sicily and Malta* (London, 1773) I, 277.

from searching for *want of money* – The King of Sicily has allowd but 600 crowns for searchg antiquities in Sicily and 200 crowns only fall to this departmt which are already expended. Perhaps no place in Sicily or Italy affords a finer field for discoveries

<The caticombs>

The enterance to the caticombs are from a small antient church or chapel. Here we found a venerable Capuchin whose wrinkled front & grey beard made him appear as one of the inhabitants of the tombs restord to life. he light[ed] two flambeaus and gave one to our guide to bear We were first shewn a subterraneous chaple & the sepulchre of a saint The walls around painted with uncouth pictures of saints & angles.

We ascended from the chaple and going thro a yard in rear of the church descended into the catacomb – Of vast extent forming a labarynth. every here & there are small chambers that appear to have had ventilators at the top – arched passages branch out in different directions large excavations for particular families having sometimes places for 60 or 70 bodies. One passage said to lead to Catania 40 miles distant. It is said that a priest & two boys undertook to explore it carrying a supply of provisions & torches. The priest & one boy died on the way and the other boy was almost sinking when he emerged into day at the foot of Mount Ætna. no bones in there at present. Walls damp with water filtering thro them.

Gardens of Latomie – belonging to a convent of Capuchins. The convent handsomely situated[.] the garden is about 100 feet below the level of the ground – go down to it by steps cut in the rock. The garden is quite a labyrinth. You pass from one part to another thro ↑a↓ immense arch formd by the falling of part of the Rocks[.] <imm> great masses of rocks remain standing in different places 70 or 80 feet high over run with foliage & with trees grown on them the sides of the rocks coverd with running vines indian fig &c The whole shelterd from wind – oranges lemons &c grow in profusion and noble large citrons[.] in two places there are remains of caves that have been cut similar to the ear of Dyonisius but the rocks have fallen or something else has intervend to prevent their being finished. in one place we were shewn the tomb of an Amer: midshipman ↑Nicholson↓ lately killd in a duel by one of his shipmates[.] he is buried in a hole dug in the side of the rock & plasterd up with an inscription in english and a cross above it. This garden is a delightful retreat <the sun being> for summer

<and> the sun being skreened by the rocks & trees. It is supposed to be the antient Quarries of Syracuse I have been told since that there are several embalmed bodies in high preservation in the caverns of this garden but I did not see them

After we left the garden we enterd the convent & asked for a glass of water[.] they shewed us to the refectory and gave us some bad wine with exortations to sobriety and repeated observations that a little wine was good but not to drink much. We had no need of this exhortation for the wine was so execrable that we could scarcely swallow it. My complaisance induced me to force down half a tumbler full but Lieut Ried could not contain himself but spit it out at the first mouthful making dreadful wry faces I was affraid the good fathers would have been displeased – When we left them we gave them what change we had left which we thought quite sufficient but they thought otherwise for we had scarcely got out of the <doo> grand gate when a young monk came after us saying the president refused to accept it[.] we told him then to keep it himself

February 6

This morning Lieut Murray of the president – <Capt> Lieut Gardner of Do.[,] Capt. Hall of the Marines of Do.[,] Capt Dent & myself sat off to see the ear of Dionysius. We sent of[f] at first a Midshipman & 4 sailors with a spar & a couple of halyards. We went to the top of the rock over the ear and fastening ourselves to the rope were lowerd over the face of the rock into a small hole at the top of the ear The persons lowerd were Murray Hall the Midshipman & myself. The <hole th> channel of the ear at the top runs to this hole but the front of the rock is broken down so as to destroy the <ch> connexion of one side of the channel – <Hole> passage from hole began to be cut to run into the interior but finishes at the distance of 15 feet. Gardner fired off a pistol repeatedly but it did not seem to make a greater noise than when below. One person speaking just above a whisper at the extremity of the cave was heard very distinctly by me and appeard to be just behind me. I could likewise hear him distinctly when he spoke low in any other part of the cave near to the wall[.] I could hear him even when he whisperd but could not distinguish the words. I doubt much that <intent of this cave opinion that> this cave was intended for the purpose generally ascribed to it. three or four persons speaking at a time in it would create a confusion. An antiquarian here supposes it was intended for a place of torture & that the echoes would make such horrible noises as too intimidate all the other untorturd prisoners[.] this does not satisfy me either but I do not know a better one.

<Ampith> Theater cut in the rock of a great size

– Saw at an Antiquarians the statue of Venus lately dug up. It is a beautiful figure. <One> In an inclined posture something <life> like the Venus of Medici One hand is covering the left breast and the left hand has hold of some robes that are round her feet and raisd up to her middle – A statue of Archmedes[11] is more common made of coarse alabaster.

In the evening visited the cathederal formerly a temple of Minerva The two rows of vast pillars with their capitol & cornice still remain & are masond into the walls of the church In the church they have several curiosities [–] an Amber Cup ↑chalice↓ of beautiful workmanship on which is worked in relief the grand actions of our Saviour The cover has carved on it the last supper in a space about the bigness of a Dollar the figures &c all perfect – An antique sandal of leather & red velvet among other curiosities[.] they shew a large bomb shell which they say fell thro the roof of the church during the time it was beseiged by the spaniards & never burst. This was owing to the interposition of St Lucie a lady of extraordinary piety who had died some time before and who was seen by some person or persons in the church to appear and extinguish the fuse of the shell She was accordingly sainted and made the patroness of the City!! What chiefly pleased me in the church was a very fine alto relievo of the lords supper on an alter in one of the side chapels and a painting over the high alter. I do not know the name of either of the authors.

Dined this day on board of the President.

February 7

This morning went to engage mules for Catania. <W> I shall have very good company thro Sicily <C> Hall Capt of Marines on board of Presdt. accompanies me – he is orderd to search thro <Ital> Sicily for a band of music & is determind <at least> not to find one at least till he gets to Palermo

<The purs> he is a young fellow of [*blank*][12] & very gentlemanlike

11. In the notebook and journal entries of February 5, Irving identified the second statue as one of Aesculapius.

12. Apparently Irving intended to supply the name of Hall's home city, Charleston, South Carolina (see journal entry of February 11, 1805).

& agreeable. The purser of the Presdt also accompanies us who is likewise a clever fellow & perhaps <to> one or two – more. We have two servants & shall all be well armd.

Syracuse is a most miserable hole – It is incredible the vast swarms of poor wretches – filth & vermin abound. The nobility are poor & man[y] great beggars. When entertaind on board of our ships they often fill their pockets with sugar &c

Syracuse <is only> stands but on a small portion of its antient scite – the island of Ortigia. Since the Americans have made this their Rendezvous the trade has briskned & a number of ↑mercht↓ vessels are constantly in the harbor. –

The Americans are constantly attended by a ragged retinue in the streets[.] they are charged exhorbitantly for every thing[.] they are very much respected & feard – formerly attacks were frequent in the streets at night on our officers but now they take care to <giv> keep clear of any one who speaks english <The nobility are always glad to be invited>

February 8

Paid <a> visits to Different nunneries this morning in company with Capt Hall Wadsworth Baker & Lieut Cargill – The first we saw was the convent of St Lucie The church is very neat and prettily painted. At one end of the church is a gallery for the nuns defended by a <gil> handsome <gilt> grating of gilt Iron They enter it by a door from the convent. After having viewd the church for some time we returned to the parlour. <There are different> Here visitors to the nuns or abbess may be permitted to talk to them thro double Iron gates but as we had no particular business with them we could not claim that indulgence. A skreen hung before the grating on the other side[.] <two> some of the young nuns lifted it to peep at us but on our advancing to speak with them They droppd it and we could hear them tittering & laughing among themselves. At some of the other <churches> ↑nunneries↓ we were more fortunate[.] we were readily admitted to a view of the church and in one a nun happned to come into the gallery – As soon as she saw us she ran & calld some of her companion[s] and we enjoyed a kind of conversation with them by signs[.] two or three of them were quite handsome. They appeard exceedingly delighted with our visit. At another convent we went to a machine that turns in an aperture in the wall to recieve & deliver things for the convent. It turns on a pivot & is a round hollow box open on one side into which you put what you wish to deliver & by a turn of the box the open place turns to the inside of the convent[.] here there was a <small hole> little peep hole <to look thro> thro which we could see the nuns employed within in a large room sewing &c &c Several were young with health beauty & innocence blooming in their countenances. They soon percieved us and ran up to the machine We talked with them in what little italian we knew and they seemed as highly pleased as the nuns had been at the other convents. In like manner we visited sevral more

The poor girls are glad to see any strange face particularly gentlemen & americans. Our officers have had handkerchiefs waved to them sevral times by nuns from the tops of the convents

February 9

Walked about

Sunday, February 10

Nuns on tops of the convents talking with Baker Lieut Morris & myself – & making lascavious gestures – dined at Gnl Birches[?].[13] evening Masquerade in character of an old man

February 11

Sat off for Catania in company with Capt Hall – Purser wadsworth of presdt & Wynn of congress & servt. Wyn & Wadsworth in a Latiga. the rest on horses. made a cavalcade of 11 men & 7 horses. Country level & stoney Caverns in the rocks about syracuse. passed <one> a circular hole in the ground that appeared to decend into a cavern of a great depth dangerous to travellers in the night. Beautiful prospect One a vista of olives Aetna in the distance – Stoppd at a convent of capuchins to dine. Old fathers met us with much civility and produced a pitcher of good white wine[.] we had provided some beef & pork & made a hearty meal[.] we then went thro the convent which appeard to be very poor One of the monks shewed us some wax work <of an> that he had made that was extremely well done. We quitted the convent in high spirits having dispatched a <cop> couple of pitchers of wine of the good friars and a few glasses of their Rosolio for which we gave

13. Possibly the Samuel Ogden Birch mentioned on the last page of this journal.

them a good recompense. Passed in sight of <Catan> Augusta – the antient Megara. Castle in the sea In evening after sun down arrived at a miserable village called Povereto del Mondo[.] inhabitants livd in miserable cabins[.] guides wished to stop here but we refused – they detailed bad roads &c &c but the moon promised to shine brilliantly & we proceeded. rugged rocks[.] passed a number of caverns where the people live who tend cattle. Put up for the night at Lentini. Antient city of Leontini. Hercules gave them a lion for a standard Settled by the Nassi. tolerable inn for Sicily – beds clean

February 12[14]

In morning set out again. beautiful plains antiently termed the Lestrigonian – reminded me of views in America. Lake Beverio said by the antients to be made by Hercules abounds with fish & wild fowl The eels are extremely fine. Passd over a hill on which were some antient remains but I could [not] ascertain whether they were the reliques of an aqueduct or not. About two Oclock arrived at Catania. The Day was cloudy so that we could not enjoy a fine prospect. Ætna shrouded in clouds. lava around catania. put up at Hotel of Gold Lion splendid carriages & liveries. Feast of St Agatha the patroness of this city. The cathederal was finely illuminated. We went there after dark and found it crowded with people. We bustled thro the crowd and at last found ourselves <opp> in front of the chapel of St Agatha which is seperated from the rest of the church by a gilt iron grate[.] we were looking thro when an old gentleman who was seated within with two ladies came and spoke to the guard at the door who opened it and desired us to walk in. We complid and the old gentleman was extremely particular in shewing us the place[.] one of the ladies spoke french extremely well & I had a long conversation with <them>her. They appeared to be people of distinction from the respect & attention shewn them. They procured us admition into an inner room where <were> we were shewn <the> a <small min> Gothic building in minature within which was the heart of St. Agatha. A little while after a grand procession was made by the priests bearing around the church the image of this saint under a velvet canopy. Mob enthusiastic in their exclamations <holding up> stretching their arms towards it & throwing up their hats. It was brot & deposited in the inner room where we were admitted to a sight of it. It is coverd with jewels to an immense amount –

14. The dateline has been supplied by the editor. There is no break in the manuscript at this point, but "12th" is written before "In."

and I never before saw such an assemblage of precious stones. Returnd thanks to the persons who had been so polite & took our leave

P.S This afternoon the Chevalier Landolini to whom we had brought letters called upon us very politely He is a Knight of Malta and related to some of the first families in the place He has offerd his services to escort us to see the curiosities of the town

[For Irving's "Traveling Notes" from February 13 through March 6, 1805, see pages 204–23, above.]

March 7

This morning <at d> early I arose and found that we were within the bay of Naples. Mount Vessuvius still continued luminous – by degrees the day broke. the objects were gradually lighted up[.] I remaind earnestly gazing around endeavoring to trace places that I had often read discriptions of – At length the heavens were brilliantly illuminated. The sun appeard diffusing the richest rays among the clouds & gilding every feature of the prospect.

Then it was that I had a full view of this lovely bay – The classic retreats of Baia – Puzzoli. The supurb city of Naples – The delightful towns of Portici &c that skirt the Mount Vessuvius The mountain itself vomiting an immense column of smoke – with the coast <of> that terminates the bay beyond the mountain affording the most picturesque scenery – The view of Naples from the sea is truly magnificent & imposing – As soon as I landed & had <changed> arranged matters at the health office & changed my clothes I went to deliver some of my letters At Degens I found letters for me from Storm at Genoa enclosing letters from America – At Valen Roaths & Co I found more letters from Storm and at Mr Falconet & Co I found two paquets that had come <for me> from <?borde?> America via Bordeaux[.] by this time my pockets were cramd like a post boys knapsack so I hastened home to enjoy them

Dined at Valen Roaths & Co Valentine is a very clever fellow – found there several honest american Captains. In the evening returned to finish the perusal of my letters.

March 9

I have kept in doors chiefly since my arrival busy engaged in writing letters – from my window I have a fine view of Mount Vessuvius the other side of the bay which <has not yet ceased fr> has lately made a considerable eruption and still emits vast volumes of smoke & considerable streams of lava [–] at night the red hot lava is very visible. My window likewise looks on a large square crow[d]ed with <obj> people coaches &c. &c. on the other side is a large castle of antient structure and extremely picturesque – This evening took a walk on the principal promenade but it was too late to see any thing.

March 10

Arrived this day the brig Jersey Capt Blagg from New York via Leghorn[.] I went along side of her but did not dare to go on board as she is Quarantined for 28 days Saw on board Mr Philips of New York who is making the tour of Europe[.] he goes the same route with myself so that we shall be travelling companions – Dined with Degen & Schwartz both very clever fellows – Ps. The people in Naples like in all other parts of italy live very high up stairs – Stairs & entrances announce mean & dirty houses so that a stranger is surprized to enter into magnificent appartments. In evening to an oratorio – called David[15] – the part of David by a Eun[u]ch [–] spight of the contempt & prejudice I had imbibed against these poor devils I was delighted with his singing – first singer of women is cousin to Mr Caffarena of Genoa and I have a letter of introduction to her – Scenery very excellent at opera

March 11

This morning I was visited by Mr Norbert Hadrava a german old gentleman who I had seen at Mr Schwartz yesterday where he played on the piano forte in a masterly manner. I had admired some pieces of music of his composing and he was so well pleased with it that he brought me copies of some of them viz Yankee Doodle & Hail Columbia with very excellent variations and a <?swa?> sweet little german song. The old gentleman breakfasted with me and I was very well amused with him.

At eleven Oclock Mr Degen calld on me & introduced me to a Mr Cabal of Virginia and Col Mercer one of the commissioners of claims sent out to france. They arrived the day before yesterday from Rome. I was highly pleasd with Cabal whom I had heard particular mention of before.

15. So many oratorios have this title that it does not seem possible to identify this one. Among the composers who produced a *David* are Scarlatti, Mozart, and Federici.

<bar> Barracks for soldiers
218 paces
Theatr[e]
Excursion to Herculaneum Pompeii
Portici & Vessuvius –[16]

March 24

Sat off for <Naples> ↑Rome↓ in compy with Mr Cabell – a Italian who sp<ea>oke french fluently is our fellow passenger in voiture[.] he is a very good humourd civil fellow. After leaving Naples we passed along fine roads thro <charm> fertile plains These grew more interesting as we approached Capua – Wheat green & gives a very verdant appearance to the fields. Beautiful hills. Appenine (spurs) mountains coverd with snow[.] Capua a decent town. demanded our passport at the gate – fortified in modern style – Antient Capua stood two miles off. We had a convincing proof that this one did not inherit its luxuries in the miserable meal we made of eggs & cheese in a wretched inn – leaving Capua we found the road more diversified by gentle Hills among which we had the most romantic & gentle scenery – every thing smiling at the reviving touch of Spring. Peasants dressed in an uncouth style [–] as it was Sunday they were all in their *Gala* suits The same taste for shew & glitter prevails from the highest to the lowest grades only the latter exhibit with more simplicity & less taste They are very fond of glaring colours scarlet purple yellow &c[.] the hats of the men are steeple crownd and they think themselves happy if they have a peacocks feather to stick in them or a bunch of gay flowers glaring ribbons &c The women have their scarlet bodices decorated with tinsel &c &c

In evening arrivd at St Agatha and put up for the night in a wretched inn – it is painful to see so fine a count[r]y in the hands of so weak & negligent a government & such miserable people

March 25

Sat off before day break – After Sunrise arrived at the river Gare-gliano antiently the Liris [–] crossed the river in a scow – Very pic-

16. The last five lines are crossed out with six diagonal lines.

turesque view – the river runs thro an extensive plain [–] Hills that used to produce the falernian wine – old towers on the river where the scow passes to [*blank*][17] Sphinx in a wall of the town – ruins of the antient town of Minturnum consisting of ampitheatre aqueduct &c On the river in the marshes near Minturnum it was that Marius took refuge from the vengeance of Sylla This river was an antient boundary of Latium

From hence we continued thro a most charming count[r]y to Mola – situated in Gulph of Gaeta – romantic scenery [–] Villages with towers & rising out of the sea. Mola was antiently Formæ built by the Listrigonians or man eaters

Breakfasted here and walked after breakfast among charming olive fields & vineyards. Country girls have much native beauty twist their hair with ribbons &c in coils on the backs of their heads.

The town of Gaeta with the chateau[18] is very picturesque.

Beyond <Ga>Mola we passd some ruins on each side of the Appian road [–] from these houses decinded a gentle slope coverd with olives to the sea[.] here it was that Cicero was murdered[.] to the left of the road we passed a high picturesque tower called The tomb of Cicero. A German Colonel accosted us at Mola & said his servt had robbd him & he wanted to have a place in the voiture, we did not like him and went off without him – fine road & beautiful prospects to fondi which has antient towers[.] here our trunks were searched & our passports examined. in the neighborhood is a cave where Sejanus concealed Tiberius. town square with two streets crossing each other.[19] After leaving Fondi we passed a beautiful river of Fontana di Petrono. The ruins of a castle where a Princess of the house of Collonna was carried off by the Pirate Barbarossa

Terracina a fine town the new part well built Walked to the old town on a hill Cathederal built on scite of an old Temple [–] portico has pillars of an old temple [–] large vase where Christians were roasted. At the gate aloft is the scull of a Murdrer who killd another in a fit of Jealousy.

17. Presumably Traetto (since 1890, Minturno).

18. Dating from Roman times, it was enlarged in 1440 by Alfonso of Aragon.

19. The principal street in Fondi is Via Appia Claudio. Two streets converge on it: the former Via dell'Angelico (now Via Tommaso d'Aquino) and Via del Campanile (now Via Onorato II Caetani).

March 26

Sat off before daylight – arrived on the Pontine marshes[.] present Pope has made a fine road on the remains of the old appian way that ran thro the marshes. The lat[t]er are draind & in some places cultivated but are not very fertile[.] they yield sustenance to herds of horses & other cattle – <About noon we> the promontory of Circe where she detaind Ulysses & his companions is just beyond Terracina and distinctly seen from the Marshes[.] it is a high rocky promontory tho homer made it an Island[.] it still retains the name of Circeii – road borderd by trees

At noon arrived at end of the marsh. here is a large convent & an inn the latter miserable in the extreme We took a repast in our carriage on cold meat and wine. Just facing the convent are several broken columns & a <mil> Roman mile stone standing with Cæsars name cut on it A little farther on is an obelisk tumbled from its pedestal with the inscript[io]n on one side *nunc ager Pontinus* & on the other *olim pontina palus* We rode on thro a level country the Appenines still to our right rising from the plain with towns scatterd among their heights. in the evening we arrived at Villetre situated on an eminence and surrounded with vinyards & plantations of olives. This town gave birth to Augustus. The inhabitants pride themselves on it and his portrait embellishd the sign of the wretched tavern where we put up for the night – Women wear vast clumsy stomachers & stays – <Ruins of roman mi at ?sermter tina?> at Sermoneta a town which we passd we saw the scull of another man exposed aloft (in a kind of Iron cage) who had committed murder.

Country neglected – people superstitiously religious & consequently ignorant & poor. Veletri antient capitol of the Volsques

March 27

Left Velletri this morning in a heavy storm of Rain – passd thro the little town of Riccia – founded by Archelous, Siccilus 500 years before the Trojan war and called by him Hermina[.] before we enterd Albano we passed an antient tomb adornd with 5 cones or pyramids calld the tomb of the Curiatii. Albano is said to have been originally founded by Ascanius son of Æneas 40 years before the foundation of Rome & destroyd by the romans but rebuilt. It stands on an eminence & from hence we had a view of Rome & the Campania around it. We arrived at rome about 1½ oclock.

[*p. [93] blank*]

From Rome to Bologna, April 14, 15, 16[20]

– first night slept at Civita Castellano

Second night at Terni –

morning – left Terni early. Our road wound for a long way thro the deep gullies & defiles of the Appenines which assume Grander hights & appearance. Coverd with Trees, oaks &c dry bed of a torrent – Wild solitary scenery – Weather unsettled & rainy. After riding some time we came to where the road ascends the mountain They furnish us with oxen at a house at the foot of the mountain to draw the carriage over. <the Pass> This pass is called il somma being the highest on this side Views confined to the neighboring mountain[.] descend again and after riding some time Spoletto breaks upon us. Old castle on a hill aqueduct. Picturesque appearance of a high mountain behind the hill clothed with trees with the white walls of convents &c appearing among them Spoletto a neat town well paved. Inn very decent [–] one of the best on this route.

Sign of the angel – sulky people – walked out after breakfast to see the curiosities – Gate with an inscription mentioning that Hannibal was repulsed by the inhabitants after the battle of Thrasymenes. Aqueduct over a deep gully said to be roman but evidently gothic. <badly> bad architecture – beautiful hill before mentiond with white convents peeping among the deep green trees. Cleared up to give us a view of the valley below this town. The old castle & a gothic church fine objects in the foreground. Valley as lovely as ever I saw waterd by the smooth Clitumnus – coverd by villages &c – renowned for its fertility – the antient[21] romans chose their victims of sacrifice from this vally – the cattle generally white – Antients pretended it was caused by drinking the white waters of this river. river chalky – All these classic streams are foul – Appenines surround the valley – Threatned a showr – we regaind the town precipitately. People enjoying the holliday of easter reminded me of America – boild eggs – men & boys cracking them as in America – Men discover taste & fancy in italy – place gay flowers in their hats appearance of sentiment

17<7> lubberly fellows in one cart drawn by a miserable horse

Passd the night at Foligni

20. The dates have been supplied by the editor from internal evidence; no date is given for this entry in the notebook.

21. "antien" is at the end of one line and "t" at the beginning of the next.

April 17

this night slept at Valcimarra in the Appenines

April 18

In the morning left Valcimarra before day break. Solitude of the mountains – beautiful sun rise brightening the snowy tops of the mountains. transparent sky – beautiful clouds – gradually descended into a beautiful valley – river that we had followd wound thro it. The town of Tolentino neat & clean [–] took coffee in a handsome caffe – resumed our route thro the valley – scenery more tranquil gently sloping hills. Appenines at a distance behind us their snowy tops rising over the hills. Contrast between the cold of the mountains & the delicious air of the valley. charming weather [–] got out of the carriage & walkd [–] fragrant smell of blossoms Country people well clad and working cheerfully in the fields [–] women working there also a sign of indolence among the men. Castle in the valley [–] beautifull birds singing [–] beautifully situated town of Macerata[22] passed it and <stopped> crossing the river on a wooden bridge we stopped at a tavern near the ruins of the antient town of [*blank*] [.][23] ruind ampitheatre [–] lovely valleys waterd by rivers, towns on eminences Appenines in the distance

Slept at Loretto

Santa Casa stripped of its treasures by the french. Golden lamps replaced by brass ones – Walls of brick. Pilgrims

April 19

Sat off early for Ancona handsome country – Country girls pretty [–] Ancona beautiful harbor [–] fine mole [–] Arch of Augustus [–] City full of business crowded & stinking Well built [–] greek taylors – galley slaves

jusque a Catania[?][24]
300 In porture[?]
piece dure 88:

22. "Macerata" is in ink.

23. Recina.

24. These jottings, on an otherwise blank page, are in ink, except "300," which is in pencil, and to the left of "piece" the number "85," which is written vertically and in pencil. The words appear to be French, but the meaning of the note, or notes, is not clear, partly because the handwriting is not in Irving's characteristic style.

Lake Maggiore, May 3

Morning rather overcast. climate delicious. <Seat> Embark on the Lake at Sesto – beautiful banks to the river Tesino. Birds singing nightingale &c – Swallows skimming over the lake – Water very clear [–] plenty of fish – trout &c Low coast on one side – Sheep & cattle – on the other side more abrupt & coverd with trees – gentle hills – hig[h]er ones alps in the background – beautiful promontories with <towns> villages – churches & convents peeping among the trees. Villages & convents on the sides of the mountains[.] before leaving the Tesino we pass a picturesque castle on a bluff. Luxurient vegetation.

white sails of little barks[25]

View from the statue of St Charles lake winding among mountains <Their> bold contours of mountains the snowy summits of the distant ones shrouded in clouds [–] to the right on the opposite side the fine promontory of the Rock of [*blank*][26] with its castle – below it a small village the whole reflected in the lake – Small boats gliding along – fishing boats – Mountains cultivated enriched by trees – Small village of [*blank*][27] at the foot of a distant mountain – lake fringed by trees – Mountains varied by white cottages chapels convents &c half shrouded in trees – lake ruffled in some places by a gentle breeze in others tranquil reflecting the scenery – Air <serene>[28] mild and salubrious. The repose of the scenery only interrupted by the melody of innumerable little birds the nightingale robin &c and the distant song of the peasant or the innocent mirth of peasant children sporting on the hills

Statue of St Charles gigantic of Bronze – little birds <?flin?> have formed their nests in its ears and on its eyelids – Said to be as large as the famous Colossus of rhodes but I do not put any faith in this observation. We laid down on the grass and enjoyed the delicious scenery sending off the man with orders for the boat to come for us to the foot of the hill.

difference of the mountains Some rising <ap> abruptly others by gentle gradations – Some directly from the water edge others skirted by beautiful plains ado[r]ned with groves of poplar & <elms>oaks. The Statue stands on a mound to which you ascend by an avenue of beautiful horse chestnuts

25. A leaf has been removed from the notebook at this point.

26. Angera.

27. Possibly Arona.

28. Between this word and the next, two pages (pp. [102, 103]) intervene on which is written the poem beginning "Why should we with cares perplex us" (see page 534).

– Peasants working at a new road that is to cross the Simplon one of the grand passes into Switzerland. They were blowing rocks [–] the explosions seemd like cannon and thunderd in repeated echoes among the mountains

– Quarries of Granite from which they furnish the great quantity of that stone that is used in Milan – Mountains coverd with mulberry trees

Changes in the temperature of the atmosphere

Why should we with cares perplex us
  Why should we not happy be
Since on earth theres naught to vex us
  drinking sets our hearts all free
  Lets have drinking without measure
Lets have wine while life we have
  Join to follow follow follow pleasure
  Theres no drinking &c.

Life at best is but a season
  time is ever on the wing
Lets the present moment reason
  Who knows what the next may bring
All our time by mirth we'll measure
  All dull care we will dispose
  Join &c
  To be merry to be wise
When death comes &c.
  Heres a glass come sit by me
Drink old boy until youre mellow
then like us you will be free

Death dont hurry we have leizure
Drinking cant be hurried so
  Join &c
When our wine is out we'll go[29]

May 4

rainy morning – We thought of remaining all day at the island in hopes of having better weather tomorrow We had agreed – upon hiring the boat that in case the weather was bad we should remain till it cleard – at Isola bella. the boatmen however who (like all people of their class in Italy) had no honesty or conscience demanded a <louis d'or> ↑4 crowns↓ per day if they stopped – As we did not wish to

29. This drinking song, presumably not by Irving, has not been identified.

have any al[t]ercation with them we offerd them 2 dollars Our servt brot. us back word that they refused and would at least have 4 livres a peice – We had determined not to indulge them so as soon as we had breakfasted we sent John to tell them either to <take> remain at 2 dollers pr day or to come up & take our trunks to the boat & we would proceed – they did the latter and entering the room pretended to busy themselves about the trunks but evidently waited In hopes we would comply with their price – We however pulld on our boots threw our great coats about our shoulders and orderd them to dispatch After a slight consultation they at length offerd to stay at our terms but it was too late – we had obse[r]ved that the boat was well coverd & dry and determined to punish them for their extortion We therefore told them that they should have complied at first we were resolved to proceed – the scoundrels grumbled but shoulderd the trunks and as they marchd down stairs I heard one reproaching the others for not immediately complying with our price. <Mo>

Mountains enveloped in mist[30] & fog. Isola Madre less beautiful at a distance than Isola bella but far more pleasing on an approach. The west end is extremely picturesque. Nature is not torturd as at Isola bella and tho far less expense is laid out the Island is infinatly more interesting than the latter.

Stopped at the village of Intri for our men to breakfast. Good hotel.

Thermom at night 55 deg

[*p. [108] blank except for unfinished sketch of Ear of Dionysus and jottings written upside down (Figure 12)*]

5000
250
nunc ager pontinus
olim pontina palus.[31]

[*p. [109] shows page-size drawing of Ear of Dionysus (Figure 13)*]

May 5

In morning early 60

Beautiful morning – cloudless sky – <f> the Inn keeper extortionate – John had failed in making a bargain with him yesterday as he was

30. Between this word and the next, two pages (pp. [108, 109]) intervene which contain only drawings and a few jottings (see below).

31. See journal entry of March 26, 1805, n. 278.

represented to him as an honest man – We were punishd for deviating from our customary rule of bargaining before hand 28 livres for a wretched dinner bed & breakfast for ourselves & servants

So much for an honest inn keeper –

Scenery beautiful – Passd the little temple on the promontory [–] it is charmingly situated & is a small rotunda of the Tuscan order all of white granite. Within is placed a statue of St Francisco – very judicious to preserve it from the abuses of the peasantry. the whole was erected by a Marquis of Milan merely thro fancy he having no house near the spot. Continued our voyage – rather windy – Mountains rocky & sterile – cultivated about the skirts dotted with white cottages & convents the former had usurped spots of soil high up on the mounts – The mountains green around the base but dry & arid as they ascended distant ones crownd with snow About 10 oclock the boatmen run into a beautiful cove where they <took shelter from the> rested for the contrary wind to subside – N.B. Mountains are of Granite large masses of which strew the shore. of Difft colours.

Castragovanne – old castle – tower of the ville – lake on summit of a mountain.

Caltageronne – a handsome town – much nobility

Caltanecetta – handsome city – <exchange>[32]

---

bottom of the mounts laid out in vine – Lake makes frequent bays and is from one to three miles wide – little fishermens hamlets & villages with the boats drawn up on the beach or shelterd by small moles. On opening points the convents erected on bluffs and the <tower> spires of village churches have a beautiful effect prospect continually changing

Encounterd a Swiss botanist & his servt who came ashore in the small boat. Took him aboard of us as he appeard very sociable. left the cove. Men draggd the boat – proceeded sometimes on foot ashore sometimes in the boat to Canova a small village situated at the foot of a mountain – Mountain sprinkled over with cottages. The wind was so high that we had to stop at this village Village children came to

32. The manuscript page begins with these notations about three Sicilian towns. Irving apparently did not visit either Caltagione or Caltanisetta, both south of the route he followed from Cantania to Palermo.

us in a kind of procession. One a pretty little girl bore a branch of a tree decorated with ribbons and little lables &c sung a song – and asked for money for a mass – gave them a few sous – Took dinner at the village <poor> indifferent little place – the Inn kept by an old man & his wife who were very honest – Botanist appeared to shuffle a little.

Slept at Canobia

May 6

Arrived at Bellinzona & passed the night

May 7

Our Letters of great service to us in procuring good mules sat off at ½ after six – Beautiful features of the valley – Chest nuts – Wall nuts &c the Tesino winding thro it. rich pasturages coverd with flowers. Mountains featherd[?] with trees. green about the bottom brown higher up[.] Mountains vast [–] Torrents – Charnel houses [–] peasants working at the road honest people – picturesque convents among the mountains – Goats on the precipices – Our mules good dismounted sometimes & walked lingering on the banks of the river in beautiful situations – Several peasants of both sexes passd – with their knapsacks on their backs. joind them & conversed with them [–] they were returning from Milan to their homes in the valley [–] they had been three days on the journey. A young fellow of the party told me of his relations settled in difft. parts all chocolate makers – His exultation at gaining sight of his native mountain –[33]

Valley grows more narrow. The <tessino> Tesino also diminishes Valley cultivated Numerous crosses Mountains of granite vast masses tumbled into the plain torrents rushing down them Mountains peaked & bristled with pines. Villages very poor [–] cliffs & precipices. Men angling for trout. Arrived at the miserable village of Jornico very hungry – hotel poor the dinner very bad – C—— could not eat any – houses of wood dirty – Landlady had a Goiture – Wild scenery of the valley houses perchd up among the cliffs. Landlady & her ↑two↓ daughter[s] came in after Dinner. The names of the latter Marianne & Rosa [–] the latter <young> the youngest & quite pretty & delicate. They shewd

33. On the remaining fourth of the manuscript page is the following, written upside down and canceled:

young earthquake – church
church bells cornfield girl
in crater of etna

the honesty & goodness of the Swiss character. Cabal asked the woman about the Goiture or swelling She said it did not come from <snow> drinking snow water as many said – she drank nothing but wine & milk but it came from child bearing – C told her Alors il ne faut pas faire les petites – Ah monsieur Cabell vous savez bien quand on est marrie il faut fair les petites par force – et alors viennet les grand Goitures en bas said C laughing Ah mon dieu said Marianne Je ne me marrieai Jamais pour cela. The good folks wished us to stay all night & they would have a dance. had our arrangements permitted it we would have done so with pleasure – Shook hands at parting as I mounted my horse Marianne calld to me from the window to stop there when I repasd <al> & alors je vous trouverai marie avec un grand Goiture said I

The valley narrowd as we ascended till it became a complete gorge with the torrent roaring thro it – awful <deflels> defiles. Vast mountains blocks of Granite – Torrents. Bridges [–] crosses. Very hot in the middle of the day – At Dusk all still except the roaring of the torrents & the sound of convent & village church bells among the mountains – moonlight beautiful road over shadowd by pines. Gloomy defile under vast Rocks. Mount St Goatherd appears more grand [–] summit of a snowy mountain glistening in the moonbeams – extremely cold – Got to the inn at nine oclock at night slow muleteer – Inn wood. room low with pannel work large granite stove – people extremely worthy fine old Lady Young man very intelligent talkd of politics of Europe & America – Manly & candid – true Swiss character ["]Libertie en chaine" – It seemed to me as if I was again in America[34]

Avalanches tumble both winter & at present Snow disappears in summer which is hot but eased by breeses Chamois bears

Canton of Ticino

May 8

Thermometer 36 at ½ past five Our Landlady told us of their troubles during the contests with the french Their family had been

34. In the left corner at the top of the next manuscript page are listed the names of four Sicilian towns:

Catania
Pedara
Zavaranne [Zaffarana]
Nicolosa [Nicolosi].

dispersed. She & her motherinlaw took refuge among the mountains wading thro snow Her son narrowly escaped with his life. This part of Swiss was fiercely democratic – <worthy> Amiable manners of the people. Ascent of the mountain Snow frozen horses slip & fall – peasants assist us Ascent steep & fatiguing – Very warm. Clouds about the points of the mountains Narrow valley dangerous for avalanches[35] – No trees[36] [–] dessolate appearance of the mountains – posts to direct travellers – Arrive at the hospice formerly inhabited by benevolent monks – honest old police officer old soldier – depart – descend long dreary difile – Vista of mountains their rocky summits peeping thro the snow – Glacier no trees – Warm – PS at 8 oclock thermom 38 deg at hospice – Peasant woman could hardly be prevaild on to take a reccompence for her trouble – her gratitude – attended us to the foot of the mountain Neat village – clean windows [–] another village – Neat hotel [–] frank manners of the people [–] family at dinner like our farmers in America <houes> houses of wood.

Lad that tended at table very intelligent Said Swiss had no reason to love the french the latter had stripped them of their things

<Passage> Valley 9 miles long 11,000 inhabitants. Go[i]tures effects of bad air Pasture land – Cheese Passage thro rock [–] Devils Bridge Steep descent – country wild dreary & sublime. long vista of barren mountains coverd partly with snow. Reuss roaring along like a Torrent Avalanches <app> gradual appearance of trees – Mountains fringed with pines – trees budding – over hanging rocks – <Country becom> road runs along precipices [–] beautiful valley at the bottom of Defile [–] pastures orchards river [–] fields well enclosed houses neat & clean [–] romantic mountains fine moonlight arrive at Altdorf – ruind houses.

Countenances of the Swiss

[*p. [121] blank*]

[*For pp. 122–29, see below, pages 540–45*]

[*p. [130] blank except for word "Canaro" written upside down*]

35. In the bottom margin below "avalanches" appears the word "torrents."

36. The manuscript page which begins with "trees" and ends with "wood" contains some eight lines written in pencil underneath this portion of the entry for the day. Only the last word in these lines, "women," is legible.

May 9[37]

Altorf – Battle of French & Austrians [–] gaiety of Swiss fled. Oppression <Ex> requisitions – French took their cattle &c as in time of Wm Tell – Cantons united [–] Swiss families about to embark for America Swiss mountaineers – food – Chamois hunters attacht. to native home – Swiss affected by songs of their country – sight of cattle &c – Swiss soldiers home sick cured by Swiss cheese –

Therm at [*blank*]

May 10

leave altorf at 8 oclock parting with the honest Landlord & his wife cold morning Snowy mountains – Therm 41

[*Irving's record of his expenses from Rome to Zurich appears on pp. [122–29] of the notebook and reads upside down in a pattern of facing pages as noted. For the convenience of the reader the editor has transferred the accounts to the end of the dated diary entries and has arranged them in normal chronological order.*][38]

[*p. [125]*]

Lent Mr Cabell	$20
Paid for our chambers at rome 16 days at 8 pauls prd. fire 3 pauls prd.	17.6[39]
Cooks bill	31.2
Buono mano to servt	2.—
Pd. for Mr Cabell	$ 5.4.8
Joseph valet deplace 3 livres pr day	11.4
Buono mano	2.
paper	.1
Chamber maid	2.—

37. The editor has supplied the dateline from internal evidence. This entry and the one of May 10 are on p. [131] in the notebook.

38. The writing is in blue ink over pencil unless otherwise noted.

39. In the figures on the remainder of this manuscript page (which total $86.83) and on the next (which total $104.65), Irving wrote a single digit or a digit and a half to the right of the dollars column to indicate the number of pauls expended. Since a paul was worth 10 cents, a cipher should be considered added to the numeral, and "½" to equal 5 cents.

<Lent Mr Cabell>	<paid	5>
Monk[?]		4
Driver at Civita Castellana		5.—
Garcon at Do.		3
Glass.		1
x		
Carriage to the Cascade of Terni		2.—
Buono mano to Postillion		.4
Ditto to the *Keeper of the Cascade*		3
Ditto to ragged Cicerone		3
<T> Wine at Terni		<3>1½
Garcon		1½
Coffee at Spoletto		3
Driver at Terni		5.
Breakfast at Spoletto		4
Garcon		.½
Cicerone at Foligno		2
		86.8.3

[p. [124]]	86.<6>8.3
Foligni Garcon	2
Apple's	1
Driver at Valcimarra	10.—
repaid John	2½
Buono mano garcon[?]	2
Coffee at Tolentino	2
Loretto cicerone	3
Garcon	1½
repaid John	2½
Breakfast Ancona	1.
Buono mano Garcon	<2>1
Garcon at Senegallia	3
Cicerone at Fano	2
Theatre at Ditto[40]	2
breakfast at Ditto & Garcon	5½
Ancona – house[?] on the road	2

40. The Teatro della Fortuna was built between 1665 and 1677 by Jacopo Torelli and restored in 1718 by Ferdinando Bibiena. It was closed in 1839 and demolished a few years later.

Item	Amount
Ditto at La Cattolico To officer 4 4 to porter <4>	8
repaid John	1
Custom officer on the confines of the popes territories	3
pd Driver at La Catolica	10.
Inn at La Catolica	2½
Coffee at Rimini	4
Ditto at Forli	2
buono mano to Garcon	1½
Charity at Forli	1
Porters at Bologna	2
	104.6.3[41]

[*p.* [127]]

Item	Amount
	104.65[42]
Paid the residue of voiturinos bill at Bologna – 30 $ & $1\frac{50}{100}$ for his horses one day at Rome	<31> 31.<7>50
	136.15
Charity	4.—
Lent Mr Cabell	1.
Mending boots	20
Paid John	<6>65
buono mano at the convent on the hill – 3 pauls	30
Church of St. Paul[43]	12
Palace Zampieri	30
Theatre	32
Washerwoman	87

41. Apparently the total should be $113.53. Posssibly Irving counted the canceled 2 pauls of the buono mano to the garcon at Ancona and counted the $10 paid to the driver at Cattolica as $1 because it was run into the pauls column.

42. Apparently in carrying over this amount Irving read his "6.3" as "6.5."

43. S. Paolo was built in 1611 by Giovanni Magenta.

Palace National[44] (buono mano)	40
Reading room	20
<2>	144 51
	<72.25>
	<5.48>
	<1>
Mr C's share	<78.73>
	<20. >
	<98 73>

	144.51
lent Mr C.	6.48
2	138. 3
	69. 1
	6.48
	75.49
lent Mr C.	20.

Mr Cs. Acct. <95.49 Settled>

[*p. [126]*]

<Valet de place – 3 days at 5 livres french per day>	<1.60>
Garcon	1
Porters	20
John	20
Custom house officer	12
	152[45]

Boat from Sesto to Magadino	2 Louis —
Buono mano to boatmen considering that we staid one day at Intra	1<2>6 francs
Horse from Magadino to Bellinzona	6 fr. francais

44. Presumably the Palazzo Publico, or del Governo, begun in 1290. It is ornamented with statues on the outside and frescoes and statues on the inside.

45. This line and the preceding four lines are in pencil.

Cart for Ditto & buono Mano }	6 fr.

Purse Recd. from Mr C & myself at Bellinzona }	2 Louis
a french Louis from here to Milan makes 37.6 Liv. Spanish dollar 8.5	
Hotel at Bellinzona supper bed & breakfast & 10 liv to waggoner }	26.10
Johns bill	2.10
Garcon	1.10
Dinner at Giornico	14.
Servant	1.

We each paid 4 louis one share <for> of 8 louis the price of 4 horses to cross the mountain

[*p. [129]*]

Airolo[46] – Dinner bed & breakfast for us & John }		$2.50
Police ticket for three	<30> ↑liv↓	1.10
Garcon		1.10
Duties on trunks		4
Purse recd. at Mt. St Goatherd from Mr C & myself		2 Louis
Expences – toll &c	↑liv↓	6.5
Buono mano to driver	2 $ french	
Capuchin	1 french	
Recd. from J. & C. at Altorf	2 louis	
Do. Do.	2.	
Bill at Altorf	33.16	

46. The manuscript page which begins with "Ariolo" and ends with "See three leaves back" contains some five lines in pencil, written with the notebook held right side up, over which the expense account is written. Four of the lines are partly legible, as follows:

> While you are [*unrecovered*] med[?] Doctr
> Gates[?] I have enjoyed [?] two delightful
> breezes [*four unrecovered words*]
> & may it [*unrecovered*]

The top nine lines of the expense account are in ink over pencil.

Domestic 2.4
Cart from Altorf to Fluellen 1 $ french
Toll livres 1.5
repast &c at Gersau 3 liv
Boat from Fluellen to Lucerne
3 men – Price 2½ $ ↑ea↓ buono mano ½ 3<louis>↑fr. crowns↓
Genl. Pfiffers plan – ½ crown
Swiss dresses ½
Church organ
about ½

See three leaves back[47]

[*p. [128] blank*]

[*p. [123] blank*]

[*p. [122]*]

Lucerne May 13
Purse recd. from C & J 2 louis'dor
Do – do 2 . . .
bill at cheval blanc for 3 days 54 livres
Valet deplace 6 livres
Garcon about 6
<Basl> Zurich 14
Purse recd. from C & J. 2 louis
Paid for carriage from Lucerne 6 crowns
Drink gelt to driver ½
P.S. pd yesterday at the village of [*blank*][48]
1 crown for horses (2) to draw the carriage up several hills
refreshments at the same place – 40 sous.

[*pp. [132–35] blank*]

[*p. [136] blank except for word "Canaro" written upside down*]

[*p. [137] blank*]

47. The next entry, on p. [122], is three leaves back from this entry.
48. Horgen (see journal entry of May 13, 1805, n. 201).

[*p. [138] blank except for the beginnings of an unrecognizable sketch*]

[*p. [139] blank*]

[*p. [140]*]

A reath of sweet flowerets they sportive ↑twine↓
for me
In vain the gay syrens wreathe chaplets
for my heart &c
Full oft I reflect on my indigent state
But reflection & reason comes ever too late
They tell me I sigh for too beauteous a fai[r]
& fill my sad bosom with doubts & despair
Then hope sweetly smiling averts their decree
For my heart &c
When the shrill pipe & tabor pro[c]laims the ↑glad dance↓
With transport I view my dear mary advance
Such grace she displays as she trips midst the throng
That each shepherd with rapture to her tunes his song
But none shes beloved <by> with such truth as by me
For my heart[49]

[*p. [141] blank*]

[*p. [142] blank except for drawing of the head of a soldier (Figure 14)*]

[*p. [143] blank except for "Valen Roth"*]

[*p. [144–47] blank*]

[*p. [148]*]

The sea was calm the sky serene
& gently blew the western gale
When Anna seated on a Rock
Watchd the lavinias lessening sail.
To heaven thus her prayer addressd
Thou who canst save or canst distroy

49. This poem is presumably by Irving.

From each surrounding danger guard
My much lovd little sailor boy.

When tempests oer the oceans howl
And even sailors shrink with dread
Be some protecting angel <nigh> near
To hover oer my williams head
He was belovd by all the plain
His fathers pride his mothers joy
Then safely to their arms restore
Their much lovd little sailor boy.

May no rude foe his course impede
Conduct him safely oer the waves
Oh may he never be compelld
To fight for powr or mix with slaves
May smiling peace his steps attend
Each rising hour be crownd with joy
As blest as that when I again
Shall meet my much lovd sailor boy.[50]

[*p. [149] blank*]

[*pp. [150–51] show two-page drawing of a building and a bridge (Figure 15)*]

[*p. [152]*]

Syra[cuse] Cat[ania] – 11
Sundries 5

[*p. [153]*]

16
24.32
———
40.32
11.20
9
———
60.52
1.30
———
59.22

50. This poem is presumably not by Irving. It has not been identified.

[*pp. [154–59] blank*]

[*p. [160]*]

11 shirts
12 cravats
3 coll[?]
2 Pocket Hdks
1 silk
4 vests[?]
1 flannel shirt[51]

[*p. [161] shows page-size drawing of a building (Figure 16)*]

[*p. [162] shows page-size drawing of a seaport with the caption "Scylla" (Figure 17)*]

[*p. 163*]

Messieur Dalph of house of Dalph & Co.
loire[?][52]

[*pp. [164–70] blank*]

[*p. 171*]

M – OCVLATIUS – M – T VIRUS
II Vir – Pro ludis[53]

[*p. [172]*]

There was an old sow & she had a wee blathe,
& the sow she jumped over the barn wall
The old sow learnt the pigs to grunt
The pigs they lay

51. This penciled list has been erased. Below it are eight more lines in pencil erased, of which only a few words are legible: "vases . . . aromas of difft . . . Catania . . . obelisk."

52. Both lines are written in ink.

53. See journal entry of March 14, 1805, and n. 224.

The sow she learnt
The sow fell in love &c
The old sow shot[?] in the flummery bi<t>bul[?]
He was Dorothee wiggin[?][54]

[*p. [173]*]

Tho far removed from friends & home
Tho <might> countless waves between us roll[55]

[*pp. [174–78] blank*]

[*p. [179] blank except for "Mr amici[?]"*]

[*Irving's record of his exchanges of credit from Messina to Lucerne and his expense accounts from January to May 14, 1805, on the following pages, begin on p. [189] and read upside down from back to front of the notebook, ending on p. [180]. For the convenience of the reader the editor has arranged them in normal order.*][56]

Recd. at Messina from Jn Gaspd Chapeaurouge[57] on acct of Letter of credit from J J Bosc & Co	$100
Recd. on above letter at Palermo	50
Recd. on above letter at Naples	100
Recd. on letter of Kuhn & Co[58] at Naples –	38
Rd. at Rome the remainder of Mr De La Rues letter of credit from the Marquis Torlonia	237

54. These lines are written quarter turned on the page. They have not been identified.

55. These lines are presumably by Irving.

56. The writing is in blue ink over pencil unless otherwise noted.

57. Probably Jean Gaspard Chapeaurouge, a Frenchman. The name of Giovanni Gaspare de Chapeaurouge, a banker, appears in a document dated February 26, 1806, in Volume 1062 of the Fondo Notarile of Messina (information furnished by the Director Archivio de Stato, Messina).

58. Presumably the firm in Genoa which in 1807 was Kuhn, Green and Company ("Peter Irving's Journal," ed. Leonard Beach, Theodore Hornberger, and Wyllis F. Wright, *Bulletin of the New York Public Library*, XLIV, 1940, 602). Presumably the head was Peter Kuhn, Jr., of Philadelphia, brother-in-law of T. H. Storm and American consul in Genoa from 1805 to 1807 (see journal entry of September 14, 1804, n. 187).

& Recd. <March> May 1, of Messr. Balabio & Bessana[59] of Milan 50 Ducats – <Common purse &c. make it 52 ¼ on the letter> of credit from the Marquis Torlonia and recd a letter of credit on Mr Balthassare Falcini[60] of Lucerne for 550 ducats } 6$

Left Milan with 21 Lou[i]s in my pocket and above half a Louis in the common purse[61]

Lucerne recd of Mr Balthazar Falcini 46 louis & three or four livres with a Letter of credit for <borowd of Cabell 5 ↑5↓ $ – Apr 3[?]>[62] 50 louis on Messr. Rougemont & Scherer of Paris being the remainder of my letter of credit from Balabio & Bassana of Milan

	<Paid Capt>	
Jany		
28	Passage on the Am. ship Matilda from Genoa to Messina and sea stores &c	28 —
	Pd. for Antonio ditto	14 —
	Boatmen	25
	health officer	12
	Pd. for fruit while at Quarantine & buono mano to the waterman	3
	Cabin boy &c.	2.
		47.37
Feby	Syracuse	
3	Mask	36
	boatmen &c	50
4	<expences>[63]	<7>
5	Mask & dress	1
6	Expences at Dionysius ear &c	50
7	Washerwoman	1.50
10	Masquerade	1.50
11	Washing	50

59. No record of this firm seems to have been preserved in the archives of Milan.

60. Xavier Balthasar Falcini (1777–1844), money changer, was the son of a silk merchant who migrated from Italy to Switzerland (information furnished by the Director of the Stadtarchiv of Lucerne).

61. "Left Milan . . . purse" is in pencil.

62. The canceled passage is inserted diagonally. The inserted "5" is written directly below the first "5" and is not canceled.

63. The canceled word is in pencil.

	Boy at Hotel	50
	Hotel	8 —
Catania[64]		
13.	Amber	1
15	Servant	50
17	Theatre	3.
		18 86
	February amt. bt over	18.86
18	bolline[65] &c.	10.
	Expences from Syracuse to Catania	11
	Sundries at Catania	5
	Palermo	
	Paid my proportion of expences	59.22
26	from Syracuse to this place &c. including stay at Catania	
	Theatre	1
27	Conversazione	1
	Expences	2
	Hat	3
28	Hotel expences	19
	Provisions to take on board	1
	Gibb's Servt.	1.50
	Footman	1.50
	Louis &c &c	5
		139. 8
March		
1	Supper at auberge near Castelazzo	40
2	Dinner & supper at do.	42
3	Bed &c	30
5	Hotel bill at Palermo	3.16
	Boatmen	16
7	Boatmen	1.—

64. Above "Catania" Irving drew a short line.
65. "Stamps."

	Sailors	1.30
	Coachman	72
	Passage from Palermo to Naples	7.25
		14.71

	Naples	14.71
7	Postage of letters	.50
8	Coachman	50
	paper	10
9	Ticket for opera	50
	present to a monk	50
	Visiting cards	60
10	Charity	1.—
11	Expences for boatmen &c	30
15	Expences	2.
	Gloves – (fine)	1.—
	Supper bed & breakfast at Portici & guides & mules to ascend ye mountain	5.—
	Carriage (proportion of) to Pompei &c	2.—
	buono mano at Virgils tomb & Pompeii	1.75
	Carriage (proportion of) to Baia	2.—
	Buono mano &c	1.75
2<2>1	Fencing master	2.50
2<3>2	Grotto del Cane (carriage & buono mano) –	1.—
	Antiques[66] at Baia 5 ↑centimes↓ Mending gaiters 1 Letter 3 Magnesia 2 (gr. Travelling cap. 3.5 ——— 14.5	1..2<8>0
2<4>3	Small trunk	1.18
	Gloves	40
	Boatmen &c	12

66. In the left-hand margin beside "Antiques" Irving has made two small lines.

	Views &c of Naples		1.64
	Washing		1.60
			43.85

	March continued		43.85
23	Taylors bill	Ducats	
	For a suppr. cloth coat	28	
	For putting buttons on a frock coat	—2	25..
		30	
	Commissions &c on Bill of exch for 500$ From Degen & Co—	—Ducats	6.53
	Ditto on 120 Ducats from Falconnet		2—
	Postage of Letters		1.56
	Hotel <expences> Bill		41.10
	Valet deplace for 1 <7> 6 days & Buono mano (½ dol pr day		9..
	Servt at Hotel		1.50
	Degens Servt		50
	Butter for the route		50
			131.54
	Place in voiture from Naples to Rome		10
	Buono mano to Voiturier		2
	Custom house &c &c.		1
	Expences on Route		1—
28.	Hotel bill at Rome – &c.		2..50
30 –	Expences		3.—
			151.4

March	--	*Rome*	151
30	Silk Stockings		2.—
	Hotel bill for lodgings 1 day & fire &c.		1.—
			154

April 1805

1.	Boots	6. .
2	Expences	2. . .
3	Expences	2.75
	<ch>Carriage to St. Paul without the wall &c	2.
4	Expences	3.—
7	Do.	2.2
	Trip to Frescati	2.60
10	Expences	4.44
	Engravings of Ariosto & Raphæl	.60
	3 books of views of rome – vases &c at 2$ each	6.—
	Map of modern rome	60
	Portrait & <casts> mould &c.	16.—
14	Blank book	40
	postage of Letters	1.—
	Expences	4.58
		53.99

		53.99
<Bolgna> Bologna April 23.	My share of difft expences for Rooms &c in Rome and of expences from ↑thence to↓ Bologna Carriage with 3 mules for 15 Louis – one repast a day & lodging at night – for Mr C myself & servt included and of expences at Bologna <&c.>	6<3>9.1
	Mending boots	10
	Theater last night – about	16
	2 pr cot hose – 7 pauls pr pr.	1.40
– 24 –	Institute – – – 7 Do.	70
25	My share for valet de place 3 days at 3 livres french pr day	. . 80
	paid for mending my pistol 2½ pauls	25

26	bill at Hotel at Bologna – dinner at 8 paul pr day breakfast – 3 lodgin[g] for 2 & servt 3 days 40 p. fire – 20		7.48
	Expences. Garçon &c – – –		— —.75
	Share of Johns bill		50
	Expences for route		2.—
27	Ditto		1
	Petrarchs works (parma)[67]		2
29	Theatre – – (– 3 livres)		
30	Paid Voiturier for my share of a carriage from Bologna to Milan at 8 louis the carriage a repast per day & lodging included – –		– 18
			158.14

April			158
30.	Buono mano to voiturier		3.
—	Moores France Swisserland & Germy[68] 2 vols. at 10 livres de milan	about	1.40
—	Gallery of paintings		23
	Expences on the road & since <our arrival> 13 livres 7 sous of Milan	about	2. .
	Expences 13.17. liv – –	about	2
<May> <1>	<Money> 2 pr. linen drawers at 5 french franks pr. pair – 10 fr Mending my coat – 1 fr.	11 fr	abt. 2
			$168.63

May. 1st. 1805.

Postage of letters	6.7 ↑livres de Milan↓ about 1.
Ambrosian Library	2.

67. See journal entry of April 27, 1805, n. 104.
68. *Ibid.*, May 23, 1805, n. 29.

	<Cicerone> Valet deplace	1.10
	My share of Hotel bill for 3 days at 92 livres the whole	46 liv
	Coffee bill at 9.15 ↑liv.↓	4.17
	Buono mano to caffetier[69]	.15
	Do. to camerier[70]	1.15
	——— Garcon	1.15
	——— to Custom officers	3.15
	Gloves	3.
	Washing	2.18
	Theatre	3.—
	Commissions of Exchg	5.13
May 2d.	Expences for route	5.10
	Paid the purse for room	16.
3	My share of carriage hire from Milan to Sesto at 3 louis the whole – 1 louis & ½	
	Pd common purse	15.15
5	My share of boat hire from Sesto to Magadina at 2 louis the boat – 1 Louis	31.10
	buono mano	8.

May 6.

	Paid common purse – about	Milan 12 liv.
	——— Ditto 1 Louis.	
	Paid in advance my share for 4 horses to cross Mount St G. at 2 louis pr horse	4 louis.
7	Paid purse 1 Louis	
9	Do. at Altorf 2 "	
12	Commissions of Exchg. of 450$ – at Lucerne –	122.7 liv de Milan

69. Coffeehouse man.
70. Houseman.

	Commiss on changing silver for gold 28 livres		1$
13	Lucerne pd purse	1 Louis	
14	<Basle> ↑Zurich↓ ditto	1 "	

[*p. [190]*][71]

Saml Ogden Birch[72]

James Broadbent

I had a hearty laugh at the apprehensions of one of the men of the health office. They had opened a small wicket window over the lower steps of the stoop and the man told the our C[apt]. that he must stand at this window & talk to those within. The captain who did not unde[rstand] him thot that he said he must go inside[?] & was about advg. up the stoop when the fellow half frightened to death[?] shrank back and hallood for him to keep back. The capt. stopd in astoni[shment] The fellow made several attempts to get <hold upon> our wicket of the stoop but as often started back[?] as if the iron was red hot[.] at last he succeeded in jerking it shut and run into the house trembling at the risk he had[?][73]

[*inside back cover*]

Grandosh

Due John 2$[74]

22[75]

71. The writing on this last page in the notebook is upside down.
72. Apparently he was not related to the Ogden family to which T. L. Ogden belonged.
73. For the same incident, see the journal entry of January 5, 1805.
74. These two lines are written in ink.
75. "22" is written in ink upside down at the bottom of the page.

MISCELLANEOUS NOTES, 1805–1806

Paris–London–
Aboard Ship for New York

The manuscript notebook is in the Manuscript Division of the New York Public Library, No. 5 in the Seligman Collection. It consists of 62 pages written in pencil and ink, of a blue paper-covered notebook of 126 pages, measuring 2¾ x 4⅜ inches. Pp. [17, 30, 36–37, 40–41, 43, 46, 50–51, 56, 62, 64–67, 69–70, 72–74, 76–79, 81–82, 86, 88, 90–95, 100–102, 109] are blank.

[*inside front cover*]

21. 4£ 3 p[1]

Tonnettine[?][2]
2 16

Pigshead[3]

[*p. 1*][4]

plants look perpendic[,] horozontal, radicules[5] horizontal <h> Sometimes the same direction[.] former *traçante*[6] – racine[7] tracant[.] racine in good soil[,] radicules divide[?] pine poplar &c racine tracent

1. This line is written in ink. Below it appears a sketch of trees, in pencil (Figure 18).
2. "Tonnettine[?] . . . Pigshead" is in pencil. Possibly Irving intended to write "Tontine," a scheme named after Lorenzo Tonti, a Neapolitan banker who originated it about 1653, in which subscribers to a common fund share an annuity with the benefit of survivorship. It was often used at this period for raising money for building projects. The Jerusalem and East India Coffee House had a Tontine Office (John Feltham, *The Picture of London for 1803,* London, 1803).
3. Possibly a nickname for the Boar's Head Tavern in Eastcheap, where Falstaff and Prince Hal in Shakespeare's *1 Henry IV* were said to carouse. It was destroyed in the fire of 1666, was rebuilt, and finally was torn down in 1831. Irving described his search for it in the chapter "The Boar's Head Tavern" in *The Sketch Book.*
4. Irving's botanical notes (pp. [1–14]) are in pencil except as noted.
5. "Radical."
6. "Running."
7. "Root."

divide[?] in rich ground[?] ground well waterd – More corps[8] in[?] radicule and many radicules[?]

<?When a soil? is radially [*illegible*]> canal[9] may radiate[?] of the same direction long & narrow[?] and divided [*illegible*][.] ground less [*word or more illegible*] that has roots [*rest of line illegible*] cut frequently downwards[?] over earth on mountains the trees pines look small but at [*illegible*] horizontal roots of trees <?deep?> ↑?corps?↓ pivot[10] straight[?] out of the earth[?] roots not proportion to the stem. Grown trees pines &c have short racines more common fusian – carrot – radicules &c radicule ↑?distinct?↓ tuberus & bulbous – potatoe ball – <m> radicule and collet[11] not easily distinguished[,] cheveleux[12] tubrous & bulbous may be confounded – racine tubrous resemble in ball carrot &c[?] terminal radicule – Bulbous one sees no cheveleux from exam[.] onions of lilly tulip have radicule inferior – exception only of the cheveleux[.] racine bulbous not properly a root two sides one towards sky other earth former has hair – fatter [latter] numerous of leaves bourgon de feull[13] – leaf not develloped – Onions are a collection of leaves feulle radicule – plantain flures radicule – bulb an assemblage of leaves and bulbets[?] – parts of a bulb[,] disk superior scales or leaves inferior radicules[.] 3 sorts of bulbs – solid – tunique[14] – scaly 1.2 or 3 scales. *tulips* – scales thick & hard. 2 scales are numerous as onion – thin towards surface closed – 3 circular[?] or in embrica[?] when like scales exterior do not envelope [?stem?]

Palmee root divides like an hand (radicules divide)

Bistorte – root twisted

Tronquee – radicule is short & terminates bluntly.

Articuler – chain of corps

ex

Seal of Solomon

Faisceau[15] on Back when the radicules over hang & large – diverging

greneau chain of little balls globular saxefrage

Cheveliu full of small radicules – strawberry

8. "Caudex."
9. "Duct."
10. "Taproot."
11. "Neck."
12. "Beard" of the root.
13. Bourgeon à feuilles ("bud of leaves").
14. "Tunicate."
15. "Bundle."

Fibrous where the radicules are a little larger than the preceding *pea* – unnecessary distinction

---

necessai[r][?]	racine
fusiform[e]	tubrous
bulbous	palme
bistorte	tronque articular
enfaiseur[16]	grenue
chevaliu	10 varietés
bulbous	most necessary
platane	the [*illegible*] root
bulbous	

---

roots sometimes run out of the ground 7 or 8 feet called extortse[?] exorhizes cypress chauve[17] these <?oilv?> trees for the sand hold the earth and give it a consistance – take up wind[?] of other plants in holand plant the plants which have a great cover[?] to fix the earth

---

Tige[18]

Tige buried & root in the air former becomes root latter branches &c. loose their original characters to assume opposites

Tige (caulis)[19] – plant sans tige (acaulis)[20]

Plant can be without Tige flowrs & leaves are radical

Plants with tige most numerous – nomenclature didactic –

1. Hampe sans feulle ou rameaux[21]

2. *Chaume* creusse[22] – knots from whence proceed leaves – bind it to the ground near knots – Racines part from knots – knots hardest part Others where the knots are weak – do not give roots

3. Collomn[23] (Forms) when the trunk <of>is of same size – Palm.

Tronque Stems of trees conical –

Tige *herbacée* – *Ligneuse*[24]

16. En faisceaux(?) ("in bundles").
17. "Bald."
18. "Stem."
19. "Stem" (Latin form).
20. "Without stem" (French and Latin).
21. "Stalk without leaves or branches."
22. "Culm hollow."
23. Colonne ("column").
24. "Herbaceous – Ligneous."

Tige – solid creuse – rempli de moelle[25] – 2 polileuse[?][26] & spongeuse[27]

position

perpendicular
– couchée sans projection[28]
roots avoine[29]
rampante when there are little roots from the joints
Tracante (Stolonafere)[30]
reclining with branches from each branch receive
<or stolonefere>
reclinée Tige inclines in form of an arch very rare
Penchee when the superior extremity bends

form

1. round[31] – common *accacia*
2. comprimé flat – borders rounding
3. Tranchante – sharp edges
4. Triangular &c &c &c
5. Carrée[32]
6 Pentagone Hexagon &c 5. 6. 7. sides
7 Cannellée ou Sillonee former small canals – latter large
8 Striée – canals light & minute
9 Lisse (Globar) Smooth – lily
10 Raboteuse (Scabre) rough
11 Crevasée (Rimosus)[33] full of crevices
12. Flexeuse – tige bends two or 3 times in Zig Zag
13. Noueuse (intersected by knots –) wheat rye &c
14 Articulée – resembling noueuse but knots are fragile

25. "Filled with pith."
26. Folliculeuse(?) ("Folliculous").
27. "Spongy."
28. "Lying without projection."
29. "Oats." Lines in the manuscript direct that this word be transferred to a position two lines earlier after "perpendicular."
30. "Stoloniferous."
31. "round," "comprimé," "Tranchante," "Triangular," and "Carrée" are in ink.
32. "Square."
33. This word is the Latin form of "crevasée."

15 Enspiral[34] or surmountin[g] ex vine
16 Grimpante – holding by tendrils[35]

vacuolum[?][36]

feeble annual – twine around others – not toughend enough – <vine>
Granpante – when the fillaments shoot from the branches
When the paccule[?][37] is spiral or twisted grampante by the roots number of forms 17.

Division[38]

Simple quand le tige n'est pas divisee[39]
Rameuse quand le tige a des rameaux vien[t] petite tiges[40]
Bifurque quand le tige se divisee en deux parties[41]
Dichotome quand chaque Rameau se divise en deux[42]
Prolefer quand les rameaux partent des different <?partes?> points de la surface de tige ou des rameaux[43] in pines always from the ends of branches.

Position

Des Rameaux
<*illegible word or words*>

Reason of lower branches being larger than upper because they are older.

ELIZA[44]

Woman's the stronger genl blessing
from sulley[?] adieu to the Po[45]

34. En spirale ("spirally").
35. Nos. 8–16 are in ink written over pencil.
36. Vasculum(?) ("small vessel").
37. Fascicule(?) ("fascicle").
38. "Division," "*Simple*," "*Rameuse*," "Bifurque," "Dichotome," and "*Prolefer*" are in ink.
39. "When the stem is not divided."
40. "*Branchy* when the stem grows small stems from the branches."
41. "Bifurcated when the stem is divided in two parts."
42. "Dichotomous when each branch is divided in two."
43. "*Proliferous* when the branches come from different points on the surface of the stem or the branches."
44. Probably the woman of this name, apparently English, who was a fellow-passenger of Irving's on the *Remittance* from London to New York in 1806 (see pages 580–82; see also the earlier appearance of the name, page 397).
45. This quotation has not been identified.

Position of the
Branches[46]

1 alternes,
2 opposes
3 Verticilles – forming rays
4 opposés en croix[47] – (Ash)
5 Divergens (diverg) from ye trunk
6 Ramassis[48] – (orange)
7 Serrés[49] – (Poplar cypress)
8 Penchés[50] – (sun flower)
9 Pendans[51] – (weeping willow[ )]
10 Etalés (scatterd – asparagus)

Situation of the flowers

1 Pedoncule – branch supporting several flowers
2 Pedicelle – little branch sustaning a single flower
Pedoncules proceed sometimes from root
often from aisselles – (stems of leaves[ )]

1 Panicule (Panicula)[52] when the branches which sustain ye flowers are scatterd pointing dift. ways as in the asparigus – oats maize – Rubarb.
2 Thyrse (thyrsus) flowers close forming an oval (Lilac [ )]
3 Grappe (Racemus) flowers are supported by little rameaux attached laterally to a <little> common pedoncule (ex vine goosberry)
4 Epi (spica) floures situated on common pedoncule – Ex wheat –
5 Chaton (Amentum) situated on pedoncule but with shells or scales. (ex Walnut)
6. Verticille (Verticillus) pedoncules disposed circularly forming rings round the stems – (ex – Sage)
7. Ombelle (umbella) pedoncules part from a common center di-

46. The notes on "Position of the Branches" and "Situation of the flowers" are in ink.
47. "Opposite crossways."
48. "Clustered."
49. "Serrated."
50. "Bending."
51. "Hanging down."
52. This word and the first words in parentheses in nos. 2–7 are the Latin forms.

vided into pedicelles ex – sweet william –
8 Cephalanthe – thick close & grouped on summit of tige in form of a sphere – *fleurs en tetes*[53] – ex. the onion

[*p. 15*]
Rue Mandar
No. 3.
fronting beaureau
of Lottery between
Rue Montmatre &
Montorgeuil

[*p. 16*][54]
Rue Verneuil – corner Rue
du barriere Maison du
papier 781 Quatrevent
Simon[55]

[*p. [17] blank*]

[*p. 18*]
Boisselieu[56]
next to Recamier[57]

[*p. 19*][58]
Isabella or fatal marriage[59]

53. "Flowers in heads."
54. A leaf is torn out of the notebook between pp. [16] and [17].
55. A Simon is listed a few years later as a "fab de papiers pients, boulev des Italiens 29," in the same neighborhood (*Almanach de 25,000 Adresses de Paris, pour l'Année 1817,* Paris, 1817).
56. Probably "Boisselier." Two persons of this name – one a merchant and one a painter – were living in Paris a few years later (*ibid.*).
57. Three Recamiers – one a physician, one (J.) a banker, and one (L.) without a designated profession – were living in Paris a few years later, but none seems to have had an address next to a Boisselier (*ibid.*).
58. From this page to p. [35] the entries are in ink.
59. *The Fatal Marriage* (1694), a tragedy by Thomas Southerne, was revived (with alterations) by David Garrick under the title *Isabella, or the Fatal Marriage* (1757).

Zanga[60]
Othello (at both houses)[61]
Macbeth – Do
Venice preservd[62] (Kemble Jaffier
Hargrave[63] pierre
Mrs Siddons Bel[)]
Do Chas Kemble Jaffier
John Kemble Pierre
Romeo & Juliet (*Drury lane*[)]
Mr Elliston.[64] Romeo. Mrs H Siddons[65] Juliet

Honey Moon[66] – D L

Richd. III ↑c g↓ Cooke[67] Richard

---

1 Part King Henry 4. Hotspur by Kemble – Falstaff – Cook – Prince Henry C Kemble

---

60. The chief character in *The Revenge* (1721) by Edward Young.

61. The two chief theaters in London at this time were the Drury Lane (D.L.) and the Covent Garden (C.G.).

62. *Venice Preserved; or, a Plot Discovered* (1682) by Thomas Otway. The chief characters were Jeffier, Belvidera, and Pierre.

63. Hargrave was an unsuccessful English actor, who played principally in London and in Dublin; for several years after 1796 he was in the army (*The Thespian Dictionary*, London, 1805).

64. Robert William Elliston (1774–1831), English actor, was a member of the Drury Lane Company between 1804 and 1809, 1812 and 1815, and 1819 and 1826, and manager of the theater during the last period. He also wrote several plays.

65. Harriet Murray Siddons (1783–1844), English actress, daughter of the actor and dramatist Charles Murray and sister of the actor and manager William Henry Murray, married Henry Siddons, the son of Sarah K. Siddons, in 1802. She made her debut in London in 1798, and played at Drury Lane from 1805 to 1809, when she moved to Edinburgh.

66. *The Honey Moon* (1796) by William Linley.

67. George Frederick Cooke (1756–1811), English actor, first appeared on the stage in 1776. Though highly successful in some roles, he was often too intoxicated to perform.

Mercht. Venice. Shylock Cook Mercht. J. Kemble. Gratiano C Kemble. Launcelot Munden[68] Portia Miss Smith[69]

London

Octr <12>7		
<put in pocket>		
Dr to cash		£ 2
16	do	2
		1
17	"	6
	"	2
19	"	12
21	"	6
22	"	1
26	"	3
28	"	2
—		2
Novr.		
1		2
2		2
6		2
7		<4>8
		£53

	Octr. 14	
	Carriage hire	5..
15	Breakfast	1.6
	Shaving case	1. 11.6
	Washing	3.6
	Circulating Library 1 month	4—
	Catalogue	1
	Dinner (Maidenlane)	9.6

68. Joseph Shepherd Munden (1758–1832), English actor, was the most celebrated comedian of his day; he first acted in London in 1790.

69. Sarah Smith (1783–1850), English actress, was the chief rival of Mrs. Sarah Siddons; she married George Bartley in 1814.

	play ½ price	3.—
	Pd. Massie for money lent for my journey from Paris to London	12—. .—. .
	2 eights of lottery tickets	5. 13.—
	Dinner	3
	Play – pit	3.6
	Dinner	6—
	Charity	1
	Hessian Boots	2. 4.—
	Card case	3
	2 Pr cot hose – 4/9	9.6
	Vest pattern	10.6
	1 months lodging &c	6. 7.6
	Novr.	53
11	Dr to Cash	£ 2.—
16		2.
19		5.
28		5 —
		67
	Decr. 10	
	Cash from Prize	2. 9.6
	12	
	Recd from Mr Main[70] on acct of Carters letter	32. 13.8
	<Novr>	
	November	
7.	pd servt. maid for 1 month	12.6
	Man servt. do	10.
	<Dinner>	<4>
8.	Dinner	4.<6>
	<theatre>	<3.6>

70. Andrew and James Main are listed as merchants in the New York city directories for 1803–1806.

9	Dinner	4.6
	Theatre	3.6
10	Dinner	8.
	expences	7.6
11	Sundries as bread butter &c	5.8
	Dinner	2.3
	Theatre (Macbeth CG)	3.6
	book of the play	.6
12	Washing	2.9
	Boatman (dock)	—6
	Dinner	3.6
	Play Venice presd. CG)[71]	3.6
13	Sandwich	1—
	Dinner (Bettys)[72]	2.6
	Monument	6
	Play (Delinquent CG)[73]	3.6
	Pastry	1.—
		4. 0.8

	Novr.	
14.	Brot over	4. 0.8
	Dinner for 2 at the Cock[74]	.10.6
15	Sandwich	1.—
	Dinner (Mitre)[75]	3.6
	Play	3.6
16	Dinner &c	
17	Dinner	5.2
	Charity	2.6
18	Dinner	3
	Sandwich	1..

71. The name of the play and the theater are in pencil under the ink.

72. Betty's Chop House, 315 Strand (Feltham, *Picture of London*, p. 357).

73. *The Delinquent; or, Seeing Company* (1805), by Frederic Reynolds. The name of the play and the theater are in pencil under the ink.

74. The Cock eating house, behind the Royal Exchange, was celebrated for its turtle, gravy, and soups (Feltham, *Picture of London*, p. 356).

75. Possibly that located on Fish Street Hill (*ibid.*).

19	Shoes (Ker)[76]	12.6
	Carriage	1.6
	Do	2
	Bar Woman at theatre (DL Seige of Belgrade)[77]	1
20	Mending boots new tops &c	14
	Servts. Bill	5.7
	Soup	—6
	Dinner	. 3.6
		7.11.5
21	Brot over	7.11.5
	Soup for 2	2.6
	<fl>	
	Under waistcoat of flannel –	8.6
	Do. of Linen	8
	Washing	7.6
22.	Dinner	3.6
	Play (Country-girl[78] DL)	3.6
	Charity	1
23	Music	3.
	Dinner	2.10
	Play ... DL (Haunted Towr)[79]	3.6
24.	Dinner (Maiden Lane)	5.
	Carriage	1.6
25	Dinner	4
	Shaving brush	9
26	Dinner	2.6
	Theatre (man ↑CG↓ of world)[80]	3.6
	Supper	2.6

76. Probably Thomas Ker, who had a boot and shoe warehouse at 190 Strand (William Lowndes, *London Directory*, London, 1799).

77. *The Seige of Belgrade* (1791) by James Cobb.

78. *The Country Girl* (1766) was an adaptation by David Garrick of William Wycherley's *The Country Wife* (1675).

79. *The Haunted Tower* (1789) by James Cobb.

80. *The Man of the World* (1781) by Charles Macklin.

27	Dinner	3.
	Play (Hamlet) CG	3.6
	Book of do	1
		£11. 2.5

	Novr.	11. 2.5
28.	Servants bill	10—0
	1 Marseilles vest	1.— —
	1 Colored Jean do	.15 —
	Dinner	4. .
	Play (Richd III)	3.6
29	Gloves	2.6
	Washing	5.5
	Dinner	3.
	Play (Mountaineers[81] <DL>CG)	3.6
	Supper	2.—
30.	Sandwich	1
	Dinner (public – Masonic Tav.[82])	14
	Coffee &c	1.6
	Servt. & coach	1.6
		15. 9.4

	Decr. 1	
	Coach	1
	Servt.	1.6
2	Dinner (N. E. C. H.)[83]	4.
	<coach lent>	1.—
3	Dinner	3 —
	Play (John Bull[84] CG)	3.6
4	Pidcocks Museum[85] &c	5. .

81. *The Mountaineers* (1793) by George Coleman the younger.

82. Possibly the Freemasons' Tavern and Hall in Great Queenstreet (Thomas Tegg, *Tegg's New Picture of London*, London, 1843, p. 343).

83. Probably the New Exchange Coffee House, 69 Strand (Lowndes, *London Directory*).

84. *John Bull; or, The Englishman's Fireside* (1803) by George Coleman the younger.

85. It occupied three apartments over Exeter Change in the Strand and was said to have "a collection of divers beasts and birds, not exceeded in rarity even by the royal managerie in the Tower" (Thomas Pennant, *London; being a Complete*

	Morlands Gallery[86] & catalogue	1.6
	Dinner	3.6
	Play (CG 1 part Henry IV)	3.6
5	Attendant at Greenwich.	1.
	2 seats in coach to London	3.—
	Dinner (Imperial hotel)[87]	— 12. .
6.	Boots	2. 3.—
	Charity	1
	Dinner	3.6
	Play (Beaux Strat[88] & Sleeping beauty[89] DL[)]	3.6
7.	2 pr cot Drawers	11.—
	Grumoon[?][90] (books)	4.6
	Dinner	2.10
	Charity	1.
	Play (mercht Venice & Wags of Windsor[91])	3.6
		5.17.4
	Brot over	5.17.4
Decr.		
8	Dinner (Maidenlane)	6.
	Carriage	1.6
	Postage [( ]letter from Edinburgh)	1 —
9	Dinner (N.E.C.H.)	5.6

Guide to the British Capital, 4th ed., London, 1814, p. 143).

86. Presumably that in the establishment of Henry Morland, a picture dealer, at 10 Dean St., Soho (*Holden's Triennial Directory, 1802, 1803 and 1804,* London, 1804, p. 248).

87. In London.

88. *The Beaux Stratagem* (1707) by George Farquhar.

89. *The Sleeping Beauty* (1805) by Sir Lumley St. George Skeffington.

90. No person of this name seems to be identifiable, but a "Ganeau & Co." were booksellers in Albemarle Street (Feltham, *Picture of London,* p. 238).

91. The only entertainment of this title which seems to be recorded was produced at the Royalty Theatre November 26, 1810 (Allardyce Nicoll, *A History of English Drama 1660–1900,* Cambridge, 1959, VI, 550).

	Theater (CG Hamlet)	3.6
	Coach &c	4.6
10	Dinner	3.6
	Play (DL School for Friends[92]	3.6
11.	Dinner	6.6
	Play (CG II part of King Henry IV & peeping Tom[93]	6.—
12.	Carriage hire	3
	Dinner	3.6
	Play (Lovers ↑CG.↓ Vows[94] & <laugh> Love laughs &[95]	6.
13.	Dinner	3.6
	Mending Boots	7
14.	Pd. 5 weeks lodging	10.10 —
	Coals	1.15
	Washing	3
	Washerwoman	7.3
	Newspaper & boy	9

[*expenses continue on page 573*]

[*p. [29] blank except for drawing of two women (Figure 19)*]

[*p. [30] blank*]

[*p. 31*]

Nebuchadnezer <on donn>
Ne buchadonnozer
Nay by God I dont know sir

Hack at Tom Pooley
Hacatompool<y>i

92. *The School for Friends* (1805) by Marianne Chambers.

93. Probably *Peeping Tom of Coventry* (1784) by John O'Keeffe.

94. Probably the adaptation (1798) by Mrs. Elizabeth Inchbald of *Das Kind der Liebe* (1798) by August von Kotzebue.

95. Probably *Love Laughs at Locksmiths* (1803) by George Coleman the younger.

Martial Music –
fond of general music –

Ireland will be the richest country in the world for its capital is always doubling (dublin).

All that sign painting could express
or youthful glaziers fancy &c
il y a de putty la dedans[96]

The wag replied &c

[*For pp. [32–34], see below, pages 576–78*]

[*p.* 35]
December 14 contind

Servts Bill	8.5
gave chamber maid	14
man servt.	12.6

[*pp. [36, 37], blank*]

[*p.* 38][97]
19 12. 0

M[98] Dr to Purse	8
I[99] – do	3

[*p.* 39]

Decr 14

Carriage hire	3—
Bar men	1
Purse	1.0.0

96. "There is putty on the inside."
97. Two leaves have been torn from the notebook between pp. [38] and [39].
98. Probably the Mr. Mumford of New York who accompanied Irving on his trip to Oxford, Bath, and Bristol (PMI, I, 163).
99. Irving.

x Do 1
Coach from London[100] to Oxford } 1.5
Place to Bath 1.8[101]
[*expenses continue below*]

[*pp. [40, 41] blank*]

[*p. 42*]
Home
Beebee
William
Swartwoort
Custom house
Hoffman
Ship[102]

[*p. [43] blank*]

[*p. 44*][103]
<What we love much & wish little>

---

grace gd passeth all understanding.[104]

Ce que nous aimons beaucoup mais que nous voudrions peu[105]

[*p. 45*]
14 Post book 8
Tea for 2 & attendce. 3.6

100. See note 98, above.
101. This line is in ink.
102. "Beebee" was Alexander Beebee, a fellow law student of Irving's in the office of J. O. Hoffman, who eventually settled in Utica (Irving to Beebee, September 18–October 27, 1804; Moses Mears Bagg, ed., *Memorial History of Utica, New York,* Syracuse, 1892, p. 191). "William" was presumably William Irving. "Swartwoort" was Samuel Swartwout (1783–1856), a native of New York state, closely associated with Aaron Burr after 1804; probably Irving knew him through Peter Irving, who was a close friend of Burr. "Hoffman" was presumably J. O. Hoffman.
103. This page is in ink.
104. "And the peace of God, which passeth all understanding, shall keep your hearts and minds through Christ Jesus" (Phil. 4:7).
105. "What we love much but wish little."

	fee to coach & Gd.	8.6
15	Hairdresser	4 —
16	turnpike[?]	8
	Gate opener	1
	China Gallery	1.6
	Palace	3.6
	Porter	2 —
	Post chaise	16.6
	Postillion	5 —
	<B> Tavern	6
	Servt	1
17	Barber 2 days	3
	Chapel[106] of New College[107]	1.6
	Charity	6
	Bodleian liberary & Gallery[108]	2.
	Theatre	1.6
	Oxford Guide	2.—
	2 places to Bath	2.16.
	7.19.8	6. 7.8
	2.12	1.12
	10.11.8	7.19.8

[*p. [46] blank*]

[*p. 47*]

	Decr. 18	
	Bill at Angel[109] 4 days 5 nights	3. 6.10
	Waiter	8
	Chambermaid	8
	Porter & Boots	5 —
19	Breakfast at Cirenchester	4.
	Coachman	2.

106. Beginning with "Chapel" the rest of the entry is in ink.

107. New College in Oxford was founded in 1379. The chapel is one of the earliest buildings in England in the perpendicular style.

108. The library was founded in 1450, opened in 1488, rebuilt in 1602.

109. The Angel Inn, Oxford.

	Bath Coachman & Guard – }	5
	Barber	2
	Theatre (boxes)	10.
	Chairmen	4.
20	Barber	1.
	Bath guide	1 6
21	Theatre	10
22	Places to Bristol.	7.
	coachman	2
	Expences there & back }	2.16.

[*p. 48*][110]

23	Ball ticket	10 —
	Sundries	6
	guide &c	
2	Chapeau bras	4. 2 6
	Case	1 6
	Gloves	1 6
	<?gaiters?>	1

[*The editor has transferred two pages (pp. [32, 33]) of accounts for January, written in ink, and one page (p. [34]) noting an expense for the Christmas season, also in ink, to this position for the convenience of the reader.*]

Recd. of Mr Main
Jany 1st. 1806 <6>
65.5.10 in full
of Carters letter of credit.

	Jany 1.	
	Dr to Cash	7<.6.0>
4	Do	5

Man of world & Harlequins Mag[111]
cg.

110. This page also contains a small drawing of a profile (Figure 20).
111. *Harlequin's Magnet; or, the Scandinavian Sorcerer* (1805) by T. J. Dibdin.

– Spanish dollars[112]

Play Romeo & Juliet & <Harlequins Mag>
C G. Betty[113] Romeo. Smith Juliet
Opera – Clemenza di Scipione[114]
Hamlet DL. Master Betty.

Jany 1. 1806

	Pd. Mumford[115]		
	cash borrowd at Bath		5.
	Coach		6.
	Dinner		4
	Play. School friends & Sleeping beauty } –		3.6
2	Gave a poor girl		17.—
	Dinner		6.—
3.	2 pr. elastic gaiters 3/6		7
	2 – cot hoze – <4/9>		9.6
	Dinner		3.
	Play (as you like it CG)		3.6

Douglas[116] C. G. Betty & Cook
Soldiers Daughter[117] D.L.
Mysterious Husband.[118] C G.

. . . . . .

2 pr lace sleeves	4/6	9.
1 " Lambs wool leather gloves		3.6
1 pr Beaver do		2.
1 " cot <Suspenders> Braces		5 —
1 Rasor strop		2.6

112. *Spanish Dollars; or, the Priest of the Parish* (1805) by Andrew Cherry.

113. William Henry West Betty (1791–1874), English actor known as the "Young Roscius," made his debut in Belfast in 1803. His final performance as a boy was in 1808, but he continued acting until 1824.

114. *La Clemenza di Scipione* (1778) by J. C. Bach.

115. See note 97, above. This was possibly John P. Mumford, New York merchant, listed in New York city directories from 1803–1804 through 1820–1821. This Mumford was, in any case, a fellow passenger of Irving's on the *Remittance* (see entry of January 17, 1806, n. 2).

116. *Douglas* (1756) by John Home.

117. *Soldier's Daughter* (1804) by Andrew Cherry.

118. *The Mysterious Husband* (1783) by Richard Cumberland.

1 likeness of Miss DC[119]	2.6
Mattrass & Blanket	1. 7.
Waiters Christmas box at NE Coffeehouse	10.6

[*p. 49*]
Her soul was made of softness & her tongue
was soft & <?flowerd?> ↑gentle↓ as her soul[120]

[*pp. [50, 51] blank*]

[*The editor has introduced here for the convenience of the reader the dated journal entries for January that appear farther on in the notebook (pp. [104–6]). They read upside down from the back of the notebook to the front.*]

Friday, January 17

Left London in Post chaise with Mumford for Gravesend to sail in the ship Remittance Capt Law for New York –[121]

Saturday, January 18

Strong wind in morning vessel taking in Ponda[?ge?][.] went on board in the evening weighd anchor but did not proceed above three miles when we anchord again

Sunday, January 19

Weighd anchor at day break and proceeded to the Nore where we anchord in the afternoon.

119. Maria Theresa or Marie Thérèse De Camp (1774–1836), English actress, married Charles Kemble in 1806. Irving brought a letter of introduction to her from Mrs. John Johnson and dined at her house, where he met Charles Kemble (PMI, I, 162).

120. Presumably the lines are by Irving.

121. The *Remittance* carried a cargo of dry goods to James Robertson, its owner, and, among others, to Ogden and Harrison, William Leffingwell, and J. P. Mumford, who bore family names known to Irving (New York *Morning Chronicle*, March 24, 1806). The ship's captain was presumably Richard Law, listed in New York city directories from 1804 to 1818–1819 as shipmaster.

Apparently Irving took aboard with him "one trunk, two boxes, small portmanteau, one bag, bed and bedding," according to his baggage certificate at the time of his landing, March 24, 1806 (STW, I, 397).

Sunday <20>19
Weighd anchor and in the afternoon came to anchor in the Downs

Monday, January 20[122]
Detaind at the Downs by a continuance of the strong west<ern> wind that has prevald for two months past

Tuesday, January 21
This afternoon a squally breeze sprung up from the east We immediately got underway & left the downs. the breeze died away in the night and towards morning sprung up ahead.

Wednesday, January 22
All day beating against a strong head wind.

Thursday, January 23
This morning at day break we <put about> wore ship and stood back for the downs where we anchord about 11 oclock

[*At this point the dated journal entries end (p. [104]). The account of Irving's crossing on the* Remittance *continues with the following undated description of life aboard ship (pp. [52, 53, 58–61]), which must have been written sometime between January 23 and March 24, when the ship reached New York.*]

6 oClock Turnd out put on grego[123] mounted companion way [–] door is shut [–] peepd over [–] fine morning – smacking breeze Second mate on deck in high glee singing a doleful ditty. Good morning Mr. Williams[124] – rolld his quid returnd my salutation and finishd his song. Six oclock pump ship – pump sucks – hold the reel [–] glass clear – clear glass – turn – stop – how many knots Mr W[–] 9 & an half by Gd. pulld up his trowsers squirted out tobacco juice lookd pleasd & whistled Barbara Allen. Sea broke over our quarter [–] had a salt salute over the head & shoulders [–] dodgd my head laughd and said nothing – hes a fool who cant take a hint so descended into cabin. <Washd> Shaved

122. Irving first wrote and then canceled "Tuesday 20 after t."
123. A short jacket made of heavy, coarse cloth with an attached hood, worn by Greeks and others in the Levant.
124. Possibly either Henry Williams, boatman, or Thomas Williams, pilot, listed in the New York city directory for 1800. A Joseph Williams is listed as a shipmaster.

washd face & hands cleand teeth – poor don Pedro[125] mounted companion way As he peepd out sea broke over & completely sousd him from head to foot – So much the better – he'll have to change his clothes & be clean in spight of himself. tie on my cravat put on <bo> cap & once more mount companion ladder Ladies there – Wish them good morning – put my arms round their waists & hug them tight to keep them from falling – What it is to be careful! Steward calls to breakfast great havoc among coffee ham & hot cakes Breakfast table dull. Admiral sick couzin John[126] & the Doctor in bed. myself too busy to talk. After breakfast go to after cabin Miss B. wishes tune on flute [–] I play – Little Guitar & admiral sings most hideously Ladies cover their ears – Miss Bayley scolds [–] Eliza[127] laughs – Miss B requests a serious sentimental tune – play her Yankee Doodle for half an hour till she is sufficiently satisfied with the concert. Hard work to kill time – Deck wet – Cabin too warm – go and sit in Jolly boat over the stern and finish a volume of Virgil – return into cabin <turn> nothing to do set down & scribble this nonsense

Cabin employments Mr Rogers[128] making a little boat for Dick. Dick lying on his back on carpet & Captain Law[?] sitting on sofa talking to him.

Fitch reading *Three Brothers*[129] – Shakes his head & looks glum at the book Don Pedro flaunting about in a great coat & wet underclothes too lazy to change them Clark[130] reading a book of childrens fables Eliza reading Naval Manners[131] – Miss Bayly holding her work in one hand the other arm on admirals shoulder who is seatd on my trunk in

125. No passenger list of the *Remittance* seems to have been preserved, so that it does not seem possible to identify with certainty Irving's fellow passengers.

126. Possibly Mumford, who was said to have been at first a grave but later a popular shipmate on the *Remittance* (PMI, I, 163). However Irving referred in his letter to Henry Brevoort, March 15, 1816, to meeting in London "little cousin John, alias Tophet," presumably an Englishman who had visited in New York several years earlier and had held several positions in Trinidad; possibly he was the passenger on the *Remittance.*

127. Apparently an Englishwoman (see the poem in which the name appears, page 581, and the earlier references to an Eliza, pages 397, 562).

128. Several Rogerses resided in New York at this period: Benjamin, Henry, Moses, Nehemiah, and I., all merchants.

129. "Fitch" was possibly William Fitch, listed in the New York city directory for 1800 as a merchant. Probably he was reading *The Three Brothers; a Romance,* by Joshua Pickersgill (London, 1803).

130. Nathaniel and Ransom Clark are listed as merchants in the New York city directory for 1800.

131. Probably a descriptive name; no work with this title has been identified.

his dirty robe de chambre reading out of a book of selections & making comments as he reads. Couzin John washing himself in gang way & making hideous faces[132]

[*pp.* 54–55]
Tho england's sons are <honest> ↑noble gentle kind[?] great↓ <?brave?>
Their hearts <?fair?> ↑brave↓ warm & true
Yet english hearts youl find can ↑beat dwell↓
In foreign bosoms too

<Sigh not eliza that you leave
Old england's shores behind>
The good remittance <?gaily goes?> ↑proudly rides↓
And woos the favring gale
that lightly curls the glassy wave
And fills the swelling sail

Sigh not eliza tho I leave
Old Englands shores behind
For other shores may prove as fair
& other climes as kind

<Tho there you leave>

<Kind be your lot wherere you roam
May joy your steps attend
each
Be theirs the task to hail you home>

Fair virtues plant is not confind
In englands soil to keep
Kind heaven conveyd its wandring ↑seed↓
Across the Atlantic deep
There may you find a happy ↑home↓
each stranger prove a friend
Peace be your lot wherere you ↑roam↓
& joy your steps attend.[133]

132. The remaining half of the manuscript page is occupied by a drawing of the group Irving has just described (Figure 21).

133. Presumably these lines are by Irving. The *Remittance* was the ship on which he sailed from London to New York in 1806, and an Eliza was one of the passengers (see entry of January 17 and that between January 23 and March 24, 1806).

[*p. [56] blank*]

[*p. [57] blank except for drawing of a woman in a chair (Figure 22)*]

[*For pp. [58–61], see above, page* 579]

[*p. [62] blank*]

[*p. [63] shows page-size drawing of a landscape (Figure 23)*]

[*pp. [64–67] blank*][134]

[*p. 68*][135]
Oh fond delusion

[*pp. [69, 70] blank*]

[*p. 71*][136]

passport	10.10
Cart	1.10
Taylor	22
361	

[*pp. [72–74] blank*]

[*p. 75*][137]
Cheaulieu[138]
Gerard Street
Soho Square

The poem indicates that this woman was English (see also the earlier references to an Eliza, pages 397 and 562). Probably the poem was written during the voyage, between January 23 and March 24, 1806.

134. A leaf has been torn out of the notebook between pp. [66] and [67].

135. Part of this page has been torn away.

136. The writing on this page is upside down.

137. The writing on this page is upside down.

138. Probably Saulieu's Coffee House at 3 Gerrard Street, Soho. This address was occupied from 1793 to 1803 by Francis Saulieu as a coffee house and continued to be referred to by this name for several years afterward (information furnished by City Librarian, City of Westminster, London).

[*pp. [76–79] blank*]

[*p. [80] blank except for drawing of a half-reclining figure (Figure 24)*]

[*pp. [81, 82] blank*]

[*p. [83] blank except for drawing, upside-down, of a soldier with a sword (Figure 25)*]

[*p. [84] blank except for drawing of a group with a flag (Figure 26)*]

[*p. 85*]
Blakes Hotel
German Street[139]
St James

[*p. [86] blank*]

[*p. [87] blank except for drawing, upside down, of an old man with a parrot (Figure 27)*]

[*p. [88] blank*]

[*p. [89] blank except for drawing of a man seated shaving (Figure 28)*]

[*pp. [90–95] blank*]

[*p. 96*]
a wench severe she was

[*p. [97] blank except for drawing, upside-down, of a profile (Figure 29)*]

[*p. 98*][140]
Miss Mills –[141]
Mitre Court
Leadenhall Street

139. Blake's Family Hotel on Jermyn Street.
140. The writing on this page is upside down.
141. No person named "Miss Mills" appears in the London city directories of the time.

(it is on the left hand
side below the
India House)

[*p.* 99][142]
Queen Ann St last –
price £2 for a night –
Suffolk St –
No. 2 – 3 – 4 – 5 – 6 – 7 – 8
9 – 10 – 11 – same price
Mrs. Courtney[143] –
Jane – Charles St –
Soho Sqr Fitzroy Sqr –
Herford St. No. 3 – 4 –
5 – Grt. Alyph[144]
St. No 41 – 42 – 51 –

[*pp. [100–102] blank*]

[*p. 103*][145]
19.9 –
4.12 –

[*For pp. [104–6], see above, page 578*]

[*Pp. [107–24] are devoted almost entirely to drawings of people, which with one exception are all upside-down on the pages of the notebook in its normal position: p. [107] small profile (Figure 30); p. [108] man with high coat collar (Figure 31, drawing right side up); p. [109] blank; p. [110] side view of man in peruke (Figure 32); p. [111] side view of man in coat and hat (Figure 33); p. [112] back view of man and the words "since then im doomd" (Figure 34); p. [113] seated man in broad-brimmed hat (Figure 35); p. [114] partial sketch of face (Figure 36);*

142. The writing on this page is upside down.
143. B. Courtney, perfumer, had the address 2 Charles St., Soho Square, a few years later (B. Critchett, *The Post-Office Annual Directory for 1813,* London, 1813).
144. Great Ayliff.
145. The numerals on this page are upside down in ink.

p. [115] back view of standing man in broad-brimmed hat (Figure 37); p. [116] profile (Figure 38); p. [117] three small profiles (Figure 39); p. [118] back views of two men (Figure 40); p. [119] large number "3"; p. [120] side view of soldier with sword (Figure 41); p. [121] man in full-skirted coat (Figure 42); p. [122] side view of man in cocked hat (Figure 43); p. [123] side view of man in cocked hat with long sword (Figure 44); p. [124] side view of woman standing (Figure 45).]

[*p. 125*][146]

Lent B –	10 fr
Mr. Lowebach[147] –	6 fr
Bank	10
	5
	2 8
	— 8

[*p. 126*][148]

Rue du Regard
Cherche midy[149]
Vanderlyn 1.4
2.9
H. Nicolle[150] rue petits
Augustins No. 33
rue d Orleans[151]
rue d Eveque
14
24
en dimanche[152]

[*inside back cover*][153]

2 gloves 25

Vanderlyn

146. The writing on this page is upside down.
147. Rougemont de Loewenberg.
148. The writing on this page, except "en dimanche," is upside down.
149. Rue de Cherche-Midi.
150. Four Nicolles, including a landscape painter, were living in Paris a few years later (*Almanach de 25,000 Adresses de Paris, pour l'Année 1817*, Paris, 1817).
151. This line and the next are erased.
152. "On Sunday."
153. The page is written upside down, in pencil.

3 6
6

6
3
12
2[154] 20
48
24
———
26.12

Hotel de l'empire
Rue Cerutti
Bankd. 12 Livres 12 sous
3 bills[?]
2 Dinners[155]

154. "2" is in ink. At its right "Irving" is written sideways on the page.
155. Faint traces of additional writing can be seen to the left of the column of figures, but none of it is legible.

INDEX